DRUG USE AND ABUSE

A Comprehensive Introduction

SEVENTH EDITION

Howard Abadinsky
St. John's University

WADSWORTH
CENGAGE Learning·

Australia · Brazil · Japan · Korea · Mexico · Singapore · Spain · United Kingdom · United States

WADSWORTH
CENGAGE Learning

Drug Use and Abuse: A Comprehensive Introduction, **Seventh Edition**
Howard Abadinsky

Publisher/Executive Editor: Linda Schreiber-Ganster

Acquisitions Editor: Carolyn Henderson Meier

Assistant Editor: Erin Abney

Editorial Assistant: John Chell

Marketing Manager: Michelle Williams

Marketing Communications Manager: Tami Strang

Content Project Manager: Pre-PressPMG

Creative Director: Rob Hugel

Art Director: Maria Epes

Print Buyer: Judy Inouye

Rights Acquisitions Account Manager, Text: Roberta Broyer

Rights Acquisitions Account Manager, Image: Dean Dauphinais

Production Service: Pre-PressPMG

Photo Researcher: Pre-PressPMG

Cover Designer: Riezebos Holzbaur/Angelyn Navasca

Cover Image: Getty Images © Garry Gay

Compositor: Pre-PressPMG

For product information and technology assistance, contact us at **Cengage Learning Customer & Sales Support, 1-800-354-9706.**
For permission to use material from this text or product, submit all requests online at **cengage.com/permissions.**
Further permissions questions can be emailed to **permissionrequest@cengage.com.**

Library of Congress Control Number: 2010922177

ISBN-13: 978-0-495-80991-3

ISBN-10: 0-495-80991-8

Wadsworth
20 Davis Drive
Belmont, CA 94002-3098
USA

Cengage Learning is a leading provider of customized learning solutions with office locations around the globe, including Singapore, the United Kingdom, Australia, Mexico, Brazil, and Japan. Locate your local office at **www.cengage.com/global**.

Cengage Learning products are represented in Canada by Nelson Education, Ltd.

To learn more about Wadsworth, visit **www.cengage.com/Wadsworth**

Purchase any of our products at your local college store or at our preferred online store **www.cengagebrain.com**.

Printed in the United States of America
1 2 3 4 5 6 7 14 13 12 11 10

*This book is dedicated to the memory
of James A. Inciardi, an outstanding drug researcher and wonderful
colleague who will be missed.*

BRIEF CONTENTS

CONTENTS

Preface

Most of the numerous texts on drug use and abuse focus on a particular aspect or aspects of the issue: pharmacology, psychology, sociology, treatment, the business of drugs, prevention, laws and law enforcement, or policy. This book is different in that it provides the reader with a thorough understanding of drug use and abuse, examining distinctions between *use* and *abuse*; drug history; biological, psychological, and sociological explanations; various types of treatment and prevention programs; the business of drugs; and drug laws and law enforcement. Without an understanding of these topics, an informed discussion of drug policy—the focus of Chapters 13 and 14—is not possible. And without an understanding of the dynamics of drugs, a discussion of the problem becomes an exercise equivalent to the proverbial blind men attempting to describe an elephant—each can accurately portray only that part he can touch. Hence the logic for the comprehensive nature of this book.

Because the subject of drugs transcends so many disciplines—history, law, neuropharmacology, political science, social work, counseling, psychology, and sociology—the literature is massive and diverse. Putting together all aspects of drug use abuse in a single book is a daunting task. This Seventh Edition nonetheless maintains the comprehensive approach for which the book is known.

AN OVERVIEW OF THE SEVENTH EDITION

Drug Use and Abuse: A Comprehensive Introduction is organized into 14 chapters using a syllabus format for ease of classroom presentation. Each chapter ends with an extensive summary and numerous review questions.

- *Chapter 1* explores the drug use continuum from abstinence to dependence and the slippery term *drug abuse*. Categories of drugs and methods for estimating their prevalence are explained, as well as the relationship between drugs, crime, and violence. The Seventh Edition provides new data on drug use and drug users and an expansion of the role of tobacco and alcohol as "gateway drugs;" the relationship between crime and the choice of drugs abused; and the often fatal dangers involved in the abuse of prescription painkillers.

- *Chapter 2* presents a history of the drugs of abuse, beginning with the temperance movement and Prohibition, the patent medicine problem, and the intertwining of foreign affairs in the Opium Wars and the Harrison Act. The chapter reviews the opiates, the erratic popularity of cocaine in its various forms, the marijuana saga, the history of artificial depressants and stimulants, and natural and artificial hallucinogens. There is an examination of U.S. policy as it moved from indifference to the "war on drugs." The chapter has an update on international conventions concerned with drugs of abuse and, in particular, the surge in amphetamine use and the re-emergence of the medical profession in dealing with substance abuse.

- *Chapter 3* explores the complex world of neurology—but explanatory diagrams and easily understood prose reveal that it is "science for poets." This prepares the student for examining how specific drugs manipulate the organism to produce their effects in Chapters 4, 5, and 6. This chapter examines the disease model, arousal theory, and genetic predisposition, as well as the roles of setting and expectations in producing a drug's effects. The chapter has been updated with the latest biological findings—often the result of advances in brain imaging—and streamlined for ease of understanding. It also adds information on the relationship between the neurology of adolescence and risky behavior.

- *Chapter 4* focuses on depressants, from opiates to alcohol and sedatives to inhalants. It identifies the role of neurotransmitters: while they can produce profound positive effects (euphoria, stress inhibition, pain reduction), they can also lead to dependence, addiction, and death. The chapter has been updated to reflect the latest on the pharmacology of psychoactive substances, including a discussion of the purported health benefits of alcohol and issues surrounding the misuse of artificial opiates OxyContin and fentanyl, and includes changes in heroin and the heroin market as the drug moves into suburban America. Information on propofol (the "Michael Jackson drug") has been added to this chapter.

- *Chapter 5* focuses on stimulants, ranging from caffeine and nicotine to cocaine and methamphetamine. The chapter explores how certain neurotransmitters play a major role, both in producing positive effects such as euphoria, increased energy levels, enhanced mood, and lessening of depression, while also leading to dependence, damage to critical organs, and death. The chapter has been updated with the latest information on cocaine and nicotine, such as use of water pipes and e-cigarettes, and new controls over tobacco products given to the FDA.

- *Chapter 6* examines hallucinogens and marijuana, which has depressing, stimulating, and hallucinogenic characteristics. So-called *psychedelics* overwhelm the nervous system's ability to modulate sensory input and produce altered perceptions of reality, sensory illusions, and hallucinations. These substances range from those used in religious ceremonies by Native Americans, to LSD, PCP, and the so-called "club drugs" MDA, MDMA/ecstasy, and added to this section, BZP. The chapter has expanded to reflect growing concern over prescription drug abuse with a new section that includes neuroenhancers such as piracetam, Adderall, and modafinal (Provigil), and the section on hallucinogens now includes salvia.

- *Chapter 7* examines sociological studies and theories that consider psychoactive drugs in their social context, characterizes their stages, and suggests explanations for their abuse. Material on the HFA ("high functioning alcoholic") has been added and the recent phenomenon of a progression from prescription drugs to heroin use. Combined with the biological views of Chapters 3 to 6, this chapter and the psychological views expressed in Chapter 8 provide the full range of knowledge critical to an informed view of the causes of drug abuse and their policy implications.

- *Chapter 8* moves the study of drug abuse to the field of psychology whose theories provide the basis for treatment discussed in Chapter 10. The chapter examines the two major branches of that discipline, one based on psychoanalytic theory and the other on behavior/learning theory, and their explanations for drug abuse.

- *Chapter 9* explores the relatively new and often illusory field of drug abuse prevention through a critique of basic premises and a description of the leading programs. Research on prevention is analyzed and the alternative harm reduction approach discussed. An expanded discussion of drug testing has been moved to this chapter from Chapter 13.

- *Chapter 10* reviews the various treatment approaches to drug abuse, reflecting drug abuse causes explored in Chapters 3 through 8. Programs ranging from methadone to mandatory, private and public, in- and outpatient, twelve-step, and the therapeutic community are described and their theoretical underpinnings discussed. There is an analysis of the difficulty of evaluating drug program effectiveness and the lack of research support for much of what is offered as substance abuse treatment. Discussion of cognitive behavior therapy has been expanded to reflect the popularity of this approach in psychology, and the *Florida Model* has been added as has discussion of the popular drug courts. There is additional critique of private drug treatment programs and a discussion of the elements that go into most treatment programs. There is an expansion of the use of medications in substance abuse treatment.

- *Chapter 11* provides a tour of the drug economy as characterized by free-wheeling capitalism that responds only to market conditions of supply and demand and as influenced by competitive violence and law enforcement efforts. There is an examination of the business of drugs: a world filled with private armies and violence, from its highest (international) levels down through mid-level wholesalers and finally to the retail (street) level. The chapter ends with a discussion of a critical element in the wholesale drug business: the various methods used to launder money. Updates in this chapter reflect increasing concern over Mexican drug cartels and their level of violence, a threat to both Mexico and the United States; increased coverage of the connection between terrorists and drug trafficking, particularly in Afghanistan; and an update on changes in the drug trade in Colombia.

- *Chapter 12* looks at the law enforcement response to the business of drugs as constrained by the U.S. Constitution and jurisdictional limitations. There is an examination of the various statutes used to investigate and prosecute drug offenders, such as conspiracy, RICO, tax, and money-laundering laws, as well as the investigative agencies and the techniques of drug law enforcement. The chapter concludes with an analysis of these techniques. The chapter has been expanded with additional material on street-level enforcement and forfeiture.
- *Chapters 13 and 14* have been updated and expanded to better compare the U.S. model with those of countries in Western Europe and Canada. *Chapter 13* ties together all of the previous chapters with an examination and critical analysis of U.S. policy with respect to drug abuse. There is expanded discussion of racism and the drug "war," contrasting approaches in other countries such as Iran, and the prosecution of pregnant women for using illegal drugs.
- *Chapter 14* extends the drug policy issue beyond our borders by examining the approach taken in Great Britain and the European alternative referred to as *harm reduction*. The chapter concludes with a comparative critique of drug decriminalization. As part of the discussion, in the Seventh Edition there is additional material on needle exchange programs, contrasting approaches used in Western Europe, especially Austria, Switzerland, and, most important, Portugal, where in 2001 all drugs were decriminalized; and information about policy changes in Canada as it moves more toward a harm reduction policy. There is expanded discussion of the medical marijuana issue.
- Because the language of drugs and drug abuse can be confusing, an extensive *glossary* is presented after Chapter 14.

INSTRUCTOR'S EDITION

Designed just for instructors, the Instructor's Edition includes a visual walkthrough that illustrates the key pedagogical features of this text, as well as the media and supplements that accompany it. Use this handy tool to learn quickly about the many options this text provides to keep your class engaging and informative.

INSTRUCTOR'S RESOURCE MANUAL WITH TEST BANK

The manual includes learning objectives, key terms, a detailed chapter outline, a chapter summary, discussion topics, student activities, media suggestions, and a test bank. Each chapter's test bank contains questions in multiple-choice, true false, fill-in-the-blank, and essay formats, with a full answer key. The test bank is coded to the learning objectives that appear in the main text, and includes the page numbers in the main text where the answers can be found.

PPTs

These handy Microsoft PowerPoint slides, which outline the chapters of the main text in a classroom-ready presentation, will help you in making your lectures engaging and in reaching your visually oriented students. The presentations are available for download on the password-protected website and can also be obtained by e-mailing your local Cengage Learning representative.

ExamView® Computerized Testing

The comprehensive Instructor's Manual described above is backed up by ExamView, a computerized test bank available for PC and Macintosh computers. With ExamView you can create, deliver, and customize tests and study guides (both print and online) in minutes. You can easily edit and import your own questions and graphics, change test layouts, and reorganize questions. And using ExamView's complete word-processing capabilities, you can enter an unlimited number of new questions or edit existing questions.

ABOUT THE AUTHOR

 Howard Abadinsky is professor of criminal justice at St. John's University, Jamaica, NY. He was an inspector for the Cook County (IL) Sheriff's Office for eight years and a New York State parole officer and senior parole officer for 15 years. He holds a B.A. from Queens College of the City University of New York, an M.S.W. from Fordham University, and a Ph.D. from New York University. He is the author of several books, including *Probation and Parole*, Tenth Edition, *Organized Crime*, Ninth Edition, and *Law and Justice*, Sixth Edition.

Dr. Abadinsky can be reached at abadinsh@stjohns.edu and encourages comments about his work.

Our society makes artificial distinctions among addictive drugs. We foster the false impression that because nicotine and alcohol are legal, they must be less dangerous and less addictive than the illicit drugs.

Avram Goldstein (2001: 4)

AN INTRODUCTION TO DRUG USE AND ABUSE

CHAPTER **1**

© Bruno Ehrs/Corbis

This book is concerned with *psychoactive* drugs that have the potential to harm their users, who might in turn harm others, such as occurs when people drive while intoxicated. While statutes distinguish between lawful drugs such as nicotine and alcohol and illegal drugs such as heroin and cocaine, biology recognizes no such distinction. Nicotine is a drug that meets the rigorous criteria for abuse liability and dependence potential, and "cigarettes are one of the major drugs of addiction in the United States and in the world and are responsible for more premature deaths than all of the other drugs of abuse combined" (Schuster 1993: 40).

NICOTINE AND ALCOHOL

Nicotine dependence is the most common substance use disorder in the United States. Approximately 60 percent to 80 percent of current smokers fulfill classic criteria for drug dependence: they have difficulty stopping, have symptoms of withdrawal when they stop, show increasing tolerance levels, and continue usage despite knowledge of personal harm. Nicotine appears to have a dependence potential at least equal to that of other drugs. For example, among people who experiment with alcohol, 10 to 15 percent will meet criteria for alcohol dependence at some point in their life. Among people who experiment with cigarettes, 20 to 30 percent will meet criteria for nicotine dependence in their lifetime (American Psychiatric Association 1995). If addiction is defined as compulsive drug-seeking behavior, even in the face of negative health consequences, than tobacco use is certainly addiction (National Institute on Drug Abuse 2001d): the drug kills an estimated 440,000 persons annually, more than alcohol, illegal drug use, homicide, car accidents, and AIDS combined (*Tobacco Addiction* 2009).

According to scientific and pharmacological data used to classify dangerous substances for the protection of society, **alcohol** should be a Schedule II narcotic, a Drug Enforcement Administration (DEA) category referring to a substance that is highly addictive and available only with a government narcotic registry number. The cost of alcohol abuse is twice the social cost of all illegal drug abuse. Alcohol is reputed to be the direct cause of 80,000 to 100,000 deaths annually, and alcohol-related auto accidents are the leading cause of death for teenagers (Wicker 1987; Li, Smith, and Baker 1994). Alcohol disturbs behavior in a way that "threatens the safety of others even when used occasionally and not compulsively" (Goldstein 2001: 5).

But alcohol for recreational use is permitted to be legally manufactured, imported, sold, and possessed. Because of this reality, while it has been associated with a myriad of social problems, since the repeal of Prohibition in 1933 trafficking in alcohol has not been associated with rampant violence and corruption. Indeed, the repeal of Prohibition resulted in a dramatic decrease in the murder rate in the United States, which began to increase in the 1960s along with the prevalence of illicit drug use (Myers 1995).

THE GATEWAY TO ILLEGAL DRUG USE

"Both tobacco and alcohol share a role as 'gateway drugs' that presage use of other psychoactive drugs; in other words, alcohol and/or tobacco use precedes most subsequent use of marijuana and cocaine" (Shiffman and Balabanis 1995: 18). Thus, "there is a fairly consistent progression of adolescent substance use beginning with the licit drugs alcohol and/or cigarettes, moving on to illicit substances initiating with marijuana and progressing to cocaine and 'harder,' more problematic drugs" (P. Johnson, Boles, and Kleber 2000: 79).

"Each day, more than 3,000 young persons smoke their first cigarette, and the likelihood of becoming addicted to nicotine is higher for these young smokers than for those who begin later in life" (Zickler 2002: 7). Nearly one in four high school seniors smokes every day, and more than one in eight smokes a half-pack or more each day (National Institute on Drug Abuse 2000). "Young people age twelve to seventeen who smoke are about twelve times more likely to use illegal drugs and sixteen times more likely to drink heavily than youths who did not smoke. Young people use alcohol more than illegal drugs and the younger a person is when alcohol use begins, the greater the risk of developing alcohol abuse or dependence later in life.... Alcohol use among the young strongly correlates with adult drug use. For example, adults who started drinking at early ages are nearly eight times more likely to use cocaine than adults who did not drink as children" (Office of National Drug Control Policy 2000: 10).

Distinctions between alcohol and other psychoactive drugs reflect neither reality nor science (N. Miller 1995). Indeed, heroin users have typically used marijuana and alcohol while adolescents, and from-heavy-alcohol-use-to-injecting-heroin is a typical sequence for most addicts (Inciardi, McBride, and Surratt 1998).

With these incongruities serving as a backdrop, this opening chapter will begin by describing the problems inherent in defining terms such as *drugs* and **drug abuse**, the drug use continuum from abstinence to dependency, measuring the extent of drug use, and the connection between drugs and crime.

DRUGS: REACHING A DEFINITION

The term *drug* is derived from the fourteenth century French word *drogue*, meaning "a dry substance"—most pharmaceuticals at that time were prepared from dried herbs (Palfai and Jankiewicz 1991). There is no completely satisfying way of delineating what is and what is not a drug—for example, the differences between water, vitamin supplements, and penicillin (Goode 1989). Therefore, some feel it appropriate to refer to chemical or **substance abuse**. Imprecision in the use of the term *drug* has had serious social consequences.

Because alcohol is excluded from most people's definition of what is a drug, the public is conditioned to regard a martini as something fundamentally different from a marijuana cigarette, a barbiturate capsule, or a bag of heroin. Similarly, because the meaning of the word drug differs so widely in therapeutic and social contexts, the public is conditioned to believe that "street" drugs act according to entirely different principles than "medical" drugs, alcohol, and nicotine do, with the result that the risks of the former are exaggerated and the risks of the latter are overlooked (Uelmen and Haddox 1983).

"In contemporary society the word drug has two connotations—one positive, explaining its crucial role in medicine, and one negative, reflecting, not the natural and synthetic makeup of these chemicals, but the self-destruction and socially deleterious patterns of misuse" (K. Jones, Shainberg, and Byer 1979: 1). In this book the term *drug* will refer to substances that have mood-altering, psychotropic (or psychoactive) effects. This definition includes caffeine, nicotine, and alcohol, as well as illegal chemicals such as marijuana and heroin.

DRUG USE, ABUSE, AND ADDICTION

Drug addiction is defined by the National Institute on Drug Abuse as "a chronic, relapsing brain disease that is characterized by compulsive drug seeking and use, despite harmful consequences" (*Science of Addiction* 2007: 5). In contrast, *drug abuse* implies the misuse of certain substances; it is a moral, not a scientific, term: "An unstandardized, value-laden, and highly relative term used with a great deal of imprecision and confusion, generally implying drug use that is excessive, dangerous, or undesirable to the individual or community and that ought to be modified" (Nelson et al. 1982: 33). Drug abuse "implies willful, improper use due to an underlying disorder or a quest for hedonistic or immoral pleasure" (N. Miller 1995: 10). Numerous definitions of drug abuse reflect social values, not scientific insight: "One reason for the prevalence of definitions of drug abuse that are neither logical nor scientific is the strength of Puritan moralism in American culture which frowns on the pleasure and recreation provided by intoxicants" (Zinberg 1984: 33). Such definitions typically refer to:

1. the nonmedical use of a substance
2. to alter the mental state
3. in a manner that is detrimental to the individual or the community and/or
4. that is illegal.

For example, the American Social Health Association (1972: 1) defines drug abuse as the "use of mood modifying chemicals outside of medical supervision, and in a manner which is harmful to the person and the community." Other definitions, such as those offered by the World Health Organization and the American Medical Association, include references to physical and/or psychological dependency (Zinberg 1984).

The *Diagnostic and Statistical Manual of Mental Disorders, Fourth Edition* (DSM-IV), published by the American Psychiatric Association (1994: 182), refers to substance abuse as a "maladaptive pattern of substance use manifested by recurrent and significant adverse consequences related to the repeated use of substances. There may be repeated failure to fulfill major role obligations, repeated use in situations in which it is physically hazardous [such as driving while intoxicated], multiple legal problems, and recurrent social and interpersonal problems."

In fact drug abuse may be defined from a number of perspectives: "The legal definition equates drug use with the mere act of using a proscribed drug or using a drug under proscribed conditions. The moral definition is similar, but greater emphasis is placed on the motivation or purpose for which the drug is used. The medical model opposes unsupervised usage but emphasizes the physical and mental consequences for the user, and the social definition stresses social responsibility and adverse effects on others" (Balter 1974: 5).

DRUG USE CONTINUUM

The *use* of psychoactive chemicals, licit or illicit, can objectively be labeled drug *abuse* only when the user becomes dysfunctional as a consequence, for example, is unable to maintain employment, has impaired social relationships, exhibits dangerous—reckless or aggressive—behavior, and/or significantly endangers his or her health. Thus, drug *use*, as opposed to drug *abuse*, can be viewed as a continuum, as shown in Figure 1.1. At one end is the nonuser who has never used prohibited or abused lawful psychoactive drugs. Along the continuum are experimental use and culturally endorsed use, which includes the use of drugs—wine or **peyote**, for example—in religious ceremonies, and recreational use. "Regardless of the duration of use, such people tend not to escalate their use to uncontrollable amounts." For example, "long-term cocaine users have found that recreational patterns can be maintained for a decade or more without loss of control. Such use tends to occur in weekly or biweekly episodes and users perceive that the effects facilitate social functioning" (Siegel 1989: 222–223). In the United Kingdom (UK), for example, "of the 11 million people in the UK (27 percent of the population aged 16–74) who have ever used illicit drugs at some point in their life, probably no more than 300,000 (1 percent) are drug dependent" (Frisher and Beckett 2006: 127). At the far end of the drug use continuum is the drug-dependent, the compulsive user whose life often revolves around obtaining, maintaining, and using a supply of drugs. For the compulsive user, failure to ingest an adequate supply of the desired drug results in psychological stress and discomfort, and there may also be physical **withdrawal** symptoms.

Understanding the use of psychoactive substances as a continuum allows the issue of drugs to be placed in its proper perspective: There is nothing inherently evil or virtuous about the use of psychoactive substances. For some—actually many—people, they make life more enjoyable; hence the widespread use of **caffeine, tobacco,** and alcohol without serious unpleasant effects. For others, drugs become a burden as dependence brings dysfunction. In between these two extremes are a variety of drug *users*, such as the underage adolescent using tobacco or alcohol on occasion, as is very common in our society. Adults may experiment with illegal drugs—marijuana and cocaine, for example—without moving up to more frequent, that is, recreational use. The recreational user enjoys some beer or cocktails on a regular basis or ingests cocaine or heroin just before or at social events, during which the drug eases social interaction for this actor. Outside of this specific social setting, the recreational user abstains and thereby is in control of his or her use of drugs. Thus, even for cocaine, a very addictive drug, only 15–16 percent of people become addicted within ten years of first use (T. Robinson and Berridge 2003). For some, recreational use crosses into compulsive use marked by a preoccupation with securing and using drugs in the face of negative consequences, losing a job, severe disruption of social relationships, and/or involvement with the criminal justice system.

"The more spectacular consequences of cocaine abuse are not typical of the drug's effects as it is normally used any more than the phenomena associated with alcoholism are typical of the ordinary consumption of that drug" (Grinspoon and Bakalar 1976: 119). "Acknowledging potentially healthy relationships with drugs allows us to better identify unhealthy ones." Although this may sound heretical to those who

FIGURE 1.1
DRUG USE
CONTINUUM

readily categorize all illicit drug *use* as *abuse*, "the refusal to recognize healthy relationships with stigmatized drugs hinders our understanding of drug-related problems and healthy relationships with them" (Whiteacre and Pepinsky 2002: 27).

What we know about those who use psychoactive drugs is skewed toward compulsive users, particularly with respect to illegal drugs: Noncompulsive users have received very little research attention because they are hard to find: "Much data on users are gathered from treatment, law enforcement, and correctional institutions, and from other institutions allied with them. Naturally these data sources provide a highly selected sample of users: those who have encountered significant personal, medical, social, or legal problems in conjunction with their drug use, and thus represent the pathological end of the using spectrum" (Zinberg et al. 1978: 13). Such data "cannot be used to support a causal interpretation because of the absence of information on individuals who may have ingested a drug but had minimal or no negative consequences" (Newcomb and Bentler 1988: 13), such as the recreational user.

ADDICTION

Addiction is from the Latin verb *addicere*, meaning "to bind a person to one thing or another." Often used interchangeably with the term *dependence*, addiction denotes a complex illness characterized by repeated, compulsive, at times uncontrollable behavior that persists even in the face of adverse social, psychological, and/or physical consequences. For many people addiction becomes chronic, with relapse possible even after years of abstinence. The elements are the same no matter whether the addiction is to alcohol, tobacco, controlled substances, or sex: compulsion and continuation despite adverse consequences. Norman Miller (1995) avoids use of the term *drug abuse* and opts instead for **addiction** characterized by:

1. *Preoccupation*: The addict assigns a high priority to acquiring drugs. Social relationships and employment are jeopardized in the quest for drugs and the consequences of use.
2. *Compulsion*: The addict continues to use drugs despite serious adverse consequences. He or she will often deny the connection between the adverse consequences and the use of drugs.
3. *Relapse*: In the face of adverse consequences, addicts discontinue drugs but subsequently return to abnormal use.

In sum, "drug addiction is defined as having lost control over drug taking, even in the face of adverse physical, personal, or social consequences" (Society for Neuroscience 2002: 33).

Dennis Donovan (1988: 6) conceives of addiction as a "complex, progressive behavior pattern having biological, psychological, sociological, and behavioral components. What sets this behavior apart from others is the individual's overwhelmingly pathological involvement in or attachment to it, subjective compulsion to continue it, and reduced ability to exert personal control over it…. The behavior pattern continues despite its negative impact on the physical, psychological, and social function of the individual."

DEFINITION DETERMINES RESPONSE

A variety of lawful substances are addicting and have been abused by any number of "respectable persons," including top government officials, not to mention people in sports, entertainment, and the popular media. Social expectations and definitions determine what kind of drug-taking is appropriate and the social situations that are approved and disapproved for drug use. The use of drugs is neither inherently bad nor inherently good—these are socially determined values (Goode 1989). Thus, Mormons and Christian Scientists consider use of tea and coffee "abusive," while Moslems and some Protestant denominations have the same view of alcohol, although they permit tobacco smoking. The National Commission on Marijuana and Drug Abuse (1973: 13) argues that the term *drug abuse* "must be deleted from official pronouncements and public policy dialogue" because the "term has no functional utility and has become no more than an arbitrary codeword for that drug use which is presently considered wrong." As the history in Chapter 2 informs us, moderate use of a drug will be defined as *abuse* (and illegal) or it will be considered socially acceptable (and lawful) as society determines, regardless of the actual relative danger inherent in the substance. In other words, how society *defines* drug abuse determines how society *responds* to drug use.

PSYCHOACTIVE DRUGS

Later in this book (Chapters 4, 5, and 6) we will examine psychoactive drugs in each of three categories according to their primary effect on the central nervous system (CNS): depressants, stimulants, and hallucinogens. (Some chemicals, such as cannabis and MDMA, also known as ecstasy, have a combination of these characteristics.) A drug can have at least three different names: chemical, generic, and trade; and drugs that have a legitimate medical use may be marketed under a variety of trade names. Trade names begin with a capital letter, while chemical or generic names are in lowercase (see Table 1.1).

DEPRESSANTS

Depressants depress the CNS and can reduce pain. The most frequently used drug in this category is alcohol; the most frequently used illegal drug is the **opiate** derivative **heroin**. Other depressants, all of which have some medical use, include **morphine**, codeine, **methadone, OxyContin, barbiturates,** and **tranquilizers**. These substances can cause physical and psychological dependence—a craving—and withdrawal results in physical and psychological stress. Opiate derivatives (heroin, morphine, and codeine) and opiumlike drugs such as methadone and OxyContin are often referred to as **narcotics**.

STIMULANTS

Stimulants elevate mood—produce feelings of well-being—by stimulating the CNS. The most frequently used drugs in this category are caffeine and **nicotine**; the most frequently used illegal stimulant is **cocaine** that, along with **amphetamines**, has some limited medical use.

TABLE 1.1 | COMMONLY ABUSED DRUGS

Substances: Category and Name	Examples of Commercial and Street Names	DEA Schedule/How Administered	Intoxication Effects/Potential Health Consequences
Cannabinoids			
hashish	boom, chronic, gangster, hash, hash oil, hemp	I/swallowed, smoked	*euphoria, slowed thinking and reaction time, confusion, impaired balance and coordination*/cough, frequent respiratory infections; impaired memory and learning; increased heart rate, anxiety, panic attacks; tolerance, addiction
marijuana	blunt, dope, ganja, grass, herb, joints, Mary Jane, pot, reefer, sinsemilla, skunk, weed	I/swallowed, smoked	
Depressants			
barbiturates	*Amytal, Nembutal, Seconal, Phenobarbital:* barbs, reds, red birds, phennies, tooies, yellows, yellow jackets	II, III, V/injected, swallowed	*reduced anxiety; feeling of well-being; lowered inhibitions; slowed pulse and breathing; lowered blood pressure; poor concentration*/fatigue; confusion; impaired coordination, memory, judgment; addiction; respiratory depression and arrest; death
benzodiazepines (other than flunitrazepam)	*Ativan, Halcion, Librium, Valium, Xanax:* candy, downers, sleeping pills, tranks	IV/swallowed, injected	Also, for barbiturates—*sedation, drowsiness*/depression, unusual excitement, fever, irritability, poor judgment, slurred speech, dizziness, life-threatening withdrawal
flunitrazepam	*Rohypnol:* forget-me pill, Mexican Valium, R2, Roche, roofies, roofinol, rope, rophies	IV/swallowed, snorted	for benzodiazepines—*sedation, drowsiness*/dizziness
GHB	*gamma-hydroxybutyrate:* G, Georgia home boy, grievous bodily harm, liquid ecstasy	I/swallowed	for flunitrazepam—*visual and gastrointestinal disturbances, urinary retention, memory loss for the time under the drug's effects*
methaqualone	*Quaalude, Sopor, Parest:* ludes, mandrex, quad, quay	I/injected, swallowed	for GHB—*drowsiness, nausea*/vomiting, headache, loss of consciousness, loss of reflexes, seizures, coma, death for methaqualone—*euphoria*/depression, poor reflexes, slurred speech, coma increased heart rate and blood pressure, impaired motor function/memory loss; numbness; nausea/vomiting

Category and Name	Examples of Commercial and Street Names	DEA Schedule/How Administered	Intoxication Effects/Potential Health Consequences
Dissociative Anesthetics			
Ketamine	Ketalar SV: cat Valiums, K, Special K, vitamin K	III/injected, snorted, smoked	Also, for ketamine—at high doses, delirium, depression, respiratory depression and arrest
PCP and analogs	phencyclidine: angel dust, boat, hog, love boat, peace pill	I, II/injected, swallowed, smoked	for PCP and analogs—possible decrease in blood pressure and heart rate, panic, aggression, violence/loss of appetite, depression
Hallucinogens			
LSD	lysergic acid diethylamide: acid, blotter, boomers, cubes, microdot, yellow sunshines	I/swallowed, absorbed through mouth tissues	altered states of perception and feeling; nausea; persisting perception disorder (flashbacks)
mescaline	buttons, cactus, mesc, peyote	I/swallowed, smoked	Also, for LSD and mescaline—increased body temperature, heart rate, blood pressure; loss of appetite, sleeplessness, numbness, weakness, tremors
psilocybin	magic mushroom, purple passion, shrooms	I/swallowed	for LSD—persistent mental disorders for psilocybin—nervousness, paranoia
Opioids and Morphine Derivatives			
Codeine	Empirin with Codeine, Fiorinal with Codeine, Robitussin A-C, Tylenol with Codeine: Captain Cody, Cody, schoolboy; (with glutethimide) doors & fours, loads, pancakes and syrup	II, III, IV, V/injected, swallowed	pain relief, euphoria, drowsiness/nausea, constipation, confusion, sedation, respiratory depression and arrest, tolerance, addiction, unconsciousness, coma, death Also, for codeine—less analgesia, sedation, and respiratory depression than morphine
fentanyl and fentanyl analogs	Actiq, Duragesic, Sublimaze: Apache, China girl, China white, dance fever, friend, goodfella, jackpot, murder 8, TNT, Tango and Cash	I, II/injected, smoked, snorted	for heroin—staggering gait

TABLE 1.1 | (CONTINUED)

Substances: Category and Name	Examples of Commercial and Street Names	DEA Schedule/How Administered	Intoxication Effects/Potential Health Consequences
heroin	*diacetylmorphine:* brown sugar, dope, H, horse, junk, skag, skunk, smack, white horse	I/injected, smoked, snorted	
morphine	*Roxanol, Duramorph:* M, Miss Emma, monkey, white stuff	II, III/injected, swallowed, smoked	
opium	*laudanum, paregoric:* big O, black stuff, block, gum, hop	II, III, V/swallowed, smoked	
oxycodone HCL	*OxyContin:* Oxy, O.C., killer	II/swallowed, snorted, injected	
hydrocodone bitartrate, acetaminophen	*Vicodin:* vike, Watson-387	II/swallowed	
Stimulants			
amphetamine	*Biphetamine, Dexedrine:* bennies, black beauties, crosses, hearts, LA turnaround, speed, truck drivers, uppers	II/injected, swallowed, smoked, snorted	increased heart rate, blood pressure, metabolism; feelings of exhilaration, energy, increased mental alertness/rapid or irregular heart beat; reduced appetite, weight loss, heart failure, nervousness, insomnia
cocaine	*Cocaine hydrochloride:* blow, bump, C, candy, Charlie, coke, crack, flake, rock, snow, toot	II/injected, smoked, snorted	*Also, for amphetamine—rapid breathing/* tremor, loss of coordination; irritability, anxiousness, restlessness, delirium, panic, paranoia, impulsive behavior, aggressiveness, tolerance, addiction, psychosis
MDMA (methyl-enedioxymeth-amphetamine)	Adam, clarity, ecstasy, Eve, lover's speed, peace, STP, X, XTC	I/swallowed	
methamphetamine	*Desoxyn:* chalk, crank, crystal, fire, glass, go fast, ice, meth, speed	II/injected, swallowed, smoked, snorted	*for cocaine—increased temperature/chest* pain, respiratory failure, nausea, abdominal pain, strokes, seizures, headaches, malnutrition, panic attacks

methylphenidate (safe and effective for treatment of ADHD)	*Ritalin:* JIF, MPH, R-ball, Skippy, the smart drug, vitamin R	II/injected, swallowed, snorted	*for MDMA—mild hallucinogenic effects, increased tactile sensitivity, empathic feelings*/impaired memory and learning, hyperthermia, cardiac toxicity, renal failure, liver toxicity
nicotine	cigarettes, cigars, smokeless tobacco, snuff, spit tobacco, bidis, chew	not scheduled/smoked, snorted, taken in snuff and spit tobacco	*for methamphetamine—aggression, violence, psychotic behavior*/ memory loss, cardiac and neurological damage; impaired memory and learning, tolerance, addiction *for nicotine*—additional effects attributable to tobacco exposure: adverse pregnancy outcomes; chronic lung disease, cardiovascular disease, stroke, cancer; tolerance, addiction
Other Compounds inhalants	*Solvents (paint thinners, gasoline, glues), gases (butane, propane, aerosol propellants, nitrous oxide), nitrites (isoamyl, isobutyl, cyclohexyl):* laughing gas, poppers, snappers, whippets	not scheduled/inhaled through nose or mouth	*stimulation, loss of inhibition; headache; nausea or vomiting; slurred speech, loss of motor coordination; wheezing*/ unconsciousness, cramps, weight loss, muscle weakness, depression, memory impairment, damage to cardiovascular and nervous systems, sudden death

Source: National Institute on Drug Abuse.

HALLUCINOGENS, "CLUB DRUGS," MARIJUANA/CANNABIS, INHALANTS, AND PRESCRIPTION DRUGS

Hallucinogens alter perceptual functions. The term *hallucinogen* rather than, for example, *psychoactive* or *psychedelic*, is a value-laden one. The most frequently used hallucinogens are **LSD** (lysergic acid diethylamide) and **PCP** (**phencyclidine**); both are produced chemically, and neither has any legitimate medical use. There are also organic hallucinogens, such as **mescaline**, which is found in the peyote cactus. The lawful use of peyote is limited to the religious ceremonies of the Native American Church, which some, but not all, states exempt from their controlled substances statutes.

Club drugs is a term used to characterize psychoactive substances associated with dance parties or *raves*, in particular **MDMA**, known as **ecstasy**.

Cannabis, frequently used in the form of marijuana, exhibits some of the characteristics of hallucinogens, depressants, and even stimulants. Its lawful use (in the liquid form of **tetrahydrocannabinol**, or **THC**, its psychoactive ingredient) is limited to the treatment of glaucoma and to reduce some of the side effects of cancer chemotherapy.

Inhalants include a variety of readily available products routinely kept in the home, such as glue, paint thinner, hair spray, and nail polish remover. They produce vapors that, when inhaled, can cause a psychoactive response.

Prescription drugs are available lawfully only with a doctor's prescription and include opiates such as codeine and morphine as well as drugs used to treat depression and other disorders.

ESTIMATING THE EXTENT OF DRUG USE

Most information on drug use in the United States is derived from five indicators, each providing a different perspective on the problem, and they complement one another. Although the indicators have recognized limitations and deficiencies that affect the quality of information, the agencies that prepare them believe the data can reliably portray general trends. Richard Rosenfeld and Scott Decker (1999) found a high correlation between drug use measurements that rely on the criminal justice system (Arrestee Drug Abuse Monitoring) and those based on reports from hospitals and medical examiners (Drug Abuse Warning Network). The fact that these two different indicators tell basically the same story raises confidence in their validity. Those indicators using self-reports (National Survey on Drug Use and Health), however, raise questions, since they have been found to be least valid for the more stigmatized drugs such as heroin and cocaine (General Accounting Office 1998).

Efforts to determine the prevalence of heroin use have a long history, with precise estimates remaining difficult to determine. Standard methods of measuring prevalence such as household surveys are inadequate; for instance, heroin use is rare in the general population, so only a small number of users would be included in a household survey. Survey-based estimates substantially underestimate prevalence because of difficulties in locating heroin abusers (many of them are not living in stable households). In addition, because heroin use involves an illegal activity, heroin users might not accurately report their use. Despite the shortcomings in data reliability, in 2003 the

Drug Enforcement Administration (DEA) stated that since the 1970s overall illegal drug use is down "by more than a third" (2003: 4), with about 123,000 Americans who use heroin at least once a month and 1.7 million who use cocaine at least once a month. By way of comparison, the DEA noted 109 million using alcohol and about 66 million using tobacco at least once a month. Of course, smokers and drinkers are easy to find and more likely to be forthcoming about their use of these substances. For example, I am one of those consuming alcohol at least once a month—actually, a glass of wine once a week—but I do not use tobacco.

NATIONAL SURVEY ON DRUG USE AND HEALTH

Called the National Household Survey on Drug Abuse (NHSDA) before 2002, the National Survey on Drug Use and Health (NSDUH) is funded by the Substance Abuse and Mental Health Services Administration of the U.S. Department of Health and Human Services. NHSDA was conducted every two or three years between 1972 and 1990 and has been conducted annually since 1990. The survey provides data on incidence, prevalence, and trends of drug use for individuals age 12 and older living in households. Results are based on interviews with people randomly selected from the household population, who record their responses on self-administered answer sheets. The NHSDA sample was increased to more than 30,000 interviews in 1991 and to 70,000 interviews in 1999.

The resulting data are used in conjunction with Monitoring the Future survey data (discussed below) to describe levels of drug use in specific segments of the population. The NSDUH data may also be used in conjunction with DAWN data (discussed below) to describe long-term trends in drug abuse. In the past, self-report surveys on drug use have been found to be reasonably trustworthy (Oetting and Beauvais 1990), but questions have been raised (General Accounting Office 1998) about their accuracy.

Survey limitations include the fact that the homeless and people living in military installations, dormitories, and institutions such as jails, prisons, and hospitals are not covered, although the survey attempts to approximate these populations by using a controversial "imputation" procedure (General Accounting Office 1993). Also, some people refuse to participate. Because the survey is voluntary and the questionnaires are self-administered, the results may be biased (and probably understate the scope of the drug problem). Concern has also been expressed over privacy and comprehension issues. During the interviews of 25–30 percent of respondents ages 12 to 17 at the time the survey was administered, a third person was present. And any numbers of people have difficulty with English or with understanding the drug use jargon employed by the survey (General Accounting Office 1993). One observer (Whiteacre 2005: 7) is skeptical of respondent veracity: "It seems quite unlikely that wealthy 'respectable' community members, having more to lose, would come forward about their drug use when surveyed" by the NHSDA.

MONITORING THE FUTURE

The Monitoring the Future (MTF) study is conducted by the Institute for Social Research at the University of Michigan for the National Institute on Drug Abuse.

Annual surveys of high school seniors began in 1975, and eighth- and tenth-grade students were added in 1991. The survey population is chosen to be representative of all students in U.S. public and private schools. About 50,000 students located in more than 400 public and private schools complete questionnaires in their classrooms every spring.

Primary uses of the data include (1) assessing the prevalence and trends of drug use among high school seniors and (2) gaining a better understanding of the lifestyles and value orientations associated with patterns of drug use and monitoring how these orientations are shifting over time. Follow-up surveys of representative subsamples of the original graduates that have been conducted for over a decade provide data on young adults and college students.

The survey has several limitations. High school dropouts (about 30 percent of students), who are associated with higher rates of drug use, are not part of the sampled universe. Chronic absentees, who may also have higher rates of abuse, are less likely to be surveyed (L. Liu 1994). In Texas, for example, youths entering that state's detention facilities are nearly twelve times as likely to have used cocaine as are youngsters in school (Fredlund et al. 1990). Conscious or unconscious distortions in self-reporting information can also bias results. In addition, new trends in drug abuse, such as the use of crack, might not be initially detected because the survey is designed to measure only drugs that are abused at significant levels. Questions about crack cocaine were asked for the first time in the 1986 survey, and questions about ecstasy (MDMA) were first asked in 1996. There is also concern over the lack of anonymity: The name, address, and telephone number of the respondent appear on the questionnaire's cover sheet to facilitate follow-up surveys.

DRUG ABUSE WARNING NETWORK

The Drug Abuse Warning Network (DAWN), which was initiated in 1972 and is funded by the National Institute on Drug Abuse, is a large-scale drug abuse data collection system designed as an early-warning indicator of the nation's drug abuse problem. An episode report is submitted for each drug abuse patient who visits the emergency room of a hospital participating in DAWN and for each drug abuse death encountered by a participating medical examiner or coroner. In a single emergency room episode, a patient might mention having ingested more than one drug. DAWN records each drug a patient reports having used within four days before the hospital visit and relays the information to the DEA. Data are collected from a non-random sample in about twenty selected metropolitan areas throughout the country, representing approximately one third of the U.S. population.

While standard definitions and data collection procedures exist, variations among individual reporters may occur. Incomplete reporting, turnover of reporting facilities and personnel, and reporting delays of up to one year (primarily for medical examiner data) are some of the system's limitations. For hospital emergencies the National Narcotics Intelligence Consumers Committee (NNICC) has used data from the DAWN Consistent Panel rather than data from the Total Panel. The Consistent Panel includes only hospitals that report on a consistent basis (specifically, 90 percent or more of each year). Data representing the total DAWN system were not used for trend analysis by NNICC because of reporting fluctuations. While data from medical examiners and coroners are not subject to the same inconsistencies, these reports are so small in comparison with the total DAWN system that they are not considered a valid trend indicator.

NNICC NARCOTICS INTELLIGENCE ESTIMATES

The National Narcotics Intelligence Consumers Committee is a federal interagency mechanism for coordinating drug intelligence collection requirements and producing joint intelligence estimates. NNICC issues periodic reports on the worldwide illicit drug situation. The report contains estimates of illegal drug production and availability and discusses four major drug categories: marijuana, cocaine, opiates, and synthetic drugs. The report also contains information on drug-trafficking routes and methods and on the flow of drug-related money. Estimates of illegal drug quantities are very difficult to make because little reliable data exist. NNICC obtains drug production data for individual countries from host country records, local contacts, informants, and sophisticated intelligence-gathering techniques. It derives drug availability and consumption estimates from sample surveys, drug seizures, drug price and purity data, drug-related hospital emergencies, and other data. "The number of hectares [hectare = 2.47 acres] under cultivation during any given year is our most solid statistic" and we can "estimate the extent of cultivation with reasonable accuracy" (United States Department of State 2008: 30).

The price and purity levels of illegal drugs at the retail (consumer) level are key values in the NNICC estimating process. The DEA gathers these data, which are used as an indicator of drug availability. Drug prices are derived from a computerized database containing reports on purchases of, and negotiations to purchase, illegal drugs by undercover federal, state, and local law enforcement officers. Purity levels for heroin and cocaine are determined through laboratory analysis. (Purity levels are not applicable to marijuana and most synthetic drugs.) The limited number of reports and lack of randomness are problems that have plagued these indicators in the past (Comptroller General 1988). In addition, the price paid by undercover officers is affected by quantity discounts, thus underestimating the

DRUG STATS

According to the U.S. Department of Justice National Drug Intelligence Center (2009):

- –More than 35 million individuals used illicit drugs or abused prescription drugs in 2007.
- –More than 1,100 children were injured at, killed at, or removed from methamphetamine laboratory sites from 2007 through September 2008.
- –For 2009, the federal government allocated more than $14 billion for drug treatment and prevention, counterdrug law enforcement, drug interdiction, and international counterdrug assistance.
- –In 2007, more than 1.8 million drug-related arrests in the United States were carried out by federal, state, and local law enforcement agencies.

actual per dose retail price; or the officers might pay a premium price because they are not known to their dealers and new customers are typically charged more (Caulkins 1994).

PULSE CHECK

Since 1992 the Office of National Drug Control Policy (ONDCP) has been providing information on illegal drug use and drug markets in twenty-five major U.S. cities as derived from the perceptions of researchers, treatment providers, and law enforcement officials. According to the ONDCP, *Pulse Check* "provides a comprehensive snapshot of drug abuse patterns in communities across the country" (Office of National Drug Control Policy 2004a: 2). While *Pulse Check* offers "a rich picture of the changing drug abuse situation," it is "not intended as a quantitative measure of the prevalence of drug abuse or its consequences" (Office of National Drug Control Policy 2004a: 1).

The report provides answers to a number of concerns, such as:

How difficult is it for undercover police and users to buy drugs?

What are the prices and purity levels?

How have marketing innovations such as packaging, and tools such as use of the Internet complicated law enforcement efforts?

Have there been any changes in sellers and users?

On a scale of 0 to 100, how serious is the perceived drug problem?

How has the perceived drug problem changed: no; somewhat worse; much worse?

How available are treatment programs?

What are the most serious drug problems?

ARRESTEE DRUG ABUSE MONITORING

Arrestee Drug Abuse Monitoring (ADAM) began in New York City in 1987, and by 1990 twenty-five of the largest cities in the United States were involved. By 2000 there were thirty-nine, most of them large urban areas. ADAM was discontinued in 2004 because of a lack of funds—about $8 million annually. In 2007, the Office of Drug Control Policy launched a new, scaled-back arrestee drug-use monitoring program, ADAM II. ADAM II collects data about arrestee drug use from a probability sample of arrestees booked at facilities at ten sites selected from the original 39 ADAM sites.

Demographic, drug use and purchase, housing, method of support, and health insurance data are collected in central police booking facilities in each city. For approximately fourteen consecutive evenings each quarter, staff members obtain voluntary and anonymous urine specimens and interviews from a new sample of arrestees. In each site approximately 225 males are sampled. All female arrestees, regardless of charge, are included in the sample because of the small number of female arrestees available. Responses are consistently high: Over 90 percent agree to be interviewed, and more than 80 percent of those interviewed provided urine specimens.

To obtain samples with a sufficient distribution of arrest charges, the number of male arrestees in each sample charged with drug-related offenses (sale or possession) is limited—one out of five most likely to be using drugs at the time of their arrest—and thus undersampled. ADAM statistics are thus minimum estimates of drug use of male arrestees.

Urine samples are analyzed for ten drugs: cocaine, opiates, marijuana, PCP, methadone, benzodiazepine (Valium), methaqualone, propoxyphene (Darvon), barbiturates, and amphetamines. Except for marijuana and PCP, which can be detected several weeks after use, urine tests detect use in the previous two to three days. ADAM data reveals that marijuana is the most commonly detected substance among arrestees, cocaine is the second, and heroin remains important but far less popular; methamphetamine was most likely to be found among arrestees in Western states.

A number of validation issues arose with respect to ADAM. Central booking facilities, where the samples are selected, serve different areas of a city or county. This makes generalizing to the wider population of arrestees unreliable. The busy, if not frantic, pace of most central booking facilities makes respondent selection procedures difficult, leading to questions about sampling techniques. And a study by the General Accounting Office (1993) revealed that ADAM standards in selecting arrestees had not been applied uniformly across sites. Further, the nature of lockups in booking facilities made confidentiality difficult to achieve.

Peter Reuter (1999: 18) concluded that each of the four drug use indicators provides useful information: "Monitoring the Future provided early indications of the cocaine epidemic, while ADAM did a good job in tracking its later stages. DAWN has shown that drug problems can increase even as the rate of drug use in the population stabilizes and has provided compelling evidence that drug problems are disproportionately borne by poor and urban minority populations. The National Household Survey on Drug Abuse has provided an essential measure of the decline in drug use in the general population through the 1980s."

DRUG USE: HOW MUCH, HOW MANY?

What do the indicators reveal? About 20 million Americans aged 12 or older use illegal drugs, primarily marijuana. There are an estimated 400,000 heroin users, while about 4 million individuals have used heroin at least once in their lifetime. An estimated 2 million Americans aged 12 and older are regular users of cocaine and an additional 3 million are occasional users. Cocaine use reached a peak of 5.7 million users in 1985. About 9 million people have tried methamphetamine at least once, but the number of adolescents using methamphetamine has fallen steadily since it was first measured in 1999. Among adolescents, ages 12–17, about 2.5 million use illegal drugs, mostly marijuana whose use among teenagers has been declining—slightly more than 32 percent of twelfth graders reported past year marijuana use in 2008.

The numbers for alcohol have remained the same for years: More than 60 percent of the U.S. population age 12 and older use alcohol, while more than 55 million admit to binge drinking (drinking five or more drinks on the same occasion on at least one day in the past thirty days). About 30 percent of twelfth graders admit

Suspected of being intoxicated, a teenager attempts to walk a straight line for law enforcement. Statistics prove that youth who experiment with alcohol are most likely to use marijuana and other drugs later on.

to binge drinking and there are an estimated 11 million underage drinkers. More than 11 percent of pregnant women reported alcohol use, while drinking and driving remained a serious problem, with more than 32 million individuals reporting having been behind the wheel while intoxicated. About 40 percent of traffic fatalities involve the use of alcohol.

Nicotine-smoking rates in the United States have remained virtually unchanged for more than a decade with an estimated 70 million smokers and an additional 7 million use smokeless tobacco. This represents almost a 50 percent decline since 1965 and since 2001 there has been a significant reduction (33 percent) in the number of high school students who smoke. Still, about one in four adolescents smokes cigarettes. The highest rate of tobacco use (about 40 percent) continues to be among those aged 18 to 25. More than 10 percent of pregnant women are cigarette smokers. Adults who live below the poverty line are more likely to smoke than are those living above the poverty line, and high school dropouts are three times more likely to smoke than are college graduates. About 44.5 million adults describe themselves as smokers who had quit.

Adolescent drug use began increasing dramatically in the late 1960s, peaked in 1979, and then fell through the 1980s, hitting lows in 1991 and 1992 before beginning to climb again. By the end of the 1990s it remained steady, with only minor fluctuations. The year 2001 marked the fifth year in a row that drug and alcohol use among eighth, ninth, and twelfth graders remained stable or, in some cases such as cigarette smoking, decreased. In 2002, for the first time, smoking, drinking, and the use of illegal drugs among adolescents fell simultaneously. The use of

MDMA (ecstasy) also showed statistically significant declines for the first time. The only significant increases in drug use were crack cocaine use by tenth graders and use of sedatives by twelfth graders. From 2001 to 2007 there was almost a 20 percent decline in illicit teen drug use, and while the decline in smoking had leveled off, it was at the lowest rate in the thirty years. The 2007 statistics revealed that while the decline in drug—mostly marijuana—and alcohol use was continuing, the decrease in daily cigarette smoking ended, and an increase in the misuse of prescription drugs such as OxyContin and Vicodin was continuing.

The "good news" found in these indicators contrasts markedly with data on drug-related deaths that increased 400 percent in two decades, reaching 28,000 in 2004, a year when there were 940,000 drug-related hospital emergency cases (Males 2006). In 2005, the most recent year for which data is available, there were 22,400 overdose deaths. Prescription painkillers were implicated in nearly 40 percent of these deaths (Office of National Drug Control Strategy 2009a).

These drugs are popular because even without a doctor's prescription, access is increasing. Restocking trips are often taken to Mexico, where the black market continues to grow. It is estimated that Tijuana alone has about 1,700 pharmacies, many of which sell controlled substances illegally over the counter. And in some instances doctors in Mexico sell prescriptions (Kirsebbaum 2002). Diversion from lawful sources, often the result of "doctor shopping" or overprescribing, has gained more attention in recent years (Querna 2005). One aspect of this problem is trafficking in the synthetic opiate **OxyContin**, particularly in rural areas of the United States that have not heretofore had a drug problem. In the rural Appalachian region, which has many miners with injuries and a shortage of doctors, prescribing of the drug has often been indiscriminate. A similar situation has occurred among injured steelworkers in Eastern Ohio. The result has been diversion to the black market. In these areas, a number of doctors have been convicted for overprescribing (Bowman 2005).

One physician set up a pain management practice in Portsmith, Ohio. At about the same time police noticed a startling rise in drug-related crime. Undercover agents were dispatched to the pain clinic. With little or no physical examination, each paid $200 and was given a prescription for OxyContin, the powerful synthetic opiate. In a subsequent raid agents found almost $500,000 in cash and passbooks for offshore accounts ("'Poor Man's Heroin'" 2001). In 2002 a 55-year-old Florida medical doctor received a sentence of sixty-two years in prison after a manslaughter conviction that involved running an OxyContin "pill mill" that was linked to several overdose deaths (Associated Press 2002).

The National Institute on Drug Abuse estimates that 48 million Americans over age 12 have used prescription drugs for nonmedical reasons in their lifetime and approximately 7 million individuals aged 12 or older are current (past month) nonmedical users of prescription-type psychotherapeutic drugs: opioid pain relievers, tranquilizers, sedatives, or stimulants (National Drug Intelligence Center 2009b). About 10 percent of high school students report nonmedical use of prescription drugs. "The elderly are among those most vulnerable to prescription abuse or misuse because they are prescribed more medications than their younger counterparts" (National Institute on Drug Abuse 2005: 1).

In 2003 it was revealed that methadone, often prescribed for treating chronic pain, is being diverted to the black market and abused by recreational drug users, often with deadly consequences. There has been an alarming number of methadone overdose fatalities, which since 1997 have surpassed those from heroin. Methadone is usually taken when the drug of choice, heroin or OxyContin, is not readily available (Belluck 2003).

In 2005 people who used prescription drugs nonmedically were asked how they obtained the drugs they used most recently. Almost 60 percent got the drugs from "a friend" for free; about 17 percent were prescribed the drugs by a doctor; about 4 percent purchased them from a dealer or other stranger; and about 1 percent bought them over the Internet (*SAMHSA News* 2006).

A related issue is the abuse, usually by adolescents, of over-the-counter medications, in particular cough medicines containing **dextromethorphan** (DXM). Although DXM is generally recognized as safe when used appropriately, when taken in large amounts, it produces hallucinations and a "high" similar to that of PCP.

DRUGS AND CRIME

A great deal of the concern over drugs is their connection to crime. The traditional way of considering the question of drugs and crime is the tripartite model offered by Paul Goldstein (1985):

1. *Pharmacological*: offenses that are psychopharmacology induced, that is, the result of a response to the intoxicating effects of a drug, including biological features discussed in Chapter 3
2. *Economic-compulsive*: crime driven by a need to buy drugs
3. *Systemic/Lifestyle*: drug use as part of a pattern of criminal behaviors but not driven by or the result of drug use, for example, violence associated with the business of drugs

The outlawing of certain drugs creates criminal opportunity for those daring enough to enter this market (discussed in Chapter 11). They become part of a business that has no mechanisms for resolving disputes except violence. The outlawing of certain drugs also makes the people who use these chemicals (actually, the crime is "possession" of the drugs) criminals while substantially inflating the cost of the substances to the consumer. To secure their preferred substance, abusers of illegal drugs typically target salable property but will also commit robbery and/or sell drugs. There is a criminal population whose nondrug law violations are based only on their desire to secure drugs. However, it is also clear that an unknown percentage, perhaps a majority, of drug users, particularly those addicted to heroin, were criminals whose drug use is simply part of a pattern of hedonistic and antisocial behavior. George Vaillant (1970: 488) reports that no matter what their class origins, most people who use narcotics "have a greater tendency than their socioeconomic peers to be delinquent," and even drug-abusing physicians "are relatively irresponsible before drug addiction."[1]

---

[1]Concern over the abuse of morphine by medical doctors dates back to at least the latter part of the nineteenth century (Mattison 1883), and in 1961 Charles Winick wrote of the physician addict, a loner who does not knowingly associate with other addicts. In fact, drug abuse is a significant problem for the medical profession, with the addiction rate for physicians estimated at anywhere from 30 to 100 times that for the population at large (Grosswirth 1982; Kennedy 1995; McDougal 2006).

In a study of drug addicts in a treatment (DATOS) program, drug use played an earlier role than it did in offender-based studies. But among the general population, other forms of deviance or criminality precede the onset of illicit drug use. However, "those who began committing crimes after initiating regular drug use were much less likely to engage in predatory (relative to victimless) crime than those for whom criminality preceded regular drug use" (Farabee, Joshi, and Anglin 2001: 217).

A Canadian study revealed that the choice of drugs influences involvement in crime: high frequency crack use, for example, was correlated with property crime, sex work, and drug dealing, while high frequency heroin use was associated with property crime and sex work; high frequency cocaine use was associated with sex work only, and the use of prescription opioids was not related to any type of crime (Fischer and Rehm 2007). Another study found that polydrug users have a higher rate of offending than those whose pattern of use is narrower; a lifestyle explanation appears to be the best fit (Bennett and Holloway 2005).

RESEARCH ON ADOLESCENTS

Research has determined that "youngsters who have conduct problems are more likely than others to be exposed to illicit drugs" (Swan n.d.: 1). Adolescents with emotional and behavioral problems are more likely to abuse alcohol, tobacco, and illicit drugs, according to a study by the Substance Abuse and Mental Health Services Administration (1999). The study found that adolescents who were inclined toward substance abuse admitted to delinquent behaviors such as stealing, cutting classes or skipping school, and hanging around with others who get into trouble. They also reported poor peer and parental relations and such problems as difficulty concentrating in school or focusing attention on tasks at home, at part-time work, or even when involved in sports.

When compared to adolescents having fewer or less serious behavioral problems, adolescents who repeatedly stole, showed physical aggression, or ran away from home were seven times as likely to be dependent on alcohol or illicit drugs. They were more than four times as likely to have used marijuana in the past month and seven times more likely to have used other illicit drugs. They were nearly three times as likely to have used alcohol in the past month, three times as likely to have smoked cigarettes in the past month, and nearly nine times as likely to need treatment for drug abuse. According to the 2001 National Household Survey on Drug Abuse (discussed earlier), youths who engaged in violent behaviors during the past year were more likely to report past month alcohol and illicit drug use than were youths who did not engage in violent behaviors during the past year.

A study of male adolescent ninth- and tenth-graders in Washington, D.C., found that for about half of those who used drugs (mostly marijuana), criminal behavior preceded use; for the other half criminal behavior followed drug use. However, "those both using and selling drugs were more than twice as likely to have started using drugs before committing crimes as were those using but not selling drugs" (Brounstein et al. 1990: 3–4). In fact, we cannot be sure whether drug abuse leads to crime or criminals tend to abuse drugs (or perhaps neither); there

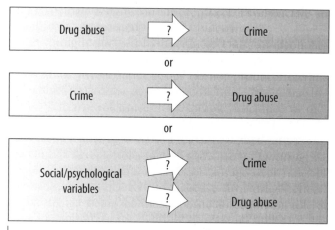

FIGURE 1.2 | RELATIONSHIP BETWEEN DRUGS AND CRIME: THREE POSSIBILITIES

are variables that lead to drug abuse, and the same variables lead to crime (see Figure 1.2) (McBride and McCoy 1981; see also Speckart and Anglin 1985, 1987). Indeed, areas with high levels of delinquency and crime also have high levels of drug usage, while the reverse is also true. In their study, Cheryl Carpenter and her colleagues (1988) found that the most seriously delinquent adolescents also abused drugs, but crime and drug use appeared to be independent of one another, both apparently being related to other causal variables. In fact, extensive research informs us that a relatively small segment of youths commit a disproportionate amount of juvenile crime, and "the majority of serious crimes committed by youths are concentrated among serious delinquents who are also heavy users of alcohol and other drugs" (B. D. Johnson et al. 1991: 206). For these individuals both drug use and crime appear to be part of a troubled lifestyle.

RESEARCH ON ADULTS

There is undoubtedly a high correlation between drug use and nondrug crime (e.g., Gandossy et al. 1980; B. D. Johnson et al. 1985; Nurco et al. 1985; Inciardi 1986; Wish and Johnson 1986). One study found that more than half of the men arrested in twelve major cities tested positive for recent use of illicit drugs (Kerr 1988). "A strong consensus has emerged in the research literature that the most frequent, serious offenders are also the heaviest drug users" (Visher 1990: 330). However, is it drug use that leads to criminal behavior?

The question of whether crime is a predrug use or postdrug use phenomenon is actually an oversimplification, and James Inciardi (1981: 59) argues that "the pursuit of some simple cause-and-effect relationship may be futile." His data found:

> Among the males there seems to be a clear progression from alcohol to crime, to drug abuse, to arrest and then to heroin use. But on closer inspection the pattern is not altogether clear. At one level, for example, criminal activity can be viewed as predating

one's drug-using career, because the median point of the first crime is slightly below that of first drug abuse and is considerably before the onset of heroin use. But at the same time, if alcohol intoxication at a median age of 13.3 years were to be considered substance abuse, then crime is clearly a phenomenon that succeeds substance abuse. Among the females the description is even more complex. In the population of female heroin users criminal activity occurred after both alcohol and other drug abuse and marijuana use but before involvement with the more debilitating barbiturates and heroin.

A study of heroin addicts in Wilmington, Delaware, revealed criminal and drug careers were rather independent of one another, the two merging as the use of heroin become overarching (Faupel and Klockars 1987).

This issue has serious policy implications. If drug abusers simply continue in crime after they have given up drug use, efforts to reduce crime by reducing drug abuse are doomed to fail. As James Q. Wilson (1975: 137) points out, perhaps "some addicts who steal to support their habit come to regard crime as more profitable than normal employment. They would probably continue to steal to provide themselves with an income even after they no longer needed to use part of that income to buy heroin" or any other illegal substance. M. Douglas Anglin and George Speckart (1988: 223) found, however, "that levels of criminality after the addiction career [is over] are near zero, a finding that is compatible with data presented by other authors and is illustrative of the 'maturing out' phase of the addiction career 'life cycle.'"

In fact, the sequence of drug use and crime has produced contradictory findings (Huizinga, Menard, and Elliott 1989). For example, James Vorenberg and Irving Lukoff (1973) found that the criminal careers of a substantial segment of the heroin addicts they studied antedated the onset of heroin use. Furthermore, they found that those whose criminality preceded heroin use tended to be more involved in violent criminal behavior. Anglin and Speckart (1988) report that between 60 and 75 percent of the addicts in their samples had arrest histories that preceded addiction. Paul Cushman (1974: 43) found, however, that the heroin addicts he studied were predominantly noncriminal before addiction and experienced "progressively increased rates of annual arrests after addiction started." (Of course, this finding could be the result of addicts being less adept at crime.) Whatever the relationship—drug abuse leading to crime or criminals becoming drug abusers—some researchers (McGlothlin, Anglin, and Wilson 1978; Ball et al. 1979; B. D. Johnson, Lipton, and Wish 1986a) have found that the amount of criminality tends to be sharply reduced when people who have been narcotic addicts are no longer addicted. Furthermore, Bruce Johnson and his colleagues (1985, 1989) and Anglin and Speckart (1988) found that the more frequent the drug use, the more serious the types of crimes committed, for example, burglary and robbery instead of shoplifting and other larcenies.

The question of the relationship between crime and drug abuse has typically been related to the abuse of heroin, not cocaine. During the time that this writer was a parole officer in New York (1964–1978), offenders who had used cocaine were rare, while studies by the New York State Division of Parole indicated that those who had used heroin were a substantial majority of parole clientele in the New York City area. Almost four decades ago, Troy Duster (1970: 42) was able to state that "cocaine usage is rare in the United States." However, during the 1980s the abuse of cocaine dramatically increased in the same populations that have traditionally been the major consumers of heroin. During these years cocaine use crossed social class lines, and the age of onset dropped considerably. Furthermore,

> [u]ntil recently, it has been assumed that cocaine was not a criminogenic force toward income-generating crime because cocaine does not have the physiological addictive power of heroin and because cocaine users were viewed as unlikely to come from population groups with high crime rates. Cocaine was thought to be a drug of the middle and upper classes. These assumptions appear to be unjustified. Weekly and daily cocaine use is associated with high levels of illegal income. (J. Collins, Hubbard, and Rachel 1985: 759)

During the 1980s cocaine (in the smokable form known as crack), not heroin, became the "in" drug among 18- to 25-year-old young adults in the low-income areas of New York City. This was a dramatic change from the drug scene of the late 1960s and 1970s, when heroin was the major problem. Furthermore, heroin abusers typically use cocaine, many as frequently as they do heroin, in a combination known as a speedball. The use of these substances, David Smith (1986) notes, is part of a lifestyle that also includes abuse of alcohol, marijuana, barbiturates, and amphetamines—and crime. In one study of 105 drug abusers, cocaine was the primary drug of choice, and 50 percent also abused alcohol (B. D. Johnson, Anderson, and Wish 1989). And one study found that the business of crack is crime-intensive in that it "leads serious delinquents to become even more seriously involved in crime" (Inciardi and Pottieger 1991: 268). It appears that crack intensifies the criminal behaviors in which users were actively involved before initiation into crack use, except for women; they moved from property crimes to prostitution (Chin and Fagan 1990). Indeed, the significant drop in homicides in some major cities, New York in particular, is, at least in part, attributed to the decline in crack use by young people.

The National Institute of Justice concludes: "Assessing the nature and extent of the influence of drugs on crime requires that reliable information about the offense and the offender be available, and that definitions be consistent. In face of problematic evidence, it is impossible to say quantitatively how much drugs influence the occurrence of crime" (1995a: 3). While "there is a generally consistent overall pattern of positive and sometimes quite strong associations between illegal drug use and criminal behavior of other types," research has not been able to validate a causal link between drug use and criminal behavior (Anthony and Forman 2000: 27). While many different data sources establish a raw correlation between drug use and criminal offenses, correlation does not equal causation. Thus, drug use might cause (promote or encourage) crime, or criminality might cause (promote or encourage) drug use, and/or both may be caused (promoted or encouraged) by other variables—environmental, situational, and/or biological (MacCoun, Kilmer, and Reuter 2002).

DRUGS USE AND VIOLENCE

According to the Drug Enforcment Administration (2003: 16), "there is ample scientific evidence that demonstrates the links between drugs, violence, and crime. Drugs often cause people to do things they wouldn't do if they were rational and free of the influence of drugs." More than three decades ago, Edwin Schur (1965) argued that narcotic addiction in the United States seems to reduce the inclination to engage in violent crime. However, a more recent research effort found that heroin users (not necessarily addicts) are at least as violent as, and perhaps more violent than, their non-drug-using or non-heroin-using criminal counterparts (B. D. Johnson, Lipton, and Wish 1986a), which is consistent with the writer's experience as a parole officer. In fact, the researchers report, "About half of the most violent criminals are heroin abusers" (B. D. Johnson, Lipton, and Wish 1986b: 3). It is difficult to determine whether this is simply a problem of changing definitions or one of a changing drug population. While there is no evidence that crime results from the direct effects of heroin itself—indeed, the substance appears to have a pacifying effect—the irritability resulting from withdrawal symptoms has been known to lead to violence (P. Goldstein 1985).

This writer dealt with heroin addicts for fourteen years and found many, if not most, to be quite capable of committing violent acts, including homicide—they were frequently convicted of violent crimes. In addition, as we shall discuss in Chapter 11, the heroin distribution subculture at every level—from wholesaling to street sale—is permeated with extreme levels of violence. And, as was noted earlier, many drug abusers use more than one psychoactive chemical (polydrug abuse), thus expanding the possible behavioral effects of the different combinations. If the additional substance is alcohol, which is relatively inexpensive, the drug-crime nexus is mitigated, at least for income-generating crimes; a great deal of violent noneconomic crime is known to be linked to alcohol intoxication. Crimes against persons and violence by drug users are often related to their use of alcohol (Dembo et al. 1991; P. Goldstein et al. 1991). And a Canadian study found that alcohol-dependent prison inmates were twice as likely to have committed violent crimes as their most serious crime compared with prisoners who were dependent on other drugs ("Canadian study quantifies link between substance abuse and crime: alcohol abuse associated with violent offenses" 2002). Similar findings were reported by Susan Martin and her colleagues (2004), who found that while cocaine was not associated with violent crime, alcohol was. While violence associated with cocaine involved dealing, alcohol-related violence was usually the result of interpersonal disputes—insults and arguments involving intoxicated offenders.

Alcohol is an important element in a great deal of crime: Drunk driving is the cause of about 16,000 deaths annually; more than 60 percent of homicides involve alcohol use by both offender and victim; and about 65 percent of aggressive sexual acts against women involve alcohol use by the offender. More than 30 percent of men who murder or attempt to murder their intimate partners are problem drinkers who were using alcohol at the time of the offense (Sharps et al. 2003).

Research has revealed that the pharmacological effects of alcohol can cause aggression in some people and that alcohol is a factor in nearly half of the murders, suicides, and accidental deaths in the United States; it is a factor in nearly 40 percent of violent crimes ("Coming to Grips with Alcohol" 1987; Chermack and Taylor 1995; Associated Press 1998, 1999a; Greenfeld 1998).

More than 20 percent of prison inmates incarcerated for violent crimes were under the influence of alcohol when they committed their crime (National Center on Addiction and Substance Abuse 1998). But is there a causal link: Would the crimes have been committed in the absence of alcohol? Was alcohol used to provide "courage" for an act that was already being planned? One study found that "intoxication primarily affects adolescents who already have violent tendencies. These are the 'mean drunks'" (Felson, Teasdale, and Burchfield 2008: 137). We know that alcohol consumption can lead to disinhibition, but what distinguishes "the life of the party" from the felonious assailant? Alcohol can also impair the processing of information and judgment, thus causing a misinterpretation of events or the behavior of others, resulting, for example, in assault and/or aggressive sexual behavior such as "date rape."

Other drugs (e.g., PCP and cocaine) may involve otherwise normal people in violent behavior. The Detroit medical examiner's office reported that 37 percent of that city's homicide victims had cocaine in their blood samples (Franklin 1987), indicating that cocaine users either engage in dangerous behavior or expose themselves to places or situations in which violence is likely to occur. And people who are intent on committing violent crimes, such as robbery, may ingest alcohol or stimulants for courage—alcohol in small doses acts as a stimulant (W. A. Hunt 1983). "The relationship between drugs and violence has been consistently documented in both the popular press and in social scientific research" (P. Goldstein 1985: 494).

Research has found that crack users are more likely to commit crimes against persons than against property. Crack sellers also appear to be more violent than other drug sellers, and their violence is not limited to drug transactions (Belenko and Chin 1989; Fagan and Chin 1991). There was a surge in children beaten and killed by their crack-abusing parents (Kerr 1988). However, a study in Kansas City, Missouri, of almost 1,500 arrestees, about half of whom abused cocaine, found "no reason to believe that drug using offenders, especially those characterized by heavy or addictive use, are more likely to be arrested for serious or violent offenses than nondrug using offenders. At the very least, it appears that nondrug using offenders commit a relatively higher rate of violent and predatory crimes" (Whitlock, Collings, and Burnett 1990: 21).

Now that we have introduced the topic, in Chapter 2 we will examine the history of drugs and drug abuse.

SUMMARY

- Statutes distinguish between lawful drugs such as nicotine and alcohol and illegal drugs such as heroin and cocaine, but biology recognizes no such distinction.
- Nicotine is a drug that meets the rigorous criteria for abuse liability and dependence potential, and cigarettes are one of the major drugs of addiction in the United.
- Both tobacco and alcohol share a role as "gateway drugs" that presage use of other psychoactive drugs.
- The *use* of psychoactive chemicals, licit or illicit, can objectively be labeled drug *abuse* only when the user becomes dysfunctional as a consequence; for example, if he or she is unable to maintain employment, has impaired social relationships, exhibits dangerous, reckless, or aggressive behavior, and/or significantly endangers his or her health.
- What we know about those who use psychoactive drugs is skewed toward compulsive users, particularly with respect to illegal drugs. Noncompulsive users have received very little research attention because they are hard to find.

- Addiction denotes a complex illness characterized by repeated, compulsive, at times uncontrollable behavior that persists even in the face of adverse social, psychological, and/or physical consequences.
- Psychoactive drugs can fit into three categories according to their primary effect on the central nervous system: depressants, stimulants, and hallucinogens.
- Most information on drug use in the United States is derived from five indicators.

- The connection between drug use and crime can be: 1. pharmacological; 2. economic compulsive; and 3. systemic/lifestyle.
- We cannot be sure whether drug abuse leads to crime or criminals tend to abuse drugs; if there are variables that lead to drug abuse, and the same variables lead to crime.
- Alcohol is an important element in a great deal of crime, but not necessarily the cause.

Review Questions

1. What is the most common substance abuse disorder in the United States?
2. What are the elements of the definition of drug addiction?
3. How does polydrug use make the issue of drug abuse more complicated?
4. Why can tobacco and alcohol be defined as "gateway drugs?"
5. What are the social consequences of the imprecision of defining "drugs?"
6. Why is *drug abuse* not a scientific term?
7. What are the criteria for labeling drug use as drug *abuse*?
8. What are the two extremes in the drug use continuum?
9. What characterizes a recreational drug user?
10. Why is our knowledge of those who use psychoactive drugs skewed toward compulsive users?
11. Why have noncompulsive drug users received little research attention?
12. Explain: How a society defines drug abuse determines how society responds to drug use.
13. What are the three categories of psychoactive substances and what is the basis for their classification?
14. What are the two most frequently used stimulants?
15. What is the primary affect of a hallucinogen?
16. What are the problems in trying to determine the extent of illegal drug use?
17. What are the three possible connections between drug use and crime?
18. What are the possible connections between alcohol use and violent behavior?
19. What policy implications flow from the relationship between drugs and criminal behavior?

The United States of America during the nineteenth century could quite properly be described as a dope fiend's paradise.

Edward M. Brecher (1972: 3)

| # DRUG USE, DRUG ABUSE, AND DRUG LEGISLATION: A HISTORY

The history of drug use and attempts at its control provide insight into the complexity of more contemporary control, enforcement, and social issues on this subject. As with many attempts at historical analyses, we are handicapped by the lack of adequate data on a number of items, particularly the extent of drug abuse at earlier periods in our history and of alcohol use during Prohibition. Providing an empirically based analysis of changing policies with respect to drugs is difficult without the ability to measure the effect of these changes, and in fact, we cannot provide such measurements. Even today the number of people abusing various substances, from alcohol to heroin, is the subject of debate.

Policy decisions, as we shall see in this chapter, have frequently been based on perceptions, beliefs, and attitudes with little empirical foundation. They have often reflected popular prejudices against a variety of racial and ethnic groups: "What we think about addiction very much depends on who is addicted" (Courtwright 1982: 3). And sometimes policy has reflected concern over issues of international, rather than domestic, politics. Because the earliest drug prohibitions in the United States reflected a concern with alcohol, we will begin our examination with a history of that substance.

ALCOHOL AND THE TEMPERANCE MOVEMENT

Drinking alcoholic beverages for recreational purposes has an ancient history, with records of such use dating back more than 5,000 years. The Bible records that Noah planted a vineyard and drank of the wine "and was drunken" (*Genesis* 9: 21). Later we are told that the daughters of Lot made their father drunk with wine to trick him into propagating the family line (*Genesis* 19: 32–36). This unseemly use of alcohol could certainly serve as an object lesson against its use, but the practice of drinking alcoholic beverages appears near universal.

The citizens of the United States have traditionally consumed large quantities of alcohol. "Early Americans drank alcohol at home and at work, and alcohol was ever-present in colonial social life" (W. L. White 1998: 1). When he retired from politics, George Washington started a whiskey business. In 1785 Dr. Benjamin Rush, the Surgeon General of the Continental Army and a signer of the Declaration of Independence, authored a pamphlet decrying the use of high-proof alcohol, which he claimed caused, among other maladies, moral degeneration, poverty, and crime. This helped to fuel the move toward prohibition and inspired the establishment in 1808 of the Union Temperance Society, the first of many such organizations (Musto 1998). The Society was superseded by the American Temperance Union in 1836, and the work of the Union was supported by Protestant churches throughout the country. But the movement was divided over appropriate goals and strategies: Should moderation be preached, or should abstinence be forced through prohibition? "Between 1825 and 1850, the tide turned toward abstinence as a goal and legal alcohol prohibition as the means" (W. L. White 1998: 5).

The abstinence view differs from the modern alcoholism movement in that it maintained that alcohol is inevitably dangerous for everyone: "Some people might believe they can drink moderately, but it is only a matter of time before they encounter increasing problems and completely lose control of their drinking." Thus, "as strange as it seems to us today, the temperance message thus was that alcohol is inevitably addicting, in the same way that we now think of narcotics" (Peele 1995: 37).

Opposition to alcohol was often intertwined with **nativism**, and efforts against alcohol and other psychoactive drugs were often a thinly veiled reaction to minority groups. (The early temperance movement, however, was strongly abolitionist.) Prohibitionists were typically rural, white Protestants antagonistic to urban Roman Catholics, particularly the Irish, who used the social world of the saloon to gain political power in large cities such as New York and Chicago (Abadinsky 2010).

The temperance movement made great progress everywhere in the country, and it often coincided with the anti-immigrant sentiment that swept over the United States during the 1840s and early 1850s. In 1843 this led to the formation in New York of the American Republican Party, which spread nationally as the Native American Party, or the "Know-Nothings." (Many clubs were secret, and when outsiders inquired about the group, they were met with the response "I know nothing.") Allied with a faction of the Whig Party, the Know-Nothings almost captured New York in 1854, and they did succeed in carrying Delaware and Massachusetts. They also won important victories in Pennsylvania, Rhode Island, New Hampshire, Connecticut, Maryland, Kentucky, and California. In 1855 the city of Chicago elected a Know-Nothing mayor, and prohibition legislation was enacted in the Illinois legislature (but was defeated in a public referendum that same year [Asbury 1950]). By 1855 about a third of the United States had prohibition laws, and other states were considering their enactment (Musto 1998). Slavery and abolition and the ensuing Civil War subsequently took the place of temperance as the day's most pressing issue (Buchanan 1992).

In 1869 the Prohibition Party attempted, with only limited success, to make alcohol a national issue. In 1874 the Women's Christian Temperance Union was established. Issues of temperance and nativism arose again strongly during the 1880s, leading to the formation of the American Protective Association, a rural-based organization that was strongly anti-Catholic and anti-Semitic.[1] In 1893 the Anti-Saloon League was organized.

Around the turn of the century, these groups moved from efforts to change individual behavior to a campaign for national prohibition. After a period of dormancy, the prohibition movement was revived in the years 1907–1919 (Humphries and Greenberg 1981). By 1910 the Anti-Saloon League had become one of the most effective political action groups in U.S. history; it had mobilized Protestant churches behind a single purpose: to enact national prohibition (Tindall 1988). In 1915 nativism and prohibitionism fueled the rise of the Ku Klux Klan, and this time the KKK spread into Northern states and exerted a great deal of political influence. During World War I an additional element, anti-German xenophobia, was added because brewing and distilling were associated with German immigrants (Cashman 1981).

---

[1]For an excellent history of nativism in the United States, see Bennett (1988).

Big business was also interested in prohibition. Alcohol contributed to industrial inefficiency, labor strife, and the saloon, which served the interests of machine politics:

> Around 1908, just as the Anti-Saloon League was preparing for a broad state-by-state drive toward national prohibition, a number of businessmen contributed the funds essential for an effective campaign. The series of quick successes that followed coincided with an equally impressive number of wealthy converts, so that as the movement entered its final stage after 1913, it employed not only ample financing but a sudden urban respectability as well. Substantial citizens now spoke about a new discipline with the disappearance of the saloon and the rampaging drunk. Significantly, prominent Southerners with one eye to the Negro and another to the poorer whites were using exactly the same arguments. (Wiebe 1967: 290–291)

Workmen's compensation laws also helped to stimulate business support for temperance. Between 1911 and 1920 forty-one states had enacted work-men's compensation laws, and Sean Cashman (1981: 6) points out: "By making employers compensate workers for industrial accidents the law obligated them to campaign for safety through sobriety. In 1914 the National Safety Council adopted a resolution condemning alcohol as a cause of industrial accidents."

NATIONAL PROHIBITION

Acrimony between rural and urban America, between Protestants and Catholics, between Republicans and (non-southern) Democrats, between "native" Americans and more recent immigrants, and between business and labor reached a pinnacle with the 1919 ratification of the Eighteenth Amendment. According to William Chambliss (1973: 10), **Prohibition** was accomplished by the political efforts of an economically declining segment of the American middle class: "By effort and some good luck this class was able to impose its will on the majority of the population through rather dramatic changes in the law." Andrew Sinclair (1962: 163) points out that "in fact, national prohibition was a measure passed by village America against urban America." We could add that it was also passed by much of Protestant America against Catholic (and, to a lesser extent, Jewish) America: "Thousands of Protestant churches held thanksgiving prayer meetings. To many of the people who attended, prohibition represented the triumph of America's towns and rural districts over the sinful cities" (Sinclair 1962; Gusfield 1963; Coffey 1975: 7). Mississippi was the first state to ratify Prohibition.

The Eighteenth Amendment to the Constitution was ratified by the thirty-sixth state, Nebraska, on January 16, 1919. According to its own terms, the amendment became effective on January 16, 1920. Ten months after ratification, over a veto by President Woodrow Wilson, Congress passed the National Prohibition Act, usually referred to as the **Volstead Act** after its sponsor, Congressman Andrew Volstead of Minnesota. The Volstead Act strengthened the language of the amendment and defined as intoxicating all beverages containing more than 0.5 percent alcohol; it also provided for federal enforcement. Thus, the Prohibition Bureau, an arm of the Treasury Department, was created, soon becoming notorious for employing agents on the basis of political patronage.

In addition to being inept and corrupt, bureau agents were a public menace. By 1930, 86 federal agents and 200 civilians had been killed, many of them innocent women and children. Prohibition agents set up illegal roadblocks and searched cars; drivers who protested were in danger of being shot. Agents who killed innocent civilians were rarely brought to justice; when they were indicted by local grand juries, the cases were simply transferred, and the agents escaped punishment (Woodiwiss 1988). The bureau was viewed as a training school for bootleggers because agents frequently left the service to join their wealthy adversaries.

The response of a large segment of the American population also proved to be a problem. People do not necessarily acquiesce to new criminal prohibitions, and general resistance can be fatal to the new norm (Packer 1968). Moreover, primary resistance or opposition to a new law such as Prohibition can result, secondarily, in disregard for laws in general—negative contagion. During Prohibition, notes Sinclair (1962: 292), a "general tolerance of the bootlegger and a disrespect for federal law were translated into a widespread contempt for the process and duties of democracy." This was exemplified by the general lawlessness that reigned in Chicago:

> Banks all over Chicago were robbed in broad daylight by bandits who scorned to wear masks. Desk sergeants at police stations grew weary of recording holdups—from one hundred to two hundred were reported every night. Burglars marked out sections of the city as their own and embarked upon a course of systematic plundering, going from house to house night after night without hindrance.... Payroll robberies were a weekly occurrence and necessitated the introduction of armored cars and armed guards for the delivery of money from banks to business houses. Automobiles were stolen by the thousands. Motorists were forced to the curbs on busy streets and boldly robbed. Women who displayed jewelry in nightclubs or at the theater were followed and held up. Wealthy women seldom left their homes unless accompanied by armed escorts. (Asbury 1950: 339)

The murder rate in the United States went from 6.8 per 100,000 persons in 1920 to 9.7 in 1933, the year Prohibition was repealed (Chapman 1991c), after which it began to decline. And while the United States had local organized crime before Prohibition, there were no large crime syndicates (King 1969). Pre-Prohibition crime, insofar as it was organized, centered on corrupt political machines, vice entrepreneurs, and, at the bottom, gangs. The "Great Experiment" of Prohibition provided an opportunity for organized crime, especially violent forms, to blossom into an important force. Prohibition acted as a catalyst for the mobilization of criminal elements in an unprecedented manner, unleashing a heightened level of competitive violence and reversing the order between the criminal gangs and the politicians. It also led to an unparalleled level of criminal organization (Abadinsky 2010). In 1933, when the repeal of Prohibition left a critical void in their business portfolios, these criminal organizations turned to the drug trade.

OPIUM: A LONG HISTORY

The earliest "war against drugs" (other than alcohol) in the United States was a response to **opium**, a depressant and pain reliever. Opium is the gum from the partially ripe seedpod of the opium **poppy**. There is no agreement on where the plant originated, and a great deal of debate surrounds its earliest use as a drug, which might date back to the Stone Age. The young leaves of the plant have been used as an herb for cooking and as a salad vegetable, and its small, oily seeds, which are high in nutritional value, can be eaten, pressed to make an edible oil, baked into poppy seed cakes, ground into poppy flour, or used as lamp oil. As a vegetal fat source "the seed oil could have been a major factor attracting early human groups to the opium poppy" (Merlin 1984: 89). Archaeologists have discovered ancient art relics that may depict opium use in Egyptian religious rituals as early as 3500 B.C.E. (Inverarity, Lauderdale, and Field 1983). By 1500 B.C.E. the Egyptians had definitely discovered the medical uses of opium: It is listed as a pain reliever in the Ebers Papyrus (Burkholz 1987). From Egypt its use spread to Greece (R. O'Brien and Cohen 1984). Opium is discussed by Homer's works, the *Iliad* and the *Odyssey* (circa 700 B.C.E.), and the term opium is derived from the Greek word *opion*, meaning the juice of the poppy (Bresler 1980). Hippocrates (460–357 B.C.E.), the "father of medicine," recommended drinking the juice of the white poppy mixed with the seed of the nettle.

Opium was used by doctors in classical Greece and ancient Rome, and Arab traders brought it to China for use in medicine. Later, the Crusaders picked it up from Arab physicians and brought it back to Europe, where it became a standard medicine. Opium is mentioned by Shakespeare in *Othello* and by Chaucer, Sir Thomas Browne, and Robert Burton. In the early sixteenth century the physician Paracelsus made a tincture of opium—powdered opium dissolved in alcohol—that he called *laudanum*, and until the end of the nineteenth century it proved to be a popular medication (R. O'Brien and Cohen 1984). De Quincey (1952) noted that opium was often cheaper than alcohol.

Two centuries ago, opium was generally available as a cure for everything. It was like aspirin; every household had some, usually in the form of laudanum. Naturally, the general availability of opium and the medical profession's enthusiasm for it helped to create addicts, some of them very famous; Samuel Taylor Coleridge (1772–1834) and Thomas De Quincy (1785–1859) are the best known. At the time medicine was primitive, doctors had no concept of addiction, and opium became the essential ingredient of innumerable remedies dispensed in Europe and America for the treatment of diarrhea, dysentery, asthma, rheumatism, diabetes, malaria, cholera, fevers, bronchitis, insomnia, and pain of any kind (Fay 1975). There was nothing to alert patients to the dangers of the patent medicines they were prescribed or to prepare them for the side effects. As a result no more stigma was attached to the opium habit than to alcoholism; it was an unfortunate weakness, not a vice. Wherever it was known, opium use was both medicinal and recreational (Alvarez 2001).

In explaining the popularity of opium, Charles Terry and Mildred Pellens (1928: 58) state: "When we realize that the chief end of medicine up to the beginning of the [nineteenth] century was to relieve pain, that therapeutic agents were directed at symptoms rather than cause, it is not difficult to understand the wide popularity of a drug which either singly or combined so eminently was suited to the needs of so many medical situations."

Opium is a labor-intensive product. To produce an appreciable quantity requires repeated incisions of a great number of poppy capsules: about 18,000 capsules—one acre—to yield 20 pounds of opium (Fay 1975). Accordingly, supplies of opium were rather limited in Europe until the eighteenth century, when improvements in plantation farming increased opium production. Attempts to produce domestic opium in the United States were not successful. While the poppy could be grown in many sections of the United States, particularly the South, Southwest, and California, labor costs and an opium gum that proved low in potency led to a reliance on imported opium (H. W. Morgan 1981).

As the primary ingredient in many "**patent medicines**" (actually secret formulas that carried no patent at all) opiates were readily available in the United States until 1914, and quacks prescribed and promoted them for general symptoms as well as for specific diseases. People who were not really ill were frightened into the patent medicine habit (Young 1961). Patients who were actually sick received the false impression that they were on the road to recovery. Of course, because there was often little or no scientific medical treatment for even the mildest of diseases, a feeling of wellbeing was at least psychologically, and perhaps by extension physiologically, beneficial. However, babies born to opiate-using mothers were often small and experienced the distress of withdrawal. Harried mothers often responded by relieving them with infant remedies that contained opium.

The smoking of opium was popularized by Chinese immigrants, who brought the habit with them to the United States. During the latter part of the nineteenth and early twentieth centuries they also operated commercial opium dens that often attracted the attention of the police, "not because of the use of narcotics but because they became gathering places for thieves, footpads [highwaymen] and gangsters." In fact, "opium dens were regarded as in a class with saloons and, for many years, were no more illegal" (Katcher 1959: 287).

MORPHINE AND HEROIN

At the end of the eighteenth century (Latimer and Goldberg 1981) or early in the nineteenth (Bresler 1980; Nelson et al. 1982; Merlin 1984; Musto 1987) a German pharmacist poured liquid ammonia over opium and obtained an alkaloid, a white powder that he found to be many times more powerful than opium. Friedrich W. Serturner named the substance *morphium* after Morpheus, the Greek god of sleep and dreams; ten parts of opium can be refined into one part of morphine (Bresler 1980). It was not until 1817, however, that articles published in scientific journals popularized the new drug, resulting in widespread use by doctors. Quite incorrectly, as it turned out, the medical profession viewed morphine as an opiate without negative side effects.

By the 1850s morphine tablets and a variety of morphine products were readily available without prescription. In 1856 the hypodermic method of injecting morphine directly into the bloodstream was introduced to U.S. medicine. The popularity of morphine rose during the Civil War, when the intravenous use of the drug to treat battlefield casualties was rather indiscriminate (Terry and Pellens 1928). Following the war, morphine use among ex-soldiers was so common as to give rise to the term *army disease*. Nevertheless, "Medical journals were replete with glowing descriptions of the effectiveness of the drug during wartime and its obvious advantages for peacetime medical practice" (Cloyd 1982: 21). Hypodermic kits became widely available, and the use of unsterile needles by many doctors and laypersons led to abscesses or disease (H. W. Morgan 1981).

In the 1870s morphine was exceedingly cheap, cheaper than alcohol, and pharmacies and general stores carried preparations that appealed to a wide segment of the population, whatever the individual emotional quirk or physical ailment. Anyone who visited nearly any physician for any complaint, from a toothache to consumption, would be prescribed morphine (Latimer and Goldberg 1981), and the substance was widely abused by physicians themselves. Morphine abuse in the latter part of the nineteenth century was apparently widespread in rural America (Terry and Pellens 1928).

Starting in the 1870s, doctors injected women with morphine to numb the pain of "female troubles" or to turn the "willful hysteric" into a manageable invalid. By the 1890s, when the first drug epidemic peaked, female medical addicts reportedly made up almost half of all addicts in the United States. In the twentieth century the drug scene shifted to underworld elements of urban America, the disreputable "sporting class": prostitutes, pimps, thieves, gamblers, gangsters, entertainers, active homosexuals, and youths who admired the sporting men and women (Stearns 1998).

In 1874 a British chemist experimenting with morphine synthesized diacetylmorphine, and the most powerful of opiates came into being: "Commercial promotion of the new drug had to wait until 1898 when the highly respected German pharmaceutical combine Bayer, in perfectly good faith but perhaps without sufficient prior care, launched upon an unsuspecting world public this new substance, for which they coined the trade name 'heroin' and which they marketed as—of all things—a 'sedative for coughs'" (Bresler 1980: 11). Jack Nelson and his colleagues (1982) state that heroin was actually isolated in 1898 in Germany by Heinrich Dreser, who was searching for a non-habit-forming pain reliever to take the place of morphine. Dreser named it after the German word *heroisch*, meaning large and powerful.

Opiates, including morphine and heroin, were readily available in the United States until 1914. In 1900, 628,177 pounds of opiates were imported into the United States (Bonnie and Whitebread 1970). The President's Commission on Organized Crime (1986) notes that between the Civil War and 1914 there was a substantial increase in the number of people using opiates. This was the consequence of a number of factors:

- The spread of opium smoking from Chinese immigrants into the wider community
- An increase in morphine addiction as a result of its indiscriminate use to treat battlefield casualties during the Civil War
- The widespread administration of morphine by hypodermic syringe
- The widespread use of opium derivatives by the U.S. patent medicine industry
- Beginning in 1898, the marketing of heroin as a safe, powerful, and nonaddictive substitute for the opium derivatives morphine and codeine

CHINA AND THE OPIUM WARS

Until the sixteenth century, China was a military power whose naval fleet surpassed any that the world had ever known. A fifteenth-century power struggle ultimately led to a regime dominated by Confucian scholars; in 1525 they ordered the destruction of all oceangoing ships and set China on a course that would lead to poverty, defeat, and decline (Kristoff 1999).

In 1626 a British warship appeared off the coast of China, and its captain imposed his will on Canton (now Guangzhou) with a bombardment. In response to the danger posed by British ships the Emperor opened the city of Canton to trade, and Britain granted the British East India Company a monopoly over the China trade. Particularly important to this trade was the shipping of tea to England. By the 1820s the trade situation between England and China paralleled trade between the United States and Japan. Although British consumers had an insatiable appetite for Chinese tea, the Chinese desired few English goods. The British attempted to introduce alcohol, but a large percentage of Asians have enzyme systems that make drinking alcohol extremely unpleasant. Opium was different (Beeching 1975). Poppy cultivation was an important source of revenue for the Mughal emperors (Muslim rulers of India between 1526 and 1857). When the Mughal Empire fell apart, the British East India Company salvaged and improved the system of state control of opium. In addition to the domestic market, the British supplied Indian opium to China.

Opium was first prohibited by the Chinese government in Peking (Beijing) in 1729, when only small amounts of the substance were reaching China. Ninety years earlier, tobacco had been similarly banned as a pernicious foreign article. Opium use was strongly condemned in China as a violation of Confucian principles, and for many years the imperial decree against opium was generally supported by the population (Beeching 1975). In 1782 a British merchant ship's attempt to sell 1,601 chests of opium in China resulted in a total loss, as no purchasers could be found. By 1799, however, a growing traffic in opium led to an imperial decree condemning the trade. Dean Latimer and Jeff Goldberg (1981) doubt that opium addiction was extensive or particularly harmful to China as a whole. The poorer classes, the authors note, could afford only adulterated opium, which was unlikely to produce addiction. "Just why the Chinese chose to obtain their supplies from India," states Peter Fay (1975: 11–12), "is no clearer than why, having obtained it, they smoked it instead of ate it." In the end, he notes, the Chinese came to prefer the Indian product to their own. However, because the preference was to smoke opium, it had to be specially prepared by being boiled in water, filtered, and boiled again until it reached the consistency of molasses, thereby becoming "smoking opium."

Like the ban on tobacco, the one on opium was not successful (official corruption was endemic in China). As consumption of imported opium increased and the method of ingestion shifted from eating to smoking, official declarations against opium increased, and so did smuggling. "When opium left Calcutta, stored in the holds of country ships and consigned to agents in Canton, it was an entirely legitimate article. It remained an entirely legitimate article all the way up to the China Sea. But the instant it reached the coast of China it became something different. It became contraband" (Fay 1975: 45). In fact, the actual shipping of opium to China was accomplished by independent British or Parsee merchants. Thus, notes Beeching, "the Honourable East India Company was able to wash its hands of all formal responsibility for the illegal drug trade" (1975: 26).

Opium furnished the British with the silver needed to buy tea. Because opium was illegal in China, however, its importation—smuggling—brought China no tariff revenue. Before 1830 opium was transported to the coast of China, where it was offloaded and smuggled by the Chinese themselves. The outlawing of opium by the Chinese government led to the development of an organized underworld; gangs became secret societies—triads—that still move heroin out of the Far East to destinations all over the world (Latimer and Goldberg 1981). (This will be discussed in Chapter 11.) The armed opium ships were safe from Chinese government intervention, and the British were able to remain aloof from the smuggling itself.

In the 1830s the shippers grew bolder and entered Chinese territorial waters with their opium cargo. The British East India Company, now in competition with other opium merchants, sought to flood China with cheap opium and drive out the competition (Beeching 1975). In 1837 the emperor ordered his officials to move against opium smugglers, but the campaign was a failure, and the smugglers grew even bolder. The following year the emperor changed his strategy and moved against Chinese traffickers and drug abusers, as only a total despot could do, helping to dry up the market for opium. As a result, the price fell significantly (Hanes and Sanello 2005).

THE FIRST OPIUM WAR

In 1839, in dramatic fashion, Chinese authorities laid siege to the port city of Canton, confiscating and destroying all opium awaiting offloading from foreign ships. The merchantmen agreed to stop importing opium into China, and the siege was lifted. The British merchants petitioned their own government for compensation and retribution. The reigning Parliamentary Whig majority was very weak, however, and compensating the opium merchants was not politically or financially feasible. Instead, the cabinet, without Parliamentary approval, decided on a war that would result in the seizure of Chinese property (Fay 1975).

In 1840 a British expedition attacked the poorly armed and poorly organized Chinese forces. In the rout that followed, the Emperor was forced to pay $6 million for the opium his officials had seized and $12 million as compensation for the war. Hong Kong became a Crown colony, and the ports of Canton, Amoy (Xiamen), Foochow (Fuzhou), Ningpo, and Shanghai were opened to British trade. Opium was not mentioned in the peace (surrender) treaty, but the trade resumed with new vigor. In a remarkable reversal of the balance of trade, by the mid-1840s China had an opium debt of about 2 million pounds sterling (Latimer and Goldberg 1981). In the wake of the First Opium War, China was laid open to extensive missionary efforts by Protestant evangelicals, who, although they opposed the opium trade, viewed saving souls as their primary goal. Christianity, they believed, would save China from opium (Fay 1975). Unfortunately, morphine was actively promoted by Catholic and Protestant missionaries as an agent for detoxifying opium addicts (Latimer and Goldberg 1981).

THE SECOND OPIUM WAR

The Second Opium War began in 1856, when the balance of payments once again favored China. In that year a minor incident between the British and Chinese governments was used as an excuse to force China into making further treaty concessions. This time the foreign powers seeking to exploit a militarily weak China included Russia, the United States, and particularly France, which was jealous of the British success. Canton was sacked, and a combined fleet of British and French warships sailed right up the Grand Canal to Peking and proceeded to sack and burn the imperial summer palace, 200 buildings spread over eighty square miles of carefully landscaped parkland with extensive libraries and priceless works of art (Hanes and Sanello 2005).

The Emperor was forced to indemnify the British 20,000 pounds sterling, more than enough to offset the balance of trade which was the real cause of the war. A commission was appointed to legalize and regulate the opium trade (Latimer and Goldberg 1981) that increased from less than 59,000 chests a year in 1860 to more than 105,000 by 1880 (Beeching 1975). Until 1946 the British permitted the use of opiates in its Crown colony of Hong Kong, first under an official monopoly and, after 1913, directly by the government (Lamour and Lamberti 1974). During Japan's occupation of China, which began a few years before its attack on Pearl Harbor, large amounts of heroin were trafficked by the Japanese army's "special services branch," which helped to finance the cost of the occupation (Karch 1998).

THE CHINESE PROBLEM AND THE AMERICAN RESPONSE

Chinese laborers were originally brought into the United States after 1848 to work in the gold fields, particularly in those aspects of mining that were most dangerous because few white men were willing to engage in blasting shafts, placing beams, and laying track lines in the gold mines. Chinese immigrants also helped to build the Western railroad lines at pay few whites would accept—known as "coolie wages." After their work was completed, the Chinese were often banned from the rural counties; by the 1860s they were clustering in cities on the Pacific coast, where they established Chinatowns—and where many of them smoked opium.

The British opium monopoly in China was challenged in the 1870s by opium imported from Persia and cultivated in China itself. In response, British colonial authorities, heavily dependent on a profitable opium trade, increased the output of Indian opium, causing a price decline that was aimed at driving the competition out of business. The resulting oversupply increased the amount of opium entering the United States for the Chinese population.

Beginning in 1875, there was an economic depression in California. As a result, the first significant piece of prohibitionary drug legislation in the United States was enacted by the city of San Francisco. "The primary event that precipitated the campaign against the Chinese and against opium was the sudden onset of economic depression, high unemployment levels, and the disintegration of working-class standards of living" (Helmer 1975: 32). The San Francisco ordinance prohibited the operation of opium dens, commercial establishments for the smoking of opium, "not because of health concerns as such, but because it was believed that the drug stimulated coolies into working harder than non-smoking whites" (Latimer and Goldberg 1981: 208). Throughout the latter part of the nineteenth century, Chinese-Americans were demonized, particularly in the West (Pfaelzer 2007).

Depressed economic conditions and xenophobia led one Western state after another to follow San Francisco's lead and enact anti-Chinese legislation that often included prohibiting the smoking of opium. The anti-Chinese nature of the legislation was noted in some early court decisions. In 1886 an Oregon district court, responding to a petition for habeas corpus filed by Yung Jon, who had been convicted of opium violations, stated: "Smoking opium is not our vice, and therefore it may be that this legislation proceeds more from a desire to vex and annoy the 'Heathen Chinese' in this respect, than to protect the people from the evil habit. But the motives of legislators cannot be the subject of judicial investigation for the purpose of affecting the validity of their acts" (Bonnie and Whitebread 1970: 997).

"After 1870 a new type of addict began to emerge, the white opium smoker drawn primarily from the underworld of pimps and prostitutes, gamblers, and thieves" (Courtwright 1982: 64). During the 1890s Chicago's Chinatown was located in the notorious First Ward, whose politicians grew powerful and wealthy by protecting almost every vice known to humanity. But First Ward alderman John "Bathhouse" Coughlin "couldn't stomach" opium smokers and threatened to raid the dens himself if necessary. There was constant police harassment, and in 1894 the city enacted an antiopium ordinance. By 1895 the last of the dens had been raided out of business (Sawyers 1988).

Anti-Chinese efforts were supported and advanced by Samuel Gompers (1850–1924) as part of his effort to establish the American Federation of Labor. The Chinese served as scapegoats for organized labor that depicted the "yellow devils" as undercutting wages and breaking strikes. Anti-opium legislation was also fostered by stories of white women being seduced by Chinese white slavers through the use of opium.[2] In 1882 the Chinese Exclusion Act banned the entry of Chinese laborers into the United States. (It was not until 1943, when the United States was allied with China in a war against Japan, that citizenship rights were extended to Chinese immigrants, and China was then permitted an annual immigration of 105 individuals.)

In 1883 Congress raised the tariff on the importation of smoking opium. In 1887, apparently in response to obligations imposed on the United States by a Chinese-American commercial treaty negotiated in 1880 and becoming effective in 1887, Congress banned the importation of smoking opium by Chinese subjects. Americans, however, were still permitted to import the substance, and many did so, selling it to both Chinese and American citizens (President's Commission on Organized Crime 1986). The Tariff Act of 1890 increased the tariff rate on smoking opium to $12 per pound, resulting in a substantial increase in opium smuggling and the diversion of medicinal opium for manufacture into smoking opium. In response, in 1897 the tariff was reduced to $6 per pound (President's Commission on Organized Crime 1986).

During the nineteenth century opiates were not associated with crime in the public mind. While some people may have frowned on opium use as immoral,

> employees were not fired for addiction. Wives did not divorce their addicted husbands or husbands their addicted wives. Children were not taken from their homes and lodged in foster homes or institutions because one or both parents were addicted. Addicts continued to participate fully in the life of the community. Addicted children

---

[2]Similar anti-Chinese hysteria, especially the diatribe that they used opium to seduce white women, led to anti-opium legislation in Australia at the end of the nineteenth century (Manderson 1999).

and young people continued to go to school, Sunday School, and college. Thus, the nineteenth century avoided one of the most disastrous effects of current narcotics laws and attitudes: the rise of a deviant addict subculture, cut off from respectable society and without a road back to respectability. (Brecher 1972: 6–7)

THE PURE FOOD AND DRUG ACT

National efforts against opiates (and cocaine) were part of a larger campaign to regulate drugs and the contents of food substances; in 1879 a bill was introduced in Congress to accomplish national food and drug regulation. These efforts were opposed by the Proprietary Association of America, which represented the patent medicine industry. The medical profession was more interested in dealing with quacks within the profession than with quack medicines, and the American Pharmaceutical Association was of mixed mind: Its members, in addition to being scientists, were merchants who found the sale of proprietary remedies bulking large in their gross income (J. H. Young 1961). Toward the end of the nineteenth century the campaign for drug regulation was assisted by agricultural chemists who decried the use of chemicals to defraud consumers into buying spoiled canned and packaged food. In 1884 state-employed chemists formed the Association of Official Agricultural Chemists to combat this widespread practice. They began to expand their efforts into non-foodstuffs, including patent medicines.

The nation's newspapers and magazines made a considerable amount of money from advertising patent medicines. Toward the turn of the century, however, a few periodicals, in particular *Ladies Home Journal and Collier's*, began vigorous investigations and denunciations of patent medicines. Eventually, the American Medical Association (AMA, founded in 1847), which was a rather weak organization at the close of the nineteenth century because the vast majority of doctors were not members (Musto 1973), began to campaign in earnest for drug regulation.

U.S. Senate hearings on the pure food issue gained a great deal of newspaper coverage and aroused the public (J. H. Young 1961). The dramatic event that quickly led to the adoption of the Pure Food and Drug Act, however, was the 1906 publication of Upton Sinclair's *The Jungle* (1981/1906). Sinclair, in a novelistic description of the meat industry in Chicago, exposed the filthy, unsanitary, and unsafe conditions under which food reached the consumer. Sales of meat fell by almost 50 percent, and President Theodore Roosevelt dispatched two investigators to Chicago to check on Sinclair's charges. Their "report not only confirmed Sinclair's allegations, but added additional ones. Congress was forced by public opinion to consider a strong bill" (Ihde 1982: 42). The result was the Pure Food and Drug Act, passed later that same year, which required medicines to list certain drugs and their amounts, including alcohol and opiates.

CHINA AND THE INTERNATIONAL OPIUM CONFERENCE

The international U.S. response to drugs in the twentieth century is directly related to its trade with China. To increase its influence in China and thus improve its trade position, the United States supported the International Reform Bureau (IRB), a temperance organization representing over thirty missionary societies in the Far East, which was seeking a ban on opiates. As a result, in 1901 Congress enacted the Native Races Act, which prohibited the sale of alcohol and opium to "aboriginal tribes and uncivilized races." The provisions of the act were later expanded to include "uncivilized elements" in the United States proper: Indians, Eskimos, and Chinese (Latimer and Goldberg 1981).

As a result of the Spanish-American War in 1898, the Philippines were ceded to the United States. At the time of Spanish colonialism opium smoking was widespread among Chinese workers on the islands. Canadian-born Reverend Charles Henry Brent (1862–1929), a supporter of the IRB, arrived in the Philippines as the Episcopal bishop during a cholera epidemic that began in 1902 and that reportedly had led to an increase in the use of opium. As a result of his efforts, in 1905 Congress enacted a ban against sales of opium to Filipino natives except for medicinal purposes. Three years later the ban was extended to all residents of the Philippines. It appears that the legislation was ineffective, and smoking opium remained widely available (Musto 1973). "Reformers attributed to drugs much of the appalling poverty, ignorance, and debilitation they encountered in the Orient. Opium was strongly identified with the problems afflicting an apparently moribund China. Eradication of drug abuse was part of America's white man's burden and a way to demonstrate the New World's superiority" (H. W. Morgan 1974: 32).

Bishop Brent proposed the formation of an international opium commission, to meet in Shanghai in 1909. This plan was supported by President Theodore Roosevelt, who saw it as a way of assuaging Chinese anger at the passage of the Chinese Exclusionary Act (Latimer and Goldberg 1981). The International Opium Commission, chaired by Brent and consisting of representatives from thirteen nations, convened in Shanghai on February 1. Brent was successful in rallying the conferees around the U.S. position that opium was evil and had no nonmedical use. The commission unanimously adopted a number of vague resolutions, the most important being (Terry and Pellens 1928):

1. That each government take action to suppress the smoking of opium at home and in overseas possessions and settlements
2. That opium has no use outside of medicine and, accordingly, that each country should move toward increasingly stringent regulations concerning opiates
3. That measures should be taken to prevent the exporting of opium and its derivatives to countries that prohibit its importation

Only the United States and China, however, were eager for future conferences, and legislative efforts against opium following the conference were generally unsuccessful. Southerners were distrustful of federal enforcement, and the drug industry was opposed. Efforts to gain Southern support for antidrug legislation focused on the alleged abuse of cocaine by African Americans—the substance was reputed to make them uncontrollable. Although tariff legislation with respect to opium already existed, Terry and Pellens (1928) note that its purpose was to generate income. The first federal legislation to control the domestic use of opium was passed in 1909 as a result of the Shanghai conference. "An Act to prohibit the importation and use of opium for other than medicinal purposes" failed to regulate domestic opium production and manufacture, nor did it control the interstate shipment of opium products, which continued to be widely available through retail and mail order outlets (President's Commission on Organized Crime 1986).

A second conference was held in the Hague in 1912, with the United States, Turkey, Great Britain, France, Portugal, Japan, Russia, Italy, Germany, Persia, the Netherlands, and China in attendance. A number of problems stood in the way of an international agreement: Germany wished to protect her burgeoning pharmaceuticals industry and insisted on a unanimous vote before any action could be agreed upon; Portugal insisted on retaining the Macao opium trade; the Dutch demanded to maintain their opium trade in the West Indies; and Persia and Russia wanted to keep on growing opium poppies. Righteous U.S. appeals to the delegates were rebuffed with allusions to domestic usage and the lack of laws in the United States (Latimer and Goldberg 1981). Nevertheless, the conference managed to put together a patchwork of agreements known as the International Opium Convention, which was ratified by Congress on October 18, 1913. The signatories committed themselves to enacting laws aimed at suppressing the abuse of opium, morphine, and cocaine as well as drugs prepared or derived from these substances (President's Commission on Organized Crime 1986). On December 17, 1914, the Harrison Act, which represented this country's attempt to carry out the provisions of the Hague Convention, was approved by President Woodrow Wilson. After World War II, the United Nations took up the torch, with Opium Protocols in 1946, 1948, and 1953, and in 1961 the Single Convention consolidated all previous international conventions, protocols, and treaties.

With the exception of synthetic opiates, the 1961 Convention did not cover the synthetic drugs which proliferated in the decade that followed its adoption, and so a second convention became necessary ten years later: the Convention on Psychotropic Substances. In 1988, the United Nations Convention against Illicit Traffic in Narcotic Drugs and Psychotropic Substances consolidated and rationalized a number of agreements and declarations into a coherent system of international controls. Today, they enjoy near universal adherence with over 180 countries as parties to the Conventions. The 1988 Convention included a focus on money laundering and the control of precursor chemicals for the manufacture of synthetic drugs (*World Drug Report* 2008).

THE HARRISON ACT

The Harrison Act provided that any person who was in the business of dealing in drugs covered by the act, including the opium derivatives morphine and heroin, as well as cocaine, was required to register annually and to pay a special annual tax of $1. The statute made it illegal to sell or give away opium or opium derivatives and coca or its derivatives without a written order on a form issued by the commissioner of revenue. People who were not registered were prohibited from engaging in interstate traffic in the drugs, and no one could possess any of the drugs who had not registered and paid the special tax, under a penalty of up to five years imprisonment and a fine of no more than $2000. Rules promulgated by the Treasury Department permitted only medical professionals to register, and they had to maintain records of the drugs they dispensed. Within the first year more than 200,000 medical professionals registered, and the small staff of

Treasury agents could not scrutinize the number of prescription records that were generated (Musto 1973).

It was concern with federalism—constitutional limitation on the police powers of the central government—that led Congress to use the taxing authority of the federal government to control drugs. While few people today would question the Drug Enforcement Administration's right to register physicians and pharmacists and control what drugs they can prescribe and dispense, at the beginning of the twentieth century federal authority to regulate narcotics and the prescription practices of physicians was generally thought to be unconstitutional (Musto 1998). In 1919, use of taxing authority to regulate drugs was upheld by the Supreme Court (*United States* v. *Doremus* 249 U.S. 86):

> If the legislation enacted has some reasonable relation to the exercise of the taxing authority conferred by the Constitution, it cannot be invalidated because of the supposed motives which induced it…. The Act may not be declared unconstitutional because its effect may be to accomplish another purpose as well as the raising of revenue. If the legislation is within the taxing authority of Congress—that is sufficient to sustain it.

The Harrison Act was enacted with the support of the AMA and the American Pharmaceutical Association, both of which had grown more powerful and influential in the first two decades of the twentieth century, since the medical profession had been granted a monopoly on dispensing opiates and cocaine. The Harrison Act also had the effect of imposing a stamp of illegitimacy on the use of most narcotics, fostering an image of the immoral and degenerate "dope fiend" (Bonnie and Whitebread 1970). At this time, according to Courtwright's (1982) estimates, there were about 300,000 opiate addicts in the United States. But, he notes, the addict population was already changing. The medical profession had, by and large, abandoned its liberal use of opiates—imports of medicinal opiates declined dramatically during the first decade of the twentieth century—and the public mind, as well as that of much of the medical profession, came to associate heroin with urban vice and crime. In contrast with opiate addicts of the nineteenth century, opiate users of the twentieth century were increasingly male habitués of pool halls and bowling alleys, denizens of the underworld, and they typically used heroin (Kinlock, Hanlon, and Nurco 1998; Acker 2002). As in the case of minority groups, this marginal population was an easy target of drug laws and drug law enforcement.

The commissioner of the Internal Revenue Service was placed in charge of upholding the Harrison Act, and in 1915, 162 collectors and agents of the Miscellaneous Division of the Internal Revenue Service were given the responsibility for enforcing drug laws. In 1919 the Narcotics Division was created within the Bureau of Prohibition with a staff of 170 agents and an appropriation of $270,000. The Narcotics Division, however, was tainted by its association with the notoriously inept and corrupt Prohibition Bureau and suffered from a corruption scandal of its own: "The public dissatisfaction intensified because of a scandal involving falsification of arrest records and charges relating to payoffs by, and collusion with, drug dealers" (President's Commission on Organized Crime 1986: 204). In response, in 1930 Congress removed drug enforcement from the Bureau of Prohibition and established the Federal Bureau of Narcotics (FBN) as a separate agency within the Department of the Treasury. "Although the FBN was

The first significant piece of prohibitionary drug legislation in the United States was enacted by the city of San Francisco in 1875; the ordinance prohibited the operation of opium dens, commercial establishments for the smoking of opium.

primarily responsible for the enforcement of the Harrison Act and related drug laws, the task of preventing and interdicting the illegal importation and smuggling of drugs remained with the Bureau of Customs" (President's Commission on Organized Crime 1986: 205).

CASE LAW RESULTS

In 1916 the Supreme Court ruled in favor of a physician (Dr. Moy) who had provided maintenance doses of morphine to an addict (*United States* v. *Jin Fuey Moy* 241 U.S. 394). In 1919, however, the Court ruled (*Webb* v. *United States* 249 U.S. 96) that a prescription for morphine issued to a habitual user not under a physician's care that was intended not to cure but to maintain the habit is not a prescription and thus violates the Harrison Act. However, private physicians found it impossible to handle the large drug clientele that was suddenly created; they could do nothing "more than sign prescriptions" (Duster 1970: 16).

In *United States* v. *Behrman* (258 U.S. 280, 289, 1922) the Court ruled that a physician was not entitled to prescribe large doses of proscribed drugs for self-administration even if the addict was under the physician's care. The Court stated: "Prescriptions in the regular course of practice did not include the indiscriminate doling out of narcotics in such quantity as charged in the indictments." In 1925 the Court limited the application of *Behrman* when it found that a physician who had prescribed small doses of drugs for the relief of an addict did not violate the Harrison Act (*Linder* v. *United States* 268 U.S. 5). In reversing the physician's conviction the Court distinguished between *Linder* and excesses shown in the case of *Behrman*:

> The enormous quantities of drugs ordered, considered in connection with the recipient's character, without explanation, seemed enough to show prohibited sales and to exclude the idea of *bona fide* professional activity. The opinion [in *Behrman*] cannot be accepted as authority for holding that a physician, who acts *fide bona* and according to fair medical standards, may never give an addict moderate amounts of drugs for self-administration in order to relieve conditions incident to addiction. Enforcement of the tax demands no such drastic rule, and if the Act had such scope it would certainly encounter grave constitutional guarantees.

In fact, the powers of the Narcotics Division were clear and limited to the enforcement of registration and record-keeping regulations. "The large number of addicts who secured their drugs from physicians were excluded from the Division's jurisdiction. Furthermore, the public's attitude toward drug use," notes Donald Dickson (1977: 39), "had not much changed with the passage of the Act—there was some opposition to drug use, some support of it, and a great many who did not care one way or the other. The Harrison Act was actually passed with very little publicity or news coverage."

Richard Bonnie and Charles Whitebread (1970: 976) note the similarities between the temperance and antinarcotics movements: "Both were first directed against the evils of large scale use and only later against all use. Most of the rhetoric was the same: These euphoriants produced crime, pauperism and insanity." However, "the temperance movement was a matter of vigorous public debate; the anti-narcotics movement was not. Temperance legislation was the product of a highly organized nationwide lobby; narcotics legislation was largely ad hoc. Temperance legislation was designed to eradicate known evils resulting from alcohol abuse; narcotics legislation was largely anticipatory." In fact, notes H. Wayne Morgan (1981), comparisons between alcohol and opiates—until the nature of addiction became clear—were often favorable to opium. It was not public sentiment that led to antidrug legislation; nevertheless, the result of such legislation was an increasing public perception of the dangerousness of certain drugs (Bonnie and Whitehead 1970). As we will see, this perception was fanned by officials of the federal drug enforcement agency.

NARCOTIC CLINICS AND ENFORCEMENT

Writing in 1916, Pearce Bailey (1974: 173–174) noted that the passage of the Act "spread dismay among the heroin takers":

> They saw in advance the increased difficulty and expense of obtaining heroin as a result of this law; then the drug stores shut down, and the purveyors who sell heroin on the street corners and in doorways became terrified, and for a time illicit trade in the drug almost ceased.... Once the law was established the traffic was resumed, but under very different circumstances. The price of heroin soared [900 percent, and was sold in adulterated form]. This put it beyond the easy reach of the majority of adherents, most of whom

do not earn more than twelve or fourteen dollars a week. Being no longer able to procure it with any money that they could lay their hands on honestly, many were forced to apply for treatment for illness brought about by result of arrest for violation of the law.

Beginning in 1918, narcotics clinics opened in almost every major city. Information about them is sketchy (Duster 1970), and there is a great deal of controversy over their operations. While they were never very popular with the general public, most clinics were well run under medical supervision (H. W. Morgan 1981). While some clinics were guilty of a variety of abuses, the good ones enabled addicts to continue their normal lives without being drawn into the black market in drugs (Duster 1970). The troubled clinics, however, such as those in New York, where the number of patients overwhelmed the medical staff, generated a great deal of newspaper coverage, resulting in an outraged public.

Following World War I and the Bolshevik Revolution in Russia, xenophobia and prohibitionism began to sweep the nation. The United States severely restricted immigration, and alcohol and drug use was increasingly associated with an alien population. In 1922 federal narcotics agents closed the drug clinics and began to arrest physicians and pharmacists who provided drugs for maintenance. At issue was Section 8 of the Harrison Act, which permitted the possession of controlled substances if prescribed "in good faith" by a registered physician, dentist, or veterinarian in accord with "professional practice." The law did not define "good faith" or "professional practice." Under a policy developed by the federal narcotics agency, thousands of people, including many physicians—more than 25,000 between 1914 and 1938 (W. L. White 1998)—were charged with violations: "Whether conviction followed or not mattered little as the effects of press publicity dealing with what were supposedly willful violations of a beneficent law were most disastrous to those concerned" (Terry and Pellens 1928: 90). "Once a strict antidrug policy had been established, both the public's and policymakers' curiosity about the details of a drug's biological effects faded. Federal scientists also feared their research findings might conflict with official policies, so they avoided some areas of investigation" (Musto 1998: 62).

The medical profession withdrew from dispensing drugs to addicts, forcing them to look to illicit sources and giving rise to an enormous illegal business in drugs. People who were addicted to opium smoking eventually found their favorite drug unavailable—the bulky smoking opium was difficult to smuggle—and turned to the more readily available heroin that was prepared for intravenous use and would produce a more intense effect (Courtwright 1982). The criminal syndicates that resulted from Prohibition added heroin trafficking to their business portfolios. When Prohibition was repealed in 1933, profits from bootlegging disappeared accordingly, but drug trafficking remained as an important source of revenue for organized criminal groups. (The business of drugs is discussed in Chapter 11.) Law enforcement efforts against drugs have proven as ineffectual as efforts against alcohol during Prohibition, with similar problems of corruption.

The federal government shaped vague and conflicting court decisions into definitive pronouncements reflecting the drug enforcement agency's own version of its proper role: "American administrative regulations took on the force of ruling law" (Trebach 1982: 132). The drug agency also embarked on a vigorous campaign to convince the public and Congress of the dangers of drugs and thereby to justify its approach to the problem of drug abuse. According to Bonnie and Whitebread (1970: 990), the existence of a separate federal narcotics bureau "anxious to fulfill its role as crusader against the evils of narcotics" has been the single major factor in the legislative history of drug control in the United States since 1930.

The actions of the federal government toward drug use must be understood within the context of the times. The years immediately following World War I were characterized by pervasive attitudes of nationalism and nativism and by a fear of anarchy and communism. The Bolshevik Revolution in Russia, a police strike in Boston (see Russell 1975), and widespread labor unrest and violence were the backdrop for the infamous Palmer Raids of 1919, in which Attorney General A. Mitchel Palmer, disregarding a host of constitutional protections, ordered the arrest of thousands of "radicals." That same year the Prohibition Amendment was ratified, and soon legislation ended large-scale (legal) immigration. Drug addiction—morphinism/heroinism—was added to the un-American "isms" of alcoholism, anarchism, and communism (Musto 1973). In 1918 there were only 888 federal arrests for narcotics law violations; in 1920 there were 3,477. In 1925, the year the clinics were closed, there were 10,297 (Cloyd 1982). "During the 1920s and 1930s," notes Susan Speaker, "newspaper and magazine accounts of narcotics problems, and the propaganda of various anti-narcotics organizations used certain stock ideas and images to construct an intensely fearful public rhetoric about drugs. Authors routinely described drugs, users, and sellers as 'evil,' described sinister conspiracies to undermine American society and values, credited drugs with immense power to corrupt users, and called for complete eradication of the problem" (Speaker 2001: 1).

According to William White (1998: 113), Treasury Department opposition to prescribing drugs for addicts was based on a belief in the prevailing propaganda of the day with respect to alcohol treatment. "The Treasury Department opposed ambulatory treatment because, for many patients, it turned into sustained maintenance, and also because the remaining inebriate hospitals and asylums of the day were still boasting 95% success rates. After all, leaders of the Treasury Department argued, why should someone be maintained on morphine when all he or she had to do was to take the cure? It was through such misrepresentation of success rates that the inebriate asylums and private treatment sanitariums contributed inadvertently to the criminalization of narcotic addiction in the U.S."

In 1923 legislation was introduced to curtail the importation of opium for the manufacture of heroin, resulting in a virtual ban on heroin in the United States. (In 1956 Congress declared all heroin to be contraband.) Among the few witnesses who testified before Congress, all supported the legislation. The AMA had already condemned the use of heroin by physicians, and the substance was described as the most dangerous of all habit-forming drugs, some witnesses arguing that the psychological effects of heroin use serve as a stimulus to crime. Much of the medical testimony, in light of what is now known about heroin, was erroneous, but the law won easy passage in 1924 (Musto 1973). A pamphlet published the same year by the prestigious Foreign Policy Association summarized contemporary thinking about heroin (cited in Trebach 1982: 48):

- It is unnecessary in the practice of medicine.
- It destroys all sense of moral responsibility.

■ | **THE LEGAL APPROACH**

> "Drug laws reflect the decision of some persons that other persons who wish to consume certain substances should not be permitted to act on their preferences. Nor should anyone be permitted to satisfy the desires of drug consumers by making and selling the prohibited drug.... [The] most important characteristic of the legal approach to drug use is that these consumptive and commercial activities are being regulated by force." Randy Barnett (1987: 73)

- It is the drug of the criminal.
- It recruits its army among youths.

The use of opiates, except for narrow medical purposes, was now thoroughly criminalized, both in law and in practice. The law defined drug users as criminals, and the public viewed heroin use as the behavior of a deviant criminal class.

THE UNIFORM DRUG ACT

Until 1930, efforts against drugs were primarily federal. Only a few states had drug control statutes, and these were generally ineffective (Musto 1973). At the urging of federal authorities, many states enacted their own antidrug legislation. By 1931 every state restricted the sale of cocaine, and all but two restricted the sale of opiates. State statutes, however, were far from uniform. As early as 1927, this lack of uniformity, combined with the growing hysteria about dope fiends and criminality, resulted in several requests for a uniform state narcotics law. The diversity of state drug statutes was not an anachronism. The need for greater uniformity in state statutes was recognized in the first half of the nineteenth century, when a prominent New York attorney, David Dudley Field (1805–1894), campaigned for a uniform code of procedure for both civil and criminal matters. During the 1890s the American Bar Association set up the National Conference of Commissioners on Uniform State Laws, whose efforts resulted in a variety of uniform codes that were adopted by virtually all jurisdictions (Abadinsky 2007).

A uniform drug act for the states was the goal of both the Committee on the Uniform Narcotic Act and representatives of the AMA because doctors wanted uniformity of legal obligations. Their first two drafts copied a 1927 New York statute that listed coca, opium, and cannabis products as habit-forming drugs to be regulated or prohibited. Because of opposition to its inclusion on the habit-forming list, cannabis was dropped from later drafts with a note indicating that each state was free to include cannabis or not in its own legislation without affecting the rest of the act. The final draft also used the 1927 New York statute as a model and included suggestions from the newly appointed commissioner of the FBN, Harry Anslinger. The draft was adopted overwhelmingly by the National Conference of Commissioners on Uniform State Laws, to which each governor had appointed two representatives. By 1937 thirty-five states had enacted the Uniform Drug Act, and every state had enacted statutes relating to marijuana. Despite propagandizing efforts by the FBN, "The laws went unnoticed by legal commentators, the press and the public at large" (Bonnie and Whitebread 1970: 1034).

The lack of public concern is related to the demographics of drug abuse, which was concentrated in minority, lower-class areas and the criminal subculture. Before the Harrison Act there was considerable use in rural areas; the South, where drugs often substituted for alcohol in dry areas, used more opiates than other parts of the country. After the Harrison Act addicts in rural areas were attended to quietly by sympathetic doctors. Heroin was heavily concentrated in urban areas of poverty. For example, during the early decades of the twentieth century heroin use in New York was heaviest in the Jewish and Italian areas of the Lower East Side. As these two groups climbed up the economic ladder and moved out, they were replaced by African Americans looking for affordable housing; this group then became the basis of the addict population (Helmer 1975). Demographics intensified the problem; African Americans had a higher birthrate than Jews and Italians, and an extraordinary number of youngsters were 16 years old, the age of highest risk for addiction. After World War II the white ethnic population became increasingly suburban, and the inner city became increasingly black and Hispanic—a new vulnerable population in a drug-infested environment.

The contemporary heroin market has moved well past its urban roots, becoming established in America's suburbs where it is abused by adolescents (C. Buckley 2009). Sources of the drug vary, but can be grouped into three broad categories: 1. Local suburban youngsters who search out heroin connections for personal use in inner-city locations. Eventually, they begin to bring additional quantities back home for sale. This phenomenon has been seen in suburban Nassau County, on New York's Long Island (Wolvier, Martino, Jr., and Bolger 2009). "The heroin being sold on Long Island is deadlier and cheaper than ever. A bag on the street costs about $6 or $7, cheaper than a pack of cigarettes. What makes the situation even more dangerous is the misconception among users that snorting or sniffing heroin, rather than injecting it, will not lead to addiction" ("Heroin on Long Island" 2009: 22). 2. Low-level urban dealers who recognize suburban locations as both lucrative and less competitive, markets they can more easily monopolize. This phenomenon has been experienced in suburbs across the Northeast (Calefati 2008). 3. Mexican drug cartels that dispatch small cells to take advantage of fertile suburban markets. The cells take orders over disposable mobile phones and use a system of dispatchers to deliver the drugs to various rendezvous points such as a shopping center parking lot. Cell members, often-illegal immigrants, stay in one location for four or five months and are then rotated as replacements arrive. This has been experienced in suburban Ohio locations (Archibold 2009b).

Pointing to the similarities between the prohibition against alcohol and that against other drugs, David Courtwright (1982: 144) asks why, since both reform efforts had ended in failure, did the public withdraw its support for one and increase its support of the other? "One factor (in addition to economic and political considerations) must have been that alcohol use was relatively widespread and cut across class lines. It seemed unreasonable for the government to deny a broad spectrum of otherwise normal persons access to drink. By 1930 opiate addiction, by contrast, was perceived to be concentrated in a small criminal subculture; it did not seem unreasonable for that same government to deny the morbid cravings of a deviant group."

World War II had a dramatic impact on the supply of heroin in the United States. The Japanese invasion of China interrupted supplies from that country, while the disruption of shipping routes by German submarines and attack battleships reduced the amount of heroin moving from Turkey to Marseilles to the United States. When the United States entered the war, security measures "designed to prevent infiltration of foreign spies and sabotage to naval installations made smuggling into the United States virtually impossible." As a result, "at the end of World War II, there was an excellent chance that heroin addiction could be eliminated in the United States" (A. W. McCoy 1972: 15). Obviously, this did not happen (the reasons will be discussed later and in Chapter 11), and "by the 1980s, an estimated 500,000 Americans used illicit opioids (mainly heroin), mostly poor young minority men and women in the inner cities" (Batki et al. 2005: 13).

Distributors in New Jersey are targeting customers in smaller towns and rural areas to gain market share. Heroin availability has increased in Upstate New York, which has led to a corresponding increase in the number of urban and suburban youths from outlying rural counties traveling to Albany, Erie, Monroe, and Onondaga Counties to obtain the drug for personal use (National Drug Intelligence Center 2009f).

COCAINE

Cocaine is a stimulant, an alkaloid found in significant quantities only in the leaves of two species of coca shrub that are indigenous to certain sections of South America, though they have been grown elsewhere.[3] "For over 4,000 years among the native Andean population the coca leaf has been used in ancient rituals and for everyday gift giving. Holding spiritual, economic, and cultural significance, coca is seen as an important medium for social integration and human solidarity in the face of adverse conditions" (Wheat and Green 1999: 42). To the Incas the plant was of divine origin and was reserved for those who believed themselves descendants of the gods. In Bolivia it is drunk as *mate* (coca tea), and the leaves are chewed for hours by farmers and miners along with an alkaloid that helps to release the active ingredients. "The result is similar to a prolonged caffeine or tobacco buzz. But it is more than that. It improves stamina, is a sacred symbol central to community life and provides essential nutrients" (Wheat and Green 1999: 43).

European experience with chewing coca coincided with Spanish exploration of the New World. While the early Spanish explorers, obsessed with gold, referred to coca leaf chewing with scorn, later reports about the effects of coca on Indians were more enthusiastic. Nevertheless, the chewing of coca leaves was not adopted by Europeans until the nineteenth century (Grinspoon and Bakalar 1976). A "mixture of ignorance and moral hauteur played an important role in the long delay between the time Europeans first became acquainted with cocaine—in the form of coca—and the time they began to use it" (Ashley 1975: 3). The coca leaves tasted bitter and were favored by pagans—Peruvian Indians—"an obviously inferior lot

---

[3]During the 1920s, Indonesia exported more coca leaf than did Latin America (Karch 1996).

who had allowed their great Inca Empire to be conquered by Pizarro and fewer than two hundred Spaniards." Early records indicate that the effects of coca—stamina and energy—were ascribed not to the drug but to a pact the Indians had made with the devil or simply to delusion—the Indian is sustained by the *belief* that chewing coca gives him extra strength.

COCAINE IN THE NINETEENTH CENTURY

Alkaloidal cocaine was isolated from the coca leaf by German scientists in the decade before the American Civil War, and the German chemical manufacturer Merck began to produce small amounts (Karch 1998). Scientists experimenting with the substance noted that it showed promise as a local anesthetic and had an effect opposite that caused by morphine. Indeed, at first cocaine was used to treat morphine addiction, but the result was often a morphine addict who was also dependent on cocaine (Van Dyke and Byck 1982). Enthusiasm for cocaine spread across the United States, and by the late 1880s a feel-good pharmacology based on the coca plant and its derivative cocaine emerged, as the substance was hawked for everything from headaches to hysteria. "Catarrh powders for sinus trouble and headaches—a few were nearly pure cocaine—introduced the concept of snorting" (Gomez 1984: 58). Patent medicines frequently contained significant amounts of cocaine.

One very popular product was the coca wine *Vin Mariani*, which contained two ounces of fresh coca leaves in a pint of Bordeaux wine; another, *Peruvian Wine of Coca*, was available for $1 a bottle through the 1902 Sears, Roebuck catalog. The most famous beverage containing coca, however, was first bottled in 1894, and an advertisement for Coca-Cola in *Scientific American* in 1906 publicized the use of coca as an important tonic in this "healthful drink" (May 1988b: 29). A 1908 government report listed more than forty brands of soft drinks containing cocaine (Helmer 1975). In contrast to the patent medicines, however, these beverages, including wine and Coca-Cola, contained only small, typically trivial, amounts of cocaine (Karch 1998).

In 1884 Sigmund Freud began taking cocaine and soon afterward began to treat his friend Ernst von Fleischl-Marxow, who had become a morphine addict, with cocaine. The following year, von Fleischl-Marxow suffered from toxic psychosis as a result of taking increasing amounts of cocaine by subcutaneous injection, and Freud wrote that the misuse of the substance had hastened his friend's death. Although Freud continued the recreational use of cocaine as late as 1895, his enthusiasm for its therapeutic value waned (Byck 1974). Influenced by the writings of Sigmund Freud on cocaine, William Stewart Halstead, surgeon-in-chief at Johns Hopkins Hospital and the "father of American surgery," began experimenting with the substance in 1884. When he died in 1922 at age 70, Dr. Halstead was still addicted to cocaine despite numerous attempts at curing himself (W. L. White 1998).

After the flush of enthusiasm for cocaine in the 1880s its direct use declined. Cocaine continued to be used in a variety of potions and tonics, but unlike morphine and heroin, it did not develop a separate appeal (H. W. Morgan 1981). Indeed, it gained a reputation for inducing bizarre and unpredictable behavior.

COCAINE IN THE TWENTIETH CENTURY

After the turn of the century, cocaine, like heroin, became identified with the urban underworld and, in the South, with African Americans. "As with Chinese opium, southern blacks became a target for class conflict, and drug use became one point of tension in this larger sociopolitical struggle" (Cloyd 1982: 35). The campaign against cocaine took on bizarre aspects aimed at winning support for antidrug legislation among Southern politicians, who traditionally resisted federal efforts that interfered with their concept of states' rights. Without any research support, a spate of articles alleged widespread abuse of cocaine by African Americans, often associating such abuse with violence and the rape of white women (Helmer 1975). Ultimately, notes Jerald Cloyd (1982: 54), "Southerners were more afraid of African-Americans than of increased federal power to regulate these drugs." At the time of the Harrison Act there was considerable discussion—but no evidence—of substantial cocaine use by blacks in Northern cities (H. W. Morgan 1981).

As with opiates, the legal use of cocaine was affected by the Pure Food and Drug Act of 1906 and finally by the Harrison Act in 1914. Before this federal legislation many states passed laws restricting the sale of cocaine, beginning with Oregon in 1887. By 1914 forty-six states had such laws, while only twenty-nine had similar laws with respect to opiates (Grinspoon and Bakalar 1976). With its dangers well known, by the end of World War I the medical community had largely lost interest in cocaine (Karch 1998), and in 1922 Congress officially defined cocaine as a narcotic and prohibited the importation of most cocaine and coca leaves. This caused an increase in law enforcement efforts, and the price of cocaine increased accordingly. In 1932 amphetamines became available, and this cheap, legal stimulant helped to further decrease user interest in cocaine (Cintron 1986).

In the United States, from 1930 until the 1960s there was limited demand for cocaine and, accordingly, only limited supply.[4] Cocaine use was associated with deviants at the fringes of society—jazz musicians and the denizens of underworld—and sources were typically diverted from medical supplies. During the late 1960s and early 1970s attitudes toward recreational drug use became more liberal because of the wide acceptance of marijuana. Cocaine was no longer associated with deviants, and the media played a significant role in shaping public attitudes:

> By publicizing and glamorizing the lifestyle of affluent, upper-class drug dealers and the use of cocaine by celebrities and athletes, all forms of mass media created an effective advertising campaign for cocaine, and many people were taught to perceive cocaine as chic, exclusive, daring, and nonaddicting. In television specials about cocaine abuse, scientists talked about the intense euphoria produced by cocaine and the compulsive craving that people (and animals) develop for it. Thus, an image of cocaine as being extraordinarily powerful, and a (therefore desirable) euphoriant was promoted. (Wesson and Smith 1985: 193)

Cocaine became associated with a privileged elite, and the new demand was sufficient to generate new sources. Refining and marketing networks outside of

---

[4]This was not the case in Europe and the Far East, where major drug firms provided cocaine—often surreptitiously—for sale in the drug black market (Karch 1998).

medical channels led to the development of the Latin-American criminal organizations discussed in Chapter 11.

During the 1980s a new form of cocaine—called **crack**—became popular in a number of cities, particularly New York. Its popularity dramatically altered the drug market at the consumer level: Both users and sellers were much younger than was typical in the heroin business. Younger retailers and a competitive market increased the level of violence associated with the drug business. The appearance of this new form of cocaine, which is smoked (as opposed to the powdered form that is typically sniffed), set off a frenzy of media interest and public alarm—a *drug scare*. Elected officials responded by increasing penalties for this form of the substance.

Steven Belenko (1993: 24) reports that drug scares have four common elements:

1. The scope of the problem is never as great as originally portrayed in the media.
2. Despite the media portrayals, compulsive use and addiction are not inevitable consequences of using the drug.
3. The violent behavior associated with the use of the drug is not as common as initially believed, nor is it necessarily caused by the drug.
4. The popularity of the particular drug waxes and wanes over time, and prevalence rates do not continue to increase.

By 1987 the rapid expansion of crack use stopped, and by 1989 its popularity began to diminish. The hysteria with which the media and public officials had greeted this "new scourge" was subjected to research and reflection: "Crack itself was never instantly addictive or totally devastating as asserted by the media, political speeches, and statements of public policy. In particular, it did not draw the naive and young in droves into this new and dangerous lifestyle." Indeed, crack use was centered in those populations in which drug abuse has always been endemic: the urban underclass (B. D. Johnson, Golub, and Fagan 1995: 291).

Cocaine has very limited medical use as a local anesthetic for ear, nose, and throat surgery. Its early use, however, led to the development of procaine (Novocain), which in 1905 was introduced into medicine and continues to be used today, particularly in dentistry (Snyder 1986). Novocain and other synthetic drugs have, for the most part, replaced cocaine as a local anesthetic. Coca leaves are legally imported into the United States by a single chemical company, which extracts the cocaine for pharmaceutical purposes. The remaining leaf material, which contains no psychoactive agents, is prepared as a flavoring for Coca-Cola.

MARIJUANA

Cannabis sativa L., the hemp plant from which marijuana and **hashish** are derived, grows wild throughout most tropical and temperate regions of the world; it has been cultivated for at least 5,000 years for a variety of purposes including the manufacture of rope and paint. There is interest in the cultivation of hemp for its fiber, particularly in the American apparel and paper industries.

Marijuana's use as an intoxicant was brought to Africa by Arab traders, and the plant was introduced into Brazil through the slave trade in the 1600s. The word **marijuana** (sometimes spelled "marihuana") is derived from the Spanish term for any substance that produces intoxication: *maraguano*. Until the early 1900s recreational use of marijuana was popular chiefly among Mexican laborers in the Southwest and certain fringe groups such as jazz musicians (Weisheit 1990).

When the dried leaves of the marijuana plant are smoked like tobacco, perceptual changes occur that vary widely according to the strength of the substance, the person smoking the marijuana, and the environmental conditions. In the past most of the cannabis growing wild in the United States derived from plants originally cultivated for their fiber rather than their drug content, so their psychoactive potency was quite weak (Peterson 1980). Entrepreneurial horticulturists in the United States now produce more powerful strains of the plant.

EARLY MARIJUANA LEGISLATION AND LITERATURE

As has already been discussed in this chapter, race, religion, and ethnicity have been closely identified with the reaction to drugs in the United States: the Irish and alcohol; the Chinese and opium; African-Americans and cocaine; and, finally, Mexicans and marijuana. Bonnie and Whitebread (1970) state that the most prominent influence in marijuana legislation was racism: State laws against marijuana, they argue, were often part of a reaction to Mexican immigration. Before 1930 sixteen states with relatively large Mexican populations had enacted anti-marijuana legislation. "Chicanos in the Southwest were believed to be incited to violence by smoking it" (Musto 1973: 65). Jerome Himmelstein (1983: 29) argues, however, that the "crucial link between Mexicans and federal marihuana policy was not locally based political pressure from the Southwest, but a specific image of marihuana that emerged from the context of marihuana use by Mexicans and was used to justify anti-marihuana legislation. Because Mexican laborers and other lower-class groups were identified as typical marihuana users, the drug was believed to cause the kinds of antisocial behavior associated with those groups, especially violent crime." Because of marijuana's association with suspect marginal groups—Mexicans, artists, intellectuals, jazz musicians, bohemians, and petty criminals—it became an easy target for regulation (Morgan 1981). In the eastern United States marijuana was erroneously believed to be addictive and there was fear that it would serve as a substitute for narcotics that were outlawed by the Harrison Act.

In light of more contemporary research into marijuana (which will be reviewed in Chapter 6), the hysterical anti-marijuana literature that was produced during the 1930s can often seem amusing. Earle Rowell and Robert Rowell (1939: 49) wrote, for example, that marijuana "seems to superimpose upon the user's character and personality a devilish form. He is one individual when normal, and an entirely different one after using marijuana." According to these authors, marijuana "has led to some of the most revolting cases of sadistic rape and murder of modern times." In 1936 the FBN presented a summary of cases that illustrate "the homicidal tendencies and the generally debasing effects which arise from the use of marijuana" (Uelmen and Haddox 1983: 1–11). The 1936 motion picture *Reefer Madness* showed a horrifying portrait of the marijuana user and was often featured at college marijuana parties during the 1960s.

"It is clear," note Bonnie and Whitebread (1970: 1021–1022), "that no state undertook any empirical or scientific study of the effects of the drug. Instead they relied on lurid and often unfounded accounts of marijuana's dangers as presented in what little newspaper coverage the drug received." By 1931 twenty-two states had marijuana legislation that was often part of a general-purpose statute against narcotics (Bonnie and Whitebread 1970). Despite its being outlawed, marijuana was never an important issue in the United States until the 1960s: "It hardly ever made headlines or became the subject of highly publicized hearings and reports. Few persons knew or cared about it, and marihuana laws were passed with minimal attention" (Himmelstein 1983: 38).

The FBN, operating on a Depression era budget, was reluctant to take on the additional responsibilities that would result from outlawing marijuana at the federal level. Harry J. Anslinger, FBN commissioner from 1930 until his retirement in 1962, hoped that the states would act against marijuana, leaving the bureau free to concentrate on heroin and cocaine. To get the states to act, the FBN dramatized the dangers of marijuana. But in such trying economic times, the states were reluctant to take on additional work, and the FBN's own propaganda forced it to act (Himmelstein 1983).

At the urging of Anslinger, Congress passed the Marijuana Tax Act of 1937. Because of uncertainty about the federal government's ability to outlaw marijuana, the act placed an exorbitant tax on cannabis—$100 an ounce—rather than prohibiting the substance outright. This tax act was a result of three days of congressional hearings that Bonnie and Whitebread (1970: 1054) characterize as "a case study in legislative carelessness." Commissioner Anslinger was able to orchestrate an undocumented and hysterical presentation before the House Ways and Means Committee on the dangers of marijuana, and the floor debate on the bill, Bonnie and Whitebread argue, represented a near-comic example of dereliction of legislative responsibility. Anslinger (with Tompkins 1953: 20–21) maintained that marijuana was "a scourge which undermines its victims and degrades them mentally, morally, and physically." The AMA's opposition to the bill was ridiculed by members of the Ways and Means Committee. Marijuana was being treated as just another narcotic (Bonnie and Whitebread 1970). The states followed the federal lead and increased their penalties for drug violations, including marijuana. In 1951 penalties for possession and trafficking in marijuana were substantially increased—along with those for other controlled substances—with the passage of the Boggs Act (discussed below).

COUNTERCULTURE USE AND CHANGING LAWS

During the 1960s public attitudes toward marijuana underwent considerable change. A nonconformist counterculture, whose members were often from the white middle class, emerged. The rebellious nature of the hippies encouraged greater experimentation with sex and drugs, marijuana in particular. In fact, note Charles Lidz and Andrew Walker (1980), marijuana use helped to tie together diverse interests: civil rights, antiwar, and antiestablishment groups and individuals. Its primary importance was as a membership ritual for an otherwise very diffuse and disorganized culture. No longer confined to minority or subcultural groups—Chicanos, African Americans, beatniks, musicians—marijuana soon found widespread acceptance among people of the middle and upper classes. This led to significant scientific inquiry into the effects of marijuana, and toward the latter part of the 1960s it became clear that whatever its dangers might be, the substance was simply not in the same class as heroin or cocaine on any important pharmacological dimension. Young, white, middle-class users, however, like their ghetto counterparts, were being subjected to the significant penalties that obtained for heroin and cocaine.

The rise of middle-class marijuana users offered the public a new view of the phenomenon in *Life* magazine's October 31, 1969, issue. Marijuana was the lead story, and the magazine presented photographs of white, middle-class people enjoying marijuana in a variety of congenial social settings. Also included was an in-depth story of a young man from Nashville, Tennessee, a long-distance runner and prep school graduate attending the University of Virginia on an athletic scholarship. He was arrested for possession of three pounds of marijuana and in a Virginia state court received a sentence of twenty years in prison. The same issue of *Life* contains an article by the former director of the U.S. Food and Drug Administration, James L. Goddard, who stated: "Our laws governing marijuana are a mixture of bad science and poor understanding of the role of law as a deterrent force. They are unenforceable, excessively severe, scientifically incorrect and revealing our ignorance of human behavior" (1969: 34). The following year Robert Kennedy, Jr. and R. Sargent Shriver III, juveniles at the time, were arrested for possession of marijuana. Public pressure soon caused legislators to reconsider state and federal penalties for marijuana.

"As of 1965, marihuana laws still bore the mark of the harsh legislation of the 1950s. Simple possession carried penalties of two years for the first offense, five for the second, and ten for the third" (Himmelstein 1983: 103). By the end of the 1960s penalties on the state level had been significantly reduced. However, the Comprehensive Drug Abuse Prevention and Control Act of 1970 established five schedules for controlled substances, and marijuana, along with heroin, was placed in the highest category, Schedule I, which has the following features:

1. The drug or other substance has a high potential for abuse.
2. The drug or other substance has no currently accepted medical use in treatment in the United States.
3. There is a lack of accepted safety for the use of the drug or other substance under medical supervision.

While the penalties remained as high as imprisonment for five years for non-narcotic drugs (i.e., marijuana), such sentences are reserved for possession of large amounts with intent to sell—for wholesale traffickers, the only type of offender traditionally of interest to federal drug law enforcement. Simple possession was made into a misdemeanor, a crime punishable by imprisonment for not more than one year. The major elements of the federal law were copied by most states.

In 1972 the presidentially appointed National Commission on Marijuana and Drug Abuse recommended that possession of marijuana for personal use or noncommercial distribution be decriminalized. The following year Oregon became the first state to abolish criminal penalties for the possession of one ounce or less of marijuana, replacing incarceration with relatively small fines. In 1975 California made possession of one ounce or less of marijuana a citable misdemeanor with a maximum penalty of $100, and there were no increased penalties for recidivists. By 1978 eleven states had decriminalized marijuana, a position supported by President Jimmy Carter (Himmelstein 1983) but opposed by the President's Commission on Organized Crime (1986), which was appointed by President Ronald Reagan. As a result of a ballot initiative in 1990, Alaska, after fifteen years, made marijuana possession illegal again.

In more recent years there has been some medical use of the active ingredient in marijuana—but not marijuana itself—to control the side effects of chemotherapy and to treat glaucoma. Despite vigorous opposition at the federal level, in 1997 voters in California and Arizona passed referenda authorizing physicians to prescribe marijuana. Maine voters did the same in 1999.

AMPHETAMINE

Manufactured under the trade name Benzedrine, in 1932 amphetamine was marketed as an inhalant, and subsequently in tablet form, for use as a nasal decongestant. It was introduced into clinical use during the 1930s and eventually offered as a "cure-all" for just about every ailment. Between 1932 and 1946 there were thirtynine generally accepted medical uses for amphetamines, including the treatment of schizophrenia, morphine addiction, low blood pressure, and caffeine and tobacco dependence (D. E. Smith 1979). "Amphetamines were unique: never before had a powerful psychoactive drug been introduced in such quantities in so short a period of time, and never before had a drug with such a high addictive potential and capability of causing long-term or irreversible physical and psychological damage been so enthusiastically embraced by the medical profession as a panacea or so extravagantly promoted by the drug industry" (Grinspoon and Hedblom 1975: 13).

By the end of the decade, as their stimulating properties became widely known amphetamines were used primarily as analeptics—stimulating drugs. Many amphetamine-based inhalants appeared on the market and were widely available without prescription. These quickly became the subject of widespread abuse. During World War II, British, German, and Japanese governments issued amphetamines to soldiers to elevate mood and to counteract fatigue and pain, and U.S. military personnel were exposed to their use through contact with the British military. During the Korean conflict the United States authorized the distribution of amphetamines to military personnel. The first major wave of abuse appeared when American servicemen in Korea and Japan mixed the substance with heroin to create "speedballs," which were taken intravenously (Grinspoon and Hedblom 1975).

Dextroamphetamine, a more potent version of Benzedrine, was marketed as Dexedrine. **Methamphetamine**, manufactured under the trade name Methadrine, is an even more potent analeptic. Currently the drug of choice for street abusers, who refer to it by the brand name Methadrine or as "meth," **"crank," "speed,"** or "ice," methamphetamine is injected, snorted, or smoked. Reports of its abuse by businessmen and athletes appeared as early as 1940, and a black market in the substance—"pep pills"—began to develop. It was (and perhaps still is) particularly popular among long-distance truck drivers and college students trying to stay awake. Amphetamines were widely prescribed in the 1950s and 1960s as an aid in dieting, leading to abuse by housewives taking "diet pills." Ralph Weisheit and William White (2009: 29) note that a surge in amphetamine use in the United States began with a core of people exposed through medicine or the military and then "spread outward into the mainstream population through new forms of the drug, excessive drug supply (from overproduction), and overprescribing." "Pep pills" moved from the beatnik subculture, to students and truck drivers, and then to the wider population.

In the 1960s the Food and Drug Administration launched a widespread anti-amphetamine campaign with the slogan "Speed Kills" (R. O'Brien and Cohen 1984), and in 1971 federal laws restricted the conditions under which amphetamines could be prescribed. During the late 1980s the smokable crystal methamphetamine called *ice* appeared on the drug scene. Media and political concern over the possible spread of this new form of drug led to a new drug scare. Widespread abuse continues, particularly in more rural parts of the country where the drug is often manufactured.

BARBITURATES

Barbiturates are sedating drugs synthesized from barbituric acid. Barbituric acid was first synthesized in Germany in 1863 by Nobel Prize–winning chemist Adolf von Baeyer. The first barbiturate was synthesized in 1882 but not marketed until 1903 (McKim 1991). Accounts vary as to how barbituric acid acquired its name. In 1903 it was released under the trade name Veronal, a name derived from the Italian city of Verona. It is known generically in the United States as barbital (Wesson and Smith 1977).

Barbiturates were used to induce sleep, replacing other aids such as alcohol and opiates. Since the appearance of phenobarbital in 1912, thousands of barbituric acid derivatives have been synthesized, although only about a dozen are commonly used; these are marketed under a variety of brand names. Barbiturates were widely prescribed in the United States during the 1930s, when their toxic effects were not fully understood. By 1942 there were campaigns against the nonmedical use of barbiturates, and by the 1950s barbiturates were one of the major drugs of abuse among adults in the United States. In the 1960s barbiturate abuse quickly spread to the youth population (R. O'Brien and Cohen 1984). Nonmedical abuse of barbiturates is usually the result of diverting licit supplies through theft or burglary, forged prescriptions, or illegal manufacture in other countries, particularly Mexico. Supplies diverted from licit sources may be repackaged in nondescript capsules, thus disguising their source (Wesson and Smith 1977).

TRANQUILIZERS AND SEDATIVES

Along with amphetamines and barbiturates, many doctors in the 1960s routinely prescribed a variety of substances to reduce anxiety. Tranquilizers or **sedatives** such as Miltown and Valium enabled millions of housewives to "get by with a little help from their friends." These substances were the subject of heavy advertising, much of it depicting women in need of relief from tension and anxiety, by drug companies that offered their products as aids in coping with the normal problems of life. Consumers often became so dependent on these substances that they could not function without them, having lost the ability to deal with normal levels of stress. As a result of unfavorable attention by health and consumer organizations and a congressional hearing in 1979, the manufacturers of Valium and other tranquilizers shifted their focus to promote these substances' ability to ease the stress of modern living. In 1980 the Food and Drug Administration required tranquilizers to be labeled as generally not appropriate for anxiety or tension associated with the stress of everyday life. Nevertheless, they continue to be widely prescribed for patients experiencing "troubling times."

HALLUCINOGENS

Hallucinogens such as LSD became popular during the 1960s, particularly among rebellious college students and people who identified themselves as antiestablishment. Lester Grinspoon (1979: 57) states: "It is impossible to write an adequate history of such an amorphous phenomenon [LSD] without discussing the whole cultural rebellion of the 1960s." LSD was first synthesized in Switzerland in 1938, but its hallucinogenic qualities did not become apparent until its discoverer took his first "trip" in 1943. During the 1950s the U.S. Army and the Central Intelligence Agency conducted LSD experiments on soldiers and civilians, without their knowledge or consent, to test its suitability for chemical warfare and its utility as a "truth serum" (Henderson 1994a).

Although LSD arrived in the United States from Europe in 1949 for experimental use in treating psychiatric disorders (Stevens 1987), it was virtually unknown before 1962 except to a small number of psychiatrists and psychologists (Brecher 1972). Two psychologists, Timothy Leary and Richard Alpert of Harvard College, were experimenting with the hallucinogenic mushroom **psilocybin**. While the "Psilo-cybin Project" began as a scientific endeavor, it ended as casual use of the drug by many friends and acquaintances, including a small clique of psychedelic enthusiasts such as the authors Aldous Huxley (*Brave New World*) and Ken Kesey (*One Flew Over the Cuckoo's Nest*) and the poet Allen Ginsberg (see Wolfe [1968] for a look at Kesey and his Merry Pranksters' psychedelic world). Experiments that Leary and Alpert conducted on inmates at Concord State Prison suggested that aggressive and hardened inmates became introspective and caring under the influence of psilocybin. Leary began encouraging his psychology students to use psilocybin. Word of their activities spread beyond the Harvard community when it was picked up by newspapers as a result of a story in the *Harvard Crimson*. Federal agencies began making inquiries. School officials were anxious to rid themselves of Leary and Alpert, so their research and control over psilocybin were placed under a faculty committee while the school awaited the expiration of Leary and Alpert's teaching contracts. No matter, they had been introduced to LSD.

"In a major city like Los Angeles," notes Jay Stevens (1987: 171), "it was as easy to go on an LSD trip as it was to visit Disneyland. Interested parties could either contact the growing number of therapists who were using LSD in practice, or they could offer themselves as guinea pigs to any of the dozens of research projects that were under way at places like UCLA." Therapists were using LSD "to heighten the traditional psychotherapeutic values of recall, abreaction, and emotional release," in most cases with apparent success and without negative side effects (Stevens 1987: 180). However, the reaction of mainstream, establishment medicine and psychiatry toward LSD was generally negative, particularly when it was used by nonphysicians such as psychologists. Stevens refers to the resulting conflict as a turf war between medically trained practitioners and all other therapists. LSD was also widely used without the guise of any therapeutic milieu, such as at the "LSD colony" in Hollywood, where, according to Leary (R. Rosenbaum 1988: 135), "Cary Grant was the high cardinal."

In 1962 Congress enacted legislation that gave the Food and Drug Administration control over all new investigational drugs. Although aimed at amphetamines, the legislation also applied to LSD (Stevens 1987). That same year Leary, Alpert, and thirty-five disciples moved to Zihuatanejo, Mexico, where they used LSD freely. The two psychologists established the International Foundation for Internal Freedom and "Freedom Center" at a small hotel in Zihuatanejo. A second headquarters was opened in Newton, Massachusetts, just outside of Boston. Their goal was to "turn on America." Leary popularized the use of LSD, and as a result of his Harvard connection, LSD gained the attention of the mass media (Grinspoon 1979). As a self-appointed High Priest of LSD (the title of Leary's book), he traveled widely and lectured on the virtues of using acid to "turn on, tune in, and drop out." Acid rock songs such as "White Rabbit" by the Jefferson Airplane, "Sunshine Superman" by Donovan, and the Beatles' "Magical Mystery Tour" and "Lucy in the Sky with Diamonds" became top hits. The books of Nobel Prize winner Hermann Hesse (1877–1962) were very popular among the youth of the 1960s, and his work helped to popularize the "psychedelic" experience (Engel 1974). Psychedelic jargon and colors became fashionable, and the media reported on the activities of hippies in New York's Greenwich Village and San Francisco's Haight-Ashbury district. LSD use became part of the counterculture and the antiwar movement.

In 1963 an editorial attacking LSD appeared in the *Journal of the American Medical Association*, and in 1965 LSD was outlawed in the United States. In 1963 Leary and Alpert were discharged from Harvard. That same year, the Mexican authorities closed down Freedom Center, and Leary was deported. In 1965 Leary was returning to the United States from a trip to Mexico with three other people, one of whom had secreted marijuana in her undergarments. When the drug was discovered during a strip search, Leary blurted out, "I'll take responsibility for the marijuana." At the time possession of marijuana was a serious crime in Texas. Despite his defense that the use of drugs was part of his religious liberty, Leary was convicted and sentenced to thirty years in prison. Leary appealed; in the meantime his harassment by law enforcement agencies resulted in numerous arrests. In 1969 the U.S. Supreme Court ordered Leary's marijuana case to be retried. In 1970 he was convicted again and sentenced to ten years. Leary appealed, but several weeks later he was convicted of another drug-related charge in California, where he received a one- to ten-year sentence. He was immediately remanded to a minimum-security prison.

Facing further trials in other states, later that year the 49 year-old Leary escaped from prison and subsequently reappeared in Algeria, where he found refuge with the Black Panthers. After being placed under house arrest for purposes of "revolutionary discipline," Leary fled again, this time to Switzerland. Eventually, he made his way to Afghanistan, where he was captured by U.S. drug enforcement agents. Leary wound up in the maximum-security prison at Folsom, California. After reportedly agreeing to provide information to the government, Leary was released in 1976 (R. Rosenbaum 1988). For a number of years he was popular on the collegiate lecture circuit, often appearing with G. Gordon Liddy, of Watergate fame, who was responsible for much of the harassment to which Leary had been subjected (Stevens 1987). In 1996, at age 75, Leary died of prostate cancer (Mansnerus 1996).

GOVERNMENT ACTION AFTER WORLD WAR II

In the years immediately before World War II the FBN seemed to have the drug problem well under control. Commissioner Anslinger released statistics indicating a significant drop in the addict population. Then came the war. Opiate smuggling dwindled, and Americans of an age most susceptible to drug use were in Europe and Asia. Drug use was viewed as unpatriotic as well as illegal. Alcohol, barbiturates, and amphetamines were the substances most widely abused during the war years, when the price of opiates increased dramatically. The addict population appeared to reach an all-time low.

At the end of the war there was fear of an epidemic of drug use as U.S. soldiers began to return from Far Eastern locations where opiate use was endemic. The epidemic failed to materialize. The FBN became a victim of its own propaganda and apparent success, and Congress would not increase the drug-fighting budget (H. W. Morgan 1981). Then in 1950 and 1951 a spate of news stories on drug abuse reported that the use of heroin was spilling out of the ghetto and into middle-class environs, where it was poisoning the minds and bodies of America's (white) youth. Musto (1973) points out a parallel between the periods following World War I and World War II: Both were characterized by an atmosphere of hostility to radicals and Communists, and both led to punitive sanctions against drug addicts. Any expression of tolerance for radical political ideas or drug addicts was un-American. In a timely stroke of political genius the FBN linked heroin trafficking to Red China.

Anslinger accused the People's Republic of China of selling opium and heroin to the free nations of the world to finance overseas ambitions (Cloyd 1982). As we shall see in Chapter 11, Far Eastern heroin was, and continues to be, the business of Chinese Nationalists, triads, Thais, and Burmese insurgents—not the People's Republic, which routinely executes drug traffickers. Indeed, "at the time of the Communist takeover in 1949, China was the world's largest producer and consumer of narcotic drugs" (Lee 1995: 194). The 1949 takeover of the Chinese mainland by the forces of Mao Zedong and the Communist Party eventually led in the elimination of domestic opium production in China.

On the basis of statistics showing that between 1946 and 1950 there had been a 100 percent increase in the number of arrests related to narcotics laws and that over a five-year period the average age of people committed to Public Health Service hospitals had declined from 37.5 to 26.7 years, Congress concluded that drug addiction was increasing and that penalties for drug trafficking were inadequate.

In 1951 Congress passed the Boggs Act, which increased penalties for violations of drug laws. Once again, using rather dubious statistical data, Congress concluded that the increased penalties of the Boggs Act had been quite successful in reducing drug trafficking. As a result, in 1956 Congress passed the Narcotic Control Act, which further increased the penalties for drug violations, for example, the sale of heroin to individuals under 18 years of age was made a capital offense; the Act also increased the authority of the FBN and agents of the Customs Bureau (President's Commission on Organized Crime 1986). State legislatures, responding to the federal initiative, significantly increased penalties for drug violations.

"Public concern over the problem of drug abuse, which had been relatively dormant during the 1940s and 1950s, flared again during the 1960s. The intensification of national concern resulted in increasing pressure for federal initiatives in the area. In response to this development, a White House Conference on Narcotics and Drug Abuse was convened in 1962, which resulted in the establishment of the President's Advisory Commission on Narcotics and Drug Abuse (Prettyman Commission) on January 15, 1963" (President's Commission on Organized Crime 1986: 215). The commission recommended discarding the antiquated legal notion that drug control was simply a taxing measure, and they suggested that the responsibilities of the FBN be transferred to the Department of Justice. On the other hand, the commission recommended that the regulation of marijuana and lawful narcotic drugs be transferred from the FBN to the Department of Health, Education, and Welfare (HEW). It also recommended increasing the number of federal drug agents and enacting legislation for the strict control of nonnarcotic drugs capable of producing psychotoxic effects when abused.

In the 1960s concern increased over the diversion of dangerous drugs from licit sources. As a result, Congress passed the Drug Abuse Control Amendments of 1965, which, among other things, mandated record-keeping and inspection requirements for depressant and stimulant drugs throughout the chain of distribution, from the basic manufacturer to (but not including) the consumer. Enforcement of the 1965 legislation was left to a newly created agency within HEW's Food and Drug Administration: the Bureau of Drug Abuse Control. The Treasury Department's monopoly over drug enforcement had ended (President's Commission on Organized Crime 1986).

A TURN TOWARD TREATMENT

During the 1960s the medical profession began to reassert itself on the issue of drug abuse in both treatment and research. Treating disciplines—psychology and social work—and researchers in sociology and public health began to focus on the drug issue as a social problem, not simply a law enforcement problem. The social activism of the 1960s also influenced the perspective on drug abuse (H. W. Morgan 1981), and a new strategic approach was implemented: reducing demand by rehabilitating large numbers of drug addicts. Arnold Trebach (1982: 226) argues that this approach was facilitated by the resignation of Harry Anslinger as commissioner of the FBN ("which had been accomplished with the active encouragement of the Kennedy brothers"). Anslinger was replaced by Harry Giordano, a pharmacist, and the pendulum of drug policy began to shift away from a law enforcement model toward a treatment model. The 1963 Prettyman Commission recommended the relaxation of mandatory prison sentences for drug convictions, greater research, and the dismantling of the FBN, whose functions were to be divided between HEW (prevention and treatment), and the Department of Justice (law enforcement).

In 1961 California established a civil commitment program in which drug addicts were taken into custody and committed—like mentally ill people in need of hospitalization—to a nonpunitive period of confinement and drug treatment. Confinement was followed by a period of aftercare (parole supervision). In 1966 New York established the Narcotic Addiction Control Commission, a large-scale effort whose goal was to confine as many drug addicts as possible under civil commitment statutes. As in California, whose lead New York was following, confinement was followed by a period of parole supervision. (This writer was employed briefly as a senior narcotics parole officer for the Narcotic Addiction Control Commission. This agency, which expended billions of dollars, was dismantled during the 1970s as a very costly failure.) In 1966 Congress passed the Narcotic Addict Rehabilitation Act, which in lieu of prosecution authorized federal district courts to order the voluntary and involuntary civil commitment of certain defendants who were found to be drug addicts and mandated the Surgeon General to establish rehabilitation and posthospitalization care programs for drug addicts. The legislation also authorized the financing of state efforts to treat addicts.

Between 1969 and 1974 the number of federally funded drug rehabilitation programs dramatically increased from 16 at the beginning of 1969 to 926 in 1974. Federal expenditures on drug treatment rose from about $80 million to about $800 million during that period. About half of the 80,000 clients in these programs were being maintained on methadone (Moss 1977), a synthetic opiate. During the 1960s a pilot program of methadone maintenance was initiated at Rockefeller University in New York. The drug, which was taken orally, prevented withdrawal symptoms in heroin addicts who were maintained with daily doses. Trebach (1982: 227) refers to this approach to heroin addiction as the "greatest theoretical and practical departure in American rehabilitation strategies and clinical attitudes since the early 1920s." While the program was successful in aiding the rehabilitation of certain kinds of drug users, methadone when ingested intravenously produces a heroinlike euphoria, and by the early 1970s large quantities had been diverted to the illegal street market. In response, Congress passed the Narcotic Treatment Act in 1974, which required annual registration by practitioners dispensing narcotic drugs and imposed new standards for the legal dispensing of dangerous drugs (President's Commission on Organized Crime 1986).

The 1960s and 1970s also experienced a rise in the popularity of the therapeutic-community approach to treating addiction, the best known being Synanon in California and Daytop Village in New York. Operated by recovered addicts, these drug-free centers use a variety of talking and confrontational therapies mixed with aspects of behavior modification. (Methadone, therapeutic communities, and other approaches to the treatment of drug abusers will be discussed in Chapter 10.)

COMPREHENSIVE DRUG ABUSE PREVENTION AND CONTROL ACT OF 1970

As the turn of the decade approached, alarming statistics (of dubious validity) about drug abuse were publicized. The drug problem was quickly becoming a major political issue. In 1968 President Lyndon Johnson decried the fragmented approach to drug law enforcement. With congressional approval the President abolished the FBN and the Bureau of Drug Abuse Control and transferred their responsibilities to a newly created agency, the Bureau of Narcotics and Dangerous Drugs (BNDD), in the Department of Justice. Revenue and importation aspects of drug trafficking remained within the Treasury Department's Internal Revenue Service and Bureau of Customs. In 1970 President Richard Nixon clarified the responsibilities of the federal agencies involved in drug control, announcing that BNDD "controls all investigations involving violations of the laws of the United States relating to narcotics, marijuana and dangerous drugs, both within the United States and beyond its borders." Several months later guidelines were promulgated that provided increased authority for customs officials at ports and borders.

The two-pronged approach to dealing with drug abuse—*reducing availability* by investigating and prosecuting traffickers and *reducing demand* by preventing addiction and treating addicts—was now firm policy. The Comprehensive Drug Abuse Prevention and Control Act of 1970 authorized HEW to increase its efforts at prevention and rehabilitation through a program of grants to special projects and made the HEW National Institute on Drug Abuse, the agency with primary responsibility for drug education and prevention activities. The legislation also established five schedules into which all controlled substances could be placed according to their potential for abuse (discussed in Chapter 12); imposed additional reporting requirements for manufacturers, distributors, and dispensers; promulgated new regulations for the importation of controlled substances; and established the Commission on Marijuana and Drug Abuse. BNDD was authorized to increase its strength by 300 agents.

The 1970 legislation represented a new legal approach to federal drug policy. It was predicated not on the constitutional power to tax, but on federal authority over interstate commerce. The President's Commission on Organized Crime (1986: 228) notes that this shift had enormous implications for the way in which the federal government would approach drug enforcement in the future. The act "set the stage for an innovation in federal drug law enforcement techniques. That innovation was the assigning of large numbers of federal narcotic agents to work in local communities. No longer was it necessary to demonstrate interstate traffic to justify federal participation in combating illegal drug use." The new approach was upheld by decisions of the Supreme Court, and the National Conference of Commissioners on Uniform State Laws drafted a model act based on the 1970 statutes, which has been adopted by most states.

A 1973 reorganization plan led to the creation of the Drug Enforcement Administration (DEA) within the Department of Justice. All investigative and enforcement responsibilities for drug control, except those related to ports of entry and borders, were given over to the new agency. In 1982 the Federal Bureau of Investigation (FBI) was given concurrent jurisdiction with the DEA for drug investigation and law enforcement. In addition, the DEA director was required to report to the director of the FBI, who was given responsibility for supervising drug law enforcement efforts and policies. That same year the Department of Defense Authorization Act contained a provision outlining military cooperation with civilian authorities. This provision was aimed at improving the level of cooperation by delineating precisely what assistance military commanders could provide. It also permits military personnel to operate military equipment that had been loaned to civilian drug enforcement agencies (President's Commission on Organized Crime 1986). (In 1988 the military's role in drug law enforcement was substantially increased; this is discussed in Chapter 12.)

DRUG SCARE OF THE 1980s

As 1980 approached, the lack of public interest in and even tolerance of drug use began to shift as grassroots parent groups began to influence the political landscape. A mother "who later presided over the National Federation of Parents for Drug-Free Youth, attended a rock concert in 1978 with her two young children and discovered rampant drug use all around them. Her anger, shared by others she contacted, apparently was a major factor in the defeat of her Congressman, ... who had sponsored a bill favoring the decriminalization of an ounce of marijuana. That a broad base of parents were antagonistic to drugs and that they were now organizing their political power had been demonstrated" (Musto 1987: 271). With encouragement from Dr. Robert L. DuPont, then director of the National Institute on Drug Abuse, an "antipot" handbook for parents was published. The antidrug theme was soon picked up by the Reagan Administration.

The issue of drug abuse is politically safe and useful because no one is in favor of it. During the presidency of Ronald Reagan drugs again became a major political issue. On June 19, 1986, Len Bias, a basketball star from the University of Maryland, died of a cocaine overdose; on June 27, Don Rogers, a defensive back for the Cleveland Browns, also died of a cocaine overdose. These widely reported incidents, occurring within a short time of each other and less than five months before congressional elections, led to an intensification of antidrug efforts, a widespread public relations effort utilizing sports and entertainment personalities whose message to television viewers was "Just Say No!" (to drugs). Not to be outdone, Congress responded with huge allocations to combat this scourge, and politicians scrambled for partisan advantage. "Len Bias' death brought together the political and human aspects of drug abuse. His death accentuated that attention placed on drugs after the announcement of the 'war on drugs.' Although consensus about the need to 'do something' was generally accepted, politicians continued to argue over the best approach" (Merriam 1989: 25). With the elections over and Congress in the hands of the Democrats, the President significantly scaled back the allocations.

The fight against drugs and drug abuse was an important issue in the presidential campaign of 1988. The heat of the national campaign led to the enactment of an omnibus drug bill (the Anti-Drug Abuse Act of 1988) in the final days of the 100th Congress. The legislation states: "It is the declared policy of the United States Government to create a Drug-Free America by 1995." The bipartisan measure, which was approved overwhelmingly, increased antidrug spending, earmarking 50 percent for treatment, a figure that was to increase to 60 percent over the next few years. On both federal and state levels penalty distinctions between marijuana and drugs such as heroin and cocaine have been erased—"zero tolerance" (Pollan 1993).

The statute mandated greater controls over **precursor** chemicals and devices used to manufacture drugs, such as encapsulating machinery. It also created a complex and extensive body of civil penalties aimed at casual users, including fines and ineligibility for federal benefits such as educational loans and mortgage guarantees and/or the loss of a maritime, pilot, or stockbroker license for a number of years. Penalties were enhanced for selling drugs to minors, and a judge was empowered to impose the death penalty for murders committed as part of a continuing criminal enterprise or for the murder of a law enforcement officer during an arrest for a drug-related felony.

The legislation also established the Office of National Drug Control Policy headed by a director ("drug czar") appointed by the President. The director is charged with coordinating federal drug supply reduction efforts, including international control, intelligence, interdiction, domestic drug law enforcement, treatment, education, and research, and serves as a liaison between the federal government and state and local drug control efforts. The first director was William J. Bennett, who served as drug czar for twenty-two months, using the position primarily as a rhetorical platform to focus attention on the issue of drug abuse as seen by the administration. His approach attracted extensive media attention, but the powers of the director are so circumscribed that he accomplished little else.

The medical profession returned to a role in responding to drug abuse. Addiction medicine grew rapidly between the 1960s and 1980s, largely due to the efforts of physicians from New York, California, and Georgia—many were themselves recovering addicts (Freed 2007). Their efforts led to the establishment of the American Society of Addiction Medicine. Psychiatrists also responded, arguing that substance abuse was often part of a co-occurring psychiatric disorder—comorbidity—that they were uniquely qualified to treat. In 1985, psychiatrists established what is now known as the Academy of Addiction Psychiatry, and by 1991 addiction psychiatry became a board-recognized subspecialty under the American Board of Psychiatry and Neurology (Freed 2007). In 1989, the American Society of Addiction Medicine was admitted to the American Medical Association (AMA), and the AMA added addiction medicine to its list of designated specialties the following year.

THE TWENTY-FIRST CENTURY

The 1990s began a remarkable period of a lack of political interest in drug abuse. Indeed, as officials began to recognize the extent of prison overcrowding resulting from state and federal drug policies, statutory and administrative remedies were formulated that placed more drug offenders in diversion or drug treatment programs, on probation, and on parole. Laws providing significantly greater prison sentences for the sellers of crack cocaine than for sellers of powdered cocaine came under fire because the former substance is more likely to be used by minorities, the latter by middle-class whites. There is a mandatory five-year minimum for selling 5 grams of crack or 500 grams of powdered cocaine and ten years for selling 50 grams of crack or 5,000 grams of powdered cocaine.

The cocaine market was affected by crack, because many crack users were purchasing the powdered form (cocaine hydrochloride) in large doses and converting it to crack themselves, reducing the demand for street-level crack, which many users believed inferior to what they could produce themselves. The use of methamphetamine increased, with new supplies coming from Mexico. In some areas methamphetamine was almost as popular as cocaine. Marijuana remained readily available, and both its use and sale transcend ethnic, racial, and gender boundaries. Users of marijuana tend to be under 20 years old (Office of National Drug Control Policy 1995).

While cocaine remained the dominant (illegal) drug of abuse, heroin, prepared for smoking and snorting, made a comeback, particularly outside its typical core clientele, the urban poor. This revival, which was fueled by the availability of high-grade heroin, particularly from Colombia, is following a pattern set by cocaine in the 1970s. The abundance of heroin is reflected in the purity levels found at the retail level.

The twenty-first century has experienced a rise in the use of methamphetamine in rural parts of the United States, while in urban areas crack use has ceased to be an epidemic. Concern over the nonmedical use of prescription medicine has led the government to focus on that problem.

In sum, this country has moved from a century of permissiveness to draconian sanctions as the result of foreign affairs, the policy of a single federal agency, and a volatile mix of racism and politics. This has led to two drug problems in the United States:

1. The drug problem of the affluent: "It is by no means insignificant, and it has caused more than its share of personal tragedies. But it is a manageable problem, and it has been steadily decreasing for several years, for reasons unrelated to the war on drugs" (Currie 1993: 3).
2. The drug problem of America's have-nots: "That problem has grown malignantly in the face of the drug war—and it is much further from solution than it was when that war began" (Currie 1993: 3).

Now that we have completed our review of the evolution of the problem of drug abuse in the United States, in the next chapter we will examine the biology of psychoactive substances.

SUMMARY

-   Historical analysis is handicapped by the lack of adequate data on the extent of drug abuse at earlier periods in our history and of alcohol use during Prohibition.
-   What we think about addiction very much depends on who is addicted and attitudes have often reflected popular prejudices against a variety of racial and ethnic groups.

-   The citizens of the United States have traditionally consumed large quantities of alcohol.
-   Opposition to alcohol was often intertwined with nativism, and efforts against alcohol and other psychoactive drugs were often a thinly veiled reaction to minority groups.

- Big business was also interested in prohibition because alcohol contributed to industrial inefficiency and labor strife, and the saloon, which served the interests of machine politics.
- The Eighteenth was ratified in 1919 and in 1920 Congress passed the Volstead Act which strengthened the language of the amendment.
- The Prohibition Bureau, an arm of the Treasury Department, was created, and became notorious for its ineptitude and corruption.
- Primary resistance or opposition to Prohibition resulted in negative contagion.
- To fill the income void, when Prohibition was repealed in 1933, criminal organizations turned to the drug trade.
- Two centuries ago, opium was generally available as a cure for everything: like aspirin, every household had some.
- As the primary ingredient in many "patent medicines," opiates were readily available in the United States until 1914, and prescribed and promoted for general symptoms as well as for specific diseases.
- The smoking of opium was popularized in the United States by Chinese immigrants, who brought the habit with them.
- The popularity of morphine rose during the Civil War, when the intravenous use of the drug to treat battlefield casualties was rather indiscriminate.
- Physicians prescribed morphine for any complaint, and the substance was widely abused by physicians themselves.
- Opium furnished the British with the silver needed to buy tea and balance its trade with China.
- Anti-opium efforts by China and British efforts to balance trade resulted in two wars, which China lost.
- Anti-opium legislation was steeped in nativism and aimed at Chinese immigrants.
- While people may have frowned on opium use during the nineteenth century, addicts were not subject to discrimination.
- National efforts against opiates (and cocaine) were part of a larger campaign to regulate drugs and the contents of food substances and to address the problem of patent medicines.
- The dramatic event that quickly led to the adoption of the Pure Food and Drug Act was the 1906 publication of Upton Sinclair's *The Jungle*.
- American efforts to improve trade with China led to international opium conferences in 1909 and one in the Hague in 1912.
- Delegates to the 1912 conference agreed that their governments would take action to suppress opium use and as a result the United States enacted the Harrison Act in 1914.
- Harrison Act rules promulgated by the Treasury Department limited the possession and dispensing of opiates to medical professionals.
- The Supreme Court ruled that physicians could prescribe maintenance doses of morphine to addicts, but the federal narcotics agency began arresting physicians who did and closed the clinics established for that purpose.
- The medical profession withdrew from dispensing drugs to addicts, forcing addicts to look to illicit sources and giving rise to an enormous illegal business in drugs.
- World War II had a dramatic impact on the supply of heroin in the United States.
- Cocaine, a stimulant, is an alkaloid found in significant quantities only in the leaves of two species of coca shrub that are indigenous to certain sections of South America.
- Patent medicines frequently contained significant amounts of cocaine.
- After the flush of enthusiasm for cocaine in the 1880s its direct use declined. Cocaine continued to be used in a variety of potions and tonics, but unlike morphine and heroin, it did not develop a separate appeal.
- In the United States, from 1930 until the 1960s there was limited demand for cocaine and, accordingly, only limited supply.

- During the 1980s, by publicizing and glamorizing the lifestyle of cocaine users, the mass media created an effective advertising campaign for cocaine and the new demand was sufficient to generate new sources. This led to the development of Latin-American criminal organizations.
- During the 1980s crack became popular in a number of cities, altering the drug market at the consumer level: users and sellers were much younger than was typical in the heroin business.
- By 1987 the rapid expansion of crack use stopped, and by 1989 its popularity began to diminish.
- State laws against marijuana were often part of a reaction to Mexican immigration.
- Marijuana was never an important issue in the United States until the 1960s when nonconformist counterculture, whose members were often from the white middle class, emerged.
- There has been some medical use of the active ingredient THC in marijuana to control the side effects of chemotherapy and to treat glaucoma. Despite vigorous opposition at the federal level, in 1997 voters in California passed a referendum authorizing physicians to prescribe marijuana; several other states have followed.
- Between 1932 and 1946 there were thirty-nine generally accepted medical uses for amphetamine.
- During World War II and the Korean conflict, governments issues amphetamine to their military personnel to counteract fatigue.
- In 1971 federal laws restricted the conditions under which amphetamines could be prescribed.

- Methamphetamine appeared on the drug scene in the late 1980s and widespread abuse continues, particularly in more rural parts of the country where the drug is often manufactured.
- Barbiturates are sedating drugs synthesized from barbituric acid and in medicine have largely been replaced by sedatives.
- Hallucinogens such as LSD became popular during the 1960s, particularly among rebellious college students and people who identified themselves as antiestablishment.
- Public concern over the problem of drug abuse, which had been relatively dormant during the 1940s and 1950s, flared again during the 1960s.
- During the 1960s the medical profession began to reassert itself on the issue of drug abuse in both treatment and research.
- The two-pronged approach to dealing with drug abuse—*reducing availability* by law enforcement and *reducing demand* by preventing addiction and treating addicts—became policy.
- The 1980s experienced another drug scare leading to the creation of the White House Office of National Drug Control Policy.
- The medical profession returned to a role in responding to drug abuse and addiction medicine experienced a dispute between psychiatrists and physician addiction specialists.
- The 1990s began a remarkable period of a lack of political interest in drug abuse that continued into the twenty-first century.
- In the twenty-first century, cocaine remained the dominant illegal drug of abuse, while heroin, prepared for smoking and snorting, made a comeback. The popularity of methamphetamine increased in rural parts of the country.

Review Questions

1. What handicaps attempts to provide an historical analysis of drug use?
2. With respect to goals, how was the temperance movement divided?
3. Which of the goals finally won out?
4. How did the temperance view of abstinence differ from the modern alcoholism movement?

5. What was the connection between efforts against alcohol and other drugs and nativism?
6. What were the demographics of prohibitionists?
7. Why did big business support Prohibition?
8. In what year was the Eighteenth Amendment ratified?
9. What was the purpose of the National Prohibition/Volstead Act?
10. Why was the Prohibition Bureau of the Treasury Department notorious?
11. How did Prohibition lead to *negative contagion*?
12. How did criminal organizations that developed during Prohibition react to its repeal.
13. Why did ancient civilizations use opium?
14. What were "patent medicines?"
15. What led to the popularity of morphine?
16. What led to the imbalance of trade between China and Britain?
17. How did the British attempt to balance trade with China?
18. How did the Chinese government react to the opium trade?
19. What caused the First Opium War?
20. What was the cause of the Second Opium War?
21. Why were Chinese laborers originally brought into the United States?
22. How did attitudes toward Chinese immigrants influence opium laws?
23. What events led to the passage of the Pure Food and Drug Act?
24. How did the Pure Food and Drug Act affect patent medicines?
25. What was the relationship between trade with China and U.S. efforts to curtail opium trafficking?
26. What led to the formation of the International Opium Commission?
27. How did the second international opium conference in the Hague influence U.S. laws with respect to drugs?
28. Why was the Harrison Act enacted?
29. Why did Congress originally use its taxing powers to control drugs?

30. How did the Harrison Act influence attitudes toward narcotic users?
31. What did the Supreme Court rule with respect to physicians providing morphine for addicted patients?
32. How did efforts to ban alcohol differ from those to ban drugs?
33. How did the federal drug enforcement agency influence the direction of drug policy in the United States?
34. How did the actions of federal narcotics agents influence U.S. drug policy?
35. How did the medical profession react to federal enforcement activity?
36. What was the primary reason for the Uniform Drug Act?
37. How did World War II impact on heroin use in the United States?
38. Why were Spanish explorers in the Americas unenthusiastic about the use of coca leaves?
39. What was the result of using cocaine to treat morphine addiction?
40. How did racism influence the campaign against cocaine?
41. During the 1960s, how did the popular media influence attitudes toward cocaine?
42. How did crack change the consumer market in cocaine?
43. What are the four elements of a *drug scare*?
44. What has replaced cocaine as a local anesthetic?
45. What is the connection between racism and marijuana legislation?
46. What was the role of the Federal Bureau of Narcotics in bringing about marijuana laws?
47. What is the relationship between changes in attitude toward marijuana and changes in the social class of users?
48. Why were amphetamines used by various militaries during wartime?
49. What explains the popularity of methamphetamine among students and truck drivers?
50. What is the medical use for barbiturates?
51. What is the danger of overprescribing sedatives such as Valium?
52. What explains the popularity of hallucinogens such as LSD during the 1960s?

53. Why did the problem of drug abuse appear to be under control in the years immediately following World War II?

54. What was the connection between the People's Republic of China and heroin trafficking?

55. What was the new approach to drug use that was influenced by the social activism of the 1960s?

56. What was the two-pronged approach to drug abuse that resulted from the Comprehensive Drug Abuse Prevention and Control Act of 1970?

57. What is the basis of the claim by psychiatrists that they should be the physicians who deal with drug addiction?

Brain imaging techniques enable researchers to observe drug effects while they are occurring in the brain and compare brain structure, function, and metabolism in drug-abusing and non-abusing individuals. The results to date have firmly established that drug addiction is a disease of the brain, causing important derangements in many areas, including pathways affecting reward and cognition.

Joanna S. Fowler, Nora D. Volkow, Cheryl A. Kissed, and Linda Chang (2007: 14).

CHAPTER **3** | # THE BIOLOGY OF DRUG USE AND ABUSE

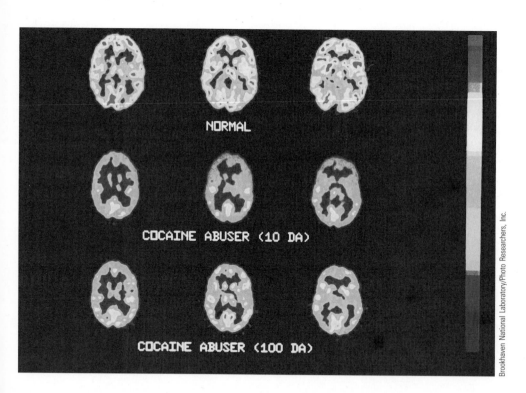

Many people do not understand why individuals become addicted to drugs or how drugs change the brain to foster compulsive drug abuse. They mistakenly view drug abuse and addiction as strictly a social problem and may characterize those who take drugs as morally weak. One very common belief is that drug abusers should be able to just stop taking drugs if they are only willing to change their behavior. What people often underestimate is the complexity of drug addiction—that it is a disease that impacts the brain and because of that, stopping drug abuse is not simply a matter of willpower.

National Institute on Drug Abuse (2008: 1a)

Distinctions between the biology and pharmacology (discussed in Chapters 3, 4, 5, and 6) of drug use, the sociology (Chapter 7) of drug use, and the psychology (Chapter 8) of drug use are quite artificial (Peele 1985). Although the explanatory value of each by itself is limited, the interaction of these three dimensions can explain drug use. Their separation into different chapters is therefore for pedagogical rather than scientific purposes. (The biology of drug use also has important treatment and policy implications—topics of subsequent chapters.) In this chapter we will examine how psychoactive drugs affect the central nervous system. In subsequent chapters we will apply this information to specific drugs—depressants, stimulants, hallucinogens, "club drugs," marijuana, and prescription drugs.

BIOLOGICAL THEORIES OF DRUG USE AND ABUSE

A **theory** helps us to explain events. It organizes events so that they can be placed in perspective; explains the causes of past events; and predicts when, where, and how future events will occur. "A theory consists of a set of assumptions; concepts regarding events, situations, individuals, and groups; and propositions that describe the interrelationships among the various assumptions and concepts" (Binder and Gees 1983: 3). Theory is the basic building block for the advancement of human knowledge. In the physical sciences, such as chemistry and physics, theory can usually be subjected to rigorous testing and replication. However, testing biological theories of drug abuse is limited to working with laboratory animals and observing and examining current users. We could not give non-drug-using human beings varying doses of drugs to find out how their central nervous system responds (which might also require an autopsy).

Thus, our discussion of the biology of psychoactive drugs will necessarily have limitations, since there is a great deal that is not known about the details of how these drugs actually affect the nervous system of a specific person. There is evidence, for example, the same substance can have a different impact on different people. The social context (the setting in which the drug is ingested) and the user's expectations can influence a drug's effects (Becker 1967, 1977; Schnoll 1979). Whether a person will interpret the effect of a drug such as marijuana, LSD, or an opiate, especially the first few times he or she takes it, as euphoria or pleasurable depends very much on the setting and other complex psychological and social conditions (Grinspoon and Hedblom 1975). In other words, use of the substances discussed in this book is not automatically pleasurable. Many, if not most, people who have been exposed to morphine or heroin, for example, find the initial experience distinctly unpleasant: "not everyone responds to the analgesic experience the same way. Some people find a narcosis tremendously alluring, while others report that the sensations of helplessness are disturbing and distinctly unappealing" (Peele 1980: 143). Thus, "one person's dysphoria may be another person's euphoria" (Schnoll 1979: 256). Some people get "high" from dangerous pursuits, others from chemicals; still others seek to avoid both. "Drug effects are strongly influenced by the amount taken, how much has been taken before, what the user wants and expects to happen, the surroundings in which it is taken, and the reactions of other people. All of these influences are themselves tied up with social and cultural attitudes and beliefs about drugs as well as more general social conditions. Even the same person will react differently at different times" (Institute for the Study of Drug Dependence 1987: 1).

DRUG EFFECTS

The effects of any drug depend on the:

- amount taken
- user's past drug experience
- manner in which the drug is taken
- circumstances under which the drug is taken (the place, the user's psychological and emotional stability, the presence of other people, the simultaneous use of alcohol or other drugs)

Source: Alcoholism and Drug Addiction Research Foundation, Toronto.

Further clouding the picture is the *placebo effect*: an inert compound triggering a drug-like response. When patients expect a drug to diminish their pain, the mere expectation results in brain activity that causes the release of pain-dampening chemicals (neurotransmitters). Thus, the power of thought processes to influence the central nervous system serves to confound our understanding of the effect of psychoactive substances.

Laboratory studies, which form the basis for much of our knowledge of psychoactive drugs, fail to reproduce social context, and their results are accordingly limited. The dependence potential of various drugs is typically based on laboratory studies with monkeys and rats, although research has discovered that there are interspecies differences in the effects of cocaine on the brains of rodents and primates. The discrepancy in findings between rodents and primate studies illustrates the limitations of animal models of drug abuse (Bolla, Cadet, and London 1998). For example, the effects of opiates vary with species: in cats and horses morphine produces intense stimulation and is sometimes used (illegally) to "dope" race horses for a better performance (Harris 1993). Furthermore, in experimental environments these animals can also become addicted to stinging electric shocks delivered to the tail or the paws (Bennett 1988). Indeed, researchers have discovered that with animals "almost any environmental stimulus can serve as a reinforcer or punisher under the right environmental conditions" (Dworkin and Pitts 1994: 106).

Experimentation on human subjects is obviously limited by ethical considerations. Thus, with respect to alcohol, a lawful drug, "because of ethical considerations, prospective studies of ethanol reactivity in children and young adolescents (before they have initiated regular drinking) have not been conducted" (Sher 1991: 86). And laboratory studies also cannot actually replicate street use in which any of the substances under discussion may be abused with alcohol or in some other combination. This leads to our next topic.

POLYDRUG USE

Understanding the biology of psychoactive drugs is complicated by the phenomenon of **polydrug use**—abusers consuming more than one type of psychoactive chemical. Research shows overwhelmingly that compulsive users use more than one drug, a major difficulty in studying drug use. Heroin addicts are very often polydrug users (Vaillant 1970; B. D. Johnson, Lipton, and Wish 1986b; McFarland 1989); they use heroin in combination with other drugs, especially cocaine and alcohol (Epstein and Gfroerer 1997). Bruce Johnson and his colleagues found that 90 percent of the heroin addicts they studied also abused alcohol and cocaine (Johnson, Lipton, and Wish 1986b), and a study of heroin addicts in San Antonio revealed that 100 percent used alcohol, almost half on a daily basis (Maddux and Desmond 1981). Almost 19 percent of the people admitted for heroin abuse treatment in Colorado also reported the use of cocaine (Colorado Alcohol and Drug Abuse Division 1987) and more than 35 percent of cocaine users admitted for treatment reported the use of alcohol (Mendelson and Harrison 1989). Mark Gold and his colleagues (1986: 55) found that "most cocaine abusers are concurrently abusing alcohol or other sedative-hypnotics to alleviate the unpleasant side effects of cocaine." Crack users frequently "administer heroin because it enhances the euphoric effect while ameliorating the intense stimulant effects of cocaine" (Drug Enforcement Administration 1994b: 1), and alcohol is frequently used to moderate the effects of cocaine. When cocaine and alcohol are ingested together the liver combines them to produce a third substance, **cocaethylene,** which intensifies cocaine's euphoric effects and is associated with a greater risk of sudden death than cocaine alone (National Institute on Drug Abuse 2008b).

The New York State Division of Substance Abuse Services (1986: 14–15) reported that the "use of more than one substance continues to be the predominant pattern of abuse. Both heroin and cocaine are commonly used with one drug ameliorating the undesired effects of the other; PCP is used by some heroin abusers to heighten the effect of heroin. Alcohol use is almost always involved." In San Antonio, Texas, approximately two thirds of substance-related deaths have involved both cocaine and heroin (Spence 1989). In Minnesota, polydrug use, which includes alcohol, is widespread among that state's chemical-abusing population (Minnesota Department of Human Services 1987). With respect to methadone patients, thirty years ago most abused only heroin. "In New York today, approximately 30 percent abuse other substances as well, including alcohol, cocaine, methamphetamine, benzodiazepines, and marijuana" (Marion 2005: 26). In Nebraska, persons singularly dependent on methamphetamine are rare; the majority of methamphetamine users can best be classified as general substance abusers: "Misuse of alcohol and other drugs almost inevitably precedes the experimentation which produced the addict's eventual dependency on methamphetamine. As the highs and cravings of the methamphetamine habit gradually monopolize the user's attention and resources, the desire for some drugs may diminish, but the pharmacological effects of others, especially alcohol, simply complement the experience" (Robinson 2006: 7).

Criss-crossing (alternately inhaling lines of cocaine and heroin) is popular among drug enthusiasts, and some users are snorting heroin and smoking crack in combination. The primary drug in this combination is believed to be crack, heroin being used to ease the agitation associated with crack. Finally, drug users who are unable to secure their preferred substance because of insufficient funds or connections when the supply is scarce often seek available substitutes.

The neurological effects of mixing drugs can be (Schnoll 1979):

1. **Additive:** Two drugs that have similar actions are ingested, and the effect is cumulative $(1 + 1 = 2)$.

2. **Synergistic:** Two drugs that have similar actions are ingested, but the effect of their joint action is more than cumulative $(1 + 1 = 3)$.
3. **Potentiating:** Two drugs have different actions, but when they are taken together, one enhances the effects of the other $(1 + 1 = 4)$.
4. **Antagonistic:** Two or more drugs are taken together, and one counteracts the effects of the other(s) $(1 + 1 = 0)$.

Drugs that are prepared for street sale are typically impure or a mixture of psychoactive chemicals. "The users of illegally purchased drugs are often totally unaware of the actual chemical substance, the dose being purchased, and the contaminants that may be present in the sample." Many of these contaminants can produce toxic reactions in their own right (Schnoll 1979: 257).

THE DISEASE MODEL

Drug abuse is often discussed in terms such as "overpowering desire," "compulsion," or even "enslavement," as if the substance had a power all its own to "hook" people foolish enough to ingest it. Such theories emphasize the involuntary nature of drug use—use based on a craving—that has found some support in laboratory experiments with animals. Indeed, with the exception of marijuana and hallucinogens, animals will abuse the same chemicals that humans do (Friedman 1993). According to this approach, sometimes referred to as the **disease model**, the drug-dependent person is a victim of forces beyond his or her control. This theoretical approach has treatment implications. For example, it would support two very different approaches to substance abuse: the use of methadone maintenance and the Alcoholics Anonymous (AA) chemical-free approach that emphasizes a need for total abstinence. (Methadone and AA will be discussed in Chapter 10.)

Some psychoactive chemicals alter the central nervous system, creating what appears to be a compulsion to use the drug to restore a sense of wellbeing. Prolonged opiate use, for example, causes pervasive changes in brain function that persist long after the individual stops taking the drug. Heroin addicts themselves state that they take the drug to "feel normal." Thus, to the heroin addict, notes John Irwin (1970: 19), "it is the fix that cures the sickness, and it is the fix that is central to the whole dope life." After a period of abstinence an addict who returns to heroin use is likely to make statements such as "'It makes me feel normal again'—that is, it relieves the ex-addict's chronic triad of anxiety, depression, and craving" (Brecher 1972: 14). While drug use might begin through experimentation, dependence would be the inevitable result of these physiological changes. In sum, drugs that were taken initially to achieve pleasurable effects ("highs") are taken after addiction to avoid withdrawal ("lows"). However, craving for the pleasurable effects appears to be a better motivator, since addicts often relapse after being free of withdrawal (Robinson and Berridge 2003).

While environmental factors may determine whether a person is exposed to drugs, genetics may help to explain why only some of those who are exposed become drug dependent.

GENETIC PREDISPOSITION

More than a century ago, genetic explanations were proposed to explain addiction: The addict inherits a nervous system that has more energy or perhaps more actual nerve fiber. Drugs provide such nervous systems with a substance that is necessary but deficient; when the user finds that a drug satisfies this deficiency, repeated drug use naturally follows. A complementary theory views drug users as having an inherited predisposition to "nervous weakness," for which the use of drugs compensates. Other observers conceived of a lack of hereditary endowments that leaves some people ill equipped to deal with the fast pace of societal change; for them drug use provides chemical compensation.

In more contemporary times the National Institute on Drug Abuse (NIDA) has been funding studies on this issue, and evidence uncovered reveals that an individual's genetic makeup is a major factor in vulnerability to drug abuse (Volkow 2006). NIDA-funded researchers found that although family and social environmental factors determine whether an individual will begin using drugs, progression from use to dependence was largely dependent on genetic factors, particularly for males, and the genetic influence for heroin addiction surpassed that of any other drug (Zickler 1999). In response to the question: "What makes certain individuals particularly vulnerable to addiction and others relatively resistant?" extensive epidemiological studies reveal that roughly half of a person's risk for addiction is genetic. "This degree of heritability exceeds that of many other conditions that are considered highly heritable, such as type 2 (non-insulin dependent) diabetes, hypertension, and breast cancer" (Nestler 2005: 8–9).

While drug abuse is the result of a complex interplay of environmental, social, psychological, and biochemical factors, genetic factors play an important role in the vulnerability to drug abuse: The more severe the abuse, the greater is the role of genetic factors (Comings 1996; Crabbe 2002). Interaction between genetics and the environment is complex, since "environmental factors can alter the expression of genes involved with the way the brain works and responds to the environment, thus influencing the behavior of the individual" (Volkow 2006: 70).

Some biological theories describe the drug abuser as a person whose body is malfunctioning with respect to the production of crucial neurotransmitters (discussed below), making drug use self-medicating. According to this view, the user's choice of drug is the result of an interaction between its pharmacological properties and the primary feeling state experienced. Thus, according to **arousal theory**, those whose central nervous system quickly habituates to incoming stimuli owing to a neurotransmitter malfunction are most apt to be reinforced for engaging in antisocial behavior and less likely to learn alternative behavior patterns. Subjectively, such people regard many ordinary environments as boring and unpleasant and would therefore be more motivated than most people to seek novel and/or intense sensory stimulation. The behavior of such people would include impulsivity, risk taking, and an inclination to use psychoactive substances (Ellis 1990).

PSYCHOACTIVE SUBSTANCES AND THE CENTRAL NERVOUS SYSTEM

The body consists of cells organized into tissues, and specialized cells along the surface of the body receive information about the environment that is translated into electrochemical signals that we experience as sight, sound, smell, and touch. Information from the internal and external environment—collectively known as *stimuli*—is received by the **central nervous system (CNS)**, consisting of the brain and the spinal cord, whose cells—**neurons**—send information to a specific processing center of the brain.

Psychoactive chemicals influence the brain's communication system by disrupting the way neurons normally send, receive, and process information. They imitate the brain's natural chemical messengers (**neurotransmitters**) and overstimulate the **reward circuit** of the brain: "Almost all abused drugs produce pleasure by activating a specific network of neurons called the brain reward system. The circuit is normally involved in an important type of learning that helps us to stay alive. It is activated when we fulfill survival functions, such as eating when we are hungry or drinking when we are thirsty. A strain of mice deficient in the neurotransmitter dopamine do not seek food even when it is readily available and eventually starve to death. In turn, our brain rewards us with pleasurable feelings that teach us to repeat the task. Because the drugs inappropriately turn on this reward circuit, people want to repeat drug use" (Society for Neuroscience 2002: 33).

Some drugs, such as marijuana and heroin, have a structure similar to neurotransmitters that are naturally produced by the brain. This similarity allows them to "fool" the brain's **receptors** (neurons programmed to receive neurotransmitters) into sending abnormal messages—they "hijack" a normally occurring process. Stimulating drugs such as cocaine or methamphetamine cause ("trick") neurons to release abnormally large amounts of neurotransmitters and prevent the normal process by which these neurotransmitters are recycled (called **reuptake**) for later use and, thus, deactivated. Without reuptake, these neurotransmitters continue to flood brain circuits.

Psychoactive drugs typically impact the brain's reward system by triggering release of the neurotransmitter **dopamine**. Dopamine is associated with regions of the brain that, among other important functions, produce the sensations associated with such pleasures as eating and sex. When the user recognizes this connection, drug use is likely to be repeated. The desire for drugs is largely a desire to reexperience the intense pleasure recalled from past episodes of drug use, memory of which is stored in a brain region (*nucleus accumbens*) that enables people to recall actions that led to the pleasures associated with dopamine release, such as sexual orgasm or a drug high (Zickler 2004; Nestler 2005). Repetition, however, can lead to a diminishing of dopamine—going to the well once too often—and lessens the ability of the drug to produce euphoria, to which the user may respond by increasing dosage (National Institute on Drug Abuse 2008). Diminished dopamine is believed to be related to the intense craving associated with withdrawal in drug-dependent humans. This subjective experience of craving is related to relapse into drug-taking behavior following a bstinence and therefore is an important factor in drug addiction.

THE BRAIN

The brain, a dense mass weighing about 3 pounds and consisting of 10 billion to 50 billion anatomically independent but functionally interrelated neurons, is connected to the spinal cord by fibers and cells (the peripheral nervous system) that carry sensory information and muscle commands to the rest of the body (Figure 3.1). "This single organ controls all body activities, ranging from heart rate and sexual function to emotion, learning and memory" (Society for Neuroscience 2002: 5). After receiving and processing information, the brain sends commands to muscles and glands.

As noted earlier, the brain contains areas that produce pleasurable sensations—reward pathways. The pharmacological activation of brain reward systems is largely responsible for producing a psychoactive chemical's potent addictive properties. Direct electrical stimulation of the medial forebrain bundle produces intensely

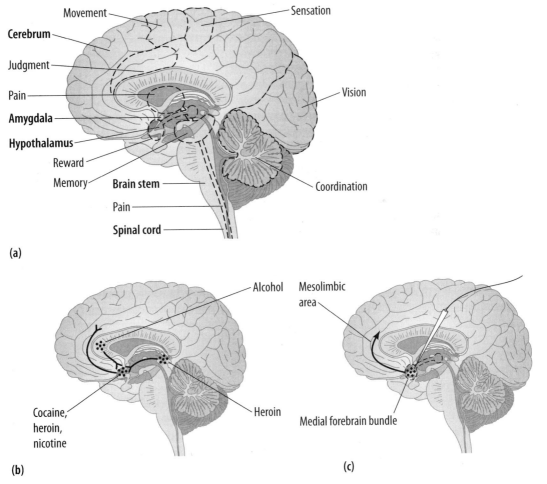

(a)

(b)   (c)

FIGURE 3.1 | THE BRAIN: (A) PARTS AND FUNCTIONS OF THE HUMAN BRAIN; (B) ACTIVATION OF THE REWARD PATHWAY OF THE BRAIN BY ADDICTIVE DRUGS; (C) EFFECTS OF ELECTRIC STIMULATION ON THE BRAIN

rewarding effects, while stimulants and depressants can activate this reward system by their pharmacological actions.

THE ADOLESCENT BRAIN AND DRUGS

The immature brain of adolescents can explain their risky behavior. Different regions of the brain develop on different timetables. One of the last parts of the brain to mature deals with the ability to make sound judgments and calm unruly emotions. Along with surges in testosterone at puberty, this could account for the rise in aggressiveness and irritability seen in adolescents

Until early adulthood, that part of the brain where planning, reasoning, and impulse control occur (prefrontal cortex) remains immature. As a result, when determining risk versus reward, the immature adolescent brain tends to emphasize benefits while discounting dangers (Reyna and Farley 2006). Research also reveals that the adolescent brain is more responsive to drugs and thus more vulnerable to drug abuse than the adult brain (Whitten 2007a). "Thus, introducing drugs while the brain is still developing may have profound and long-lasting consequences" *Science of Addiction* (2007: 10).

The developing adolescent brain drives an interest in novelty that vastly exceeds that of children or adults. The choice of "novelty" often depends on the youngster's environment: Middle-class youths are more likely to have access to activities such as skiing and scuba diving, while for many others, crime, sex, and drugs are the most viable outlets (Brownlee 1999).

NEURONS

A neuron is the basic working unit of the central nervous system, a specialized cell designed to transmit information from the brain to other nerve cells or to muscle or gland cells. Neurons come in many sizes and shapes and form chains of specialized and excitable cells. They differ from other body cells in that they can conduct information in the form of electrical impulses over long distances. There are over 100 billion neurons in the body and across them, from neuron to neuron, move signals or impulses—information in the form of electrical activity. A neuron consists of a cell body (**soma**) containing the nucleus and an electricity-conducting fiber; the **axon**, which also gives rise to many smaller axon branches before ending at nerve terminals; **synapses**, contact points where one neuron communicates with another; and **dendrites**, which appear as branches of a tree and extend from the neuron cell body and receive messages from other neurons (see Figure 3.2). "The dendrites and cell body are covered with synapses formed by the ends of axons of other neurons" (Society for Neuroscience 2002: 7). Each neuron has multiple dendrites that form structural networks for receiving information from another neuron or from the environment in the form of light, sound, smell, and so on and converting it (*transduction*) into electrical activity that is transmitted to the axon.

Axons may be long or short. Neurons in the brain stem have axons that extend down into the spinal cord, where they divide into thousands of branches, making contact with different receiving neurons. The microscopic complexity of this system

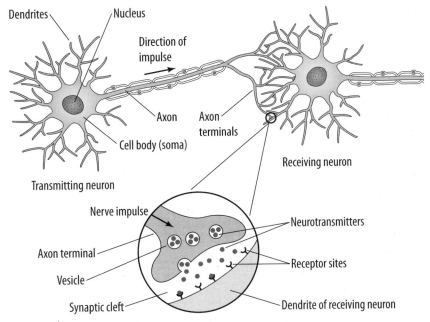

Dendrites   Nucleus

Direction of impulse

Axon   Axon terminals

Cell body (soma)

Receiving neuron

Transmitting neuron

Nerve impulse   Neurotransmitters

Axon terminal

Vesicle   Receptor sites

Synaptic cleft   Dendrite of receiving neuron

FIGURE 3.2 | NEURON, SHOWING SYNAPSE, NEUROTRANSMITTERS, AND RECEPTOR SITES

explains why a spinal injury cannot usually be repaired. The axon conducts ("fires") electrical impulses to terminals, which react by releasing neurotransmitters that are stored in synaptic buttons, vesicles at the end of the axon. These neurotransmitters move across the synaptic gap to receptor sites on the dendrites of a neuron on the other side, triggering activity in that neuron. Through this mechanism an impulse is directed neuron by neuron to the spinal cord and into the proper circuit for transmission to the brain. The process is similar to that of car battery, producing electricity through the action of chemicals; indeed, our bodies are low-wattage batteries. A dead battery is one whose chemicals no longer produce electric energy, just as in humans.

Neurons do not interlock but instead are separated by synapses, fluid-filled microscopic gaps (0.0002 mm) that provide a chemical bridge for signals in the form of charged particles (ions) from one neuron to another. A neuron may have over 10,000 synapses. There are two functional types of synapses: (1) *excitatory* synapses, which enhance electrical impulses, and (2) *inhibitory* synapses, which retard electrical impulses. Depressants reduce synaptic transmission by inhibiting nerve impulse conduction at synapses; this causes a reduction in sensory pain signals received by the brain (Tortora 1983). Stimulants facilitate synaptic transmission. A large concentration of positively charged particles entering a receiving neuron signals the neuron to pass on the message. On the other hand, a large concentration of negatively charged particles entering the neuron will inhibit it from passing on the message to the brain (Society for Neuroscience 2002). That is why powerful depressants like morphine reduce pain sensations.

"Nerve signals often travel over long distances in the body. For example, if you step barefooted on a sharp object, the sensory information is relayed from your foot all the way to the brain; from there, nerve signals travel back to the leg muscles and cause them to contract, drawing back the foot. Dozens of neurons can be involved in such a circuit, necessitating a sophisticated communication system to rapidly convey signals between cells. Also, because individual neurons can be up to three feet long, a rapid-relay mechanism within the neurons themselves is required to transmit each signal from the site where it is received to the site where it is passed on to a neighboring cell." ("Principles of Nerve Cell Communication" 1997: 107).

NEUROTRANSMITTERS

Neurotransmitters are stored in sacs (vesicles) clustered in the synaptic terminals at the end of axons of neurons. When activated by electrical charges, neurotransmitters cross over the synaptic gap where they bind to receptors on the surface of an adjoining neuron—a lock and key action. Each neurotransmitter has a receptor site designed to receive it. Depending on the type of neurotransmitter, electrical charges from the adjoining neuron are either inhibited or enhanced: dopamine, epinephrine, norepinephrine, excite (speed firing), and others (**endorphins**) inhibit (slow firing). The body uses these chemicals to trigger such effects as anger or to regulate the operation of different organs.

Dopamine, one of about 100 neurotransmitters found in the central nervous system, has received special attention because of its apparent role in the regulation of mood and affect and because of its role in motivation and reward processes. Studies have revealed that the reinforcing effects of psychoactive drugs in humans are associated with increases in brain dopamine (Volkow et al. 1999b). Dopamine is necessary to sustain life. This neurotransmitter "acts as a pacesetter for many nerve cells throughout the brain. At every moment of our lives, dopamine is responsible for keeping those cells operating at the appropriate levels of activity to accomplish our needs and aims. Whenever we need to mobilize our muscles or mind to work harder or faster, dopamine drives some of the involved brain cells to step up to the challenge" (Nestler 2005: 5).

A dopamine deficiency is believed to cause **Parkinson's disease**,[1] an excess is believed to cause Tourette syndrome.[2] The brains of schizophrenics are high in dopamine, and antischizophrenic (narcoleptic) drugs work because of their ability to block dopamine (Snyder 1986). Cocaine and amphetamine can cause schizophrenic symptoms because these drugs interfere with the reuptake of dopamine, increasing the concentration of dopamine in the brain (Palfai and Jankiewicz 1991; Bloom 1993).

---

[1]Clinical studies of cocaine users in their thirties show an increase in symptoms of Parkinson's disease—tremors or stiffness—apparently the result of a decrease of dopamine receptors (Hartel 1993). Flupentixol, a drug that blocks dopamine, reduces the effects of cocaine but cannot be used for drug treatment because it also produces symptoms of Parkinson's disease (Bloom 1993).

[2]Tourette syndrome is an incurable genetic affliction whose symptoms can range from mild tics to coprolalia—periodic outbursts of often foul language (Brody 1995).

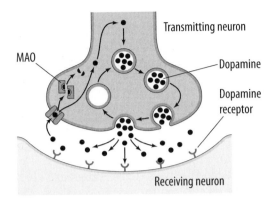

FIGURE 3.3 | DOPAMINE'S NORMAL ACTION

Dopamine is constantly released in small amounts in order to "keep the receiving cells in each brain region functioning at appropriate intensities for current demands—neither too high or too low—the dopaminergic cells continuously increase and decrease the number of dopamine molecules they launch" (Nestler 2005: 5). Neurotransmitter level is controlled by chemicals in the presynaptic terminal known as **monoamine oxidases (MAO)** that deactivate neurotransmitters in order to maintain equilibrium (Figure 3.3). In some individuals an excess of MAO lowers the amount of dopamine, norepinephrine, and serotonin, which results in depression (Sunderwirth 1985). **Serotonin,** a neurotransmitter involved in sleep, mood, depression, and anxiety, serves to moderate primitive drives, such as aggression, sex, and food seeking, while improving the ability to interact socially. The medically prescribed anti-depressant Prozac (fluoxetine) inhibits the reuptake of serotonin. **Norepinephrine** is a neurotransmitter that governs arousal reactions and appears to play a role in elevating mood.

Receptor sites, where neurotransmitters attach (the lock-and-key effect) causing chemical substances to interact and produce pharmacological actions, distinguish between substances. Only upon receiving the correct substance (creating a chemical fit) will they transmit signals that bring about pharmacological action. Some psychoactive drugs (**agonists**) can mimic the action of neurotransmitters and "fool" the receptor into accepting it. Competing drugs (**antagonists**—substances that inhibit the action of a receptor site) can counteract the effect of an agonist by their ability to occupy receptor sites without triggering activity, providing a basis for using chemicals to deal with drug abuse (discussed in Chapter 10).

Once they have performed their assigned task—conveying messages to nearby neurons—neurotransmitters are recycled by the sending neuron in a process called reuptake. This process conserves the neurotransmitters by bringing them back into the presynaptic terminal for storage so that they can be used again. Proteins called **transporters,** located on the surface of the sending neurons, latch onto the neurotransmitters and transport them back inside for use at a later time. Psychoactive substances not only cause the release of neurotransmitters, but may also inhibit the transporters from performing their reuptake task so that the neurotransmitters continue to stimulate the receiving neuron. In sum, after being released into the synapse, a neurotransmitter attaches to receptor sites on the receiving neuron and then is either quickly recycled by a transporter or broken down by MAO. Or, if the transporter and/or MAO is inhibited by a psychoactive substance, the neurotransmitter will continue to impact the receptor site until it is finally exhausted—used up.

DRUG INGESTION

The entire volume of human blood—11.6 pints for an average-sized adult male, 9.5 pints for an average-sized adult female—makes a complete circulation about every sixty seconds. Psychoactive drugs are absorbed into the bloodstream and quickly carried to the central nervous system. Eventually, they pass through the **blood-brain barrier,** causing the release of neurotransmitters in the brain. The barrier acts as a gatekeeper, preventing certain substances from entering brain tissue, for example, penicillin (because it would cause convulsions), but readily admits psychoactive substances (and general anesthetics). Since their blood-brain barrier has not matured, infants are particularly vulnerable to the effects of psychoactive chemicals.[3]

Drugs enter the bloodstream in one of three ways, and the route of administration affects how fast the substance will enter the brain and thus assert a psychoactive response:

1. *Oral ingestion:* The substance is swallowed and enters the bloodstream through the gastrointestinal tract, the slowest route of administration.
2. *Inhalation:* The substance is sniffed and rapidly reaches the bloodstream through mucous membranes of the nose or sinus cavities, or it is smoked and quickly absorbed through the linings of the lungs, which are surrounded by capillaries.
3. *Injection:* The substance is injected into a vein (**intravenous**), and all of the drug enters the bloodstream. Some is carried directly to the brain, producing an effect within seconds. Injecting a drug under the skin (**subcutaneous**) increases the time required for the substance to enter the bloodstream and thus produces a delayed and reduced effect.

Some drugs can be ingested in a number of ways; for example, different forms of heroin and cocaine can be sniffed, smoked, or injected.

A drug that is taken intravenously is carried to the right chamber of the heart, where it mixes with blood returning from the rest of the body, and it is then pumped through the lungs, returns to the heart, and is then delivered to the brain. This takes about sixteen seconds, and when the drug arrives at the brain, it is greatly diluted. A substance that is smoked results in some passing directly into the bloodstream through membranes of the mouth. With deep inhalations, however, most of the drug will spread though the fine membranes of the lungs (all of

---

[3]A fetus is also vulnerable because the placental barrier is more permeable than the blood-brain barrier is. Infants lack a fully functioning liver and therefore cannot readily deactivate and eliminate psychoactive chemicals.

the blood in the body moves through the lungs) and pass directly into the blood stream, carrying drug molecules to the left side of the heart, where it is pumped directly to the brain without dilution; this takes about three seconds. Each breath produces an immediate drug spike in the brain, an immediate euphoric effect that is more powerful than the intravenous route. Inhalation also avoids the danger of overdose. Oral ingestion results in slow **absorption** from stomach and intestine and is the method least favored by drug abusers (A. Goldstein 2001).

The amount of time it takes for a substance to be eliminated from the body is measured in terms of **half-life**, the time it takes for one half of the drug to be eliminated through the liver and primarily into the kidneys for urination. The half-life of some drugs may be as short as a few minutes, while traces of other drugs may remain in the system for several weeks. Drugs that are lipid-soluble (insoluble in water, but) will be absorbed by body fat and subsequently released into the bloodstream in small doses over a relatively longer period of time, thus having a greater half-life. This explains why the percentage of body fat is a factor in the effect of drugs. The greater the half-life, the less severe are the withdrawal symptoms after use of the drug has been discontinued. The longer a drug remains in the bloodstream, the less likely it is that tolerance will occur.

TOLERANCE

The continued use of certain drugs, particularly depressants, produces **tolerance**, "a progressive increase in the ability of the body to adapt to the effects of a drug that is used at regular and frequent intervals. It is manifested in two ways: (1) progressively larger doses must be administered to produce the same effects; and (2) eventually as much as ten or more times the original lethal dose can be safely taken" as the metabolism adapts to the substance (Ausubel 1978: 14).

> Tolerance develops as the body becomes progressively immune to the chemical effects of the drug at the cellular level. Should usage continue, a physiological dependence on the narcotic will occur as the affected tissues and cells accommodate the chemically induced processes that result from the introduction of the drug. The *homeostatic* processes of the body adjust to the narcotic and bring about a new physiological equilibrium. If the equilibrium and normal functioning are to be maintained at the physiological level, regular and stable amounts of the drug [or a similar drug—**cross-tolerance**[4]] must be taken. (Biernacki 1986: 9; italics added)

Homeostasis refers to a state of equilibrium achieved through the self-adjusting characteristics of the body. Through homeostasis complex organisms adapt themselves to changes in the environment by means of, for example, changes in body temperature, blood sugar level, and heart rate. The physiology and biochemistry of the body change according to information received and processed by the central nervous system (and the endocrine system—glands such as the thyroid and adrenal). With respect to both neurotransmitters and receptors, the brain behaves as if trying

---

[4]Cross-tolerance refers to the ability of one drug (an agonist) to substitute for another.

to maintain all its operating systems on an even keel. Psychoactive substances upset this normal balance (A. Goldstein 2001).

The toxicity of a drug is affected by tolerance. Thus, an alcoholic—someone addicted to alcohol—can ingest quantities of alcohol that would be potentially fatal for an occasional user. Some psychoactive drugs do not produce tolerance (marijuana), while others may produce various degrees of tolerance, from hardly perceptible to severe. There is also **selective tolerance**; for example, tolerance to the "nod" experienced by heroin users develops rapidly, while the "rush" will always be experienced by heroin users no matter how high their level of tolerance (discussed in Chapter 4). There is also evidence of **reverse tolerance**, referred to as *kindling*, to certain drugs: becoming more sensitive to the same or a lesser dosage over time. Pharmacologists use the term **sensitization** to refer to this increase in a drug's effect with repeated administration, the change being in the opposite direction of tolerance (Robinson and Berridge 2003).

When tolerance develops, the failure to ingest enough of a drug on a timely basis will disrupt homeostasis and cause the onset of withdrawal symptoms. These symptoms can manifest themselves in a number of ways, all of them unpleasant to the person being subjected to them, usually taking the form of being directly opposite of the effects produced by the drug—overacting by a system that was originally suppressed. Thus, chronic heroin use can induce constipation, whereas in withdrawal, in direct contrast to the initial condition, the addict suffers stomach cramps and diarrhea. "During withdrawal from alcohol, delirium tremens may develop into convulsions owing to over activity of the central nervous system" (Taylor 2002: 138). While in withdrawal, the addict may experience extreme anxiety, hyperactivity, shaking, cold sweat, and severe depression—all of which can be alleviated by ingesting a sufficient amount of the drug, thus restoring equilibrium.

DRUG CUES

Brain imaging and other modern technologies show that the addicted brain is distinctly different from the nonaddictive brain; the differences are manifested by changes in brain metabolic activity, receptor availability, gene expression, and responsiveness to environmental cues (Fowler et al. 2007). It appears that the intensity of the drug euphoria burns emotional memories into brain circuits, making that person vulnerable to the appearance of drug cues. These memories are encoded into a part of the brain (*amygdala*) that operates outside of conscious control to cause intense cravings for re-creating the euphoric experience. Research has discovered a connection between cues and reversion to drug use (Childress et al. 1999). Even tolerance and withdrawal symptoms in laboratory animals are affected by environmental cues (Hinson 1985; Bloom 1993). Indeed, a person who has been removed from his or her drug-seeking environment to treat addiction but then is returned to the former environment gets secondary associations that can induce the person to relapse, go back to using drugs (Bloom 1993).

"Cocaine abusers may experience a powerful urge to take the drug when they encounter environmental cues such as people, places, or paraphernalia that they associate with drug use. This cue-induced behavior may be accompanied by physical sensations—light-headedness, increased heart rate, or mild drug like 'high'—like those produced by cocaine" (Zickler 2001: 1). In approximately two thirds of cocaine-dependent subjects in a laboratory setting, drug cues increased craving for cocaine (Avants et al. 1995). In another research effort, cocaine users who viewed items related to their drug use, such as a glass crack pipe, a mirror, razor blade, a straw, a rolled $20 bill, lactose powder, and simulated crack rocks, elicited a high degree of craving, as measured by brain scans (Bonson et al. 2002). In alcoholics, alcohol-associated cues can trigger craving for that substance (Heinz et al. 2003).

Drug abuse is characterized by a pattern of sexual dysfunction. The same brain regions that are activated by cocaine cues are also activated by sexual activity. Drugs can substitute for sexual activity through corresponding stimulation of these same pleasure regions. Many drugs enter the brain in high concentrations at the blood-rich hypothalamus, creating initial autonomic effects on consciousness and mood. The **hypothalamus**, a small gland located near the base of the brain, integrates information from many sources and is the control center for the autonomic nervous system. It is also the primary point of contact between the nervous system and the endocrine system, sending messages in the form of impulses to appropriate control centers to restore normal levels of blood chemicals in line with the homeostatic needs of the body.

The hypothalamus controls such basic drives as sexual activity. It regulates the release of hormones from the pituitary gland, located directly below. These hormones act directly on the adrenal glands, testes, and ovaries. Disruptions in the normal flow of hormones, the result of drug use, from the pituitary can adversely affect sexual function, and chronic drug use upsets hormonal balance by decreasing dopamine secretion from the hypothalamus ("Sexual Dysfunction and Addiction Treatment" 2000).

If addiction is, at its core, a consequence of fundamental changes in brain function, a goal of treatment must be to either reverse or compensate for those brain changes (J. Cooper 1998). Although drug addicts might not be able to control their cravings, through behavior therapy (discussed in Chapter 10) they may be able to control the way they respond to the cravings (Grady 1998).

SUMMARY

- Research into drug abuse is limited by ethical considerations.
- Drug addiction is essentially a disease of the brain.
- A theory organizes events so that they can be placed in perspective; explains the causes of past events; and predicts when, where, and how future events will occur.
- The same substance can have a different impact on different people depending on the setting in which the drug is ingested and the user's expectations.
- Understanding the biology of psychoactive drugs is also complicated by polydrug use.

- Mixing drugs can result in four different effects: additive, synergistic, potentiating, antagonistic.
- The disease model refers to drug abuse as a compulsive behavior.
- A person's genetic makeup is a major factor in vulnerability to drug abuse.
- Arousal theory explains why some people are more likely to use drugs.
- The immature brain of adolescents can explain their risky behavior.
- The central nervous system consists of the brain and the spinal cord, whose neurons send information to a specific processing center of the brain.

- Psychoactive chemicals trigger the release of dopamine and/or overstimulate the brain's reward pathways.
- Neurons communicate through alternating chemical and electrical activity.
- Neurotransmitters can excite or inhibit the transmission of information to the brain.
- Almost all drugs of abuse affect dopamine.

- Drugs can block the reuptake of neurotransmitters.
- The greater the half-life of a drug, the less severe are its withdrawal symptoms.
- Drugs that produce tolerance require larger doses to overcome homeostasis and achieve a prior level of impact.
- Drug cues can influence drug use and relapse.

Review Questions

1. What is a theory?
2. Why is it difficult to test a biological theory of drug abuse?
3. What nonbiological factors influence the effects of a drug?
4. How does polydrug use complicate understanding the biology of drug use?
5. What is the disease model of drug use?
6. How is drug use influenced by genetics?
7. How can brain development explain the risky behavior of adolescents?
8. How does arousal theory explain drug use?
9. What comprises the central nervous system?
10. How do drugs "trick" the central nervous system?
11. What is the connection between drug use and the neurotransmitter dopamine?
12. What function does a neuron perform?
13. What are synapses?
14. How can a depressant reduce pain sensations?
15. How is a human body similar to a car battery?
16. What is the difference between an agonist and an antagonist?

17. How can an antagonist provide the basis for treating drug abuse?
18. What is the purpose of MAO?
19. What is the effect of drugs that inhibit MAO?
20. What is the function of a neuron's transporters?
21. What is the role of the blood-brain barrier?
22. What is the slowest form of drug ingestion?
23. Why do substances with a greater half-life cause less severe withdrawal symptoms?
24. What is meant when a drug produces "tolerance"?
25. What is cross-tolerance?
26. What is meant by homeostasis?
27. What is the relationship between homeostasis and tolerance?
28. What is reverse tolerance?
29. What is selective tolerance?
30. What form do withdrawal symptoms usually take?
31. How can drug cues influence relapse?
32. Why can drugs substitute for sexual activity?

In determination of a drug's status, more than abuse potential should be considered. What are the toxicities of the drug? What are the chances of becoming dependent on the drug? Is dependency on a drug necessarily bad? Sometimes these questions are difficult to answer. Certainly, two of the most toxic drugs we know are alcohol and tobacco (nicotine).... Dependency to both of these drugs develops, as it does to caffeine.

Sidney H. Schnoll (1979: 255)

DEPRESSANTS

CHAPTER **4**

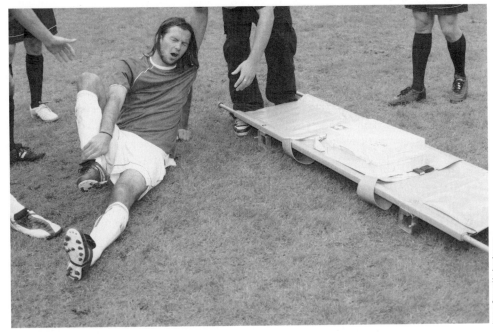

Image Source/Jupiter Images

Depressants are a category of drugs that includes alcohol, barbiturates, sedatives/ tranquilizers, and the narcotics. The latter may be natural (opium derivatives such as morphine and codeine), semisynthetic (such as heroin), or synthetic (such as methadone, Demerol and OxyContin).[1] Depressants are typically addicting, and studies have indicated a relationship between certain chemical deficiencies and the propensity for addiction to depressants.

ENDORPHINS

During the 1970s a number of scientists, working independently, discovered analgesics in brain and body tissues generally referred to as *endorphins*, a contraction of the term *endogenous morphine*. Three families of endorphins (enkephalins, dynorphins, and beta-endorphins) have many of the characteristics of morphine, and the body contains receptor sites that are programmed to receive these neurotransmitters. When they reach the receptor sites in the central nervous system (CNS), endorphins relieve pain. Pain is the result of a trauma experienced by the body, information about which is detected by sensors that send impulses along the nervous system, through neurons and across synapses as they move toward the brain. The subsequent release of endorphins in the brain inhibits pain impulses. Eventually, endorphins are destroyed by enzymes.

When people stub a toe or injure a finger, they usually grit their teeth and clench their fists, activities that apparently cause the release of these naturally occurring opiates that reduce sensations of pain. The athlete's ability to overcome pain during competition and the soldier's ability to perform heroic feats while severely wounded can be explained by the endorphin-receptor phenomenon, as can success in treating pain with acupuncture (Snyder 1977, 1989; Davis 1984; J. Goldberg 1988).[2] These receptor sites are programmed to receive endorphins, but they are also receptive to external chemicals such as opiates.

These opioid receptors are found in the brain's reward pathways and are distributed widely throughout the nervous system and in the nerves that supply the extremities, the skin, the blood vessels, and most internal organs. These receptors are found along pain pathways and, when activated, interrupt the pain pathway to the brain, diminishing the perception of pain (A. Goldstein 2001).

Endorphins also enable the organism (including many animals) to deal with psychological stress by curbing an autonomic overreaction and producing calm: They slow breathing, reduce blood pressure, and lower the level of motor activity (Davis 1984). A "deficiency in an endorphin system that ordinarily would support feelings of pleasure and reinforcement might lead to feelings of inadequacy and sadness" (Levinthal 1988: 149), a phenomenon that would make the use of depressants essentially a form of self-medication. As was noted in Chapter 3, the use of

---

[1] In contrast to depressants, which act centrally on the brain, analgesics such as acetaminophen (e.g., Tylenol, Panadol, Anacin-3), ibuprofen (e.g., Nuprin, Mediprin, Advil), and aspirin relieve pain via localized action. They are not addictive (Brody 1988).

[2] In one study, treating drug abusers with acupuncture was not found to be beneficial (Latessa and Moon 1992). Another study found it effective in detoxification treatment (Brewington, Smith, and Lipton 1994).

psychoactive substances does not automatically produce a pleasurable response. However, people who are at risk for addiction may suffer from an endorphin deficiency. For such people, addiction would be the result of a genetically acquired deficiency or of a temporary or permanent impairment of the body's ability to produce endorphins. "This point of view would help account for the puzzling variability from individual to individual in the addictive power of opiate drugs. If an endorphin deficiency exists, however, the question would still remain as to what precipitating circumstances would lead to such a deficiency and whether these circumstances were environmental, inherited genetically, or a product of both" (Levinthal 1988: 154).

The ingestion of large amounts of heroin or some other opiate can also cause this deficiency (Snyder 1977). Thus, an abstaining addict would be unusually sensitive to feelings of pain or stress and would be inclined to use narcotic drugs again. In other words, receptors become increasingly dependent on external depressants, which in turn further reduce the production of endorphins, leaving the receptors increasingly dependent on substances from the outside. "If the opiate drug is later withdrawn, the receptors are now left without a supply from any source at all, and the symptoms of withdrawal are a consequence of this physiological dilemma" (Levinthal 1988: 156).

STRESS AND ADDICTION

Depressants such as heroin inhibit stress hormones (such as cortisol and adrenalin) and stress-related neurotransmitters. A person who is having difficulties dealing with stress and is exposed to opiates is likely to find them rewarding and thus become addicted. In the absence of stress, many people who take heroin over long periods of time do so without becoming addicted, and hospital patients who self-administer morphine for pain do not increase their intake over time, nor do they suffer from a morphine craving when the pain subsides and they no longer have access to the drug (Peele 1985; E. Rosenthal 1993). One study found that only four out of more than 12,000 patients who were given opioids for acute pain became addicted to the drugs. Even long-term morphine use has limited potential for addiction. In a study of thirty-eight chronic pain patients, most of whom received opioids for four to seven years, only two patients actually became addicted, and both had a prior history of drug abuse (National Institute on Drug Abuse data). A study of 11,882 hospital patients who had been treated with pain-killing drugs revealed that only four became addicted. A study of more than 10,000 burn victims who received injections of narcotics for weeks or months found not a single case of addiction attributed to this treatment (Melzack 1990). Russell Portnoy, director of analgesic studies in the Pain Service at Sloan-Kettering Memorial Hospital, points out, "Just as the vast majority of people who drink do not become alcoholics, those who are treated with opioid for pain do not become addicts" (Goleman 1987: 10; Brownlee and Schrof 1997).

Drug addicts who are trying to remain off drugs can often resist the cravings brought on by seeing reminders (cues) of their former drug life. For months they can walk past the street corner where they used to buy drugs and not succumb. But then there is a sudden relapse that addicts explain with statements such as

"Well, things weren't going well at my job" or "I broke up with my girlfriend." Sometimes the problem is as simple as a delayed unemployment check. That they often relapse, apparently in response to what most people would consider mild stressors, suggests that addicts are perhaps more sensitive than nonaddicts to stress. This hypersensitivity "may exist before drug abusers start taking drugs and may contribute to their initial drug use, or it could result from the effects of chronic drug use on the brain, or its existence could be due to a combination of both" (Jeanne Kreek quoted in Stocker 1999: 12). Chronic use of heroin, however, may increase hypersensitivity to stress and trigger a cycle of continued drug use when the effects of heroin wear off.

Research has shown that during withdrawal the level of stress hormones rises in the blood, and stress-related neurotransmitters are released in the brain. These chemicals trigger emotions that are perceived as highly unpleasant, driving the addict to take more drugs. Because the effects of heroin last only four to six hours, addicts often experience withdrawal three or four times a day. This constant switching on and off of the stress systems of the body heightens whatever hypersensitivity these systems might have had before the person started taking drugs. The result is that these stress chemicals are on a sort of hair-trigger release, surging at the slightest provocation (Kreek in Stocker 1999).

The body reacts to stress by secreting two types of chemical messengers: hormones in the blood and neurotransmitters in the brain. Some of the hormones travel throughout the body, altering the metabolism of food so that the brain and muscles have sufficient stores of metabolic fuel for activities, such as fighting or fleeing, that help the person to cope with the source of the stress. In the brain the neurotransmitters trigger emotions, such as aggression or anxiety, that prompt the person to take action. U.S. Navy researchers found that prompt treatment with morphine cuts the chances in half of injured personnel subsequently suffering from post-traumatic stress disorder (Carey 2010).

Normally, stress hormones are released in small amounts throughout the day, but when the body is under stress, the level of these hormones increases dramatically. Endorphins inhibit these stress hormones, thereby restraining stressful emotions. Heroin and morphine inhibit the stress hormone cycle and presumably the release of stress-related neurotransmitters just as endorphins do. Thus, when people take heroin or morphine, the drugs add to the inhibition already being provided by the endorphins.

HEROIN

The opium poppy,[3] *Papaver somniferum*, requires a hot, dry climate and very careful cultivation (Wishart 1974). It grows best in loamy soil that retains moisture and nutrients. To grow opium poppies, the seeds are scattered across the surface of freshly cultivated fields. Three months later, when the poppy is mature, the green stem is topped by a brightly colored flower. Gradually, the flower petals fall off leaving a seedpod about the size of a small egg. Incisions are made in the seedpod

---

[3]Sale of poppy seeds for cultivation has been illegal in the United States since 1970. Sale for culinary use is legal; poppy seeds often appear on bagels.

just after the petals have fallen but before it is fully ripe, a labor-intensive process. A milky-white fluid oozes out and hardens on the surface into a dark brown gum, which is raw opium. It is collected by scraping the pod with a flat, dull knife, another labor-intensive process. "Because the yield per acre is small and because laborious care is required in collecting the juice, it can only be grown profitably where both land and labor are cheap" (Ausubel 1978: 9). Because the plant matures only one time, that is, it does not regenerate, new seed must be planted each season.

Raw or cooked opium contains more than thirty-five different alkaloids, including morphine and codeine. In the mainland countries of Southeast Asia, the morphine alkaloid alone accounts for approximately 10 percent of the total weight of opium. Heroin manufacturers must first extract the morphine from the opium before converting the morphine to heroin. The extraction is a simple process, requiring only a few chemicals and a supply of water. Morphine is sometimes extracted from opium in small clandestine laboratories which are typically set up near the opium poppy fields. Because the morphine base has about one tenth the weight and volume of raw opium, it is desirable to reduce the opium to morphine before transporting the product from the field to a heroin laboratory.

The process of extracting morphine from opium involves dissolving opium in boiling water; adding lime (calcium oxide), slaked lime (calcium hydroxide), or limestone (calcium carbonate) to precipitate nonmorphine alkaloids; and then pouring off the morphine in solution. Ammonium chloride is then added to the solution to precipitate morphine from the solution. The chemicals that are used to process opium to morphine have a number of legitimate purposes and are widely available on the open market. An empty oil drum, some cooking pots, and filter cloths or filter paper are also needed.

The conversion of morphine to heroin base is a relatively simple and inexpensive procedure. The necessary chemicals for conversion to heroin are commonly available as industrial chemicals. The equipment is very basic and quite portable. Heroin conversion laboratories are generally located in isolated, rural areas because of the telltale odors of the laboratory's chemicals. Acetic anhydride, in particular, is a key chemical with a very pungent odor resembling that of vinegar. Thai speakers in the Golden Triangle Area commonly refer to acetic anhydride as *nam-som* (vinegar).

Heroin synthesis from morphine (either morphine base or morphine hydrochloride) is a two-step process that requires between four and six hours to complete. Heroin base is the intermediate product. Typically, morphine hydrochloride bricks are pulverized, and the dried powder is then placed in an enamel pot. Acetic anhydride is added, which then reacts with the morphine to form heroin acetate. (This acetylation process will work with either morphine hydrochloride or morphine base.) The pot lid is tied or clamped on, using a damp towel for a gasket. The pot is carefully heated for about two hours, below boiling, at a constant temperature of 185° Fahrenheit. It is never allowed to boil or to become so hot as to vent fumes into the room. The mixture is agitated by tilting and rotation until all of the morphine has dissolved. When cooking is completed, the pot is cooled and opened. During this step, morphine and the anhydride become chemically bonded, creating an impure form of diacetylmorphine (heroin).

Water is added to the thick, soupy mixture, and the mixture is stirred as the heroin dissolves in the solution. Sodium carbonate (a crystalline powder) is dissolved in hot water and then added slowly to the heroin solution until effervescence stops. This precipitates heroin base, which is then filtered and dried by heating in a steam bath. For each kilogram of morphine, 685–937 grams of crude heroin base is formed, depending on the quality of the morphine.

The tan-colored heroin base (about 70 percent pure heroin) may be dried, packed, and transported to a heroin-refining laboratory, or it may be purified further before conversion to heroin hydrochloride (a water-soluble salt form of heroin) at the same site. In the mainland countries of Southeast Asia, heroin base is an intermediate product that can be further converted to either "smoking heroin" (heroin no. 3) or "injectable heroin" (heroin no. 4), a powder that is between 80 and 99 percent pure. Heroin is either heroin salt or heroin base. Heroin salt dissolves readily in water, so it is easy to inject or sniff. Heroin base is easy to smoke but needs to be mixed with an acid like vitamin C in order to dissolve. If it is mixed with a certain amount of caffeine, heroin will vaporize at a lower temperature facilitating smoking and inhaling.

Lawfully produced morphine is usually harvested by the more modern industrial poppy straw process of extracting alkaloid from the mature dried plant. The extract may be either liquid, solid, or powder (Drug Enforcement Administration 1989). In equivalent doses, heroin is about two and a half times as potent as morphine because heroin more easily penetrates the blood-brain barrier. Once heroin reaches the brain, however, it is converted back into morphine (Royal College of Psychiatrists 1987). The Drug Enforcement Administration (DEA) reports that more than 400 tons of opium or its equivalent in poppy straw concentrate are legally imported each year into the United States. Part of this quantity is used to extract codeine (an opiate alkaloid that is about 20 percent as potent as morphine), an ingredient used in many cough medicines.

MORPHINE: USES AND EFFECTS

Classification: Narcotic

CSA Schedule: Schedule II

Trade or Other Names: Duramorph, MS-Contin, Roxanol, Oramorph SR

Medical Uses: Analgesic

Physical Dependence: High for nonmedical use, low for medical patients in pain

Psychological Dependence: High

Tolerance: Yes

Duration (hours): 3–6

Usual Method: Oral, smoked, injected

Possible Effects: Euphoria, drowsiness, respiratory depression, constricted pupils, nausea

Effects of Overdose: Slow and shallow breathing, clammy skin, convulsions, coma, possible death

Withdrawal Syndrome: Watery eyes, runny nose, yawning, loss of appetite, irritability, tremors, panic, cramps, nausea, chills, and sweating

Source: U.S. Drug Enforcement Administration.

Pure heroin is a white powder with a bitter taste and little odor, but street heroin comes in many different forms, depending on how it was made and what has been added to it. Street heroin can be white, tan, brown, gray, or black. It can be a fine, fluffy powder; coarse like sand; chunky; or a solid mass that is either gummy or rock hard (black tar heroin). It can smell like vinegar, vitamins, or medicine—or have no smell. No matter what its color or form, all heroin is either heroin salt or heroin base. Heroin salt dissolves easily in water, so it is easy to inject or sniff. Heroin base (like cocaine base) is easy to smoke but needs to be mixed with an acid such as vitamin C to dissolve. White powder and black tar heroin are usually heroin salt, and brown heroin is usually heroin base. The term *white powder* refers to heroin salt, which is mostly snorted or injected ("China White," Number 4). The term *brown base* refers to heroin base (Persian, Brown Sugar, Pakistani), which can be smoked but needs to be heated in a solution of water and mild acid to inject. The term *black tar* refers to the black, sticky, gumlike form of heroin (Chiva, Mexican Tar, or Black Tar Heroin), mostly smoked or injected (Harm Reduction Coalition 1998). Mexico is also the source of "cheese heroin," a powdered blend of black tar heroin, acetaminohen, and diphenhydramine hcl, a sedative-hypnotic prescribed as an antihistimine.

For street sale heroin is typically diluted ("stepped on" or "cut") with any powdery substance that dissolves when heated, such as lactose, quinine, flour, or cornstarch. Until the 1990s consumer-available heroin prepared for intravenous use usually had a purity of less than 5 percent. In recent years the purity level of retail heroin sold in New York City has averaged above 60 percent, revealing that

CODEINE: USES AND EFFECTS

Classification: Narcotic

CSA Schedule: Schedule II, III, V

Trade or Other Names: Tylenol w/Codeine, Empirin w/Codeine, Robitussin A-C, Fiorinal w/Codeine, APAP w/Codeine

Medical Uses: Analgesic, antitussive (cough suppressant)

Physical Dependence: Moderate

Psychological Dependence: Moderate

Tolerance: Yes

Duration (hours): 3–6

Usual Method: Oral; injected

Possible Effects: Euphoria, drowsiness, respiratory depression, constricted pupils, nausea

Effects of Overdose: Slow and shallow breathing, clammy skin, convulsions, coma, possible death

Withdrawal Syndrome: Watery eyes, runny nose, yawning, loss of appetite, irritability, tremors, panic, cramps, nausea, chills, and sweating

Source: U.S. Drug Enforcement Administration.

heroin is being subjected to little cutting before it reaches the consumer. Increased purity makes smoking and sniffing feasible; the substance prepared for sniffing or smoking is generally 40 percent heroin. The increased purity and the concern about AIDS may be causing the shift from injecting to smoking and sniffing among heroin users (Epstein and Gfroerer 1997; Adrade, Sifaneck, and Neaigus 1999). Numerous reports have suggested a rise in heroin use in recent years, attributed to young people who are smoking or sniffing rather than injecting.

EFFECTS OF HEROIN

Heroin has analgesic and euphoric properties. Although brief, sharp, localized (phasic) pain is poorly relieved by opiates, they do effectively relieve duller, more chronic, and less localized (tonic) pain (Snyder 1977; R. Melzack 1990). As with all opiates, heroin "acts chiefly on the central and autonomic nervous systems and, to some extent, directly on smooth muscles. Effects on the central nervous system are primarily depressant, although larger doses may bring out stimulant properties, especially at the spinal level of reaction.... The depressant actions include analgesia (relief of pain, sedation, freedom from anxiety, muscular relaxation, decreased motor activity), hypnosis (drowsiness and lethargy), and euphoria (a sense of well-being and contentment). Unlike anesthetics, opiates are able to produce marked analgesia without excessive drowsiness, muscular weakness, confusion, or loss of consciousness" (Ausubel 1978: 11).

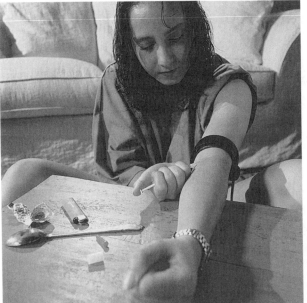

Hugh Burden/Taxi/Getty Images

Heroin users come in all types, including adolescents from upper-middle-class homes. Psychologists say that immature drug-dependent personalities ignore longterm negative consequences of behavior and opt for the shortterm positive reinforcement that drugs provide.

Heroin is typically ingested intravenously, a method that has a ten-second onset, although some users inject it just under the skin ("skin-popping"), a method that has a delayed onset of five to eight minutes. To be prepared for injection, powdered heroin is placed in a "cooker"—usually a spoon or bottle cap. A small amount of water is added, and the mixture is heated with a match or lighter until the heroin is dissolved. The mixture is drawn up into a hypodermic needle and inserted into a vein that has been distended by being tied with a tourniquet (or under the skin). The intravenous heroin user might bring blood back into the hypodermic, where it can mix with the heroin, a process known as "booting." Heroin can also be sniffed like cocaine and even smoked. When smoked ("chasing the dragon"), heroin is heated and the fumes are inhaled, usually through a small tube; the effects peak in ten to fifteen minutes.

Michael Agar (1973) points out that the heroin user can experience four different effects from ingesting heroin:

1. *The rush.* Heroin produces euphoria, referred to as the "rush": "About 10 seconds after the beginning of an injection of heroin the subjects had a typical narcotic 'rush,' including a wave of euphoric feelings, visceral sensations, a facial flush and a deepening of the voice" (Dole 1980: 146). Heroin and cocaine activate brain systems that are responsible for the reinforcing properties of such natural rewards as food and sex; male and female users describe the euphoric rush produced by heroin and cocaine as similar to, but several times stronger than, sexual orgasm (National Institute of Drug Abuse 1997b). Agar (1973) notes that while heroin is believed to have no effect on an addict after his or her tolerance builds up, heroin users actually experience the rush no matter how addicted they are. Addicts frequently describe the rush in sexual terms: "I felt like I died and went to heaven. My whole body was like one giant fucking incredible orgasm" (Inciardi 1986: 61). Indeed, heroin use substitutes for sex, in which the addict usually has little or no interest. Typically, the onset of heroin-using behavior coincides with adolescence, and remission usually occurs, with or without treatment, as the sex drive diminishes with age; there are few heroin addicts among people older than forty years of age.

2. *The high.* Described by addicts as a feeling of general well-being, the high decreases with increased tolerance; thus, increasing dosages are required to achieve the high. Whereas the rush is experienced over a period of seconds, the high can last for several hours.

3. *The nod.* This is described by addicts as being "out of it," in a state of unawareness, oblivious to one's surroundings—an escape from reality. The nod ranges from a slight dropping of the eyelids and jaw to complete unconsciousness: "they become calm, contented, and detached. They appeared to be quite uninterested in external events" (Dole 1980: 146). One addict provides this description: "It just knocks you completely into another dimension. The nod is like—you know, it's not describable. There's not words to express the feeling. The feeling is *that* good. So good that once hooked you never really live the feeling down" (Rettig, Torres, and Garrett 1977: 35). Tolerance affects the nod dramatically, and doses greater than that required for the high are needed to sustain the nod.

4. *Being straight.* This is how addicts describe their condition when they are not sick, that is, not suffering the onset of withdrawal symptoms; that is, when

their bodies are homeostatic. Unless tricked into buying a "blank," addicts will get a rush and get straight, although they will not necessarily experience a high or the nod (Agar 1973).

Heroin impairs homeostatic body functions. There is a slight decrease in body temperature, although dilation of blood vessels gives the user a feeling of warmth. The body retains fluids. There is also a decrease in the secretion of digestive fluids, and a depression of bowel activity, and the user suffers from constipation. Heroin also causes a constriction of the pupils, which explains why addicts frequently wear sunglasses. At relatively high doses, the sedating effects cause a semistuporous, lethargic, and dreamy state ("nodding"), in which there is a feeling of extreme contentment. Unlike alcohol, heroin depresses aggression. It also stimulates the brain area that controls nausea and vomiting, and instead of euphoria, some initial users experience nausea and vomiting: "I got such a bad pain in my head that I thought I was fucking brain damaged. I puked my guts out" (Inciardi 1986: 61). However, the vomiting caused by opiates "is not accompanied by the usual adverse feelings that nausea and vomiting produce in most people" (Harris 1993: 87).

A very dangerous side effect of heroin is that it depresses the respiratory centers in the brain. Thus, an overdose can result in respiratory arrest and death from lack of oxygen to the brain. (Physicians use the antagonist Naloxone to undo the heroin-induced depressed respiration rate.) It is believed that there are millions of occasional users of heroin—*chippers* or *weekenders*, whose use parallels that of people who drink heavily only on weekends or at parties; they appear to avoid addiction.

TOLERANCE FOR HEROIN

Tolerance to some aspects of heroin use, in particular the high, requires an increase in the dosage in order to gain the same level of response. In other words, a maintenance dose of morphine or some other narcotic will prevent physical withdrawal symptoms. Those seeking the high, however, must keep increasing the dosage until it is no longer feasible (i.e., economically possible) to do so. They might then seek some way to reduce the level of tolerance, possibly by entering a drug rehabilitation program. With a lowered level of tolerance, the addict can resume low-dose usage and gain the sought-after response. There is also cross-tolerance; that is, tolerance to heroin carries over to other narcotic drugs, such as morphine and methadone (which will be discussed in Chapter 10), but not to other depressants, such as alcohol or barbiturates. (But because of cross-tolerance, alcohol withdrawal symptoms—delirium tremens, convulsions, and hallucinations—can be relieved by barbiturates or sedatives.) However, as was mentioned earlier, rapid physical tolerance does not develop in medical patients who take morphine for physical pain (Melzack 1990).

HEROIN WITHDRAWAL

The neuroadaptation that we refer to as *tolerance* often results in *rebounding* when the substance is withdrawn; that is, the withdrawal symptoms tend to be the opposite of effects produced by the drug. "Thus, withdrawal from a depressant drug will give rise to brain excitation as adrenergic neurons that have been unnaturally

Signs and Symptoms of Opioid Withdrawal

The signs and symptoms of withdrawal from opioid drugs, in temporal order of appearance, are as follows (Ginzburg 1985):

1. Several hours after last use: anxiety, restlessness, irritability, drug craving
2. Eight to fifteen hours since last use: yawning, perspiration
3. Sixteen to twenty-four hours since last use: sneezing, sniffles, anorexia (severe appetite loss), vomiting, abdominal cramps, bone pains, tremors, weakness, insomnia, goose flesh, convulsions (very rarely), cardiovascular collapse

inhibited by a drug such as heroin in its absence become hyperactive and cause anxiety, shaking, and cold sweat" (Royal College of Psychiatrists 1987: 34) and sometimes spontaneous orgasm. Heroin depletes the neurotransmitter dopamine, and in withdrawal the dramatic increase in dopamine activity intensifies other unpleasant symptoms (Fishbein and Pease 1990). Physicians often use clonidine, a nonaddicting drug (discussed in Chapter 10), to slow down these neurons and thereby relieve withdrawal symptoms (Davis 1984). Withdrawal symptoms, as David Ausubel (1978: 16) notes, while undoubtedly uncomfortable, "are seldom more severe than a bad case of gastrointestinal influenza." Symptoms peak in twenty-four to forty-eight hours and subside in about a week, although the psychological symptoms may persist indefinitely. While never fatal to otherwise healthy adults, heroin withdrawal can cause the death of the fetus in a pregnant addict (National Institute of Drug Abuse 2005b).

An addict describes withdrawal as follows: "The first twenty-four hours are totally fine; you feel like you're getting a cold. The next day is fucking terrible—constantly shitting, pissing, spitting, everything just flowing out of you. You feel achy, twitchy. You can't focus and the restlessness is intolerable. Every nerve ending is flared up; everything feels raw. You're consumed with this one idea: You need to get drugs because this isn't working" (Anonymous 2006: 126 [edited]).

Children born to addicted mothers, in addition to having a host of other physical problems, such as small size, anemia, heart disease, hepatitis, and pneumonia, also suffer from withdrawal symptoms (O'Brien and Cohen 1984). The National Institute on Drug Abuse reports that infants who are born to heroin-abusing mothers frequently suffer from neonatal abstinence syndrome—withdrawal symptoms that may require medication. This view has been challenged by Stanton Peele (1985), who argues that the symptoms exhibited by the newborn of heroin addicts—undue crying and ineffective feeding, followed cyclically by restless periods of sleep—are not symptoms of heroin withdrawal but result from the cumulative effects of the mother's unhealthy lifestyle.

Medical Use of Heroin

Since 1924 heroin has been virtually banned in the United States, even for medical use as an analgesic. The prohibition against the use of heroin under any circumstances, even to alleviate the intractable pain experienced by some cancer patients,

HEROIN: USES AND EFFECTS

Classification: Narcotic

CSA Schedule: Schedule I

Trade or Other Names: Diacetylmorphine, horse, smack

Medical Uses: None in United States, analgesic, antitussive

Physical Dependence: High

Psychological Dependence: High

Tolerance: Yes

Duration (hours): 3–6

Usual Method: Injected, sniffed, smoked

Possible Effects: Euphoria, drowsiness, respiratory depression, constricted pupils, nausea

Effects of Overdose: Slow and shallow breathing, clammy skin, convulsions, coma, possible death

Withdrawal Syndrome: Watery eyes, runny nose, yawning, loss of appetite, irritability, tremors, panic, cramps, nausea, chills, and sweating

Source: U.S. Drug Enforcement Administration.

is controversial. Arnold Trebach (1982: 79) argues that heroin should be made available under such circumstances. "For some patients, heroin is superior to other medicines for the control of pain, anxiety, and related conditions." John Kaplan (1983b) states that while most patients cannot tell the difference between heroin and morphine in equivalent doses, patients in England, where such use is legal, who take the drug intravenously tend to prefer heroin. The greater euphoric effect of intravenous heroin appears to provide some relief for terminal patients whose painful existence is often measured in weeks, days, or hours. However, heroin is not the most powerful of the narcotics. The synthetic chemical etorphine is 5,000–10,000 times more potent than morphine. Because of its potency, etorphine is usually used only by veterinarians to immobilize large wild animals (Snyder 1977; Drug Enforcement Administration 1989).

DANGERS OF HEROIN USE

Ingesting heroin that is significantly more pure than the user's level of tolerance leads to overdose reactions that can include respiratory arrest and death. And because heroin is illegal, there is no way for the user to determine the level of purity. Indeed, the "hot shot"—a dose of heroin pure enough to be fatal—is used as a relatively easy way of eliminating addicts who have become police informers. Another danger is that heroin cut for street sale might contain adulterants that can be harmful to the user. Even if the heroin is not adulterated, the user might mix it with other drugs, such as the stimulants cocaine and amphetamine, to enhance the euphoric reaction (potentiating effect); such combinations can be fatal.

Users also face the dangers associated with diseases that are transmitted by shared hypodermic needles, particularly hepatitis and AIDS. In New York City, where there are believed to be about 200,000 heroin addicts, as many as 60 percent of them might be infected with the AIDS virus, and addicts are the leading cause of the spread of AIDS. In addition to transmission by shared needles, infected addicts spread the disease through sexual relations with nonaddicts.

OXYCODONE/OXYCONTIN

Oxycodone, a synthetic version of morphine, is a DEA Schedule II drug that was first introduced in 1995 and marketed under the trade name of OxyContin. OxyContin is prescribed for chronic or long-lasting pain. The medication's active ingredient oxycodone, is also found in medications such as Percodan and Tylox. However, OxyContin contains between 10 and 80 milligrams (mg) of oxycodone in a timed-release tablet, while painkillers such as Tylox contain 5 mg and often require repeated doses to bring about pain relief because they lack the timed-release formulation. People who abuse OxyContin either crush the tablet and ingest or snort it, or dilute it in water and inject it. Crushing or diluting the tablet disarms the timed-release action of the medication and causes a quick, powerful high ("OxyContin: Prescription Drug Abuse—2008 Revision": 1). In 2005 a federal appeals court ruled that the patent for OxyContin is invalid, opening the door for generic versions.

Oxycodone, a synthetic version of morphine, is a DEA Schedule II drug that was first introduced in December 1995 and marketed under the trade name of Oxy-Contin. Oxycodone is sold in tablets that contain 40–160 milligrams in a time-released formulation. The 160-milligram tablet is intended to work for up to twelve hours (Clines and Meier 2001). This powerful depressant is prescribed for severe and chronic pain, but it has been linked to numerous overdose fatalities—the result of diversion to the substance abuse market.

In 2007, several executives of the Purdue Pharma of Connecticut, the company that produces OxyContin, pleaded guilty to misleading doctors and patients by claiming that the drug was less likely to be abused than heroin. In fact, experienced drug users and novices alike quickly discovered that by crushing the pills and swallowing, inhaling, or injecting the powder produces an immediate and intense reaction (Meier 2007). So far the most famous abuser of OxyContin has been conservative talk radio host Rush Limbaugh, who reportedly took as many as thirty pills a day (Adler 2003). The popularity of black market OxyContin in Appalachia led to its being dubbed "hillbilly heroin" (Meier 2007).

BARBITURATES

There are about 2,500 derivatives of barbituric acid and dozens of brand names. Lawfully produced barbiturates are found in tablet or capsule form; illegal barbiturates may be found in liquid form for intravenous use because barbiturates are poorly soluble in water. Classified as sedative/hypnotics, they include amobarbital (e.g., Amytal), pentobarbital (e.g., Nembutal), pheno-barbital (e.g., Luminal), secobarbital (e.g., Seconal), and the combination amobarbital-secobarbital (e.g., Tuinal).

EFFECTS OF BARBITURATES

"Barbiturates depress the sensory cortex, decrease motor activity, alter cerebellar function, and produce drowsiness, sedation, and hypnosis" (*Physicians Desk Reference* 1987: 1163). They inhibit seizure activity and can induce unconsciousness in the form of sleep or surgical anesthesia. Unlike opiates, barbiturates do not decrease reaction to pain and may actually increase it. They can produce a variety of alterations in the CNS, ranging from mild sedation to hypnosis and deep coma. In high enough dosage they can induce anesthesia, and an overdose can be fatal. Although they are CNS depressants, in some people they produce excitation (*Physicians Desk Reference* 1988). The user's expectations can have a marked influence on the drug's effect: "For instance, the person who takes 200 mg of secobarbital and expects to fall asleep will usually sleep, if provided with a suitable environment. Another individual, who takes the same amount of secobarbital and expects to have a good time in a stimulating environment, may experience a state of paradoxical stimulation or disinhibition euphoria" (Wesson and Smith 1977: 28).

Barbiturates are often used for their intoxicating effects. Some people take them in addition to alcohol or as a substitute. Heavy users of other drugs sometimes turn to them if their usual drugs are not available or to counteract the effects of large doses of stimulants such as amphetamines or cocaine. Barbiturates are known generally on the street as "downers" or "barbs." Many are named for the colors of their brand-name versions: blues or blue heavens (Amytal), yellow jackets (Nembutal), red birds or red devils (Seconal), and rainbows or reds and blues (Tuinal).

BARBITURATES: USES AND EFFECTS

Classification: Depressant

CSA Schedule: Schedule II, III, IV

Trade or Other Names: Amytal, Florinal, Nembutal, Seconal, Tuinal, phenobarbital, pentobarbital

Medical Uses: Anesthetic, anticonvulsant, sedative, hypnotic, veterinary euthanasia agent

Physical Dependence: High to moderate

Psychological Dependence: High to moderate

Tolerance: Yes

Duration (hours): 5–8

Usual Method: Oral, injected

Possible Effects: Slurred speech, disorientation, drunken behavior without odor of alcohol

Effects of Overdose: Shallow respiration, clammy skin, dilated pupils, weak and rapid pulse, coma, possible death

Withdrawal Syndrome: Anxiety, insomnia, tremors, delirium, convulsions, possible death

Source: U.S. Drug Enforcement Administration.

A small dose (e.g., 50 mg or less) may relieve anxiety and tension. A somewhat larger dose (e.g., 100 to 200 mg) will, in a tranquil setting, usually induce sleep. An equivalent dose in a social setting, however, can produce effects similar to those of drunkenness—a "high" feeling, slurred speech, staggering, slowed reactions, loss of inhibition, and intense emotions often expressed in an extreme and unpredictable manner. High doses characteristically produce slow, shallow, and irregular breathing and can result in death from respiratory arrest. Barbiturate use during pregnancy has been associated with birth defects.

Barbiturates are classified according to the speed with which they are metabolized (broken down chemically) in the liver and eliminated by the kidneys: slow, intermediate, fast, and ultrafast. In low doses, barbiturates may actually increase the reaction to painful stimuli. The fast-acting barbiturates, particularly Nembutal (pentobarbital sodium), Amytal (amobarbital sodium), Seconal (secobarbital sodium), and Tuinal (secobarbital sodium and amobarbital sodium combined), are most likely to be abused (O'Brien and Cohen 1984). Exactly how barbiturates cause their neurophysiological effects is not fully understood, but the substance impairs the postsynaptic action of excitatory neurotransmitters (McKim 1991). Barbiturates serve as a positive reinforcer for laboratory animals.

TOLERANCE FOR BARBITURATES

As with opiates, tolerance develops to barbiturates; but in contrast to opiates there is a fatal dosage level, and the margin between an intoxicating dosage and a fatal dosage becomes smaller with continued use. "Tolerance to a fatal dosage, however, does not increase more than twofold. As this occurs, the margin between an intoxicating dosage and a fatal dosage becomes smaller" (*Physicians Desk Reference* 1988: 537). Drinking alcohol can further reduce that margin because alcohol "enhances the absorption and produces an additive CNS depression." When under the influence of small amounts of barbiturates or a combination of alcohol and barbiturates, a "person may 'forget' that he has already taken barbiturates and continue to ingest them until he reaches a lethal dose." Such overdoses often appear, incorrectly, to be suicidal (Wesson and Smith 1977: 24).

BARBITURATE WITHDRAWAL

Withdrawal symptoms range from the mild—muscle twitching, tremors, weakness, dizziness, visual distortion, nausea, vomiting, and insomnia—to the major—delirium, convulsions, and possibly death (*Physicians Desk Reference* 1987).

MEDICAL USE OF BARBITURATES

Barbiturates are used primarily as sedatives for the treatment of insomnia and as anticonvulsants to help prevent or mitigate epileptic seizures. The ultrafast barbiturates—the best-known being sodium pentothal—are used to induce unconsciousness in a few minutes. At relatively high dosages, they are used as anesthetics for minor surgery and to induce anesthesia before the administration of slow-acting barbiturates.

Because of the risks associated with barbiturate abuse and because new and safer drugs such as the tranquilizers/benzodiazepines are now available, barbiturates are less frequently prescribed than in the past. Nonetheless, they are still available both by prescription and illegally.

DANGERS OF BARBITURATE USE

As already noted, tolerance to barbiturates will build up beyond the level of a fatal dosage. Short of that, the disinhibition euphoria that can follow intake is what makes barbiturates appealing as intoxicants (Wesson and Smith 1977). Intoxication results in slurred speech, unsteady gait, confusion, poor judgment, and a marked impairment of motor skills. Unlike opiates, barbiturates make it dangerous to operate a motor vehicle. With continuous intoxication at high doses the user typically neglects his or her appearance, bathing infrequently and becoming unkempt and dirty as well as irritable and aggressive (McKim 1991). Like opiates, barbiturates are addicting, with both psychological and physiological dependence. High doses characteristically produce slow, shallow, and irregular breathing and can result in death from respiratory arrest. "Following a large overdose of secobarbital or phenobarbital (short-acting barbiturates), an individual may be in coma for several days" (Wesson and Smith 1977: 20).

Taking barbiturates with other CNS depressants, for example, alcohol; tranquilizers such opioids as heroin, morphine, meperidine (Demerol), codeine, or methadone; or antihistamines (found in cold, cough, and allergy remedies), can be extremely dangerous, even lethal. Over the long term, high dosage produces chronic inebriation; the impairment of memory and judgment; hostility, depression, or mood swings; chronic fatigue; and stimulation of preexisting emotional disorders, which can result in paranoia or thoughts of suicide. The prescribing of barbiturates has declined notably since the safer benzodiazepine tranquilizers (discussed below) were introduced.

BENZODIAZEPINES

Benzodiazepines (ben-zo-di-az-a-pins), which are minor tranquilizers or sedatives—referred to pharmacologically as *sedative-hypnotics*—are among the most widely prescribed of all drugs. One of earliest, Valium (diazepam), was approved by the Food and Drug Administration in 1963 to treat anxiety. Others now include Librium (chlordiazepoxide) and Equanil and Miltown (meprobamate). Prozac is a more recent and more widely prescribed selective serotonin reuptake inhibitor (SSRI), and the newer and longer-acting Klonopin is believed to have fewer withdrawal problems because it is metabolized more slowly and leaves the body gradually. The full extent of the nonmedical use of sedatives is not known, although it appears that their abuse often occurs in combination with other controlled substances. They produce effects that are subjectively similar to those of alcohol and barbiturates, but unlike these other depressants, benzodiazepines have few effects outside the CNS (McKim 1991). Major or antipsychotic tranquilizers such as Thorazine (chlorpromazine) do not produce euphoria and therefore are rarely used nonmedically.

BENZODIAZEPINES: USES AND EFFECTS

Classification: Depressant

CSA Schedule: Schedule IV

Trade or Other Names: Ativan, Dalmane, Diazepam, Librium, Xanax, Serax, Valium, Tranxene, Verstran, Versed, Halcion, Paxpam, Restoril

Medical Uses: Antianxiety, sedative, anticonvulsant, hypnotic

Physical Dependence: Low

Psychological Dependence: Low

Tolerance: Yes

Duration (hours): 4–8

Usual Method: Oral, injected

Possible Effects: Slurred speech, disorientation, drunken behavior without odor of alcohol

Effects of Overdose: Shallow respiration, clammy skin, dilated pupils, weak and rapid pulse, coma, possible death

Withdrawal Syndrome: Anxiety, insomnia, tremors, delirium, convulsions, possible death

Source: U.S. Drug Enforcement Administration.

EFFECTS OF TRANQUILIZERS

Minor tranquilizers or SSRIs are absorbed into the bloodstream and affect the CNS, slowing down physical, mental and emotional responses. The CNS contains benzodiazepine receptors that (through a complex process involving GABA receptors) inhibit the brain's limbic system, which regulates emotions (Smith and Wesson 1994). Although it has yet to be discovered, scientists believe that the body produces its own benzodiazepine-like substance that controls anxiety.

MEDICAL USE OF BENZODIAZEPINES

Minor tranquilizers are usually prescribed for anxiety or sleep problems. They can be used to treat panic disorders and muscle spasms. Sometimes referred to as "sleeping pills," these CNS depressants have largely replaced barbiturates, which reportedly have a significantly greater potential for abuse and risk for fatal overdose. In laboratory animals benzodiazepines have proven to be less effective reinforcers than barbiturates (National Institute on Drug Abuse 1991). Benzodiazepines have an upper limit of effectiveness; after a certain point, increasing the dosage will not increase the effect, and overdoses are rarely fatal (McKim 1991): "Even when a benzodiazepine is taken in an overdose of 50–100 times the usual therapeutic dose, fatalities from repertory depression is rare" (Smith and Wesson 1994: 180).

Valium is often prescribed to relieve stress, because it produces a sense of calm and well-being. It is also addictive. Benzodiazepines are not effective for treating anxiety beyond four months, and Valium can generate intense and severe secondary anxiety. Therefore, if the underlying cause of the anxiety is not treated, benzodiazepines may worsen the condition and increase the risk of suicide (Miller and Gold 1990). Valium has a very long half-life (twenty-four to forty-eight hours), which means that even after it is discontinued, it stays in the system, metabolizing slowly (Bluhm 1987). A benzodiazepine known as Versed is ten times more potent than Valium and is used to induce "twilight sleep" for surgery patients who need to be relaxed but conscious.

TOLERANCE FOR BENZODIAZEPINES

When benzodiazepines are used as sleeping pills, tolerance develops rapidly, and effectiveness may wear off after three nights. Because of tolerance, even if the dosage is increased, benzodiazepines are not effective for treating anxiety beyond four months.

WITHDRAWAL FROM BENZODIAZEPINES

Repeated use leads to dependence, and discontinuing tranquilizers can produce withdrawal symptoms, although it is unclear in what proportion of users. Symptoms include anxiety, insomnia, agitation, anorexia, tremor, muscle twitching, nausea/vomiting, hypersensitivity to sensory stimuli and other perceptual disturbances, and depersonalization. Discontinuing use after prolonged exposure to high doses can produce hallucinations, delirium, grand mal convulsions, and, on rare occasions, death (National Institute on Drug Abuse 1987; Smith and Wesson 1994). Valium withdrawal symptoms may first appear after seven to ten days and may be quite serious and even life-threatening (Bluhm 1987). Someone using minor tranquilizers under medical supervision for more than two or three weeks is usually withdrawn gradually over a period of months.

DANGERS OF TRANQUILIZER USE

Common short-term effects of tranquilizer use include drowsiness, dizziness, confusion, and mood swings. Common long-term effects include lethargy, irritability, nausea, loss of sexual interest, increased appetite, and weight gain. Regular use of minor tranquilizers can produce both psychological and physical dependence. Combining minor tranquilizers with alcohol, painkillers, or drugs containing antihistamines, such as cough, cold, and allergy medications, can result in unconsciousness and failure to breathe. A life-endangering CNS depression can result when benzodiazepines are used in conjunction with alcohol. In some people benzodiazepines can induce hostility and even aggression (McKim 1991). Valium overdose is the second leading cause of drug-related emergency room admissions in the United States. Some tranquilizers block receptors for the neurotransmitter dopamine, which can lead to symptoms of Parkinson's disease. In 2005 it was revealed that babies born to women who take SSRIs late in pregnancy often exhibit jitteriness, irritability, and serious respiratory problems. Although the symptoms were generally mild, some babies required hospitalization and intensive care (Associated Press 2005).

METHAQUALONE

Such drugs as glutethimide (Doriden), methyprylon (Noludar), ethchlorvynol (Placidyl), and methaqualone (found in Mandrax) were introduced as barbiturate substitutes in the belief that they would be safer. It was soon found, however, that they shared problems similar to those of barbiturates, including abuse leading to overdose and interaction with other CNS depressants. The caution that is necessary in using barbiturates therefore applies to these other sedative/hypnotics as well.

Methaqualone was first synthesized in 1951 in India, where it was introduced as an antimalarial drug but proved to be ineffective. At the same time its sedating effects caused it to be introduced in Great Britain as a safe, non-barbiturate "sleeping pill." The substance subsequently found its way into street abuse, and similar patterns occurred in Germany and Japan. In 1965 methaqualone was introduced into the United States as the prescription drugs Sopors and Quaalude without any restrictions—it was not listed as a scheduled (controlled) drug. By the early 1970s "ludes" and "sopors" were part of the drug culture. Physicians were overprescribing the drugs for anxiety and insomnia, believing that they were safer than barbiturates. Street sales were primarily diversions from legitimate sources.

Eight years after methaqualone was first introduced into the United States, the drug's serious dangers had become evident, and in 1973 it was placed on the DEA's Schedule II list. Although the drug is chemically unrelated to barbiturates, methaqualone intoxication is similar to barbiturate intoxication. Addiction develops rapidly, and an overdose can be fatal. However, though similar to barbiturates in its effect, methaqualone produces an even greater loss of motor coordination, which is why it is sometimes referred to as a "wall-banger." Methaqualone is now illegally manufactured in Colombia and smuggled into the United States.

ALCOHOL

Alcohol[4] is a potentially dangerous drug that is used by mainstream religions such as Judaism and Catholicism (though alcohol consumption is prohibited by Islam and several Protestant denominations) and whose recreational use in moderation is an accepted part of American culture: Two out of every three adult Americans consume alcohol.

Alcohols are compounds used in perfumes, paints, and many other products. Ethyl alcohol (ethanol) is used as a beverage and often added to gasoline. A natural substance, ethyl alcohol is formed by the **fermentation** that occurs when sugar

---

[4]Unless otherwise noted, information in this section is from the Office of Substance Abuse Studies, University of Maryland; Missouri Division of Alcohol and Drug Abuse; Alcoholism and Drug Addiction Research Foundation, Toronto, Canada; Canadian Centre on Substance Abuse, Ottawa, Canada; and the Centre for Education and Information on Drugs and Alcohol in New South Wales, Australia.

reacts with yeast. It can be made by distillation or by fermenting fruits, vegetables, or grains. In pure form, the substance is colorless and has a bitter taste. Although some people apparently enjoy the taste of beverages that contain alcohol, many others ingest the drug *despite* its taste. The substance can produce feelings of well-being, sedation, intoxication, or unconsciousness, depending on the amount and the manner in which it is consumed.

Some research indicates that alcohol taken in moderate amounts—one drink daily for women, two for men (more than 5 grams but not more than 30 grams of pure alcohol)[5]—can help protect against heart disease by raising the level of high-density lipoproteins (HDL, the so-called good cholesterol) that help to cleanse the arteries of fatty deposits (Burros 1996; Angier 1991). Research has revealed that as little as a single glass of wine or beer per week can significantly reduce the risk of ischemic stroke, which is the most common type of stroke and is caused by clots that reduce blood flow to the brain. An estimated 600,000 people in the United States suffer a stroke each year (Greenberg 1999).

However, the purported health benefits of moderate drinking have been challenged because they have not been subjected to randomized long-term clinical studies. It may just be, critics argue, that moderate drinkers tend to lead a healthier lifestyle—good diet, exercise, good medical care—and that lifestyle, not moderate use of alcohol, explains their better health. Critics state that it may be that people who are abstainers are so because of poor health ("sick quitters") or because they are elderly (people tend to reduce drinking as they age) and thus more likely to suffer from illness (Rabin 2009).

Alcohol is a *regulated* rather than *controlled* substance; that is, it can be purchased and possessed with only a few restrictions. There are three major classes of alcoholic beverage:

1. *Beer.* Beer is produced by the fermentation (brewing) of barley malt or other grains. It is usually flavored with hops or other aromatic bitters. In the United States beer generally contains no more than 5 percent alcohol (10 proof), although some "ice" beers contain closer to 6 percent and some (mostly foreign) brews contain 7 percent. A variant of beer known as "malt liquor" can contain 8 percent alcohol (16 proof). There are also "light" beers (about 4 percent alcohol), low-alcohol beer (less than 4 percent alcohol), and non-alcoholic beers (about 0.05 percent alcohol).[6]
2. *Wine.* Wine is obtained from the fermentation of the juice of grapes (and sometimes other fruits). It usually contains 6–14 percent alcohol (12–28 proof). Wine coolers, mixtures of wine and fruit juice, range from 5 percent to 8 percent alcohol. There are also fortified wines that have had additional alcohol added. Port and sherry wines are examples of high-quality fortified wines. Low-priced fortified wines are produced by adding grain alcohol to

---

[5]A six-ounce glass of wine has about eleven grams of alcohol; a twelve-ounce can of beer has about thirteen grams; and a one-ounce shot of liquor has about fifteen grams.

[6]In 1935, fearing that beer manufacturers would attempt to lure customers by raising the amount of alcohol in their brews, Congress enacted legislation that prohibited the listing of alcohol content on beer labels. In 1995 the Supreme Court ruled that law unconstitutional.

low-grade wine; these are often sold in screw-top bottles and are favorites of low-income alcoholics and of youths, since these wines produce more intoxication at less cost than other types of alcoholic beverage.

3. *Liquor.* When alcohol produced by fermentation (of corn, malt, other grains, molasses, or potatoes) reaches about 15 percent, it kills the alcohol-producing yeast cells. To obtain higher concentrations of alcohol, **distillation** is necessary: The mix is heated—alcohol has a lower boiling point than the other liquids—and its cooling vapors are collected. After several distillations nearly pure alcohol can be obtained. The colorless liquid is usually mixed with water, coloring, and flavoring agents. It contains at least 25 percent alcohol (50 proof) but may be as high as 50 percent alcohol (100 proof). This category includes whiskey (including the Kentucky version known as bourbon and the Scottish version known as Scotch as well as Tennessee, Irish, Canadian, and rye whiskeys), brandy, rum, gin, and vodka.

A relatively recent category, *caffeinated alcoholic drinks*, combines malt liquor with caffeine and fruit juices and contains about ten percent alcohol. Popular among college students, the caffeine in these drinks can provide false confidence in the ability to perform tasks such as driving, that the drinker is too impaired to undertake. There are about 30 manufacturers of these drinks that resemble nonalcoholic "energy drinks" (Harris 2009).

Distilling alcohol involves the danger of working with flammable liquids and requires licensing by the state and federal governments.

Alcohol is absorbed primarily through the small intestine. The rate of absorption depends on the type and amount of foods in the stomach, if any; foods, especially solid and fatty foods, slow the absorption process. Body weight and gender also influence the effects of alcohol: Heavier people have more bodily fluids and thus dilute more of the substance; women have less gastric acid and will absorb about 30 percent more alcohol than men. Once absorbed into the bloodstream, alcohol moves to wherever there is water in the body, including inside cells of the CNS.

THE BASICS OF BOURBON

In 1776 Virginia named its western frontier Kentucky County. After the American Revolution, the county was divided, and one part was named Bourbon County in honor of France's help in the war. Later, the state of Kentucky was formed largely from what had been Bourbon County. One of the chief products of Kentucky was corn whiskey, which became popularly known as bourbon. Bourbon, which by law must be derived from at least 51 percent corn—as distinct from rye whiskey—receives its color and almost all of its taste from the charred barrels in which it is stored for at least two years. For the substance to be labeled *bourbon*, according to U.S. law, the barrels can be used only once. Bourbon whiskey's cousin, Tennessee whiskey, sold under the brand names Jack Daniel's and George Dickel, is the result of slow filtering over the course of several days through maple charcoal (Allen 1998).

Scotch whiskey is aged for three years in used barrels, mostly bourbon barrels imported from Kentucky (Allen 1998; Kummer 1999).

Alcoholic women are more vulnerable than alcoholic men to many of the medical consequences of alcohol use. Alcoholic women develop cirrhosis of the liver, alcohol-induced damage of the heart muscle (cardiomyopathy), and nerve damage (peripheral neuropathy) after fewer years of heavy drinking than do alcoholic men (National Institute on Alcohol Abuse and Alcoholism 2004).

EFFECTS OF ALCOHOL

Alcohol is a psychoactive (mind-altering) chemical that, like heroin and tranquilizers, depresses the CNS. It is an efficient tranquilizer with the ability to reduce short-term anxiety (Willoughby 1988). However, alcohol first affects the part of the brain that controls inhibitions: Drinkers talk more, exude self-confidence, and may get foolish or even rowdy; there is a general loss of self-restraint (Valenzuela 1997).

The mechanism by which alcohol does this involves two receptors: GABA receptors restrain neuron activity so that chaotic communication is avoided; NMDA receptors promote communication necessary to encode memories, generate thoughts, and make decisions. Alcohol reinforces GABA activity while reducing NMDA activity, thereby slowing communication between neurons (Kotulak 2002b). As the dose increases, so do the effects, the brain experiencing greater difficulty communicating with nerves and muscles. This results in slurred speech, staggering, and a loss of emotional control. Further ingestion can lead to stupor from which arousal is difficult, severe respiratory depression, coma, and possibly death.

A common problem among college students, binge drinking is defined as having at least five drinks (for men) or four drinks (for women) in a two-hour period. This causes a rapid rise in the blood alcohol level, placing the person at risk for experiencing a blackout during which he or she might engage in potentially dangerous behavior such as driving and unprotected sex that the inebriated person might not remember (National Institute on Alcohol Abuse and Alcoholism 2004).

Alcohol is a complex substance that affects a number of neurotransmitter and receptor systems in the brain: endorphin, dopamine, serotonin, and glutamine. When alcoholics imbibe, their brains release elevated levels of endorphins, triggering rewarding sensations that entice the person to drink more. However, at low doses, alcohol acts as a stimulant, and initially, the user of alcohol often experiences it as an energizer with euphoric effects (Bukstein, Brent, and Kaminer 1989). As with most other psychoactive substances, this is the result of alcohol stimulating the dopaminergic reward pathway in the brain (Dettling et al. 1995).

As with other drugs the influence of alcohol is mediated through setting and expectations. Imbibers at a funeral will act differently than they would if they imbibed at a wedding or other happy occasion. The two effects— stimulation and sedation—appear to be influenced by the degree of excitability of the CNS at the time of ingestion, which depends on the setting in which alcohol is used as well as the personality of the user. In a quiet environment the excitatory influence may be impaired, and alcohol produces sedation and drowsiness. If the environment is loud and lively, the drinker demonstrates excitement.

Similar reactions have been found with respect to alcohol and sexual arousal. Except at very low doses, alcohol makes it more difficult for males to maintain an erection sufficient for intercourse and retards their ability to achieve orgasm. These effects increase with increased alcohol consumption (George and Stoner 2000). While increasing doses of alcohol suppresses physiological arousal for both men and women, subjective sexual arousal is affected not only by blood alcohol concentration, but also by a person's beliefs about the effects of alcohol. Thus, in men, but not women, the culturally transmitted connection between sex and alcohol enhances arousal. Culturally transmitted beliefs and expectations exert a powerful influence over sexuality in drinking situations. That is, expectations about the relationship between alcohol and sex generated by the culture influence how a person believes he or she will respond to sexual stimuli while under the influence of alcohol (George and Norris n.d.).

Regular use of moderate daily amounts of alcohol can produce psychological dependence, the lack of alcohol resulting in anxiety and mild panic attacks. Prolonged or chronic drinking produces both psychological and physical dependence. The stronger depressant effect lasts about two hours, while a weaker stimulation of the CNS lasts about six times as long. As the time since the last drink increases, the longer-lasting stimulating effect becomes dominant, and the drinker becomes agitated—the "morning-after hangover." This is the start of the drinker's withdrawal syndrome. Because of alcohol's primary depressant effect, calm can be temporarily restored by more drinking. For the alcoholic the morning drink has a calming effect that is part of a vicious cycle of continued alcohol use.

At age 65, the body's ability to respond to alcohol is quite different from that at age 45. Thus, older adults can get into trouble after drinking an amount of alcohol that would not be considered immoderate at a younger age. As people age, they lose muscle, bone, and lean body mass and acquire a greater percentage of body fat. As a result, there is a decrease in body water, in which alcohol is soluble, replaced by fat, in which alcohol is not soluble. Aging also results in a decline in a stomach enzyme that breaks down alcohol before it reaches the bloodstream. As a result, there is greater burden on the liver, where most alcohol metabolism takes place. Advancing age also causes a decline in the blood flow through the liver, so alcohol is eliminated more slowly from the blood. Thus, blood alcohol levels in older people are 30–40 percent higher than those in younger people (Wald 2002).

As was noted in Chapter 1, alcohol is associated with a great deal of violence and crime. Alcohol causes some people to become very aggressive. Males under the influence of alcohol are more easily provoked and more likely to react in a violent manner than are males who are not under influence of alcohol (Hoaken, Campbell, Stewart, and Phil 2003).

Asians often carry a gene that makes them physically ill and flushed before they can consume an addicting amount of alcohol (Brody 2003).

Blood Alcohol Level   Almost all alcohol is burned as fuel. Unlike other drugs of abuse, alcohol provides calories and is technically a food with some eliminated through the lungs and in urine. Breathalyzer tests measure the **blood alcohol level**—the amount of alcohol in the blood—because alcohol in the air exhaled closely parallels concentrations in the blood. In most states, a blood alcohol level of 0.10 is the legal standard for intoxication, although a number of states have lowered the level to 0.08. Tables 4.1a and 4.1b show the degrees of impairment at different blood

TABLE 4.1A | ALCOHOL IMPAIRMENT CHART, MEN

Body Weight[2]	Approximate Blood Alcohol Percentage[1]								
Drinks[3]	100	120	140	160	180	200	220	240	
0	.00	.00	.00	.00	.00	.00	.00	.00	Only safe driving limit
1	.04	.03	.03	.02	.02	.02	.02	.02	Impairment begins
2	.08	.06	.05	.05	.04	.04	.03	.03	Driving skills significantly affected
3	.11	.09	.08	.07	.06	.06	.05	.05	
4	.15	.12	.11	.09	.08	.08	.07	.06	
5	.19	.16	.13	.12	.11	.09	.09	.08	Possible criminal penalties
6	.23	.19	.16	.14	.13	.11	.10	.09	
7	.26	.22	.19	.16	.15	.13	.12	.11	Legally intoxicated
8	.30	.25	.21	.19	.17	.15	.14	.13	
9	.34	.28	.24	.21	.19	.17	.15	.14	Criminal penalties
10	.38	.31	.27	.23	.21	.19	.17	.16	

TABLE 4.1b | Alcohol Impairment Chart, Women

Body Weight[2]	Approximate Blood Alcohol Percentage[1]									
	90	100	120	140	160	180	200	220	240	
Drinks[3]										
0	.00	.00	.00	.00	.00	.00	.00	.00	.00	Only safe driving limit
1	.05	.05	.04	.03	.03	.03	.02	.02	.02	Impairment begins
2	.10	.09	.08	.07	.06	.05	.05	.04	.04	Driving skills significantly affected
3	.15	.14	.11	.10	.09	.08	.07	.06	.04	
4	.20	.18	.15	.13	.11	.10	.09	.08	.06	
5	.25	.23	.19	.16	.14	.13	.11	.10	.08	Possible criminal penalties
6	.30	.27	.23	.19	.17	.15	.14	.12	.11	
7	.38	.32	.27	.23	.20	.18	.16	.14	.13	Legally intoxicated
8	.40	.36	.30	.26	.23	.20	.18	.17	.15	
9	.45	.41	.34	.29	.26	.23	.20	.19	.17	
10	.51	.45	.38	.32	.28	.25	.23	.21	.19	Criminal penalties

[1]Subtract .01% for each 40 minutes of drinking.
[2]In pounds.
[3]One drink is 1.25 ounces of 80 proof liquor, 12 ounces of beer, or 5 ounces of table wine.

Source: Data supplied by the Pennsylvania Liquor Control Board.

alcohol levels for men and women, respectively, and the numbers of drinks typically required to reach these levels. Alcohol use produces tolerance, and people with high levels of alcohol tolerance can perform tasks with a blood alcohol level that would render a nontolerant person a "falling-down drunk." Alcohol has a cross-tolerance with barbiturates and benzodiazepines. It appears to act on the CNS in the same manner as benzodiazepines; that is, it acts on benzodiazepine receptors, which are inhibitory.

Genetic Influence on Alcohol Use   A wide variety of studies clearly indicate that genetic factors influence the development of alcoholism, but the studies differ in their estimate of the degree of genetic influence. Although genes (segments of chromosomes that code for the production of specific proteins) are important in the control of behavior, they do not directly cause a person to become alcoholic or drug-dependent, although genes are believed to produce a tendency or predisposition to respond to drugs (including alcohol) in a certain manner. "If you are the son of a male alcoholic who began his alcoholism in early adolescence or early adulthood, the chance of your becoming an alcoholic is 7 to 10 times greater than that of the average population. If you are the twin of a male alcoholic, the chance of your becoming an alcoholic is about 70 percent. This means there is some factor, or factors, passed to the male offspring that make them more vulnerable to the actions of alcoholism" (Bloom 1993: 24). Research that compared fraternal and identical male twins supports the role of genetic factors in alcoholism. The researchers also found that environmental factors had little influence on the development of alcoholism (Prescott and Kendler 1999).

Studies have revealed that some people with particular inherited characteristics are at greater risk for addiction than are people without these characteristics. "Researchers have identified as important influences such inherited characteristics as how an individual metabolizes alcohol, hormonal and behavioral effects of alcohol and tolerance of high levels of alcohol in the blood" (Brody 1987: 14; also see Tarter, Alterman, and Edwards [1985] and Tarter [1988] for a review of research on behavioral traits and predisposition to substance abuse). Studies have shown that first-degree relatives of alcoholics are more likely to be alcoholics than are close blood relatives of nonalcoholics. Adopted children with alcoholic natural parents are more likely to become alcoholics than are adopted children with nonalcoholic natural parents (Schuckit 1985). Identical twins are about twice as likely as fraternal twins to resemble each other in terms of the presence of alcoholism (National Institute on Alcohol Abuse and Alcoholism 2003).

Research reveals that the genetic component of alcoholism appears to be related to an abnormality of a dopamine receptor gene (Blum et al. 1990). People who have this defect are at potentially greater risk for the disease than is the general population. Research has identified a specific genetic (dopamine-related) abnormality associated with susceptibility for alcoholism (Dettling et al. 1995; Guardia et al. 2000). It has been shown that another stimulating neurotransmitter, serotonin, also influences drinking behavior (Gulley et al. 1995), and a deficiency in serotonin or serotonin receptors has been linked to a predisposition to alcoholism (Goleman 1990). The ability of alcohol to produce both depressant and

UNDER THE INFLUENCE

After one drink, a person weighing 120 pounds has a blood alcohol level of about .04; a person weighing 140 pounds has a blood alcohol level of about .03; and a person weighing 240 pounds has a blood alcohol level of about .02. Following are the effects of alcohol at different blood levels:

.02–.03: Slight euphoria and loss of inhibition

.04–.06: Feeling of well-being and relaxation, sensation of warmth, minor impairment of reasoning and lowering of caution

.07–.09: Slight impairment of balance, motor coordination, vision, and self-control; slurred speech

.10–.12: Significant impairment of motor coordination, balance, vision, and reaction time; loss of good judgment

.30–.40: Loss of consciousness and possible death from respiratory arrest

stimulant effects may be related to the fact that, in contrast to other psychoactive substances, alcohol can affect many different parts of the CNS (Kotulak 1997).

ALCOHOL TOLERANCE AND WITHDRAWAL

Although tolerance does not develop to alcohol's rewarding effects, people who drink on a regular basis become tolerant to many of the unpleasant effects of alcohol and are thus able to drink more before suffering these effects (National Institute on Alcohol Abuse and Alcoholism 1997). Even with increased consumption many such drinkers do not appear intoxicated.

In the liver, alcohol is converted to acetaldehyde, which in high levels causes permanent liver damage. In the alcoholic—though not in people who are not addicted to alcohol—acetaldehyde builds up and is transported through the blood-brain barrier, where it combines with neurotransmitters to produce tetrahydroisoquinolines (TIQs). TIQs attach to CNS receptors to produce a feeling of well-being similar to that produced by morphine. This activity causes brain cell membranes to become abnormally thickened and to require a constant supply of alcohol. Thus, the brain cells have become addicted to alcohol. In its absence, membranes function poorly, and the alcoholic experiences withdrawal symptoms (Catanzarite 1992; Kotulak 2002b).

A physically dependent alcoholic who abruptly stops drinking will experience a withdrawal syndrome that can range from very mild to life threatening. If large amounts of alcohol are consumed for a long time, withdrawal symptoms will often be severe and far more dangerous than withdrawal from heroin. By contrast, the morning-after hangover—nausea, shakiness, and headache—may result from a single bout of alcohol abuse.

In the typical course of withdrawal, symptoms begin within the first twenty-four hours after the last drink, reach their peak intensity within two or three days, and disappear within one or two weeks. As the blood alcohol level begins to drop, the person may experience headaches, anxiety, involuntary twitching of muscles, tremor of hands, weakness, insomnia, nausea, anxiety, rapid heart rate, and increased blood pressure. At this point the alcoholic usually craves alcohol. The second stage of alcohol withdrawal includes hallucinations; these are usually visual but may include auditory or olfactory as well. If hallucinations develop, they may persist for hours, days, or even weeks.

The third stage occurs during the next forty-eight hours as symptoms become progressively more intense. There may be a fall in blood pressure; fever; delirium characterized by disorientation, delusions, and visual hallucinations; and convulsions similar to those exhibited in grand mal epileptic seizures. The fever, delirium, and convulsions are the most serious symptoms and can be fatal.

If the person remains untreated, the syndrome may progress to **delirium tremens** (DTs): profound confusion, disorientation, hallucinations, hyperactivity, and extreme cardiovascular disturbances. Without close medical management the person may harm himself or herself or others or could die from the medical complications. Prevention of the DTs involves the use of sedatives such as Valium, since once the DTs begin, no known medical treatment is able to stop them. If left untreated, DTs can be fatal.

DANGERS OF ALCOHOL USE

Alcohol has a pervasive effect on the body's gastrointestinal tract, liver, bloodstream, brain and nervous system, heart, muscles, and endocrine system. Some harmful consequences are primary; that is, they result directly from prolonged exposure to alcohol's toxic effects (such as heart and liver disease or inflammation of the stomach). Others are secondary, indirectly related to chronic alcohol abuse; these include loss of appetite, vitamin deficiencies, infections, and sexual impotence or menstrual irregularities. Because alcohol can be utilized as a source of energy, this supply of calories often suppresses appetite, leading to dietary deficiencies that may be responsible in part for the pathologic conditions that are seen in chronic alcoholism. The risk of serious disease increases with the amount of alcohol consumed:

- Loss of control of eye muscles
- Hypoglycemia (low level of glucose in the blood)
- Gastritis (chronic inflammation of the stomach)
- Increased susceptibility to infections
- Cardiac arrhythmia (irregularity)
- Anemia (red blood cell deficiency)
- Neuritis (nerve inflammation)
- Pancreatitis (inflammation of the pancreas)
- Increased blood pressure
- Cardiomyopathy (heart muscle disorder)
- Cancer of the tongue, mouth, pharynx, hypopharynx, esophagus, and liver
- Decreased white blood cells
- Weakened immune system
- Depletion of vitamins and minerals
- Lowered hormone levels, leading to sexual dysfunction

Wernicke-Korsakoff Syndrome   Most long-term alcoholics suffer from Wernicke-Korsakoff syndrome, a deficiency in thiamine (vitamin B1), an essential nutrient required by all tissues, including the brain. Wernicke-Korsakoff syndrome consists of two separate syndromes, a short-lived and severe condition called Wernicke's encephalopathy and a long-lasting and debilitating condition known as Korsakoff's psychosis. The symptoms of Wernicke's encephalopathy include mental confusion, paralysis of the nerves that move the eyes (oculomotor disturbances), and difficulty with muscle coordination. Victims might be too confused to find their way out of a room or might not even be able to walk.

About 80 to 90 percent of alcoholics with Wernicke's encephalopathy also develop Korsakoff's psychosis, a chronic and debilitating disease characterized by persistent learning and memory problems, being forgetful and quickly frustrated, and having difficulty with walking and coordination. Although these patients have problems remembering old information (retrograde amnesia), it is their difficulty in "laying down" new information (anterograde amnesia) that is the most striking. For example, these patients can discuss in detail an event in their lives, but an hour later they might not remember ever having the conversation (National Institute on Alcohol Abuse and Alcoholism 2004).

Liver and Brain Damage   About one out of five heavy drinkers develop fatty liver (steatosis), which usually produces no clinical symptoms except an enlarged liver. Although the condition can be reversed if alcohol consumption is significantly reduced, it can eventually be fatal. Heavy drinkers may also suffer from alcoholic hepatitis, the symptoms of which include a swollen liver, nausea, vomiting, and abdominal pain. They may also experience jaundice, bleeding, and liver failure. If severe drinking continues, there is about a 50 percent chance of mortality, or the person will probably develop cirrhosis.

Cirrhosis results in scar tissue replacing normal liver tissue, causing a disruption of blood flow through the liver, preventing it from working properly. Symptoms include redness of the palms caused by capillary dilation, shortening of muscles in the fingers caused by toxic effects or fibrous changes, white nails, thickening and widening of the fingers and nails, liver enlargement or inflammation, and abnormal accumulation of fat in normal liver cells. About 10–15 percent of people with alcoholism develop cirrhosis, but many survive it. Many are unaware that they have it; about 30–40 percent of cirrhosis cases are discovered at autopsy. When late-stage cirrhosis develops, that is, when jaundice, accumulation of fluid in the abdomen, or gastrointestinal bleeding has occurred, the survival rate is only 60 percent for those who stop drinking and 35 percent for those who do not (Mann, Smart, and Govoni 2004).

Prolonged liver dysfunction, such as liver cirrhosis, can also harm the brain, leading to a serious and potentially fatal brain disorder known as hepatic encephalopathy (Tuma and Casey 2004). Research has found serious brain deficits in alcoholics, but there is no conclusive evidence that can link this to any one variable. The most plausible explanation is some combination of prolonged use of alcohol and individual vulnerability to some forms of brain damage (Oscar-Berman and Marinkovic 2004).

Fetal Alcohol Spectrum Disorders   Fetal alcohol spectrum disorders are a variety of conditions that result from a mother who drinks during pregnancy. Foremost among them is fetal alcohol syndrome (FAS). The serious effects of FAS include mental retardation, growth deficiency, head and facial deformities, joint and limb abnormalities, and heart defects. (When the symptoms of FAS are present without the characteristic facial features, the disorder is referred to as *fetal alcohol effects.*) When a FAS baby is born, he or she may experience withdrawal from alcohol, exhibiting tremors, irritability, fits, and a bloated stomach. Why some pregnant women who drink heavily give birth to normal babies while others have babies who are severely damaged is not known. But there are an unknown number of babies who, while affected by their mother's drinking, appear relatively normal but subsequently develop behavioral and learning problems (Carroll 2003). Whether an individual child will have FAS appears to depend on a number of factors in addition to alcohol, including parental health, other drug use, lifestyle, and other socioeconomic factors. Some of the factors contributing to FAS may be male-mediated. This influence may occur biologically through damage to the sperm or physically and psychologically through violence or other abuse to the mother before and during pregnancy.

Alcohol-related birth defects include malformations in the skeletal and major organ systems, while alcohol-related neurodevelopmental disorder involves CNS deficits (Substance Abuse and Mental Health Services Administration 2004). Researchers have discovered that even moderate drinking by a pregnant woman can impair the child's intellectual ability in school (Goleman 1989), and alcohol has been linked to a tenfold increased risk of developing leukemia during infancy ("New Hazard of Drinking in Pregnancy Is Found" 1996). Because alcohol affects so many parts of the brain, it is viewed as the most harmful drug of abuse that a pregnant mother can use. Indeed, much of the damage ascribed to cocaine, particularly crack, appears to be primarily the result of the mother using alcohol as well (Carroll 2003).

The fetus is at greatest risk of harm during the first three months of pregnancy, as the major organs and limbs are starting to form during that time. Research indicates that ethanol induces the destruction of large numbers of neurons from several regions of the developing brain (Ikonomidou et al. 2000). A 2004 study indicates that just two cocktails consumed by a pregnant woman can kill developing brain cells in a fetus and thus can lead to a lifetime of neurological problems (Associated Press 2004b).

ANALOGS AND DESIGNER DRUGS

Many chemical variations, or **analogs**, of the drugs discussed in this chapter have been found or developed. These include semisynthetic opiates such as hydromorphine, oxycodone, etorphine, and diprenorphine and synthetic opiates such as pethidine, methadone, and propoxyphene (Darvon). The synthetic drug **fentanyl** citrate, which is often used intravenously in major surgery, works exactly like the opiates: It kills pain and produces euphoria and, if abused, leads to addiction.

Fentanyl was first synthesized by a Belgium pharmaceutical company in 1960 for use as an intravenous anesthetic. Shortly after its introduction into the

FENTANYL: USES AND EFFECTS

Classification: Narcotic

CSA Schedule: Schedule I, II

Trade or Other Names: Innovar, Sublimaze, Alfenta, Sufenta, Duragesic

Medical Uses: Analgesic, adjunct to anesthesia, anesthetic

Physical Dependence: High

Psychological Dependence: High

Tolerance: Yes

Duration (hours): 10–72

Usual Method: Injected, transdermal patch

Possible Effects: Euphoria, drowsiness, respiratory depression, constricted pupils, nausea

Effects of Overdose: Slow and shallow breathing, clammy skin, convulsions, coma, possible death

Withdrawal Syndrome: Watery eyes, runny nose, yawning, loss of appetite, irritability, tremors, panic. cramps, nausea, chills, and sweating

Source: U.S. Drug Enforcement Administration.

United States in 1968, there was a wave of abuse by medical professionals who had access to the drug in hospitals. In 1979, a still unidentified rogue chemist created an even more powerful version that was soon being sold on the streets; overdoses became common. Its use remained relatively rare until the late 1990s when a simple method of manufacture was posted online. "For the first time, anyone with a basement lab and a chemistry degree could make his own synthetic heroin" (Higginbotham 2007: 215).

Fentanyl compounds are often sold as "China White," the street name for the finest Southeast Asian heroin, to addicts who cannot tell the difference. Those who know the difference may actually prefer fentanyl because it is usually cheaper than heroin and more readily available, and some users believe that it contains fewer adulterants than heroin (Roberton 1986; K. Johnson 2006). In Chicago, in 2006, after a wave of fentanyl overdoses was in the news, the police department distributed a flyer explaining its often fatal dangers: in response, heroin users "began showing up brandishing the Police Department's flyer, asking dealers for the drug it described" (Higinbotham 2007: 217).

Fentanyl compounds are quite potent and difficult for street dealers to cut properly, a situation that can lead to overdose and death. One derivative, 3-methyl fentanyl, is extremely potent (approximately 3,000 times as potent as morphine) and is thought to have been responsible for a number of overdose deaths. In 1988 3-methyl fentanyl led to the death of eighteen people in the Pittsburgh area. A local chemist without a criminal record was found to be the source; he apparently got the idea from a television news report. In 1991 the drug killed ten people in one weekend in four Northeastern cities (Nieves 1991). In 2006 fentanyl mixed with and sold as heroin was responsible for killing hundreds of people in cities from Chicago to Philadelphia (Associated Press 2006; K. Johnson 2006). Some of the victims had snorted the drug (Santora 2006). Fentanyl has been used (illegally) to "dope" race-horses because the substance is very difficult to detect in urine or blood.

Analogs designed by underground chemists (**designer drugs**) to mimic controlled substances are an emerging problem: "These chemists change the molecular structure of a drug and thus make the drug legally unrestricted. Since the passage of the Anti-Drug Abuse Act of 1986 all analogs of controlled substances have themselves become controlled substances. The changes in chemical structure may also change its potency, length of action, euphoric effects, and toxicity" (National Institute on Drug Abuse 1987: 27).

SUMMARY

- Depressants are typically addicting, and studies have indicated a relationship between certain chemical deficiencies and the propensity for addiction to depressants.
- Endorphins have many of the characteristics of morphine; they relieve pain and enable people to deal with psychological stress.
- A person who is having difficulties dealing with stress and is exposed to opiates is likely to find them rewarding and thus become addicted.
- Consumer heroin is either "smoking heroin" (heroin no. 3) or "injectable heroin" (heroin no. 4).
- Pure heroin is a white powder with a bitter taste and little odor, but street heroin comes in many different forms, depending on how it was made and what has been added to it.
- Heroin has analgesic and euphoric properties. The user can experience four different effects: the rush, the high, the nod, and being straight.
- Heroin depresses the respiratory centers in the brain. An overdose can result in respiratory arrest and death from lack of oxygen to the brain.
- Tolerance to some aspects of heroin use requires an increase in the dosage in order to gain the same level of response.
- Withdrawal symptoms tend to be the opposite of effects produced by the drug.
- Oxycodone (OxyContin) is a synthetic version of morphine.

- Barbiturates are powerful sedatives classified according the speed of their action.
- While tolerance develops to the effects of barbiturates there is a fatal dose level.
- Barbiturates are prescribed for the treatment of insomnia and as anticonvulsants to help prevent or mitigate epileptic seizures.
- Benzodiazepines are minor tranquilizers or sedatives which have largely replaced barbiturates.
- The purported health benefits of moderate drinking have been challenged because they have not been subjected to randomized long-term clinical studies.
- While alcohol is an efficient tranquilizer with the ability to reduce short-term anxiety, at low doses it acts as a stimulant.
- Initially alcohol affects the part of the brain that controls inhibitions.
- Alcohol is an addicting drug whose withdrawal symptoms can be fatal.
- Genetic factors influence a person's risk of suffering from alcoholism.
- Chronic alcohol use can result in fatal liver disease—cirrhosis.
- Alcohol use during pregnancy can result in fetal alcohol syndrome.
- Many chemical variations or analogs of psychoactive drugs have been found or developed, such as fentanyl, which is quite potent and difficult for street dealers to cut properly.

Review Questions

1. What are endorphins?
2. What purpose do endorphins serve?
3. What would be the effect of a deficiency in endorphins?
4. How does the ingestion of large amounts of opiates affect receptor sites?
5. How can use of opiates be explained by stress?
6. Why do patients prescribed morphine for long-term pain rarely develop a craving for the drug?
7. How can cues affect a recovering heroin addict?
8. How can heroin result in hypersensitivity to stress?
9. Why can't the chemicals needed to produce heroin be outlawed?
10. What is the difference between no. 3 and no. 4 heroin?
11. What are the methods of heroin ingestion?
12. For heroin users, what are the differences between the rush, the high, and the nod?
13. How does heroin impair homeostatic body functions?
14. What is the most dangerous side effect of heroin?
15. What is the rebounding effect resulting from heroin withdrawal?
16. What is OxyContin?
17. What are the effects of barbiturates?
18. How do barbiturates differ from opiates?
19. What are the medical uses of barbiturates?
20. How does the user's setting influence the effect of barbiturates?
21. What is the basis for classifying barbiturates?
22. Why is barbiturate use more dangerous than opiate use?
23. What substances have largely replaced barbiturates in medicine?
24. For what are they prescribed?
25. How does methaqualone affect the user?
26. What are the purported health benefits of moderate alcohol use?
27. What are the arguments of those who are critical of the purported health benefits of alcohol?
28. Why is alcohol likely to produce more intoxication in women than in men?
29. How does alcohol differ from other central nervous system depressants?
30. How does the setting influence the effects of alcohol?
31. What is the influence of genetics on alcoholism?
32. Why is withdrawal from alcohol addiction potentially more dangerous than withdrawal from heroin addiction?
33. How does heavy drinking impact the liver?
34. What is fetal alcohol syndrome?
35. What are analogs and designer drugs?
36. What are the dangers of using fentanyl nomadically?

Stimulants produce profound subjective well-being with alertness. Normal pleasures are magnified and anxiety is decreased. Self-confidence and self-perceptions of mastery increase. Social inhibitions are reduced and interpersonal communication is facilitated. All aspects of the personal environment take on intensified qualities but without hallucinatory perceptual distortions. Emotionality and sexual feelings are enhanced.

Frank H. Gawin, M. Elena Khalsa, and Everett Ellinwood, Jr. (1994: 113)

CHAPTER **5** | # STIMULANTS

Chris Rout/Alamy

As the term *stimulant* indicates, substances in this category stimulate the central nervous system (CNS). In moderation they enhance mood, increase alertness, and relieve fatigue. Two commonly used stimulants are nicotine, which is found in tobacco products, and caffeine, an active ingredient in coffee, tea, and some soft drinks. Used in moderation, these substances tend to relieve malaise and increase alertness.

More powerful stimulants, such as cocaine and methamphetamine, are taken orally, sniffed, smoked, or injected. Smoking, snorting, or injecting stimulants produces a sudden sensation known as a "rush" or a "flash." The high from snorting is relatively slow but can last fifteen to thirty minutes; effects from smoking are more immediate but may last only five to ten minutes. Abuse is often associated with a pattern of binge use, that is, consuming large doses of stimulants sporadically. Heavy users might inject themselves every few hours, continuing until they have depleted their drug supply or reached a point of delirium, psychosis, and physical exhaustion. During this period of heavy use, all other interests become secondary to re-creating the initial euphoric rush. Tolerance can develop rapidly, and both physical dependence and psychological dependence occur. Abrupt cessation, even after a weekend binge, is commonly followed by depression, anxiety, drug craving, and extreme fatigue ("crash").

It has been hypothesized that stimulants such as cocaine and amphetamine compensate for a deficiency in three neurotransmitters—dopamine, norepinephrine, which acts with epinephrine (adrenaline), and serotonin—that can otherwise result in apathy and depression (Khantzian 1985; Nunes and Rosecan 1987), bolstering the theory of drug use as being self-medication. Cocaine increases serotonin transmission, a neurotransmitter that influences essential behaviors such sleep, eating, mood, and cognitive processes (Whitten 2007b).

As noted in Chapter 3, in the presynaptic terminals of normal people, monoamine oxidases (MAO) control the level of neurotransmitters. As a result of dysfunction, an excess of MAO can lower the amount of dopamine, norepinephrine, and serotonin, causing depression (Sunderwirth 1985). Indeed, MAO-inhibiting drugs such as Nardil (phenelzine) are medically prescribed to treat depression. The use of powerful stimulants by some people and not others, given that both groups have equal access to these drugs, can be explained by physiological deficiencies, much as the use of insulin by diabetics can be explained: Nondiabetics will not find the ingestion of insulin a positive experience. The users of stimulants, according to this view, are attempting to reduce inner tension and increase energy and activity levels (see, e.g., Fishbein, Lozovsky, and Jaffe 1989).

At the other extreme, in people who are highly extroverted, perhaps even manic, stimulants make more dopamine available to the brain and are thus highly rewarding even in small doses, making such people susceptible to addiction (Goleman 1990). In 1995 a variant of the dopamine receptor D^4 was found to be associated with novelty seeking; people with this genetic factor tend to be extroverted, quick-tempered, impulsive, and easily bored (Angier 1995). Several teams of researchers working independently reported that such people possess a gene that makes them especially responsive to dopamine, and this is believed to be related to participation in extreme sports such as skydiving and ice climbing, as well as drug use (Koerber 1997).

Scientists have also discovered a mechanism that appears to account for the different levels of euphoria people experience when they take a stimulant. People who have lower levels of dopamine D^2 receptors in their brains were found to be more inclined to like the effects of a mild stimulant than were those who have higher levels of these receptors, who were found to dislike the drug's effects (National Institute on Drug Abuse 1999f). Dopamine deficiencies in the brain cannot be remedied by introducing corrective substances because the blood-brain barrier prevents most substances from reaching it.

COCAINE

Coca is a flowering bush or shrub (*Erythroxylon* coca) that in cultivation stands three to six feet high and yields at most four ounces of waxy, elliptical leaves that are about 1 percent cocaine by weight. Conversion into cocaine hydrochloride—powdered cocaine—requires several steps. Immediately after being harvested, the leaves are pulverized, soaked, and shaken in a mixture of alcohol and benzene (a coal tar derivative) for about three days. After the liquid has been drained, sulfuric or hydrochloric acid, depending on the alkaloid content of the leaves, is added, and the solution is again shaken. Sodium carbonate is added, forming a precipitate, which is washed with kerosene and chilled, leaving behind crystals of crude cocaine known as **coca paste**, which is allowed to dry.

Between 200 and 500 kilograms of coca leaves are required to make one kilo of paste; two and one-half kilos of coca paste are converted into one kilo of cocaine base—a malodorous, rough, greenish yellow powder of more than 66 percent purity—and finally into cocaine hydrochloride by being treated with ether, acetone, and hydrochloric acid. One kilo of cocaine base is synthesized into one kilo of cocaine hydrochloride, a white crystalline powder that is about 95 percent pure. Those who process the substance are exposed to noxious fumes and the real danger of an explosion.

In the United States cocaine hydrochloride is "cut" (diluted) for street sale by adding sugars (such as lactose, inositol, and mannitol) or talcum powder, borax, or other neutral substances, as well as local anesthetics such as procaine hydrochloride (Novocain) or lidocaine hydrochloride. (Novocain is sometimes mixed with mannitol or lactose and sold as cocaine.) After cutting, cocaine typically has a consumer sale purity of less than 20 percent, although huge increases in the availability of cocaine can result in a level as high as 50 percent and a concomitant increase in the number of emergency room admissions for cocaine overdoses.

EFFECTS OF COCAINE

Cocaine typically enters the bloodstream by being snorted into the nostrils through a straw or rolled paper or from a "coke spoon." "Because cocaine is a vasoconstrictor, it inhibits its own absorption, and the time it takes to reach peak concentration gets longer as the dose gets larger" (Karch 1996: 19). Some abusers will take it intravenously, which is the only way to ingest 100 percent of the drug. Because this is a more efficient method, users with limited funds sometimes buy and inject cocaine as a group, a method that can spread HIV/AIDS. Cocaine can also be absorbed

COCAINE: USES AND EFFECTS

Classification: Stimulant

CSA Schedule: Schedule II

Trade or Other Names: Coke, flake, snow, crack

Medical Uses: Local anesthetic

Physical Dependence: Possible

Psychological Dependence: High

Tolerance: Yes

Duration (hours): 1–2

Usual Method: Sniffed, smoked, injected

Possible Effects: Increased alertness, excitation, euphoria, increased pulse rate and blood pressure, insomnia, loss of appetite

Effects of Overdose: Agitation, increased body temperature, hallucinations, convulsions, possible death

Withdrawal Syndrome: Apathy, long periods of sleep, irritability, depression, disorientation

Source: U.S. Drug Enforcement Administration.

through genital or rectal application, during which its anesthetic properties prolong vaginal intercourse or suppress the discomfort of anal intercourse. This extremely dangerous practice can lead to seizure, coma, and death (Karch 1998). When the drug is inhaled, its effects peak in fifteen to twenty minutes and disappear in sixty to ninety minutes. Intravenous use results in an intense feeling of euphoria that crests in three to five minutes and wanes in thirty to forty minutes. (Smoking crack cocaine is discussed later in the chapter.)

Neurological Effects "Smoked, snorted, or injected, cocaine rapidly enters the bloodstream and penetrates the brain. The drug achieves its main immediate psychological effect—the high—by causing a buildup of the neuro-chemical dopamine" (Nestler 2005: 5). The drug binds to specific receptor sites on brain membranes and triggers the release of dopamine but also serotonin and norepinephrine. These neurotransmitters enhance mood and, at high enough doses, produce feelings of euphoria by activating the sympathetic nervous system, giving rise to increased heart rate, blood pressure, breathing rate, body temperature, and blood sugar (Washton 1989). A deficiency in serotonin was found to be linked to a desire for cocaine, and genetically altered mice continued to find cocaine rewarding even when it failed to increase their (already high) levels of dopamine (Blakeslee 1998; Parsons, Weiss, and Koob 1998; Rocha et al. 1998; National Institute on Drug Abuse 1999e). The substance also acts on the hypothalamus to decrease appetite and reduces the need for sleep by inducing the release of stimulant neurotransmitters.

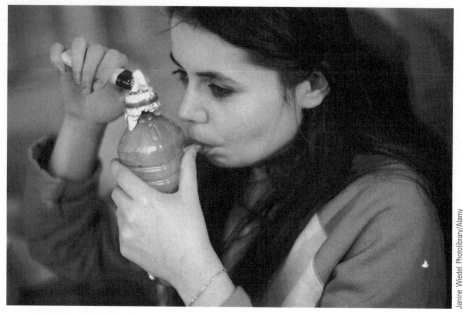

Janine Wiedel Photolibrary/Alamy

Cocaine cooked in a mixture of sodium bicarbonate (baking soda) and water becomes hard when heat-dried, and is called crack. The soaplike substance is then cut into bars or chips. This freebase cocaine can be crushed and smoked in a special glass pipe or sprinkled on a tobacco or marijuana product. The term crack refers to the crackling sound heard when the mixture is smoked (heated).

In addition to stimulating their release, cocaine blocks or inhibits the reabsorption of dopamine, norepinephrine, and serotonin by the discharging neurons by preventing a reuptake transporter from performing its usual function (Figure 5.1). As a result, neurotransmitters continue to bombard their receptor sites. The neurons remain in a state of excitement, the brain is stimulated accordingly, and euphoria increases (Sunderwirth 1985; Holloway 1991). This "initial, short-term effect—a buildup of the neurochemical dopamine—gives rise to euphoria and a desire to take the drug again" (Nestler 2005: 4).[1]

As the supply of dopamine depletes, however, depression sets in. Research has discovered that cocaine-dependent people have fewer dopamine receptors than do normal controls, which also helps to explain why they feel depressed when not on cocaine (Holloway 1991). Depletion of both dopamine and serotonin in specific brain regions that control drive and affect may contribute to the craving and depression that are evident in the aftermath of cocaine abuse, "but when cocaine is readministered, frontal brain regions may be reactivated, again contributing to the compulsion to use cocaine" (Bolla, Cadet, and London 1998: 281). Although the case for dopamine's centrality remains airtight, another neurotransmitter, glutamate (or mGluR5), appears to play an independent role in the rewarding

---

[1] A strain of mice bred for the absence of the dopamine transporter is impervious to cocaine; these mice are also highly active, fail to eat, and often die from exhaustion (Grady 1996).

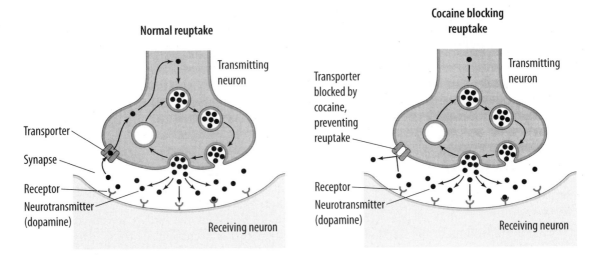

FIGURE 5.1 | COCAINE BLOCKING REUPTAKE OF NEUROTRANSMITTERS. BLOCKED NEUROTRANSMITTERS CAN INCLUDE DOPAMINE, NOREPINEPHRINE, AND SEROTONIN. THIS RESULTS IN THEIR ACCUMULATION IN THE SYNAPSE, STIMULATING THE RECEIVING NEURON.

qualities of cocaine. Indeed, research in Geneva, Switzerland, reveals that glutamate's role in cocaine dependence is even more central than dopamine's (Hollon 2002).

There are regions within the brain that, when stimulated, produce feelings of pleasure. One neural system that appears to be most affected by cocaine originates in such a region (the **ventral tegmental area**, or **VTA**), located deep within the brain. Cocaine short-circuits the reward pathways of the brain (Dunwiddie 1988), and in laboratory animals cocaine has usurped other rewards, such as food and sex. In laboratory tests, monkeys pressed a bar as many as 12,800 times for an infusion of 0.5 milligram of cocaine. "No other drug, including opiates and amphetamine, has been reported to be more potent than cocaine in such tests" (Geary 1987: 31). The ultimate consequence of unlimited access to cocaine is death. Without unlimited access, however, monkeys are able to self-regulate their cocaine use (Siegel 1989).

Would monkeys in the wild succumb to the allure of unlimited amounts of cocaine? Laboratory conditions do not replicate the animals' natural environment, nor are the results of such experiments readily generalizable to humans, who have such species-exclusive traits as a sense of values and a desire for self-control (Peele 1985). Some dopamine agonists are self-administered by and rewarding to animals but do not produce euphoria in humans (Rothman 1994). Furthermore, we know that the use of cocaine is related to behavioral stress (National Institute on Drug Abuse 1997b), and monkeys in the laboratory setting are under considerable stress.

Physiological Effects   In small doses cocaine will bring about extreme euphoria and indifference to pain, along with illusions of increased mental and sensory alertness and physical strength: "A few hundredths of a gram of cocaine hydrochloride, chopped finely and arranged on a smooth surface into several lines, or rows of powder, can be snorted into the nose through a rolled piece of paper in a few seconds. The inhalation shortly gives rise to feelings of elation and a sense of clarity or power of thought, feelings that pass away for most people in about half an hour" (Van Dyke and Byck 1982: 128). At higher doses, however, the drug has the potential "to produce megalomania and feelings of omnipotence in most individuals" (Gold et al. 1986: 44). Cocaine causes the body to feel as if there were an impending threat, a response to stimuli that causes the release of stimulating neurotransmitters (dopamine and norepinephrine): "In essence the cocaine stimulated reactions in the body are mimicking a natural physiological stress response; the generalized adrenergic discharge stimulates the energy producing mechanisms to prepare the CNS and skeletal muscles for 'fight' or 'flight.' The body feels the chemistry of fright, tension and anxiety but the brain gives the message that everything is better than fine" (Gold et al. 1986: 38).

Studies suggest that cocaine actually heightens the body's sensitivity to stress, although the user fails to recognize that this is occurring. Cocaine activates stress systems, much like what occurs when an opiate addict goes into withdrawal, but the person perceives this as part of the cocaine rush because cocaine is also stimulating the parts of the brain that are involved in feeling pleasure. When cocaine's effects wear off and the addict goes into withdrawal, the stress systems are again activated. This time, the cocaine addict perceives the activation as unpleasant because cocaine is no longer stimulating the pleasure circuits in the brain. Because cocaine switches on the stress systems both when it is active and during withdrawal, these systems rapidly become hypersensitive (Kreek 1997).

Chemically similar substances such as lidocaine (Xylocaine) and procaine (Novocain), as dental patients recognize, eliminate all feeling when applied topically or subcutaneously. Single small doses of procaine, when taken intranasally or smoked, produce the same euphoric response as does cocaine in experienced cocaine users. Users cannot distinguish between the two substances, and tests indicate that laboratory animals will work as hard for procaine as they will for cocaine (Van Dyke and Byck 1982). In laboratory tests with animals, however, while procaine served as a reinforcer similar to cocaine, lidocaine did not (Balster 1988).

COCA PASTE AND COCAINE COMBINATIONS

Versions of the drug other than cocaine hydrochloride have become popular among certain abusers. Coca paste, which is typically smoked with either tobacco or marijuana products, is used extensively in cocaine-processing countries. Because it requires less processing than cocaine, coca paste—called *bazuco*—is popular among low-income groups in these countries and has become a major abuse problem in Colombia. In the late 1980s the substance made its way into the United States, where it became known as "bubble gum" to young abusers because of the phonetic association of the word *bazuco* with Bazooka bubble gum. The substance usually results from an error in the water/sulfuric acid ratio. The paste has at least traces of a host of dangerous chemicals used in its production, including kerosene, sulfuric acid, leaded gasoline, and potassium permanganate, which can cause irreversible damage to the liver, lungs, and brain.

Some intravenous abusers combine cocaine with heroin—a practice known as "speedballing." This was the combination that led to the death of comedian John Belushi in 1982. It appears that heroin enhances the subjective effects of cocaine, although the neurobiology of the interaction is unclear. Because heroin and cocaine work on different parts of the mesolimbic dopamine neurons, they can be combined to produce even more intense dopamine activation. The heroin increases cell firing and dopamine release, while the cocaine keeps the released dopamine in the synaptic cleft longer, thereby intensifying and prolonging its effects. Users show very rapid psychological and physiological deterioration. Although speedball use produces extremely intense activation of brain reward systems, it is often short-lived because this drug combination is associated with a very high fatality rate. The combination of cocaine and heroin is perhaps the most dangerous form of illicit substance use (Addiction Research Unit 1998). Some cocaine users also ingest heroin to soften and prolong the impact of cocaine.

Some users mix cocaine and alcohol consumption, a dangerous combination that increases the euphoric effects.

CRACK

Crack, the drug abuser's answer to fast food, became popular among young men and women during the 1980s. The drug is relatively cheap, five to ten dollars a "rock," although users hooked on crack report spending between $100 and $200 a day on the substance. Crack is generally sold on the street in small glass vials or tiny plastic bags. Versions of crack may contain any combination of freebase residue, concentrated caffeine, or different amphetamines.

Although cocaine hydrochloride cannot easily be smoked—the melting and vaporization point is very high (195° Celsius)—freeing the alkaloid from the hydrochloride attachment (**freebase**) will produce purified crystals of cocaine base that readily vaporize at 98 degrees Celsius. Cocaine cooked in a mixture of sodium bicarbonate (baking soda) and water becomes hard when heat-dried and is called **crack**. The soap like substance is then cut into bars or chips (sometimes called quarter rocks) and smoked. This freebase cocaine can be crushed and smoked in a special glass pipe or sprinkled on a tobacco or marijuana product. The term *crack* refers to the crackling sound heard when the mixture is smoked (heated), presumably from the sodium bicarbonate.

Dennis Watlington (1987), a former crack user, states that crack is typically smoked in a glass pipe about five inches long and a quarter inch in diameter with a metal screen at the top to hold a small clump of the substance. When lit, the substance melts and clings to the screen; some of it oozes down inside the stem where it dries and forms a hard residue that can later be scraped off and smoked. "The most satisfying way to smoke crack," Watlington notes, "is to insert this stem into a glass bowl the size of an espresso cup. Through a second pipe inserted into the side of the bowl, the smoker pulls the smoke after it collects in quantity in the bowl" (1987: 150).

Because crack is inhaled directly into the lungs, bypassing much of the circulatory system en route to the brain, it takes about five seconds to take effect—even faster than intravenous ingestion. When "crack is heated, the drug crosses the blood-brain barrier in only a few seconds, providing a virtually instantaneous 'high' and intense gratification, often described as a 'sexual euphoria,' or orgasm" (McCoy, Miles, and Inciardi 1995: 172). "Crack can excite sexual desires while inhibiting the ability to achieve orgasm, creating sexual encounters that are prolonged and more conducive to the spread of AIDS" (Drug Enforcement Administration 1994a: 3).

The vapors first produce a potent **rush**: "This 'rush' lasts a few seconds, and is replaced by a euphoric excitation that lasts for several minutes. A five- to twenty-minute period of less pleasurable hyperexcitability follows. Then the 'ultimate high' degenerates into the ultimate low" (National Institute on Drug Abuse 1986: 4). "After smoking crack repeatedly, the user develops an intense craving for more. Although it can take months or even years for a nasal cocaine user to progress from recreational to compulsive use, this can happen within days to weeks with crack" (Rosecan, Spitz, and Gross 1987: 299).

Interviews with crack users in drug treatment programs revealed the apparent power of this substance (Frank et al. 1987: 12):

> Despite the many years of using other drugs, the experience with Crack was quite different. Most respondents had been in control of their drug use, even those who had been using very heavily. The majority (63 percent) had never needed treatment for their drug use before using Crack. The experience with Crack, however, was very much a jolt, for which these users were not prepared in spite of their past experience. For many it was a very frightening experience. Respondents remembered feelings and behaviors under the influence of Crack that they had never experienced before—the irritability, rage, and aggression. Most of the clients had held jobs and valued the money they earned. Now, in retrospect, the loss of so much spent on Crack was incomprehensible to them.

Females who become compulsive users frequently exchange sex for the drug.

That crack is smoked rather than injected has increased its appeal. Indeed, it constitutes the first psychoactive drug experience of many young abusers, who try it even before alcohol and marijuana (Rosecan, Spitz, and Gross 1987). Unfortunately, "because of the large, concentrated doses that reach the brain, seizures are more likely to occur from smoking cocaine than from snorting it, and smoking can lead more easily to respiratory failure and/or cardiac arrest" (Washton 1989: 16). It was crack that led to the death of college basketball star Len Bias, age 22 years, and professional football player Don Rogers, age 23 years.

Reports—some would say hysteria—about the power of crack to produce dependence have subsided, and today it is rarely mentioned in the media. Although crack is admittedly a strongly dependence-producing substance, recent research indicates that it is not the all-powerful drug the media had portrayed. Crack appears to be less addictive than nicotine, though more addictive than alcohol (Kolata 1989b; Egan 1999a). A study of 79 crack users in Toronto revealed a "lack of strong evidence to support the view that use of the drug is necessarily compulsive. Over half of the respondents had never or rarely experienced a craving to take crack" (Cheung, Erickson, and Landau 1991: 133). There has been a dramatic change in the crack-using population as adolescents began to reject the substance, and "crackheads," no longer considered "cool," became outcasts.

Crack users today are more likely to be older (in their late twenties or early thirties) males.

COCAINE TOLERANCE

After frequent and high doses of cocaine, the failure to continue ingestion produces a withdrawal syndrome characterized by psychological depression, irritability, extreme fatigue, and prolonged periods of restless sleep. Roger Weiss and Steven Mirin report a form of reverse tolerance: "long-term users may experience more excitatory effects from the same, or even smaller, doses of the drug," a phenomenon referred to as **kindling** (1987: 48).

Many researchers have reported that tolerance to the euphoric effects occurs with repeated use, although the biological basis underlying sensitization or tolerance to cocaine is not yet fully understood (O'Brien and Cohen 1984; Grinspoon and Bakalar 1985; Zahniser et al. 1988; Izenwasser and Unterwald 1994). This tolerance causes the abuser to increase the dosage. "Chronic users often find themselves caught in a futile, obsessive chase to recapture the original cocaine 'high,' but as dosages and frequency increase, so does the user's tolerance to the euphoric effects" (Washton, Stone, and Henrickson 1988: 367). And "in face of dose escalation, one might eventually achieve blood levels of cocaine high enough to induce toxic local anesthetic effects" that include panic attacks and the risk of seizures (Post and Weiss 1988: 232). However, Steven Karch (1996), a medical examiner, reports that because of tolerance, chronic cocaine users can consume massive amounts without apparent ill effects. There is evidence of cocaine tolerance in binge-type ingestion (Kreek 1997).

COCAINE WITHDRAWAL

After frequent and high doses of cocaine the failure to continue ingestion produces a withdrawal syndrome characterized by psychological depression, irritability, extreme fatigue, and prolonged periods of restless sleep. James Inciardi (1986: 79) states that this syndrome is not necessarily physiological; it might simply be the result of an emotional letdown that results when heavy abusers try to discontinue the drug: "they *think* they have a physical need for cocaine."

Strong cravings for the substance and the malaise that follows cessation are possibly brain-mediated behavioral changes indicating physical dependence, and the elevation in reward thresholds as a result of cocaine use could trigger a withdrawal effect after use is discontinued (Koob et al. 1994). "When the cocaine- or amphetamine-dependent person is not taking one of these drugs, dopamine release will be diminished to levels lower than normal, which could contribute to the anhedonia [inability to enjoy routine pleasures], dysphoria [chronic discontent], and other symptoms of withdrawal that motivate repeated drug taking" (Hyman and Nestler 1996: 158). Chronic overstimulation of postsynaptic DA receptors could lead to a new adaptive state, so continued use of the drug would be required to maintain homeostasis (Bolla, Cadet, and London 1998). Despite the lack of signs of physical dependence, animals that are given free access to cocaine will continue to self-administer the drug until death, something they will not do for opiates

(Geary 1987). The *Merck Manual* (Berkow 1982: 1427) refers to cocaine as "probably the best example of a drug to which neither tolerance nor physical dependence develops, but to which psychic dependence develops that can lead to addiction." While the cocaine withdrawal syndrome does not generally require medical treatment or pharmacotherapy, the risk of relapse is highest during withdrawal (McCance 1997).

"Withdrawal in [cocaine-] dependent subjects is not characterized by the obvious physical signs like those observed with opiates or sedative-hypnotics" (Koob et al. 1994: 7). Indeed, "there is no withdrawal syndrome after abruptly stopping cocaine. That is, the body has never developed a need for cocaine to maintain homeostasis" (Washton and Stone-Washton 1993: 17). "The absence of a clear-cut withdrawal syndrome and serious medical risk following abrupt cessation of the drug use obviates the need either for switching the cocaine-dependent patient to a substitute drug or for having to detoxify the patient by means of a gradual withdrawal procedure, as is routinely done in the treatment of heroin addicts and severe alcoholics" (Washton, Stone, and Henrickson 1988: 376). However, one study found evidence of cardiac and mood-related symptoms during short-term abstinence from chronic crack use that could indicate specific withdrawal phenomena (Kajdasz et al. 1999).

Although tolerance can mask sensitization to cocaine-induced euphoria, craving persists. During early abstinence, persisting tolerance masks sensitization, but as tolerance wears off, sensitization becomes manifest as craving based on environmental cues increase (Bonson et al. 2002). Thus, abstinent cocaine users who are no longer experiencing withdrawal symptoms develop craving on returning to environments linked to the use of cocaine (discussed in Chapter 3). Research has revealed that cocaine-addicted patients respond to these cues "as if they were stressful situations, with the release of adrenaline and other hormones that increase pulse rate and blood pressure," and these responses take a long time to normalize, indicating that cocaine heightens sensitivity to stress (Whitten 2005: 1).

MEDICAL USE OF COCAINE

In addition to its anesthetizing qualities, cocaine constricts blood vessels when applied topically. It is the only local anesthetic that has this effect, and cocaine was the anesthetic of choice for eye surgery because of this ability to limit the flow of blood. However, when it was discovered that the reduced flow could damage the surface of the eye, cocaine was no longer recommended for use in ophthalmology. It continues to be used in surgery of the mucous membranes of the ear, nose, and throat and for procedures that require passing a tube through the nose or throat (Van Dyke and Byck 1982), about 200,000 operations a year (P. White 1989). Plastic surgeons use it for nose alterations.

DANGERS OF COCAINE USE

In "very small and occasional doses," argues Inciardi, "cocaine is no more harmful than equally moderate doses of alcohol or marijuana" (1986: 79). One research effort found that "experimental use of cocaine during adolescence has benign consequences over a one-year period," although the researchers could not deny the possibility of long-term negative consequences (Newcomb and Bentler 1986: 273). Large doses of cocaine, however, intensify each of the drug's reactions and can sometimes cause irrational behavior. In heavy abusers the euphoria is often accompanied by intensified heartbeat, sweating, dilation of pupils, and a rise in body temperature. After the initial euphoria, depression, irritability, insomnia, and, in more serious instances, paranoia may result. Extreme reactions, such as delirium, hallucinations, muscle spasms, and chest pain, may appear. In a small of number of people—the risk appears to be genetically determined—high levels of cocaine ingestion leads to a psychosis syndrome characterized by bizarre, paranoid agitation that frequently ends in death (Karch 1998).

Research indicates that cocaine users are four times more likely to develop a coronary aneurysm than are nonusers. Although coronary aneurysms rarely burst, they could set up cocaine users for a heart attack. The reasons are unclear, but researchers suspect that cocaine weakens the artery wall by causing sharp spikes in blood pressure and damaging cells in the inner walls of the heart's arteries (Altman 2005).

Chronic users can also suffer from "cocaine bugs" (**formication**, known as Magnon's syndrome), a sensation similar to that of bugs crawling under the skin. In extreme cases, the sensation can become so great that the user will cut open his or her skin to get at "them." Less extreme reactions cause the user to scratch and pick at the "bugs," causing sores.

When people mix cocaine and alcohol consumption, they are compounding the danger each drug poses and unknowingly performing a complex chemical experiment within their bodies. Researchers have found that the human liver combines cocaine and alcohol and manufactures a third substance, cocaethylene, which intensifies cocaine's euphoric effects while possibly increasing the risk of sudden death (National Institute on Drug Abuse 2001a).

The detrimental effects of heavy cocaine use—two or more grams a week—on an individual's manual dexterity, problem solving, and other critical skills can last for up to a month after the drug was taken last. In one study, heavy cocaine users were outperformed by moderate users and nonusers on most tests measuring verbal memory, manual dexterity, and other cognitive skills. Although the intensity (measured in grams per week) of cocaine use was more closely associated with decreased performance than was duration of use, all cocaine users studied experienced reduced cognitive function. Dose-related effects were seen primarily on tasks involving the prefrontal cortex, which is the area of the brain most responsible for attention, concentration, planning, and reasoning. The heaviest cocaine users showed slower median reaction times and poorer attention and concentration (National Institute on Drug Abuse 1999g).

Cardiac and Circulatory Dangers   Cocaine causes blood vessels to constrict and increases heart rate and blood pressure. As a result, the heart requires more oxygen-rich blood to nourish its muscle cells (Karch 1996). In people whose coronary arteries are narrowed by atherosclerosis, reactions can range from mild angina to a fatal heart attack. Even in people with normal coronary arteries, the ingesting of cocaine has resulted in angina and heart attacks that are believed to be consequences of spasms that reduce or shut off the flow of the oxygenated blood that nourishes the heart.

There is also evidence that cocaine can painlessly and permanently damage heart muscles: "Cocaine causes vascular disease. Vessels throughout the body can be involved, but the brunt of the injury is borne by the heart" (Karch 1996: 83). Several thousand people a year die as the result of sudden cardiac death induced by cocaine; the exact number is unknown because diagnosing the cause of death in such cases is quite difficult and the mechanism causing this fatal outcome is unknown (Karch 1996). Using advanced brain-scanning techniques, researchers have found that the temporary narrowing of blood vessels caused by cocaine results in a cumulative effect: More cocaine use leads to more narrowing of the arteries. This suggests that heavy cocaine users are susceptible to strokes, bleeding inside the brain, thinking and memory deficits, and other brain disorders (Bolla, Cadet, and London 1998; National Institute on Drug Abuse 1998d). The American Heart Association (1999) reports that cocaine use can lead to the development of aneurysms—ballooning-out of the wall of an artery—in heart arteries. An aneurysm in a heart artery can lead to a heart attack; an aneurysm in an artery of the brain could burst and trigger a stroke. Some aneurysms do not cause symptoms; others may cause chest pain and other coronary artery disease symptoms. The lack of judgment, unreliability, poor foresight, difficulty making decisions, disinhibition, apathy, euphoria, and irritability exhibited by chronic cocaine abusers appear to be related to damage the drug causes in the part of the brain (the prefrontal lobe) that controls or modifies these behaviors (Bolla, Cadet, and London 1998).

Crack Babies   Cocaine use by pregnant women has been linked to various abnormalities in their infants because the substance reduces the supply of blood and oxygen to the fetus (e.g., Mayes 1992; Woods 1993). Children born to crack-abusing mothers exhibit serious emotional difficulties that can hinder their psychological and social development (Blakeslee 1989).

But these difficulties are more likely caused by poor prenatal nutrition and health than by the pharmacology of cocaine. Researchers have had difficulty isolating maternal drug use from the typically negative environment in which the children are raised: "If you grow up in such a lousy environment, things are so bad already that cocaine exposure doesn't seem to make much difference" (Barry Lester quoted in Begley 1999: 62). More recent research has revealed that "snow babies" are neither the emotional and cognitive cripples that many predicted nor the perfectly normal kids that others have claimed. "Worries that 'crack babies' would never be able to function in society have turned out to be unfounded for the great majority" (Leshner 1999b: 3).

Crack or cocaine exposure in utero has not been demonstrated to affect physical growth and does not appear to independently affect developmental scores in the first six years of life (although there are insufficient data to assess this for infants born preterm). Findings are mixed regarding early motor development, but any effect appears to be transient and might, in fact, reflect tobacco exposure (Chavkin 2001). Preschool children of crack-using mothers do not appear to suffer any language or cognitive development problems. However, in one controlled study, they exhibited higher rates of emotional and behavioral problems than did children from similar backgrounds whose mothers did not use cocaine. It was not determined whether this is a function of the drug or the postnatal environment (Hawley, Halle, Drasin, and Thomas 1995). "The 'crack baby' became a convenient symbol for an aggressive war on drug users because of the implication that anyone who is selfish enough to irreparably damage an innocent child for the sake of a quick high deserves retribution. This image, promoted by the mass media, makes it easier to advocate a simplistic punitive response than to address the complex causes of drug use" (Chavkin 2001: 1627). The bottom line: Cocaine use is undoubtedly bad for the fetus, "but experts say its effects are less severe than those of alcohol and are comparable to those of tobacco" (Oakie 2009: D1).

Because cocaine causes blood vessels to constrict, snorting can cause the cartilage in the middle of the nose to be deprived of oxygen. When the drug wears off, the tissue swells, which is why cocaine users frequently have stuffy, runny noses. Eventually, gradual deterioration of the nasal cartilage can cause the nose to collapse. The constriction of blood vessels in the nose also means a delay in the absorption of cocaine. Thus, intravenous injection of the drug is more efficient and quickly produces a powerful rush; it can also cause abscesses on the skin. This form of ingestion "produces the more debilitating effects of psychoses and paranoid delusions" (Inciardi 1986: 81) and is more likely than other forms of ingestion to have fatal results.

Cocaine and Sex   Although cocaine has the reputation of being an aphrodisiac, heavy use can cause male abusers to become impotent or incapable of ejaculation, and females can experience difficulty in reaching an orgasm. Freebasing and intravenous use increase sexual desire but not performance. In fact, cocaine may produce spontaneous ejaculation without sexual activity and can replace the sex partner of either gender (M. Gold et al. 1986). Arnold Washton and Nanette Stone-Washton (1993) report that cocaine produced hypersexuality and sexual compulsivity in their patients, and "sexual feelings and fantasies often trigger powerful urges and cravings for cocaine." Crack cocaine has been associated with the spread of sexually transmitted diseases, especially AIDS, often the result of young women having unsafe sex with multiple partners in exchange for crack (Chitwood, Rivera, and Inciardi 1996).

Cocaine has anesthetic properties, however, and is sometimes applied directly to the head of the penis or to the clitoris to anesthetize the tissues, prolonging intercourse by retarding orgasm.

AMPHETAMINES

"Among the commonly used psychoactive drugs," note Grinspoon and Peter Hedblom (1975: 258), "the amphetamines have one of the most formidable potentials for psychological, physical, and social harm." Unlike cocaine, amphetamines are products of the laboratory—they are synthetic drugs. Although their chemical structures are distinctly different (Snyder 1986) and amphetamine has no anesthetic properties, the effects of cocaine and amphetamines are similar. In fact, experienced intravenous cocaine users frequently identified amphetamine incorrectly as cocaine. In animal studies, cocaine and amphetamines often substitute for one another and have similar reinforcing patterns of self-administration (Balster 1988).

The high from amphetamine lasts hours, rather than the fraction of an hour for cocaine. And amphetamine, particularly methamphetamine (discussed shortly), can be taken in pill form; cocaine is not effective when taken orally. Although legally produced amphetamine is taken in the form of tablets or capsules, some abusers will crush the substance, dissolve it in water, and ingest it intravenously.

There are three basic types of amphetamine, the methyl-amphetamines having the greatest potential for abuse because they are fast acting and produce a rush. There are three types of methyl-amphetamine: dextro-methamphetamine (D-methamphetamine), dextro-levo-methamphetamine (D,L-methamphetamine), and levo-methamphetamine (L-methamphetamine). D-Methamphetamine is the most potent and widely abused form of methamphetamine in the United States today. It is a white, odorless, bitter-tasting crystalline powder that easily dissolves in water or alcohol.

According to the World Health Organization, methamphetamine is second only to marijuana as the most abused drug in the world. In the United States, methamphetamine use began in the West, and "it is in the West [often in rural communities] where methamphetamine remains the biggest problem," (Weisheit and White 2009: 10).

Methamphetamine is known by many street names, such as "speed," "crank," "go," "crystal," "crystal meth," and "poor man's cocaine." It can be used by all of the common routes of illicit drug administration (inhalation, intranasal snorting, intravenous injection, or orally) but must be purified before it can be smoked. *Ice* is a purified form that is frequently sold as large crystals (rocks) that are smoked. Like rock salt in size and appearance, ice produces a high that is reputed to last from seven to twenty-four hours. Because of its purity, ice exaggerates all of the effects of methamphetamine. Overdoses are more common with ice because it is difficult for smokers to control the amount being inhaled. The substance could easily substitute for crack.

Ice rocks are made by melting methamphetamine crystals using a variety of techniques; "the turkey bag method" is the most popular: Dry methamphetamine crystals are placed in an aluminum turkey-roasting bag, which is then closed and dipped into boiling water until the methamphetamine melts. The melted material is then placed in cool water or in the refrigerator until it solidifies as a large crystal. The crystal is then cut into rocks that fit the various glass pipes that are used for smoking ice. Methamphetamine is usually smoked by inhaling it from a sheet of aluminum foil or through a glass pipe. When foil is used, the drug is heated in a crease of the foil until it vaporizes; it is then inhaled via a straw. Pipes for smoking D-methamphetamine differ from those used for smoking crack; methamphetamine vaporizes at a much lower temperature than crack does, so smoking it in a crack pipe at high heat would destroy it. Methamphetamine pipes have a large glass ball at the end for holding the methamphetamine, and a lighter is held under the ball to vaporize the drug. Airflow is regulated by a finger placed over a hole on the top of the pipe. Some users reportedly prefer glass pipes for smoking methamphetamine because they fear developing Alzheimer's disease from using aluminum foil (Lukas 1996).

With $500 worth of chemicals, laboratory glassware, and a rudimentary knowledge of chemistry, an outlaw chemist can easily produce a pound of methamphetamine worth $20,000 to $30,000. As a result, hundreds of clandestine laboratories have sprung up in remote regions throughout the United States. Recipes for manufacturing methamphetamine are widely available through pamphlets and the Internet. The clandestine manufacturing process has undergone substantial changes over the years. Phenyl-2-propanone (P2P), which was originally used in illegal manufacturing, is now controlled by the Drug Enforcement Administration as a bulk "immediate precursor" of methamphetamine. Accordingly, lab operators shifted to ephedrine, an ingredient common in over-the-counter cold and allergy remedies. Subsequent regulatory efforts led manufacturers to switch to the use of pseudoephedrine tablets. The yield from both methods is typically 70 percent of the precursor. Thus, one kilogram of ephedrine yields 700 grams of methamphetamine. The federal Combat Methamphetamine Epidemic Act of 2005 requires that over-the-counter pseudoephedrine products such as nasal decongestants be kept behind the counter. Purchasers must show a photo ID and can buy only a limited supply. Purchases are logged so that law enforcement agencies can monitor the amount of pseudoephedrine being purchased at a particular location.

During the 1980s, clandestine manufacturers using the precursor chemical pseudoephedrine created D-methamphetamine. For the user, D-methamphetamine not only is significantly more potent than other forms, but also has fewer adverse side effects. D-Methamphetamine eventually became the predominant form of methamphetamine illegally manufactured in the so-called superlabs in the Central Valley of California or by Mexican polydrug trafficking organizations (discussed in Chapter 11). The rest, about 20 percent, is produced in the small labs of rural America (Butterfield 2005).

D-Methamphetamine is clandestinely manufactured by using the ephedrine or pseudoephedrine reduction method, producing quantities of up to 200 pounds at a time. The manufacturing process is fairly simple, though quite dangerous, and almost all the necessary ingredients are easily attainable either through commercial sources or by producing the chemicals clandestinely. Some chemists die as a result of the toxic fumes produced or from explosions that can easily be ignited by a tiny spark or even the flip of a light switch. Illegal methamphetamine production also poses a serious environmental problem, because outlaws dump the chemical wastes into local streams or lakes or bury it in ditches. Methamphetamine labs are so contaminated that they pose a risk to the law enforcement officers who seize them. Home-based labs present a danger to all who live anywhere in the house, particularly children (Butterfield 2004a).

A mixture of methamphetamine and caffeine, called *yaba*—"crazy medicine" in Thai—is popular in some Asian communities in the United States where is usually sold and ingested in tablet form. These tablets are usually brightly colored and sometimes flavored like candy. Some users place the tablet on aluminum foil and heat it from below. As the tablet melts, vapors rise and are inhaled. The tablet may also be crushed into powder, which is then snorted or mixed with a solvent and injected (National Drug Intelligence Center n.d.).

AMPHETAMINE/METHAMPHETAMINE: USES AND EFFECTS

Classification: Stimulant

CSA Schedule: Schedule II

Trade or Other Names: Biphetamine, Desoxyn, Dexedrine, Obetrol, ice

Medical Uses: Attention–deficit/hyperactivity disorder, narcolepsy, weight control

Physical Dependence: Possible

Psychological Dependence: High

Tolerance: Yes

Duration (hours): 2–4

Usual Method: Oral, injected, smoked

Possible Effects: Increased alertness, excitation, euphoria, increased pulse rate and blood pressure, insomnia, loss of appetite

Effects of Overdose: Agitation, increased body temperature, hallucinations, convulsions, possible death

Withdrawal Syndrome: Apathy, long periods of sleep, irritability, depression, disorientation

Source: Drug Enforcement Administration.

EFFECTS OF AMPHETAMINES

Methamphetamine accelerates the body's metabolism and produces euphoria, increases alertness, and gives the abuser a sense of increased energy. It can enable a shy person to become more outgoing and a tired person to become energized. Its ability to produce intensified feelings of sexual desire can, at least in part, explain its popularity. Although methamphetamine can impair the ability to operate a motor vehicle, truck drivers often abuse it to keep them awake during long hauls. The driver risks suddenly being rendered unconscious during the "crash" stage of methamphetamine use (discussed later).

Experiments have shown that when given a choice, animals will readily operate pumps that inject them with amphetamine and will work hard to get more of the drug. Rhesus monkeys that are given unlimited access to amphetamine will continually ingest the substance day and night, going almost completely without water, food, or sleep for six to eight days, until they collapse into exhausted sleep for two days. On waking, they show an immediate interest in food and water and then embark on another week-long binge of amphetamine. When access to the drug is discontinued for a few weeks and the monkeys are returned to their cages, they will push the (now nonoperative) buttons for amphetamine an average of 4,000 times, indicating that a significant level of craving exists even in the absence of physiological dependence. When the substance is heroin, the monkeys will press the nonoperative buttons an average of 2,000 times, indicating that the craving for amphetamine is higher than that for heroin (Grinspoon and Hedblom 1975). As noted in Chapter 4, while the novice typically finds the first experience with heroin unpleasant and, therefore, has to learn to enjoy its effects, the methamphetamine experience is pleasurable "right out of the box"—on first dose (Weisheit and White 2009).

Methamphetamine stimulates by triggering the release of dopamine, serotonin, and norepinephrine while inhibiting their reuptake (Selden et al. 1993). Thus, like cocaine, methamphetamine mimics naturally occurring substances and causes a biochemical arousal—a "turn on"—without the presence of sensory input requiring such arousal. The body becomes physiologically activated, but it is a false alarm. Because reuptake is blocked, the depletion of the body's stimulating neurotransmitters is believed to be responsible for the crash that results after the ingestion of high doses of amphetamine. The abuser becomes almost lifeless for one or more days, and the body uses the crash to replenish its depleted supply.

As with cocaine, in small doses methamphetamine results in illusions of increased mental and sensory alertness and physical strength, an indifference to pain, and a "rush" or "flash" that lasts a few minutes and is described as extremely pleasurable. The rush is the initial response the user feels when smoking or injecting methamphetamine and is the aspect of the drug that low-intensity users do not experience when snorting or swallowing the drug. During the rush, the user's heartbeat races and metabolism, blood pressure, and pulse soar, and the user can experience feelings that have been described in terms of multiple orgasms. Unlike the rush associated with crack cocaine, which lasts for approximately two to five minutes, the methamphetamine rush can continue for five to thirty minutes. The rush is a result of methamphetamine triggering the adrenal gland to release epinephrine (adrenaline), a hormone that puts the body in a fight-or-flight mode. As with cocaine, the body feels the chemistry of fright, tension, and anxiety, but the brain gives the message that everything is better than fine because methamphetamine causes the explosive release of dopamine in the pleasure center of the brain. After the rush, a high ensues, during which the user feels euphoric, energized, and aggressively smarter; he or she may become argumentative, often interrupting other people and finishing their sentences. The high can last four to sixteen hours. Snorting or oral ingestion produces a high but not an intense rush. Snorting produces effects within three to five minutes, and oral ingestion produces effects within fifteen to twenty minutes.

Methamphetamine and Sex   Taken episodically and in low doses, methamphetamine can enhance sexual drive and performance; used habitually at high dosage, it can impair sexual functioning. In some abusers it provides a substitute for sex (D. E. Smith 1979). Grinspoon and Hedblom (1975: 103) state that although some people experience improved sexual performance, which might be an important reason for its popularity, "amphetamines are particularly dangerous in the hands of people whose sexuality is abnormal or overtly perverse" because the drugs appear to obliterate conventional restraints. One of the ways in which methamphetamine (MA) use can be distinguished from other drug and alcohol addictions, notes T. Hank Robinson (2006: 20), is the out-of-control sexual activity which appears to be a key element in its use. Users report a loss of control over their sexual expression, describing sex as "compulsive" and "obsessive." "The disinhibitory affects of MA (and Ice in particular) have been strongly associated with sexual behaviors that put men at high risk of sexually transmitted and blood-borne disease, including HIV infection." The "crystal meth" version has proven popular in the gay community and is associated with the transmission of HIV/AIDS among gay males who take it with Viagra or similar drugs and engage in unprotected sex with multiple partners.

Anal insertion of methamphetamine, known in the gay community as "booty-bumping," results in the substance passing quickly though anal tissue, causing physical and psychological stimulation that leads to a likelihood of hypersexual anal activity (Halkitis, Parsons, and Wilton 2003).

METHAMPHETAMINE TOLERANCE AND WITHDRAWAL

Tolerance does not develop to all effects of methamphetamine at the same rate; indeed, there may be increased sensitivity to some of them. For the high-intensity user, each successive rush becomes less euphoric, and it takes more methamphetamine to achieve it. Likewise, each high is not quite as strong as the one before, and the user needs more methamphetamine more often to get a high that is not as good as the last one. "Because tolerance for methamphetamine occurs within minutes—meaning that the pleasurable effects disappear even before the drug concentration in the blood falls significantly—users try to maintain the high by binging on the drug" (National Institute on Drug Abuse 1999b: 3–4).

The most common symptoms of withdrawal among heavy amphetamine users are fatigue, long but troubled sleep, irritability, intense hunger, and moderate to severe depression, which can lead to suicidal behavior. Fits of violence may also occur. These disturbances can be temporarily reversed if the drug is taken again. Less systematic users experience no acute, immediate symptoms of physical distress during methamphetamine withdrawal, a stage that the abuser might enter slowly. Often, thirty to ninety days must pass after the last drug use before the abuser realizes that he or she is in withdrawal. First, without really noticing, the individual becomes depressed, loses the ability to experience pleasure, becomes lethargic, and has no energy. Then the craving for more methamphetamine hits.

MEDICAL USE OF AMPHETAMINES

Because amphetamines appear to act on the hypothalamus to suppress the appetite—although other CNS or metabolic effects may be involved—at one time the drugs were widely prescribed to treat obesity. In contrast to more natural forms of dieting, however, the appetite returns with greater intensity after withdrawal from the drug, and it is only as a last resort that methamphetamine hydrochloride (Desoxyn) is used to treat obesity as one component of a weight reduction regimen; even then, the treatment is limited to only a few weeks.

As it became known that most of the benefits from treating many ailments with amphetamine were due to the drug's ability to elevate mood, medically accepted uses declined. Besides obesity, there are only two such uses in the United States: for treating narcolepsy, a sleeping disorder that affects about 250,000 Americans and is usually treated with Dexedrine, and certain types of hyperactivity—hyperkinetic syndrome—in children with minimal brain damage or adolescent attention deficit/hyperactivity disorder (ADHD) when other remedies have proven insufficient. About 3 to 5 percent of the general population has ADHD, which is characterized by agitated behavior and an inability to focus on tasks. Paradoxically, in children with ADHD these drugs produce a calming effect, and tolerance does not develop; these children have no exceptional risk for drug abuse problems in later life.

Methamphetamine is structurally similar to the neurotransmitter dopamine, but it is quite different from cocaine. Although these stimulants have similar behavioral and physiological effects, there are some major differences in the basic mechanisms of how they work at the level of the nerve cell. However, the bottom line is that methamphetamine, like cocaine, results in an accumulation of the neurotransmitter dopamine, and this excessive dopamine concentration appears to produce the stimulation and feelings of euphoria that the user experiences. In contrast to cocaine, which is quickly removed and almost completely metabolized in the body, methamphetamine has a much longer duration of action, and a larger percentage of the drug remains unchanged in the body. This results in methamphetamine being present in the brain for a longer time, which ultimately leads to prolonged stimulant effects (National Institute on Drug Abuse 2002a).

Amphetamine continues to have military uses; for instance, the U.S. Air Force provided it to aircrews during the Persian Gulf War. "More than sixty percent of the pilots who used the drug said it was 'essential' to accomplishing their mission" (Groopman 2001: 53; Rosenkranz 2003).

DANGERS OF METHAMPHETAMINE USE

A small amount of methamphetamine can increase breathing and heart rates, cause heart palpitations, and provoke anxiety or nervousness. Higher doses can make these effects more intense. Headaches, dizziness, and a rapid or irregular heartbeat can occur. Some users become hostile and aggressive. Methamphetamine often causes hypothermia with renal failure that can be fatal. Although less commonly than with cocaine, methamphetamine use can lead to heart failure (Karch 1996). Using amphetamines over a long period of time can cause some health problems. With increased doses, users may become talkative, restless, and excited and may feel a sense of power and superiority. With prolonged use, the short-term effects are exaggerated.

Because methamphetamine suppresses appetite, chronic heavy users generally fail to eat properly and thus develop various illnesses related to vitamin deficiencies and malnutrition. They may also be more prone to illness because they are generally run down, lack sleep, and live in an unhealthy environment. Chronic heavy users may also develop a drug-induced psychosis, a mental disturbance that is very similar to paranoid schizophrenia. The condition is an exaggeration of the short-term effects of high doses. Symptoms include hearing voices and paranoia—delusions that other people are threatening or persecuting the person. Heavy users may be prone to sudden, violent, and irrational acts. Herbert Meltzer (1979: 156) notes that "normal volunteers screened to exclude any subjects with schizophrenic symptoms will become psychotic within 1 day if given repeated doses of amphetamine totaling several hundred milligrams." Symptoms of psychosis at an abated level can persist for some time after the drug is discontinued (Institute for the Study of Drug Dependence 1987).

In rural America, where methamphetamine has had a significant impact, dentists have been treating the ravaged teeth of the drug's abusers. Although it is not clear what is causing this condition, there are hypotheses: The substance causes dry mouth, and the lack of saliva promotes the growth of bacteria; the drug causes thirst, and users crave a constant supply of sugary drinks that spur decay; caustic ingredients used in the drug's manufacture contribute to the damage when "meth" users tend to grind and clench their teeth nervously, aggravating already damaged gums and teeth (Davey 2005).

The heightened feelings of energy combined with a significant lowering of social restraints on unconventional or aggressive behavior can, in some people and/or in some situations, lead to extremely violent behavior: "Under the influence of speed even the most normally lethargic person *must* do something, even if it is as boring and repetitious as stringing beads for hours. When such a deep and insistent need to do *something* is thought to be disapproved or blocked, the speed abuser may attack the perceived thwarter with murderous rage" (Grinspoon and Hedblom 1975: 204). The symptoms usually disappear within a few days or weeks after drug use is stopped. Methamphetamine increases the libido and is associated with rougher sex that might lead to bleeding and abrasions, increasing the danger of HIV/AIDS transmission (National Institute on Drug Abuse 1998a).

Methamphetamine poisoning or overdose can cause brain hemorrhage, heart attack, high fever, coma, and occasionally death; however, most methamphetamine-associated deaths are due to accidents while the person is under the influence of the drug. Methamphetamine may contain substances that do not easily dissolve in water. When users inject the drug, these particles can pass into the body and block small blood vessels or weaken the blood vessel walls. Kidney damage, lung problems, strokes, or other tissue injury can result. There is also the danger of acute lead poisoning because a common method of production uses lead acetate as a reagent (National Institute on Drug Abuse 1998a).

Methamphetamine at doses abused by humans leads to dopamine transporter reductions in the brain, and this reduction is associated with the functional impairment experienced by those with Parkinson's disease (Volkow et al. 2001). Research indicates that methamphetamine also causes damage to nerve endings of dopamine-containing cells and persists for years after drug use has stopped. The damage is similar to that caused by Parkinson's disease but less extensive.

In laboratory experiments, a single exposure to methamphetamine at high doses or prolonged use at low doses destroyed up to 50 percent of the brain cells that use dopamine. Although this damage might not be immediately apparent, scientists believe that with aging or exposure to other toxic agents, Parkinson symptoms may eventually emerge. These symptoms begin with lack of coordination and tremors and may eventually result in a form of paralysis. Methamphetamine users risk long-term brain damage, since methamphetamine amplifies a process known as *apoptosis*, by which the brain culls defective cells, to the point at which healthy cells are also eliminated (Mathias 2000; Zickler 2000a). These results provide evidence that methamphetamine at dose levels taken by human abusers of the drug leads to dopamine transporter reduction that is associated with motor and cognitive impairment (Volkow et al. 2001).

Little research has been done in humans into the effects of amphetamine use on pregnancy and fetal growth, although experiments with animals suggest that use during pregnancy might produce adverse behavioral effects.

NICOTINE

Nicotine is one of more than 4,000 chemicals found in the smoke from tobacco; smokeless tobacco also contains a high level of nicotine (National Institute on Drug Abuse 1998b). About 1 percent of the weight of tobacco leaf is nicotine, and if all the nicotine in one cigarette were absorbed quickly into the body, the effect would be toxic and even fatal (A. Goldstein 2001). Most American cigarettes contain at least ten milligrams of nicotine, and the average smoker, through inhalation, takes in one to two milligrams per cigarette. Nicotine is absorbed through the skin and mucosal lining of the mouth and nose by inhalation into the lungs (National Institute on Drug Abuse 2001d).

EFFECTS OF NICOTINE

After each inhalation from a cigarette, within ten seconds the brain is swamped by a new drug spike (A. Goldstein 2001). Immediately after ingestion there is a "kick" that results in part from stimulation of the adrenal glands and resulting discharge of epinephrine (adrenaline). Depending on the level of CNS arousal and the dose of nicotine taken, as with alcohol, nicotine can also exert a sedative effect (National Institute on Drug Abuse 2001d).

The manner in which nicotine produces behavioral and cognitive effects is quite complex (see, e.g., McGehee et al. 1995). Like other stimulants, particular CNS receptors have an affinity for nicotine. As is the case with other psychoactive drugs, nicotine attaches to these (nicotinic cholinergic) receptors located on the surface of neurons, triggering the release of stimulating neurotransmitters such as acetylcholine and glutamate. In addition, nicotine indirectly causes a release of dopamine in the brain regions that control pleasure and motivation. This reaction

"E-SMOKING"

Resembling a normal cigarette, electronic cigarettes use a battery-powered device to deliver a smokeless and odorless dose of nicotine. When the user inhales, a sensor heats a cartridge that dispenses nicotine and produces imitation smoke using propylene glycol, a product used to create smoke or fog in theatrical productions. Manufactured in China, the Food and Drug Administration (FDA) has refused to allow e-cigarettes into the country, but they are, nevertheless, available on the Internet (Zezima 2009a). And despite claims by their manufacturers to the contrary, an FDA analysis revealed that electronic cigarettes contain traces of toxic substances and carcinogens (Zezima 2009b).

is similar to that seen with other drugs of abuse, such as cocaine and heroin, and is thought to underlie the pleasurable sensations that many smokers experience.

Immediately after exposure to nicotine, there is a "kick" that is caused in part by the drug's stimulation of the adrenal glands and resulting discharge of epinephrine (adrenaline). The rush of adrenaline stimulates the body and causes a sudden release of glucose as well as an increase in blood pressure, respiration, and heart rate. Nicotine also suppresses insulin output from the pancreas, so smokers are always slightly hyperglycemic. "In addition, nicotine indirectly causes a release of dopamine in the brain regions that control pleasure and motivation" (Society for Neuroscience 2002: 33). Nicotine also acts on a group of regulatory cells whose job is to control the dopamine response. When these mechanisms are disabled, the reward system continues to operate long after it should normally have shut down, causing a high that can last an hour (Kotulak 2002a). Furthermore, a non-nicotine tobacco smoke ingredient decreases levels of the MAO enzyme, which exists in forms A and B. Cigarette smokers have a 40 percent MAO-B deficiency, causing the dopamine triggered by nicotine to remain active and thus enhancing its impact (National Institute on Drug Abuse 2001d).

The characteristics of smoking cigarettes indicate that nicotine might be a **gateway drug** leading to addiction to other drugs of abuse (Glassman and Koob 1996). Cigarette use typically precedes the use of illegal substances (Clymer 1994), and people who abuse heroin and cocaine are more likely to be tobacco smokers than is the rest of the population (Zickler 2000b). Research has revealed that children who have never smoked are certain not to use heroin or cocaine, while a significant proportion of children who smoke heavily have used these drugs, and many have become drug-dependent (Center on Addiction and Substance Abuse 1994). The stimulating effects of nicotine are followed by depression and fatigue, leading the user to seek more nicotine, an explanation for chain-smoking (National Institute on Drug Abuse 2004).

As with other psychoactive substances, research has revealed that the use of nicotine might be a form of self-medication, smokers using nicotine to ward off depression; antidepressants can often help hardcore depressed smokers to quit (Brody 1997). And as is the case with alcohol, discussed in Chapter 4, genetics seem to play a role in the predisposition to nicotine dependence: "People with a gene variant in a particular enzyme metabolize or break down nicotine in the body more slowly and are significantly less likely to become addicted to nicotine

HOOKAH

The use of water pipes, popular in the Middle East, has become part of the college scene. Flavored and sweetened tobacco is heated over charcoal and then cooled as it passes through a bowl of water. While many enthusiasts believe that it is safer than smoking cigarettes, in fact the hookah may expose users to more toxic materials than do cigarettes: "Each puff has as much as 100 times the smoke as a puff from a cigarette" and smokers are also inhaling fumes from the charcoal ("Despite Dangers, Hookahs Gain Favor" 2008: 6).

than people without the variant" (Mathias 1999: 5; see also Zickler 2003). Research has discovered that prenatal exposure to tobacco is a significant risk factor for early substance abuse among preadolescents (National Institute on Drug Abuse 1997c).

Secondhand Smoke Smoking is also a hazard to those who are exposed to secondhand smoke, a 1986 finding by the U.S. Surgeon General that was confirmed in 2006:

- There is no safe level of secondhand smoke, and even brief exposure can be harmful, especially to children, pregnant women, and those with respiratory diseases.
- For nonsmoking adults exposure to secondhand smoke raises the risk of heart disease by 25 percent and the risk of cancer by 20 to 30 percent (O'Neil 2006).

According to the American Lung Association, environmental tobacco smoke (ETS, sometimes referred to as secondhand smoke) is believed responsible for 35,500 nonsmoker deaths a year from heart disease. ETS can cause irritation of the eyes, nose, throat, and lungs, which can lead to coughing, an achiness in the chest, and excessive phlegm production. People who are exposed to secondhand smoke are more likely to have serious health problems, including lung cancer, cardiovascular disease, low birth weight, sudden infant death syndrome, asthma, bronchitis, pneumonia, middle ear infections, and nasal and eye irritation.

Children whose bodies are still developing are especially vulnerable to ETS; effects include ear infections, croup, bronchitis, tonsillitis, and even cancer and leukemia. ETS is a risk factor for child behavior problems such as acting out, hyperactivity, and disruptive types of behaviors. Children who are exposed to higher levels of ETS exhibit more depression, withdrawal, and anxiety-type behaviors. Exposure to secondhand smoke was also found to negatively affect a child's reading and math skills (Kirkey 2006). There is also the problem of passive secondhand smoke, which is a major source of indoor air contaminants.

In 2007, researchers revealed that the craving for nicotine appears to be contained in the *insula*, a prune-size region under the frontal lobs of the brain near the ear. Chronic smokers who have suffered a stroke that injured the insula no longer have any desire to smoke cigarettes (Carey 2007). Injury to the insula can also lead to apathy and loss of libido. The insula is important for anticipating events and becomes activated when an addict experiences stimuli associated with drug use (Blakeslee 2007).

In contrast to cocaine and amphetamine, nicotine can also exert a sedative effect, depending on the level of the smoker's nervous system arousal and the dose of nicotine taken. At high doses there is evidence that nicotine might actually block cholinergic transmission, preventing the release of the neurotransmitter acetylcholine and producing sedation. Many users report a calming effect; this might be related to nicotine's ability to activate cells in the spinal cord that reduce muscle tone and thus serves as a muscle relaxant. It also reduces appetite, although this might be at least partially offset by a decrease in metabolic rate.

Cigarette smoking "produces a rapid distribution of nicotine to the brain, with drug levels peaking with 10 seconds of inhalation. The acute effects of nicotine dissipate in a few minutes, causing the smoker to continue dosing frequently throughout the day to maintain the drug's pleasurable effects and prevent withdrawal." A typical smoker "will take 10 puffs on a cigarette over a period of 5 minutes that the cigarette is lit. Thus, a person who smokes about 1.5 packs (30 cigarettes) daily, gets 300 'hits' of nicotine to the brain each day" (National Institute on Drug Abuse 2001d: 2).

The addictive nature of nicotine is highlighted by the difficulty smokers exhibit in attempting abstinence. Fewer than 7 percent of smokers who try to quit on their own achieve more than one year of abstinence, and most relapse within a few days of attempting to quit. As humorist Will Rogers (1879–1935) quipped: "Quitting smoking is easy; I've done it hundreds of times." Chronic use of nicotine products such as cigarettes produces physiological and/or psychological dependence. These smokers experience heightened stress between cigarettes, and smoking briefly restores their stress levels to normal; the apparent mood benefits reflect relief of withdrawal symptoms (Parrott 1999).

Addiction to nicotine is influenced by gender. For men, the "compulsion to smoke is driven more strongly by nicotine's pharmacological effects on the brain, while women's addiction owes more to the visual, tactile, taste, and olfactory sensations" (G. R. Hanson 2002a: 4).

NICOTINE TOLERANCE AND WITHDRAWAL

Repeated exposure to nicotine results in the development of tolerance, and higher doses of the drug are required to produce the same initial stimulation. Nicotine is metabolized fairly rapidly, disappearing from the body in a few hours. Although some tolerance is lost overnight, smokers often report that the first cigarette of the day is the strongest and/or the "best," indicating that it relieves the discomfort of withdrawal. As the day progresses, acute tolerance develops, and later cigarettes have less effect. Tolerance produces withdrawal symptoms when the consumption of nicotine ceases: slowing of brain activity, restless sleep, decreased heart rate and thyroid functioning, anxiety, anger, cognitive and attentional deficits, and increased appetite (J. R. Hughes 1990).

Withdrawal may begin within a few hours after the last cigarette, and symptoms peak within the first few days and may subside within a few weeks. For some people, however, symptoms persist for months or longer (National Institute on Drug Abuse 1997c). "Dramatic changes in the brain's pleasure circuits during withdrawal from chronic nicotine use rival the magnitude and duration of similar changes observed during withdrawal from other abused drugs such as cocaine, opiates, amphetamines, and alcohol" (National Institute on Drug Abuse 1998c: 1). Failure to continue the ingestion of nicotine causes severe craving, which can last for six months or longer—a major reason for relapse (National Institute on Drug Abuse 1998b).

The craving for nicotine is an important but poorly understood component of the withdrawal syndrome that has been described as a major obstacle to successful abstinence. Although the withdrawal syndrome is related to the pharmacological effects of nicotine, many behavioral factors also can affect the severity of withdrawal symptoms. For some people the feel, smell, and sight of a cigarette and the ritual of obtaining, handling, lighting, and smoking the cigarette are associated with the pleasurable effects of smoking and can make withdrawal or craving worse. Although nicotine gum and patches may alleviate the pharmacological aspects of withdrawal, cravings often persist.

DANGERS OF NICOTINE USE

The medical consequences of nicotine exposure result from effects of both the nicotine itself and how it is taken. About 440,000 people die annually from the deadly effects of tobacco smoke. Smoking cigarettes accounts for one third of all cancers, particularly lung cancer. Cigarette smoking has been linked to about 90 percent of all lung cancer cases, and lung cancer is the nation's single leading cause of death and disability (Brody 2001). Smoking also causes lung diseases such as chronic bronchitis and emphysema, and it has been found to exacerbate asthma symptoms in adults and children. Smoking is also associated with cancers of the mouth, pharynx, larynx, esophagus, stomach, pancreas, cervix, kidney, ureter, and bladder. The overall rates of death from cancer are twice as high among smokers as among nonsmokers, heavy smokers having rates that are four times greater than those of nonsmokers (National Institute on Drug Abuse 2004). In 1999 it was revealed that cigar smokers are twice as likely to get cancer of the mouth, throat, and lungs as nonsmokers are (Associated Press 1999d).

Nicotine is a vascoconstrictor—constricts blood vessels—that causes the heart to work harder to maintain a sufficient level of oxygen. Cigarette smoking releases carbon monoxide which reduces the body's supply of oxygen and causes shortness of breadth—it is why participants in high-energy sports are advised to avoid smoking. A chronic oxygen-deficit can damage the heart. The relationship between cigarette smoking and coronary heart disease was first reported in the 1940s. Since that time, it has been well documented that smoking substantially increases the risk of heart disease, including stroke, heart attack, vascular disease, and aneurysm. It is estimated that nearly one fifth of deaths from heart disease are attributable to smoking (National Institute on Drug Abuse 2004). Research has revealed that even occasional smoking causes considerable artery damage, making the smoker vulnerable to cardiovascular disease (Parker-Pope 2008).

The relationship between cigarette smoking and coronary heart disease was first reported in the 1940s. Since that time, it has been well documented that smoking substantially increases the risk of heart disease, including stroke, heart attack, vascular disease, and aneurysm. It is estimated that nearly one fifth of deaths from heart disease are attributable to smoking (National Institute on Drug Abuse 2004). Research has revealed that even occasional smoking causes considerable artery damage, making the smoker vulnerable to cardiovascular disease (Parker-Pope 2008).

Preliminary research has linked cigarette smoking by fathers to an increased risk of brain cancer and leukemia in their offspring, and children whose parents smoke are three to four times more likely to develop serious infectious diseases. An estimated 5,600 infant deaths are caused by smoking among pregnant women (Associated Press 1995). Nicotine affects the blood vessels in the placenta, interfering with oxygen supply to the fetus (A. Goldstein 2001). According to a study by Laurence Namur, newborns whose mothers smoke during pregnancy have the same nicotine level as adult smokers and spend the first few days of life going through withdrawal (Associated Press 1997a). In addition, research in 2001 found that prenatal exposure to smoke could predispose children to early smoking experimentation. The researchers speculate that maternal smoking during pregnancy causes disturbances in the neurophysiological functioning of the fetus (Thomas 2001). There is also considerable research indicating that children whose mothers smoke during pregnancy are at much greater risk than other children for drug abuse and conduct disorder (Varisco 2000). The toxic effects of prenatal exposure to nicotine has been found to include lower IQ and increased risk of ADHD (Williams 2004).

Nicotine causes blood vessels in the skin to constrict, reducing blood and oxygen supplies to the extremities—an obvious detriment in high-energy sports—and might be the reason why the skin of cigarette smokers tends to be more wrinkled than that of nonsmokers of the same age. As with heroin, nicotine stimulates centers of the brain cell that control vomiting, and new smokers may experience nausea.

According to researchers at the Centers for Disease Control and Prevention, because cigarette smoke makes it harder for the lungs to expel foreign material and easier for bacteria to stick, smokers are four times more likely than nonsmokers to get life-threatening blood infections or meningitis from bacteria that usually causes pneumonia. And the more cigarettes a person smokes, the higher is the risk of an infection. The researchers noted that former smokers have an increased risk of the infection for at least ten years after they quit (McConnaughey 2000).

CHEWING TOBACCO

He was one of the world's best saddle bronco riders on the rodeo circuit. When he died at age 47, his throat cancer was so bad that it had wrapped around his jugular vein and got into his brain. His family brought a lawsuit against the nation's leading manufacturer of chewing tobacco, which is also the oldest sponsor of rodeos (Egan 2004).

"SOFT" ON SMOKING

Men who smoke a pack or more per day have a 40 percent greater risk of erectile dysfunction. Nicotine is a vasoconstrictor (i.e., it tightens blood vessels and restricts blood flow) that has been shown to cause permanent damage to arteries. Because a man's erection depends on blood flow, researchers theorized that smoking would affect erections, and studies have confirmed this. Although young male smokers might not notice negative effects, their sexual futures could be limp.

The Family Smoking Prevention and Tobacco Control Act of 2009 authorizes the Food and Drug Administration (FDA) to regulate the tobacco industry. The FDA subsequently banned marketing cigarettes as "light" or "low tar," and prohibited candy- fruit- and other flavored cigarettes that appeal to children.

HERBAL STIMULANTS

Herbal substances are used by young people as a "safe" alternative to illegal drugs The 1994 Dietary Supplement Health and Education Act was passed as the result of an effective lobbying campaign by the food supplement industry. The statute deregulated the industry and now permits the marketing of any supplement until the FDA is able to prove that it is unsafe. The law also enables companies to make unrestrained and unjustified health claims.

So-called herbal stimulants, particularly **ephedra** (also known by its Chinese name *ma huang*), were sold in the form of pills in many health food stores under a variety of brand names. Ephedra contains **ephedrine**, which is an amphetamine precursor and is produced as a stimulant in nonprescription asthma and some cold and allergy medicine. Sometimes other ephedra derivatives and caffeine were added to increase its stimulating properties. Within twenty minutes of taking the substance, there is a jump in the heart rate and blood pressure. One popular brand is called Herbal Ecstasy, although it is not related to MDMA (ecstasy) (discussed in Chapter 6). In 2004, the Food and Drug Administration banned the sale of dietary supplements containing ephedra because of "an unreasonable risk of illness or injury."

CAFFEINE

Caffeine—found in tea, coffee, many cola drinks, cocoa products, and pain relievers—is the most widely used psychoactive drug; about 90 percent of the adult North American population ingests caffeine regularly. After ingestion of caffeine, the chemical's compounds dissolve in the bloodstream and travel to the brain. Caffeine molecules are almost identical to those of the neurotransmitter adenosine, which controls the release of chemicals that excite the central nervous system and thus acts as a natural "sleeping pill" (Reid 2005). Caffeine occupies adenosine receptor sites in the brain, neutralizing this function.

The result is an elevation of mood, a decrease in fatigue, and, in high doses, insomnia and a racing heart. Abrupt withdrawal of caffeine can result in headaches, lethargy, and depressionlike symptoms (Griffiths 1990; Griffiths et al. 1990; Blakeslee 1991, 1994; "Quitting Caffeine Can Bring on the Blahs" 1991)—hence a person's *need* for that first cup of coffee in the morning. Withdrawal symptoms disappear in two to four days but can last up to a week (Reid 2005). Research has revealed that drinking two cups of coffee a day has some health benefits for adults.

Caffeine is routinely served to children as an ingredient in sodas and chocolate bars. "In fact, most babies in the developed world enter the universe with traces of caffeine in their bodies, a transfer through the umbilical cord from the mother's latte or Snapple." There is no evidence, however, that caffeine in small doses is unsafe for children (Reid 2005: 13).

SUMMARY

- Cocaine and amphetamines produce a sudden sensation known as a "rush" or a "flash." Abuse is often associated with a pattern of binge use. Abrupt cessation, even after a weekend binge, is commonly followed by depression, anxiety, drug craving, and extreme fatigue ("crash").

- The use of powerful stimulants by some people and not others, given that both groups have equal access to these drugs, can be explained by physiological deficiencies.

- Stimulants such as cocaine and amphetamine compensate for a deficiency in three neurotransmitters that can otherwise result in apathy and depression—dopamine; norepinephrine, which acts with epinephrine (adrenaline); and serotonin.

- Cocaine binds to specific receptor sites on brain membranes and triggers the release of neurotransmitters that enhance mood and, at high enough doses, produce feelings of euphoria and indifference to pain, along with illusions of increased mental and sensory alertness and physical strength, along with an increased heart rate, blood pressure, breathing rate, body temperature, and blood sugar. As the supply of dopamine depletes, depression sets in.

- Substances chemically similar to cocaine, such as Novocain, eliminate all feeling when applied topically or subcutaneously, and when taken intranasally or smoked, produce the same euphoric response.

- Although cocaine hydrochloride cannot easily be smoked, freeing the alkaloid from the hydrochloride attachment ("freebase") will produce purified crystals of cocaine ("crack") that can be crushed and smoked in a special glass pipe or sprinkled on a tobacco or marijuana product.

- After frequent and high doses of cocaine, the failure to continue ingestion produces a withdrawal syndrome characterized by psychological depression, irritability, extreme fatigue, and prolonged periods of restless sleep.

- Cocaine causes blood vessels to constrict and heart rate and blood pressure to increase. In people whose coronary arteries are narrowed by atherosclerosis, reactions can range from mild angina to a fatal heart attack. Even in people with normal coronary arteries, the ingesting of cocaine has resulted in angina and heart attacks.

- Methamphetamine, synthetic stimulants with no anesthetic properties, mimics the effects of cocaine and in form purified for smoking—ice—produces a high reputed to last from seven to twenty-four hours.

- Methamphetamine stimulates by triggering the release of neurotransmitters while inhibiting their reuptake. Like cocaine, methamphetamine mimics naturally occurring substances and causes a biochemical arousal—a "turn on"—without the presence of sensory input requiring such arousal. Because reuptake is blocked, the depletion of the body's stimulating neurotransmitters is believed to be responsible for the crash that follows the ingestion of high doses of methamphetamine.

- The most common symptoms of withdrawal among heavy methamphetamine users are fatigue, long but troubled sleep, irritability, intense hunger, and moderate to severe depression, which can lead to suicidal behavior. Fits of violence may also occur. These disturbances can be temporarily reversed if the drug is taken again.

- The heightened feelings of energy combined with a significant lowering of social restraints on unconventional or aggressive behavior can, in some people and/or in some situations, lead to extremely violent behavior.

- Methamphetamine at doses abused by humans leads to dopamine transporter reductions in the brain. This reduction is associated with the functional impairment experienced by those with Parkinson's disease.

- After each inhalation from a cigarette, within ten seconds a new drug spike swamps the brain. Immediately after ingestion there is a "kick" and, as with alcohol, nicotine can also exert a sedative effect.
- Nicotine causes a release of dopamine in the brain regions that control pleasure and motivation.
- Cigarette use typically precedes the use of illegal substances.
- As with other psychoactive substances, the use of nicotine might be a form of self-medication to ward off depression.
- Smoking is also a hazard to those who are exposed to secondhand smoke.
- The addictive nature of nicotine is highlighted by the difficulty smokers exhibit in attempting abstinence. Fewer than 7 percent of smokers who try to quit on their own achieve more than one year of abstinence.
- Repeated exposure to nicotine results in the development of tolerance, and higher doses of the drug are required to produce the same initial stimulation.
- Nicotine tolerance produces withdrawal symptoms when consumption ceases that include slowing of brain activity, restless sleep, decreased heart rate and thyroid functioning, anxiety, anger, cognitive and attentional deficits, and increased appetite.

- The most deleterious effects of nicotine addiction are the result of smoking cigarettes, which accounts for one third of all cancers, particularly lung cancer.
- Nicotine causes blood vessels in the skin to constrict, reducing blood and oxygen supplies to the extremities—an obvious detriment in high-energy sports—and might be the reason why the skin of cigarette smokers tends to be more wrinkled than that of nonsmokers of the same age.
- Herbal stimulants, particularly ephedra, were sold in the form of pills in many health food stores under a variety of brand names. Ephedra contains ephedrine, an amphetamine precursor and is used nonprescription asthma and some cold and allergy medicine.
- Caffeine—found in tea, coffee, many cola drinks, cocoa products, and pain relievers—is the most widely used psychoactive drug. About 90 percent of the adult North American population ingests caffeine regularly.
- Caffeine causes an elevation of mood, a decrease in fatigue, and, in high doses, insomnia and a racing heart. Abrupt withdrawal of caffeine can result in headaches, lethargy, and depression-like symptoms that disappear in two to four days.

Review Questions

1. What are the most commonly used stimulants?
2. What is the possible relationship between a neurotransmitter deficiency and use of cocaine and amphetamine?
3. How can an excess of MAO help explain the desire for stimulant drugs?
4. How can increases in the availability of cocaine result in an increase in emergency room admissions for overdoses?
5. How does cocaine cause its main psychological effect, the "high"?
6. What is the effect on the cocaine user when the supply of dopamine depletes?
7. What is the outcome of allowing laboratory animals unlimited access to cocaine?
8. What are the physiological effects of small doses of cocaine?
9. What is the relationship between cocaine and the "fight or flight" mechanism?
10. What are the possible effects of cocaine on sexual activity?
11. What is the effect of combining heroin with cocaine?
12. How does crack differ from cocaine hydrochloride (powdered cocaine)?
13. How do withdrawal symptoms associated with cocaine differ from those of heroin?

14. How is cocaine used in medical practice?
15. What are the dangers associated with chronic use of cocaine?
16. What is the controversy surrounding "crack babies"?
17. How are cocaine and amphetamines similar and dissimilar?
18. How does methamphetamine effect the central nervous system?
19. What is the effect of methamphetamine on sexual activity?
20. What is the relationship between methamphetamine use and tolerance?

21. What are the medical uses of amphetamines?
22. What are the dangers of methamphetamine use?
23. What are e-cigarettes?
24. How is nicotine similar to other psychoactive drugs?
25. What are the dangers of secondhand smoke?
26. What are nicotine's withdrawal symptoms?
27. What are the dangers of smoking cigarettes?
28. What are the dangers of using herbal stimulants?
29. What are the withdrawal symptoms associated with caffeine?

Under the influence of hallucinogens, people see images, hear sounds, and feel sensations that seem real but do not exist.

National Institute on Drug Abuse (1999a: 1)

HALLUCINOGENS, CLUB DRUGS, MARIJUANA, INHALANTS, AND PRESCRIPTION DRUGS

CHAPTER **6**

AP Photo/Jeff Barnard

This chapter examines drugs that do fit into the categories discussed in Chapters 4 and 5; substances that combine depressant and stimulant qualities, hallucinogens, and prescription drugs that include depressants and stimulants.

HALLUCINOGENS

The American Heritage Dictionary (2000: 782) defines hallucination as a "Perception of visual, auditory, tactile, olfactory, or gustatory experiences without an external stimulus and with a compelling sense of their reality." "A hallucinogen is a drug that changes a person's state of awareness by modifying sensory inputs, loosening cognitive and creative restraints, and providing access to material normally hidden in memory or material of an unconscious nature" (Jacob and Shulgin 1994: 74). Hallucinogens can change a person's perception, making the person see or hear things that do not exist. They can also produce changes in thought, sense of time, and mood. According to Erich Goode (1972), the term *hallucinogen* implies something undesirable and suggests being "crazy." Supporters of the use of such chemicals prefer the term **psychedelic.**[1]

Hallucinogenic substances occur both naturally and synthetically. They excite the central nervous system (CNS), overwhelming its ability to modulate sensory input. Autonomic hyperactivity results in distortions of the perception of objective reality. These include:

- *Depersonalization*: "Out-of-body" experiences or misperceptions of reality
- *Synesthesia*: "Seeing" sound and "hearing" visual input
- *Hallucinations*: Perceiving sounds, odors, tactile sensations, or visual images that arise from within the person, not the environment

The sensory illusions produced by hallucinogens are often accompanied by mood alterations that are usually euphoric but sometimes severely depressive (Drug Enforcement Administration 1989) and that mimic severe mental illness (National Institute on Drug Abuse 1987). Marked impairment of judgment can lead to poor decision making and serious accidents (Berkow 1982). A number of hallucinogens produce cross-tolerance. Unlike depressants and stimulants, hallucinogens do not function as reinforcers in animals (Winter 1994). Hallucinogens apparently have their own receptors (5-HT$_2$) in the CNS (Lin and Glennon 1994).

LYSERGIC ACID DIETHYLAMIDE (LSD)

Lysergic acid diethylamide was synthesized in 1938. The first LSD "trip" was recorded by its discoverer, Dr. Albert Hofmann (1906–2008), a research chemist in Basel, Switzerland. In 1943, Hofmann accidentally ingested a minute quantity of the drug through the skin of his fingers (Grinspoon 1979). About this experience, Hofmann relates:

> I had to leave my work in the laboratory and go home because I felt strangely restless and dizzy. Once there, I lay down and sank into a not unpleasant delirium which was marked by an extreme degree of fantasy. In sort of a trance with closed eyes ... fantastic

---

[1]The term *psychedelic* was coined by research psychiatrist Humphrey Osmand in 1957.

visions of extraordinary vividness accompanied by a kaleidoscopic play of intense coloration continuously swirled around me. After two hours this condition subsided. (quoted in Goode 1972: 98–99)

Three days later, Hofmann experimented by swallowing 250 micrograms of LSD, not realizing that this was an extremely high dose. He soon became terrified, fearing that he would lose his mind or perhaps die (Grinspoon 1979). A user of LSD throughout his long life, Hofmann advocated its use in psychiatry but decried recreational use (C. Smith 2008).

In 1949, LSD was introduced into the United States as an experimental drug for treating psychiatric illnesses, but until 1954 it remained relatively rare and expensive because the ergot fungus from which it was derived was difficult to cultivate. In that year the Eli Lily Company announced that it had succeeded in creating a totally synthetic version of LSD (J. Stevens 1987); So had outlaw chemists.

Pure, high-potency LSD is a clear or white odorless crystalline material that is soluble in water. It is mixed with binding agents, such as spray-dried skim milk, for producing tablets or is dissolved and diluted in a solvent for application onto paper or other materials. Variations in the manufacturing process or the presence of precursors or by-products can cause LSD to range in color from clear or white, in its purest form, to tan or even black, indicating poor quality or degradation. To mask product deficiencies and disguise discoloration, distributors often apply LSD to off-white, tan, or yellow paper.

LSD has a slightly bitter taste and is usually taken by mouth. Commonly referred to as "acid," LSD is sold on the street in tablet, capsules and, occasionally, liquid form. LSD is often added to absorbent paper ("blotter acid") and divided into small decorated squares, each square representing one dose. It may be mixed with any number of substances, sugar, or gelatin sheets ("window panes"). It takes only 0.01 milligram for LSD to have an effect.

Just how LSD work is not completely understood. "The molecular structure of LSD is similar to that of the neurotransmitter serotonin. LSD therefore has a high affinity for serotonin receptors and interferes with the normal functioning of these receptors" (Henderson 1994a: 42). Stimulation of serotonin receptors by agonists such as LSD and the hallucinogen psilocybin inhibits the activity of a mechanism (a neural system called the raphe) that modulates sensory input into the brain stem. This mechanism would normally integrate sensory inflow and the emotional and ideational state of the organism and suppress irrelevant information. Serotonin agonists occupy serotonin receptor sites in the brain and thereby cause a backup of serotonin that exceeds the ability of MAO to control serotonin. Serotonin overloads the sensory input systems of the CNS, so normal stimuli take on distorted images—the size of the signal delivered to the cerebral cortex is greatly enlarged. This combination—inhibition of control mechanisms and increasing signal size—overloads the brain (Ray 1978). The result is actually a serotonin, rather than LSD, trip and consists of intoxication for several hours (Palfai and Jankiewicz 1991).

EFFECTS OF LSD

LSD is absorbed easily from the gastrointestinal tract and rapidly reaches a high concentration in the blood. It is circulated throughout the body and subsequently to the brain. LSD is metabolized in the liver and is excreted in the urine in about twenty-four hours. The effects of LSD range from blurred vision to a visual field filled with strange objects. Three-dimensional space appears to contract and enlarge, and light appears to fluctuate in intensity. Auditory effects also occur but to a lesser degree. All of these changes are episodic. Temperature sensitivity is altered, the environment being perceived as abnormally cold or hot. Body images are altered (out of-body experiences), and body parts appear to float. Time is sometimes perceived as running fast forward or backward. "Perceptually," notes Grinspoon (1979: 12), "LSD produces an especially brilliant and intense impact of sensory stimuli on consciousness. Normally unnoticed aspects of the environment capture the attention: ordinary objects are seen as if for the first time and with a sense of fascination or entrancement, as though they had unimagined depths of significance." There is apparently selective recall of some aspects of the LSD experience: "During the period of drug activity the subject may report that he feels less friendly, more aggressive or agitated, or depressed. Much later, he will recall the experience as illuminating and pleasurable. He will rarely recall psychotic symptoms" (Meltzer 1979: 162).

A trip begins between thirty to sixty minutes after ingestion, peaks after two to six hours, and fades out after about 12 hours. There are "good acid trips" and "bad acid trips." They appear to be controlled by the user's attitude, mood, and expectations and often depend on suggestions of those around the user at the time of the trip. Favorable expectations produce good trips, and excessive apprehension is likely to produce the opposite. Because the substance appears to intensify feelings, the user might feel a magnified sense of love, lust, and joy or anger, terror, and despair: "The extraordinary sensations and feelings may bring on fear of losing control, paranoia, and panic, or they may cause euphoria and even bliss" (Grinspoon 1979: 13). According to James MacDonald and Michael Agar (1994: 12), a good trip, when everything is touched by magic but the user remains aware that reality will return when the drug wears off, turns into a bad trip when the user "loses sight of this fact [that reality will return] for too long." The bad trip is the result of a failure to comprehend that reality has not changed, merely its perception while under the influence of LSD. Sensations and feelings change much more dramatically than do the physical signs, which are as varied as the psychological ones and include dilation of the pupils (almost always); increased heart rate, blood pressure, and body temperature; mild dizziness or nausea; chills; trembling; slow, deep breathing; loss of appetite; and insomnia (Grinspoon 1979).

> "A bad trip is actually an acute anxiety or panic reaction following the ingestion of LSD. On a bad trip, painful or frightening feelings are intensified, just as pleasurable sensations are on a good trip. Distortion of the sense of time can cause this experience to seem almost unbearably long. The person might feel that he or she has lost control of the drug and that the trip will never end; he or she might exhibit paranoia or attempt to flee. A bad trip is an acute reaction to LSD, however, and dissipates as the effects of the drug wear off (Henderson 1994b: 58)."

The user might feel several different emotions at once or swing rapidly from one emotion to another. If taken in a large enough dose, the drug produces delusions and visual hallucinations. The user's sense of time and self changes. Sensations might seem to "cross over," giving the user the feeling of seeing colors and

LSD: USES AND EFFECTS

Classification: Hallucinogen

CSA Schedule: Schedule I

Trade or Other Names: Acid, microdot

Medical Uses: None

Physical Dependence: None

Psychological Dependence: Unknown

Tolerance: Yes

Duration (hours): 8–12

Usual Method: Oral

Possible Effects: Illusions and hallucinations, altered perception of time and distance

Effects of Overdose: Longer, more intense "trip" episodes; psychosis; possible death

Withdrawal Syndrome: Unknown

Source: U.S. Drug Enforcement Administration.

hearing sounds. These changes can be frightening and can cause panic. Although LSD has been used experimentally to treat a variety of psychological illnesses, it currently has no accepted medical use.

LSD TOLERANCE AND WITHDRAWAL

Tolerance develops rapidly; repeated doses become completely ineffective after a few days of continuous use, and there is cross-tolerance to other hallucinogens. LSD is not addictive; there are no physical withdrawal symptoms (Institute for the Study of Drug Dependence 1987).

DANGERS OF LSD USE

LSD use can produce mydriasis (prolonged dilation of the pupil of the eye), raised body temperature, rapid heartbeat, elevated blood pressure, increased blood sugar, salivation, tingling in fingers and toes, weakness, tremors, palpitations, facial flushing, chills, gooseflesh, profuse perspiration, nausea, dizziness, inappropriate speech, blurred vision, and intense anxiety. Death caused by the direct effect of LSD on the body is virtually impossible. However, death related to LSD abuse has occurred as a result of the panic reactions, hallucinations, delusions, and paranoia experienced by users (Drug Enforcement Administration n.d.).

There are no known physical dangers in long-term use, although psychosis has been reported in a few instances. Some users report experiencing severe, terrifying thoughts and feelings; fear of losing control; fear of insanity and death; and despair while using LSD. For those who knowingly ingest LSD at low doses, there is usually mild euphoria and a loosening of inhibitions (Grinspoon 1979). Ingesting LSD unknowingly, however, can result in a highly traumatic experience as the victim might feel that he or she has suddenly "gone crazy" (Brecher 1972). Fatal accidents have occurred during states of LSD intoxication.

Some LSD users, fewer than 25 percent (Abrahart 1998), report recurring low-intensity trips—"flashbacks"—without having ingested the substance recently. This might be caused by LSD stored in and eventually released from fatty tissue. A flashback occurs suddenly, often without warning, and may occur within a few days or more than a year after the last use of LSD. Flashbacks usually occur in people who have used hallucinogens chronically or have an underlying personality problem; however, otherwise healthy people who use LSD occasionally may also have flashbacks. In normal (i.e., nonpsychotic) populations, more than half of those who experience flashbacks report them as pleasant (Abrahart 1998). However, it remains to be established whether there are any causal links between flash-backs and LSD use; the link could be explained by the lack of control over what an LSD user is actually ingesting. Like other illegally produced drugs, LSD may contain any variety of additives, including methamphetamine, which appears to increase the likelihood of a bad trip (Ray 1978). Medically supervised LSD research would use pharmaceutically pure LSD, but because LSD use was prohibited in 1966, most research on adverse effects involved individuals who had obtained black-market LSD, the real composition, purity, and strength of which would be unknown (Abrahart 1998).

Most users of LSD voluntarily decrease or stop its use over time. LSD is not considered an addictive drug, since it does not produce compulsive drug-seeking behavior. But because tolerance develops rapidly, some users take progressively higher doses to achieve the state of intoxication that they had previously achieved—a dangerous practice, given the unpredictability of the substance.

PHENCYCLIDINE (PCP)

Phencyclidine was initially developed as a general anesthetic for surgery. Although it produces distortions of sight and sound and feelings of dissociation from the environment and self, these mind-altering effects are technically not hallucinations and more properly known as "dissociative anesthetics" (National Institute on Drug Abuse 1999a). The drug is reported to have received the name PCP (or "peace pill") on the streets of San Francisco, where the drug was reputed to give illusions of everlasting peace. PCP is a white crystalline powder that has a distinctive bitter chemical taste. It is readily soluble in water or alcohol, and more than 100 variations (analogs) are produced easily and cheaply in clandestine laboratories (Lerner 1980). PCP can be mixed easily with dyes and turns up on the illicit drug market in liquid form and a variety of tablets, capsules, and colored powders. Like any drug sold on the street, PCP is often mixed with other psychoactive substances. It is sometimes sold as LSD. Although it can be snorted or eaten, PCP is most commonly applied to a leafy material such as mint, parsley, oregano, or marijuana ("killer joints" or "crystal supergrass") and smoked.

PCP is typically made by mixing ingredients in three buckets for several hours. This is often accomplished in the back of a van that is moving to disperse the fumes that are produced. The ingredients must be poured from one bucket to the other, leading to the term "bucket chemists." PCP is sold on the street by such names as "angel dust," "ozone," "whack," and "rocket fuel." The variety of street names for PCP reflects its bizarre and volatile effects.

EFFECTS OF PCP

PCP was first synthesized in 1956 and was found to be an effective surgical anesthetic when tested on monkeys. As a **dissociative anesthetic**, it induces a lack of responsive awareness not only of pain but also of the general environment, without a corresponding depression of the autonomic nervous system (Dotson, Ackerman, and West 1995). Experiments on humans were carried out in 1957, and although PCP proved to work as an anesthetic, it had serious side effects. Some patients manifested agitation, excitement, and disorientation during the recovery period. Some male surgical patients became violent, and some females appeared to experience simple intoxication (Linder, Lerner, and Burns 1981). "When PCP was subsequently given to normal volunteers in smaller doses, it induced a psychotic-like state resembling schizophrenia. Volunteers experienced body image changes, depersonalization, and feelings of loneliness, isolation, and dependency. Their thinking was observed to become progressively disorganized" (Lerner 1980: 14).

There is evidence of PCP receptors in the brain, suggesting that an "important relationship exists between the chemical structure of the 'phencyclidines' and receptors in the CNS related to neurotransmitters" (Burns and Done 1980: 100). Exactly how PCP acts on the body is not completely known, although it appears that the release of dopamine is a critical piece of the puzzle (French, Levenson, and Ceci 1990). In contrast to other anesthetics, PCP increases respiration, heart rate, and blood pressure, qualities that make it useful for patients who are endangered by a depressed heart rate or low blood pressure. In the 1960s, PCP became commercially available for use in veterinary medicine as an analgesic and anesthetic, but diversion to street use led the manufacturer to discontinue production in 1978.

Within thirty to sixty minutes of ingesting a moderate amount of PCP, the user experiences a sense of detachment, distance, and estrangement from his or her surroundings. Numbness, slurred speech, and a loss of coordination also occur. These symptoms, which last up to five hours, are often accompanied by feelings of invulnerability. "A blank stare, rapid and involuntary eye movements, and an exaggerated gait are among the more common observable effects" (Drug Enforcement Administration 1989: 50). Under laboratory conditions, a subject might experience a feeling of "flying with angels" and "peace and tranquility" (R. Siegel 1989: 220). At low to moderate doses, the physiological effects of PCP include a slight increase in breathing rate and a more pronounced rise in blood pressure and pulse rate. Respiration becomes shallow, and flushing and profuse sweating occur. Generalized numbness of the extremities and muscular incoordination may also occur. Psychological effects include distinct changes in body awareness, similar to those associated with alcohol intoxication.

PHENCYCLIDINE: USES AND EFFECTS

Classification: Hallucinogen

CSA Schedule: Schedule I, II

Trade or Other Names: PCE, PCPy, TCP, PCP, hog, loveboat, angel dust

Medical Uses: None

Physical Dependence: Unknown

Psychological Dependence: High

Tolerance: Yes

Duration (hours): Days

Usual Method: Oral, smoked

Possible Effects: Illusions and hallucinations, altered perception of time and distance

Effects of Overdose: Longer, more intense "trip" episodes, psychosis, possible death

Withdrawal Syndrome: Unknown

Source: U.S. Drug Enforcement Administration.

PCP TOLERANCE AND WITHDRAWAL

PCP use does not seem to result in any significant tolerance or withdrawal symptoms (National Institute on Drug Abuse 1991). "Generally 24–48 hours are required until the person again feels completely normal" (Lerner 1980: 16).

DANGERS OF PCP USE

PCP can result in mood disorders, acute anxiety, paranoia, and violent behavior. PCP-intoxicated individuals can present severe management problems to treatment staff and law enforcement personnel because the drug activates stress hormones that allow users to demonstrate remarkable strength. Some reactions are similar to those in LSD intoxication: auditory hallucinations and image distortion similar to fun house mirror images. "PCP is unique among popular drugs of abuse in its power to produce psychoses indistinguishable from schizophrenia" (National Institute on Drug Abuse 1989: 50). As a result, "the phencyclidine intoxicated patient is often improperly diagnosed and treated by well-meaning uninformed personnel" (Lerner 1980: 13).

Use of PCP among adolescents can interfere with hormones related to normal growth and development as well as with the learning process. At high doses of PCP, there is a drop in blood pressure, pulse rate, and respiration. This may be accompanied by nausea, vomiting, blurred vision, flicking up and down of the eyes, drooling, loss of balance, and dizziness. High doses of PCP can also cause seizures, coma, and death (though death more often results from accidental injury or suicide during PCP intoxication). Speech is often sparse and garbled. People who use PCP for long periods report memory loss, difficulties with speech and thinking, depression, and weight loss. These symptoms can persist up to a year after cessation of PCP use. Mood disorders also have been reported. PCP has sedative effects, and interactions with other CNS depressants, such as alcohol and benzodiazepines, can lead to coma or accidental overdose.

MUSHROOMS AND CACTUS

Some natural substances produce effects similar to those of the synthetic hallucinogens. **Mescaline** is the primary hallucinogenic ingredient of the fleshy part of the small spineless peyote cactus, referred to as *buttons*, which are the size of a quarter to several inches across. Indians in Northern Mexico have used mescaline as part of their religious rites since prehistoric times. The Native American Church, which has about 250,000 members, continues to use peyote as part of religious ceremonies for which the church has been exempted from certain provisions of the federal Controlled Substances Act. Twenty-three states also exempt the sacramental use of peyote from criminal penalties.[2] Six people are licensed by the state and federal governments to harvest peyote that grows wild (cultivation is illegal) in South Texas thirty miles east of Laredo (Milloy 2002).

Although the buttons may be chewed or boiled in water to produce a tea, peyote is usually ground into a powder and taken orally. Mescaline can also be produced synthetically. A typical dose of 350–500 milligrams produces illusions and hallucinations that last anywhere from five to twelve hours (National Institute on Drug Abuse 1989). In healthy volunteers, half a gram of mescaline produced symptoms of psychosis that were indistinguishable from those of schizophrenia (Karch 1996). There have been no reports of fatal overdoses of mescaline.

Psilocybe mushrooms have also been used for centuries in Native American religious ceremonies. The sacred or magic mushroom is typically eaten. Its active ingredients—**psilocybin** and psilocyn—are chemically similar to LSD and can be produced synthetically. Like mescaline and LSD, they affect perceptions and mood (National Institute on Drug Abuse 1989), and users cannot distinguish between psilocybin and LSD. There has been little research into this substance and virtually none on human subjects (Karch 1996).

Dimethyltryptamine (DMT) is a hallucinogenic substance that occurs naturally in many plants and is used by Caribbean and Latin American Indians; it is also found in Ololiuqui, the seeds of the morning glory plant that are used by Indian priests in Latin America to produce delirium.

Another hallucinogen is the "magic mushroom": *Amanita muscaria*. In the past it had religious significance in the culture of Siberia, and in Scandinavia it was reputedly used by Vikings to increase their ferocity in battle (Ray 1978), although Richard Blum (1969) disputes this legend. A brownish solid material that smells like mothballs, the mushroom must be smoked or injected; it is not activated

---

[2]In 1990 the Supreme Court, in an Oregon case, ruled 6-3 that states could prohibit the use of peyote by members of the American Indian Church, the First Amendment notwithstanding (Greenhouse 1990). In the wake of this decision, Congress enacted a statute providing a defense for people who use the substance "with good faith practice of a religious belief."

MESCALINE AND PEYOTE: USES AND EFFECTS

Classification: Hallucinogen

CSA Schedule: Schedule I

Trade or Other Names: Mescal, buttons, cactus

Medical Uses: None

Physical Dependence: None

Psychological Dependence: Unknown

Tolerance: Yes

Duration (hours): 8–12

Usual Method: Oral

Possible Effects: Illusions and hallucinations, altered perception of time and distance

Effects of Overdose: Longer, more intense "trip" episodes; psychosis; possible death

Withdrawal Syndrome: Unknown

Source: U.S. Drug Enforcement Administration.

when taken orally. It is typically placed at the end of a tobacco or marijuana cigarette. A single inhalation will produce a five- to ten-minute trip. There has been little research into the substance, and it is not known whether the mushroom has toxic effects (Karch 1996).[3]

CLUB DRUGS

Club drugs is a general term for a number of illicit drugs, primarily synthetic, that are most commonly encountered at nightclubs and "raves." The drugs include MDMA (ecstasy), ketamine, GHB, GBL, and Rohypnol and BZP.

ECSTASY

Ecstasy, the common name for MDMA (3,4-*m*ethylene*d*ioxy-N-*m*eth*a*mphetamine), is a synthetic drug that has stimulant and hallucinogenic properties. Although MDMA does not cause overt hallucinations, many people report distorted time and exaggerated sensory perception while under the influence of the drug (Hanson 2001). Developed in Germany in 1914 as an appetite suppressant and for some psychiatric research (Nichols and Oberlender 1989; McNeil 2002), MDMA is but one of about 200 amphetamine analogs of the methylenedioxyamphetamine (MDA) type. Accordingly, *ecstasy* is frequently used as a generic term for this family of

---

[3]For a fascinating history of hallucinogenic mushrooms, one that debunks the myths surround the fungus, see (Letcher 2007).

substances. In the 1970s it was used by some therapists to help patients explore their feelings for each other. In a controlled setting it was reputed to promote trust between patients and physicians (Karch 1996). Recent studies indicate that MDMA used in psychotherapy is beneficial for treating post-traumatic stress disorders (Palmquiest 2009).

Ecstasy (or "X-TC") proved popular among white professionals—earning its nickname as a "yuppie drug"—and individuals who consider themselves part of the New Age spiritual movement (Beck and Rosenbaum 1994). MDMA is usually ingested orally in tablet or capsule form. It is also available as a powder and is sometimes snorted and occasionally smoked but rarely injected.

While MDMA is reported to be popular on college campuses in the United States and at dance parties known as **raves,** use has spread into varying ethnic minority groups, especially the African-American community (Dew, Elifson, and Sterk 2006).

Effects of Ecstasy MDMA has a chemical structure similar to those of the stimulant methamphetamine and the hallucinogen mescaline. MDMA increases the activity levels of at least three neurotransmitters: serotonin, dopamine, and norepinephrine; this is a likely cause of the increased heart rate and blood pressure that can accompany MDMA use (National Institute on Drug Abuse 2006). Compared to the very potent stimulant methamphetamine, MDMA causes greater serotonin release and somewhat less dopamine release (Hanson 2001). During the 1950s, along with other hallucinogens, MDMA was used—unsuccessfully—by the military as a "truth serum." It was not until its "rediscovery" in the late 1970s that ecstasy received a great deal of attention because of its purported ability to produce profound pleasurable effects: acute euphoria and long-lasting

RAVES

Raves emerged in the late 1980s, starting in the party atmosphere of a Mediterranean island frequented by British youths on vacation. Rave music originated in the United States, mainly in Detroit, Chicago, and New York. The rave scene soon spread to other European countries, Australia, New Zealand, and elsewhere around the world. Raves vary in size; some draw a few hundred people, while others draw tens of thousands. They are commonly advertised in flyers distributed in clubs and music stores and on Internet Web sites.

Raves usually start late at night and continue into the morning. A well-known disk jockey is often the rave's main attraction. Ravers often wear or carry glow sticks or other brightly lit accessories and eat lollipops and candy necklaces. Some wear painters' masks with mentholated vapor rub applied to the inside to enhance ecstasy's effects. Rave culture has become increasingly commercialized since its early days and today accounts for a large part of the youth entertainment industry. So-called energy drinks (nonalcoholic beverages laced with amino acids) are often marketed at rave clubs. Bottled water is also prevalent at raves, since participants drink a lot of water to keep their bodies hydrated and their body temperatures down (Scott 2002: 20–21).

Brand X Pictures / Alamy

Rave culture has become increasingly commercialized since its early days, and today accounts for a large part of the youth entertainment industry. MDMA is a popular drug at raves; the drug can produce stimulant effects such as an enhanced sense of pleasure and selfconfidence and increased energy. Its psychedelic effects include feelings of peacefulness, acceptance, and empathy. Users claim they experience feelings of closeness with others and a desire to touch them.

positive changes in attitude and self-confidence, some symptoms resembling those caused by LSD but without the severe side effects typically associated with methamphetamine.

> The effects of MDMA usually become apparent twenty to sixty minutes following oral ingestion of an average dose (100–125 milligrams) on an empty stomach. The sudden and intense onset of the high experienced by many users is commonly referred to as the "rush" (also the "wave" or "weird period"). This phase was often (particularly during initial use) experienced with a certain degree of trepidation, tension, stomach tightness, and/or mild nausea. This discomfort was generally transitory and melted away into a more relaxed state of being. Although novice users occasionally experienced some apprehension during this initial onset, anxiety levels typically decreased with subsequent use, allowing for increased enjoyment. (Beck and Rosenbaum 1994: 63)

MDMA: USES AND EFFECTS

Classification: Hallucinogen

CSA Schedule: Schedule I

Trade or Other Names: 2,5-DMA, STP, MDA, MDMA, ecstasy, DOM, DOB

Medical Uses: None

Physical Dependence: Unknown

Psychological Dependence: Unknown

Tolerance: Yes

Duration (hours): Variable

Usual Method: Oral, injected

Possible Effects: Illusions and hallucinations, altered perception of time and distance

Effects of Overdose: Longer, more intense "trip" episodes; psychosis; possible death

Withdrawal Syndrome: Unknown

Source: U.S. Drug Enforcement Administration.

The total effects of MDMA last from three to six hours.

The drug's rewarding effects vary with the individual taking it, the dose and purity, and the environment in which it is taken. MDMA can produce stimulant effects such as an enhanced sense of pleasure and self-confidence and increased energy; as with amphetamines, it increases heart rate and blood pressure. Its psychedelic effects include feelings of peacefulness, acceptance, and empathy. Users claim that they experience feelings of closeness with others and a desire to touch them. Because MDMA engenders feelings of closeness and trust and has a short duration of action, some clinicians claim that the drug is potentially valuable as a psychotherapeutic agent.

The mechanism by which the drug exerts its unique effects in humans is not well understood (Tancer and Schuster 1997). It is known that, like amphetamine, MDMA increases serotonin in the synapses, but it inhibits reuptake several times as much as amphetamine does. To a lesser degree, MDMA inhibits dopamine reuptake. Research indicates that ecstasy destroys serotonin-producing neurons, which play a direct role in regulating aggression, mood, sexual activity, sleep, and sensitivity to pain. It is probably this action on the serotonin system that gives it the purported properties of heightened sexual experience, tranquility, and conviviality.

Ecstasy Tolerance and Withdrawal   Although tolerance to ecstasy develops, withdrawal symptoms, if any, are not known. A study of young adults found, however, that heavy users report distinct withdrawal symptoms after MDMA use, as well as greater tolerance to MDMA over time (Dew, Elifson, and Sterk 2006).

Dangers of MDMA   Ecstasy causes large increases in blood pressure, heart rate, and myocardial oxygen consumption that can increase the risk of a cardiovascular catastrophe in people with preexisting heart disease (Mathias and Zickler 2001). Additional adverse effects include muscle tension, involuntary teeth clenching, nausea, blurred vision, feeling faint, tremors, rapid eye movement, and sweating or chills (Office of National Drug Control Policy 2002d). Because many users of MDMA use other drugs at the same time and because a dose of ecstasy may contain other drugs, it is difficult to isolate out the effects of MDMA. An increasing amount of ecstasy seized at the Canadian border contained methamphetamine (Gross 2008).

In 1985, MDMA was placed in the Drug Enforcement Administration (DEA)'s Schedule I, although some medical supporters argue for its experimental use in psychotherapy. Indeed, the DEA has been criticized for placing MDMA in Schedule I, thereby precluding its use clinically, without methodical study of the substance (Shenk 1999). Scheduling hearings on MDMA were conducted in 1985, and the administrative law judge expressed his view that there was sufficient evidence for safe utilization under medical supervision and recommended Schedule III status. He was overruled by the director of the DEA, who in 1988 placed MDMA in Schedule I—high potential for abuse, no medically accepted use. Nevertheless, there is continued interest in testing the drug for such disorders as posttraumatic stress disorder (PTSD), and in 2005 the Food and Drug Administration (FDA) approved clinical trials of the drug to treat anxiety in terminally ill cancer patients and hospital patients suffering from PTSD (McNeil 2002; Conant 2005). The consensus among drug researchers is that there is no proof that ecstasy causes any permanent damage (McNeil 2003).

In small doses, MDMA can greatly reduce the body's ability to metabolize the drug, so it remains active in the body for longer periods. When users take multiple doses over a brief period, the increased toxic effects can lead to dehydration, hypothermia, and seizures (Mathias and Zickler 2001). In high doses, ecstasy may cause the body's temperature to increase markedly (malignant hyperthermia), leading to muscle breakdown and kidney and cardiovascular system failure, which in some cases has proven fatal. Although drinking water does not reduce the effects of ecstasy, it prevents dehydration. Drinking too much water, however, can lead to serious health complications in some people. Ecstasy can also produce a hangover effect: loss of appetite, insomnia, depression, and muscle aches. It can also make concentration difficult, particularly on the day after ecstasy is taken. Higher doses of ecstasy can produce hallucinations, irrational behavior, vomiting, and convulsions. Some evidence suggests that long-term use of ecstasy might cause damage to the brain, heart, and liver. "Ecstasy users at clubs and raves dance energetically in stuffy quarters, increasing the risk of exhaustion, which can result in dangerous dehydration leading to convulsions and, on occasion, death" (Stryker 2001: D5).

"MDMA gives you tons of energy to dance for five straight hours, raises your body temperature and causes dehydration. Though you are not hallucinating, you're so swept up in that terrific sense of wellbeing that you don't feel as though you're overheating, even when you are. And if you drink too much water to quench that terrific thirst," it can be fatal (Klam 2001: 43). During intense expenditures of energy, the kidneys cannot excrete excess water, causing hyponatremia.

The extra water eventually moves into neurons and causes them to swell. With no room to expand, neurons press against the skull and compress the brain stem, which controls such vital functions as breathing.

BZP (1-BENZYLPIPERAZINE)

Originally developed as an antiparasite agent for cattle, **BZP** is an artificial stimulant—dopamine and serotonin agonist—usually consumed orally but sometimes smoked or snorted. Since 2004 it has been a Schedule I substance having no accepted medical use in the United States, although in some countries usage is less restrictive and even legal. Similar to the stimulating properties of amphetamine, BZP is often taken in combination with TFMPP (1-[3-(trifluoro-methyl) phenyl] piperazine), an unscheduled hallucinogen—it is illegal in some states—in order to enhance its spectrum of effects. It has been promoted to young people as a substitute for MDMA at raves.

PARAMETHOXYAMPHETAMINE (PMA)

PMA, an illegal synthetic hallucinogen that has stimulant effects similar to those of MDMA, is sometimes sold as ecstasy. When users take PMA thinking that they are really ingesting MDMA, they often conclude that they have taken weak ecstasy because PMA's effects take longer to appear. "They then ingest more of the substance to attain a better high, which can result in overdose and death" (Office of National Drug Control Policy 2002a: 2).

KETAMINE

Ketamine is a dissociative anesthetic similar to PCP but produces less confusion, irrationality, and violence. Developed in the 1960s, ketamine is used as a surgical anesthetic for children who are typically able to avoid unpleasant reactions, for battlefield injuries in which rapid onset is critical, and for repeated procedures such as chemotherapy and treatment of burns. It is also used in veterinary medicine, primarily to immobilize cats or monkeys. Its use in human surgery has declined with introduction of safer, more-effective products.

The synthesis of ketamine is complicated, and at this time diversion of the legitimate product—particularly from burglary of veterinary facilities—is the only known source on the street. Street users often refer to the drug as "K" or "special K," and it is sold in powder, capsule, tablet, solution, and some injectable forms. Ketamine powder can be snorted like cocaine, mixed into drinks, or smoked. The liquid is injected, applied to smokable materials, or consumed in drinks. Its illegal use is associated with "acid house" music, which also makes references to other hallucinogens, such as LSD and MDMA. Less is known about the extent of the abuse and dangers of ketamine, although habituation can result in significant mental and emotional problems (Dotson, Ackerman, and West 1995).

A pharmaceutical vial of liquid contains the equivalent of about one gram of powder. A smaller quantity, called a "bump," is about 0.2 gram and costs about $20. Ketamine can produce a very wide range of effects, and users adjust the dosage depending on the desired effect. The drug's effect can be influenced by body size, tolerance, the presence of alcohol or other drugs, the method of administration, and the setting in which the drug is consumed. In the past several years, law enforcement has encountered ketamine powder packaged in small plastic bags, folded paper, aluminum foil, and capsules. These packets commonly contain 0.2 gram and more recently 0.07 gram. Some users inhale about 0.02 gram in each nostril, repeated at five- to ten-minute intervals until the desired state is reached. A dose of 0.07 gram may produce intoxication. A larger dose of 0.2 gram may result in "kland," a "mellow, colorful wonder-world." A dose of 0.5 gram can produce a so-called "K-hole" or out-of-body, near-death experience. With repeated daily exposure, users can develop tolerance and psychological dependence. In 1999, ketamine was placed in Schedule III of the Controlled Substances Act.

ROHYPNOL

The benzodiazepine **Rohypnol** (flunitrazepam), although not approved for use in the United States, where it is classified as a Schedule III drug, is prescribed in about seventy countries for the short-term (four weeks or less) treatment of insomnia; it is the most widely prescribed sedative in Europe (Office of National Drug Control Policy 1998). It is ten times as potent as Valium. The effects begin within twenty minutes of administration and, depending on the amount ingested, may persist for more than twelve hours. The drug can be detected in urine for up to seventy-two hours (Office of National Drug Control Policy 2002c).

Rohypnol is known on the street as "rophies," "roofies," "rope," "ruffies," "R2," "roofenol," "roche," and "roachies." The illegal flunitrazepam that is sold in the United States is typically diverted from legal sources in Mexico and South America. Usually sold here in the original bubble packs of one- or two-milligram tablets, the drug is taken with alcohol or marijuana to enhance intoxication and is popular in some adolescent and young adult crowds. Heroin abusers use flunitrazepam to enhance the effects of low-quality heroin, and cocaine abusers have reported using Rohypnol to ease themselves down from a cocaine or crack binge. "Like other benzodiazepines, when taken alone, it is unlikely to cause problems. But, if combined even with a small amount of alcohol, the intoxication effects may be extreme, leading to severely impaired judgment and motor skills" (Fields 2001: 57). Eight to twenty-four hours might be required for recovery, and the person might have no memory of any events that transpired while under the influence.

Lethal overdose is unlikely. As is the case with other benzodiazepines, prolonged use will result in physical dependence. Withdrawal symptoms include headache, muscle pain, and confusion. Severe withdrawal involving hallucinations and convulsions can occur. Seizures have been reported a week or more after last use. The substance, which can be ingested orally, snorted, or injected, induces muscle relaxation, short-term amnesia, and sleep. Rohypnol takes about fifteen to twenty minutes to affect the CNS, lasts more than eight hours, and induces tolerance (Navarro 1995). Adverse effects include drowsiness, hangover, dizziness, gastrointestinal upsets, confusion, and headaches.

Because Rohypnol is colorless, odorless, and tasteless, it has been implicated in cases of "date rape": People may unknowingly be given the drug, which, when mixed with alcohol, can incapacitate a victim and prevent the person from resisting sexual assault. It can also cause a blackout and little, if any, memory of the assault. In response, in 1996 Congress passed the Drug-Induced Rape Prevention and Punishment Act, which provides for severe punishment for distribution of a controlled substance to an individual without that person's knowledge or consent and with the intent to commit a crime of violence, including rape (Navarro 1995; Seligmann and King 1996). Rohypnol can be lethal when mixed with alcohol and/or other depressants.

GHB AND GBL

Similar to Rohypnol, **GHB** (gamma-hydroxybutyrate) and its precursor **GBL** (gamma-butyrolactone) are colorless, odorless, and virtually tasteless. They are typically sold as a white powder or a clear liquid; both have a salty taste. Since about 1990, GHB has been abused in the United States for euphoric, sedative, and anabolic (bodybuilding) effects. Like Rohypnol, GHB has been associated with sexual assault (National Institute on Drug Abuse 1999c).

In very low doses, these drugs are CNS depressants; in higher doses they can produce unconsciousness and even respiratory failure. GBL was widely available as a dietary supplement in health food stores until an FDA recall in 1999. GBL is used as an industrial solvent, and tens of thousands of metric tons are produced each year and sold by its chemical name, 2(3H)-furanone dihydro (E. Brown 1999). Ingredients in GBL and GHB are found in a number of dietary supplements sold in health food stores, where they are promoted to induce sleep, build muscles, and enhance sexual performance. More than two dozen states have outlawed GHB, and at the beginning of 2000 it was placed in Schedule I of the Controlled Substances Act. It is typically manufactured from caustic chemicals such as paint or furniture polish remover, and when poorly prepared, it can cause severe chemical burns of the user's throat. An error in dosage of a tiny fraction of a gram can result in coma and death. GHB has been used by sexual predators because in addition to being rendered unconscious, victims are often unable to recall what happened. Mixing GHB or GBL with alcohol is particularly dangerous, since it enhances the drug's depressant effects.

GHB has a withdrawal syndrome that has aspects of alcohol withdrawal (delirium tremens) and benzodiazepine withdrawal (long duration of symptoms). The syndrome appears to manifest itself in patients who have self-administered GHB in an around-the-clock dosing schedule; that is, users who take GHB every two to three hours are at increased risk for the emergence of severe symptoms. GHB withdrawal can occur after several months of around-the-clock use. Because of the drug's short duration of action and rapid elimination, the signs and symptoms of GHB abstinence syndrome appear rapidly, generally within one to six hours after the last dose.

Withdrawal symptoms begin with anxiety, insomnia, tremor, and episodes of tachycardia. Symptoms may rapidly progress to a state of uncontrolled delirium and agitation (Zickler 2006). Despite its apparent dangers, GHB has been useful in treating an illness experienced by about 50,000 people who also suffer narcolepsy, a serious sleeping disorder that afflicts more than 200,000 people in the

United States. That illness, cataplexy, results in muscle weakness that can cause victims to collapse without warning. Under the brand name Xyrem, GHB has been approved by the FDA for treatment of cataplexy and is sold under severe restrictions (J. Reese 2000; "FDA: Date-Rape Drug has Medical Use" 2002).

SALVIA

A herb that is a member of the mint family—sometimes referred to as the "Magic Mint"—salvia (*Salvia divinorum*) grows over three-feet in height with large green leaves and has long been associated with Mazatec shamans in Oaxaca, Mexico, and "new agers." Reputedly, it produces profound introspective states of awareness and visions, which adherents describe as "divine inebriation." Salvia can be chewed or smoked, usually in a water pipe; shamans crush the leaves to extract its juices that they mix with water. The main active ingredient in Salvia, salvinorin A, is a potent activator of opioid receptors in the brain, but these receptors differ from those activated by opioids, such as heroin and morphine (National Institute on Drug Abuse 2007). While its effects typically disappear in a few minutes, its immediate impact on a user can be intense and, for some, quite unsettling—an out-of-body/dissociative experience, The substance is not known to be addictive nor does there appear to be dangers of overdose, but few studies have actually been done on the potential long-term harm of salvia (Sack and McDonald 2008).

Salvia is promoted on and sold via the Internet, and the substance is not a regulated by the federal Controlled Substances Act, although more than a dozen jurisdictions have enacted laws criminalizing salvia—in Florida, possession for sale is a felony punishable by 15 years in prison, and in California a misdemeanor if sold to minors.

MARIJUANA

Marijuana does not fit easily into any of the categories we have already discussed, so we will consider it separately. Its scientific name, *Cannabis sativa*, Latin for "cultivated hemp," was given by the Swedish scientist Linnaeus, which accounts for the "*L.*" that is sometimes added to the term. The plant grows wild throughout most of the tropical and temperate regions of the world, including parts of the United States. It has been cultivated for the tough fiber of its stem, and its seed is used in feed mixtures and its oil in paint. The psychoactive part of the plant is an isomer of tetrahydrocannabinol, delta9-tetrahydrocannabinol (THC), which is most highly concentrated in the leaves and resinous flowering tops.

The THC level of marijuana cigarettes varies considerably: Domestic marijuana has typically had less than 0.5 percent, although more recently cultivated plants have considerably higher levels. Indeed, the domestic cultivation of marijuana has spawned a significant market in horticultural equipment. These suppliers advertise in *High Times*, a magazine devoted to marijuana use. Much of the cultivation in the United States is accomplished indoors. The plant grows best under the same conditions that favor corn. The amount of THC in Jamaican, Colombian, and Mexican marijuana ranges from 0.5 to 4 percent; and the most select product, sinsemilla (from the Spanish *sin semilla*, "without seed"), has been found to have

MARIJUANA: USES AND EFFECTS

Classification: Cannabis

CSA Schedule: Schedule I

Trade or Other Names: Pot, Acapulco Gold, grass, reefer, sinsemilla, Thai sticks

Medical Uses: None

Physical Dependence: Unknown

Psychological Dependence: Moderate

Tolerance: Yes

Duration (hours): 2–4

Usual Method: Smoked, oral

Possible Effects: Euphoria, relaxed inhibitions, increased appetite, disorientation

Effects of Overdose: Fatigue, paranoia, possible psychosis

Withdrawal Syndrome: Occasional reports of insomnia, hyperactivity, decreased appetite

Source: U.S. Drug Enforcement Administration.

as much as 8 percent THC. Male plants are killed so that the female plant, in seeking to trap pollen, produces more and more of the sticky resin that covers the buds. These buds can grow as large as a man's arm from the fingertips to the elbow. Growers concentrate on sinsemilla, selling these flowering tops; indeed, nowadays the leaves of the cannabis plant ("shake") are typically discarded. Indoor cultivation has been aided by miniaturization ("marijuana bonsai") of plants with an abundance of THC-rich buds (Pollan 1995).

Hashish, usually from the Middle East, contains the drug-rich resinous secretions of the cannabis plant, which are collected, dried, and then compressed into a variety of forms: balls, cakes, or cookie-like sheets. Hashish has a potency as high as 10 percent THC. It is usually mixed with tobacco and smoked in a pipe. Hashish oil—a misnomer—is simply the result of repeated extractions of cannabis plant materials to yield a dark, viscous liquid with a THC level as high as 20 percent. A drop or two on a tobacco cigarette has the effect of a single marijuana cigarette. Marijuana prepared for street sale may be diluted with oregano, catnip, or other ingredients and may also contain psychoactive substances such as LSD. Marijuana from Vietnam often contained opium.

EFFECTS OF CANNABIS

Cannabis preparations can be eaten or drunk in mixtures of resin and water or milk, a form known in India as *bhang*. In the United States, marijuana is usually rolled in paper or inserted into a hollowed-out cigar ("blunting") and smoked, the user typically inhaling the smoke deeply and holding it in the lungs for as long as possible. This tends to maximize the absorption of THC, about one half of which

HASHISH: USES AND EFFECTS

Classification: Cannabis

CSA Schedule: Schedule I

Trade or Other Names: Hash, hash oil

Medical Uses: None

Physical Dependence: Unknown

Psychological Dependence: Moderate

Tolerance: Yes

Duration (hours): 2–4

Usual Method: Smoked; Oral

Possible Effects: Euphoria, relaxed inhibitions, increased appetite, disorientation

Effects of Overdose: Fatigue, paranoia, possible psychosis

Withdrawal Syndrome: Occasional reports of insomnia, hyperactivity, decreased appetite

Source: U.S. Drug Enforcement Administration.

is lost during smoking. THC appears to act as a dopamine agonist while also having an opiate-like effect on the brain's receptor system (M. Gold 1994). The psychoactive reaction occurs in one to ten minutes and peaks in about ten to thirty minutes, with a total duration of about three to four hours.

In 1990, researchers discovered **cannabinoid receptors** discretely located throughout the brain to receive *endocannabinoids*, natural brain compounds similar to THC that play a role in numerous physiological processes including appetite, memory, and pain. These receptors react to compounds in cannabis, triggering similar effects. Marijuana also triggers the release of dopamine, which stimulates pleasure centers of the brain and a craving for more marijuana (Blakeslee 1997; Carroll 2002).

The most important variables with respect to the drug's impact are the individual's experiences and expectations and the strength of the marijuana. Thus, the first-time user might not experience any significant reaction. In general, low doses tend to induce restlessness, an increasing sense of well-being, and gregariousness, followed by a dreamy state of relaxation and frequently hunger, especially for sweets. Higher doses may induce changes in sensory perception, resulting in a more vivid sense of smell, sight, hearing, and taste, which may be accompanied by subtle alterations in thought formation and expression.

MARIJUANA TOLERANCE AND WITHDRAWAL

Animal and human studies conducted since the 1970s have revealed a marijuana withdrawal syndrome, which, though less severe than that for alcohol, heroin, or cocaine, is characterized by insomnia, restlessness, loss of appetite, irritability, anger, and aggression (Carroll 2002). In 1999, a study found that people who have smoked marijuana daily for many years display more aggressive behavior when they stop smoking the drug (National Institute on Drug Abuse 1999a). However, THC has a very long half-life, working its way out of the body slowly over many days and thereby obviating severe withdrawal symptoms (Markel 2002). In fact, marijuana withdrawal is similar to that experienced by cigarette smokers when they quit (Carroll 2002; Zickler 2002). "Most symptoms begin within 24 to 48 hours of abstinence, peak within 4 to 6 days, and last from 1 to 3 weeks" (Budney et al. 2007: 10).

DANGERS OF MARIJUANA USE

Caution must be exercised in determining the health effects of any drug, particularly marijuana which in the United States is at the center of a great deal of controversy that intertwines with politics.

"Doses of illicit drugs used over periods of years are difficult to quantify because of the varied dosages of blackmarket drugs and stigma in admitting to illicit drug use. Interpretation is complicated by the fact that regular cannabis users often also use alcohol, tobacco and other illicit drugs" (Hall, Degenhardt, and Lynskey 2001: xv).

The negative short-term effects of marijuana seem quite limited; there is loss of inhibition, and some users also experience a loss of self-confidence, aggressiveness, and even auditory hallucinations. High doses impair learning, short-term memory, and reaction time (Misner and Sullivan 1999). The more-potent marijuana ingested by users today, compared to that of the heady days of Woodstock and the 1960s, is more likely to bring on paranoia in some users (Markel 2002).

Marijuana causes a significant increase in heart rate; however, this increase is no more dangerous than that caused by using caffeine or nicotine. Casual use of marijuana results in the same impairments that one would expect from equal amounts of alcohol (Abel 1978). The long-range effects are more controversial, some claiming no significant physical or psychological damage and others finding the opposite. Although most marijuana users are able to quit, there appears to a small portion of that population, 10–14 percent, who become strongly dependent (Carroll 2002).

Marijuana is frequently referred to (by government and "drug warrior" sources) as a *gateway drug*. In other words, the "road to drug hell"—abuse of heroin and cocaine—begins with marijuana. Although many, if not most, users of hard drugs did at one time use marijuana (e.g., Office of National Drug Control Policy 2004), they also smoked cigarettes and used alcohol as well as caffeine, and the majority of marijuana users aged 12–17 also use alcohol (McCurley and Snyder 2008). The most obvious connection between marijuana and "harder drugs" is via the retail dealer, who is often a "walking drug store." Because marijuana is illegal, enterprising outlaws selling the substance might have a smorgasbord of products available to tempt marijuana users, possibly when their preferred substance is unavailable or from a desire for novelty.

Marijuana has use in medicine to relieve the pressure on the eyes of glaucoma patients, to control the nausea and vomiting that accompany cancer chemotherapy, and to control the muscle spasms of multiple sclerosis patients. The policy implications of "medical marijuana" are discussed in Chapter 14.

INHALANTS

Commonly abused inhalants are usually **volatile substances** such as hydrocarbon solvents produced from petroleum and natural gas; the two main exceptions are **amyl nitrite** and **nitrous oxide**. (*Volatile* means that the hydrocarbons evaporate when exposed to air; *solvents* refers to their capacity, in liquid form, to dissolve many other substances.) Inhalants include a variety of readily available products that are often kept in the home. They can be divided into four classes:

1. *Volatile solvents*, such as glue, paint thinner, cleaning fluid, nail polish remover, and gasoline
2. *Aerosols*, such as hair spray, spray paint, frying pan lubricants, and deodorants
3. *Anesthetics*, such as nitrous oxide ("laughing gas" used as a whipped cream propellant) and ether
4. *Volatile nitrates*, such as amyl nitrate, a prescription drug used to treat angina, and butyl nitrate, formerly used in room deodorizers but now illegal

Toluene (methyl benzene), a common ingredient of most solvents, has the greatest abuse potential, and some industries have added mustard oil to their toluene-rich products so that the nasal irritation it causes will deter abusers. For a long time the mechanism by which toluene attracts users was not known. In 2003, researchers at the University of Arizona discovered that the substance enhances dopamine activity in the brain's pleasure center. In other words, toluene is in the same category as other drugs that are subject to abuse (Sherman 2005).

EFFECTS OF INHALANTS AND SOLVENTS

With some exceptions, inhalants and solvents are not usually produced for their psychoactive qualities, but when used for mind-altering purposes, they are drugs. Although different in makeup, nearly all abused inhalants produce effects similar to those of anesthetics: They slow down the body's functions (National Institute on Drug Abuse 2001b). In general, these chemicals are abused by young (preadolescent and adolescent) males, although some, such as the volatile nitrites, are popular among aficionados of anal sex because they relax the sphincter muscles; they are also reputed to increase the intensity of orgasm. Inhaled vapors from solvents and propellants enter the bloodstream directly from the lungs and are then rapidly distributed to the brain and liver, the organs with the largest blood supply. Most volatile hydrocarbons are fat-soluble and are thus absorbed quickly into the central nervous system.

Immediate effects are very similar to those of alcohol and include feeling less inhibited, disoriented, and uncoordinated. After inhaling, there is a euphoric feeling, characterized by lightheadedness and exhilaration. The effects of the first brief inhalation fade after several minutes. The experienced user may prolong the effects for up to twelve hours, increasing the dose by concentrating the drug inside a plastic bag and continuing to sniff. For the majority of users, most effects disappear within an hour after sniffing is stopped, although hangovers and headaches can last several days.

Although some volatile hydrocarbons are metabolized and then excreted through the kidneys, many are eliminated from the body unchanged, primarily through the lungs. The odor of solvents may therefore remain on the breath for several hours following inhalation. The complete elimination of volatile hydrocarbons can take some time, since they are released slowly from fatty tissues back into the blood.

INHALANT TOLERANCE AND WITHDRAWAL

Regular users can become dependent on volatile substances, as the substances become important in their daily lives. But even with extended use, the possibility of developing tolerance is very small. It is also rare for withdrawal symptoms to occur when a person stops using (Hormes, Filley, and Rosenberg 1986). Very heavy users, however, may experience headaches, muscular cramps, and abdominal pain.

DANGERS OF INHALANT USE

Research evidence suggests that short-term use of volatile substances rarely causes permanent damage, and effects are reversible if the person stops using inhalants. The dangers of inhalants have often been exaggerated, but long-term use of aerosols and cleaning fluids can damage the kidneys, liver, and brain, though this is rare. Perception and coordination become impaired, and heavy use can cause unconsciousness. The "high" may be accompanied by sedation, hallucinations, and delusions. High dosage can result in vomiting, paralysis, and coma. A common method of use, a plastic bag covering the head, can lead to unconsciousness and death by suffocation.

The long-term inhaling of leaded gasoline can cause leukemia and various types of cancers, because the lead accumulates in the body. Other physical effects of gasoline sniffing can include anorexia, seizure, and "sudden sniffing syndrome." This syndrome is caused by heart failure that can happen if a person does strenuous exercise or has a sudden fright immediately after sniffing. However, this is rare and is usually associated with aerosols, butane gas, and cleaning fluid. The harms that are most associated with volatile substances depend on how and where they are sniffed. Deaths or accidents can occur as a result of sniffing in unsafe places, such as on a roof or by a railroad line (information from the Centre for Education and Information on Drugs and Alcohol in New South Wales).

Research sponsored by the National Institute on Drug Abuse (Mathias 2002) revealed that chronic inhalant abuse is associated with brain abnormalities and cognitive impairment at a considerably higher rate than that experienced by cocaine abusers.

PRESCRIPTION AND OVER-THE-COUNTER DRUG ABUSE

According to various surveys, more than seven million Americans use psychoactive prescription drugs for nonmedical purposes annually—a number greater than that for cocaine, heroin, hallucinogens, and inhalants combined. Most (about 65 percent) are young adults aged 18 to 25; more teens report abusing prescription drugs (19 percent in grades 7–12) than any illicit drug except marijuana (CESAR 2009b). In 2008, more than 15 percent of twelfth graders reported using a prescription drug nonmedically (National Institute on Drug Abuse data). The National Institute on Drug Abuse (2005: 1) estimates that 48 million Americans over age 12 have used prescription drugs for nonmedical reasons in their lifetime. About 10 percent of high school students report nonmedical use of prescription drugs. In addition, according to the National Institute of Drug Abuse, the elderly are among those most vulnerable to prescription misuse and abuse: persons 65 years of age and above comprise 13 percent of the U.S. population but are prescribed approximately one-third of all medications.

Pain relievers are the most widely abused prescription medicines. They include: codeine, fentanyl (Duragesic, Actiq), hydromorphone (Dilaudid), meperidine (Demerol), morphine (MS Contin), oxycodone (OxyContin), pentazocine (Talwin), dextropropoxyphene (Darvon), methadone (Dolophine), and hydrocodone combinations (Vicodin, Lortab, and Lorcet). "Prescription stimulants are abused to a much lesser extent, primarily by young adults who reportedly use the drugs in an attempt to enhance their academic, professional, or athletic performance" (National Drug Intelligence Center 2008a: IV).

There are three classes of prescription drugs that are most commonly abused:

Opiods, such as Darvon, Demoerol, methadone, morphine, OxyContin, Percocet, Percodan, and Vicodin, which are prescribed to treat pain.

Central nervous system depressants and barbiturates, such as Amytal, Nembutal, Seconal, and Phenobarbital, and tranquilizers such as Valium, and Xanax, which are used to treat anxiety and sleep disorders; and

Stimulants, such as Adderall, Concerta, Dexedrine, and Ritalin, which are prescribed to treat the sleep disorder narcolepsy, attention deficit hyperactivity disorder ADHD), and depression

"ADHD is characterized by a persistent pattern of inattention and/or hyperactivity-impulsivity that is more frequently displayed and more severe than is typically observed in individuals at a comparable level of development. This pattern of behavior usually becomes evident in the preschool or early elementary years, and the median age of onset of ADHD symptoms is 7 years. For many individuals, ADHD symptoms improve during adolescence or as age increases, but the disorder can persist into adulthood" (National Institute on Drug Abuse 2008c: 1).

The stimulant methylphenidate (Ritalin) has much in common with cocaine: both bind to similar sites in the brain, and when administered intravenously, they both cause a rapid and large increase in dopamine that is experienced as a rush or high. While its effects are similar to those of amphetamine, methylphenidate is less potent and often the preferred drug for treating ADHD. Researchers speculate that by amplifying the release of dopamine, methylphenidate improves attention and focus in individuals who have dopamine signals that are weak, such as persons with ADHD. Taken orally, as prescribed, Ritalin elicits a gradual and sustained increase in dopamine, "which is not perceived as euphoria and instead produces the expected therapeutic effects seen in many patients" (Nora Volkow in Drug Enforcement Administration 2008: 12). Research reveals that people with ADHD do not become addicted to stimulant medications when they are taken in the form prescribed and at treatment dosages. Indeed, one study found that boys with ADHD who are treated with stimulants such as methylphenidate are significantly less likely to abuse drugs and alcohol when they are older when compared to nontreated boys with ADHD ("Methylphenidate" 2001).

Because of its stimulant properties, methylphenidate is abused by people for whom it is not a medication. Some abuse it for appetite suppression, wakefulness,

RITALIN: USES AND EFFECTS

Classification: Stimulant

CSA Schedule: Schedule II

Trade or Other Names: Methylphenidate

Medical Uses: Attention-deficit/hyperactivity disorder, narcolepsy

Physical Dependence: Possible

Psychological Dependence: High

Tolerance: Yes

Duration (hours): 2–4

Usual Method: Oral, injected

Possible Effects: Increased alertness, excitation, euphoria, increased pulse rate and blood pressure, insomnia, loss of appetite

Effects of Overdose: Agitation, increased body temperature, hallucinations, convulsions, possible death

Withdrawal Syndrome: Apathy, long periods of sleep, irritability, depression, disorientation

Source: U.S. Drug Enforcement Administration.

increased focus/attentiveness, and euphoria. When abused, the tablets are taken either orally or crushed and snorted. Some abusers dissolve the tablets in water and inject the mixture; complications can arise from this because insoluble fillers in the tablets can block small blood vessels (National Institute on Drug Abuse 2001e). There are reports of Ritalin being used illegally by college students, often as an aid in staying awake for late night studying during exam week (Zielbauer 2000).

A recent phenomenon is leading prescription drug abusers to heroin use. At "pharm parties," adolescents share whatever they have been able to acquire (often purloined from a home medicine cabinet). Those who are determined to continue drug use must eventually find new sources. When the cost of pharmaceuticals on the black market exceeds that of heroin, the user now makes a giant leap into a new world of "junkies" (Wolvier, Martino, Jr., and Bolger 2009). "Many abusers of prescription opiates such as OxyContin [oxycodone],[4] Percocet, and Vicodin eventually begin abusing heroin because it is typically cheaper and easier to obtain, and it provides a more intense high." And "once an individual switches from prescription opiates to heroin, he or she rarely switches back to exclusively abusing prescription opiates" (National Drug Intelligence Center 2009a: 25–26).

Prescription drugs are typically abused by white people of at least middle class status for whom they are easier to acquire than their illegal street counterparts; and

---

[4]Oxycodone is the active ingredient in a number of commonly prescribed pain relief medications such as Percocet and Percodan. These medications contain oxycodone in smaller doses and are combined with other active ingredients like aspirin or acetaminophen.

TABLE 6.1 | PRESCRIPTION DRUG ABUSE CHART

Substances: Category and Name	Examples of Commercial and Street Names	DEA Schedule*/ How Administered**	Intoxication Effects/Potential Health Consequences
Depressants			*reduced pain and anxiety; feeling of well-being; lowered inhibitions; slowed pulse and breathing; lowered blood pressure; poor concentration/ confusion, fatigue; impaired coordination, memory, judgment; respiratory depression and arrest, addiction*
barbiturates	*Amytal, Nembutal, Seconai, phenbarbital;* barbs, reds, red birds, phennies, tooies, yellows, yellow jackets	II, III, V/injected, swallowed	
			Also, for barbiturates—sedation, drowsiness/ depression, unusual excitement, fever, irritability, poor judgment, slurred speech, dizziness
Benzodiazepines (other than flunitrazepam)	*Ativan, Halcion, Librium, Valium, Xanax;* candy, downers, sleeping pills, tranks	IV/swallowed	
			for benzodiazepines—sedation, drowsiness/dizziness
flunitrazepam****+	*Robypnol;* forget-me pill, Mexican Valium, R2, Roche, roofies, roofinol, rope, rophies	IV/swallowed, snorted	*for flunitrazepam—visual and gastrointestinal disturbances, urinary retention, memory loss for the time under the drug's effects*
Dissociative Anesthetics			*increased heart rate and blood pressure, impaired molar function/memory loss; numbness; nausea/ vomiting*
Ketamine	*Ketalar SV;* cat Valium, K, Special K, vitamin K	III/injected, snorted, smoked	
			Also, for Ketamine—at high doses, delirium, depression, respiratory depression and arrest
Opioids and Morphine Derivatives			
codeine	*Empirin with Codeine, Fiorinal with Codeine, Robitussin A-C, Tylenol with Codeine;* Captain Cody, Cody, schoolboy; (with glutethimide) doors & fours, loads, pancakes and syrup	II, III, IV/injected, swallowed	*Pain relief, euphoria, drowsiness/respiratory depression and arrest, nausea, confusion, constipation, sedation, unconsciousness, coma, tolerance, addiction*
			Also, for codeine—less analgesia, sedation, and respiratory depression than morphine
fentany	*Actiq, Duragesic, Sublimaze;* Apache, China girl, China white, dance fever, friend, goodfella, jackpot, murder 8, TNT, Tango and cash	II/injected, smoked, snorted	
morphine	*Roxanol, Duramorph; M,* Miss Emma, monkey, white stuff	II, III/injected, swallowed, smoked	

Substance	Examples of Commercial and Street Names	Schedule/How Administered	Intoxication Effects/Potential Health Consequences
opium	*Laudanum, paregone* big O, black stuff, block, gum, hop	II, III, V/swallowed, smoked	
Other opioid pain relievers (oxycodone, meperidine, hydromorphone, hydrocodone, propoxyphene)	*Tylox, OxyContin, Percodan, Percocet,* oxy 80s, oxycotton, oxycet, hillbilly heroin, percs *Demeral,mependine hydrochloride;* demmies, pain killer *Dilaudid;* juice, dillies *Vicodin, Lortab, Lorcet; Darvon, Darvocet*	II, III, IV/swallowed, injected, suppositories, chewed, Crushed, snorted	
Stimulants			*increased heart rate, blood pressure, metabolism; feelings of exhilaration, energy, increased mental alertness/rapid or irregular heart beat; reduced appetite, weight loss, heart failure*
amphetamines	*Biphetamine, Dexedrine;* bennies, black beauties, crosses, hearts, LA turnaround, speed, truck drivers, uppers	II/injected, swallowed, smoked, snorted	*Also, for amphetamines—rapid breathing;* hallucinations/tremor, loss of coordination; irritability, anxiousness, restlessness, delirium, panic, paranoia, impulsive behavior, aggressiveness, tolerance, addiction
cocaine	*Cocaine hydrochloride; blow,* bump, C, candy, Charlie, coke, crack, flake, rock, snow, toot	II/injected, smoked, snorted	*For cocaine*—increased temperature/chest pain, respiratory failure, nausea, abdominal pain, strokes, seizures, headaches, malnutrition
methamphetamine	*Desoxyn;* chalk, crank, crystal, fire, glass, go fast, ice, meth, speed	II/injected, swallowed, smoked, snorted	*For methamphetamine—aggression, violence, psychotic behavior/*memory loss, cardiac and neurological damage; impaired memory and learning, tolerance, addiction
methylphenidate	*Ritalin;* JIF, MPH, R-ball, Skippy, the smart drug, vitamin R	II/injected, swallowed, snorted	*For methylphenidate—increase or decrease in blood pressure, psychotic episodes/digestive problems, loss of appetite, weight loss*

*Schedule I and II drugs have a high potential for abuse. They require greater storage security and have a quota on manufacturing, among other restrictions. Schedule I drugs are available for research only and have no approved medical use; Schedule II drugs are available only by prescription (unrefillable) and require a form for ordering. Schedule III and IV drugs are available by prescription, may have five refills in 6 months, and may be ordered orally. Most Schedule V drugs are available over the counter.

**Taking drugs by injection can increase the risk of infection through needle contamination with staphylococci, HIV, hepatitis, and other organisms.

***Associated with sexual assaults.

†Not available by prescription in the United States.

Source: National Institute on Drug Abuse

Prescription Drugs and Alcohol

When alcohol and prescription drugs are used simultaneously, severe medical problems can result, including alcohol poisoning, unconsciousness, respiratory depression, and sometimes death. Passing out is a protective mechanism that stops people from drinking when they are approaching potentially dangerous blood alcohol concentrations. But if a person takes stimulants when drinking, the combination can potentially override this protective mechanism and lead to life-threatening consequences (Ashton 2008).

they may be cheaper than heroin and cocaine. The cost of an evening's worth of cocaine or heroin can run into hundreds of dollars, whereas in Miami, dealers sell Vicodin, Valium, Xanax, and OxyContin, a painkiller often given to cancer patients, for as little as three to four dollars a pill. "The only major category of illegal drug use to have risen since 2002, prescription drug abuse poses a particular challenge, as these substances are widely available to treat legitimate medical conditions and can often be obtained within the home" (Office of National Drug Control Strategy 2008: 3). Nonmedical use of prescription drugs appears, at least in part, to be related to the mistaken belief that these substances are less harmful than "illegal drugs" and, they thereby, avoid the stigma typically associated with the latter.

According to data from the national Monitoring the Future Survey, friends and family are the source of most prescription amphetamines and painkillers used non-medically by high school seniors. More than one-half of twelfth graders who used prescription drugs non-medically in the past year reported getting them for free, while more than one-third reported buying them from a friend or relative. High school seniors also report getting prescription drugs from other sources, such as from drug dealers or buying them over the Internet (CESAR 2009c):

Illegal pharmaceutical sales are promoted by Internet facilitators who have no medical or pharmaceutical training and are not DEA registrants. These facilitators start by targeting doctors who may be carrying a significant debt, such as a young doctor fresh out of medical school, or those who have retired and are looking for some extra income. The facilitator convinces these doctors that it is OK to approve the prescriptions because they will be provided with some purported "medical history" (often submitted by the "patient" through completion of an online questionnaire). What has become increasingly common is for the facilitator to provide an opportunity for the doctor to have a telephone conversation with the "patient" or for the "patient" to fax or email "medical" information to the doctor. Such communications fall far short of legitimate telemedicine-based medical consultations. The doctor then approves a prescription for a Schedule III or Schedule IV substance with the mistaken belief or "justification" that these substances are not as "dangerous" as those in Schedule II. (Note: The criminal penalties for violations involving Schedule II substances can be significantly higher than for those involving a Schedule III or IV substance.) This poorly constructed veil of medical evaluation is designed to provide added justification for the requested medicine. And for every prescription the doctor authorizes, the Internet facilitator will pay the doctor anywhere from ten to twenty-five dollars. Law enforcement has discovered Web site-affiliated doctors who authorize hundreds of prescriptions a day.

The Internet facilitators will also recruit pharmacies into their scheme. They often target small, independent pharmacies struggling to make ends meet. The Internet facilitator will tell the pharmacist that all they have to do is fill and ship these prescriptions to customers, that the prescriptions have all been approved by a doctor, and that they are only for Schedule III or Schedule IV substances. In addition to paying the pharmacy for the cost of the medicine, the Internet facilitator will also pay the pharmacy an agreed upon amount that may reach into the millions of dollars. (Rannazzisi 2008: 1)

In 2009, Drug Enforcement Administration (DEA) regulations implementing the Ryan Haight Online Pharmacy Consumer Protection Act of 2008 went into effect. The Ryan Haight Act is named after an 18-year-old who died after overdosing on a prescription painkiller he obtained on the Internet from a medical doctor he never saw. The statute amends the Controlled Substances Act (CSA) by adding several new provisions to prevent the illegal distribution of controlled substances by means of the Internet, including:

- New definitions, such as "online pharmacy" and "deliver, distribute, or dispense by means of the Internet"
- A requirement of at least one face-to-face patient medical evaluation prior to issuance of a controlled substance prescription
- Registration requirements for online pharmacies
- Internet pharmacy Web site disclosure information requirements; and
- Prescription reporting requirements for online pharmacies.

These drugs are popular because even without a doctor's prescription, access is increasing. Restocking trips are often taken to Mexico, where the black market continues to grow. It is estimated that Tijuana alone has about 1,700 pharmacies, many of which sell controlled substances illegally over the counter. And in some instances, doctors in Mexico sell prescriptions (Kirsebbaum 2002). Diversion from lawful sources, often the result of "doctor shopping" or overprescribing, has gained more attention in recent years (Querna 2005).

One aspect of this problem is trafficking in the synthetic opiate **OxyContin**, particularly in rural areas of the United States that have not heretofore had a drug problem. In the rural Appalachian region, which has many miners with injuries and a shortage of doctors, prescribing of the drug has often been indiscriminate. A similar situation has occurred among injured steelworkers in Eastern Ohio. The result has been diversion to the black market. In these areas, a number of doctors have been convicted for overprescribing (Bowman 2005). In 2009, a Dayton, Ohio, physician was sentenced to 84 months imprisonment for selling prescriptions at his storefront clinic for OxyContin, amphetamine, and methadone—700,000 dosage units in a nine-month period (FBI press release, September 11, 2009).

In 2003, it was revealed that methadone, often prescribed for treating chronic pain, is being diverted to the black market and abused by recreational drug users, with often deadly consequences. There have been an alarming number of methadone overdose fatalities, which since 1997 have surpassed those from heroin.

Methadone is usually taken when the drug of choice, heroin or OxyContin, is not readily available (Belluck 2003).

One physician set up a pain management practice in Portsmith, Ohio. At about the same time police noticed a startling rise in drug-related crime. Undercover agents were dispatched to the pain clinic. With little or no physical examination, each paid $200 and was given a prescription for OxyContin. In a subsequent raid, agents found almost $500,000 in cash and passbooks for offshore accounts ("'Poor Man's Heroin'" 2001). In 2002, a 55-year-old Florida medical doctor received a sentence of 62 years in prison after a manslaughter conviction that involved running an OxyContin "pill mill" that was linked to several overdose deaths (Associated Press 2002). In addition, significant quantities of prescription drugs are diverted from legitimate commerce through armed robbery, employee theft, and pharmacy break-ins (National Drug Intelligence Center 2009ab). Massive amounts of prescription opiates are being stolen prior to medical dispensing and potentially being fed into illicit drug markets (Fischer, Gittins, and Rehm 2008).

In 2005, people who used prescription drugs nonmedically were asked how they obtained the drugs they used most recently. Almost 60 percent got the drugs from "a friend" for free; about 17 percent were prescribed the drugs by a doctor; about 4 percent purchased them from a dealer or other stranger; and about 1 percent bought them over the Internet (*SAMHSA News* 2006).

The issue of prescription drug abuse is intertwined with the role of physicians treating patients experiencing high levels of pain: "Pain produces high levels of hormones that inflict stress on heart and lungs. Pain can cause blood pressure to spike, leading to heart attacks and strokes. "Pain can also consume so much of the body's energy that the immune system degrades" (Rosenberg 2007: 50). But a doctor prescribing high dose of pain medication, such as OxyContin, runs the risk of scrutiny by state and federal officials concerned with prescription fraud, doctor shopping, overprescribing, and the diversion of prescription drugs to the black market. Doctors receive little training in medical school about dealing with pain, and there are relatively few doctors who specialize in pain management. Unlike other ailments, pain cannot be measured with an MRI, an x-ray, or blood tests, leaving physicians in a quandary: undermedicate or risk overprescribing. And prescription monitoring by government agencies threatens to compromise the pain treatment practices which have taken a long time to be realized, bringing the war on drugs directly in opposition to the war on pain (Fischer, Gittins, and Rehm 2008).

The death of Michael Jackson in 2009 cast a spotlight on **propofol** (Diprivan), a widely used, short-acting intravenous sedative-hypnotic used in the induction and maintenance of anesthesia or sedation, that which not produce post-operative grogginess or nausea. The substance was introduced two decades ago to replace sodium pentothal, which has unpleasant side effects. A white milky liquid that is not a federally controlled substance, propofol is typically abused by medical professionals, anesthesiologists, in particular, for its ability to induce relaxation or sleep; it can also produce mild euphoria, hallucinations, and disinhibition. Because it leaves the bloodstream quickly, the substance is difficult to detect. Propofol is extremely dangerous as it depresses respiration and blood pressure to the point of death if not constantly monitored (Belluck 2009; "Propofol Abuse Growing Problem for Anesthesiologists" 2007).

Adolescents also abuse some over-the-counter (OTC) drugs, primarily cough and cold remedies that contain dextromethorphan (DXM), a synthetic drug related to codeine and used as a cough suppressant. Products with DXM include NyQuil, Coricidin, and Robitussin, among others. Although DXM is generally recognized as safe when used appropriately, when taken in large amounts, it produces hallucinations and a "high" similar to that of PCP. Side effects include blurred vision, loss of coordination, abdominal pain, and rapid heartbeat. OTC drugs taken with alcohol increased the chances of dangerous complications.

NOOTROPICS/NEUROENHANCERS

To judge by discussions on the Internet, the use of drugs developed for recognized medical conditions, such as ADHD and sleep disorders, to strengthen ordinary cognition is widespread. According to Margaret Talbot (2009: 32), these *neuroenhancers* are used by "high-functioning, overcommitted people to become higher-functioning and more overcommitted." They reputedly enhance focus and concentration, thwart sleepiness and fatigue, and improve memory. The two most popular cognitive enhancers are Adderall and Provigil (monafinil).

Adderall is the brand name for a stimulant composed of amphetamine salts that increase the amount of norepinephrine and dopamine in the brain. Adderall is a Schedule II drug under the Controlled Substance Act (CSA). *Modafinil* is a generic term for Provigil, a stimulant drug approved by the U.S. Food and Drug Administration (FDA) for the treatment of narcolepsy, shift work sleep disorder, and excessive daytime sleepiness associated with obstructive sleep apnea. Modafinil is currently classified as a nonnarcotic CSA Schedule IV controlled substance. A third, *piracetam*, and related substances, is available as a "supplement" and has not been approved by the FDA for any use in the United States.

SUMMARY

- A hallucinogen changes perceptions: the person sees things or hears sounds that do not exist. They can also produce changes in thought, sense of time, and mood.
- Hallucinogenic substances occur both naturally and synthetically. They excite the central nervous system (CNS), overwhelming its ability to modulate sensory input.
- The effects of LSD range from blurred vision to a visual field filled with strange objects. Three-dimensional space appears to contract and enlarge, and light appears to fluctuate in intensity. Auditory effects also occur but to a lesser degree. All of these changes are

episodic. Body images are altered (out-of-body experiences) and body parts appear to float. Normally unnoticed aspects of the environment capture the attention.

- There are "good acid trips" and "bad acid trips." They appear to be controlled by the user's attitude, mood, and expectations and often depend on suggestions of those around the user at the time of the trip. Favorable expectations produce good trips, and excessive apprehension is likely to produce the opposite.
- Tolerance develops rapidly; repeated doses become completely ineffective after a few

- days of continuous use, and there is cross-tolerance to other hallucinogens.
- LSD is not considered an addictive drug, since it does not produce compulsive drug-seeking behavior. But because tolerance develops rapidly, some users take progressively higher doses to achieve the state of intoxication that they had previously achieved—a dangerous practice, given the unpredictability of the substance.
- Phencyclidine (PCP) induces a lack of responsive awareness not only of pain but also of the general environment. The user experiences a sense of detachment, distance, and estrangement from his or her surroundings. often accompanied by feelings of invulnerability. PCP can result in mood disorders, acute anxiety, paranoia, and violent behavior.
- Some natural substances, such as mescaline, produce effects similar to those of the synthetic hallucinogens. Psilocybin is the primary hallucinogenic ingredient of the fleshy part of the small spineless peyote cactus.
- "Club drugs" is a general term for a number of illicit drugs, primarily synthetic, that are most commonly encountered at nightclubs and "raves." They include MDMA (ecstasy), ketamine, GHB, GBL, and Rohypnol.
- MDMA has a chemical structure similar to those of the stimulant methamphetamine and the hallucinogen mescaline.
- When MDMA users take multiple doses over a brief period, the increased toxic effects can lead to dehydration, hypothermia, and seizures. High doses of ecstasy may cause the body's temperature to increase markedly (malignant hyperthermia), leading to muscle breakdown and kidney and cardiovascular system failure, which in some cases has proven fatal.
- Rohypnol is sometimes called the "date rape" drug because it is colorless, odorless, and tasteless and can thus be administered to victims unknowingly. When mixed with alcohol, rohypnol can incapacitate a victim and prevent the person from resisting sexual assault. It can also cause a blackout, leaving little, if any, memory of the assault.
- GBL (gamma-butyrolactone) is a CNS depressant. In high doses it can produce unconsciousness and even respiratory failure. GBL was widely available as a dietary supplement in health food stores until an FDA recall in 1999.
- Marijuana triggers the release of dopamine, which stimulates pleasure centers of the brain and a craving for more marijuana.
- The most important variables with respect to marijuana's impact are the individual's experiences and expectations and the strength of the drug.
- Interpretation of the impacts of marijuana use is complicated by the fact that regular cannabis users often also use alcohol, tobacco, and illicit drugs.
- Marijuana has use in medicine to relieve the pressure on the eyes of glaucoma patients, to control the nausea and vomiting that accompany cancer chemotherapy, and to control the muscle spasms of multiple sclerosis patients.
- Inhalants include a variety of readily available products that are often kept in the home, such as glue, paint thinner, cleaning fluid, nail polish remover, and gasoline; aerosols, such as hair spray, spray paint, frying pan lubricants, and deodorants; and anesthetics, such as nitrous oxide (a whipped cream propellant).
- Immediate effects of inhalants are very similar to those of alcohol and include feeling less inhibited, disoriented, and uncoordinated.
- There are three classes of prescription drugs that are most commonly abused: opiods prescribed to treat pain; central nervous system depressants used to treat anxiety and sleep disorders; and stimulants, prescribed to treat the sleep disorder narcolepsy, attention deficit hyperactivity disorder, and depression.
- Nonmedical use of prescription drugs appears, at least in part, to be related to the

mistaken belief that these substances are less harmful than "illegal drugs" and that they thereby avoid the stigma typically associated with the latter.

- Adolescents abuse some over-the-counter drugs, primarily cough and cold remedies, to get high.

- Neuroenhancers reputedly enhance focus and concentration, thwart sleepiness and fatigue, and improve memory. The two most popular cognitive enhancers are Adderall and Provigil (monafinil).

Review Questions

1. What are the effects of ingesting a hallucinogen?
2. How do hallucinogens affect the central nervous system?
3. How do hallucinogens cause these effects?
4. What determines whether an LSD trip will be a good one or a bad one?
5. What are the effects of ingesting phencyclidine (PCP)?
6. What are dangers of PCP use?
7. What two drug properties does MDMA/ecstasy have?
8. What are the dangers of using ecstasy?
9. How is ketamine different from PCP?
10. Why is Rohypnol known as the "date rape drug?"
11. What is the medical use for GHB (gamma-hydroxybutyrate)?
12. How is mescaline produced?
13. What are the effects of peyote?
14. Why does not marijuana easily fit into the depressant, stimulant, or hallucinogen categories?
15. How does marijuana cause psychoactive reactions?
16. What are marijuana withdrawal symptoms?
17. What are the short-term and long-term dangers of marijuana?
18. How do inhalants differ from other commonly abused substances?
19. What are the dangers of inhalant use?
20. What are the three categories of commonly abused prescription drugs?
21. What are neuroenhancers?
22. Why would high-functioning persons use neuroenhancers?

In order to be motivated to continue to experiment with the use of any drug, the individual must learn to use the drug appropriately and to experience its effects as pleasurable. This may depend partly on genetic predisposition, which influences whether drug use is pleasurable, and to a large degree on contact with a peer/user network already socialized into these practices and understandings.

Advisory Council on the Misuse of Drugs (1998: 31)

CHAPTER 7 | # THE SOCIOLOGY OF DRUG ABUSE

Bruce Ayres/Stone/Getty Images

Since the discovery of drugs as a social problem (discussed in Chapter 2) attempts have been made to explain why some people become dependent on chemicals while others, even those who use the same substances, do not. These explanations go beyond simply labeling abusers as "bad" or "weak" people who are oriented toward a harmful vice: "Some believe it is a medical disease,[1] while others believe it is a behavioral problem. Some consider it to have genetic origins; others consider it to be primarily environmentally determined. Some examine it within a cultural context, others consider it to be an individual adjustment reaction. Some view it as a personality disorder, while others view it as a psychosocial problem" (Pickens and Thompson 1984: 53). In the bio-psychosocial model, drug dependence is seen as being determined by the interaction of psychological, environmental, and physiological factors (Donovan 1988).

Theories of drug use typically depend on the discipline of the observer: neurology and pharmacology (discussed in Chapters 3, 4, 5, and 6), psychology (discussed in Chapter 8), and sociology, discussed in this chapter. Although many theories of drug use presented by these disciplines might seem competitive or even conflicting, our examination will emphasize their complementary nature: Each provides a partial explanation for drug use and has important treatment and policy implications. Indeed, the "real" explanation could involve a combination of factors. For example, although we know that certain types of drug abuse are concentrated in areas of relative deprivation, most people in such areas do not abuse drugs. So perhaps what promotes drug abuse in this situation is a biologically vulnerable person—i.e., having a neurotransmitter deficiency—living in deprived social circumstances who is exposed to certain psychoactive chemicals.

SOCIOLOGICAL THEORY

Because the social or behavioral sciences are concerned with behavior that is peculiarly human, the amount of ethically based testing that can be done is limited. We can subject rats to extreme levels of physical stress and then study their reaction to morphine, but we cannot subject human beings to similar levels of stress, expose them to morphine, and then find out whether they become drug addicts. The social or behavioral sciences have to study the etiology of drug addiction in a more circuitous manner.

Sociological theory is concerned with social structures and social behavior, so it examines drug use in its social context. A sociological perspective often views drug use as the product of social conditions and relationships that cause despair, frustration, hopelessness, and general feelings of alienation in the most disadvantaged segments of the population (Biernacki 1986). The National Institute on Drug Abuse (1987) outlines factors that are associated positively with adolescent

---

[1]"Moving etiological and rehabilitative issues from the context of morals to that of medicine offered many advantages. The legitimacy bestowed on substance abuse by treating it as a disease opened the way for more humane and effective treatment of patients. In addition, this view provided the impetus for scientific research into the condition" (Siegal et al. 1995: 67).

substance abuse, factors that are frequently found in deprived socioeconomic environments (most arrested cocaine and heroin users reside in disadvantaged neighborhoods [Lo 2003]):

1. Families whose members have a history of alcohol abuse and/or histories of antisocial behavior or criminality
2. Inconsistent parental supervision, with reactions that swing from permissiveness to severity
3. Parental approval or use of dangerous substances
4. Friends who abuse drugs
5. Children who fail in school during the late elementary years and show a lack of interest in school during early adolescence
6. Children who are alienated and rebellious
7. Children who exhibit antisocial behavior, particularly aggressive behavior, during early adolescence

There is also a strong link between childhood sexual and physical abuse and substance abuse (Brems et al. 2004).

Many sociological studies have found that drug use among adolescents is motivated by intermittent feelings of boredom and depression and that, like other aspects of adolescence, drug use is typically abandoned when the person reaches adulthood. Furthermore, contrary to conventional wisdom, research has found that drug use is typically a group activity of socially well-integrated youngsters (Glassner and Loughlin 1989). That is, contrary to some psychological views, the adolescent drug user is socially competent (or ego sufficient). Sociological studies often challenge the conflicting views of the adolescent drug user as either a deviant isolate or a peer-driven conformist. Sociology also cautions us to separate drug use that is situational and transitional from drug dependence or addiction, which is compulsive and dysfunctional. In England the much smaller number of adolescents who use illicit drugs regularly, in contrast to those who have tried illicit drugs, "reminds us that because a young person has tried an illicit drugs does not mean that they will necessarily develop a pattern of long term misuse" (Advisory Council on the Misuse of Drugs 1998: xii). This has important policy implications, and treatment approaches based on sociological theories usually "stress resocialization, the adopting of prosocial values, and/or submission to a peer culture that is strongly opposed to drug use." Thus, "according to a social stress model, adolescents initiate substance use as a means of coping with a variety of stressors and influences that may arise from within the family, the school, the peer group, or the community." And adolescents "will be more resilient and, as such, less likely to engage in problematic early usage as a means of coping with these stressors if they are members of prosocial, supportive social networks" (Rhodes and Jason 1990: 396).

STAGES OF DRUG USE

Sociologists have studied and labeled the stages that alcohol, heroin, and cocaine users go through on the path to addiction—a path that is not inevitable.

ALCOHOL

The alcoholic typically passes through several stages on the way to becoming addicted to alcohol (Catanzarite 1992):

- *Social drinking*: In this initial pattern alcohol is used to enhance pleasant social situations. The drug is taken for relaxation and entertainment. For some individuals drinking alcohol has a ritualistic dimension—a glass of wine or beer or a drink with a meal or as part of a religious ritual. Others may have an alcoholic beverage after work with colleagues—"a beer with the boys." The social drinker imbibes small amounts and does not experience harmful effects such as loss of control or impaired judgment. Although social drinkers view alcohol as generating positive feelings, they do not need the substance for enjoyment. The social drinker observes societal conventions about when, where, and how much to drink.

- *Heavy drinking*: The heavy drinker uses alcohol to escape. For one type of drinker this critical step involves a circular problem: He or she experiences constantly high levels of stress and seeks relief by drinking alcohol, which creates additional stress that must be relieved by more alcohol. Another type of person resorts to heavy alcohol use when particular stressful problems are encountered and reduces drinking in the absence of stressors. By becoming intoxicated, both types of drinkers violate social conventions about the use of alcohol and suffer negative side effects with respect to family, friends, and employment. They become defensive about their drinking and deny the influence of alcohol on their lives.

- *Dependent drinking*: The person is now addicted to alcohol and suffers from many consequences, in particular an inability to function normally either socially, intellectually, or physically. He or she is not able to control drinking behavior and becomes obsessed and preoccupied with alcohol. Indeed, the person needs alcohol to "feel normal."

Sarah Benton (2009) has identified a category of persons with an alcohol problem that she refers to as the **high functioning alcoholic (HFA)**. Such persons are able to maintain respectable, if not high-profile, lives, and they are psychologically (but not physically) dependent and do not meet the *Diagnostic and Statistical Manual of Mental Disorders* (DSM)[2] criteria for alcohol abuse. Yet they are unable to control their intake, obsess about drinking, behave inappropriately when drinking, experience blackouts, and are unable to remember what took place while they were drinking. Their double life continues until a crisis intervenes, such as an arrest for DWI, being accused of unwanted sexual advances, or being asked for a divorce by a spouse no longer able to tolerate the abusive drinking. The HFA avoids treatment because they are in denial or they view seeking help as a sign of weakness (Brody 2009).

---

[2]Published by the American Psychiatric Association and currently in its fourth edition.

While many college students are focused on academics, others are learning to abuse alcohol and other drugs. The overindulgence of alcohol has become a social norm at college fraternities across America.

HEROIN AND COCAINE

Heroin and cocaine addiction have been studied extensively, with two general conclusions (Gerstein and Harwood 1990):

1. Initial use is experimental in nature and begins during adolescence
2. Very few people begin using drugs after reaching age 25 (unless drugs were not previously available).

The pattern has a familiar sequence: from tobacco and alcohol to marijuana and then to other illegal psychoactive substances such as heroin and cocaine. Although most new users do not progress very far, the earlier the onset of use, the more likely is dependence. "Individuals who do not initiate the use of alcohol or tobacco tend not to initiate the use of marijuana. Similarly, those who do not initiate the use of marijuana tend not to progress to hard drug use" (Golub and Johnson 1994: 404).

Heroin   The life of a heroin addict can be conceived of as a "career" with a number of stages:

1. *Experimentation.* The individual, usually an adolescent, experiments with a variety of substances, including alcohol, cigarettes, marijuana, and perhaps barbiturates and amphetamines, and might snort heroin or inject it subcutaneously.

2. *Initiation*. The drug abuser is initiated into intravenous use of heroin. Although the first use is often accompanied by unpleasant side effects such as vomiting, the user learns to enjoy subsequent injections. Heroin use begins to be a center of existence.

3. *Commitment*. The user is now an addict and takes on the social identity associated with the drug subculture, orienting his or her life toward the maintenance of a heroin habit.

4. *Disjunction*. The addict's life is now characterized by crime, arrest, and imprisonment, interspersed with participation in drug-treatment programs in response to court direction (to avoid imprisonment), to reduce an expensive habit to manageable size, or to deal with severe physical ailments.

5. *Maturation*. At some point, usually when the addict is closer to age 40 than to 20, he or she typically begins to use only sporadically, gives up drugs completely as a result of treatment, or simply experiences spontaneous remission—or he or she dies. Although there are relatively few addicts over the age of 50 in the heroin-using population, one California study found that among hard-core addicts, by age 50 to 60 years, half of the 242 subjects tested positive for heroin (Hser et al. 2001). The "aging out" phenomenon is also found in other types of deviant behavior, such as crime in general.

"The addict lifestyle," notes Marsha Rosenbaum (1981: 14), "rotates around taking heroin for the purposes of alleviating withdrawal symptoms and/or getting high." Heroin is quite costly and too expensive for most addicts to secure with only legitimate sources of income. Nevertheless, a habit requires intravenous use three, four, or five times daily, and the addict also requires funds for minimal life-support items such as food, clothing, and housing. The addict who is also a dealer or is sufficiently organized is able to start the day with a fix. Few addicts, however, are able to plan even for the immediate future, so they rarely keep enough heroin in reserve to begin the day with a "wake-up fix." Without funds or drugs the addict must begin the day hustling for money to get the first fix.

After a "connection" has been made and the heroin has been purchased, the drug must be ingested as part of an almost ritualistic process. A safe place must be found where the addict, often in the company of other addicts, can inject the substance using a hypodermic syringe. The addict typically allows the solution to mix with blood by bringing blood back and forth between the vein and the syringe ("booting"), an act that some researchers see as analogous to sexual intercourse and that many users describe as more pleasurable and intense than sexual orgasm. In any event, as the short-term heightened feeling of euphoria that follows ingestion—the rush—subsides, the addict begins to experience the high, a feeling of general well-being that lasts about four hours. The cycle then needs to be repeated. "This is the 'addict's cycle'—an existence almost literally from fix to fix—with the necessary heroin-related activities in between" (M. Rosenbaum 1981: 15).

The heroin user recognizes the dangers of addiction, but "it is typical of the early experience of the addict-to-be that he knows or knows of people who use narcotics and who get away with it" (Duster 1970: 192). He sees himself as indestructible: "the tendency of the ego to treat the self as exempt from the experience of personal disaster."

Some heroin users, particularly postadolescents, are attracted to unconventional media images that romanticize the "traffic beauty" of heroin users. For some, if their favorite musicians can use heroin and still maintain or even excel in their careers, a positive light is cast on heroin use. Others are attracted to "heroin chic," the thin, wan look promulgated by the fashion industry (Duterte et al. 2003).

A more recently observed phenomenon of behavior leading to heroin use is the progression from prescription drugs (discussed in Chapter 6), often purloined from a home medicine cabinet. At "pharm parties" adolescents share whatever they have been able to acquire, but those who are determined to continue drug use must eventually find new sources. When the cost of pharmaceuticals on the black market exceeds that of heroin, the user now makes a giant leap into a new world of "junkies" (Wolvier, Martino, Jr., and Bolger 2009).

Cocaine   Here are some typical steps involved in becoming dependent on cocaine (based on D. E. Smith 1986):

1. *Experimental use.* The individual begins his or her initiation out of curiosity in a social situation in which some friends offer a "taste" of cocaine. Most of the person's friends are nonusers, and the person uses cocaine only when it is offered to enhance feelings. Relationships remain normal, and no significant health or financial problems appear. There might even be an improvement in work performance and social functioning—gregariousness or extroversion.

2. *Compulsive use.* The person begins to buy cocaine and increases the number of friends who are users. Solitary use of cocaine follows, and use to enhance moods and performance and to ward off depression associated with the "crash" of coming down off cocaine continues to increase. Social disruptions appear, particularly mood swings, as well as health problems due to a lack of proper nutrition and sleep. Work performance begins to deteriorate steadily, and the user avoids non-drug-using friends. The user begins to encounter financial problems that result from supporting a growing cocaine habit.

3. *Dysfunctional use.* The abuser is preoccupied with drug use and associates only with cocaine-using friends. The abuser might begin to deal in cocaine and/or to engage in other illegal or financially damaging activities to support the dependence on cocaine. Severe disruption of social life follows, possibly including marital violence and divorce. Serious medical pathology appears, with a risk of seizure and toxic psychosis, paranoia, delusions, and hallucinations. The abuser has chronic sleep and nutritional problems as well. His or her physical appearance deteriorates; this is usually accompanied by a lack of concern about personal hygiene and dress. Compulsion, a loss of control, and an inability to stop despite adverse consequences might lead the abuser to seek treatment, often because of pressure from family, friends, and/or employer and/or because of serious legal entanglements.

Early research (e.g., Washton and Gold 1987) and journalistic sources reported that addiction to crack cocaine appeared to present a different progression because the speed with which this substance acts can lead to chronic habituation or addiction very quickly. In their research, however, Jeffrey Fagan and Ko-lin Chin (1991) found no significant difference between the addictive qualities of crack and those of powdered cocaine. However, crack users more often reported an inability to stop using it. For reasons that have not yet been determined, crack has proven to be more popular among women than heroin is, leading to a significant increase in child neglect and abuse as well as to increasing numbers of newborn children with cocaine in their urine and syphilis resulting from the rampant sexual activity of their crack-abusing mothers. A seller describes a crack house as "full of young girls—fourteen, fifteen, sixteen years old. Some of these girls stayed for days at a time, getting high and having sex with these guys," any guy who offered drugs (T. Williams 1989: 108). Smoking crack reduces inhibitions while creating a desire for more drugs, leading female users to unprotected sexual behavior and the risk of sexually transmitted diseases, including AIDS. In their research Fagan and Chin (1991: 327) found "no significant differences among those involved in crack, cocaine HCL [powdered cocaine], heroin or other drugs in the location, motivation or methods of introduction to their new drug." Most users (90 percent) were introduced to the new drug by family or friends, and most (71 percent) got it free. In their study Andrew Golub and Bruce Johnson (1994) found that older crack users were nearly all former heroin injectors or cocaine snorters, while crack tended to be the first hard drug for younger users.

Let us now examine some of the major sociological theories that help to explain drug abuse.

ANOMIE

Derived from the Greek meaning "lack of law," the term *anomie* was used by sociologist Émile Durkheim (1858–1917) to describe an abnormal social condition wherein the cohesion of society is weakened by some crisis, such as an economic depression, that causes each individual to pursue his or her own solitary interests without concern for the wider society. In 1938 Robert Merton Americanized the concept, arguing that no other society comes so close to viewing economic success as such an absolute value that the pressure to succeed tends to eliminate social constraint over the means employed to achieve success. In the United States, in this view, "good" (ambition) causes "evil" (deviance). According to Merton (1964: 218), anomie results when people, confronted by the contradiction between goals and means, "become estranged from a society that promises them in principle what they are denied in reality [economic opportunity]." This sense of strain is particularly strong among the disadvantaged segments of our population, whose use of drugs is endemic.

RESPONSE TO ANOMIE

Strain leads to anomie, suffering to which people respond in one of four ways:

1. *Conformity.* Most people scale down their aspirations and conform to conventional social norms.
2. *Rebellion.* Some people rebel, rejecting the conventional social structure and seeking instead to establish a new social order through political action or alternative lifestyles.

3. *Innovation.* Some people turn to innovation, which Merton defines as the use of illegitimate means to gain success, in particular professional and organized criminality, including drug trafficking.
4. *Retreatism.* The final response, retreatism, explains drug abuse: The individual abandons all attempts to reach conventional social goals in favor of a deviant adaptation.

The retreat into drug abuse allows the addict to expend time and energy on achieving an attainable goal: getting high. Dan Waldorf (1973: 10) notes:

> The need for heroin requires an active life. The addict *may* be, as psychologists have claimed, depressed, he may be psychopathic, and he may use drugs to escape some reality in his life, but he is active in pursuit of a demanding life that requires considerable skill and ability to sustain. Addiction is *not* some aberrant, part-time leisure activity that one indulges in from time to time but that never engages one's life. On the contrary, addiction does engage the addict in an active life that has a precise purpose and satisfies a specific physical need. Whatever the individual's motives for using heroin or the ways in which a specific addict approaches his heroin use, he most certainly experiences an absorbing or engrossing drive, lives an active life, and is very much part of a social group.

Edward Preble and John Casey (1995: 121) argue that the behavior of the heroin addict is anything but an escape: "They are actively engaged in meaningful activities and relationships seven days a week. The brief moments of euphoria after each administration of a small amount of heroin constitute a small fraction of their daily lives. The rest of the time they are aggressively pursuing a career that is exacting, challenging, adventurous, and rewarding. They are always on the move and must be alert, flexible, and resourceful."

Some heroin addicts view life as an adventure. As a San Francisco addict explained to John Irwin (1970: 19): "Cowboys and Indians at the Saturday matinee didn't have a life that was any more exciting than this. The cops are the bad guys, you are the glorious bandit.... The chase is on all day long. You awaken in the morning to shoot the dope you saved to be well enough to go out and get some more. First you have to get some money. To steal you have to outwit those you steal from, plus the police. It is very exciting." The typical heroin addict, note Bertram Sackman and his colleagues (1978: 433), "exhibits as much pride in his heroin-getting skills as does the licit craftsman. He thinks about hustling and heroin, he talks about his exploits to other addicts, and his righteousness about heroin is rewarded by his women in the admiration and respect they accord him and his skills." Being "in the life" is *reinforcing* (discussed in Chapter 8).

According to Richard Cloward and Lloyd Ohlin (1960), however, the heroin addict is actually a double failure, unsuccessful at both legitimate and illegitimate enterprises, since his or her crimes are typically high-risk, low-yield activities. In this case the first response to anomie is *innovation*; when that fails to reduce the anomic condition, the addict moves to *retreatism*.

PROBLEMS WITH THE THEORY

Isidor Chein and his colleagues (1964) used a questionnaire to examine anomic attitudes. The questionnaires were administered to classes of male eighth-grade public school students in three neighborhoods with varying rates of delinquency: low, medium, and high (though even the "low" neighborhood had a relatively high rate of delinquency). Anomie was highly correlated with heroin use. But, as was noted in Chapter 1, the drug-to-crime sequence is not at all certain. According to Cloward and Ohlin's (1960) thesis, delinquency or crime precedes drug dependence, but research has not clearly supported this contention. In any event the successful and skilled (innovative) criminal is so rare that the "double failure" thesis must be questioned (Lindesmith and Gagnon 1964).

Of course, anomie does not explain cocaine use by people who are not retreatists and who have achieved notable social and economic success in either criminal or noncriminal enterprises. Nor does it satisfactorily explain the relatively high rate of drug abuse among physicians, whose use of drugs is better explained by access than by anomie. The American Society of Addiction Medicine with about 3,000 members has approximately one-third in recovery from addiction (Freed 2007). Access, not anomie, is also put forth as an explanation for the high concentration of drug use in ghetto areas: Lack of viable economic opportunity induces more people to take the risks associated with drug trafficking, resulting in greater availability of illegal substances (Lindesmith and Gagnon 1964). Of course, greater access can be the result of anomie, drug trafficking being an innovative response to the anomic condition.

Working from a psychoanalytical model (discussed in Chapter 8), Frederic Schiffer (1988) found retreatism motivating cocaine abuse in the patients he treated, the drug taken because of a fear of failure: "Unconsciously, despair seemed familiar and inevitable, and success seemed foreign and unattainable" (1988: 134). In contrast to these views, Erich Goode declares that "anomie theory seems to explain no significant feature of drug use, abuse, or addiction" (1989: 64). For Elliott Currie (1993: 145), writing during a different economic climate, the breeding conditions for anomie are connected to drug abuse, and these conditions have grown more severe: "It is not just that material prospects have dimmed for the relatively young and poor, but that they have dimmed just when there has been an explosion of affluence and a growing celebration of material consumption at the other end." This is exacerbated by the increasing gap between this country's wealthiest citizens and its poorest: Of the sixteen most industrialized nations the United States has the widest gap between rich and poor, and its poor children are the worst off (Bradsher 1995a, 1995b, 1995c).

THE ADAPTIVE MODEL OF ANOMIE

Bruce Alexander sees drug dependence (*compulsive* as opposed to *casual* or recreational use) as functional. The addict's behavior is an attempt to deal with a failure to integrate; that is, "failure to achieve the kinds of social acceptance, competence, self-confidence, and personal autonomy that are the minimal expectation of individuals and society" (1990: 39). In the *adaptive model*, as in the retreatist perspective, the addict perceives the identity and life of an addict, with its attendant misery, ill health, and social stigma, to be less painful than the void of no identity at all. According to Alexander, people who have not failed at integration and can form social strong bonds are not in danger of drug dependence. (This view is an important part of social control theory, discussed later in the chapter.)

Drug dependence serves "as a strategy to remove the individual [a retreat] from competitive situations in which defeat is almost certain" (Alexander 1990: 45). This model contrasts with the *disease model* of drug dependence because it sees the addict as a healthy person who is a social, not biological or psychological, failure. The addict is not under the control of a drug, nor is his or her drug use "out of control"; the behavior is self-directed and purposeful, though not necessarily on a conscious level.

DIFFERENTIAL ASSOCIATION

As proposed by Edwin Sutherland (1973), differential association explains how criminal behavior is transmitted. *Differential association* complements learning theory (discussed in Chapter 8): Criminal behavior is learned, and the principal learning occurs in intimate personal groups. The effectiveness of learning depends on the degree of intensity, frequency, and duration of the association. With respect to drug use, differential association can be conceived of as a scale in balance. On each side of the scale deviant and prosocial associations accumulate; at some theoretical point drug use will be initiated when there is an excess of deviant associations (drug abusers) over nondeviant or prosocial associations.

Robert Burgess and Ronald Akers (1969) reformulated Sutherland's central premise into a differential association reinforcement theory: A person becomes delinquent if social norms or laws do not actually reinforce conforming legal behavior. Because behavior is shaped by positive reinforcement, if lawful behavior does not result in reinforcement, the strength of that lawful behavior is weakened, and a state of reinforcement deprivation results. This deprivation increases the probability that other—deviant—behaviors will be reinforced and strengthened. Members of the person's social a group also make social reinforcement, such as social approval, esteem, and status, contingent on the new deviant behavior.

In fact, initiation into drug use appears to be completely dependent on peer associations. "The first source of contact with the drug [heroin] was usually a friend," notes Troy Duster (1970: 180). The typical user receives his or her first "taste" free from relatively new users who do not have expensive habits and will therefore share their drugs. Most frequently, the user is introduced to heroin as a result of meeting a friend who was on his way to "cop" or was preparing a "fix"; "he rarely sought out the drug the first time. Thus, initiation depended more on fortuitous circumstances than on a willful act by the new user" (P. H. Hughes 1977: 84).

In their study of heroin addicts in San Antonio, James Maddux and David Desmond (1981) found that only 4 percent obtained their first heroin directly from a dealer. Similar scenarios of heroin initiation are reported by Richard Rettig, Manual Torres, and Gerald Garrett (1977) and by Chein and his colleagues (1964). Waldorf (1973: 31) found a similar pattern and notes that heroin use is a social, not solitary, phenomenon: "Persons are initiated in a group situation among friends and acquaintances." The first experience with drugs, notes Duster (1970: 183), "is usually in a group situation." In England the situation is the same; Geoffrey Pearson (1987: 9) found that "the first time someone is offered heroin it will be by a friend. Or maybe by a brother or a sister. But always by someone well known, liked and even loved."

The relationship between initiation and friendship or kinship presents a problem for preventing the first use of drugs: "In light of the decisive role of friendship networks in disseminating drugs, it is difficult to conceive of any effective form of conventionally conceived drug enforcement policy to control access at this level—quite simply, how might one be expected to police friendship?" (Advisory Council on the Misuse of Drugs 1998: 30).

What of the relationship between parental use of psychoactive substances and the use of these substances by their children? (Peer relationships might simply serve as a mediating or intervening variable.) According to the theory of differential association, parental influence is responsible for generating the type of behavior that parents explicitly condemn in their children. However, in her research Denise Kandel (1974: 235) found that "parental influence is relatively small, especially when compared with the influence of peers." Peers provide social acceptance or reinforcement for the rules governing acceptance or conforming behavior valued by the peer group. To the adolescent, this reinforcement is typically more relevant than that provided by parents. Kandel concludes, however, that parents can enhance differential association: "When their friends use illegal drugs, children of nondrug-using parents are somewhat *less* likely to use illegal drugs, whereas children of drug-using parents are *more* likely to use drugs" (1974: 235).

According to Coryl Jones and Robert Battjes (1987: 15), the use of certain drugs allows adolescents to emulate adults while at the same time rebelling against parental standards: "In emulation of their elders, adolescents use drugs to assuage immediate or anticipated discomfort, and, in rejection of their elders, they seize upon certain drugs of which their elders would disapprove. The use of illicit substances offers young adolescents the unique opportunity simultaneously to rebel against the rules their elders set down and to conform with the underlying attitudes which parental behavior manifests."

However, an extensive study found that favorable parent-adolescent relationships can offset personality risk factors for drug use and enhance personality protective factors against drug use. The study also found that peer drug use during adolescence was not a strong predictor of initiation into drug use during early adulthood (Morojele and Brook 2001).

Anomie and differential association help to explain what Patrick Hughes (1977: 88) referred to as a heroin epidemic. In a Chicago-based study he posited a theory of heroin contagion in the form of microepidemics and macroepidemics: "The multiple drug using friendship group served as fertile soil for the growth of heroin addiction" into microepidemics, while "macroepidemics generally occurred in neighborhoods that had recently undergone rapid population change, leading to a breakdown in community stability and established mechanisms of social control [anomie]. In other words, not only had heroin addiction become rampant in these neighborhoods, but so had other forms of deviance as well." Hughes states that intensive treatment and outreach efforts can nip a new heroin-using network before it burgeons into an epidemic.

Identifying oneself as a "doper," "pothead," or "cokehead" typically results from being enmeshed in a social network that includes others who are similarly situated. For some this becomes the primary reference group, and they might spend most of their time with other dopers, potheads, or cokeheads, withdrawing from non-drug-using social contacts. The substance becomes a symbol of group cohesion and unity and provides a sense of belonging, thus offering strong support for continued use (Roffman and George 1988).

SOCIAL CONTROL THEORY

Social control theorists focus on why only relatively few people engage in deviant behavior such as crime and drug abuse, and their answer is that the strength of an individual's bond to society is the determining factor. Youths who maintain strong attachments with and commitment toward parents and school are less likely to engage in deviant behavior. According to control theorists, deviance "results when an individual's bond to society is weak or broken" (Hirschi 1969: 16). The strength of this social bond is determined by internal and external restraints. In other words, internal and external restraints determine whether people move in the direction of deviance or law-abiding behavior.

Internal restraints include what psychoanalytic theory (discussed in Chapter 8) refers to as the *superego*—they provide a sense of guilt. Dysfunction during early stages of childhood development or parental influences that are not normative can result in an adult who has no prosocial internal constraints—sociopathology. (There is also evidence tying sociopathology to brain defects.) Criminal behavior, devoid of any genuine remorse, can be explained by this theory. According to social control theory, deviants are poorly socialized, and the family is the basic unit for socialization. Thus, whether they are conceived of in terms of psychology or sociology, internal constraints are linked to the influence of the family (Hirschi 1969). Adolescent involvement with drugs and/or crime is therefore "highly correlated with family estrangement" (Brounstein et al. 1990: 10), an influence that can be supported or weakened by the presence or absence of significant external restraints.

External restraints include social disapproval linked to public shame and/or social ostracism and fear of punishment. In other words, people are typically deterred from criminal behavior by the possibility of being caught and the punishment that can result, ranging from public shame to imprisonment (and in extreme cases capital punishment). However, the strength of official deterrence—force of law—is measured according to two dimensions: risk versus reward. Risk involves the criminal justice system's ability to detect, apprehend, and convict the offender. The amount of risk is weighed against the potential rewards. Both risk and reward, however, are relative to one's socioeconomic situation. In other words, the less one has to lose, the greater is the willingness to engage in risk; and the greater the reward, the greater is the willingness to engage in risk. This theory explains why people in deprived economic circumstances would be more willing to engage in certain criminal behavior. However, the potential rewards and a perception of relatively low risk can also explain why individuals in more advantaged economic circumstances would engage in remunerative criminal behavior such as corporate crime.

Social control theory does not argue that only people with weak societal ties will engage in drug use. Instead, it is the persistence of drug use that indicates a lack of societal bonds. Instead of conforming to conventional norms, through differential association some people organize their behavior according to the norms of a delinquent or criminal group with which they identify or to which they belong. This is most likely to occur in environments that are characterized by relative social disorganization, in which familial and communal controls are ineffective in exerting a conforming influence. "A similar process also helps explain why drugs are sometimes rampant in more affluent communities. Just as strong families and cultures can shield the materially deprived from drugs, so weakened families, the absence of available or concerned adults, and the pervasiveness of an insistent consumer culture can make the affluent more vulnerable" (Currie 1993: 103).

Another study revealed that family monitoring and rules, family conflict, and family bonding predict an adolescent's risk of illicit drug initiation. The researchers found that a warm and supportive family environment characterized by a strong bond to family members and a low level of family conflict predicted a lower risk for illicit drug initiation during adolescence. Thus, good parental control and supervision characterized by close parental monitoring and clear family rules for children's behavior may significantly reduce the risk of illicit drug initiation throughout adolescence by affecting children's association with peers. These findings regarding family influences are consistent with findings from previous studies (Guo et al. 2002).

In a major study of the strength of family ties and risky behavior (involving cigarettes, marijuana, and sex) by adolescents, researchers found that lower risk was closely related to a close-knit family. Family ties were found to be more important than peer relations (S. Gilbert 1997). In a longitudinal study designed to test social control theory, in particular that element relating poor interpersonal relations with deviance (in this case drug abuse), Denise Kandel and Mark Davies (1991: 459) found no relationship between integration failure and drug abuse. In fact, they found illicit drug use to be "positively associated with intimacy among members of male friendship networks, whether intimacy refers to confiding or to interacting with friends. Further, the structure of the networks of illicit users is similar to that of nonusers. To the extent that some differences occurred, they tended to indicate closer friendships for drug users than nonusers."

The researchers note that their findings tend to support subcultural (or cultural deviance) theory rather than control theory. George Vaillant (1983), a research psychiatrist, found that culture plays an important role in the genesis of alcoholism and that family practices—drinking habits into which a child is socialized, rather than a lack of social control (or even social distress)—are a dominant factor. The idea that drug abuse, in particular alcoholism, is the result of a habit learned in accord with the same principles that govern other learning experiences is consistent with the behavior/learning theory of drug abuse (Bandura 1969, 1974).

SUBCULTURES AND CULTURAL DEVIANCE

Some sociologists explain deviant behavior as the result of people conforming to subcultures to which they belong. "Subcultures are patterns of values, norms, and behavior which have become traditional among certain groups." They are "important frames of reference through which individuals and groups see the world and interpret it" (Short 1968: 11). A person without important bonds to conventional society but with strong ties to a drug-using subculture would be more likely to abuse drugs. Members of a drug subculture promote its values and norms to people who are attracted to "the life" (socialization). The person who joins must reorder his or her life in conformity with the new subculture to be accepted by others and to remain a member in good standing. The subculture provides rewards and punishments along the lines proposed by operant conditioning theory to retain the member's loyalty.

Albert Cohen (1965) argues that certain lower-class subcultures negate middle-class values, and this negation is a severe handicap because middle-class cultural characteristics are necessary to succeed in our society. These characteristics include:

1. Ambition
2. A sense of individual responsibility
3. Skills for achievement
4. Ability to postpone gratification
5. Industry and thrift
6. Rational planning, such as budgeting time and money
7. Cultivation of manners and politeness
8. Control of physical aggression
9. Respect for property
10. A sense of wholesome recreation

The norms of some lower-class subcultures, according to James Short (1968) and Walter Miller (1958), are simply not conducive to conventional types of achievement. The members of an adolescent street group adhere to the norms of a lower-class subculture, whose focal concerns are (Miller 1958):

- *Trouble*: law-violating behavior
- *Toughness*: physical prowess, daring
- *Smartness*: ability to con others, shrewdness
- *Excitement*: thrills, risk, danger
- *Fate*: being lucky
- *Autonomy*: independence of external restraint

Trouble often involves fighting or sexual adventures while drinking; troublesome behavior for women frequently means sexual involvement with disadvantageous consequences. Trouble-producing behavior is a source of status. Toughness evolves out of the significant proportion of lower-class males reared in female-dominated households and the resulting concern over homosexuality that Miller contends runs through lower-class culture.

Gambling, also prevalent in lower-class culture, is rooted in the belief that life is subject to a set of forces over which there is little or no control—fate. Autonomy is often expressed in statements such as "No one is going to push me around" and "I'm going to tell him to take this job and shove it." Such sentiments, however, often contrast with actual patterns of behavior; in other words, according to Miller, many lower-class individuals desire highly restrictive social environments such as the armed forces, prison, and drug treatment programs: "Being controlled is equated with being cared for" (1958: 13).

Chein and his colleagues note that "boys who become addicts are clearly related to the delinquent subculture. Even before they started using drugs regularly, most users have had friends who have been in jail, reformatory, or on probation" (1964: 13). Without exception they found that addicts come from homes that are devoid of a father or strong father figure—female-dominated households. These individuals are identified with what others have dubbed the *criminal underclass* subculture (B. D. Johnson et al. 1990), of which the drug subculture is an important component.

The concept of a drug subculture, notes John O'Donnell (1969: 84), implies that addicts are in contact with each other (differential association):

> In this contact, learning takes place. The learning can be of facts and techniques. For example, the neophyte can learn from more experienced addicts that his withdrawal symptoms are the result of not having his usual dose of narcotics, and will be relieved by a dose; that the intravenous route enhances the drug effect; how to obtain narcotics, or money for narcotics; new sources of narcotics; how to prepare narcotics for administration, and other knowledge of this kind. He will usually learn new attitudes too. He may learn to define himself as an addict, learn new justifications for his drug use, and new and negative attitudes toward the laws that try to prevent drug use.

As the drug user comes to define himself or herself as an addict, the wider society perceives him or her as such, in a process known as *labeling* (see the next section).

Drug cultures come in many different types. Some are linked to the use of particular substances; others seem to be part of a larger subculture. Using participant observation, Patricia Adler provides an insider's look at a marijuana- and cocaine-smuggling subculture centered in the middle- and upper-class environs of the coastal communities of Southern California. She states: "This subculture provides guidelines for their dealing and smuggling, outlining members' rules, roles, and reputation. Their social life is deviant as well, as evidenced by their abundant drug consumption, extravagant spending, uninhibited sexual mores, and focus on immediate gratification" (1985: 1).

In general, cocaine abusers do not appear to present any clearly discernible subculture. Surveys of cocaine users have revealed that there is apparently no "typical" cocaine user (President's Commission on Organized Crime 1986). Heavy cocaine users fit no easy stereotype of drug abuse:

> A large proportion are successful, well-educated, upwardly mobile professionals in their early twenties and thirties. They are stockbrokers and lawyers and architects with sufficient disposable income to sink into a diversion that even at "social" use levels can cost $100 or more an evening. Many are, for the most part, otherwise law-abiding citizens who would cringe at being labeled criminals, even though they know what they are doing is illegal. A majority are men, but a growing number are women. And, as cocaine prices fall, more and more are teenagers and others for whom the drug's exorbitant cost once kept it out of reach. (National Institute on Drug Abuse 1985: 1)

Cocaine in the form of crack, however, seems to have produced a drug subculture in poor neighborhoods of urban areas. "The subcultural patterns include an argot of terms that describes the activities having to do with crack, the various crack combinations touted and paraphernalia needed for using, and the institution of base houses [where the substance is smoked] and crack houses [where the substance is purchased]" (Frank et al. 1987: 6). Blanche Frank and her colleagues

(1987) point out that the development of this subculture helped to glamorize and thereby spread the use of crack.

Harold Finestone (1964) drew a portrait of the black heroin subculture in Chicago at the beginning of the 1950s. He found that the stereotypical addict eschewed violence, used a deliberately colorful vocabulary, and disdained work. (This contrasted with a small number of white addicts interviewed by Finestone, whose type of adjustment stressed violence.) These addicts, whom Finestone (1964: 284) calls the "cats," had a lifestyle that centered on achieving "kicks." A kick is any act considered taboo by conventional society "that heightens and intensifies the present moment of experience and differentiates it as much as possible from the humdrum routine of daily life." To the cat, heroin abuse provided the ultimate kick. A similar type of stereotypical heroin addict was found by Harvey Feldman (1977), who conducted his research in the late 1960s in a community that he called by the pseudonym "East Highland."

SYMBOLIC INTERACTIONISM/LABELING

Symbolic interactionism is a sociological approach that appears in such perspectives as labeling or societal reaction theory. Its central premise is that people make their own reality:

> Symbolic interactionists suggest that categories which individuals use to render the world meaningful, and even the experience of self, are structured by socially acquired definitions. They argue that individuals, in reaction to group rewards and sanctions, gradually internalize group expectations. These internalized social definitions allow people to evaluate their own behavior from the standpoint of the group and in doing so provide a lens through which to view oneself as a social object. (Quadagno and Antonio 1975: 33)

Symbolic interactionism does not explain drug abuse because its focus is not on the behavior of the social actor but on how the behavior or person is viewed by others—by society. Thus, Kai Erikson (1966: 6) states: "deviance is not a property *inherent* in any particular kind of behavior; it is a property *conferred* upon that behavior by people who come into direct or indirect contact with it." In Chapter 1 we noted that certain harmful substances—alcohol and tobacco—can be lawfully manufactured, distributed, and possessed, while other chemicals are outlawed and the people who choose to use them are labeled outlaws. In Chapter 2 we noted that at one time the users of certain substances—opiates and cocaine—were not seen as outcasts or criminals. After passage of the Harrison Act what had been lawful behavior became illegal, and a new class of criminals was created, as well as a lucrative new enterprise: drug trafficking. Using this perspective, Thomas Szasz (1974: 11) argues that "before 1914 [and the Harrison Act] there was no 'drug problem' in the United States." Thus, society is inclined to view those who abuse alcohol as suffering from a disease (alcoholism), while those who indulge in illegal chemicals are viewed—stigmatized—as deserving punishment. The societal interactionist view of drug use has important policy implications.

LABELING

"Young offenders in particular must be confronted with penalties that both deter them from future drug use and embarrass them among their peers. Today, many young offenders boast about their lenient treatment in the hands of the authorities and wear it as a badge of pride; corrections officials must make sure that when juveniles are caught using or selling drugs, their punishment becomes a source of shame. We need a mix of sanctions for juvenile drug use that includes school suspension, parental notification, and postponement of driver's license eligibility, and extends to weekends of 'community service' that involve arduous and unenviable public chores" (Office of National Drug Control Policy 1989: 25).

While those who abuse chemicals such as heroin and cocaine are labeled pejoratively, fired from employment, and subjected to law enforcement scrutiny, jail, and prison, the widespread acceptance of the traditional disease concept of alcoholism reduces the stigma associated with that problem. The disease model of alcoholism "provided a way for hundreds of thousands of alcoholics to make sense of their experience, to regain a measure of dignity and self-respect. And to begin to take control of and to rebuilt their shattered lives" (Wallace 1993: 70).

Societal reaction labels—stigmatizes—certain actors, which causes a damaged self-image, deviant identity, and a host of negative social expectations. Furthermore, a damaged self-image can become a self-fulfilling prophecy. Edwin Schur (1973: 124) notes that "once an individual has been branded as a wrong-doer, it becomes extremely difficult for him to shed that new identity." During adolescence "many youths engage in socially disruptive and health-endangering behavior," although "most adolescents who experiment with drugs or other health-compromising and illicit practices do not escalate their worrisome behavior" (Baumrind 1987: 14). This should caution us against unnecessarily labeling people, particularly young people. "Zero tolerance" might be politically viable, but it can significantly limit a young person's social and economic options in a way that does not encourage conforming behavior as an adult.

According to Edwin Lemert, the person who is labeled deviant reorganizes his or her behavior in accordance with the social reaction "and begins to employ his deviant behavior, or role based upon it, as a means of defense, attack, or adjustment to the overt and covert problems created by the subsequent societal reaction to him" (1951: 76). This *secondary deviance* is best exemplified by drug abusers who are forced to associate with other drug abusers and furthermore must often resort to crime (secondary deviance) in order to support their primary deviance: their drug habits.

In the next chapter we will examine psychological theories that help to explain drug use.

SUMMARY

- Some believe that drug dependency is a medical disease; others believe it is a behavioral problem. Some consider it to have genetic origins; others consider it to be primarily environmentally determined.
- Because the social or behavioral sciences are concerned with behavior that is peculiarly human, the amount of ethically based testing that can be done is limited.
- Sociological theory examines drug use in its social context. A sociological perspective often views drug use as the product of social conditions and relationships that cause despair, frustration, hopelessness, and general feelings of alienation in the most disadvantaged segments of the population.
- Sociological studies have found that drug use among adolescents is motivated by intermittent feelings of boredom and depression and that, like other aspects of adolescence, drug use is typically abandoned when the person reaches adulthood.
- Sociology separates drug use that is situational and transitional from drug dependence or addiction, which is compulsive and dysfunctional.
- According to a social stress model, adolescents initiate substance use as a means of coping with a variety of stressors and influences that may arise from within the family, the school, the peer group, or the community.
- Alcoholics pass through three stages: social drinking; heavy drinking; dependent drinking.
- The high functioning alcoholic is able to maintain a respectable life despite being unable to control intake and avoid treatment because they are in denial or they view seeking help as a sign of weakness.
- The "career" of a heroin addict has a number of stages: experimentation, initiation, commitment, disjunction, and finally, maturation (or death).
- Heroin users recognize the dangers of addiction, but know of people who use narcotics and get away with it, and thus see themselves as indestructible.
- There are three steps typically involved in becoming dependent on cocaine: experimental use; compulsive use; dysfunctional use.
- Anomie results when people become estranged from a society that promises them economic opportunity in principle but the reality is otherwise. This sense of strain is particularly strong among the disadvantaged segments of our population, whose use of drugs is endemic.
- Retreatism explains drug abuse as the individual abandoning all attempts to reach conventional social goals in favor of a deviant adaptation that allows the addict to expend time and energy on achieving an attainable goal: getting high.
- Anomie does not explain cocaine use by people who are not retreatists and who have achieved notable social and economic success in either criminal or noncriminal enterprises. Nor does it satisfactorily explain the relatively high rate of drug abuse among physicians, whose use of drugs is better explained by access than by anomie.
- Differential association can be conceived of as a scale in balance. On each side of the scale deviant and prosocial associations accumulate; at some theoretical point drug use will be initiated when there is an excess of deviant associations (drug abusers) over nondeviant or prosocial associations. Initiation into drug use appears to be completely dependent on peer associations.
- Social control theorists focus on why only relatively few people engage in deviant behavior such as crime and drug abuse, and their answer is that the strength of an individual's bond to society is the determining factor.
- Internal and external restraints determine whether people move in the direction of deviance or law-abiding behavior.
- The norms of some lower-class subcultures are not conducive to conventional types of achievement.

- As the drug user comes to define himself or herself as an addict, the wider society perceives him or her as such, in a process known as *labeling*.
- Symbolic interactionism's central premise is that people make their own reality.
- Societal reaction stigmatizes drug users which causes a damaged self-image, deviant identity, and a host of negative social expectations.
- "Zero tolerance" might be politically viable, but it can significantly limit a young person's social and economic options in a way that does not encourage conforming behavior as an adult.

Review Questions

1. What limits scientific testing in the social or behavioral sciences?
2. What are the social factors associated with adolescent drug abuse?
3. How do sociological views of the adolescent drug user differ from psychological views?
4. With respect to adolescent drug use, what caution does sociology recommend?
5. What are the stages to becoming addicted to alcohol?
6. What are the characteristics of a high-functioning alcoholic?
7. What are the stages of a "heroin career"?
8. What is the "aging out" phenomenon?
9. If heroin users recognize the dangers involved, why do they continue to use heroin?
10. What are the typical steps involved in becoming dependent on cocaine?
11. How does the theory of anomie explain drug abuse?
12. Why can a heroin addict be characterized as a "double failure"?
13. What type of drug user does anomie fail to explain?
14. How does anomie compete with "access" as an explanation for high levels of drug use?
15. What is the adaptive model of retreatism?
16. How does differential association explain the transmission of such deviant behavior as drug abuse?
17. Who is the usual source of a drug for the first-time user?
18. How does this complicate preventing first use of drugs?
19. What is the question social control theory seeks to answer?
20. How do social control theorists distinguish between internal and external restraints on such deviant behavior as drug abuse?
21. According to social control theory, what is the importance of social bonds in preventing drug use?
22. What are subcultures?
23. How can a subculture explain drug use?
24. How can the characteristics of a "lower-class subcultures" explain drug abuse?
25. What does the symbolic interactionism/labeling view mean by the premise that people make their own reality?
26. How does symbolic interactionism contribute to understanding the problem of drug abuse?
27. What is the labeling view of "zero tolerance" policy?
28. What is secondary deviance?

The addictive disorders are complex because they are influenced by genetic, familial, psychological, and socio-cultural factors.

American Psychiatric Association (1995: 5)

CHAPTER **8** | THE PSYCHOLOGY OF DRUG USE AND ABUSE

Imagesource/PhotoLibrary

The sociology of drug use, discussed in Chapter 7, notes that the phenomenon tends to be clustered in environments that are characterized by social conditions and relationships that cause despair, frustration, hopelessness, and general feelings of alienation. However, in these environments drug abusers represent only a small fraction of the populace. Why? Why do people who are exposed to the same physical environment react differently to the use and abuse of drugs? Psychology, a discipline that focuses on the individual, provides some answers. In this chapter, for pedagogical purposes psychological explanations are placed into two broad categories: clinical and behaviorist.

PSYCHOLOGY AND PERSONALITY

Psychology examines individual human behavior, and clinicians attempt to treat abnormal or dysfunctional behavior. Some psychological theories of drug abuse are based on personality: "Drug addiction is primarily a personality disorder. It represents one type of abortive adjustment to life that individuals with certain personality predispositions may choose under appropriate conditions of availability and sociocultural attitudinal tolerance" (Ausubel 1978: 77). Robert Craig (1987: 31) notes that the psychological literature supports such a conclusion: "[D]rug addicts have a paucity of major psychiatric syndromes and neuroses and a plethora of personality disorders and character disorders." An extensive review of the literature on psychological testing of heroin addicts found them to be hostile, demanding, aggressive, rebellious, irresponsible, playful, and impulsive (Craig 1987). But many of these traits are also been found in outstanding athletes. With respect to substance abusers in general, they "are characterized by disregard for established social customs, lack of control and foresight, inability to maintain lasting personal commitments, and the need for unusual and varied experiences" (Cox 1985: 233).

Part of the psychological explanation for drug abuse has been a presumed *addictive personality*, a psychological vulnerability resulting from problematic family relationships, inappropriate reinforcement, the lack of healthy role models, contradictory parental expectations, and/or an absence of love and respect. The psychologically immature drug-dependent personality seeks gratification on a primitive level or, according to the pleasure principle, finds drug use and its attendant behavior reinforcing. He or she ignores the long-term negative consequences of behavior and instead opts for the short-term positive reinforcement that drugs provide.

Unfortunately, the search for the addictive personality—psychological variables that can predict future drug abuse—has not been fruitful (see Lang 1983). Peter Nathan (1988) points out that the search for predictors of drug dependence has discovered a variety of overt acts by prealcoholic- and pre-drug abusers that reveal an unwillingness to accept societal rules. Beyond that, however, few consistent links have been found between other behaviors or personality factors and later abuse of alcohol and drugs. Furthermore, Nathan (1988) notes that large numbers of abusers have never demonstrated antisocial behavior in childhood and that a substantial number of antisocial or conduct-disordered children never develop alcohol or drug problems as adults.

Psychological theories can be broadly categorized into those that are based on a Freudian or psychoanalytic strain and those that are based on behaviorism or learning theory.

PSYCHOANALYTIC THEORY AND DRUG ABUSE

Psychoanalytic theory was "fathered" by Sigmund Freud (1856–1939). Although it has undergone change over the years, its basic proposition continues to be the influence of unconscious phenomena on human behavior. "Simply put, this concept says that people are not aware of the most important determinants of their behavior" (Cloninger, 1993: 25). According to Freud there are three types of mental phenomena:

1. *Conscious*: what we are currently thinking about
2. *Preconscious*: thoughts and memories that can easily be called into consciousness
3. *Unconscious*: feelings and experiences that have been repressed and that can be made conscious only with a great deal of difficulty and that nevertheless exert a dominant influence over our behavior

THE STAGES OF PSYCHOLOGICAL DEVELOPMENT

Freud posited that unconscious feelings and thoughts relate to stages of psychosexual development from infancy to adulthood. Psychoanalytic theory "conceives of the human being as a dynamic energy system consisting of basic drives and instincts which in interaction with the environment serve to organize and develop the personality through a series of developmental stages. Individuals from birth are pushed by these largely unconscious and irrational drives toward satisfaction of desires which are largely unconscious and irrational" (Compton and Galaway 1979: 90). Although we lack conscious memory of these stages, in later life they serve as a source of anxiety and guilt, psychoneurosis, and psychosis. The stages overlap, and transition from one to the other is gradual, the time spans noted below being approximate and dependent on individual and cultural differences. (See Figure 8.1.)

Oral Stage (Birth to 18 Months)   During the oral stage the infant organizes his or her primitive impulses around the mouth, lips, and tongue, which are the predominant sexual organs during this stage. Desires and gratifications are mainly oral—sucking and biting. The infant is unsocialized, devoid of all self-control, and narcissistic. In the normal infant, the source of pleasure becomes associated with the touch and warmth of the parent, who gratifies the infant's oral needs. When this gratification is lacking, narcissism remains predominant, and in the narcissistically disturbed adult, drugs become a substitute for maternal warmth and self-esteem.

The infant's physiological balance is precarious, so any environmental change may cause distress. The anxiety that is experienced in the helpless state of infancy is ameliorated by the discovery of a maternal object capable of providing nurture. The absence of warm mother–infant interaction and sensory deprivation during

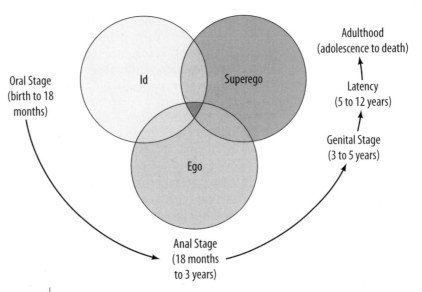

FIGURE 8.1 | STAGES OF PSYCHOSEXUAL DEVELOPMENT

this stage causes the adult to use drugs as a means of reducing anxiety; drugs serve as a substitute for maternal attachment, and drug abuse is a regression back to an unfulfilled oral stage. Experiments conducted on animals reveal that the young of many species experience separation anxiety that can be ameliorated by opiates. "For human species, the experience of social attachments and comfort becomes inevitably bound up with the euphoria of human affection, intimacy, and love." Opiates apparently provide a substitute, albeit an inadequate one, for the absent maternal object (Levinthal 1988: 145).

During this stage the infant attempts to reach a state of homeostatic peacefulness, and this requires a responsive and supportive maternal object. Because of trauma or deficiencies experienced during this stage of development, "the infant may fail to achieve homeostatic balance, in the context of an attachment to a maternal object," and this can lead to drug abuse in the adult. The "substance, be it heroin or some other narcotic or stimulant, works at a physiologic and psychological representational level to facilitate the attainment of this basic homeostatic experience" (Greenspan 1978: 74).

Anal Stage (18 Months to 3 Years)   As the infant moves into his or her second year, the "instinctual organization is beginning to organize around the mental representations concerned with anality" (Greenspan 1978: 76). The anus becomes the center of sexual desire and gratification during this stage, with pleasure closely associated with the retention and expulsion of feces. Physiologically, the child is now able to control eliminatory processes. The child typically experiences toilet training and becomes partially socialized, the beginning of a parental internalizing process that is completed during the genital stage that follows. During the anal stage children may act out destructive urges such as breaking toys or even injuring living organisms, insects, or small animals. A great deal of adult psychopathology, including violent antisocial behavior and sociopath personality disorders, is traced back to this stage. Depressants such as heroin, alcohol, barbiturates, and tranquilizers can provide a way of managing sadistic and masochistic impulses—self-medication—that were not successfully dealt with during the anal stage. Such people take depressants not for pleasure but to control internal rage. (The policy implications of this theory argue against our current response to drug use.)

If development is thwarted during this stage, the infant does not succeed in achieving "an internal sense of mastery and delineation of self from the primary other"—the maternal figure. Drugs are used in an effort to obtain a state of mastery and clear demarcation from the maternal figure that is necessary to manage the transition to the genital stage. To gain greater independence, the infant must relinquish the dependent attachment to the maternal object, and if successful, he or she can then move into the genital stage. In those who fail to accomplish this transition, substance abuse "is a defense against separation anxiety and its accompanying depression" (Greenspan 1978: 78).

Genital Stage (3 to 5 Years)   In this stage, which anticipates adulthood, the main sexual interest is assumed by the genitals and in normal people is thereafter maintained there. During this period boys experience strong attachments to their mothers (*Oedipus complex*) and girls to their fathers (*Electra complex*); both boys and girls have incestuous fantasies, although they do not fully understand the mechanics of adult sexual relations. The child must begin to relinquish the dependent maternal or paternal attachment despite feelings of sadness in doing so. Drugs provide solace to the adult who was unable to deal with the ensuing depression of separation.

As was noted in previous chapters, psychoactive drugs often affect sexual performance—by enhancing or depressing desire and/or performance. Drugs can provide a chemical means of dealing with disturbances experienced during the genital stage of development. Heroin, for example, might serve to suppress the sexual drive that is fixated in the genital stage; that is, the drug helps the person to deal with unconscious (and guilt-provoking) incestuous wishes. Heroin causes a return to the oral stage, enabling the addict to avoid dealing with conflicts that were not adequately resolved.

Adolescence/Adulthood   In this stage the individual experiences a dramatic reawakening of genital interest and awareness. The incestuous wish, however, is repressed, and sexual interest is expressed in terms of mature (adult) sexuality. As was noted above, drug use that substitutes for or enhances sexual activity allows the abuser to avoid or overcome the reawakening of incestuous sexual feelings that were never successfully reconciled during the genital stage. Furthermore, each stage is left behind but never completely abandoned. Some amount of psychic energy (*cathexis*) remains attached to earlier objects of psychosexual development. When the strength of the cathexis is particularly strong, it is expressed as a *fixation*. For example, instead of a boy transferring his affection to another woman in the adolescent/adult stage, he might remain fixated on his mother (or a girl on her father):

> At each stage, particular behaviors are important, but as we progress through the stages we use the behaviours associated with stages. So, in early stages, babies gain

satisfaction from sucking (for example, at a mother's breast to satisfy the need for food). Later, sucking can also be satisfying—for example, in the use of cigarettes, sweets or in sexual activities. However, adults have a wider range of satisfying activities to choose from. Some people become unconsciously attached to behaviour associated with particular stages (fixation). They are driven to seek that form of satisfaction to an unreasonable degree. Consequently they cannot use the full repertoire of behaviour available to them. (Payne 1997: 73)

While the individual is experiencing each of these stages of development, corresponding psychic phenomena develop.

Divisions of the Psyche

Id Each person is born with a mass of powerful drives, wishes, urges, and psychic tensions that are energized in the form of the *libido*. These seek immediate discharge or gratification. These **id** impulses are asocial, operating on the primitive level of pleasure and pain (that is, they are hedonistic), and from about birth to 7 months of age the id is the total psychic apparatus. Id drives are a central component of personality, impelling a person toward activity that leads to cessation of the tension excitement it creates, satisfying the libido. For example, the hunger drive will result in activity that eventually satisfies (gratifies the id of) the person experiencing hunger. A craving for pleasure-producing chemicals will lead the id-driven person to seek drugs at considerable risk in order to satiate his or her desire, and the feelings of omnipotence that drugs can produce reinforce this drive.

Ego Through the environment and training, infants learn to modify their expression of id drives and to delay immediate gratification. Ego development permits them to obtain maximum gratification with a minimum of difficulty; the **ego** tempers the id with reality and is the organism's contact with the real world. In normal development the child learns to relinquish primitive id demands and to adapt behavior to social demands (F. Smart 1970). The stronger the ego, the stronger is the individual's ability to tolerate frustration. Poor ego functioning, manifested by an inability to tolerate the psychological discomfort of frustration or stress, can lead to the abuse of chemicals that lower the discomfort and provide immediate gratification. Furthermore, note Henry Krystal and Herbert Raskin (1970: 31), in the ego-deficient personality "drugs are used to avoid impending psychic trauma in circumstances which would not be potentially traumatic to other persons"; in other words, drug use reflects a dysfunction in reality testing. Through drug use, notes Sandor Rado (1981), stress is alleviated and reality is avoided, but only temporarily; when the chemical reaction subsides, reality returns with renewed vigor, and the subject again seeks relief through drugs. However, the psyche now finds that the same dosage brings diminished relief—tolerance has developed—leading to increasing dosages.

As a result of disturbances in psychosexual development, a person may remain at the ego level of development; in other words, "the child remains asocial or else behaves as if he had become social without having made actual adjustment to the demands of society. This means that he has not repudiated completely his instinctual wishes but has suppressed them so that they lurk in the background awaiting an opportunity to break through to satisfaction" (Aichhorn 1963: 4). Drug use, a reversion to gratifications associated with the oral stage, is a symptom of such a disturbance. Drug use is also associated with the ego's need to be in control of the source of pleasurable feelings—it is narcissistic (Rado 1981). Edward Khantzian (1980) states that heroin use is caused by the ego's need to control feelings of rage and aggression, emotions that relate to the anal stage of development; a form of self-medication.

The choice of drugs is either ego-constricting or ego-expanding. The weak ego structure of heroin users causes them to seek quiet and lonely lives—a tranquility through ego constriction that is aided by narcotics. Cocaine and amphetamine users, on the other hand, often come from households with warm mothers and fathers who are strong and encouraging. For them, stimulant use grows out of a self-directed and intensely competitive personality: "They take cocaine to expand their egos and their self-confidence" (Spotts and Shontz 1980: 65). The user of stimulants is suffering from anxiety brought on by a lack of stimulation: The ego is disturbed by the absence of stimuli, and intense stimulation is preferred by those using amphetamines and cocaine to ward off boredom and depression (Krystal and Raskin 1970).

In the course of normal development, over time the child integrates outer (social) discipline and imposes it on himself or herself. The instinctual impulses are brought under his or her own control, and we get the beginning of a superego (F. Smart 1970).

Superego   Oversimplified as the conscience, the **superego** is a counterforce to the id, exercising a critical influence, a sense of morality that controls behavior. Tied to overcoming the incestuous feelings of the genital stage, the superego serves as an internalized parent, meaning that behavior is no longer exclusively dependent on external forces (the ego level of control). Failures in superego development may leave a person without strong internal controls over id and ego impulses and can result in behavior that is harmful or destructive. The sociopath lacks sufficient superego strength, and the ego is insufficient to control powerful id impulses.

At the other extreme is an overactive superego that cannot make distinctions between *thinking* bad and *doing* bad. Unresolved conflicts of earlier development (e.g., an Oedipus complex) and id impulses that are normally repressed or dealt with through other, less-destructive processes (such as reaction formation, discussed below) create a severe sense of guilt. This guilt is experienced (unconsciously) as a compulsive need to be punished; and to alleviate guilt, the person commits acts for which punishment is virtually certain. August Aichhorn (1963) notes that such people are victims of their own personalities. For them drugs accomplish a dual purpose: Drugs reduce the anxiety caused by unresolved inner conflicts, while the deleterious aspects of drug abuse provide external punishment. According to Leon Wurmser (1978), society assists the drug abuser in this quest by imposing shame and punishment.

According to psychoanalytic theory, unconscious forces maintain a delicate balance as the person experiences life's various sociocultural and biological aspects.

The balance is easily upset, crossing the very thin line between the normal and the neurotic or between the neurotic and the psychotic. In fact, there is only a difference of degree between the *normal* and the *abnormal*. When repressed material begins to overwhelm the psyche and threatens to enter the person's consciousness, external defense mechanisms come into play in the form of psychoneuroses and, in more serious cases, psychosis. These responses may take the form of phobias— toward heights, insects, or closed spaces, for example. In the paranoid reaction the person projects his or her thoughts onto imagined enemies; in the reaction formation the destructive urges of the anal stage can be channeled into prosocial activities— becoming a surgeon, a veterinarian, or a butcher, for example. The degree to which defense mechanisms cause the person to become dysfunctional provides an objective measurement of abnormality. The psychoneuroses, or the primitive defense mechanism that is drug abuse, allow psychic energy to be discharged without having to confront unconscious material (Wurmser 1978). In his cocaine-abusing patients, Frederic Schiffer (1988) found that drug use was a self-medication aimed at alleviating the pain of early trauma. Cocaine abuse represented an unconscious, symbolic repetition of childhood trauma. Old psychological injuries were reinflicted by the drug, which also allowed the patient to unconsciously gain a (false) sense of control over these early difficulties, providing an opportunity to struggle against them again.

©Imagesource/Photolibrary

Adolescents typically undergo periods of boredom, anxiety, anger, frustration, and even short-lived depression; a defining feature of this time is change on many levels. Research has identified these factors as well as the peer group as being associated with drug abuse. Sociopsychological growth and maturity require grappling with reality—drug use reduces social competence and adaptive behaviors, leaving adolescents ill-equipped to become adults.

DRUG USE AND ADOLESCENCE

Psychoanalytic theory views drug abuse as a symptom of neuroses that manifest themselves during adolescence. We recognize that adolescents typically undergo periods of boredom, anxiety, anger, frustration, and even short-lived depression. A defining feature of adolescence "is the rapid and far-reaching changes occurring in virtually all aspects of life and the resultant high-level stress" (Newcomb and Bentler 1988: 11). Research has identified these factors as well as the peer group as being associated with drug abuse. The typical adolescent has not had sufficient experience in dealing with feelings of psychosocial stress in a mature—that is, adult—fashion. Psychoactive drugs can be seen as a form of self-medication in response to the stressful conditions of adolescence. These frequently include affective disorders: "Drugs of abuse and medications prescribed for affective disorders have common neurochemical effects that presumably treat the abnormality" (Bukstein, Brent, and Kaminer 1989: 1139).

It is normal for an adolescent to grapple with the problems of physiological and psychological development. The struggle for identity through a progressive process of relationships and experiences enables the person to manage the complexities of adolescence. He or she becomes more competent and eventually moves into young adulthood. "Adolescence is a period of development involving transitions in the major physical, intellectual, psychosocial, and moral processes that make up a person. Transitional stages of development are by definition periods of disequilibration and disruption and, therefore, replete with opportunities for experiences that are both dangerous and growth-enhancing" (Baumrind 1987: 14).

"The adolescent addict, however, sidesteps such growth by at first simply avoiding the situations in which he can gradually acquire competence or by passively going along with the whims and decisions of others and eventually by substituting the anxiety-reducing 'normative' influence of the opiate drugs" (Chein et al. 1964: 202). As Otto Fenichel (1945) points out, euphoric substances protect against painful mental states. However, because of this, the adolescent's reality-testing ability (an ego function) remains primitive, and his or her ability to tolerate stress and frustration remains at an infantile (oral) level. Like the infant during the oral stage, the addict is motivated only by a need to immediately gratify his or her perceived needs. This type of behavior is governed only by the primitive id impulses—the pleasure principle—without any real concern for the results. As a result of their extensive longitudinal research, Michael Newcomb and Peter Bentler (1988: 240) conclude that adolescent drug use, "particularly of cannabis and hard drugs, has measurably negative effects on several critical areas of life functioning as a young adult."

Heroin use typically begins during adolescence, with the drug serving as a means for avoiding psychologically demanding—but healthier—responses to developmental crisis, stress, deprivation, and other forms of emotional pain (Khantzian, Mack, Schatzberg 1974). Sociopsychological growth and maturity require grappling with reality, as exercise aficionados will recognize: "No pain, no gain." Drug use reduces social competence and adaptive behaviors. The therapeutic community, a particular approach to treating drug abusers discussed in Chapter 10, responds to people whose use of drugs is based on an inability to deal with the frustrations of reality.

UNRESOLVED PARENTAL RELATIONSHIPS

According to Freud, "from the time of puberty onward the human individual must devote himself to the great task of freeing himself from the parents; and only after this detachment is accomplished can he cease to be a child and so become a member of the social community" (1961: 345–346). Freud points out that in neurotics, such as addicts, this detachment is not accomplished because the neurotic has a distorted pathological relationship with his or her parents. This relationship is characterized by overdependence and fear of being rejected. Although there is identification with the father (or father figure), it is "at best laden with hostility" (Frazier 1962: 97). Isidor Chein and his colleagues (1964) found that addicts, in contrast to controls from the same environment, came either from single-parent households or from families in which the father was usually distant, presented immoral models of behavior, was primarily concerned with day-to-day gratification of appetites, and impulsive. As would be expected, the fathers had unstable work histories, pessimistic and fatalistic attitudes toward the future, and low aspirations for their sons. The level of interaction between father and son was minimal. A 1999 study at Columbia University found that adolescents who do not get along well with their fathers are much more likely to use nicotine, alcohol, and illegal drugs than are even children from one-parent/mother-only households (Molotsky 1999).

The addict's relationship with his mother includes a long history of emotional deprivation (Frazier 1962: 98):

> Frequently, a tense, dominant, autistic, unhappy mother forced the child into becoming an adjunct to herself rather than allowing him to develop as an independent person. The feeling of hostility toward the mother and the inability to form any close satisfactory relationships date back to these earliest years. The addict's conflicts reflect this oral deprivation in an infantile helplessness, and the drug helps him to regress to "happy" infancy that was never really happy. The effects of the drug handle his hostility and reduce tensions that are symptoms of these lifelong conflicts. The hostility toward the mother generally remains unconscious, but it is expressed through the drug that not only "destroys" the user but also symbolically destroys the mother whom he has incorporated through identification.

EGO DEFICIENCIES

According to Robert Savitt (1963: 45), it is not euphoria that the addict seeks in narcotics but a satiated feeling reminiscent of infancy: "When an infant's basic needs for sustenance and love are fulfilled, he falls asleep." Thus, the purported use of heroin for its euphoric properties is an exaggeration: "It would appear that the elation which the heroin addict experiences has been stressed out of proportion to the sleep or stupor which often soon follows.... Like the infant who alternates between hunger and sleep, the addict alternates between hunger for a drug and narcotic stupor" (1963: 44). The adolescent addict suffers from a narcissism (self-love), an infantile level of relating to others that retards the ability to form close, warm, emotional relationships. Other people are simply instruments for the adolescent's own purposes—even his or her own mother, from whom the adolescent has not learned to differentiate as a portion of himself or herself. Interpersonal relationships, even with parents, are shallow. Groups of "junkies" are tied together only by the one thing they share: drugs. It is an easy group, without demands, deliberate structure, or goals beyond those involving continued drug use. Stanley Greenspan (1978: 74) states: "Substance abuse could emanate from the lack of this basic ability of attaching to the human object." A prominent feature of the family situation of the adolescent opiate addict "is the peculiarly close relationship between the addict and his mother. It is not a closeness of warmth or mutual regard so much as it is a clinging and feeling of being bound together" (Chein et al. 1964: 212).

Drug-dependent adolescents suffer from severe ego inadequacies. They have been found to be relatively unresponsive or indifferent to opportunities for education, work, or recreation; they have limited interests and curiosity. They appear to suffer from gross disturbances in early life, leading to a restricted pattern of responsiveness. They have poor reality testing and an inability to delay gratification or accept frustration. They react to criticism by withdrawal, giving up easily in school or employment situations, and they are unable to form realistic goal orientations. While recognizing all of the dangers inherent in heroin use, addicts are unable to exercise restraint. They use heroin to deal with frustrations and pain; they are retreatists for whom heroin relieves anxiety, by changing feelings of tenseness and restlessness into feelings of comfort, relaxation, and peacefulness (Chein et al. 1964). Heroin helps to overcome the usual tensions of adolescence. The heroin addict may also find heroin effective in thwarting feelings of intense destructiveness and sadism associated with a disturbance in the anal stage of development. The drug pacifies such drives, and the negative and punishing results of heroin addiction satisfy the superego's need to punish such feelings (Yorke 1970).

REGRESSION TO INFANT SEXUALITY

There are significant sexual implications in drug use, particularly the intravenous use of heroin. "Addicts are persons who have a disposition to react to the effects of alcohol, morphine, or other drugs in such a way that they try to use these effects to satisfy the archaic oral longings which is sexual longing, a need for security, and a need for the maintenance of self-esteem simultaneously" (Fenichel 1945: 376). This pathology has its origins in infantile sexuality, both oral and genital. "The addict uses his addiction to express or act out repressed impulses and needs," and the discharge of psychic energy is pleasurable enough to replace other pleasurable activities, such as sex and eating (Chein et al. 1964: 235). The use of heroin is autoerotic, bypassing genital sex in favor of the infantile or oral-stage eroticism (Yorke 1970).

Psychoanalytic theories of drug abuse have been criticized for their reliance on retrospective self-reports and individual case studies, which are limited methods that lack rigorous empirical grounding. This contrasts with the rigorous experimentation that underlies learning theory.

BEHAVIORISM/LEARNING THEORY

The second major school of psychological thought has its roots in the laboratory of experimental psychology with its dogs, pigeons, rats, monkeys, and mazes (see, e.g., Rachlin 1991). Behaviorists typically reject psychoanalytic theory as unscientific, that is, lacking the rigorous testing to which learning theory has been subjected. Indeed, measurement of objective behavior is intrinsic to **learning theory**, which proceeds on the basis that all forms of behavior are conditioned, the result of learned responses to certain stimuli. Disturbed behavior such as drug abuse results from inappropriate conditioning (London 1964). To the behaviorist a person is simply the sum product of his or her experience or learning, and learning is based on operant conditioning.

OPERANT CONDITIONING

The behaviorist stresses—and has been able to prove—that animal behavior can be modified through the proper application of operant conditioning: positive and negative reinforcement. Behavior is "*strengthened* by its consequences, and for that reason the consequences themselves are called 'reinforcers.'" (Skinner 1974: 40). When some aspect of (animal or human) behavior is followed by a certain type of consequence—a reward—the behavior is more likely to be repeated. The reward is called **positive reinforcement**. If the probability of a behavior goes up after the *removal* of a stimulus, then **negative reinforcement** has occurred. "A negative reinforcer strengthens any behavior that reduces or terminates it" (Skinner 1974: 47). For example, the negative reinforcement that occurs when a heroin addict fails to ingest enough heroin—withdrawal symptoms—strengthens drug-seeking behavior. Both positive and negative reinforcers increase behavioral responses; they differ in their ordering relationship: Positive reinforcers *follow* the behavior they reinforce, while negative reinforcers *precede* the behavior they reinforce. A person *works to receive* a positive reinforcer and *works to escape* a negative reinforcer. Punishment is the third general principle of operant conditioning. *Punishment* decreases the probability or frequency of a behavior (Bozarth 1994).

Behavioral psychology recognizes two basic types of processes associated with learning (Tilson 1993: 2):

Classical conditioning involves the pairing of two stimuli, one of which elicits a reflex and one of which is neutral [food and the sounding of a bell, for example]. With repeated pairing of the two stimuli, the previously neutral stimulus [bell] becomes a conditioned stimulus and elicits the response [salivating, for example] in absence of the original eliciting stimulus [food].

Operant conditioning involves the repeated presentation or removal of a stimulus following a behavior to increase the probability of the behavior (i.e., **reinforcement**). A reinforcer is a stimulus that increases the probability of a behavior. If the probability of a behavior goes up following the presentation of some stimulus, then positive reinforcement has occurred. If the probability of a behavior goes up after the *removal* of a stimulus, then negative reinforcement has occurred.

The noted behaviorist B. F. Skinner states: "Punishment is easily confused with negative reinforcement, sometimes called 'aversive control.' The same stimuli are used, and negative reinforcement might be defined as the punishment of not behaving, but punishment is designed to remove behavior from a repertoire, whereas negative reinforcement generates behavior" (1974: 63). As was noted earlier, a particular psychoactive substance will be reinforcing to some people or to most people under certain conditions—for example, opiates when one is in pain. For most people under ordinary circumstances, the same substance will not provide reinforcement—at least not reinforcement that is sufficiently positive to offset negative consequences—and they do not seek to repeat the behavior.

According to this view, drug use is merely the result of learning directly from others. Chein and his colleagues (1964) note that both the processes involved with the use of heroin, excitement and the actions of the drug itself, become reinforcing, thus shaping—that is, molding—the behavior of the addict. Alfred Lindesmith (1968: 8) argues that a continuation of heroin use is based on negative reinforcement: "persons become addicts when they recognize or perceive the significance of withdrawal distress which they are experiencing" when they cease to use heroin. Lindesmith argues that substances such as cocaine and marijuana, on the other hand, are positive reinforcers because they are taken to enhance mood rather than to stave off withdrawal. From the discussion in Chapter 4 we know that Lindesmith's assertions are questionable: The physiological discomfort of heroin withdrawal is usually no greater than a bout with the flu; discontinuing the use of cocaine can produce depression; and sudden withdrawal from alcohol can be life threatening.

BEHAVIOR MODIFICATION

The abuse of stimulants and depressants can be explained by learning theory. The use of cocaine, for example, can be quite rewarding: It elevates mood and provides a sense of well-being, strength, and energy, whereas discontinuing use provides negative reinforcement in the form of psychological depression, or the "coke blues." Likewise, heroin use can be quite rewarding to the addict: It significantly reduces perceptions of physical and psychological pain, stress, and anxiety, and provides a sense of euphoria, whereas discontinuing use provides negative reinforcement in the form of uncomfortable physical and psychological withdrawal symptoms. Although chemicals such as cocaine or heroin might initially have been used for social reasons, these substances' ability to provide physiological and psychological rewards explains why addicts seek to continue use even in the face of considerable hardship: Drugs overcome *competing reinforcers*: "The balancing of pleasurable or rewarding experiences and punishing or unpleasant experiences that occurs during the early weeks or months of drug involvement may be of critical importance. If the net impact of those experiences is highly positive, the effect or memory of that 'honeymoon' can remain remarkably strong over time, even as continuing reward diminishes and punishment increases, especially if alternative competitive behaviors are not exercised or reinforced as strongly" (Gerstein and Harwood 1990: 65).

Furthermore, while being known as a "junkie" or a "cokehead" might have negative consequences in conventional society, it often provides positive reinforcement in that it allows entry and acceptance into a small clique that is the drug subculture. Daily activities can now be focused on a clearly identifiable goal: drugs.

The sociological dimension of this concept appeared in Chapter 7 in our discussion of anomie and retreatism. Furthermore, the illegal aspects of drug abuse provide a level of excitement that some people find quite rewarding. For drug users who must engage in criminality to support their habits, success in crime also provides an important source of reinforcement, particularly when the users do not possess skills necessary to succeed in noncriminal endeavors that could offer a competing source of reinforcement.

Although a dose of intravenous methamphetamine would probably be physically pleasurable to anyone, Thomas Crowley (1981: 368) points out that not everyone who experiences the pleasure continues to use amphetamines. The person who continues use is more likely to be from an impoverished environment: "Users in impoverished environments, with few other reinforcers available, will probably seek drug reinforcement more actively. Similarly, long experience with disturbed, unloving parents seems to convince many young people that they can never achieve respect or love from others. These young people have not learned to expect reinforcement from their environment, and so they may more actively seek the predictable, regular reinforcement of drug abuse." Most people who find the intake of certain substances rewarding do not become compulsive about continued use. Thus, while some people become obese because of their eating habits, most people do not become compulsive overeaters. While certain foods are pleasing to most people—chocolate or ice cream, for example—relatively few respond by compulsive intake. Large numbers of Americans use alcoholic beverages, but most avoid dependence.

COGNITIVE LEARNING THEORY

Cognition refers to learning and memory, and while cognitive processes cannot be observed the way outward behavior can, many behaviorists believe that cognition plays a crucial role in learning theory in humans.

> An important distinction in learning theory is between observable and unobservable behavior. Many behaviorists use "behavior" only in reference to observable activity, but this is too restrictive. No matter what it is called, unobservable behavior, especially cognitive behavior, is important in people's lives.... A cognitive response is simply a thought or feeling, typically in reaction to some stimulus. But a thought or feeling may also serve as a stimulus for a subsequent response. So a cognitive event may act either as a stimulus or as a response, or as both, as these events often do. (Starkweather 1982: 37)

Cognitive behaviorists recognize that human behavior is more complex than that of other species—that, for example, human behavior is often mediated by beliefs and symbols. The readiness to fight or die for a cause—symbolized by the cross, the star of David, the crescent, or the red star—illustrates the abstract complexities of human behavior. This recognition has led to *cognitive learning theory*, the major tenets of which are that "human behavior is mediated by unobservables that intervene between a stimulus and a response to that stimulus. Beliefs, sets, strategies, attributions, and expectancies are examples of the types of mediating constructs currently considered crucial to an understanding of emotion and behavior" (S. Gold 1980: 8).

Furthermore, "the way an individual labels or evaluates a situation determines his or her emotional and behavioral responses to it." Thus, based on past learning, a twisted cross (swastika) may have a different meaning to a Jew than to a Navajo Indian (for whom it is a cosmic religious symbol). According to this approach, the drug abuser has difficulty in meeting societal demands or expectations, and this leads to anxiety. Although anxiety is a universal experience, Steven Gold notes (1980: 9), drug abusers feel that "they cannot alter or control the situation; that they are powerless to affect their environment to decrease or eliminate the sources of stress."

People who face persistent difficulties and anxieties in their lives and who are not prepared to cope with them may resort to analgesic drugs for comfort. "While enabling them to forget their problems and stress, the painkilling experience engendered by such drugs actually *decreases* the ability to cope. This is because such drugs depress the central nervous system and the individual's responsive capacity" (Peele 1980: 143). Heroin or alcohol provide relief from anxiety, and the user also attains temporary euphoria: "Under the influence of the drug the individual temporarily experiences an increased sense of power, control, and well-being." The drug acts as a powerful reinforcer—it can do for the abuser what he or she cannot do for himself or herself. However, these effects are short-lived, and after the drug wears off, the user finds that feelings of powerlessness return with full fury, which leads to further use of the drug and a cycle of continuing drug abuse: "The reliance on drugs to cope with stress therefore creates a vicious cycle; the more drugs are used, the more the individual believes they are necessary. Each drug experience serves to confirm for users the belief that they are powerless to function on their own" (S. Gold 1980: 9). Behaviorists often refer to this state of thinking as *learned helplessness*: Through inappropriate reinforcement, the drug abuser *learns* that he or she can neither escape nor avoid the stimulus leading to drug use.

Stimulants such as amphetamine and cocaine provide not only primary reinforcement as a result of their impact on the central nervous system but also secondary reinforcement as the result of drug-induced behavioral change for those who wish to increase their assertiveness. Amphetamines, for example, can produce a sense of cleverness, clear thinking, energy, alertness, and loquaciousness (Crowley 1981).

Learning theory is difficult to apply in the treatment of drug abusers. As was noted earlier, drugs are so reinforcing, providing immediate gratification for those who have *learned* to enjoy their use, that finding appropriate reinforcers that can successfully compete is quite difficult. Relapse after treatment can also be explained by learning theory, that is, the classical conditioned response: Certain cues associated with drug-taking behavior trigger a craving (Childress et al. 1993). These cues are discussed in Chapter 10. Agonists and antagonists, also discussed in Chapter 10, can be used to thwart the reinforcing quality of psychoactive substances. That chapter will also examine treatment programs that apply behavior theory, in particular the popular cognitive behavior therapy.

Stanley Greenspan (1978: 80) explains drug abuse by integrating behaviorism and psychoanalytic theory into a model that defines external experiences in terms of stimuli and reinforcers derived from psychosexual stages of development and the organization of id, ego, and superego. He states, for example, that "a substance abuser who achieves a basic and primitive homeostatic experience by using his addictive drug may be obtaining tremendous and potent reinforcement from the substance abuse.... Because of a lack of internalized control and the number of potent internal forces working from within, he tends to be vulnerable to environmental influences in rather dramatic ways and is sensitive to many potentially reinforcing events in his external environment [even though they may be destructive]."

A PSYCHOSOCIOLOGICAL DIMENSION

Drug use has a psychosociological dimension according to which the actor must *learn* that ingesting certain chemicals is desirable; intoxication, for example, is not inherently pleasurable. Expectations are based on learning and influence the direction of drug use. Thus, naive drug users, such as hospitalized patients who are given doses of morphine to relieve pain, do not experience euphoria and do not continue to seek out opiates when the pain subsides (Chein et al. 1964). Chein and his colleagues go so far as to state that opiates "are not inherently attractive, euphoric, or stimulant substances. The danger of addiction to opiates resides in the person, not in the drug" (1964: 348). Edward Brecher (1972: 13) notes that while there is "no doubt that the injection directly into a vein of a substantial dose of morphine or heroin produces a readily identifiable sensation," described by nonaddicts as a sudden flush of warmth and by addicts as a rush, few nonaddicts perceive the rush as particularly pleasurable. R. M. Gilbert (1981: 386) states that just because "a substance *can* have a pharmacological effect, it does not automatically follow that use of the substance is caused by or maintained by that effect." A 16-year-old cigarette smoker reports: "The first time I tried it, last year, I was like, 'This is totally gross.' I was coughing, and I turned green, and I thought I was going to throw up. So I had to *learn* to like it" (Verhovek 1995: 1; emphasis added). In an update of Howard Becker's (1966) work on becoming a marijuana user, however, Michael Hallstone (2002) found that most marijuana users became intoxicated the first time they smoked the substance and did not necessarily have to learn that they were intoxicated through social interaction with other users, and most found the initial experience pleasurable.

People who believe that they are drinking alcohol when actually they have been given nonalcoholic substitutes get more relaxed and outgoing, and a party atmosphere develops (D. Wood 1991). Indeed, levels of sexual arousal increase when people who are given a placebo believe that they have imbibed alcohol, although alcohol reduces sexual performance (Mendelson and Mello 1995).

The focus of psychology is on the individual and is divided into clinical and behavioral. The first is influenced by Freudian theory, which explains human behavior as being driven through processes that are largely unconscious. Drug abuse is seen as a manifestation of unresolved developmental issues related to oral, anal, or genital stages. While experiencing these stages, the person develops an id, ego, and superego, deficiencies which can be connected to adult drug use.

Drug abuse in adolescence is explained as an immature response to the stress typical of this period: The adolescent drug user circumvents the demands of maturity. Although users reach chronological adulthood, they remain psychologically preadolescent.

Behaviorism has its roots in the laboratory of experimental psychology and is based on learning theory. All forms of behavior are conditioned, the result of learned responses to certain stimuli. Behavior is strengthened by its consequences and can be modified by operant conditioning: positive and negative reinforcement. Drugs can serve as powerful reinforcers, while withdrawal symptoms provide negative reinforcement.

With these explanations in mind, in the next chapter we will examine the variety of methods that are used to treat drug abusers and prevent drug abuse.

SUMMARY

- Psychology, a discipline that focuses on the individual, provides some answers as to why people who are exposed to the same physical environment react differently to the use and abuse of drugs.
- The *addictive personality* is a psychological vulnerability resulting from problematic family relationships and inappropriate reinforcement.
- Psychological theories can be broadly categorized into those that are based on a Freudian or psychoanalytic strain and those that are based on behaviorism or learning theory.
- The basic proposition of psychoanalytic theory concerns the influence of unconscious phenomena on human behavior; that people are not aware of the most important determinants of their behavior.
- Sigmund Freud posited that unconscious feelings and thoughts relate to stages of psychosexual development from infancy to adulthood: oral, anal, genital, latency, adulthood. Each has a link to adult drug abuse.
- While the individual is experiencing each of these stages of development, three corresponding psychic phenomena develop: id, ego, and superego.
- Oversimplified as the conscience, the superego is a counterforce to the id, exercising a critical influence, a sense of morality that controls behavior.
- Failures in superego development may leave a person without strong internal controls over id and ego impulses and can result in behavior that is harmful or destructive.

- At the other extreme is an overactive superego that cannot make distinctions between *thinking* bad and *doing* bad. Drugs reduce the anxiety caused by unresolved inner conflicts, while the deleterious aspects of drug abuse provide external punishment.
- The adolescent has not had sufficient experience in dealing with feelings of psychosocial stress in a mature fashion and psychoactive drugs can be seen as a form of self-medication in response to the stressful conditions of adolescence.
- Drugs allow the adolescent to bypass dealing with stress and frustration and so the adolescent's ego function remains primitive, and his or her ability to tolerate stress and frustration remains at an infantile level.
- Learning theory proceeds on the basis that all forms of behavior are conditioned, the result of learned responses to certain stimuli. Disturbed behavior such as drug abuse results from inappropriate conditioning.
- Behavior is strengthened by its consequences, called reinforcers. When some aspect of behavior is followed by a reward, the behavior is more likely to be repeated. The reward is called positive reinforcement. The reinforcement provided by drugs can overwhelm competing reinforcers.
- Not everyone exposed to drugs finds the experience reinforcing; hospital patients do not experience euphoria when treated for pain.
- The reliance on drugs to cope with stress therefore creates a vicious cycle; the more drugs are used, the more the individual believes they are necessary.

Review Questions

1. What are the features of the addictive personality explanation for drug abuse?
2. What distinguishes psychological explanations of drug abuse from sociological explanations?
3. What has research disclosed with respect to the addictive personality thesis?
4. How can psychological theories be broadly categorized?
5. What is the basic proposition of psychoanalytic theory?
6. How can problems experienced during the oral stage of development lead to drug abuse in the adult?
7. How can the use of depressants by an adult be connected to the anal stage of development?
8. What is the relationship between difficulty during the genital stage and drug abuse in adulthood?
9. How can drug abuse be explained by id drives?
10. How can drugs compensate for ego deficiencies?
11. How can a deficiency in superego development lead to drug abuse?
12. How does psychoanalytic theory explain drug abuse during adolescence?
13. What basic belief underlies behaviorism/learning theory?
14. According to psychoanalytic theory, what are the stages of psychological development?
15. How can each of these stages be linked to drug abuse in the adult?
16. How do divisions of the psyche help explain drug use?
17. How can an overactive superego explain drug abuse?
18. How does psychoanalytic theory explain adolescent drug use?
19. Why does drug abuse cause the adolescent to remain at a primitive level of maturity?
20. Why does psychoanalytic theory consider the pursuit of euphoria as at best a minor reason for drug addiction?
21. Why is it difficult if not impossible to use psychoanalysis to treat heroin addiction?
22. How does learning theory differ from psychoanalytic theory?
23. How does operant conditioning explain drug use?
24. How is classical conditioning distinguished from operant conditioning?
25. How can being known as a "junkie" or a "cokehead" provide positive reinforcement?
26. How can drugs overwhelm competing reinforcers?
27. How does cognitive learning theory add to our understanding of drug use?
28. Why do hospital patients receiving morphine to relieve pain or experience euphoria and in the absence of pain rarely become dependent?
29. Why is it difficult to apply behavior theory in the treatment of drug abuse?
30. How do expectations based on learning influence individual drug use?

Less than 3 percent of federal and state substance abuse spending goes to prevention, treatment, or research.

Center for Substance Abuse Research (2009)

CHAPTER 9

DRUG USE AND ABUSE: PREVENTION

Prevention programs should address all forms of drug abuse, alone or in combination, including the underage use of legal drugs (e.g., tobacco or alcohol); the use of illegal drugs (e.g., marijuana or heroin); and the inappropriate use of legally obtained substances (e.g., inhalants), prescription medications, or over-the-counter drugs.

National Institute on Drug Abuse (2003b: 2)

Efforts at prevention attempt to reduce the supply of or demand for drugs of abuse. The former is the goal of drug law enforcement (see Chapter 12); the latter has been the goal of coercive legislation and education. "Considering the difficulty and cost of treating individuals with substance abuse problems, the prospect of developing effective substance abuse prevention programs has long held a great deal of appeal" (National Institute on Drug Abuse 1987: 35). Unfortunately, effective prevention has proven to be as elusive as effective treatment (and effective law enforcement).

MODELS FOR PREVENTION

On the basis of extensive research, the National Institute on Drug Abuse recommends that prevention programs be designed to enhance protective factors and move toward reversing or reducing known risk factors. Protective factors are those associated with reduced potential for drug use; risk factors are those that make the potential for drug use more likely.

Protective factors include strong and positive bonds within a prosocial family; parental monitoring; clear rules of conduct that are consistently enforced within the family; involvement of parents in the lives of their children; success in school performance; strong bonds with other prosocial institutions, such as school and religious organizations; and adoption of conventional norms about drug use.

Risk factors include chaotic home environments, particularly those in which parents abuse substances or suffer from mental illnesses; ineffective parenting, especially with children who have difficult temperaments or conduct disorders; lack of mutual attachments and nurturing; inappropriately shy or aggressive behavior in the classroom; failure in school performance; poor social coping skills; affiliations with deviant peers or peers who display deviant behaviors; and perceptions of approval of drug-using behaviors in family, work, school, peer, and community environments (National Institute on Drug Abuse 2001c: 1).

"Problematic drug use and drug use risk factors may be symptomatic of the troubled lives experienced by some young people" (Home Office 2007: 47). While there are relatively well-established associations between several risk and protective factors and problematic drug use among young people, these associations are not necessarily causal. In other words, risk factors may result in drug use, but it is also possible that "troubled lives" may result in both risk factors and drug use.

Most efforts at prevention have focused on schools, and school-based antidrug programs are widespread. These programs have been dominated by three models (Ellickson 1995):

1. *Information model.* Assuming that children and adolescents will avoid drugs when they understand their potential hazards, this model seeks to impart information. Furthermore, the model assumes that students will develop negative attitudes that will deter them from using drugs. "In short, the information

model posits a causal sequence leading from knowledge (about drugs) to attitude change (negative) to behavior change (nonuse)" (Ellickson 1995: 100). Sometimes shock or scare tactics are part of this approach, exemplified by hard-hitting antidrug videos, talks by ex-junkies, or TV and billboard campaigns that focus on the horrors of drug use (J. Cohen 1996).

2. *Affective model.* Shifting the focus away from education, this model instead seeks to affect personality. The focus is on the individual rather than drugs per se, and it is assumed that young people who have high self-esteem will not use drugs (J. Cohen 1996). "The model assumes that adolescents who turn to drugs do so because of problems within themselves—low self-esteem or inadequate personal skills in communication and decision making" (Ellickson 1995: 101). Affective model programs attempt to improve the affective skills (communication, decision making, self-assertion) that are believed to be related to drug use. In attempting to improve a student's self-image, ability to interact within a group, and problem-solving ability, the model focuses on feelings, values, and self-awareness and, in some programs, on personal values and choices.

3. *Social influence model.* Young people are seen as easy prey to peer pressure and in need of developing the skills to "Say No To Drugs." The approach assumes that young people lack the skills to make rational choices and that if they had these skills, they would not use drugs (Cohen 1996). The social influence model is centered on external influences that push students toward drug use, especially peer pressure, as well as internal influences, such as the desire to be accepted by "the crowd." To deal with adolescent vulnerabilities, the social influence model seeks to familiarize students with the pressures to use drugs, enabling them to develop resistance skills and techniques for saying no in those pressure situations.

Educating people, particularly elementary, high school, and college students (the primary population at risk), about the dangers of drug use would seem at first blush to be devoid of controversy and a sound response to the problem of drug abuse. After all, as Richard Brotman and Frederic Suffet (1975) point out, the

DRUG EDUCATION OR PROPAGANDA?

Drug education is often not based on the educational principles that underlie the teaching of other subjects but tends to skew and censor information, to give a narrow view of drug use, and to tell young people what they should think and do. This is propaganda, not education. It often results in young people not being able to talk openly and honestly. Instead, they end up saying what they think their teachers or parents want to hear rather than what they really believe. The gulf between adults and young people widens, open dialogue lessens, and young people with problems or concerns about drugs become less likely to approach adults for support. (J. Cohen 1996)

"Health education discourses have often been cleansed of any reference to the possibility that people might use drugs because they find them pleasurable." (Advisory Council on the Misuse of Drugs 1998: 36)

thinking behind the idea appears to be quite rational: Provide valid information about the harmful consequences of drug abuse, and most people will elect to avoid drugs. However, as Patricia Wald and Peter Hutt (1972: 18) note, "There is substantial uncertainty and confusion in the area of drug education and prevention" because "there is no real evidence that such educational efforts are successful." Indeed, as research by Isidor Chein and his colleagues (1964) revealed, the youngsters who have the greatest knowledge about drugs are the most likely to use drugs. In addition, there is a substantial drug abuse problem among physicians, who presumably know a great deal about the dangers of drugs (Kennedy 1995; McDougall 2006).

Michael Goodstadt (n.d.: 2) points out that informational programs typically suffer from major weaknesses that might actually encourage drug use: "The unfortunate result is that young people might become more rather than less likely to experiment with drugs." Dan Waldorf (1973) noted that during the 1960s and early 1970s, heroin in New York City was seemingly everywhere in African-American and Puerto Rican ghettos, where young people are exposed to it at an early age. They know about heroin and drug addicts through firsthand exposure; they witness the drugs being purchased and see addicts nodding on the streets and clustering in doorways, communal washrooms, and rooftops to "get off." They know that addicts steal family belongings to sell for money to buy drugs. The real question, Waldorf states, is not why so many ghetto residents become drug abusers but why a majority avoid becoming addicted to a powerful substance that provides relief from an oppressive environment (1973).

INFORMATION MODEL

The standard educational approach has been to present factual information about the dangers of substance abuse because it was assumed that increased knowledge would serve as an effective deterrent by enabling students to make rational decisions not to use drugs. Unfortunately, this information has been frequently burdened with moral judgments about drug use (Zinberg 1984). The "scare" lecture of physical education teachers or nonschool personnel such as police officers has often been integral to this approach. Although intended to frighten students away from dangerous substances, these lectures often contain so much misinformation or exaggeration that they raise students' skepticism and jeopardize all drug education efforts. Young people have often found, through their own experiences of drug use and what friends tell them, that they have been lied to, and this leads them to mistrust adult sources of information on drugs (J. Cohen 1996; Brotman and Suffet 1975).

Goodstadt (n.d.: 3) suggests acknowledging the positive reinforcements of drug use: "Drug use consequences are not all negative; if they were, nobody would continue to use drugs. Moderate use of some drugs offers physical, psychological, and social benefits for some people. Drug education programs that do not take into account this important aspect of the decision to start or continue using drugs diminish their credibility and effectiveness." Julian Cohen (1996) concludes that the research evidence shows that appropriate drug education can increase drug knowledge, develop decision-making skills, and make young people more discerning about what they actually do. This does not mean that they will not use either legal or illegal drugs. In other words, drug education can play a role in reducing drug-related harm rather than preventing drug use.

The American Social Health Association (1972: 5) states that drug education "must avoid overconcentration on 'the drug problem.' Many youngsters, knowing more about drugs than their parents and teachers, will not accept moralization but will respect realistic, valid information derived from a credible source." A different approach to educating youngsters about certain dangerous chemicals avoids exaggeration and scare tactics, relying instead on a factual presentation about dangerous substances and the body's reaction to them, both the good and the bad. The goal is to provide information so that students can make informed decisions rather than to prevent drug use, which might be too much to expect from any educational program. This approach has some implementation problems:

1. It might be opposed by public officials or parents who believe that schools should teach "proper" behavior, that is, preach on the evils of drug use.
2. A great deal is not known about drugs of abuse.
3. Depending on their ages, students might not be able to understand the information.
4. Providing greater knowledge about drugs might serve the unintended (latent) function of piquing interest in and arousing curiosity about them and might possibly encourage more daring adolescents to seek out drugs (Goodstadt n.d.; Wald and Abrams 1972; Stuart 1974).

Goodstadt (n.d.: 3) states: "Efforts to prevent drug abuse by reducing the most risky forms of drug use (for example, drinking and driving, cannabis use and gymnastics) need not condone illegal drug use." Information programs should keep in mind that an eight-year study of adolescent drug use revealed that the vast majority of teenagers who occasionally use drugs suffer no long-lasting negative effects and cannot in later years be distinguished from those who abstained from drug use (Blakeslee 1988).

Research indicates that drug addicts are quite familiar with the effects and dangers of the substances they abuse, but they either discount the risks or view them as minor and part of the "game" (see, e.g., Hendler and Stephens 1977). Troy Duster (1970: 192) reports that prospective addicts see themselves as exceptions to the pattern of addiction they see around them: "It is typical of the early experience of the addict-to-be that he knows of people who use narcotics and who get away with it ... [in that] they are neither addicted nor are they known to the police. This double victory is witnessed by probably every individual who knowingly used heroin illegally for the first time." However, although there is evidence that drug users know much more about drugs than do nonusers, "there is no evidence that increases in such knowledge stimulate use" (D. J. Hanson 1980: 273). "Simply providing the child with information about substance abuse would primarily alter the behavior of well-socialized children from cohesive families rather than those most at risk" (Dishion, Patterson, and Reid 1988: 90).

AFFECTIVE MODEL

A broad approach to drug abuse prevention involves affective or humanistic education (although the term *humanistic* is likely to trigger negative responses in people who hold certain religious and social views). Public schools have turned away from the "scare 'em" approach toward one that emphasizes the judgment and social skills that are necessary to avoid substance abuse (Berger 1989). Some research indicates that this approach shows promise only with youngsters who are not likely to become problem drug users in the first place. The U.S. Center for Substance Abuse Prevention maintains that a "life skills" approach—problem-solving skills, decision-making skills, resistance skills against adverse peer influences, and social and communication skills—"is associated with short-term reductions in substance abuse among adolescents" and recommends that "life skills curricula should be recognized as an important component of effective substance abuse prevention programs for adolescents" (Chavez and Sanchez-Way 1997: 13, 14).

These affective efforts are designed to enhance self-esteem, to encourage responsible decision making, and to enrich students' personal and social development. The conceptual grounding for this approach was discussed in Chapter 8 as part of behaviorist/learning theory: prevention through the enhancement of social competence. This approach has research support (Pentz 1985).

The bases of this approach are assumptions that (National Institute on Drug Abuse 1987: 35):

1. Substance abuse programs should aim at developing prevention-oriented decision making concerning the use of licit or illicit drugs.
2. Such decisions should result in fewer negative consequences for the individuals.
3. The most effective way of achieving these goals is by increasing self-esteem, interpersonal skills, and participation in alternatives to substance use.

These assumptions are generally implemented through communication training, peer counseling, role-playing, and assertiveness training. In the Los Angeles school system this approach has been implemented through Project D.A.R.E. and Reconnecting Youth, which are discussed below.

SOCIAL INFLUENCE/LEARNING MODEL

The *social influence approach* attempts to "inoculate" students against using dangerous substances by making the students aware of the social pressures they are likely to encounter and teaching skills that promote refusal.

The *social learning approach* views chemical abuse from the perspective of learning theory; that is, like other behavior, it is learned through modeling and reinforcement. Through instruction, demonstration, feedback, reinforcement, behavioral rehearsal (classroom practice), and extended practice through homework assignments, the youngster is taught life-coping skills that have a rather broad range of applications, including drug resistance. There is considerable variation in age groups and length of program. Some groups are led by adults; others use peer leaders.

EFFECTIVE PREVENTION STRATEGIES

Prevention strategies targeting youths have evolved over more than twenty years as evaluation research has revealed more about what works. Several strategies are used effectively, especially in combination (Indiana Prevention Resource Center at Indiana University):

- *Information dissemination.* This strategy provides awareness and knowledge of the nature and extent of alcohol, tobacco, and other drug use, abuse, and addiction and their effects on individuals, families, and communities as well as information to increase perceptions of risk. It also provides knowledge and awareness of prevention policies, programs, and services. It helps to set and reinforce norms (e.g., a policy that underage drinking and drug dealers will not be tolerated in this neighborhood).

- *Prevention education.* This strategy aims to affect critical life and social skills, including decision making, refusal skills, critical analysis (e.g., of media messages), and systematic and judgmental abilities.

- *Alternatives.* This strategy provides for the participation of targeted populations in activities that exclude alcohol, tobacco, and other drug use by youths. Constructive and healthy activities offset the attraction to, or otherwise meet the needs that are usually filled by, alcohol, tobacco, and other drug use.

- *Problem identification and referral.* This strategy calls for identification, education, and counseling for youths who have indulged in age-inappropriate use of tobacco products or alcohol or who have indulged in the first use of illicit drugs. Activities under this strategy would include screening for tendencies toward substance abuse and referral for preventive treatment for curbing such tendencies.

Dr. Matthew Hopkins, who now works to help substance abusers overcome their addictions, had to overcome his own addictions.

- *Community-based process.* This strategy aims to enhance the community's ability to provide prevention and treatment services to alcohol, tobacco, and other drug use disorders more effectively. Activities include organizing, planning, enhancing efficiency and effectiveness of services implementation, interagency collaboration, coalition building, and networking. Building healthy communities encourages healthy lifestyle choices.
- *Environmental approach.* This strategy sets up or changes written and unwritten community standards, codes, and attitudes, influencing the incidence and prevalence of alcohol, tobacco, and other drug use problems in the general population. Included are laws to restrict availability and access, price increases, and communitywide actions.

SAMPLE PROGRAMS
PROJECT D.A.R.E.

D.A.R.E. (Drug Abuse Resistance Education) has proven popular with police departments throughout the United States. Any number of departments advertise the program on their police vehicles. The Los Angeles Police Department (LAPD) and the Los Angeles Unified School District jointly sponsor Project D.A.R.E., which is designed to equip fifth, sixth, and seventh graders with the skills and motivation they need to resist peer pressure to use drugs, alcohol, and tobacco. D.A.R.E.'s instructors are uniformed police officers on full-time duty with the project. All are veteran officers and volunteers who are carefully selected by D.A.R.E. supervisory staff and fully trained by officers and specialists from the school district.

> A D.A.R.E. police officer is assigned to teach in every elementary school under the LAPD's jurisdiction, offering the 17-session core curriculum to either fifth- or sixth-grade students. A junior-high program for seventh-graders, which includes early intervention with students deemed at risk, is also at full implementation in 58 junior high schools.
>
> In bringing the core curriculum to the elementary schools, D.A.R.E. officers are assigned to five schools per semester, and they visit each classroom once a week. Beyond this, the officers conduct one-day visits at other schools for an assembly program and follow-up visits in individual classrooms; hold formal training sessions on drug abuse for teachers; and conduct evening parent meetings. (DeJong 1987a: 4)

The use of uniformed police officers as instructors is seen as a key element in the program's success: "Police have knowledge of the drug scene and its impact on both individuals and society as a whole that regular classroom teachers cannot match. Indeed, many classroom teachers frankly admit their discomfiture in teaching lessons on drug abuse. For children this age, police hold a mystique. Kids respond to them" (DeJong 1987a: 7). And because the program "involves police officers in positive, nonpunitive roles, students are more likely to develop positive attitudes toward police officers and greater respect for the law" (1987a: 17). The D.A.R.E. curriculum ends with a schoolwide assembly that includes the reading of the winning "D.A.R.E. Pledges." Each student who completes the program receives a certificate of achievement signed by the chief of police and the superintendent of schools.

RECONNECTING YOUTH

Reconnecting Youth is a peer group approach to building life skills for high school students who are at risk for dropping out. Designed to build resiliency, the program is presented in the form of a personal growth class, typically delivered in daily fifty- to sixty-minute sessions during regular school hours by specifically trained school personnel (e.g., teachers, counselors, nurses) who work with students in a small-group format with a ratio of 1:12 per class. An important component is the enhancement of learning skills: "One of the most important risk factors for substance abuse is academic failure" (National Institute on Drug Abuse 1997a: 17).

During the first two weeks students are given an overview of the course as well as rules and expectations for working together as a group. Students learn about concepts such as inner strength, self-praise, and group praise, and they set goals for their participation in the class. This overview is followed by four life skills training units:

1. *Self-esteem enhancement* provides the basis for training in the other units and includes visualization, relaxation techniques, self-praise, group praise, and liberal praise of others in the group. Students are encouraged to generate more and more positive self-portraits and, as these develop, to be able to make positive lifestyle changes.
2. *Decision making* is designed to help students enhance personal empowerment by learning to exercise greater freedom of choice and personal control over decisions. The benefits—increased self-esteem and improved mood—are emphasized. Participants examine how to make decisions in a group by reaching agreement and resolving conflicts: stopping an impulsive response, thinking of options, evaluating options in terms of whether each is helpful or hurtful, putting into action the most helpful option, and self-praise for taking these steps.
3. *Personal control* over stress, depression, and anger. Students probe for what triggers feelings of depression and destructiveness, and they explore the effect of uncontrolled aggression on themselves and others. They practice strategies for dealing with stress, anger, and depression, with an emphasis on developing a repertoire of strategies that emphasize giving and receiving support from friends and others in their social network.
4. *Interpersonal communication* focuses on skills for communicating more effectively, and students practice ways of expressing concern for and developing healthy relationships with others at school.

As they develop, issues that are raised in the group become the basis for introducing and working on specific skills. At the beginning of a personal growth class, for example, the group leader might start with a check-in to monitor all members of the group to assess how they are doing with respect to mood, school, and substance abuse control. The group works on setting the agenda for the day. The leader asks whether anyone has individual issues for which they want group support and problem-solving time. Using group work and discussion skills, the leader is able to relate the students' issues to the planned skills-training session and activities. "The challenge for the leader is to balance the students' daily needs with related skills building, skills application, and group problem-solving applied to the students' current concerns and real-life issues" (National Institute on Drug Abuse 1997a: 61).

The program provides students with opportunities for prosocial recreation and school volunteer activities, which are designed to enhance self-esteem and school bonding. During the final two weeks of the class, students review what they have learned and celebrate their experiences.

PREPARING FOR THE DRUG-FREE YEARS (PDFY)

"The goal of PDFY is to empower parents of children ages 8 to 14 years to reduce risks that their children will abuse drugs and alcohol or develop other common adolescent problems" (Haggerty et al. 1999: 1). PDFY is based on extensive research on factors that increase risk:

- Little parental supervision and monitoring
- Low degree of parent-child communication and interaction
- Poorly defined and communicated rules and expectations for children's behavior
- Inconsistent and excessively severe discipline
- Parental alcohol and drug use

Parents are recruited through public service announcements and advertisements. Since establishment of the program in 1987, more than 120,000 families have been trained in five two-hour sessions or ten one-hour sessions in more than thirty states and Canada. The focus is on strengthening family bonding (see social control theory in Chapter 7), and children join their parents for a session that focuses on risk factors, including friends who use drugs, and how to resist peer pressure to use alcohol or other drugs. Sessions are typically conducted by two trained workshop leaders from the community aided by a curriculum kit that includes videos and family activity books.

STRENGTHENING FAMILIES PROGRAM

This seven-week curriculum is designed for parents and youths ages 10–14 years. It aims at reducing substance abuse and other problem behavior during adolescence. "Intermediate objectives include improved parental nurturing and limit-setting skills, improved communication skills for both parents and youth, and youth prosocial skills development" (Molgaard, Spoth, and Redmond 2000: 2). Participants are recruited by a local family services agency that identifies a core of groups of parents and motivates them to recruit other families to the program. Recruitment material includes a motivational video and incentives such as $5 grocery certificates and fast-food coupons for youths.

There are separate skill-building sessions for parents and youths for the first hour, followed by a second hour together in supervised family activities, during which facilitators offer assistance and model appropriate skills. The separate sessions contain parallel content; for example, while parents are learning how to use consequences when youths break rules, youths are learning about the importance of following rules. In small- and large-group discussions the youth sessions "focus on strengthening goals for the future, dealing with stress and strong emotions, appreciating parents and other elders, increasing the desire to be responsible, and building skills to deal with peer pressure" (Molgaard, Spoth, and Redmond 2000: 2). Topics are presented in gamelike activities that are designed to keep participants engaged and sustain their interest while they are learning.

Parent sessions focus on understanding the developmental characteristics of young people, providing nurturing support, and dealing effectively with youths in everyday interactions. The need to set appropriate limits and to follow through with reasonable and respectful consequences is emphasized, as well as the sharing of beliefs and expectations regarding alcohol and drug use. The sessions include didactic presentations, role-playing, group discussions, and the use of videotapes. "Two-thirds of each family session is spent within individual family units in which parents and youth participate in discussions on projects. The remaining time is spent in large-group skill building activities and games" (Molgaard, Spoth, and Redmond 2000: 2).

CHILD DEVELOPMENT PROJECT (CDP)

Although billed as a substance abuse prevention effort, the Child Development Project (CDP) did not address this issue. Instead, the program focused on developing a strong sense of community in twelve elementary schools in six districts across the country as an indirect way of reducing involvement in drug use and other problem behaviors. The effort to develop this sense of community included training school staff in revised teaching practices that used cooperative learning activities, cross-grade buddy programs, and schoolwide events and activities that involved parents with their children. "Students' sense of the school as a community was associated with a wide range of positive outcomes, including increased liking for the school" and "reduced involvement in drug use and delinquent behaviors" (Brounstein and Zweig n.d.: 22).

PROJECT ALERT

This two-year classroom program starts with eleven lessons in seventh grade that specifically target alcohol, cigarettes, and marijuana, substances that middle-school youths are likely to try first. The seventh-grade lessons are reinforced with three more in the eighth grade. Program activities—videos, guided classroom discussions, small-group activities, intensive role-playing, and parent-involved homework assignments—are designed to help students identify and resist pro-drug pressures and understand the social, emotional, and physical consequences of using harmful substances.

PREVENTION RESEARCH

Research into the effectiveness of prevention programs has been at best mixed or inconclusive. According to J. Kelly Coker (2001: 1):

> In the early days of prevention education, young people were shown what drugs looked like, with warnings about what evil would befall them if these drugs were taken. In the 1980s, peers and adults were portrayed as vicious culprits exposing

innocent children to drugs in the "just say no" campaigns. The more recent focus has been on concurrently teaching refusal skills and bolstering self-esteem with the belief that these will suffice to prevent experimentation with drugs. The problem with all of these prevention approaches is that there is no firm evidence that they work.

A well-designed research effort found that a program based on a social influence model of prevention (Project ALERT) that seeks to motivate young people to resist drugs and helps them develop the skills to do so can be effective in preventing or reducing adolescent use of cigarettes and marijuana. The research effort involved randomly selected seventh-and eighth-grade students across geographic, racial, and socioeconomic lines. Students developed reasons for not using drugs and responses to internal and external pressures to use them. ALERT had clearly positive results with respect to cigarette and marijuana use with both low-risk and high-risk students. The impact on alcohol consumption was negligible; and a "boomerang effect"—increased use of tobacco—was found for confirmed smokers (Ellickson and Bell 1990; Ellickson et al. 2003).

In Kansas City, Kansas, and Indianapolis, Indiana, beginning in the sixth and seventh grades, students were exposed to information about the dangers of drug use at school, at home, and in the community. Parents were trained to reinforce the antidrug message at home, and public service announcements were carried by news organizations throughout the community. Of the high school students who participated in the program, 1.6 percent said that they had used cocaine in the last month, whereas 3.7 percent of the control group did. With respect to marijuana the figures were 14.2 percent versus 20.2 percent; for alcohol they were 36 percent versus 50 percent; and for cigarettes they were 24 percent versus 32 percent (C. Johnson et al. 1990; Treaster 1990a).

Research into eight programs that used different prevention strategies found that each of them, in its own setting and in its own manner, promoted supportive and caring relationships between youth and members of their families, their communities, and their peer groups. And each program implemented multi-faceted interventions targeting the specific needs of its audiences. Each of the programs was successful either in increasing the time before first alcohol, tobacco, and drug use; in reducing the frequency of alcohol, tobacco, and drug use; or in effectively reducing risk factors and/or enhancing protective factors related to the development of substance use (Substance Abuse and Mental Health Services Administration 2001). Research into LifeSkills Training (LST), a school-based life skills (discussed earlier) prevention program, found that its positive effects extended beyond the typical low-risk youths to those who were at higher than average risk: LST "significantly reduced initiation of drug use among urban, middle school students who were doing poorly academically and had substance-abusing friends." After one year, "these youths reported lower rates of cigarette, alcohol, and inhalant use than a comparable group of nonparticipating students" (Mathias 2003: 12).

The largest-ever study of community-based antidrug partnerships found that male residents served by Community Anti-Drug Partnerships funded by the Center for Substance Abuse Prevention had slightly lower rates—by an average of about 3 percent—of alcohol and illicit drug use than their counterparts in nonpartnership communities. The study compared rates of alcohol and other drug use in twenty-four communities that had antidrug partnership programs to those in twenty-four similar communities without such partnerships. Use rates were measured in 1994 and 1996 through a survey of 83,473 adults plus eighth- and tenth-grade students. Results for females were not nearly as encouraging: Past-month and past-year alcohol and other drug use rates were unchanged among women and girls between 1994 and 1996, and use of illicit drugs among eighth-grade girls in the partnership communities actually increased during that time period (Substance Abuse Resource Center 1999).

The Child Development Project (CDP) discussed earlier revealed positive results in a research design that paired program schools to similar ones that did not utilize the CDP. Over a four-year period, use of alcohol by students declined from 48 percent to 37 percent, while in the matched schools it rose from 36 to 38 percent; cigarette use declined in the program schools from 25 percent to 17 percent and declined in the comparison schools from 17 percent to 14 percent; marijuana use declined in the program schools from 7 to 5 percent and rose in the matched schools from 4 percent to 6 percent (Brounstein and Zweig n.d.).

A research effort—two randomized, controlled prevention trials—into preventing methamphetamine use among high school students in the rural Midwest using the Iowa Strengthening Families Program, the Preparing for the Drug Free Years, and Life Skills Training, revealed significant and positive results (Spoth et al. 2006).

Two short-term reviews of Project D.A.R.E. (Nyre 1985; Aniskiewicz and Wysong 1990) have been positive: The program enhanced antidrug attitudes and knowledge while strengthening the social skills that are believed to be important in resisting drug use. A third evaluation (DeJong 1987b) contradicted these findings but nevertheless found that the D.A.R.E. students showed significantly less drug use. A subsequent analysis by Earl Wysong, Richard Aniskiewicz, and David Wright (1994: 467), which tracked a D.A.R.E. program for five years, found "no long-term effects for the program in preventing or reducing adolescent drug use." In their review of eight D.A.R.E. studies, Susan Ennett and her colleagues (1994) did not find encouraging results. They also questioned the use of law enforcement personnel as teachers in the program, noting that there have been no studies on whether or not this is an effective use of police personnel. A controlled study of D.A.R.E. in Houston, Texas, found that drug, alcohol, and tobacco use increased among students who had been exposed to the program (Gay 1999).

Criticism of the program continued to grow. In an editorial, the conservative *Chicago Tribune* advised (August 11, 1999: 18): "It's time to show D.A.R.E. the door. Year after year, about 80 percent of the elementary schools in the country allocate resources and classroom time for a curriculum that simply doesn't work, and few of them seem to care." In response to the increasing criticism, in 2001 the leaders of D.A.R.E. acknowledged its shortcomings and proposed changing the program accordingly. A new curriculum was developed, focusing exclusively on middle and high schools, and the role of police officers was significantly reduced (Zernike 2001). Nevertheless, research-based reports continued to criticize the program, and by 2003 state funding began to dry up, and more and more resource-starved police departments and school districts began dropping D.A.R.E. (Vogt 2003).

Research has found that although it is relatively easy to increase knowledge and change attitudes, it is more difficult to bring about long-term sustained behavior change. "However, long-term changes can be achieved. The most persuasive support for this view comes from cigarette smoking. In 1972, about 46% of the British population smoked cigarettes and by 1992 this had been reduced to 30%. These gains were not won by one simple strategy nor by any interventions applied only in the short term.... Effecting health behaviour change through education is difficult but not impossible. It is likely to require perseverance, multiple approaches, and a long-term view" (Advisory Council on the Misuse of Drugs 1993: 16).

Smoking among adolescents has been declining, but the explanation has little to do with school-based antismoking campaigns. "A review of school programs that have been tested with randomized controlled trials shows no evidence of long-term effectiveness in any of them" (Bakalar 2005: F7). Instead, "[i]t has been shown over and over that kids are especially sensitive to tax increases" (Sarah Weiss quoted in Bakalar 2005: F7). Student orientation, alcohol awareness weeks, and curriculum infusion, typical interventions found on high school and college campuses, assume that people make wise choices if they know the facts about alcohol. "Although this may be true, information alone is usually insufficient to change behavior. Evaluations of these stand-alone programs have found no effect on alcohol use or alcohol-related consequences" (K. D. Johnson 2004: 43).

TECHNICAL PROBLEMS AND CRITICISMS

Difficulty in producing and implementing effective drug abuse prevention programs could be related to some of the technical aspects of these programs. It might be—and there is evidence to support such a hypothesis—that instead of intervention models based on firm theoretical and empirical foundations, drug abuse prevention programs are too often put together and implemented by well-meaning but otherwise limited people, a method that results in a naive or simplistic approach to a complex problem.

School drug education staff are often more enthusiastic about their programs' effectiveness than the empirical data warrant. An evaluation of junior high school antidrug programs in the Kansas City, Missouri area, for example, found that although school staff viewed the programs as beneficial and successful, outcome measurements did not support their optimism (Gilham, Lucas, and Siverwright 1997). In fact, support for drug prevention programs, as Aniskiewicz and Wysong (1990) note, might have more to do with politics than research. Such programs appear to rest less on clear-cut evidence of effectiveness than on their popularity as symbolic action against the "drug crisis." Being associated with such efforts can enhance the public standing of elected, police, and school officials.

Furthermore, "strategies which are adequate for preventing experimentation among those at low risk of engaging in serious antisocial behaviors may be wholly inadequate for preventing initiation and use by those who exhibit a 'deviance syndrome.' On the other hand, well-founded strategies for preventing drug abuse among those at highest risk for abuse may be inappropriate for those at risk of only becoming experimental users" (Hawkins, Lishner, and Catalano 1987: 78). Thus, a rational prevention program needs to establish and explicate its goals. "If the goal of prevention is to prevent serious maladaptive behavior associated with drug abuse in adolescence, then it may be desirable from an etiological perspective to focus prevention efforts on those youth who manifest behavior problems, including aggressive and other antisocial behaviors during the elementary grades. On the other hand, if the goal is to prevent experimentation with drugs, or to delay the age of experimentation in the general population, such highly focused efforts may by inappropriate" (Hawkins, Lishner, and Catalano 1987: 80).

Diana Baumrind (1987: 32) cautions that "when socially deviant youths are required to participate in the school setting in peer-led denunciation of activities they value, they are more likely to become alienated than converted." An eight-year study revealed that once an adolescent decides to use drugs in response to internal problems, peer-based prevention programs will not work (Blakeslee 1988). Michael Newcomb and Peter Bentler (1989: 246) recommend that prevention and intervention "focus on the misuse, abuse, problem use, and heavy use of drugs to meet internal needs, cope with distress, and avoid responsibility and important life decisions and difficulties. The youngsters facing these tasks are in need of help, education, and intervention." Newcomb and Bentler argue that it "is misleading to bask in the success of some peer programs that have reduced the number of youngsters who experiment with drugs (but would probably never have become regular users, let alone abusers) and ignore the tougher problems of those youngsters who are at high risk for drug abuse as well as other serious difficulties" (1989: 246).

An examination of the potential impact of a universal school-based prevention effort concludes that "it would not dramatically affect the course of drug use and the benefits would take years to accrue" (Caulkins et al. 1999: xxxi). However, "implementing model prevention programs seems to be justifiable in the sense that the benefits would likely outweigh the costs of the resources used" (Caulkins et al 1999: xxxii). Best estimates are that prevention reduces lifetime consumption of cigarettes by 2.1 percent, of alcohol by 2.2 percent, and of cocaine by 3.0 percent. Although these numbers might seem relatively low, even small reductions in use can cause large decreases in social costs. With only thirty hours of programming, small reductions might be all that anyone should expect from prevention ("What Kind of Drug Use Does School-Based Prevention Prevent?" 2002).

DRUG TESTING

Drug testing first appeared in the 1960s as a part of methadone maintenance programs (discussed in Chapters 2 and 10). "With the passage of the Drug Free Workplace Act (1998) and Omnibus Transportation Employee Testing Act (1991), drug testing also became a standard feature in the workplace as a way to measure worker productivity and to ensure public safety" (Paik 2006: 934). The President's Commission on Organized Crime (1986), in what has become its most controversial recommendation, suggested extensive drug testing as a device for reducing consumer demand (see Table 9.1). The U.S. Office of National Drug Control Policy has actively promoted this approach, particularly for students. However, a federally financed study of 76,000 students found that drug testing had no effect on drug use—it does not change "hearts and minds" (G. Winter 2003).

Drug testing of prospective employees has become almost routine at many large corporations: About 61 percent of major U.S. companies administer pre-employment drug tests, and more than 500 school districts have screening programs (D. Hawkins 2002). The military has extended its program of drug testing, and various levels of

TABLE 9.1 | PROS AND CONS OF VARIOUS DRUG TESTING METHODS

Type of Test	Pros	Cons	Window of Detection
Urine	• Highest assurance of reliable results. • Least expensive. • Most flexibility in testing different drugs, including alcohol and nicotine. • Most likely of all drug-testing methods to withstand legal challenge.	• Specimen can be adulterated, substituted, or diluted. • Limited window of detection. • Test sometimes viewed as invasive or embarrassing. • Biological hazard for specimen handling and shipping to lab.	• Typically 1 to 5 days.
Hair	• Longer window of detection. • Greater stability (does not deteriorate). • Can measure chronic drug use. • Convenient shipping and storage (no need to refrigerate). • Collection procedure not considered invasive or embarrassing. • More difficult to adulterate than urine. • Detects alcohol/cocaine combination use.	• More expensive. • Test usually limited to basic 5-drug panel. • Cannot detect alcohol use. • Will not detect very recent drug use (1 to 7 days prior to test).	• Depends on the length of hair in the sample. Hair grows about a half-inch per month, so a 1 1/2-inch specimen would show a 3-month history.
Oral Fluids	• Sample obtained under direct observation. • Minimal risk of tampering. • Noninvasive. • Samples can be collected easily in virtually any environment. • Can detect alcohol use. • Reflects recent drug use.	• Drugs and drug metabolites do not remain in oral fluids as long as they do in urine. • Less efficient than other testing methods in detecting marijuana use.	• Approximately 10 to 24 hours.
Sweat Patch	• Noninvasive. • Variable removal date (generally 1 to 7 days). • Quick application and removal. • Longer window of detection than urine. • No sample substitution possible.	• Limited number of labs able to process results. • People with skin eruptions, excessive hair, or cuts and abrasions cannot wear the patch. • Passive exposure to drugs may contaminate patch and affect results.	• Patch retains evidence of drug use for at least 7 days, and can detect even low levels of drugs 2 to 5 hours after last use.

Source: Office of National Drug Control Policy (2002a).

government have initiated the testing of employees in critical areas involving public safety, particularly law enforcement and transportation. Some states have reacted to increasing protests about the practice by enacting legislation barring random testing of employees, and in a number of states the practice is thwarted by constitutional provisions guaranteeing individuals' right to privacy. Vermont and Rhode Island prohibit companywide random testing, and Minnesota and Vermont require employers to offer those who test positive a first-time chance at rehabilitation (Fahmy 2007).

DRUG-TESTING PROCESS

Drug testing has spawned a growth industry. The National Institute on Drug Abuse (NIDA) certifies drug-testing firms, a necessity for securing federal contracts. NIDA has certified about fifty laboratories that must maintain stringent standards in areas such as sample collection, storage, personnel, laboratory controls, and testing procedures and accuracy. Various testing methods are used, but the most common is urinalysis.

Urinalysis   Primarily because of its low cost, the enzyme-multiplied immune test is the most frequently used urinalysis (Wish n.d.: 2): "These tests depend on a chemical reaction between the specimen and an antibody designed to react to a specific drug. The chemical reaction causes a change in the specimen's transmission of light, which is measured by a machine. If the reading is higher than a given standard, the specimen is positive for the drug." Eric Wish (n.d.: 2) notes that there have been complaints of relatively high rates of false positives using this test, sometimes as a result of commonly used licit drugs cross-reacting with the test's antibody. "Sloppy recording procedures by laboratory staff and failure to maintain careful controls over the chain of custody of the specimen can also produce serious test errors."

The most accurate test, gas chromatography/mass spectroscopy (GC-MS), notes Wish (n.d.), is relatively expensive, about $100 per specimen for screening and confirmation, but so is the cost of firing or not hiring someone because of a false positive. Drug-testing programs often use the enzyme-multiplied immune test for an initial screening and then submit all positives for GC-MS. But GC-MS is not perfect. "The test works by extracting and heating molecules from a sample and using an electric field to separate and identify them." At best, however, this is 95–99 percent accurate. Furthermore, some labs, as a cost saving device, "look for only a few fragments of the drug molecules which raises the risk of mistaking legitimate medicines, herbs, and foods like poppy seeds for illegal drugs" (Hawkins 2002: 47).

Hair Analysis   Collecting hair samples is easy and is not subject to evasive actions designed to produce false negatives; shampooing, for example, has no effect. Hair analysis has been used for some time to detect exposure to such toxic metals as mercury and lead. In a process similar to that of urinalysis, dissolved hair shafts reveal whether drugs are in the blood. Because of the unique qualities of hair growth— about one-half inch a month—it may be possible to determine the amount of drug use over a period of several months and whether it is increasing or decreasing. There are complications, however. The test can also be positive for those who come into contact with drugs in the environment, for example, via touching the skin or sweat of a user or through exposure to air where the substance has been smoked (Baumgartner, Hill, and Blahd 1989; Ropero-Miller and Stout 2009), and these contaminants can be discriminatory in their impact: "drug molecules, whether ingested or picked up from the environment, have an affinity for the pigment melanin and bind more strongly to dark hair than light" (Hawkins 2002: 48; Ropero-Miller and Stout 2009). Although it can reveal drug use within the prior three months, it cannot be used to detect recent usage. Hair analysis has been suggested as an initial screening method for drug use, positives to be corroborated by urinalysis or GC-MS (Magura, Kang, and Shapiro 1995; Mieczkowski 1995; Hawkins 2002).

Sweat Patch   For this type of test, a Band-Aid-like patch is attached to the skin to collect sweat for up to seven days and is subsequently lab-tested for drug residue. If the patch is removed, it cannot be reattached. This test is often used by probation and parole agencies. However, drug molecules from clothes or other people can penetrate the patch and trigger a false positive (Hawkins 2002).

Drug Residues   Portable devices that detect drug residues are used in the workplace and schools. They can identify vapors from minuscule particles of heroin, cocaine, and methamphetamines. Samples are gathered at such critical areas as doorknobs or desktops by cloth or vacuum cleaners and are analyzed through gas chromatography, a process that separates out compounds according to their boiling points; a readout indicates the type of substance that is detected. The Drug Wipe, which detects drug residues left on surfaces from contact with the skin or sweat of users, has been used in some schools to check locker handles, computer keyboards, vending machines, and sports equipment. Residue can be detected for up to eight weeks. There is a version for cocaine and opiates and another for marijuana and amphetamines and their derivatives.

The criminal justice system uses drug testing in making bail or pretrial release decisions and in probation and parole supervision.

TESTING PROBLEMS

At best, drug testing can determine that the subject has used a drug recently; it cannot determine when or how much. Tests cannot distinguish the casual user from a chronic one. There is also concern over the inadequacy of testing—false positives that could destroy the careers of innocent employees. In 2000 the U.S. Department of Health and Human Services revealed that the shortcomings of drug-testing laboratories were jeopardizing the jobs of innocent employees (Zuckerman 2000).

The rationale behind drug testing is confused and ironic: Employers are interested in having a drug-free workplace because controlled substances are presumed to be detrimental to job performance. If this is so, then monitoring job performance—a rather routine managerial task—makes more sense than drug testing, since some people will perform quite well even though their urine reveals drugs. People who lawfully come into contact with cocaine, such as plastic surgeons and drug law enforcement officers, will test positive for the substance, as will anyone who is exposed to crack cocaine fumes, even though the dose is far too low to produce symptoms (Karch 1996).

A standard argument is that *impaired* workers represent a work-place hazard. This might indeed be true, but drug testing does not reveal impairment, and impaired workers are most likely to be alcohol abusers. There is a lack of documentation proving that workers who test positive for illegal drugs have a higher rate of accidents (Noble 1992). Sound public relations might better explain work-place drug testing than sound public policy does.

CASE LAW RESULTS

For an intrusive act such as mandatory drug testing to be constitutional, there must be a "compelling interest." In a 1987 case a computer programmer who had been dismissed from her job for refusing to take a drug test on the grounds of personal privacy was awarded $485,000; the San Francisco jury failed to find "compelling interest." That city subsequently enacted an ordinance prohibiting mandatory testing unless an employer has reason to believe ("reasonable suspicion") that an employee is impaired because of drug use (Bishop 1987).

In 1989 the Supreme Court upheld the testing of railroad employees for drugs after an accident and ruled that personnel of the U.S. Customs Service in sensitive positions must submit to drug testing even in the absence of "individualized suspicion" (*Skinner v. Railway Labor Executives' Association*, 109 S.Ct. 1402; *National Treasury Employees Union v. von Raab*, 109 S.Ct. 1384). In a six-month study completed in 1990, slightly more than 3 percent of 65,000 U.S. transportation workers tested positive for drugs—mostly marijuana and cocaine—as did 4.2 percent of applicants for such positions (Cawley 1990). Lower federal courts have rejected the testing of *public* employees who are suspected of using drugs in a manner that does not affect job performance; the U.S. Constitution does not similarly protect *private* employees. In an Oregon case the U.S. Supreme Court (6–3) approved of the random urinalysis of public school athletes as a condition of their continued participation in sports (*Vernonia School District v. Acton*, 515 U.S. 646 [1995]).

In 2002 the Supreme Court, in a 5–4 decision (*Board of Education v. Earls*, 536 U.S. 822), extended *Vernonia* by upholding an Oklahoma school district's policy of requiring students engaged in virtually all extracurricular school activities to submit to random drug testing. The majority opinion written by Justice Clarence Thomas stated that given the epidemic of drug use by youngsters and the schools' "custodial responsibilities," drug testing was entirely reasonable. That led hundreds of school boards across the country, mostly in smaller districts, to consider proposals for testing students (Lewin 2002). While the *Earls* decision permits drug testing of students in extracurricular activities, states may enact legislation that limits or prohibits the practice.

SUMMARY

- Prevention programs are designed to enhance protective factors and move toward reversing or reducing known risk factors.

- Most efforts at prevention have focused on schools, and school-based antidrug programs have been dominated by three models: information; affective; and social influence.

- Youngsters who have the greatest knowledge about drugs are the most likely to use drugs.
- Prevention programming should acknowledge that drug use consequences are not all negative; if they were, nobody would continue to use drugs.
- Many youngsters, knowing more about drugs than their parents and teachers, will not accept moralization but will respect realistic, valid information derived from a credible source.
- D.A.R.E. (Drug Abuse Resistance Education) has proven popular with police departments throughout the United States. Research was critical of the program, and by 2003 state funding began to dry up and more and more resource-starved police

departments and school districts began dropping D.A.R.E.

- Prevention strategies that target youths have been used effectively, especially in combination: information dissemination; prevention education; alternatives; problem identification and referral; community-based process; environmental approach.
- Research has found that although it is relatively easy to increase knowledge and change attitudes, it is more difficult to bring about long-term sustained behavior change. However, long-term changes can be achieved. The most persuasive support for this view comes from cigarette smoking.
- The difficulty in producing and implementing effective drug abuse prevention programs could be related to some of the technical aspects of these programs.

Review Questions

1. What are the risk factors for making drug use more likely?
2. What are the protective factors for reducing the risks of drug use?
3. What are the three models for school-based antidrug programs?
4. How do these three models differ?
5. What is the affective or humanistic approach to drug education?
6. What is the relationship between knowledge of the dangers of drug use and drug use?
7. What drawbacks are inherent in educating youngsters about the dangers of drug abuse?
8. What are the dangers of drug education that focuses on the dangers of drug use?
9. What did research into D.A.R.E. reveal?
10. What is the goal of the Preparing for the Drug-Free Years program?
11. What is the primary reason for the reduction in smoking among adolescents?
12. What technical problems are encountered in implementing and evaluating drug prevention efforts?

That there is no single treatment for drug dependence is most likely a consequence of the multiple factors—physiological, behavioural and social—contributing to the condition.

David Taylor (2002: Internet)

CHAPTER **10** | # DRUG USE AND ABUSE: TREATMENT

COCAINE IS SUICIDE ANY WAY YOU CUT IT.
PARTNERSHIP FOR A DRUG FREE AMERICA

There are probably as many approaches to treating and preventing drug abuse as there are theories explaining the phenomenon. Unfortunately, drug abuse is unlike diseases whose etiology, and therefore treatment and prevention, appears to be clearly physiological. In fact, considering drug dependence a "disease," in the narrow sense of that term, is controversial (see, e.g., Wilbanks 1990; Maltzman 1994). As with other chronic illnesses, the National Institute on Drug Abuse recommends speaking in terms of *remission* and *improvement* rather than *cure* in discussing the treatment of substance abuse (National Institute on Drug Abuse 1987) because the problem has proven to be quite intractable.

Adding to the problem's complexity are the incongruities that were discussed in Chapter 1: The moderate use of any variety of psychoactive substances—from nicotine to cocaine—may be the focus of a treatment response, not because of properties inherent in the chemicals themselves but because of the societal definition of "abuse." Thus, in the United States moderate use of alcohol, tobacco, or coffee is seen as being within the mainstream of acceptable behavior, while even the occasional use of heroin or cocaine is often seen as requiring "treatment" (if not imprisonment). The difficulty is apparent: Patients who do not feel ill, who do not want treatment, and are not dysfunctional are coerced into "treatment" by their families, their employers, or the criminal justice system. And as Dean Gerstein and Henrick Harwood point out, "drug treatment is not designed for the low-intensity user who is readily able to control his or her level of consumption and for whom functional consequences have not yet accumulated" (1990: 69–70).

THE CURE INDUSTRY

Like the quest for an explanation of drug abuse, the search for a cure, particularly a "magic bullet" in the form of a chemical cure, has a history that cautions us to be skeptical. Opiates were once presented as a cure for alcohol dependence; morphine was offered as a cure for opiate addiction; cocaine was offered as a cure for morphine addiction (though patients became dependent on cocaine while remaining addicted to morphine); heroin was proposed as a cure for morphine addiction; and methadone was presented as a cure for heroin addiction. In fact, the "cure industry" has a long and often less than honorable history.

The medical profession "often shared the distaste for drug users that permeated the society" (Morgan 1981: 65). Furthermore, the problem of addiction was only peripheral to the practice of most doctors, who typically sought to avoid association with the failure that was so common to treating drug dependence. This left a fertile field for charlatans, and around the turn of the century the quest for a cure led to the development of an industry similar to that of patent medicines. Unregulated nostrums that were widely advertised as "cures" for drug dependence frequently contained alcohol, cocaine, and opiates. In 1906 these compounds came under regulation by the Pure Food and Drug Administration, which caused a significant decline in sales. In response quacks began to portray themselves as outsiders feared by a medical establishment centered in the eastern United States. This approach had strong appeal, particularly in the South and Midwest, where anti-Eastern feelings ran deep.

Any number of self-proclaimed doctors operated clinics for the drug dependent and grew quite wealthy from their "cures." The most famous was Charles B.

Towns, a Georgia farm boy, insurance salesman, and stockbroker. David Musto (1973) refers to Towns as the king of the cure proclaimers. After arriving in New York City in 1901, Towns spent several years as a partner in a stock brokerage that failed in 1904. Shortly afterward, he began advertising a secret formula that would cure drug addiction. The medical profession was skeptical, but Towns and his cure were widely accepted and were promoted even by federal agencies; a 1909 article in the *Journal of the American Medical Association* was also favorable. The Charles B. Towns Hospital[1] proclaimed a cure rate between 75 and 90 percent. Determining "success" was rather simple: If the patient never returned, he or she was "cured." Eventually, it was revealed that Towns's secret formula contained three ingredients: prickly ash bark, extract of hyoscyamus (henbane, a poisonous plant), and belladonna (deadly nightshade, a poisonous plant).

There were at the same time, however, sanatoriums whose approach to drug abuse was quite similar, if not identical, to that of many contemporary inpatient programs. The patient was withdrawn from drugs, sometimes with the aid of nonaddicting drugs. Before 1914 treating addiction was all the more difficult because morphine was usually available in a pure form that made withdrawal particularly painful (Morgan 1981). The patient was given frequent baths, and as soon as he or she began to function more normally, a regimen of nourishing food and exercise was initiated. The patient, now withdrawn from drugs, engaged in such tasks as reading and gardening and was given a great deal of reassurance. The extent of the treatment often depended on a patient's ability to pay (Morgan 1981). More recently, the profit that can accrue from treating certain types of substance abusers—rich and famous and/or those with appropriate health insurance—has led to the expansion of a private cure industry that is often based in health care or hospital settings. These will be discussed later in the chapter.

For alcoholics there were "inebriate homes" and asylums that operated on the fringes of religion, charity, and law enforcement. The different philosophies and treatment methods tended to merge over time, the medically oriented ones incorporating spiritual and religion-oriented remedies and those operating on moral or religious principles integrating medical and psychological treatments. And as with the profit-making sector of drug addiction treatment, the alcohol cure industry became a business that promoted dubious notions hyped by unsupported claims. Indeed, many organizations claimed success in treating both the drug- and alcohol-addicted (W. L. White 1998). Always pressed for sources of funding, these institutions were abandoned by the temperance movement and met their demise with the onset of Prohibition.

TREATMENT

Whatever the treatment approach of contemporary programs, there are three standard components: screening; assessment and diagnosis; and treatment plan (*Principles of Drug Dependence Treatment* 2008: 6 edited):

---

[1]Bill Wilson, cofounder of Alcoholics Anonymous (AA), was a patient of the Towns Hospital, where, according to AA publications, he learned that alcoholism was a malady of mind, emotions, and body.

■ ESSENTIALS OF EFFECTIVE TREATMENT

–No single treatment is appropriate for all individuals.
–Treatment needs to be readily available.
–Effective treatment attends to multiple needs of the individual, not just his or her drug addiction.
Source: National Institute on Drug Abuse (2008d).

Screening identifies individuals with hazardous or harmful drug use, or drug dependence, as well as associated risk behaviors (needle sharing, unprotected sexual activity, potential violent behavior, suicide risk). There are standardized tools to assess drug use and its severity in an individual that help determine the degree of help required. These tools can be applied in different environments (primary health care system, school health and counseling services, and employee assistance programs at work places).

Diagnosis frequently uses references common to the mental health field. If there is a diagnosis of a co-morbid psychiatric disorder, a follow-up is made by a psychiatrist, while other health care professionals identify and manage drug use disorders and associated psychiatric co-morbidity.

A comprehensive assessment takes into account the stage and severity of the disease, physical and mental health status, individual temperament and personality traits, vocational and employment status, family and social integration, and legal situation. It further considers environmental and developmental factors, including childhood and adolescent history, family history and relationships, social and cultural circumstances, and previous treatment experience.

An adequate assessment process creates the environment for the development of a therapeutic relationship to engage the client in treatment.

The **treatment plan** is developed with the client and establishes goals based on identified needs and sets interventions to meet those goals. A care or treatment plan is a written description of the treatment to be provided and its anticipated course. Care plans set the specific individual needs and how they are going to be met by the treatment program. The plan is then monitored and revised periodically as required to respond to the client's changing situation. Treatment plans may include the use of medication.

MEDICATION-ASSISTED TREATMENT

A variety of treatment approaches use chemicals, often as a supplement to or in conjunction with some other form of clinical or behavioral therapy. These medications target the pharmacological effect of a particular drug but "do nothing to counteract the effects of craving and overlearned drug-seeking behavioral responses that frequently lead to relapse" (Harwood and Myers 2004: 11). Nicotine replacement therapies, such as nicotine gum and the transdermal nicotine patch, are used in conjunction with behavioral support to relieve withdrawal symptoms. They

DRUGS TO TREAT NICOTINE ADDICTION

In 2009 the Food and Drug Administration ordered that the packaging of two smoking cessation drugs, Chantix and Zyban, include the agency's strongest safety warning regarding side effects that include depression and suicidal ideation.

produce less severe physiological alterations than tobacco-based systems and generally provide users with lower overall nicotine levels than they receive with tobacco. They have little abuse potential since they do not produce the pleasurable effects of tobacco products, nor do they contain the carcinogens and gases associated with tobacco smoke (*Tobacco Addiction* 2009).

OPIOID ANTAGONISTS

As part of the search for a "magic bullet," scientists developed a number of heroin antagonists, substances that block or counteract the effects of opiates. These substances bind with opiate receptor sites, thereby preventing stimulation, or they displace an opiate that is already at the site. Antagonists, such as **naloxone (Narcan)**, have significant side effects. A dose as small as 0.25 mg will block the effects of heroin for ten hours, but it is effective only when administered intravenously. It does not reduce the "drug hunger" of heroin addicts. Naloxone is used for testing for opiate dependence (Narcon test) before admission to a methadone program (Judson and Goldstein 1986). It has no effect on the nondependent person but causes immediate signs of heroin withdrawal in the opiate-dependent person. New Mexico, as a part of its "harm reduction" approach to drug abuse (discussed in Chapter 14), distributes naloxone to addicts in an effort to stem overdose deaths (Eckholm 2008c).

Naloxone is administered to people seeking methadone treatment because they might not be opioid-dependent or might have only minimal dependence. Their admission to a methadone program would raise ethical and legal questions since methadone is addicting (Peachey and Lei 1988). According to federal regulations, admission to methadone treatment is restricted to people who have been addicted to heroin for at least one year.

The National Institute on Drug Abuse was instrumental in developing **naltrexone** hydrochloride, a long-acting orally administered narcotic antagonist first synthesized in 1965 and marketed in tablet form as Trexan by DuPont. This non-addicting drug defeats the effects of opiates by occupying their receptor sites in the brain. It also displaces any agonists that are present, causing severe precipitated withdrawal in people who are opioid-dependent. Naltrexone users often suffer from nausea and vomiting; less common side effects include headache, anxiety or depression, low energy, skin rashes, and decreased alertness. Taken in large doses, naltrexone can cause liver damage. Discontinuing naltrexone will not cause withdrawal symptoms, but the drug does not ease the craving for heroin (Batki et al. 2005).

Like any antagonist, naltrexone is effective only with patients who are motivated to give up the feeling of euphoria that opiates can provide. The manufacturer clearly states that it is recommended for use as an adjunct in the treatment of opioid abusers (Ginzburg 1985: 5): "Treatment failure cannot be blamed on the failure of naltrexone to block opioids nor is treatment success likely to be the consequence of a use of naltrexone alone."

In 1995 the Food and Drug Administration (FDA) approved naltrexone to prevent alcohol relapse by alcohol-dependent patients, and under the brand names ReVia and Depade, naltrexone is marketed for use in treating alcoholism. Alcohol causes the release of endorphins, which are believed a major factor in causing a person to continue drinking. Naltrexone blocks the endorphin-mediated rewarding effects of drinking alcohol thereby reducing craving.

CHEMICALS FOR DETOXIFICATION

Like those in the past, contemporary treatment programs typically begin with detoxification—"a term left over from an obsolete theory that addicts suffer from an accumulation of toxins" (Dole 1980: 138)—with or without the assistance of drugs. Antagonists are sometimes used as an aid in heroin detoxification. Because of its potency, withdrawal from licit maintenance doses of methadone is generally accomplished by decreasing dosages. The antihypertension drug clonidine has been used to relieve many of the symptoms of opioid withdrawal, particularly those involving autonomic nervous system hyperactivity. The substance is non-addicting (National Institute on Drug Abuse 1987). Some physicians have recommended clonidine for the detoxification of methadone patients who are being maintained on relatively low dosages. Whereas methadone can be found in the patient's system more than a week after the last dose, clonidine has a shorter life. Thus, a clonidine patient can be placed on naltrexone immediately on detoxification, whereas a methadone patient would experience unpleasant withdrawal symptoms under similar treatment (Ginzburg 1985).

Cocaine detoxification presents a serious problem because of the patient's craving for the drug. This may be associated with the depletion of dopamine, which, as was noted in Chapter 5, is essential to maintain life. The extreme depression that occurs during the early days of abstinence, particularly in crack users, can lead to suicide. Withdrawal from opiates and cocaine can be accomplished without using other chemicals, although the patient might feel quite uncomfortable. Detoxification from sedatives can lead to seizures and cardiac arrest and therefore must be accomplished by decreasing dosages of the sedative.

The use of chemicals to facilitate drug withdrawal can serve to attract drug abusers into treatment and increases the probability that they will complete detoxification. However, at least with respect to heroin abusers, the use of chemicals has some troubling aspects: Addicts typically enter treatment when their habit is too expensive to support; at this point the addict has to work quite hard simply to prevent the onset of withdrawal symptoms, while a high level of tolerance prevents achieving the high. Under such conditions addiction is no longer fun. "Then he enters a detoxification ward and is comfortably withdrawn from heroin. Detoxification is made so easy, compared to 'cold turkey,'[2] that addicts are not confronted

---

[2]A common symptom of withdrawal is piloerection—"goose flesh" (W. L. White 1998).

with negatively reinforcing pharmacological and physiological aspects of addiction" (Bellis 1981: 139). Detoxification reduces the addict's tolerance so that the high can be enjoyed once again at an affordable price. Drug program staff "should not be surprised or miffed when addicts leave the detoxification ward and inject heroin within a few minutes or hours" (Bellis 1981: 140).

Anesthesia Assisted Rapid Opiate Detoxification, which is sometimes called Accelerated Neuro-Regulation and is often referred to as **rapid detox**, is a controversial process. Patients addicted to heroin or to synthetic opiates (such as oxycondin) are strapped to a gurney, anesthetized, and hooked up to a respirator. They then receive intravenous doses of Naltrexone that dislodge opiate molecules from their receptor sites. The patients experience instant withdrawal that is complete in about four to six hours. Being unconscious, the patients avoid experiencing the usual discomfort that accompanies withdrawal, such as vomiting, shivering, and pain. After a night in intensive care, the patients are able to leave the hospital drug-free. Some programs, in addition, offer Naltrexone implants that are inserted under the skin while patients are unconscious. This aids abstinence by blocking opiate receptors for up to two months. Other programs prescribe daily doses of Naltrexone for up to one year.

The cost of the procedure can be as high as $8,500. Detoxification, of course, is simply a first step toward abstinence, and rapid detox is criticized for its expense while having no proven benefits in comparison to less costly approaches to withdrawal (Duenwald 2001). Indeed, making withdrawal relatively easy provides little incentive for remaining drug free (although the cost of rapid detox can be seen as an incentive for remaining heroin-free).

Research conducted in 2005 revealed that there is no advantage to rapid detox, which can also be dangerous for individuals with a variety of preexisting conditions, such as diabetes or bipolar disorder. Once awakened from anesthesia, patients in the rapid detox group demonstrated and reported symptoms of discomfort comparable to those experienced by participants who were treated with traditional medical withdrawal methods (buprenorphine or clonidine). The rapid detox patients fared no better on remaining in treatment; only 18 percent remained the full twelve weeks, and the percentage who submitted opiate-positive urine samples during outpatient treatment (63 percent) was the same as with the other methods (Whitten 2006b).

OPIOID AGONISTS

Certain synthetic substances have a chemical makeup similar to that of opioids. The most widely used agonist, **methadone**, a wholly synthetic narcotic, was developed in Germany (where it was named *Dolophine* in honor of Hitler) when access to morphine was cut off during World War II. While it produces virtually the same analgesic and sedative effects as heroin and is no less addictive, orally administered methadone lasts longer. In contrast to the shorter-acting opiates such as heroin, the high it produces is less dramatic. Whereas the effects of heroin wear off in two to three hours, the effects of oral methadone continue for twelve to twenty-four hours. Methadone can be prepared in a way that makes it difficult to inject, rendering it less likely to be diverted into the black market. After World War II methadone was typically used in hospitals to systematically detoxify people addicted to opiates (Dole 1980; Gerstein and Harwood 1990). Methadone is also prescribed for treating chronic pain.

The first clinical use of methadone to treat narcotic addiction occurred at the U.S. Public Health Hospital in Lexington, Kentucky, where it was substituted for morphine and heroin to help detoxify addicted patients. Withdrawal from heroin was made relatively painless by first administering doses equivalent to the patient's street use of heroin. The doses were then lowered until the patient was no longer addicted, a process that took seven to ten days (Blackmore 1979). During the early 1960s, when narcotics addiction once again emerged as a major national concern, Vincent Dole and Marie Nyswander of Rockefeller University reported on their successful use of methadone to treat heroin addicts in a dramatically new way: through maintenance.

Methadone: Magic Bullet? In 1964 Doctors Dole and Nyswander gave twenty-two hospitalized heroin addicts increasing doses of methadone until they reached a "stabilized state," meaning that they had neither withdrawal symptoms nor a craving for further increases in the dosage: "With repeated administration of a fixed dose, methadone loses its sedative and analgesic powers. The subject becomes tolerant" (Dole 1980: 146). The patients were then released, but they returned each day for an oral dose of methadone. The following year a research report by Dole and Nyswander (1965) revealed extraordinary results from this approach, which they ascribed to methadone's ability to provide a "pharmacological block" against heroin. Furthermore, it was theorized, heroin abuse in certain addicts results in a metabolic disorder that requires the continued ingestion of narcotics if the person is to remain homeostatic. With such disorders methadone acts like any prescribed medicine, normalizing the patient's functioning.

Continuing research with additional patients provided further support for methadone maintenance: Addict patients refrained from heroin use, secured employment, and avoided criminal activity. In 1966 Dole and Nyswander established a large outpatient methadone program at Beth Israel Hospital in New York City. Other programs followed. Dole and Nyswander (1966) intimated that they had discovered the "magic bullet" because methadone allegedly provides a blockade to the effects of heroin.

The typical methadone program begins with a period of inpatient care, during which low doses of methadone are substituted for heroin. (The patient is not informed of the dosage he or she receives.) The methadone is usually mixed with orange juice (which helps to reduce its bitter taste) and is consumed in front of a nurse. Slow increases in dosage reduce the high, which disappears once tolerance develops. Addicts subsequently report daily on an outpatient basis and are given take-home doses for weekends. As they progress, less frequent than daily pickups are permitted. Patients usually provide a urine specimen before they are given methadone.

By the late 1960s a few thousand addicts were being maintained on methadone in the United States; by early 1973 there were approximately 73,000 (Danaceau 1974). This change was brought about by the Nixon administration, which was convinced that methadone could help to reduce the crime rate—a cornerstone of the "law-and-order" presidency of Richard Nixon. Experts who knew better,

Methadone clinics across the country treat as many as 180,000 ex-heroin users every day. Methadone maintenance appears to be beneficial for certain addicts—it can act as a crutch for those motivated to give up heroin.

argues Edward Jay Epstein (1974: 22), "chose not to deflate the unrealistic claim that methadone would substantially reduce crime." They hoped that such programs would lure otherwise recalcitrant hard-core heroin addicts into treatment. Eventually, however, the "bad news" came out: Methadone was not the "magic bullet." Indeed, there was no blockade but simply cross-tolerance. The patient who was maintained at significantly high doses of methadone would not experience the high from heroin, but methadone did not affect the euphoric rush. In fact, it was discovered that methadone patients, even those who were on high daily doses, were often abusing heroin as well as other drugs. Furthermore, whereas methadone maintenance was designed for heroin addicts, the problem was often one of poly-drug use. In fact, cocaine is a major drug of abuse among methadone patients (C. P. O'Brien et al. 1990). Today, there are about 180,000 methadone users nationally. (Eight states—Idaho, Mississippi, Montana, New Hampshire, North Dakota, South Dakota, Vermont, and West Virginia—prohibit methadone to treat drug dependence.) Methadone is also prescribed as a painkiller that is considerably much cheaper than OxyContin and, therefore, more likely to be covered by medical insurance (Eckholm and Pierce 2008). The increased use of methadone for pain has led to an increase in diversion to the black market.

Furthermore, research revealed that the figures given out by Dole and Nyswander were deceptive: The rate of "cure" attributed to methadone was better explained by the screening mechanisms that were used—older and more motivated addicts were preferred—and by the fact that unsuccessful cases were simply dropped from the program and from the final tabulations. Methadone clinics came under severe attack by those associated with the drug-free therapeutic

METHADONE: USES AND EFFECTS

Classification: Narcotic

CSA Schedule: Schedule I, II

Trade or Other Names: Dolophine, Methadose

Medical Uses: Analgesic, treatment of dependence

Physical Dependence: High

Psychological Dependence: High

Tolerance: Yes

Duration (hours): 12–72

Usual Method: Oral, injected

Possible Effects: Euphoria, drowsiness, respiratory depression, constricted pupils; nausea

Effects of Overdose: Slow and shallow breathing, clammy skin, convulsions, coma, possible death

Withdrawal Syndrome: Watery eyes, runny nose, yawning, loss of appetite, irritability, tremors, panic, cramps, nausea, chills and sweating

Source: Drug Enforcement Administration.

---

communities (discussed below), and by 1979 they were operating at about 90 percent of capacity (Blackmore 1979). Robert Newman (1977: xx) states that "proponents of specific treatment approaches rarely missed an opportunity to make exaggerated claims for their own modality and to vilify publicly other therapeutic efforts." Residents also strongly opposed the opening of methadone treatment centers in their communities—the NIMBY (not-in-my-backyard) syndrome.

No Magic Bullet, but Methadone Is Still Useful   This is not to say that methadone maintenance has no role in treating heroin addiction. Methadone maintenance appears to be quite beneficial to certain heroin abusers (e.g., Byrne 2000). It can act as a crutch for those who are motivated to give up heroin. The programs also attract addicts who are seeking a chemical cure, although the counseling and job assistance that are provided might be the real "cure." Even without such services, notes James DeLong (1972), methadone may have a placebo effect: The addict who believes that methadone is beneficial will find it so. To the extent that heroin addiction is explained by physiology, as discussed in Chapter 3 (e.g., people with abnormal endorphin levels compensating by ingesting heroin), methadone maintenance is the equivalent of providing insulin to diabetics.

If psychoanalytic theory is accurate, methadone might serve as an anti-aggression chemical for heroin addicts whose drug use is based on a need to control the rage and aggressive tendencies originating in a problematic anal stage of development (Khantzian 1980). In a review of evaluations of methadone maintenance programs, M. Douglas Anglin and William McGlothlin (1985: 274) conclude that "methadone maintenance has been shown to effectively reduce drug use, dealing, and income-generating crime, and to a lesser extent to increase employment and family responsibility." Furthermore, they note, methadone maintenance "appeals to a portion of the addict population that has not been amenable to other social intervention strategies." And methadone has proven to be effective in suppressing the administration of opiates in laboratory experiments with animals (Winger 1988).

There is some concern that older addicts who might have gone into remission without any intervention are nevertheless maintained on methadone and thus are still addicted. In 2005 New York had ten methadone clients over age 80 years (Marion 2005). On the other hand, "patients who terminate before they have achieved stable social functioning are very unlikely to remain abstinent," and "even patients who terminate under the best of circumstances still may have less than a 50 percent chance of remaining abstinent as long as 3 years" (Hargreaves 1986: 70). Mary Kreek (1987) reports that only 20–30 percent of former "hardcore" heroin addicts remain heroin-free for three years or more following discharge from a methadone maintenance program, which is about the same percentages generally reported for other treatment modalities, including residential drug-free or short-term methadone detoxification programs. Anglin and McGlothlin (1985: 274–275) state that although methadone maintenance has not produced the wonderful results anticipated by early researchers, it makes a "real and beneficial contribution to reducing the social and individual costs associated with addiction."

Critics of New York City's methadone programs argue that they discourage abstinence as an ultimate goal, thus prolonging dependency for those who might be able and willing to give up all drug use. They note that this dependency extends to employment: Fees from methadone patients on welfare are guaranteed, paid for by Medicaid, while patients who are employed can usually afford to pay only a fraction of what Medicaid provides. Few programs offer vocational or job skills training (Massing 1999). Furthermore, methadone maintenance is predicated on the exclusiveness of heroin use, although heroin addicts are usually polydrug users who may continue use of illegal drugs even while being maintained on methadone (Inciardi, McBride, and Surratt 1998). When they enter treatment, methadone patients "frequently bring with them an inclination to experiment with a variety of other drugs and often view themselves as connoisseurs of drug-taking experiences.... Thus, continued use of other illicit drugs is frequently a problem in the treatment of a large percentage of methadone patients" (Platt et al. 1998).

The methadone maintenance program that was established by Dole and Nyswander at Beth Israel Medical Center in New York has continued to operate ever since. Beth Israel treats more than 8,000 patients, who make more than 1 million visits annually to the center's twenty-three outpatient clinics. Most patients have been in continuous treatment for more than two years; about half for more than five years. Treatment is voluntary; the program will not take coerced patients. Patients can remain on methadone for as long as they wish, or they can opt for detoxification. For the past decade the program has operated above capacity.

Methadone has gained popularity as a prescription drug for pain management and as a much cheaper alternative to OxyContin. But faulty Food and Drug Administration guidelines and prescribing physicians with little understanding of the drug led to overdose deaths (Eckholm and Pierce 2008).

Buprenorphine Buprenorphine (pronounced "byoo-pre-NOR-feen"), marketed under the brand name Suboxone, is chemically an opioid, but is only mildly addictive. As was noted in Chapter 4, when an opioid stimulates a particular receptor (the *mu* receptor), neurotransmitters are released, reducing pain sensations and causing feelings of pleasure. Buprenorphine is only a partial agonist and thus yields the same effects as heroin or methadone with less intensity. Because buprenorphine has a great affinity for the *mu* receptor and binds so tightly, taking additional opioids will not produce additional effects because buprenorphine prevents the opioids from locking into the receptor site. Because it detaches from the *mu* receptor site slowly, buprenorphine has a longer duration than methadone: two to three days (A. O'Connor 2004). Since it is a partial agonist, buprenorphine exhibits ceiling effects (i.e., increasing the dose has effects only to a certain level). Partial agonists usually have greater safety profiles than do full agonists because they are less likely to cause respiratory depression, the major toxic effect of opiate drugs (H. E. Jones 2004).

Another benefit of buprenorphine is that the withdrawal syndrome is, at worst, mild to moderate and can often be managed without administration of narcotics. Addicts who are being maintained on high does of methadone, on the other hand, will go through withdrawal symptoms if they are suddenly switched to buprenorphine (Pérez-Peña 2003). However, since buprenorphine is a partial agonist, "in severely addicted people, it may not provide enough opiate agonist activity to treat them adequately" (Mann 2004a: 8).

In 2002 the FDA announced the approval of buprenorphine and buprenorphine-naloxone (a partial opiate agonist with an opiate blocker) under the brand name Subutex. When taken orally, buprenorphine-naloxone does not produce euphoria and if injected, makes the user feel sick. Naloxone causes an immediate withdrawal syndrome in opioid addicts and needs to be taken only every one to three days. As a result of the Drug Addiction Treatment Act of 2000 these drugs can be dispensed in a doctor's office instead of a clinic and are subject to the same restrictions on quantities as methadone. This has the added benefit of avoiding having addicts associating at clinics while they await their methadone. The statute requires doctors to take an eight-hour course on the use of buprenorphine-naloxone. Originally, each doctor or group practice was allowed to treat only thirty patients, but legislation enacted in 2005 allows each qualified doctor within a group medical practice to prescribe Suboxone up to his or her individual physician limit of thirty patients. Group medical practices include large institutions such as hospitals and health maintenance organizations, many of which have numerous doctors who have been certified to treat opioid dependence.

CHEMICAL RESPONSES TO COCAINE ABUSE

In Chapter 5 we learned that the neurotransmitters dopamine and serotonin appear to play an important role in cocaine abuse. Cocaine agonists and antagonists that typically affect these neurotransmitters have been tested as possible treatment agents, but no drug has emerged that effectively treats the cocaine-dependent patient. "Progress in understanding the neurobiology of stimulant dependence has led to the identification of several medications whose effects counter or alleviate the disordered processing that underlies patients' symptoms. Depending on their specific actions, these medications may help patients attain an initial period of abstinence or avoid relapse. Although none has yet been approved for treating stimulant dependence, several have shown encouraging results in controlled clinical trials" (Kampman 2008: 28).

Dopamine antagonists are available, but they "can produce serious and permanent motor disorders, unpleasant subjective effects, or increases rather than decreases in cocaine self-administration in experimental animals" (Winger 1988: 125). Medication can be used as an adjunct to treating cocaine abusers either to deal with the deleterious effects of cocaine use itself or to treat the underlying motivations for using cocaine. Medication might be needed by addicts who are at risk of suicide during the postcocaine "crash" period, which is characterized by a lack of energy and an inability to feel pleasure, or by those who exhibit transient psychotic states. Severe delusional states and paranoid reactions from excessive cocaine require medication.

As was noted in Chapters 3 and 5, cocaine use may be a form of self-medication for those who suffer from certain chemical deficiencies, particularly neurotransmitters that affect mood and activity levels. In fact, note Henry Spitz and Jeffrey Rosecan (1987), some cocaine abusers have been successfully treated with prescribed antidepressants, although crack addicts appear to be less amenable to such treatment (Kolata 1989a). **Tricyclic antidepressants (TCAs)** such as Tofranil (imipramine) or Prozac are used to treat depression by manipulating the level of several neurotransmitters. They are used to treat cocaine depression, particularly in patients whose cocaine use appears to be a form of self-medication to ward off depression: "[TCAs] appear to reverse some of the neurochemical effects of chronic cocaine administration" (Spitz and Rosecan 1987: 260). It is believed that TCAs could act as cocaine antagonists by displacing or blocking cocaine receptors in the central nervous system and might help to reduce the craving for cocaine.

In 1990 the National Institute of Mental Health won a patent for one TCA, **desipramine,** an antidepressant used to wean users off the drug. Desipramine does not have any of the dangerous side effects of cocaine and is believed to reduce craving (Andrews 1990). Desipramine has since become the most widely studied medication for dealing with cocaine dependence. In limited clinical trials, it has shown some ability to decrease the reinforcing effects of cocaine and to reduce the craving for it (National Institute on Drug Abuse 1991; Kosten 1993). The substance is most effective with subjects who, in addition to cocaine dependence, suffer from depression (McCance 1997). Desipramine presents a risk of suicide in patients. Lithium, a standard drug for psychotic disorders, particularly depressive states, is used with patients whose cyclothymia (mild mood swings) or bipolar disorder (extreme mood swings) preceded cocaine use.

Chronic cocaine use may deplete the neurotransmitter dopamine, causing a craving in dopamine receptors. Bromocriptine, a dopamine agonist that is used to treat Parkinson's disease, appears to bind to the dopamine receptors, thus reducing the craving for cocaine. It does, however, have serious side effects, including nausea, headaches, dizziness, abnormal involuntary movements, and psychosis. According to Rosecan and Nunes (1987), use of bromocriptine is justified only in treatment-resistant cases in which recovery is hampered by severe craving. And while bromocriptine decreased cocaine use in laboratory monkeys, its chronic administration produced toxic effects including preconvulsive signs (Winger 1988). One study (Eiler, Schaefer, and Salstrom 1995) found little benefit in using bromocriptine to treat cocaine withdrawal, but Elinore McCance (1997) states that it still has potential as a possible treatment agent.

While no medications have been approved for the treatment of cocaine and methamphetamine dependence, there are some that show promise. The most promising medication for promoting abstinence in cocaine users is *modafinil* (Provigil), which is FDA-approved to treat narcolepsy ("sleeping sickness"). The drug acts as a mild stimulant countering the energy depletion experienced during withdrawal, and it appears to block the euphoric effects of cocaine, but there are some side-effects: Modafinal can cause insomnia, exacerbate the symptoms of bipolar disorder, and cannot be used by persons with certain cardiovascular problems (Kampman 2008).

PSYCHOLOGICAL TREATMENT

Treatment based on psychological theories can be broadly divided into those that are psychoanalytically oriented—sometimes referred to as *dynamic* or *clinical*—and those that utilize some form of behaviorism. Some programs mix the two approaches.

A PSYCHOANALYTIC APPROACH

To the psychoanalyst,[3] symptoms of neurotic behavior, such as drug abuse, are tied to repressed material from early life—the developmental stages examined in Chapter 8. In this view, the symptoms will disappear when the repressed material is exposed under psychoanalytic treatment. Therefore, the psychoanalyst seeks to make unconscious affect and memories available to the patient's consciousness (Holinger 1989). Psychoanalysis and the therapies based on it aim "at inducing the patient to give up the repressions belonging to his early life and to replace them by reactions of a sort that could correspond better to a psychically mature condition." To accomplish this, a psychoanalyst uses interpretation—attempts to get the patient "to recollect certain experiences and emotions called up by them which he has at the moment forgotten or repressed" (Reiff 1963: 274). This is accomplished through dream interpretation and free association. While in a relaxed state, the patient is asked to say what comes to mind about any given element in a dream, or the therapist might ask the patient to let a proper name or even a number occur to him or her. The train of associations stirred up by the dream, the name, or the number becomes an entry point for the release of repressed material, which the analyst helps the patient to interpret.

---

[3]*Psychoanalyst* is not a restricted title like that enjoyed by psychiatrists, who are physicians, or clinical psychologists, who hold a doctorate in psychology. Although there are certifying bodies for psychoanalysts, they do not enjoy a government-supported monopoly on the use of the title. There is a great deal of acrimony between psychologists and psychiatrists over who is qualified to practice psychoanalysis (Goleman 1988).

To re-create the emotional state that was originally attached to these associations, the therapist takes advantage of transference, the development of an emotional attitude—positive or negative—by the patient toward the therapist. Thus, the psychoanalyst might be emotionally (and unconsciously) perceived by the patient as a paternal or maternal figure in a re-creation of the emotions tied to very early psychic development.

In fact, psychoanalysis is rarely used to treat substance abusers, and there is a paucity of literature on treating substance abusers using this approach. This method requires highly skilled therapists, articulate patients—because psychoanalysis and the therapies based on it are "talk therapies"—and a long period of costly treatment: Psychoanalysis typically involves three to five fifty-minute sessions a week for as long as seven years, at $75 to $200 per session. There are few published reports of successful psychoanalytic treatment of drug-dependent individuals, and those that exist deal almost exclusively with heroin addiction. As Clifford Yorke (1970: 156) pointed out more than four decades ago with respect to heroin addicts, "the number of confirmed addicts seeking psychoanalytic treatment is almost certainly very small, the number of analysts prepared to accept them even smaller, and the number of addicts who pursue their treatment to conclusion smaller still." Freud himself doubted the usefulness of psychoanalysis for treating drug addicts (Byck 1974).

Frederic Schiffer (1988) used short-term therapy based on a psychoanalytic model to treat cocaine addicts in a hospital and subsequently on an outpatient basis. He found their pathology to be based on psychologically abusive conditions covertly carried out by one or both parents during childhood. Patients were filled with a long-standing rage and pain that they could not understand. Therapy allowed the patient to understand and appreciate the cause of his (all patients were male) feelings. Finally, patients were helped to master their traumatic pasts by "reliving, in effect through the patient's memories and transference, the early trauma" (Schiffer 1988: 133). The goal of psychoanalytically oriented therapy is to foster insight and self-awareness, which helps the patient to come to grips with his or her narcissistic disturbance that plays out as drug abuse (narcissistic tranquility). Substance abusers chemically extinguish unpleasant feelings and conflicts; self-awareness enables the patient to understand these emotions and thus learn to use nonchemical responses to them (Forrest 1985).

Psychology, notes James DeLong (1972: 224), has not found a consistent pathology among drug addicts: "No psychiatric diagnosis can be shown to apply to all heroin addicts or even to a majority of them." George E. Woody and his colleagues (1983: 639) argue, however, that "studies indicate that the types of psychiatric problems observed in addicts are similar to illnesses that are often treated with psychotherapy when they occur in nonaddicted populations." In practice, while therapists might be steeped in psychoanalytic theory, they generally avoid the psychoanalytical goal of effecting personality changes in drug abusers. Instead, they focus on improving the ego level of functioning by trying to help patients maintain constructive reality-based relationships, solve problems, and achieve adequate and satisfying social functioning without drugs and within the existing personality structure. The focus of treatment is on the functions of the ego and its ability to adapt to stress and changes in the environment, despite inadequacies experienced during early stages of development. (For a comparison of the effectiveness of different forms of psychotherapy with opiate addicts, see Woody et al. [1983]; for a discussion of the techniques of psychoanalytically based therapy with addicts, see Kaufman [1994].) This is accomplished through encouragement and moral support, persuasion and suggestion, training and advice, reeducation and counseling—not psychoanalysis. The therapist maintains a substance abuse orientation and typically focuses on identifying specific needs rather than intrapsychic processes. The therapist will deal with impaired self-esteem and ability to form sound interpersonal relationships, characteristics that depend on healthy psychosocial development at early stages of life. While recognizing the unconscious etiology, the therapist focuses on the client's present and future reality. Abstinence, not intrapsychic change, is the goal. For example, at City Roads, a short-term drug treatment program in London,

> the aims of counseling are to clarify *needs* and to build up the residents' motivation to do something about their needs. The first phase involves getting to know the resident, building up confidence and trust in City Roads. The very fact of sitting down and talking to a staff member who takes an interest in the resident is in itself fruitful. The resident starts to feel that someone cares. This was for them a very positive experience, which many drug abusers are not used to.
>
> The next step is "getting to the root of the problem," exploring the personal strengths and weaknesses and their origin, and the needs or problems under investigation are seen as psychological ones. People are seen as being unable to take responsibility, unable to form relationships, depressed, bitter, angry, frustrated, and lacking in trust. The causes of these problems are thought to lie in past experiences, most commonly in an emotionally unstable childhood characterized by lack of parental care, alcoholism in the home, an institutional upbringing, which are thought to lead to deprivation of warmth, care, and stability. (Jamieson, Glanz, and MacGregor 1984: 116–117 [edited])

A rigorous study that adhered to research protocols found that a combination of intensive individual and group counseling by credentialed psychotherapists for nine months had a significant impact on drug-using behavior (Crits-Christoph et al. 1999).

BEHAVIOR MODIFICATION

Behavior modification is a treatment approach based on learning theory. The strength of psychoactive substances as positive reinforcers and the negative reinforcement associated with abstinence provide conditioned responses that can explain the key difficulty in treating drug abusers: finding reinforcers that can successfully compete with these substances. Methadone's success in treating some heroin abusers can be explained in terms of behaviorism (Stitzer, Bigelow, and McCaul 1985). Furthermore, according to operant conditioning, for behavior modification to be effective, reinforcement—negative or positive—must follow immediately after the behavior is exhibited; this instant gratification is what makes drug use so reinforcing and why it is difficult to use behavior modification techniques with chronic drug users.

Aversion Treatment   Behavior modification can also attempt to shape behavior by applying punishment or aversive stimulation. Aversive control was depicted in

Stanley Kubrick's motion picture *A Clockwork Orange.* In actual drug treatment Anectine (succinylcholine), a muscle relaxant that causes brief paralysis but leaves the patient conscious, is injected into the subject immediately following the heroin cook-up ritual. The addict-patient remains conscious but is unable to move or breathe voluntarily, conditions that simulate the onset of death. The dangers of heroin use are recited while the patient remains paralyzed.

Drug antagonists can serve a similar function by rendering opiates or other substances ineffective—lacking positive reinforcement—or extremely unpleasant—negative reinforcement or punishment. Disulfiram (Antabuse), metronidazole, or chlorpropamide can serve this purpose for alcohol abusers. **Antabuse**, the best known of these substances, disrupts the liver's metabolism, producing a severe reaction that includes stomach and head pain, extreme nausea, and vomiting. (Milder reactions can be triggered by any number of products that contain alcohol, such as cough medicine, mouthwash, or even skin lotions.) In 1990, a patent was granted for a substance that has the appearance and smell of cocaine and even produces a numbing effect but is not psychoactive. The substance is used in conjunction with an aversive chemical (Andrews 1990). Other behavioral therapies use biofeedback and relaxation training and sometimes assertiveness training to prepare drug abusers to better cope with the stress and anxiety that are believed linked to drug use.

Research has discovered a connection between cues and drug use (see Chapter 3). It is believed that the intensity of the drug euphoria burns emotional memories into brain circuits. These memories are encoded into a part of the brain—the amygdala—that operates outside of conscious control to cause intense cravings for re-creating the euphoric experience. These cravings are countered by desensitization treatment: "[P]atients are usually first relaxed, then given repeated exposure to a graded hierarchy of anxiety-producing stimuli (real or imaginal)" to provide a form of immunity (Childress, McLellan, and O'Brien 1985: 957). In voluntary patients electric shocks may be self-administered whenever a craving for the chemical arises. Some researchers report that the use of chemical or electrical stimuli has not proven effective in producing a conditioned aversion in drug abusers, while success has been reported with verbal aversion techniques in which "a patient is asked to *imagine* strongly aversive stimuli (usually vomiting) in association with imaginal drug-related cues, scenes, and/or behavior" (Childress, McLellan, and O'Brien 1985: 951). Thus, imagined aversive stimuli might be superior to real aversive stimuli with the drug-dependent person (although this appears to run contrary to a great deal of research in operant conditioning). In any event, "aversive counterconditioning is not a substitute for support for life-enhancing behavior, rather it suppresses the undesirable behavior while other modalities support positive alternatives" (Frawley and Smith 1990: 21).

In an experiment using both chemical and verbal aversive techniques, cocaine abusers were provided with a nonpsychoactive substitute that smelled like cocaine and numbed the nose. The white substance was set out with a razor blade, a straw, and mirrors for the preparation of "lines." The patient received an injection of nausea-producing drugs. Just before the onset of nausea, the patient snorted the lines of "coke." During the three-hour recovery period the patient was encouraged to dwell on the drug paraphernalia and pictures of cocaine and to pair the use of cocaine with negative consequences. After six months of in-hospital and outpatient booster treatments the abstinence rate was 78 percent. Although a few patients had used cocaine again during the six-month period, the relapses were quite brief (Frawley and Smith 1990).

Social Learning Theory Approach Social learning theory, a variant of behaviorism, focuses on cognitive mediational processes. According to this view, people are active participants in their operant conditioning processes—they determine what is and what is not reinforcing. For example, as was noted in Chapter 8, the actor must *learn* that ingesting certain chemicals is desirable. In other words, behavior is complex, and reinforcement is often abstract. Thus, notes Albert Bandura (1974: 862), "human beings can cognitively bridge delays between behavior and subsequent reinforcement without impairing the efficacy of incentive operations." People have a unique capacity to use abstractions—symbols, such as the medals and trophies that are so dear to any amateur athlete—as important reinforcers.

The drug abuser is seen as lacking the level of social competence necessary to cope adequately with a variety of situational demands. In using operant conditioning with drug abusers, the social learning theorist stresses patient analysis to discover the variables that are reinforcing. The therapist attempts to discover the situational demands and their related negative emotions that are related to the patient's drug use. The treatment begins with an assessment of the positive and negative aspects of drug use and a self-report on the type, amount, and frequency of drugs used. The assessment includes a focus on the social, physical, and emotional environments in which drug use occurs (Donovan 1988).

Three types of stimulus can trigger intense craving leading to relapse (G. R. Hanson 2002b):

Priming: Just one exposure to a formerly abused substance can precipitate rapid resumption of abuse at previously established levels or greater.

Environmental cues: Exposure to people, places, or things associated with drug use can lead to resumption of abuse.

Stress: Acute and chronic stress can contribute to the establishment, maintenance, and resumption of drug abuse.

After the assessment the role of the therapist is to enable the patient to deal with triggering behavior so that it does not lead to drug use, the patient's own report of the negative aspects of drug use serving as a motivator for adopting more positive coping strategies (Donovan 1988).

- Through a detailed examination of the antecedents and consequences of substance abuse, the therapist attempts to understand why patients might be more likely to use in a given situation and to understand the role that drugs play in their lives. This functional analysis is used to identify the high-risk situations in which they are likely to abuse drugs and thus to provide the basis for learning more effective coping behaviors in those situations.
- The therapist attempts to help patients develop meaningful alternative reinforcers, that is, other activities and involvements (relationships, work, hobbies) that serve as viable alternatives to cocaine abuse and help patients remain abstinent.

- A detailed examination of the consequences, both long-term and short-term, of cocaine and other substance abuse is used as a strategy to build or reinforce the patient's resolve to reduce or cease substance abuse.

Cognitive Behavior Therapy   The cognitive position, which has become dominant in psychology, maintains that it is necessary to look to thoughts, memory, language, and beliefs. The emphasis is on inner rather than environmental determinants of behavior. Cognitive approaches in general tend to focus not on the psychological causes of substance abuse but rather on teaching abusers to understand their cravings and to develop coping skills. This may include detailed planning on how to get from one day to the next without using drugs (Orenstein 2002). Cognitive behavior therapy (CBT) is a short-term (e.g., twelve sessions in twelve weeks) outpatient approach focused on helping patients to recognize, avoid, and cope: *recognize* the situations in which they are most likely to use drugs, *avoid* these situations when appropriate, and *cope* more effectively with a range of problems and problematic behaviors associated with substance abuse (K. Carroll 1998).

Cognitive behavior therapy (CBT) is a broad term for therapies designed to correct dysfunctional and criminogenic thinking patterns. CBT "attempts to change negative behaviors by attacking, as it were, from both ends. Clients are not only taught more positive behaviors to replace their old ways of getting through life, they are also shown how to be more attuned to the thought processes that led them to choose negative actions in the past" (Morris Thigpen in Foreword to Milkman and Wanberg 2007: vii).

Because people can monitor and change their cognitive activity—"think drugs"—and resulting behavior—"do drugs"—the therapeutic process begins with an assessment of positive and negative aspects of their behavior. The assessment includes a focus on the social, physical, and emotional environments in which the behavior occurs. After the assessment, the role of the therapist is to enable the person to deal with cues that trigger problem behavior in a manner that avoids resorting to drug use, with the patient's own report of the negative aspects (e.g., arrest) serving as a motivator for adopting more positive coping strategies (Donovan, 1988). Negative reinforcement in the form of avoidance strategies serves to prevent the occurrence of influences that trigger drug use behavior.

In a cognitive approach developed by Anna Rose Childress (1993), the therapist first conducts a study to develop a set of cues that trigger drug cravings. Patients are then taught methods of combating the urges, including a planned delay before acting on a craving, having an alternative behavior planned for this delay period, and systematic relaxation to counter drug arousal. Other techniques include listening to a recording of positive and negative craving consequences, which instructs the addict to list the three most negative consequences of relapsing into drugs and the three most positive consequences of not acting on cravings. Negative imagery is used to encourage patients to remember their worst period of addiction—a type of scare tactic.

Fred Wright and his colleagues (1993) use the Socratic method of challenging questions and answers to stimulate patients to examine and modify their drug-related beliefs. Patients are also taught to keep a log of their cravings; after each entry they write spontaneous negative thoughts. CBT patients are taught to recognize connections between thoughts, feelings, and actions that undermine attempts to become abstinent. They are taught to avoid specific situations associated with their drug use and to use techniques such as "thought stopping" to cope with cravings. But to benefit, the patient must be intact cognitively (A. Mann 2004b).

Research into CBT with cocaine abusers found a high dropout rate, ranging from 33 percent to 64 percent. The researchers believe that this is related to the impaired attention, learning, memory, reaction time, and cognitive flexibility that are biological consequences of cocaine use. They suggest modifying treatment—a "dumbing down" of the curriculum—in a way that reduces demands on memory and attention (A. Mann 2004b).

Contingency Management and Contingency Contracting   Success in modifying behavior using learning theory has been experienced in the controlled setting of a total institution (Goffman 1961) such as a prison or hospital. In such environments, important reinforcers can be manipulated by therapists, often in the form of contingency management and **contingency contracting**.

Sometimes referred to as the *token economy*, contingency management rewards residents for behavior classified as "therapeutic" by providing them with points or tokens that can be redeemed for items the patient values, such as snacks, television time, and weekend passes. Roy Pickens and Travis Thompson (1984) describe the program that is used in a drug-treatment ward at the University of Minnesota Hospital, where staff members record point transactions—added or subtracted—in a small booklet issued to each patient.

Points can be earned for engaging in personal care activities such as cleaning the room or washing clothes, for doing chores such as preparing meals, for participating in ward activities, for attending classes aimed at helping residents to think rationally about themselves, and for assertiveness and problem-solving training that improve interpersonal skills. Extra points can be earned for good-quality participation; these are given to the resident at the end of each activity: "At this time a staff person marks the points earned in the patients' point booklets and briefly describes how the quality of their participation earned them extra points, or how they might improve their participation in the class to earn extra points" (Pickens and Thompson 1984: 55). Points earned are exchangeable for various goods or services, such as snacks, soft drinks, cigarettes, or personal care items. It is obvious that contingency management is not designed to directly affect drug-using behavior but is a means of getting patients to participate in the therapeutic activities that have abstinence as a goal.

The University of Minnesota Hospital uses contingency contracting in the form of "a formalized agreement between a staff person and the patient that specifies the manner in which learning principles are applied to the modification of the patient's behavior" (Pickens and Thompson 1984: 57). The contingency contract is drafted, and the parties sign it. The contract "details the specific behaviors to be changed, how such behaviors are to be monitored, and the contingencies [rewards or punishments] to be placed on the behaviors" (Pickens and Thompson 1984: 57). Contingency contracts are also used with patients during the first several weeks after discharge. The contracts are designed to allow for the implementation of behavioral contingencies in the patient's own home environment to reduce the likelihood of a return to drug use.

Stephen Higgens and Alan Budney (1993) describe a contingency management program for outpatient cocaine abusers that provides points for drug-free urine samples: The number of points multiplies when consecutive negative samples are submitted. The points can be exchanged for a variety of gift items. At the end of three months, patients are shifted from points and gifts to lottery tickets. Cognitive behavior therapy with vouchers has been used to treat marijuana users on an outpatient basis. When a patient submits a marijuana-negative urine sample, he or she receives a voucher worth $1.50; a second consecutive negative sample earns $3.00, a third $4.50, and so on. In addition, each consecutive pair of negative samples nets a bonus voucher worth $10. A full fourteen-week run of weekly drug-free samples nets vouchers worth $570, which are redeemable for retail goods or services (Davis 2008)

Methadone clinics have used contingency management to treat patients who ingest opiates and other drugs while on methadone maintenance or methadone withdrawal programs. Rewards for a drug-free urine sample include a cash payment and methadone take-home privileges. Negative contingencies include the loss of cash payments or take-home privileges, daily urinalysis, and counseling (Stitzer et al. 1984; see also Magura et al. 1988; Kidorf and Stitzer 1996). Stephen Magura and his colleagues (1988) report that contingency management utilizing take-home privileges did not have a significant effect on most methadone patients whose poly-drug use included cocaine; cocaine was especially attractive to these patients whose drug use was resistant to behavioral modification.

Contingency contracting with negative reinforcement has been used to ensure abstinence in cocaine treatment programs: "For example, a patient participating in such a contract will agree that, in the event of relapse, a previously drafted letter will be sent to his employer informing the latter of the patient's cocaine problem" (Kertzner 1987: 145). Robert Kertzner states that negative contingency contracting has been found to be very effective with patients who agreed to participate. However, he notes, one of the limitations of this strategy is the large number of patients who decline to participate. "Others have modified this technique to include positive sanctions for continued abstinence, such as returning patients' money held in escrow" (Kertzner 1987: 146).

The use of relatively inexpensive reinforcers can improve the outcome of drug treatment. In a study that was conducted at eight community-based treatment programs across the United States, participants who submitted negative drug and alcohol urine samples were immediately able to draw from a container of chips, half with words of encouragement ("good job") and half for prizes valued at between $1 and $200 that were conferred immediately. The number of draws to which they were entitled for being drug free increased by one every week but fell back to just one after a positive sample or a missed appointment. Forty-nine percent of the reinforcement participants and 35 percent of the usual care controls completed twelve weeks of counseling. Reinforcement participants achieved an average abstinence duration of 4.4 consecutive weeks compared to 2.6 weeks for the controls and attended more treatment sessions: nineteen versus sixteen (Whitten 2006c).

GROUP TREATMENT

Treatment using psychotherapeutic techniques or behavior modification may utilize casework—one-to-one counseling—or group approaches. "Because of our need for human contact is biologically determined, we are, from the start, social creatures. This propensity to congregate is a powerful therapeutic tool" (Flores and Georgi 2005: 2). "Groups organized around therapeutic goals can enrich members with insight and guidance; and during times of crisis, groups can comfort and guide people who otherwise might be unhappy or lost" (Flores and Georgi 2005: 2). As Helen Northern (1969: 52), points out, one of the advantages of the uses of the group approach "is that stimulation toward improvement arises from a network of interpersonal influences in which all members participate." Philip Flores and Jeffrey Georgi (2005: 2) note the special value of group treatment, since "people who abuse substances often are more likely to remain abstinent and committed to recovery when treatment is provided in groups, apparently because of rewarding and therapeutic forces such as affiliation, confrontation, support, gratifications, and identification."

The basic theory underlying this approach is that peer interactions are more powerful than therapist-patient interactions in the one-to-one situation. In casework the relationship between therapist and patient can remain distant because the therapist typically lacks the all-important personal experience with drug abuse. In the group approach, the group, not the group leader-therapist, is the helping instrument, obviating the therapist's personal experience with drugs. Furthermore, many critical interpersonal behaviors that might not emerge in the casework approach will emerge in a group (Flores 1988). "Group members are more likely to try new forms of behavior if these have been demonstrated effectively by others" (Kauffman, Dore, and Nelson-Zlupko 1995: 365).

Treatment groups are typically formed around one basic trait that all members share and from which the group derives its descriptive label. For example, they might be formed around cocaine abuse, a subtrait being age or gender. In general, notes Henry Spitz (1987), the more heterogeneous the group elements, the greater is the intragroup tension that promotes interaction. The more homogeneous the group elements, the greater is the basis for inter-member trust and group cohesion. Groups may be organized at different points in the treatment process, such as intake, detoxification, inpatient, and outpatient. There may also be groups for parents, siblings, and spouses. Although group approaches have many advantages over casework, considerably fewer therapists are trained in the former than in the latter. Furthermore, "patients whose motivation for change appears highly questionable should not be accepted into a group-oriented treatment program, because they usually have a negative, demoralizing impact on other patients who may be working hard to remain abstinent" (Washton, Stone, and Hendrickson 1988: 380).

Although group approaches may vary, "most professionals who work with alcoholics and addicts on a sustained basis agree that group therapy offers the chemically dependent individual unique opportunities to (1) share and to identify with others who are going through similar problems; (2) to understand their own attitudes about addiction and their defenses against giving up alcohol and drugs by confronting similar attitudes and defenses in others; and (3) to learn to communicate needs and feelings more directly" (Flores 1988: 7). Support provided by the group enables it to act as a catalyst for abstinence. (This has been the author's experience in working with groups of adolescent drug abusers.) Some researchers, however, advise caution: Group approaches "for youth with histories of antisocial behavior may be counterproductive; participants in a group may tend to validate and legitimize the antisocial behavior of the other group members" (Chavez and Sanchez-Way 1997: 17).

DRUG TREATMENT PROGRAMS

The treatment of drug-dependent people presents an obvious problem: If we do not know the cause, how can we offer the "cure"? This problem is exacerbated by programs that fail to develop theory-centered treatment responses or to incorporate the results of research into their approach to clients. While matching patient needs with specific treatments is the norm in medicine, this approach might be missing even in drug programs that are housed in medical settings (Hester and Miller 1988). The admissions policies of some in-patient programs depend more on financial status than on matching patient needs and program resources. Often, these are relatively new programs looking for middle- and upper class patients, who are most likely to enjoy high financial status and/or have third-party or insurance support. Assessment and intake are informal or based on available space. Mounting health-related costs have caused third-party payment organizations to "require treatment organizations to further document and better justify the need for treatment" (Winters and Henly 1988: 4). Indeed, the American Society of Addiction Medicine has established minimum criteria for inpatient drug and alcohol treatment for adults:

• Severe but manageable withdrawal risk
• Need for medical monitoring and a twenty-four-hour structured setting
• High resistance despite negative consequences
• Inability of outpatient treatment to curtail drug use
• Home environment dangerous for recovery

Treatment can be accomplished in a variety of settings: voluntary, involuntary, inpatient, and outpatient. The cost of these programs varies according to whether they are inpatient or outpatient, the qualifications of their staff, and the length of treatment. A particularly vexing problem is community opposition to drug treatment programs. Let us examine the settings and treatments offered by some drug programs.

TREATMENT PROGRAMS IN THE CRIMINAL JUSTICE SYSTEM

Despite more than two decades of research that demonstrate its effectiveness, the vast majority of prisoners who could benefit from drug abuse treatment do not receive it. About half of all prisoners (including some sentenced for non-drug-related offenses) are dependent on drugs, yet less than 20 percent of inmates suffering from drug abuse or dependence receive formal treatment (National Institute on Drug Abuse 2009).

About half the states have statutory provisions for the **civil commitment** of drug abusers (Leukefeld and Tims 1988), although few make any regular use of these provisions. Civil commitment, the nonpunitive incarceration of addicts for purposes of treatment, dates back to 1935, when a federal narcotics "farm" was opened in Lexington, Kentucky. A second was opened in 1938 in Fort Worth, Texas. Addict-patients who requested commitment and involuntary patients who had been prosecuted for criminal offenses spent six months at these facilities, which followed a standard course of withdrawal—physical restoration, psychological therapy in the form of individual and group counseling, and vocational counseling—after which patients returned to their communities. The physical structure of these facilities, however, resembled that of a modified prison, and security was strict (H. W. Morgan 1981). Reviews of the program were either mixed or inconclusive, and the federal government chose not to expand civil commitment. Despite this, in 1961 California enacted a program built on the Lexington model.

California Rehabilitation Center   In 1961 the California legislature established within the Department of Corrections the California Rehabilitation Center (CRC) for the compulsory care of individuals addicted to narcotics. In 1962 the U.S. Supreme Court ruled (in *Robinson* v. *California*, 370 U.S. 660) that drug addiction was an illness and that therefore a state could not make this status a crime. In that decision the Court also suggested that the Constitution would not be offended by involuntary civil commitment for the purpose of treating the illness of addiction. A later decision gave further support to the commitment-for-treatment approach, and in 1963 the legislature amended certain sections of the California Rehabilitation Act to emphasize treatment.

California statutes provide four methods of commitment (California Narcotic Addict Evaluation Authority 1994):

1. After a person has been convicted and sentenced to prison for a felony, the judge may suspend the sentence and order the district attorney to file for a narcotic petition. If the judge subsequently determines that the person is addicted or is in imminent danger of becoming addicted, execution of the sentence can be suspended, and the offender is placed in the CRC at Norco. Most residents at the CRC fall into this category.
2. After conviction for a misdemeanor and before or after sentencing, the judge can certify the case to superior court for a commitment petition. After an examination the offender may be sent to the CRC.
3. Any interested party may report to the district attorney under oath his or her belief that another person is addicted to narcotics or is in imminent danger of becoming addicted. If sufficient evidence (probable cause) is present, the district attorney may petition the superior court for a period of commitment not to exceed twelve months.
4. Any person who believes that he or she is addicted or about to become addicted may report such belief to the district attorney, who can then petition the superior court for a period of commitment not to exceed twelve months.

The CRC is a medium-security facility of the Department of Corrections with open dormitories, double fences, and armed officers at the perimeter. CRC has remedial and high school educational facilities as well as vocational training. Residents may voluntarily join various self-help groups such as Alcoholics Anonymous and Narcotics Anonymous. Leisure activities include organized and individual athletics. Following institutional care, civil commitment residents are released to aftercare: parole supervision that includes regular testing for drug use. Those who fail to live up to the terms of release can be returned to the CRC. Composed of seven members appointed by the governor, release to aftercare/parole and return to the CRC are governed by the Narcotic Addict Evaluation Authority.

Researchers followed 581 male heroin addicts who had been admitted to the California Civil Addict Program (CAP) between 1962 and 1964. The average age of participants on admission to CAP was 25 years. More than 60 percent had started using heroin before age 20. The men were, on average, 57 years old in 1996–1997. Of the 242 subjects who were interviewed at that time, 21 percent tested positive for opiates. A total of 13.8 percent of the original 581 subjects had died by the time of the first interview; 27.7 percent had died by the time of the second interview; and 48.9 percent had died by the time of the latest interview. At the first interview, about 38 percent of the surviving sample had opiate-free urine tests; 41 percent were opiate-free at the second interview; and 56 percent were opiate-free at the last interview. The unanswered question is whether these results were caused by successful programming, aging out, or any combination of the two ("33-Year Study Shows Severe Long Term Effects of Heroin" 2001).

In any event, to ease prison overcrowding, during the 1980s the CRC began receiving felony inmates who now number about 4,500 and, thus, outnumber the approximately 1,500 civil commitments. There are also about 2,200 aftercare parolees.

A federal civil commitment program was authorized in the 1966 Narcotic Rehabilitation Act, but since the 1970s has fallen into disuse.

DRUG COURTS

Established as a result of court and prison overcrowding, special **drug courts** have proven popular. The effects of aggressively expanding punitive drug enforcement starting in the 1980s have been cited as one of the main rationales for the vigorous emergence of drug courts. "The enforcement-centred 'War on Drugs' has sent large populations of drug offenders into the criminal justice system, and has led to an unprecedented increase in the number of offenders receiving long imprisonment sentences" (Fischer 2003: 227). In 1989, a special drug court was established by judicial order in Miami, Florida. This high-volume court expanded on traditional drug defendant diversion programs by offering a year or more of court-run treatment; defendants who complete this option have their criminal cases dismissed. Between 1991 and 1993 Miami influenced officials in more than twenty other jurisdictions to establish drug courts (National Institute of Justice 1995b). While drug courts were originally a response to criminal justice overcrowding, they subsequently became part of therapeutic (as distinguished from adversarial) jurisprudence, that is, the use of the courts to deal with a range of human problems (Abadinsky 2008). Drug courts have "transformed specialized criminal courts from adversarial to therapeutic and rehabilitative" (Lurigio 2008: 15).

Although they vary widely, the approximately two thousand drug courts have common features that include a nonadversarial approach to integrating substance abuse treatment with criminal justice case processing. The focus is on early identification of eligible substance abusers and prompt placement in treatment, combined with frequent drug testing (Gebelein 2000). The goal is to facilitate drug abstinence through treatment using the threat of being expelled from the program and concomitant adjudication of the original charge court to compel cooperation. In drug court, judges assume broad supervision over a defendant and monitor progress by, for example, frequent drug tests, group meetings, and court appearances (Armstrong 2003). Participants must frequently appear in court, usually weekly for the first 90 days, before specially-trained judges during which their compliance is reviewed.

The Madison County, Illinois, drug court was fueled by a 437-percent increase in drug arrests between 1988 and 1992. The program targets individuals arrested on felony drug charges who have been diagnosed with alcohol or drug dependence that could be treated on an outpatient basis. Those who successfully complete the program have their charges dismissed. The program provides job assistance, which includes vocational training and high school equivalency education. Initially, clients are scheduled for three to five intensive three- to four-hour counseling sessions per week. As the clients progress, the number and length of sessions are reduced. Depending on a client's progress, the program can be completed in about one year or less. Random drug tests are given, and failure to comply with program requirements results in prosecution for the original felony offense (Illinois Criminal Justice Authority 1999).

In Maricopa (Phoenix) County, Arizona, the goal of drug court is considerably different: to increase the number of drug cases entering the system. Using a catchy "do drugs, do time" slogan, law enforcement agencies targeted casual users to enforce a "zero tolerance" policy. Users are "held accountable" for their illegal drug use by a policy of arrest and threatened prosecution; those who accept the treatment option—which includes paying fees—avoid further court action (Hepburn, Johnston, and Rogers 1994).

A study of drug court participants in six U.S. cities found that judicial supervision coupled with treatment is a powerful tool for responding to drug abusers, despite the fact that most participants enrolled to avoid incarceration and not for purposes of rehabilitation. Indeed, the study found that the threat of incarceration and frequent drug testing were essential to program success (National Institute of Justice 2002). A study in New York revealed that drug offenders who complete the court supervised program are less likely to commit crimes than are similar offenders who opt for prison time instead: 29 percent lower over three years (von Zielbauer 2003). Of course, drug abusers who opt for prison may be quite different from those who complete drug court treatment. Research into the Multnomah County (Portland) Oregon drug court, the second oldest in the United States, revealed that program participants experienced an almost 30 percent reduction in the incidence of re-arrest (Truitt 2007) and Doris Layton MacKenzie (2006) concludes that an examination of research into drug courts reveals that they are effective in reducing participant recidivism.

"Drug courts are premised on the idea that legal coercion to enter drug treatment is an effective means of achieving the benefits associated with treatment programs" and "stiff sanctions associated with noncompliance are used to coerce offenders to enter and remain in treatment" (Hepburn and Harvey 2007: 257). However, in their study, John Hepburn and Angela Harvey found "no support for the widely held view that the threat of incarceration is needed to motivate offenders to participate in the drug court program (2007: 271).

Reported success rates, critics argue, may be a function of the type of offender typically subject to drug court—persons without serious dependency, but looking to avoid incarceration. And, of course, drug court depends on the availability of drug treatment programs for its clientele (Eckholm 2008). That raises a more fundamental issue: Why are drug offenders in the criminal justice system rather than in treatment in the first place? (Fischer 2003). Indeed, drug court policy that substantially limits access to treatment for high-risk offenders, while likely to generate good "success stats," is not necessarily cost effective in terms of actual dollars expended or public safety (Bhati, Roman, and Chalfin 2008).

TREATMENT ALTERNATIVE TO STREET CRIME (TASC)

The federally funded Treatment Alternative to Street Crime (TASC) program initiated in 1972 to divert substance-abusing offenders out of the court system and into community treatment, stands somewhere between compulsory and voluntary treatment. Since its inception it has been expanded to include people on probation and parole. TASC identifies, assesses, and refers appropriate drug- and/or alcohol-dependent offenders accused or convicted of nonviolent crimes to community-based substance abuse treatment, as an alternative to or supplement to existing criminal justice sanctions and procedures (Cook and Weinman 1988). TASC monitors the client's progress in drug treatment and reports back to the criminal justice agency that made the referral. Those who fail to conform to program requirements face further criminal justice processing. Research into the effectiveness—reducing recidivism and drug use—of TASC, which operates in about thirty states, has generally been positive (Anglin, Longshore, and Turner 1999).

Coercive treatment, civil or criminal, appears to have a positive outcome (Anglin 1988; Anglin and Hser 1990a; D. Young 2002). Extensive research indicates that "[c]oerced involvement in community-based programs and/or corrections-based treatment can have a substantial impact on the behavior of chronic drug-abusing offenders" (Anglin and Maughr 1992: 76). George Vaillant (1970: 494) found that although the most effective motivation for abstinence is that narcotics are illegal, "the most potent treatment was compulsory supervision. Thus, if the addict is followed over time, external coercion of some kind appears a critical variable in facilitating abstinence."

This was the author's experience when as a parole officer (see Abadinsky 2009) he supervised heroin addicts in New York City. Close personal contact, unannounced home visits and searches, arm checks (for needle marks), and random urinalysis provided the ego and superego strengths for addicts to remain heroin free: "Besides offering addicts compulsory support and an 'external super-ego,' parole itself was probably a substitute for addiction in that it required ex-addicts to remain regularly employed" (Vaillant 1970: 495). The parole officer could redirect the considerable skills and energy that are required to be a successful heroin addict into seeking and maintaining legitimate employment (see also Eaglin 1986). From the behaviorist point of view, the probation or parole officer provides the basis for operant conditioning, applying positive reinforcement for abstinence and negative reinforcement for relapse.

In a study of compulsory treatment—residential treatment or imprisonment for felony offenders—Douglas Young (2002) found that mandatory treatment programs and progressively higher perceived legal pressure can increase treatment retention and that such retention is directly related to a positive treatment outcome for participants. MacKenzie (2006) states that although drug treatment in general is effective in reducing the recidivism of drug-involved offenders, the research literature does not reveal which interventions are most effective.

But in some locales there is a paucity of interventions available for voluntary or court-ordered abusers. In the relatively affluent Long Island, New York counties of Nassau and Suffolk, for those without sufficient funds or medical insurance there are only 20 beds available for the 5-day detox and 28-day therapy program at Nassau University Medical Center, although the hospital's outpatient methadone program services about 650 patients daily (Martino, Jr. 2009).

THERAPEUTIC COMMUNITY

Therapeutic community (TC) is a generic term for residential, self-help, drug-free treatment programs that have some common characteristics, including concepts adopted from Alcoholics Anonymous (AA): "There is no such thing as an ex-addict, only an addict who is not using at the moment; the emphasis on mutual support and aid; the distrust of mental-health professionals; and the concept of continual confession and catharsis. However, the TC has extended these notions to include the concept of a live-in community with a rigid structure of day-to-day behavior and a complex system of punishment and rewards" (DeLong 1972: 190–191). "The primary aims of the therapeutic community are a global change in lifestyle reflecting abstinence from illicit substances, elimination of antisocial activity, increased employability, and prosocial attitudes and values. A critical assumption in TCs is that stable recovery depends upon a successful integration of these social and psychological goals. The rehabilitative approach, therefore, requires multidimensional influences and training that, for most clients, can only occur after an extended period of living in a 24-hour residential setting" (De Leon 1986b: 69).

The TC "views drug abuse as deviant behavior, reflecting impeded personality development and/or chronic deficits in social, educational and economic skills" (De Leon 1986a: 5; see also DeLeon 2000). "A considerable number of [TC] clients never have acquired conventional lifestyles. Vocational and educational deficits are marked; mainstream values either are missing or unpursued. Most often, these clients emerge from a socially disadvantaged sector where drug abuse is more a social response than a psychological disturbance. Their TC experience can be termed *habilitation*—the development of a socially productive, conventional lifestyle for the first time in their lives" (De Leon 1994: 19). "According to the TC treatment perspective, drug abuse is a disorder of the whole person; the problem is the person, not the drug, and the *addiction* is only a *symptom* and not the essence of the disorder" (Nielsen and Scarpitti 1997: 280).

TC Models   The TC becomes a surrogate family and a communal support group for dealing with alienation and drug abuse that derives from it. Its purpose, notes Mitchell Rosenthal (1973), is to strengthen ego functioning. Therapy, except for

███

THE THERAPEUTIC COMMUNITY IN SUM

"TCs are drug-free residential settings that use a hierarchical model with treatment stages that reflect increased levels of personal and social responsibility. Peer influence, mediated through a variety of group processes, is used to help individuals learn and assimilate social norms and develop more effective social skills. TCs differ from other treatment approaches principally in their use of the community, comprising treatment staff and those in recovery, as key agents of change" (National Institute on Drug Abuse 2002b: 1).

the time spent asleep, is total. James DeLong (1972) notes that there is a quasi-evangelistic quality to the "TC movement." The day at a therapeutic community is varied but regimented. A typical day begins at 7:00 A.M. and ends at 11:00 P.M. "and includes morning and evening house meetings, job assignments, groups, seminars, scheduled personal time, recreation, and individual counseling. As employment is considered an important element of successful participation in society, work is a distinctive component of the TC model. In the TC, all activities and interpersonal and social interactions are considered important opportunities to facilitate individual change" (National Institute on Drug Abuse 2002b: 5).

The residences are often similar to the communes that were popular during the late 1960s and 1970s counterculture movement, except that they generally have a strict hierarchy and insist on rigid adherence to norms even more stringent than those of the proverbial middle class. The model of all therapeutic communities, note Jerome Platt and Christina Labate (1976), is Synanon, founded in 1958 by Charles E. Dederich[4], a former alcoholic who was a participant in and advocate of the Alcoholics Anonymous twelve-step approach to substance abuse. (AA is discussed later in this chapter.) The Synanon Foundation expanded rapidly into several states, with facilities run almost entirely by ex-addicts. Treatment programs based on twelve-step/drug-free approaches frequently have an antimedication bias (Harwood and Myers 2004).

Therapeutic communities such as Odyssey House, however, have been more receptive to using professionals and even medicine-assisted withdrawal. The director of the New York–based Phoenix House, the largest private, nonprofit drug-treatment institution in the country—with ninety programs serving more than 5,000 clients—has long had a psychiatrist, Mitchell Rosenthal, as its executive director, and the program now uses buprenorphine for withdrawing patients from heroin (Horton and McMurphy 2004). David Bellis (1981: 155) is critical of therapeutic communities that resist professional involvement and that instead use untrained staff and residents, "many hardly off heroin themselves," who, under no

---

[4]Dederich eventually transformed Synanon into a cultlike phenomenon. In 1980 he pled guilty to plotting to murder one of his Synanon critics, a lawyer representing former Synanon members who maintained that they were held against their will. In poor health, Dederich received a sentence of five years' probation and was banned from participating in Synanon. In 1997, at age 83, Dederich died of a heart attack.

PHOENIX HOUSE

At Phoenix House in the Bronx, every day begins the same. After a thirty-minute breakfast starting at 7:00 A.M., there is an hour-long meeting that includes inspirational songs and skits written and performed by the residents. The rest of the day consists of seminars, classes to prepare for the general equivalency diploma, rap sessions, job assignments, and more meals and meetings. There is little free time until 9:00 P.M. Lights are out at 11:00 P.M. The 185-word Phoenix House philosophy is recited from memory at least twice a day. The weekend schedule is slightly more relaxed, with rented videos available and highly supervised trips into New York. Most of the residents are between 20 and 40 years old and on welfare, which helps to pay for their stay at the program. They typically have lengthy criminal records (Marriott 1989).

legal or professional oversight, unleash their own brand of "therapy" on addicts, many of whom are undergoing mandatory treatment because of a plea bargain, probation, or parole status. In his study of a failed therapeutic community Robert Weppner (1983) points out that being a poorly educated ex-addict does not endow one with treatment skills.

Although Synanon requires a lifetime commitment, most TCs have abandoned or modified this aspect of the Synanon model. The TCs frequently offer vocational training and education to prepare residents to live in the community without continuous help from the TC. Indeed, George De Leon describes the TC as "community as method": "*the purposive use of the peer community to facilitate social and psychological change in individuals*" (1995: 9 [italics in original]).

Life in the Therapeutic Community   A prominent feature of the TC has been the stiff entry requirement: a devastating initial interview that tests an applicant's motivation by focusing on his or her inadequacies and lack of success. Successful applicants must invest completely in the program, which encourages the resident to identify with the former addicts who run it and become resocialized into embracing a drug-free existence. The new resident is isolated from all outside contacts, including family and friends. The withdrawal process is accomplished without drugs but with the support of other residents. Once withdrawal has been accomplished, a program of positive and negative reinforcement is implemented. The resident is assigned menial work projects, such as cleaning toilets, but is given an opportunity to earn more prestigious assignments and greater freedom through conformity with the program. Transgressions are punished by public humiliation such as reprimands, shaved heads, and wearing a sign indicating the nature of the violation. Those who leave, relapse, and return are required to wear a sign announcing their situation. Shame and guilt are constantly used to force the addict to conform and to change his or her view of drugs (Platt and Labate 1976). There is little privacy. Drug use, physical violence, and sexual activity between residents are punished with expulsion.

Residents are kept busy in a highly structured environment that offers little time for idleness or boredom. They are expected to be active in all aspects of the

ODYSSEY HOUSE

Odyssey House operates a TC on New York's Wards' Island for pregnant women and those with young children. Residents include about two dozen women and children. Some of the women are pregnant, and most have been abusing crack. The facility is underfunded and must depend on private donations to make up for inadequate government support. As a result, children's clothing and nursery toys are in short supply. The residents "participate in rigorous therapy, they are given parenting courses including such essentials as how to hold a baby and they must work at jobs. The overbearing and obnoxious scrape plates, while the shy and withdrawn are given pretty clothes and work as front-desk receptionists. But the most prized assignments are in the nursery.... Graduation requirements are stiff. Along with conquering addiction, women must complete the equivalent of high school, secure a driver's license and find a full-time job" (D. Martin 1990: 13).

TC program. Failure to do so becomes the subject of criticism at the encounter session, a central feature of the therapeutic process. The encounter is a relatively unstructured, leaderless group session in which members focus on a particular resident (who occupies the "hot seat") and bombard him or her with criticisms about attitude and behavior. The target is encouraged to fight back verbally, although the goal of such sessions is to destroy the rationalizations and defenses that help to perpetuate irresponsible thought patterns and behavior—a resocialization process. The ex-addict counselor at San Francisco's Center Point TC addresses one of the residents at a group session: "You like to present yourself as a middle-class white woman with a *little* drug and alcohol problem who some stuff happened to and now you're here to get your life back.... [But] you are a homeless dope fiend with no education who chose drugs over your kids" (Orenstein 2002: 37).

"The style of the encounter, with its abrasive attacks and its permitted verbal violence ... is designed to encourage the spewing out of pent-up hostility and anger, to force the patient to confront his maladaptive emotional response and behavior patterns" (M. Rosenthal 1973: 91). "TCs are successful because they provide the setting and the mechanisms for clients' learning new roles, attitudes, skills, and definitions of self. The most important mechanism for change is the community of peers who confront the client when old values or behaviors are displayed, who provide positive and negative reinforcements to elicit appropriate behavior, and who serve as role models for lifestyle changes" (Nielson and Scarpitti 1997: 281).

Dan Waldorf (1973) points out that the TC is an exciting, friendly, and highly moral—almost utopian—environment. But, notes Mitchell Rosenthal (1984: 55), it is not for all abusers: "Severe disturbances may be exacerbated by the TC regimen and may have an adverse effect not only on the disturbed client but also on the treatment environment and the progress of others in the treatment population. Also unsuitable for treatment are candidates whose drug involvement is of so limited a nature as to require a less rigorous intervention or who—despite the deleterious effects of drug abuse—are able to function with the help of a positive support network (e.g., family or significant others)."

TCs in Prisons   TCs have been established in prisons in New York, California, and a number of other states (Pendergast et al. 2002). In these so-called "Stay 'N Out" therapeutic communities inmates are recruited at state correctional facilities and housed in units that are segregated from the general prison population, although they eat and attend morning activities with other prisoners. The program, which lasts from six to nine months, is staffed by graduates of community TCs and by ex-offenders with prison experience who act as role models demonstrating successful rehabilitation.

As with its community-based counterpart, the prison-based TC program provides an intensive, highly structured prosocial environment that differs from other treatment principally in its use of the TC community as the key agent of change. "Peer influence, mediated through a variety of group processes, is used to help residents learn and assimilate social norms and develop more effective social skills.... Strict and explicit behavioral norms are emphasized and reinforced with specific contingencies (rewards and punishments) directed toward developing self-control and responsibility" (Welsh 2007: 1482).

> During the early phase of treatment, the major clinical thrust involves observation and assessment of client needs and problem areas. Orientation to the prison TC procedures occurs through individual counseling, encounter sessions, and seminars. Clients are given low-level jobs and granted little status. During the later phase of treatment, residents are provided opportunities to earn higher-level positions and increased status though sincere involvement in the program and hard work. Encounter groups and counseling sessions are more in-depth and focus on the areas of self-discipline, self-worth, self-awareness, respect for authority, and acceptance of guidance for problem areas. Seminars take on a more intellectual nature. Debate is encouraged to enhance self-expression and to increase self-confidence. (Wexler and Williams 1986: 224)

Do TCs Work?   There has been a great deal of controversy over the success rate of TCs, and most research has been inadequate or inconclusive. Many TCs release statistics that cannot withstand scrutiny by disinterested researchers. The arduous screening process keeps out many drug abusers who would probably fail the program, and an abuser's graduation from a TC does not necessarily mean that the program has succeeded. In a study of two TCs, researchers found that while participants who complete the programs showed positive treatment effects, a 50 percent drop-out rate may indicate that successful residents have unique characteristics— commitment to change, for example--that explain the results (Klebe and O'Keefe 2004).

The TC insists on behavioral change that is not only away from antisocial behavior, that of the street addict, and toward the norms of the larger society, "but toward norms accepted in the group alone" (Weppner 1983: xi). Those who need to manage in the community without the continuing support of the group are at risk because they will return to the same environment that led to drug dependence in the first place, and they often bring with them all of the educational and vocational deficiencies they had on entering. Those who enter the TC with a greater degree of mental health, with limited or no attachment to a criminal subculture, and with employment skills are obviously better equipped to deal with post-TC existence.

Prison-based TC research has generally revealed positive outcomes among seriously drug-involved offenders, but effectiveness remains unclear because of methodological limitations that include selection and attrition biases and dissimilar outcome measures (Welsh 2007). Research into the effect of the prison TC on parole success found that while it reduced recidivism (Wexler, Lipton, and Foster 1985; Wexler, Falkin, and Lipton 1990; Lipton 1995; Wexler et al. 1999; Welsh 2003, 2007) and significantly lowered the likelihood of reincarceration, it did not necessarily prevent drug relapse.

CHEMICAL DEPENDENCY PROGRAMS

Short-term residential programs, often referred to as chemical dependency units, are often based on the *Minnesota Model* of treatment for alcoholism. These programs involve a three- to six-week inpatient treatment phase, followed by extended outpatient therapy or participation in twelve-step self-help groups such as Narcotics Anonymous or Cocaine Anonymous. "Chemical dependency programs for drug abuse arose in the private sector in the mid-1980s with insured alcohol and cocaine abusers as their primary patients" (National Institute on Drug Abuse 2003s: 1). Some are for-profit, and others are nonprofit; many call themselves "therapeutic communities," although they differ dramatically from the TCs discussed above. There are approximately 11,000 privately operated substance abuse treatment programs in the United States, of which about 25 percent are for-profit.

These programs typically share a number of features: They do a great deal of outreach—most employ a marketing person—and often advertise for clients who are likely to have health insurance, such as employed alcohol and cocaine abusers, as opposed to heroin addicts, because the costs can run over $1,000 a day for inpatient care. Many CD programs are located in a health care facility, which can increase the cost of treatment. Adding a chemical dependency program to a health care facility can help to reduce the number of otherwise vacant beds that can be costly to any hospital. The treatment approach usually includes individual and group counseling, and the model tends to be eclectic rather than doctrinal.

"Primarily they serve the more socially advantaged substance abusers whose fee for service is generally covered by insurance, in contrast to the major modalities whose costs are mostly tax subsidized. The treatment orientation of these programs is also

PRIVATE HOSPITAL DRUG TREATMENT

"Parents are often frightened by media hype or hospital treatment center advertisements that they have seen on television. Insurance coverage and the parents' willingness to have someone else deal with the 'abuser' are also factors. As a result, what may be experimental adolescent behavior becomes a reason to place an adolescent in an inpatient hospital treatment program. Such treatment programs are one of the few large-scale sources of profit for private hospitals. Managers of these programs have become desperate for adolescent admissions because of the vast overbuilding of these facilities that occurred during the 1980s" (Lawson 1992: 4).

varied, but mainly reflects a mix of traditional mental health and twelve-step perspectives [discussed below]. They offer a broad menu of services such as education, nutrition, relaxation training, recreation, counseling-psychotherapy, psychopharmacological adjuncts, and self-help groups" (De Leon 1995: 5). "CD programs do not require patients to perform housekeeping duties.... [and they] are especially attractive to patients with greater initial functional and social resources who can afford the better facilities and amenities" (Gerstein 1994: 56).

The typical program is a three- to six-week intensive and highly structured inpatient regimen:

> Clients begin with an in-depth psychiatric and psychosocial evaluation and then follow a general education-oriented program track of daily lectures plus two to three meetings per week in small task-oriented groups. Group education teaches clients about the disease concept of dependence, focusing on the harmful medical and psychosocial effects of illicit drugs and excessive alcohol consumption. There is also an individual prescriptive track for each client, meetings about once a week with a "focal counselor," and appointments with other professionals if medical, psychiatric, or family services are needed. (Gerstein and Harwood 1990: 171)

A class of super-luxury rehabilitation centers in California— ocean-view mansions where the patients often come from the world of show business—charge from $40,000 to $100,000 for a 30-day stay (J. Adler 2007). Malibu, population 13,000, has 29 licensed, mostly for-profit rehab establishments (Fortini 2008). Passages Malibu, an exception to the prevalent twelve-step approach, presents itself as a "cure center" with a success rate above 84 percent (Waxman 2007). Like similar programs, it offers luxury with therapy—"a sprawling 10-acre private sanctuary estate overlooking the ocean in Malibu, California," with "gourmet-organic chefs, gym, tennis courts, pools, [and] Jacuzzis." It also promises 60 one-on-one treatment sessions in 30 days. And like similar programs, its clientele must be able to afford this approach: Passages charges $78,550; similar programs about $50,000. In common with other CD programs, the manner of determining "success" is less than rigorous and fails to meet standards required of sound research.

The *Florida Model* of substance abuse treatment (Florida has an abundance of private substance abuse rehabilitation programs) consists of residential treatment followed by living in a halfway house with "recovery employment" in a low-wage job. One program (Behavioral Health of the Palm Beaches) notes the draw of Florida: "The weather in Florida is beautiful, especially in the winter. Nice warm weather makes the concept of going to alcohol or drug rehab in Florida a comfortable idea." And "Florida and the ocean is a beautiful, natural environment. Many of the best alcohol treatment centers are on or near the Atlantic Ocean, creating a natural atmosphere of peace and serenity."

Delray Beach, on Florida's Atlantic coast, with a year-round population of about 65,000, is the "recovery capital of America," so-called because it has abundant halfway houses and more than 5,000 people who attend twelve-step meetings each week; it has its own recovery radio show. The critical mass of recovering substance abusers in Delray Beach constitutes a society within a society. The halfway houses, some established by former substance abusers, are unregulated. They are typically modest bungalows that "provide structure and supervision—curfews, random drug tests, the requirement that tenants have jobs and attend meetings"

(Gross 2007: 24). Some owners put rule-breakers on the street and without alternative housing, raising the ire of neighborhood homeowners.

Harvey Siegal and his colleagues (1995: 69) are critical of CD programs: "Since it is the treatment professional who retains all responsibility for prescribing and implementing the necessary therapeutic activity, patients may have difficulty achieving ownership of their recovery program." And **aftercare**—treatment and services following discharge—is typically meager. "Aftercare is considered quite important in CD [28-day] treatment, but relatively few program resources are devoted to it" (Gerstein 1994: 56).

Although treatment at most inpatient chemical dependency programs in the United States is based on a disease model built around an AA twelve-step approach, there is an almost total lack of relevant research data on their effectiveness (Gerstein and Harwood 1990; Galaif and Sussman 1995; Ogborne and Glaser 1985). Furthermore, most of these programs provide no aftercare but refer patients to AA, which deals with the problems of drinking but not with related or contributing problems such as unemployment and interpersonal skills or with drug use as a form of self-medication.

ALCOHOLICS ANONYMOUS (AA) TWELVE-STEPS

The **Alcoholics Anonymous (AA)** approach of using public confession and commitment and mutual aid concepts can be found in a number of nineteenth century temperance organizations (W. L. White 1998). Alcoholics Anonymous was established during the 1930s by William ("Bill W.") Wilson (1895–1971), a financial investigator and alcoholic, and Robert ("Dr. Bob") Holbrook Smith (1879–1950), a physician and alcoholic. Nan Robertson (1988b) presents a rather unflattering view of the two, particularly of Wilson (see also Cheever 2004), whom she refers to as a Wall Street hustler and compulsive womanizer. Bill W. had joined the Oxford Group (renamed Moral Re-Armament in 1939), an international religious movement, as the result of the influence of another alcoholic whose religious experience appeared to act as a cure. Bill W. was influenced by the work of William James (1842–1910), a psychologist and philosopher, particularly his *Varieties of Religious Experience*, published in 1902.[5] As part of the Oxford Group Bill W. began dedicating his activities to curing alcoholics, an effort that was quite unsuccessful until he met Dr. Bob, also a member of the Oxford Group, in 1935 while on a business trip to Akron, Ohio. He helped Dr. Bob to become abstinent, and the two recognized that success in helping alcoholics was not to be found in preaching abstinence but rather in a fellowship in which each alcoholic simply relates his or her story of drunkenness and conversion to a nonalcoholic lifestyle. The "listening" was as important as the "telling." "There could not have been just one founder of A.A.," notes Robertson (1988b: 34), "because the essence of the process is one person telling his story to another as honestly as he knows how."

---

[5]It is ironic that William James typically found his religious and philosophical insights while intoxicated from nitrous oxide (Tymoczco 1996).

Early in 1939, Bill W. published *Alcoholics Anonymous*, which explained the philosophy and methods—the **twelve steps** of recovery—of his small association of alcoholics and contained case histories of some thirty recovered members. They became known as Alcoholics Anonymous after the title of Wilson's book, which AA members often refer to as "the Big Book" (it was quite bulky when originally published). Wilson, who died in 1971, was supported by the substantial royalties the book eventually generated.[6] His home in Bedford Hills, New York, is listed on the National Register of Historical Places. His wife, Lois Burnham, who died in 1988 at age 97 years, established **Al-Anon** for the family members of alcoholics. She was a nonalcoholic who patterned her organization on the AA model (Pace 1988). There are now similar groups for the family and friends of cocaine users (Co-Anon) and of users of heroin and other narcotics (Nar-Anon).

THE AA PROGRAM

The AA program requires an act of surrender—an acknowledgment of being an alcoholic and of the destructiveness that results—a bearing of witness, and an acknowledgement of a higher power. Although AA is nondenominational, there is a strong repent-of-your-sins revivalism; groups begin or end their meetings holding hands in a circle and reciting the Lord's Prayer or the Serenity Prayer: "God grant me the serenity to accept the things I cannot change; courage to change the things I can; and wisdom to know the difference" (DuPont and McGovern 1994: 27). As in Protestant revival meetings, the alcoholic/sinner seeks salvation through personal testimony, public contrition, and submission to a higher authority (Peele 1985; Delbanco and Delbanco 1995). Courts have ruled that Alcoholics Anonymous is a religion for purposes of separation of church and state, thus rendering what transpires at AA meetings subject to the same protection as clergy-parishioner exchanges (Worth 2002). AA also provides "an important social network through which members learn appropriate behavior and coping skills in drinking situations and become involved in various (nondrinking) leisure activities with other recovering alcoholics" (McElrath 1995: 314).

According to the organization's publications, AA recognizes the potency of shared honesty and mutual vulnerability openly acknowledged. The AA group supports each member in his or her effort to remain alcohol-free. According to AA literature, "Maintenance of sobriety depends on our sharing of our experiences, strength and hope with each other, thus helping to identify and understand the nature of our disease." AA offers a biological explanation for alcohol addiction, and the AA conceptual model is that alcoholism is a disease, a controllable disability that cannot be cured—thus, there are no ex-alcoholics, only recovering alcoholics. AA members are encouraged to accept the belief that they are powerless over alcohol, that they cannot control their intake, and that total abstinence is required. New members are advised to obtain a sponsor who has remained abstinent and who will help the initiate work through the twelve steps that are the essence of the

---

[6]The original version of Bill Wilson's *Alcoholic's Anonymous*, a typewritten manuscript with a multitude of annotations, sold at auction in 2004 for $1.576 million.

"BEEN THERE"

"A man falls into a hole so deep he can't get out. A doctor walks by, and the man calls for help. The doctor writes a prescription, tosses it into the hole, and walks on. A priest walks by, and the man tries again. The priest writes a prayer, tosses it into the hole, and walks on. Finally a friend walks by, and again the man asks for help. To his surprise, the friend jumps in with him. 'Why did you do that?' the man asks. 'Now we're both in the hole.' 'Yes,' the friend responds, 'But I've been in this hole before, and I know the way out'" (Clay 2004: 1).

AA program. Those who are successful "twelfth steppers" carry the AA message and program to other alcoholics—they become "missionaries" for AA.

AA and groups based on the AA approach "attempt to instill the substitution of more adaptive attitudes to replace habitual dysfunctional ones. The extreme use of denial and projection of responsibility for chemical dependency onto other people, circumstances, or conditions outside oneself is an example of a target behavior strongly challenged in the substance abuse self-help group. The familiar opening statement of 'I'm an alcoholic and/or drug addict' epitomizes the concrete representation that defense mechanisms of projection and denial run counter to the group culture and norms" (Spitz 1987: 160).

Because of their fear of losing employment, recovering alcoholics were often unwilling to admit their problem in front of others; therefore, strict anonymity became part of the AA approach. AA never uses surnames at meetings or in its publications. According to an AA publication: "Individual anonymity is paramount. No AA member has the right to divulge the identity or membership of any other member. We must always maintain personal anonymity at the level of press, radio, TV and film" (hence the use of the names "Bill W." and "Dr. Bob"). However, "as a result of AA's popular success and the acceptance of the disease viewpoint," Stanton Peele (1995: 46) notes that "prominent alcoholics today do not place the emphasis on anonymity that AA officially demands of its members: many public figures have described their alcoholism and their treatment before the camera."

AA ORGANIZATION

More than 50,000 AA groups are registered in the United States (Delbanco and Delbanco 1995). AA has minimal formal organization. The basic AA unit is the local group, which is autonomous except in matters that affect other AA groups or the fellowship as a whole. According to AA literature, "No group has powers over its members and instead of officers with authority, groups rotate leadership." A secretary chosen by the members plans the meetings and sets the agenda. In most local groups the position is rotated every six months. Delegates to the General Service Conference serve two years. There are twenty-one trustees, of whom seven are nonalcoholics who are often professionals in social work or medicine and who may serve for up to nine years; alcoholic trustees may serve only four years.

There are no entry requirements or dues; "the hat is passed" at most meetings to defray costs. Some of this money goes to support a local service committee and the General Service Office in New York. AA does not engage in fund raising, and no one person is permitted to contribute more than $1,000. The sale of publications generates considerable income. The financial affairs of the General Service Office are handled by nonalcoholics: "The reason is that Bill Wilson and the early A.A.s were afraid that if anybody running A.A. fell off the wagon, that would be bad enough, but if he were handling finances as well, the results could be disastrous" (Robertson 1988a: 57).

AA members typically attend four meetings a week for about five years, after which attendance is less frequent, or they might drop out completely when capable of functioning comfortably without alcohol. "The movement works in quiet and simple ways. Members usually give of themselves without reservation; exchange telephone numbers with newcomers; come to help at any hour when a fellow member is in crisis; are free with tips on how to avoid that first drink" (Robertson 1988a: 47).

The AA approach has been criticized because of its emphasis on total abstinence and its lack of research support: "The erstwhile abstainer who, for whatever reason, takes a drink may in effect be induced to go on a spree by the belief that this is inevitable. Spree drinking could also be induced by the fact that status in A.A. is correlated with length of sobriety. Years of sobriety with their attendant symbols and status can be obliterated by one slip, so the social cost of a single drink is as great as the cost of an all-out binge" (Ogborne and Glaser 1985: 176). Some twelve-step groups "do not consider members 'clean and sober' when they are using any psychoactive medication. Cases of adverse treatment consequences, even suicide, have resulted from well-meaning twelve-step members dissuading individuals from taking prescribed medications" (DuPont and McGovern 1994: 56).

Many, if not most, substance abuse treatment programs are based wholly in or part of the twelve-step model.

NARCOTICS ANONYMOUS

Nan Robertson (1988b) notes that some AA groups are less than accepting of people who are addicted to substances other than alcohol. Bill Wilson was opposed to allowing heroin addicts to become part of AA. However, there are self-help groups for drug abusers based on the twelve-step approach, such as Narcotics Anonymous (NA) and Cocaine Anonymous (CA). According to its website, NA "sprang from the Alcoholics Anonymous Program of the late 1940s with meetings first emerging in the Los Angeles area of California, USA, in the early Fifties." There are more than 20,000 registered NA groups holding over 30,000 weekly meetings in more than 100 countries. Attendance records are not kept either for NA's own purposes or for others. Because of this, it is sometimes difficult to provide interested parties with comprehensive information about NA membership.

NA membership is open to all drug addicts, regardless of the particular drug or combination of drugs used. When adapting AA's First Step, the word "addiction" was substituted for "alcohol," thus removing drug-specific language while maintaining

THE TWELVE STEPS OF NARCOTICS ANONYMOUS

1. We admitted that we were powerless over our addiction, that our lives had become unmanageable.
2. We came to believe that a Power greater than ourselves could restore us to sanity.
3. We made a decision to turn our will and our lives over to the care of God as we understood Him.
4. We made a searching and fearless moral inventory of ourselves.
5. We admitted to God, to ourselves, and to another human being the exact nature of our wrongs.
6. We were entirely ready to have God remove all these defects of character.
7. We humbly asked Him to remove our shortcomings.
8. We made a list of all persons we had harmed, and became willing to make amends to them all.
9. We made direct amends to such people whenever possible, except when to do so would injure them or others.
10. We continued to take personal inventory and when we were wrong promptly admitted it.
11. We sought through prayer and meditation to improve our conscious contact with God as we understood Him, praying only for knowledge of His will for us and the power to carry that out.
12. Having had a spiritual awakening as a result of these steps, we tried to carry this message to addicts, and practice these principles in all our affairs.

NA publishes a monthly journal, *The NA Way*, which is filled with brief personal stories, news, and opinion (available from Narcotics Anonymous World Service Office, PO Box 9999, Van Nuys, CA 91409; telephone: 818-780-3951). Local AA and NA chapters can be found in the telephone book.

the "disease concept" of addiction. As in AA, there are no dues or fees for membership, although most members contribute in meetings to help cover expenses. Medications prescribed by a physician and taken under medical supervision are not seen as compromising a person's recovery in NA (NA website).

THE MINNESOTA MODEL

One of the best examples of the AA approach in private inpatient chemical dependence treatment is the so-called **Minnesota model**, which integrates the twelve-step approach into the medical treatment of addiction (DuPont and McGovern 1994: xxii). The Hazelden Foundation in Center City, Minnesota, has inspired many similar programs in the United States and England in which substance abuse is seen as an incurable but controllable disease. Total abstinence and lifestyle improvement are the treatment goals. The 28-day program begins with an admissions assessment and detoxification following medical protocol. Individual counseling is provided by abusers who are "in recovery" and professional staff, including physicians, social workers, nurses, and clergy. Therapy groups take various forms, all of which are present and future oriented, including problem solving, personal issues, and decision making related to substance use, family sessions, and confrontations similar in process to those of the therapeutic community. Cost for the nonprofit Hazelden is $27,000 for a 28-day stay. Rounding out the program are lectures and videos on a variety of related topics, including AA/NA, the social and psychological aspects of substance abuse, and techniques for handling substance abuse problems, as well as reading and writing assignments. Aftercare usually involves attendance at AA or NA meetings (Cook 1988a).

In a review of research on the Minnesota model, Christopher Cook concludes: "Despite exaggerated claims of success, it appears to have a genuinely impressive 'track record' with as many as two-thirds of its patients achieving a 'good' outcome at 1 year after discharge" (1988b: 746). This treatment-rich private sector approach to substance abuse is obviously expensive, and patients, who include such luminaries as Betty Ford and Elizabeth Taylor, are therefore representative of the economically successful.

The Minnesota model is used by central Ohio's Maryhaven, whose staff is made up primarily of former twelve-step participants in recovery. "Maryhaven integrates twelve-step-related practices and interventions into all of its basic services to assist the patient with the goals of self-diagnosis, acceptance of addiction as an illness, [and] acceptance of abstinence" (Brigham 2003: 46). At Maryhaven substance abuse is viewed as a chronic illness; therefore, treatment is focused on abstinence, not moderation.

ALTERNATIVES TO AA

The spiritual dimension of AA and its insistence on a disease model of alcoholism—alcoholics cannot help themselves—have encountered opposition and led to the establishment of alternative groups, such as Rational Recovery (RR) and Secular Organization for Sobriety. Although it is a voluntary self-help group in the AA mode, RR rejects the twelve-step approach as fostering dependency and instead argues that alcoholic participants are not powerless but fully capable of overcoming their addiction (T. Hall 1990). According to RR, alcoholism is not a disease but an individual shortcoming. Their approach emphasizes taking personal responsibility for behavior—there isn't any treatment for addiction other than voluntary abstinence.

RR uses "the Big Plan," a commitment never to drink again. It focuses on planning to prevent relapses and attempting to gain insight into how self-defeating beliefs encourage drinking behavior. Various strategies are discussed to deal with high-risk situations in which temptations may run high (Galaif and Sussman 1995).

There are also groups, such as Moderation Management (MM), that reject the total abstinence proviso of AA and instead emphasize sobriety—drinking in moderation. A national support organization, MM is designed for people who want to limit, rather than eliminate, their drinking. While an estimated 30 percent of their members are on abstinence-based programs, most participants seek a way to control but not eliminate their use of alcohol. "An important MM recommendation is to go 30 days without alcohol" (Condor 2002a: Sec. 13: 1, 2002b). A similar program, Drink Wise, suggests two to three weeks without imbibing to reduce tolerance and gain control over the habit. Both programs call for keeping a "drink diary" to become more fully aware of alcohol consumption patterns and temptations (Condor 2002b).

MM and Drink Wise promote tactics that lead to self limits on alcohol consumption (Condor 2002a, 2002b).

- Delay drinking by not having any alcohol until sitting down for dinner
- Stay with beer or wine and avoid mixed drinks
- Alternate between alcoholic drinks and other beverages—club soda with a splash of lemon or lime, for example
- Never drink alcoholic beverages when you are thirsty
- Develop a plan for drinking, such as one or two drinks and leaving after two hours at a party or bar

EVALUATING TREATMENT EFFECTIVENESS

How well do drug treatment programs perform? A straightforward answer to this question is not possible. A variety of programs—hospitals, public health agencies, and independent organizations—offer treatment using an array of methodologies ranging from the twelve steps to drug-free therapeutic communities to methadone maintenance, and the intensity of services and staff qualifications vary significantly. The client population is similarly complex: "They vary in age, social and economic background, number and types of drug abused, health status, and psychological well-being. Some have lengthy histories of addiction and treatment, while others are entering treatment for the first time in the early stages of dependence. Clients may be highly involved in criminal activity or may not have committed any crime other than drug possession" (Hubbard et al. 1989: 9). In general, high-intensity (long-term residential) treatment for high-severity users produces favorable outcomes for at least five years. For low-severity users, brief, low-intensity services have proven adequate and more cost-effective (D. Simpson 2002).

There are additional problems with measuring the effectiveness of treatment for adolescents, as there are with providing them with appropriate programs: Adolescents go through distinctive developmental stages, and their substance abuse patterns differ from those of adults (Hser et al. 2001).

Many or most programs that purport to treat specific types of substance abuse are not based on a scientific approach to such problems. They are not organized and structured according to controlled studies with random assignment, and they often are not eager for independent evaluation that could affect their bottom line—their finances. Evaluation requires a measurement of success, such as being drug free for a certain period of time. Tracking individuals who complete treatment is often difficult if not impossible. Programs have different criteria for "completion." Some use length of time; others use number of visits or regularity of attendance. This makes it difficult to compare programs (E. E. Simpson 1989).

Evaluating drug treatment requires a comparison with a similar population that is not being treated or with other programs treating similar populations. In fact, any research efforts that do not include a control group are suspect, because in "the absence of a control group, it is difficult to determine whether unanticipated bias occurred in selecting the subjects for study, and whether the resulting experimental group is sufficiently representative for generalizations to be made about the outcome findings. Furthermore, without comparison groups, behavioral changes during and after treatment that result from the passage of time may wrongly be attributed to program activities" (Anglin and Hser 1990b: 408). However, withholding treatment from control groups has ethical, political, and legal dimensions (De Leon, Inciardi, and Martin 1995; P. J. Cohen 2002).

Some private treatment programs are quite selective. Their patients are required to have financial resources or employment that provide third-party coverage, which are social indicators of a better prognosis. Other programs accept patients with a host of social, psychological, and economic problems that are likely to affect their prognosis. "In the real world of drug abuse treatment," say George De Leon, James Inciardi, and Steven Martin (1995: 88), "program staff choose the clients they feel are ready for treatment and are appropriate for a particular treatment modality."

Patrick Biernacki (1986: 191) notes the serious problems in gauging the success of drug treatment programs. He asks, for example, what a 50 percent rate of success means: Would some, most, or all of the people who were "successful" have abandoned drug addiction without treatment? In fact, he points out, drug treatment programs might be successful only with those individuals who have resolved to stop using drugs: "Once addicts voluntarily have resolved to stop using drugs, treatment programs may then be able to help them realize their resolutions to change" (Biernacki 1986: 191). (For a review of drug treatment outcome research and its methodological shortcomings, see Anglin and Hser 1990b; Moras 1993; De Leon, Inciardi, and Martin 1995.)

Drug dependence might best be viewed as a career requiring treatment that is similarly oriented. "Many researchers, practitioners, and clinicians have assumed that treatment should occur once and should result in a cure if it is to be termed effective. Substance abuse does not appear to be the kind of problem that makes this orientation pragmatic. When the community in which people live is so strongly pro-intoxication, it is not surprising that treated persons are recruited back into the drug lifestyle." Therefore, "while treatment does not need to be applied forever, repeated episodes of treatment are probably necessary for most who develop serious problems with intoxicants" (Senay 1986: 143).

There is no clear research evidence on the effectiveness of short-term inpatient or outpatient treatment: "Given what is known about the importance of length of stay in treatment and the complexity of the recovery process in addiction, there is little likelihood that twenty-eight-day clinics or short-term modalities (one to six months) will yield positive outcomes" (De Leon 1990: 125). In fact, it might be the availability of legitimate economic opportunity rather than the mode of treatment that predicts posttreatment success. Without such opportunity clients in disadvantaged groups will remain enmeshed in the drug abuse subculture and continue to rely on income-generating crime (Anglin and Hser 1990b). In any event, after noting shortcomings in the research—they question the accuracy of self-reports by drug abusers—the General Accounting Office (the research arm of Congress) concludes (1998) that while the effectiveness might be overstated, drug abuse treatment can in fact be effective.

MEASURING AA/TWELVE-STEP EFFECTIVENESS

Evaluations of AA encounter definitional problems from the start. Programs and studies vary in their definitions and measurement of recovery, of success and failure, even of the term *alcoholism* itself (McElrath 1995). William R. Miller and Reid K. Hester (1980: 47), in a review of AA evaluation literature, state:

> Attempts to evaluate the effectiveness of A.A. have met with considerable, if not insurmountable, methodological problems, among them the very anonymity of members, which precludes systematic follow-up evaluation. Most studies have failed to include control groups (a near impossibility because of the availability of A.A. to all who are interested), have relied almost entirely upon self-report (often via mailed questionnaires) and upon abstinence as the sole criteria for success, have been plagued by sizable attrition rates and large selection confounds, and have failed to use single-blind designs, thus remaining open to criticisms of interviewer bias (particularly when the investigators have been "insiders"—members of A.A. themselves).

Although AA contends that upward of 75 percent of its members maintain abstinence, the evidence that is used to make this claim is typically testimonials of long-term, abstinent participants and ignores dropouts, who may be more likely to continue or resume drug and alcohol use. Approximately 50 percent of AA participants will drop out within the first three months of attendance, and only about 13 percent of initial attendees will maintain a long-term relationship with AA (Fiorentine 1999).

In his careful research Geary Alford (1980) found that a residential treatment program for alcoholics that used the AA approach was highly effective. Two years after discharge from the program approximately 50 percent of the patients who had completed inpatient treatment remained largely abstinent, were employed or otherwise functioning productively, and had healthy social relationships. The figure increased to 56 percent if those who drank only very lightly were included. Alford and his colleagues (1991: 122) report that an AA/NA model inpatient treatment program for adolescents whose drug use was primarily alcohol or marijuana was successful: "Some 71% of male treatment completers and 79% of female treatment completers were found to be chemically abstinent or essentially abstinent at 6 months after discharge." However, two years after treatment, the figure for men dropped to 40 percent, while 37 percent of the males who dropped out of the program were also found to be abstinent or essentially abstinent. Thirty percent of female noncompleters were abstinent or essentially abstinent after two years. As with the research reviewed by Miller and Hester (1980), Alford's studies did not utilize a control group. In fact, AA successes appear to be concentrated among middle- and upper-class people who had relatively stable lives before the onset of a drinking problem (Alexander 1990).

In an extensive research effort Robert Fiorentine (1999) reports that any participation in twelve-step programs is associated with lower levels of drug and alcohol use and that the magnitude of the association is about the same for both illicit drug and alcohol use. Less-than-weekly participants, who were more likely to be problematic drinkers, had levels of drug and alcohol use that were no different from those of nonparticipants. Fiorentine's findings suggest that weekly or more frequent twelve-step participation is associated with drug and alcohol abstinence.

However, *commitment* to attend a twelve-step program might be a predictor of success; the program itself might actually do little or nothing to generate abstinence. A study comparing the results of AA with those of other forms of treatment found that twelve-step programs were neither more nor less effective than, for example, the cognitive approach discussed earlier (Bakalar 2006).

Despite the paucity of research on its effectiveness, the twelve-step approach is very popular, some arguing that it has become a fad. The rise in the number of twelve-step programs and members and the inclusion of twelve-step philosophy in treatment programs are, of course, evidence only of its popularity, not of its effectiveness (Fiorentine 1999). Groups such as Gamblers Anonymous, Over-eaters Anonymous, Debtors Anonymous, and Sex Addicts Anonymous have been formed to address a host of social problems. While they claim inspiration from the AA twelve-step approach, critics see them as groups for whiners who want an audience to dwell on their injured self (Delbanco and Delbanco 1995).

SUMMARY

- The moderate use of any variety of psychoactive substances—from nicotine to cocaine—may be the focus of a treatment response, not because of properties inherent in the chemicals themselves but because of the societal definition of "abuse."
- Contemporary programs have standard components: screening, assessment and diagnosis, and the treatment plan.
- Chemicals as a supplement to or in conjunction with some other form of clinical or behavioral therapy target the pharmacological effect of a particular drug but do not counteract the effects of craving and learned drug-seeking behavioral responses that frequently lead to relapse.
- Chemicals used to treat drug abusers can be classified as antagonists, detoxification agents, agonists, and antidepressants.
- The opium agonist methadone has been used for detoxification and maintenance.
- Treatment can be based on psychoanalytic or learning theory/behavior modification.
- The strength of psychoactive substances as positive reinforcers and the negative reinforcement associated with abstinence provide conditioned responses that can explain the key difficulty in treating drug abusers.

- Research has discovered a connection between cues and drug craving. These cravings are countered by desensitization.
- In the social learning approach drug abuser is seen as lacking the level of social competence necessary to cope adequately with a variety of situational demands.
- Cognitive approaches focus on teaching abusers to understand their cravings and to develop coping skills.
- Sometimes referred to as the *token economy*, contingency management rewards patients for behavior classified as "therapeutic."
- Group approaches are based on the theory that peer interactions are more powerful than therapist-patient interactions in the one-to-one situation.
- About half the states have statutory provisions for the civil commitment of drug abusers, the nonpunitive incarceration of addicts for purposes of treatment.
- Drug courts, established in response to court and prison overcrowding, have common features that include a nonadversarial approach to integrating substance abuse treatment with criminal justice case processing.
- Drug courts are premised on the idea that legal coercion to enter drug treatment is an effective means of achieving the benefits associated with treatment programs.

- Reported success rates, critics argue, may be a function of the type of offender typically subject to drug court—persons without serious dependency.
- The therapeutic community is a residential, self-help, drug-free treatment program that includes concepts adopted from Alcoholics Anonymous; peer influence, used to help individuals learn and assimilate social norms and develop more effective social skills.
- Chemical dependency programs may be for-profit or nonprofit, but they seek clients who are likely to have health insurance because their costs can run over $1,000 a day for inpatient care.
- The Alcoholics Anonymous (AA) approach uses public confession and commitment and mutual aid.
- The AA/twelve-step program requires an act of surrender—an acknowledgment of being an alcoholic and of the destructiveness that results—a bearing of witness, and an acknowledgement of a higher power.
- Evaluating drug treatment requires a control group, often absent in drug treatment evaluation research.

Review Questions

1. Why has the medical profession historically avoided dealing with the problem of drug abuse?
2. Why was the medical professional generally not interested in treating drug addicts?
3. What was the basis for the famous Charles B. Towns Hospital declaring a cure rate of between 75 and 90 percent?
4. What are the standard components of contemporary drug treatment programs?
5. What is the role of opioid antagonists in drug treatment?
6. What is the purpose of a Narcon test for those seeking admission to a methadone treatment program?
7. How does naltrexone defeat the affects of opiates?
8. Why does detoxification from cocaine present special problems?
9. What is rapid detox? Why is it controversial?
10. What are the advantages and disadvantages of methadone maintenance?
11. What are the advantages of using buprenorphine instead of methadone in treating heroin addiction?
12. To the psychoanalyst, what is the source of drug abuse?
13. Why is psychoanalysis rarely used to treat drug abuse?
14. Instead of psychoanalysis, how does the therapist treat drug abusers?
15. How does psychoanalytic theory differ from learning theory?
16. How does learning theory explain drug abuse?
17. Why is it difficult to apply behavior theory in the treatment of drug abuse?
18. What is aversion treatment?
19. How is Antabuse used to treat alcoholics?
20. What is the role of cues in drug abuse?
21. What is desensitization treatment?
22. What are the three stimuli that can lead to relapse?
23. How does social learning theory view the drug abuser?
24. How is social learning theory implemented in drug abuse treatment?
25. What is the cognitive behavior therapy approach to drug abuse?
26. What is the contingency contract approach to drug abuse?
27. How do methadone clinics use contingency management?
28. What are the advantages of using group treatment?
29. What is the civil commitment approach to drug abuse?
30. What is the "drug court" response to court and prison overcrowding?

31. What are the criticisms of the drug court approach?
32. What are the characteristics of the therapeutic community approach to drug abuse?
33. What is the controversy over the success rates therapeutic communities?
34. What are the features of a chemical dependency program based on the Minnesota model?
35. What is the *Florida model* approach to drug treatment?
36. What are the features of the Alcoholics Anonymous/12-step approach to substance abuse?
37. Why is it difficult to determine the rate of success of Alcoholic Anonymous?
38. Why is the Alcoholics Anonymous criticized?
39. What was the reason for the establishment of Narcotics Anonymous?
40. What are features of the Minnesota model?
41. How does Rational Recovery and Moderation Management differ from Alcoholics Anonymous?
42. What are the difficulties of determining the effectiveness of drug treatment programs?

Regardless of what we think we are trying to do, when we make it illegal to traffic in commodities for which there is an inelastic demand, the effect is to secure a kind of monopoly profit to the entrepreneur who is willing to break the law. In effect, we say to him: "We will set up a barrier to entry into this line of commerce by making it illegal and, therefore, risky; if you are willing to take the risk, you will be sheltered from the competition of those who are unwilling to do so. Of course, if we catch you, you may possibly (although not necessarily) be put out of business; but meanwhile you are free to gather the fruits that grow in the hothouse atmosphere we are providing for you. **Herbert L. Packer** (1968: 279)

CHAPTER **11** | # THE BUSINESS OF DRUGS

Kimberly White/Bloomberg/Getty Images

While opium used to be produced in a huge belt, stretching from China to Indochina, Burma, India, Persia, Turkey and the Balkan countries, the illegal production of opium is now concentrated in Afghanistan (92%). Same for coca. Its leaves used to be cultivated not only in the Andean region but also in several Asian countries including Java (Indonesia), Formosa (Taiwan) and Ceylon (Sri Lanka). Today coca leaf production is concentrated in three Andean countries: Colombia, Peru and Bolivia.

Antonio Maria Costa (2009: 3)

This chapter examines the international and domestic traffic in illegal drugs which, by any estimate, is a multibillion-dollar-a-year industry with enormous profit-to-cost ratios. For example, heroin can be purchased in 700-gram units in Bangkok, Thailand, for between $7,500 and $9,500 and sold in the United States for $60,000–$70,000. Because the product is illegal but nevertheless in great demand, drug trafficking is characterized by a level of free enterprise that Adam Smith never envisioned. It is a market totally devoid of legal constraints in which prices and profits are governed only by the law of supply and demand.

The business of illegal drugs shares some elements with the business of selling legal products: "It requires lots of working capital, steady supplies of raw materials, sophisticated manufacturing facilities, reliable shipping contractors and wholesale distributors, the all-important marketing arms and access to retail franchises for maximum market penetration" (Brzezinski 2002: 26).

As in any major industry there are various functional levels: manufacturers, importers, wholesalers, distributors, retailers, and consumers. Workers in the drug business range from leaders of powerful international cartels to street dealers whose activities support a personal drug habit. At the manufacturing and importation levels, the drug business is usually concentrated among a relatively few people who head major trafficking organizations; at the retail level, it is filled with a large, fluctuating, and open-ended number of dealers and consumers. Because people at the highest levels of the drug trade are often connected by kinship and ethnicity, we will frequently refer to the ethnicity of criminal organizations in this chapter.

Drugs are smuggled into the United States from both source and transshipment countries. Traffickers may use circuitous routes to avoid the suspicion that is normally generated by shipments from source countries. For example, cocaine might be shipped from Colombia to Africa and move from there to Europe and the United States as part of legitimate maritime cargo. Indeed, "traffickers are increasingly using Africa, both east and west, to smuggle cocaine from Latin America into Europe" (Lacey 2006: 4; *Cocaine Trafficking in West Africa* 2007; *World Drug Report* 2008). Pleasure crafts and fishing vessels blend in with normal maritime traffic, and low-profile vessels made of wood or fiberglass and measuring up to 40 feet in length are difficult to spot and do not readily appear on radar. Smugglers also use aircraft, landing on isolated runways and even highways or dropping their cargo from the air. Motor vehicles use land routes across Canada and Mexico and onto Indian reservations bordering the United States. Often with the aid of Native American criminal groups, the traffickers then move the drugs across national borders into the United States for distribution (Kershaw 2006; National Drug Intelligence Center 2008a). The Tohono O'odham Nation reservation in Arizona straddles 75 miles of the U.S.-Mexican border and has emerged as a major transit point for drug smuggling, particularly marijuana, a bulky product that cannot be safely smuggled through official border checkpoints. The once placid reservation is now home to tribal members enticed by the financial rewards or fearful of declining the smuggler's offers (Eckholm 2010). "In addition to the 43 legitimate border crossing points, the Southwest border includes thousands of miles of open desert, rugged mountains, the Rio Grande River, and maritime transit lanes into California and Texas" (Office of National Drug Control Strategy 2009b: 13).

INTERNATIONAL DRUG TRAFFICKING

For decades heroin trafficking in the United States was controlled principally by traditional organized crime groups that lived and operated inside the country. In a drug-trafficking network that became known as the French Connection, New York City–based Mafia "Families" purchased heroin from Corsican sources working with French sailors operating from Marseilles to transship the drug directly to the United States. The heroin was distributed throughout the United States by other Mafia Families to street-level dealers working in low-income, minority communities. However, in 1972 French and U.S. drug agents effectively dismantled the French Connection, ending the domestic Mafia's monopoly on heroin distribution in the United States.

The demise of the French Connection coupled with the subsequent emergence of criminal syndicates based in Colombia marked a significant evolution in the international drug trade. These new traffickers introduced cocaine into the United States on a massive scale, launching unparalleled waves of drug crimes and violence. Throughout the 1980s and 1990s the international crime syndicates continued to increase their wealth and dominance over the U.S. drug trade, overshadowing the domestic Mafia Families.

Today, traffic in illegal drugs at the highest wholesale levels is controlled by international organized crime syndicates from Colombia, Mexico, and other countries. From their headquarters overseas, foreign drug lords produce and distribute unprecedented volumes of cocaine, methamphetamine, and heroin. The international nature of the drug business is highlighted by the 2006 seizure by Colombian authorities of tons of potassium permanganate, a chemical that is necessary for producing cocaine, that was being smuggled from the Republic of Korea to Colombia by Korean nationals.

These traffickers maintain tight control of their workers through highly compartmentalized cell structures that separate production, shipment, distribution, money laundering, communications, security, and recruitment. Traffickers have at their disposal the most technologically advanced aircraft, boats, vehicles, radar, communications equipment, and weapons that money can buy. They have also established vast counterintelligence capabilities and transportation networks. There is also the connection between drug trafficking and terrorism.

THE TERRORISM[1] CONNECTION

Any number of terrorist groups use drug trafficking to further political ends: overthrowing governments and imposing their worldview. "It is not particularly uncommon for terrorist groups to recruit some of their members among criminal elements, particularly among individuals who may have special skills or common criminals who contribute to its goals in instrumental, training, and other matters" (Préfontaine and Dandurand 2004: 16). Terrorist and drug-trafficking groups share

---

[1]As defined by the U.S. Department of State, terrorism is premeditated, politically motivated violence perpetrated against non-combatant targets by subnational groups or clandestine agents, usually intended to influence an audience.

some attributes, in particular organizational structure such as *compartmentaliza-tion* (Figure 11.2). Terrorist groups and criminal organizations often have similar requirements for moving people, money, material, and weapons across borders and often operate under a similar set of contingencies. The distinction between drug trafficking and terrorism is becoming increasingly blurred, and we see an overlapping, symbiotic relationship between terrorism, drugs, and organized crime (Perl 2000). For example, leftist guerillas in Colombia benefit from dealing cocaine, as do their right-wing paramilitary enemies.

Taliban insurgents in Afghanistan have been using heroin to finance their efforts. In 2005 at age 47, Afghan drug lord Baz Mohammad was extradited to the United States for heading an organization that controlled poppy fields in Afghanistan, heroin-processing plants in Pakistan, and a trafficking network that smuggled millions of dollars worth of drugs into the United States. In a partnership with the Taliban Mohammad told supporters that they would be committing jihad by selling heroin to Americans (McFadden 2005; Zambito 2005). The Taliban tax poppy farmers and the traders who collect opium paste from them for transport to labs where it is converted into heroin. Truckers pay a transit tariff when heroin is smuggled out of Afghanistan and drug trafficking organizations make large regular payments to the Quetta Shura, the Taliban's governing body (Schmitt 2009).

In Southeast Asia's Golden Triangle there is a long-standing tradition of using heroin trafficking to support insurgencies. According to John Walters, Director of the Office of National Drug Control Policy, "Almost half of the State Department's list of known terrorist organizations are known to have, at one point or another, trafficked in drugs" (2003: 9). This gives rise to the term *narcoterrorism*—terrorist acts carried out by groups that are directly or indirectly involved in cultivating, manufacturing, transporting, or distributing illegal drugs.

The links between terrorist organizations and drug traffickers can take many forms, ranging from facilitation—protection, transportation, and taxation—to direct trafficking by the terrorist organization itself to finance its activities. Traffickers and terrorists have similar logistical needs in terms of materiel and the covert movement of goods, people, and money. Relationships between drug traffickers and terrorists are mutually beneficial. Drug traffickers gain from access to terrorists' military skills and weapons supply; terrorists gain a source of revenue and expertise in illicit transfer and laundering of proceeds. Both bring corrupt officials whose services provide mutual benefits, such as greater access to fraudulent documents, including passports and customs papers. Drug traffickers can also gain considerable freedom of movement when they operate in conjunction with terrorists who control large amounts of territory (Beers and Taylor 2002).

COLOMBIA

When Fidel Castro overthrew the corrupt dictatorial regime of Fulgencio Batista early in 1959, he expelled American gangsters who operated gambling casinos in Havana. Many of their Cuban associates fled to the United States, along with *narcotraficantes* who had distributed cocaine in Cuba. They settled primarily in the New York, New Jersey, and Miami areas and began to look for new sources of income. Many Cubans who fled with, or soon after, the Batista loyalists were organized and trained by the Central Intelligence Agency (CIA) in an effort to dislodge Castro. After the Bay of Pigs debacle in 1961, members of the CIA-organized Cuban exile army were supposed to disband and go into lawful businesses. Elements of these exile groups (they often overlapped) began to enter the cocaine business. At first they imported only enough cocaine to satisfy members of their own community, but by the mid-1960s the market had expanded way beyond the Cuban community, and so they began to import the substance in greater quantities.

Until the early 1970s, the importation of cocaine into the United States was largely a Cuban operation, although the suppliers were Colombians. During the latter half of the 1960s, Colombians began emigrating to the United States in numbers sufficient to establish communities in Miami, Chicago, Los Angeles, and New York. Colombian traffickers became highly organized both in the United States and at home and by 1973, independent foreign nationals could no longer "deal drugs" in Colombia. In 1976, the Colombians became dissatisfied with their Cuban agents in the United States, who were reportedly making most of the profits and short-changing the Colombians. Enforcers were sent in and systematically executed Cubans in Miami and New York. By 1978, Cubans remaining in the cocaine business had become subordinate to the Colombians.

Colombians have been able to dominate the cocaine industry for a number of reasons. The President's Commission on Organized Crime (PCOC) (1986: 78–79) notes, "Colombia is well-positioned both to receive coca from Peru and Bolivia and to export the processed drug to the United States by air or by sea." And "the country's vast central forests effectively conceal clandestine processing laboratories and air strips, which facilitate the traffic." The Colombians "have a momentum by benefit of their early involvement in the cocaine trade. "In 1968, in an attempt to bolster its domestic economic performance, Colombia proudly established the Institute of Advanced Chemical Research in Bogotá, which started to train top-class chemists, who were later to find lucrative work in the employ of the Medellín and Cali cartels" (Glenny 2008: 245). And, there is a Colombian reputation for violence that serves to maintain discipline and intimidate would-be competitors (PCOC 1986: 78–79). The propensity to use violence led to domination of potential Bolivian and Peruvian rivals in the cocaine business.

Colombia is the only country in the world where the three main plant-based illegal drugs—cocaine, heroin, and marijuana—are produced in significant amounts (Thoumi 2002). A nation of about 45 million persons, Colombia is the only South American country that has both Pacific and Caribbean coastlines (see Figure 11.1). The high Andes divide the country into four ranges, with most of Colombia's population concentrated in green valleys and mountain basins that lie between the Andes ranges; travel between populated areas is difficult (Buckman 2004).

Control of most of the world's cocaine industry remains in the hands of Colombian organizations. It is a nation that has been torn by political strife, with civil wars in 1902 and 1948. *La Violencia*, as the civil war of 1948–1958 is known, cost the lives of about 300,000 people (Riding 1987). It ended when the Liberals and the Conservatives formed the National Front, but several Marxist insurgencies continued to threaten the stability of the central government. Not only was murder

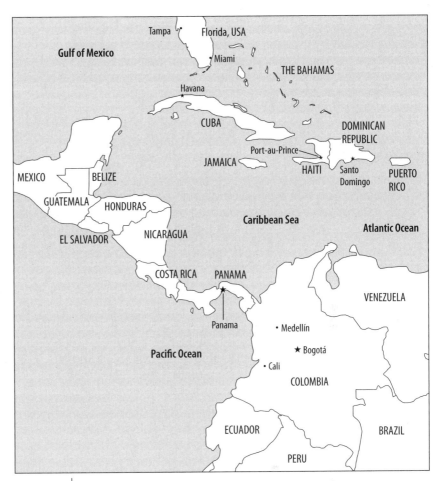

FIGURE 11.1 | COLOMBIA, CENTER OF THE WORLD'S COCAINE TRAFFICKING

frequent, but the methods that were used were often sadistic, such as the *corte de corbata*—the infamous "Colombian necktie"—in which the throat is cut longitudinally and the tongue is pulled through to hang like a tie. Another practice, no *dejar la semilla* ("don't leave the seed"), includes the castration of male victims and the execution of women and children (Wolfgang and Ferracuti 1967).

***La Violencia:* The Violence That Never Ended**   In Colombia drug traffickers exemplify a lack of belief in the legitimacy of the country's political and economic institutions. "Breaking the law—any law—is justified, and not just for the usual economic reasons that criminals favor. For traffickers, the law, law-enforcement officials, U.S. drug operatives, and drug-control organizations all represent the traditional elite, international imperialism, or other international competitive economic interests, none of which has any historical moral standing in their eyes. Therefore, moralistic arguments about restraining violent behavior do not capture these people's attention ... [and] allows traffickers to garner enthusiastic support in some areas" (Tullis 1995: 66).

"At the root of Colombia's easy violence is an extraordinary indifference toward death" (Romoli 1941: 37). The homicide rate is ten times higher than that of the United States (Rohter 2000a, 200b). Murder is the leading cause of death for Colombian males aged 15 to 44 years (Schemo 1997). The country has the highest child murder rates in the world; street children kill each other, and hundreds are murdered by vigilante groups as part of their campaign of "social cleansing" (Luft 1995). *La Violencia* "debased the incipient development of judicial and police apparatuses, as well as the moral foundations of political action" (Palacios 2007: 138).

In this sociopolitical atmosphere bandits have roamed freely, engaging in a combination of brigandage, terrorism, and revolution. In a country where drug barons act as a state within a state, dozens of armed paramilitary groups "ply their murderous trade in the cities and countryside, sometimes selling themselves to the highest bidder as outmanned and intimidated judges and government officials feel helpless to stop them" (de Lama 1988: 5; Duzán 1994). These paramilitaries are sometimes allied with—and sometimes fighting against—the drug traffickers, and they receive financial backing from wealthy landowners. In coca-growing regions "guerilla and paramilitary groups substitute for the state in imposing a very authoritarian regime, defining and applying their own laws and regulations, and providing education, police, and civil justice to solve conflicts among the population. In exchange, these groups charge coca production and cocaine export taxes" (Thoumi 2002: 106).

For many decades coca leaf was converted to cocaine base in Bolivia and Peru and smuggled by small aircraft or boats into Colombia, where it was refined into cocaine in jungle laboratories. Laboratories have relocated to cities far from cultivation sites to be closer to sources of precursor chemicals and because improved law enforcement methods have facilitated the detection of jungle laboratories. Precursor chemicals are usually manufactured in the United States and Germany; Panama and Mexico serve as major transit sources. Colombian cartels, using dummy companies and multiple suppliers, pay up to ten times the normal prices for these chemicals. Traffickers have also been stealing precursor shipments in transit from the point of entry into Colombia en route to a legitimate end-user.

Some Colombian traffickers set up laboratories in other Latin American countries and even the United States in response to increased law enforcement in Colombia and the increasing cost of ether, sulfuric acid, and acetone in Colombia. Acetone, sulfuric acid, and ether are widely available for commercial purposes in the United States. While sulfuric acid and acetone have wide industrial use in Colombia, ether does not, and each kilo of cocaine requires 17 liters of ether. The cost of these chemicals has increased as a result of controls imposed by the Colombian government on their importation and sale and of U.S. Drug Enforcement Administration efforts to disrupt the supply of chemicals that are essential in the cocaine refinement process (Hall 2000).

In the past because Colombian coca was significantly lower in quality than that grown in Peru and Bolivia, Colombia had not been a major coca producer. Success in eradicating coca in Bolivia and Peru led to a major increase in Colombian coca cultivation, and in 1998 Colombia became the world's leading coca producer (Goering 1998; Krauss 2000). Colombian traffickers achieved extraordinary levels of efficiency in extracting cocaine from their coca crops (*International Narcotics Control Strategy Report* 2000).

By 2002, however, coca was making a comeback in Peru, driven by a combination of poverty and soaring prices for coca. In Bolivia coca production shot up in 2005, the result of a backlash against U.S.-financed eradication programs that had helped to destabilize the country and topple several governments (Forero 2002, 2005). Indeed, in 2005 Bolivia elected Juan Evo Morales Ayma as president. A leftist critic of the United States, Morales had been a leader of *cocalero* movement, coca growers opposed to U.S. eradication efforts. In Peru, *Marxist Sendero Luminoso*, Shining Parth, a brutally violent Maoist-inspired guerilla organization, had been largely dormant since 2000. Copying Colombia's rebels, Shining Path "has reinvented itself as an illicit enterprise, rebuilding on the profits from Peru's thriving cocaine trade" (Romero 2009b: 1). Colombia, Peru, and Bolivia produce an estimated 1,000 tons of cocaine annually, most of which is shipped to 10 million users in the United States and Europe (Office on Drugs and Crime 2008).

About three quarters of the coca that is grown in Colombia comes from six rural provinces about the size of Kansas, with a population of about 6 million, southwest of the capital, Bogotá. The area is desperately poor and plagued by left- and right-wing paramilitary groups (Forero 2001a). Indeed, Colombia is the only country in Latin America that is still fighting a major guerilla insurgency. At the end of 1998, in an effort to advance peace negotiations with the main Marxist guerilla group, the Revolutionary Armed Forces of Colombia (FARC), with about 18,000 fighters, the Colombian government evacuated its security forces from a swath of central Colombia, conceding an area about the size of Switzerland. FARC acts as a "labor organizer in the coca fields, keeping the price of a bushel up while taking a hefty percentage from the farmers" (Howe 2000: 38; Schemo 1999). In FARC-controlled areas, the economy is built on coca, and coca paste often serves as the local currency. Because paper currency is in short supply, "it is not unusual for people to be paid for their work in coca. They, in turn, pay for the necessities with the paste, which is soft and powdery like flour" (Forero 2001b:12). The traffickers buy the paste, process it into cocaine, and ship it by the ton to the United States, while FARC taxes the trade. "To prevent narcotraffickers from ripping off farmers, the rebels set a minimum price for a kilo of coca paste. They also tax the traffickers for protection of smuggling routes, the use of clandestine runways, the importation of cocaine-processing chemicals, and the export of every kilo of refined cocaine shipped from the region" (Semple 2001: 61; Guillermoprieto 2002).

Colombia is a relatively large country, and many regions have only a weak federal presence. "While Colombian authorities built suburbs and major highways between cities, they ignored vast sections of the country; much of rural Colombia is isolated by hilly, trackless terrain" (Duzán 1994: 63). Three steep mountain ranges run the length of Colombia, and impenetrable jungle covers the south: "The government didn't lose control of this half of Colombia; it never had it" (Robinson 1998a: 39). The vacuum left by the central government has proved ideal for coca cultivation and cocaine manufacture because it left areas where only local officials had to be bribed, a cheaper and less risky action than bribery at the federal level (Thoumi 1995). In 1998, Colombia became the world's leading coca producer; Peru had fallen to second place (Goering 1998). However, Colombian coca was significantly lower in quality than that grown in Peru and Bolivia. In response, traffickers have imported the type of coca that is native to Peru and, with the help of agronomists, grafted it onto the weaker Colombian species to create a powerful hybrid (Rohter 1999a).

Although it originated as a Marxist militia, in more recent years FARC has resembled organized banditry, operating its own coca farms and laboratories in rural Colombia (Brooke 1995). FARC has also collected taxes from traffickers and has permitted them to operate in jungle areas that FARC controls. In 1996 there were mass protests against the government's campaign to eradicate both coca and poppy crops in response to U.S. pressure. Colombia has been spraying herbicides from the air in several rural provinces. In support of these protests, FARC launched an attack on military and police installations, destroying two police stations and killing and abducting dozens of soldiers and police officers.

Contesting the FARC and other leftist militias are right-wing paramilitaries that often receive assistance from wealthy landowners, ranchers, and the Colombian military (Forero 2001c; Romero 2007). They are part of a loose-knit coalition, the United Self-Defense Forces of Colombia (AUC), about 11,000 strong, that is fighting Marxist guerillas for control of poppy- and coca-producing regions. Ranchers who had been under siege from the guerillas helped to transform this group of outlaws into a formidable army (Forero 2001c; Guillermoprieto 2002). The militias have proven to be more effective against the guerillas than government forces, and this has endeared them to elements of the population at risk. The militias have reinforced this support by building roads and schools in the areas from which they have driven the guerillas (Forero 2001c; Guillermoprieto 2002).

In exchange for not being prosecuted, beginning in 2003, paramilitary leaders agreed to disarm, and many turned to politics to maintain power. They have elected governors and mayors across northern Colombia by bribing, murdering, or intimidating opposing candidates and boast of having influence over one-third of the Colombian congress (Forero 2005d). In some areas, their candidates succeed by winning more than 90 percent of the votes or run unopposed. The militias are also being reshaped into criminal networks that traffic in cocaine, smuggle cheap subsidized petrol from Venezuela, extort from businesses, and loot local governments (Forero 2006). Some have adopted exotic names—Black Eagles (*Aguilas Negras*) and New Generation Organization (*Organización Nueva Generación*— ONG). While there is no consensus on what the new groups actually are and to what extent they continue the AUC, and although all are involved criminal activity, organization and modus operandi vary from region to region. Some are headed by paramilitaries who did not demobilize, while others are commanded by former mid-ranking AUC leaders who took up arms again; still others are the armed wing of drug-trafficking organizations that have existed for years, or even combinations of all these. Some, such as the ONG, continue the tradition of wearing military-style uniforms, while others, such as the Black Eagles, prefer civilian garb (*Colombia's New Armed Groups* 2007; Romero 2010).

Pushed westward by Colombian military successes into jungle areas populated primarily by indigenous Indians, some former paramilitary and cocaine trafficking groups—the two often overlap—abandoned their ideological bent and have forged alliances with their former left-wing enemies. The same groups in other parts continue their violent struggles, but now the goal is control over the cocaine trade (Romero 2009a).

Growing and Trafficking Cocaine in Colombia The economic modernization of Colombia failed to bring about a corresponding respect for government. Delegitimization of government and *La Violencia* "left legacies which have worked to permit, if not encourage, the development of the cocaine industry" (Thoumi 1995: 84). Delegitimization spurred the development of smuggling, particularly export of cattle, emeralds, and coffee out of Colombia and into Venezuela and Ecuador, providing experience in contraband trade and money laundering. The propensity to use violence led to domination of potential Bolivian and Peruvian rivals in the cocaine business. "Aside from their disdain for Colombian institutions and their long criminal records, Colombian traffickers share other characteristics. They appear to be great believers in fate and providence and seem unmoved by normal considerations of personal danger. It is a perspective unaltered by normal law-enforcement efforts and one that makes dealing with or trying to control them such a dangerous enterprise" (Tullis 1995: 67). Speculative capitalism with a focus on very high short-term profits, a feature of Colombia's financial elite, provided the resources for development of a cocaine industry (Thoumi 1995).

Cells and Cartels Colombia-based cocaine trafficking groups in the United States continue to be organized around "cells" that operate within a given geographic area. Because these cells are based on family relationships or close friendships, outsiders who attempt to penetrate the cell run a high risk of arousing suspicion. Some cells specialize in a particular facet of the drug trade, such as cocaine transport, storage, wholesale distribution, or money laundering. Each cell, which may comprise ten or more individuals, operates with little or no knowledge about the other cells. In this way, should one of the cells be compromised, the operations of the other cells would not be endangered (Figure 11.2).

A rigid top-down command and control structure is characteristic of these groups. The head of each cell reports to a regional director, who is responsible for the overall management of several cells. The regional director, in turn, reports directly to one of the top drug lords or his designate, based in Colombia. Trusted lieutenants of the organization in the United States have discretion in day-to-day operations, but ultimate authority rests with the leadership in Colombia (Ledwith 2000).

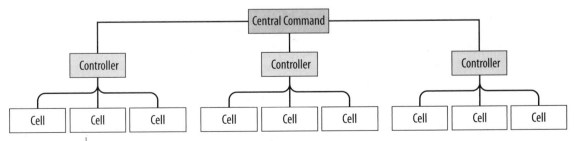

FIGURE 11.2 | COMPARTMENTALIZED ORGANIZATION

Traffickers from Colombia use state-of-the-art encryption devices to translate their communications into indecipherable code. This evolving technology presents a significant impediment to law enforcement investigations of criminal activities. In the past the necessity for frequent communication between drug lords in Colombia and their surrogates in the United States made the drug-trafficking organizations vulnerable to law enforcement wiretaps. Now, however, through the use of encryption technology, the traffickers can protect their electronic business communications from law enforcement interception and hide information that could be used to build criminal cases against them.

Colombian managers dispatched to the Dominican Republic and Puerto Rico operate these command and control centers and are responsible for overseeing drug trafficking in the region. Puerto Rico, a 110-mile-long island with the third busiest seaport in North America, is ideal for smugglers, who have fewer problems getting their goods to the United States because shipments from Puerto Rico are not searched by customs agents. In 2009, DEA agents arrested 23 people, including 8 employees of American Airlines in Puerto Rico, for using commercial aircraft to transport in excess of 9,000 kilograms of cocaine to the United States (DEA press release, September 15, 2009).

These groups also direct networks of transporters that oversee the importation, storage, exportation, and wholesale distribution of cocaine destined for the continental United States. They have franchised to criminals from the Dominican Republic a portion of the midlevel wholesale cocaine and heroin trade on the East Coast of the United States. The Dominican trafficking groups, already firmly entrenched as low-level cocaine and heroin wholesalers in the larger northeastern cities, were uniquely placed to assume a far more significant role in this multi-billion-dollar business. However, the Colombian groups remain in control of the sources of supply.

The Dominican traffickers operating in the United States, not the Colombians, are now the ones who are subject to arrest, while the top-level Colombians control the organization with sophisticated telecommunications. This change in operations reduces profits somewhat for the syndicate leaders but reduces their exposure to U.S. law enforcement. If arrested, the Dominicans will have little damaging information that can be used against their Colombian masters. Reducing their exposure, together with sophisticated communications, puts the Colombian bosses closer to their goal of operating from a political, legal, and electronic sanctuary.

Heroin Trafficking in Colombia   Colombian entry into heroin is based on demographics. During the 1980s, the popularity of cocaine began to fade among urban professionals, and "cokeheads" tend to burn out after five years. With this dwindling consumer base, the Colombians expanded into Europe but with only limited success—heroin was the hard drug of choice and that market was dominated by Pakistani and Turkish groups. So the Colombians diversified, importing poppy seeds, equipment, and expertise from Southwest Asia (Golden Crescent). By 1999, Colombians had become major heroin wholesalers, often selling cocaine and heroin to wholesalers as part of a package deal. Colombian market advantages include geographic proximity to the United States and established distribution networks. They required their Dominican cells in the United States to take a couple of kilos of heroin for every 100 kilos of cocaine to give out free samples to customers—and the strategy worked, creating an entirely new client base for heroin. The purity level of their heroin permits it to be prepared for smoking, ridding the product of its dirty needles and HIV reputation (Brzezinski 2002). Smoking is a less efficient way of ingesting than intravenous use because a lot of the drug literally goes up in smoke. Therefore, only when it is relatively cheap and therefore plentiful will smoking heroin predominate.

Since the 1980s Colombia has become a leading poppy grower, and Colombians have become major heroin wholesalers. At the end of 1991 police raids in Colombia disclosed thousands of acres of poppy plants ("Colombian Heroin May Be Increasing" 1991). On the mountain slopes of Colombia's Andean rain forests guerrillas and drug traffickers grow significant crops. On the hillsides of a reservation in the southern Colombian state of Cauca, at an altitude of 9,000 feet, Guambiano Indians cultivate their most precious crop. Gum from their poppies brings about $115 a pound and represents the difference between food and hunger. Nine other states are known to have poppy plantations (Tamayo 2001).

By 1998 Colombian heroin accounted for more than 50 percent of the drug smuggled into the United States. The high purity level of Colombian heroin—it passes through fewer hands from "the farm to the arm" than the Asian variety—enables ingestion by sniffing and smoking. By 1999 Colombia was believed the source of 70 percent of the heroin sold on the East Coast. In New York Colombians caused a glut on the heroin market, with declining prices and street-sale purity as high as 90 percent, whereas in the early (pre-Colombian) 1980s the purity was barely 5 percent (Wren 1999a).

During the 1980s the Colombian drug lords relied heavily on organized groups from Mexico to transport cocaine into the United States after it was delivered to Mexico from Colombia. Currently, the greatest proportion of cocaine available in the United States is still entering the United States through Mexico. Using their skills as seasoned drug traffickers with a long tradition of polydrug smuggling, crime lords from Mexico soon established cocaine-trafficking routes and contacts. In the late 1980s Colombia-based organizations, which had paid transporters from Mexico cash for their services, began to pay them in cocaine—in many cases up to half of the shipment. As a result the organizations from Mexico evolved from mere transporters of cocaine to major cocaine traffickers in their own right, and today they pose a grave threat to the United States. Mexican organized crime syndicates control the wholesale distribution of cocaine in the western half and the Midwest of the United States and they dominate the drug trade in the Northwestern United States (National Drug Intelligence Center 2009h, 2009). The dismantling of major Colombian cartels in Medellín and Cali created opportunities for their Mexican colleagues who began forging direct links with cocaine sources in Bolivia and Peru. In their weakened state, Colombians now have to compete with Mexican organizations for the U.S. market. Mexican organizations "are the greatest drug trafficking threat to the United States" (National Drug Intelligence Center 2009: 45).

MEXICO

Mexican drug trafficking organizations "control most of the U.S. drug market and have established varied transportation routes, advanced communications capabilities, and strong affiliations with gangs in the United States," overseeing drug distribution in more than 230 U.S. cities (National Drug Intelligence Center 2009: 45).

The popular culture of Mexico is infused with songs and ballads—known as *narcocorridos*—glamorizing drug trafficking (Downes 2009). Major *narcotraficantes* are celebrated, along with their subculture of violence. Many songs contain references to an outlaw code of behavior, and *narcocorrido* music videos depict violence, including torture and the murder of police officers (Dillon 1999a). Mexicans distrust the police while fearing the traffickers, who have resorted to beheadings to terrorize the public. "Along with the widespread fear comes a certain respect. Big-time mobsters are treated like folk heroes in their home regions, their stories told and retold in popular songs" (J. C. McKinley 2007: 10). In the Pacific seaside resort town of Mazatlán, in Sinaloa State, home of the notorious Sinaloa cartel, tourists can enjoy a "narco-tour." Tourists—almost all are Mexicans from other parts of the country—pay about $15 an hour to visit the homes of *narcotraficantes* and scenes of some of their bloody shootouts (Lacey 2009a).

Charles Bowden (2009) refers to two Mexicos. The first is where the Mexican president is fighting a valiant war on drugs, aided by the Mexican Army and $1.4 billion in U.S. aid. The second is where there is a war for control of drugs, where the police and the military fight for their share of the business. Even imprisonment does little to impede their drug business. Indeed, prisons often serve as a base of cartel operations: "For drug lords, flush with money, life on the inside is often the free-spirited existence they led outside. Inmates look up to them. Guards often become their employees" (Lacey 2009c: 6). In 2009, guards at a northern Mexican prison allowed 53 dangerous inmates, including about a dozen who were drug cartel suspects, to walk out. Once outside, the inmates were met by eight men wearing jackets with the federal police insignia who escorted them to police cars with flashing lights. The incident was captured on video by prison security cameras (Associated Press 2009a).

Mexico is a nation of more than 100 million people, 75 percent of who live in urban areas. Independence from Spanish rule in 1821 was followed by a series of revolutions, rigged elections, and general turmoil. There was a war with the United States in 1848 and a French invasion and occupation from 1863 to 1867. In still another violent overthrow, Porfirio Diaz came to power in 1876 and ruled Mexico for thirty-five years. Out of the revolution that ousted Diaz emerged Mexico's dominant political party, *Partido Revolucionario Institucional* (PRI; pronounced *pree*).

For decades after its founding, the PRI "was a tool of successive presidents using authoritarian methods to insure one-party rule" (Dillon 1999b: 1). The police forces—federal, state, and local—that evolved out of this atmosphere have been deployed not to protect but to control the population. Furthermore, police officers have been poorly paid, and it is understood that they can supplement their pittance with bribes as long as they remain loyal to the government (Dillon 1996). The PRI ruled Mexico for more than seventy years without any strong opposition, during which time corruption became endemic.

When it ruled Mexico as an elective dictatorship, the PRI "accommodated but regulated the drug cartels" (Padgett 2009: 39). The decline of the PRI and political reform in Mexico brought unintended consequences: In the wake of his election in

2006, President Felipe Calderón declared war on the drug cartels and dispatched the military in what has become an increasingly bloody campaign as the traffickers fought back ferociously.

In the employ of the Gulf cartel—one of several operating in Mexico—is an assassination unit of former Mexican special forces (*Grupo Aeromovil de Fuerzas Especiales*) trained in the United States and known as Los Zetas, named after the radio call name of their original leader who was killed in 2002. In 2004, the unit's chief was captured after a gunfight with Mexican agents who found a cache of military-grade automatic weapons and grenades (McKinley 2004a). That same year, a well-organized jailbreak freed five suspected cartel gunman who were being held on murder charges (Reuters 2004a). Their leader, Heriberto Lazcano, 29, known as "El Verdugo," The Executioner, is reported to have fed victims to the lions and tigers he keeps on his ranches. Lazcano was part of an elite special forces unit sent to combat drug trafficking on the eastern border that, instead, began working for Gulf cartel in the late 1990s. In place of their military pay of $700 a month, they are paid $15,000 a month. Their military discipline, training, arsenal, and wiretap capability make the Zetas a formidable organization that has expanded into ransom kidnapping and extortion from businesses (Padgett 2005). In 2008, Mexican federal agents arrested six Zetas who were guarding suitcases stuffed with $6 million in cash (McKinley 2008c).

The lethality of the Zetas has been strengthened by their recruitment of Mexican-American teenagers, some as young as thirteen, who are trained for months on the use of assault rifles and hand-to-hand combat and placed in comfortable houses on both sides of the border. While awaiting assignments, youngsters receive a retainer of $500 a week and from $10,000 to $50,000 per assassination. There are also perks such as parties with attractive women and luxury cars for outstanding work (McKinley 2009b). Los Zetas has since expanded beyond its enforcement and security services to become fully engaged in trafficking illicit drugs to the United States" (National Drug Intelligence Center 2009d: 9). Along with other trafficking organizations, Los Zetas have extended their portfolios to include a variety of businesses such as spas and day-care centers. Zetas wholesale pirated movies and CDs under their own label containing the organization's unicorn logo (McKinley, Jr., and Lacey 2009).

On the night of May 17, 2008, dozens of men with assault rifles rode into the small Mexican town of Villa Ahumada, population less than 9,000, a way station along a major drug route to the border city of Ciudad Juárez. They killed the police chief, two officers, and three civilians. When they left, they carried off ten civilians while the entire police force quit. The federal government responded by sending more than 300 troops and state police officers, but the "who and why" for the attack remains a mystery (McKinley 2008a). Nine months later, in response to death threats and the assassination of police officers, the police chief of Juárez resigned.

In 2005, hours after being sworn in, a businessman who had volunteered to become Nuevo Laredo's police chief—no one else wanted the job—was assassinated by men firing assault rifles from an SUV. The federal government responded by sending in the military (Jordon and Sullivan 2005). Later that year, federal authorities arrested fifteen Laredo police officers for abducting people on orders from the Gulf cartel (Iliff 2005). In 2008, gunmen killed the head of the federal organized crime division, and two weeks later the chief of the federal police. Mexican authorities subsequently charged six men with links to the Sinaloa cartel including the man who hired the shooter, a federal police officer (McKinley 2008f, 2008g). "Mexico has never been particularly adept at bringing criminals to justice," notes Marc Lacey (2009e 1), and "the drug war has made things worse. Investigators are now swamped with homicides and other drug crimes that they will never crack. On top of the standard obstacles—too little expertise, too much corruption—is one that seems to grow by the day: fear of becoming the next body on the street."

Cartel militarization and the Mexican government's military response have resulted in fierce gun battles. Gunmen have refused to surrender and have ambushed soldiers and police officers. They have corrupted local police departments and assassinated honest police commanders. In 2008, after a violent gun battle with soldiers and police officers in Rio Bravo, Mexican authorities arrested three U.S. citizens who were gunmen working for the Gulf cartel and who had been recruited from across the border (McKinley 2008h). A few days later in Tijuana, government forces fought a three-hour battle with gunmen who used heavy machine guns and rocket-propelled grenades (McKinley 2008d, 2008e). The group acquired military-grade weapons, including assault weapons and ammunition, in the United States and smuggled them back into Mexico.

At the end of 2009, in a two-hour shootout, Mexican marines killed the wanted drug lord Arturo Beltran Leyva; six other traffickers and one marine were also killed. Several hours after the dead marine's mother attended his memorial service in Mexico City, where she received the Mexican flag covering her son's coffin, gunmen armed with assault rifles broke into the marine's home and killed his mother, his aunt, and two siblings (Associated Press 2009c).

In 2009, after the arrest of a ranking member of *La Familia Michoacána*, notorious cult-like methamphetamine traffickers noted for beheading enemies and head-quartered in the southwestern state of Michoacán, a series of retaliatory attacks ensued resulting in the killing three federal officers and two soldiers. Several days later, the bodies of twelve military intelligence officers who were investigating *La Familia* were found bound, blindfolded, and tortured (Malkin 2009; "12 Mexican Intelligence Agents Tortured, Slain" 2009).

Core leaders of *La Familia* regularly attend church services and their leader carries a Bible and espouses a pseudoreligious philosophy whose stated goal is to protect Mexicans from the influence of drugs: the group claims it opposes the sale of drugs to Mexicans, but supports its consumption by Americans. *La Familia* recruits members as young as 14 who are inculcated with a religious doctrine that demands loyalty and a commitment to kill rivals as "divine justice." The group has an extensive distribution network in the United States (Booth and Fainaru 2009; McKinley 2009d: 1, 24) and in 2009 more than 300 persons in 19 states were arrested for being part of that network: Officials seized 550 pounds of cocaine, 729 pounds of methamphetamine, 967 pounds of marijuana, and $8 million (Archibold 2009c; FBI press release, October 22, 2009).

Mexicans civilians require permission from the military to buy firearms and they are not permitted to own large caliber rifles or high-powered handguns, which are considered military weapons. Mexican drug dealers purchase such arms in the United States and smuggle them back to Mexico along with their drug profits. They are particularly partial to assault rifles such as the AK-47 (McKinley 2009a).

In 2009, John Hernandez, a resident of Houston, Texas, was sentenced to eight years imprisonment for unlawfully purchasing firearms that were smuggled into Mexico. The firearms included 15 assault rifles and additional weapons chambered in ammunition known in Mexico as *mata policias* ("police killers") because of their reputed ability to defeat body armor worn by the police. Hernandez also recruited other "straw buyers" who purchased more than 100 firearms. Many of these weapons were subsequently recovered at crime scenes involving assaults and murders committed by Mexican drug cartels—victims included police officers (U.S. Department of Justice press release, April 17, 2009).

The Mexican military has been mobilized to combat the drug cartels, but critics claim the army is a major part of the problem: There is a history of collusion between the armed forces and drug traffickers and the military has been responsible for widespread human rights abuse (Caputo 2009). Amnesty International, Human Rights Watch, Mexican human rights groups, as well as the U.S. Department of State, have accused the Mexican military of widespread human rights violations that include kidnappings and extra-legal killings (Lacey 2009f). Meanwhile, violence between feuding Mexican drug cartels has spilled over the border. A renegade unit of the Arellano-Felix cartel, *Los Palillos* ("The Toothpicks"), for example, has been responsible for numerous murders and kidnappings in the United States (Moore 2009b).

FROM HEROIN TO COCAINE

The poppy is not native to Mexico but was brought into the country at the turn of the twentieth century by Chinese laborers who were helping to build the railroad system. Chinese immigrants dominated heroin trafficking until anti-Chinese riots and property confiscations during the 1930s caused the trade to pass into Mexican hands (Lupsha 1991). Poppy fields are generally small and difficult to detect, although larger fields cultivated by more sophisticated growers have been discovered. The poppies are grown in remote areas of the Sierra Madre states of Durango, Sinaloa, and Chihuahua as well as in Sonora (the Mexican state just south of Arizona) (see Figure 11.3). Opium gum is then transported to nearby villages. *Acaparadores* (gatherers) travel around the countryside buying large quantities of opium gum, which is flown to secret laboratories that are owned and operated by major heroin organizations. The conversion process takes about three days (although with special equipment and trained personnel it can be accomplished in one day). Once the chemists are finished, the heroin is moved to large population centers. From there Mexican couriers transport the heroin to members of the trafficking organization in the United States. Law enforcement officials have identified more than 200 U.S. cities where Mexican cartels maintain distribution networks or where they supply drug to distributors, particularly street gangs (Archibold 2009a).

Mexican heroin smuggled into the United States is transported to metropolitan areas in the western and southwestern states with sizable Latino populations.

Mexican heroin is also transported to primary markets in Chicago, Denver, and St. Louis. Attempts to find markets for Mexican black tar heroin in East Coast cities, such as Boston and Atlanta, failed (Marshall 2001). "Brown" or "black tar" heroin is a less refined form of the substance that gained a foothold in the U.S. drug market after the demise of the French Connection. Whereas white heroin from the Golden Triangle and the Golden Crescent in Southwest Asia can approach 100 percent purity, Mexican brown generally ranges from 65 to 85 percent pure.

On the Mexican side of the border across from Laredo, Texas, Nuevo Laredo, a city of more than 300,000, has been turned into a "Little Baghdad" by warring drug organizations—the Gulf cartel versus the Sinaloa cartel—attempting to control this critical distribution center. In contrast to Colombia, Mexican traffickers typically do not fight over territory or production: they battle to control smuggling routes used to move drugs and money. Victims have included journalists and police officers (G. Thompson 2005a). Assassins are often adolescents, and some are U.S. citizens, trained by instructors from the Mexican military in the employ of the cartels.

In the early 1990s the Mexicans struck a deal with the Colombians whose cocaine they were moving from Mexico into the United States on a contract basis: For every 2 kilograms of smuggled cocaine the Mexicans would keep 1 kilogram

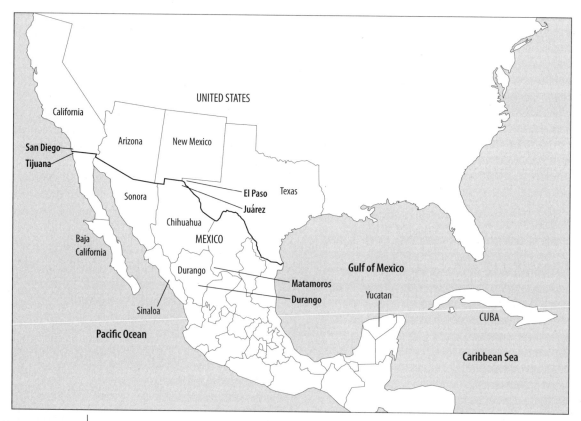

FIGURE 11.3 | MEXICO AND THE STATES THAT BORDER IT

Not "Short" on Wealth

In 2009, *Forbes* magazine listed Joaquín Guzmán, known as "El Chapo" ("Shorty"), head of Mexico's feared Sinaloa cartel, as one of the richest men in the world. In 2001, before he could be extradited to the United States, Guzmán escaped from prison and the United States offered a $5 million reward for his capture.

as payment in kind (O'Brien and Greenburg 1996; Wren 1996). Both sides benefited. The Colombians had an abundance of cocaine, and the Mexicans had a distribution network in the United States that they had previously used for heroin. This arrangement was aided by the North American Free Trade Act, which further opened the already porous borders between the United States and Mexico.

The relationship with the Colombians also led to structural changes as some Mexican drug groups modeled their organizations along Colombian lines: compartmentalized units operating independently of each other but controlled hierarchically. More recently, however, Mexican trafficking organizations (DTO) "appear to have moved away from traditional hierarchical structures in favor of decentralized networks of interdependent, task-oriented cells. The diversity of the individual cells provides operational flexibility to Mexican DTOs and reduces the risk of apprehension for DTO leaders" (2009k: 4).

The arrangement had significant benefits to the Mexican traffickers: Profits increased five to ten times. It also led to a dramatic increase in payments to public officials to protect the lucrative business (Golden 1997). This arrangement also had a certain logic for the Colombia-based traffickers, who in 1989 had been stunned by four costly cocaine seizures. Under the new payment plan, if a shipment was seized in a U.S. warehouse, the losses to the Colombia-based traffickers would be cut by half.

The markups for drug sales were so great that the new arrangement offered the traffickers from Mexico an opportunity to make far greater sums of money than they could have made being mere transporters for the traffickers from Colombia. More revenues meant more profits to invest in new distribution strategies. Eventually, the United States became divided into two marketing areas: the Mexico-based traffickers controlling the Midwest and West and the Colombia-based traffickers controlling the East. As a result, organized crime figures from Mexico began using their long-established contacts to emerge as major cocaine traffickers in their own right.

The drug trade is big business in poverty-wracked Mexico. Large traffickers have traditionally received protection from the highest levels of government and law enforcement. Indeed, some important traffickers have backgrounds in law enforcement. As Peter Lupsha notes, "For some of Mexico's top enforcement officials entrance into drug trafficking has simply been a lateral transfer" (1990:12). This ugly facet of the drug trade was dramatically revealed when several Mexican law enforcement officers were implicated in the torture-murder of a U.S. drug agent. They were acting on orders from drug kingpin Rafael Caro Quintero. When Quintero and other members of his Guadalajara cartel were arrested, they were

■ | ## DIGGING FOR DOPE

> Since authorities began keeping records in 1990, dozens of dope tunnels have been found along the Mexican border with the United States—24 were discovered in 2008 (Office of National Drug Control Policy 2009b). In 2006, federal agents discovered a tunnel 60-feet below ground that stretched from a warehouse near the international airport in Tijuana to a vacant industrial building in Otay Mesa, California, about 20 miles southeast of downtown San Diego. The tunnel was outfitted with a concrete floor, electricity, lights, ventilation, and groundwater pumping systems. On the Mexican side, officials found a pulley system at the entrance and several thousand pounds of marijuana (Archibold 2006). In 2007, authorities uncovered a 1,300-foot tunnel some 50 feet below the ground linking Tecate, Mexico, with the city of the same name in California. The tunnel began in the floor of a building in Mexico and ended in a large shipping container in California. Passages were illuminated by fluorescent light, and carefully placed pumps kept the tunnel dry. "The neatly squared walls, carved through solid rock, bear the signs of engineering skill and professional drilling tools" (Archibold 2007: 18).

carrying credentials identifying them as agents of the Dirección Federal de Seguridad, the Mexican equivalent of the FBI. Sicilia Falcón, another leading Mexican trafficker, carried similar credentials (Lupsha 1991). In Rafael Quintero's hometown of Sinaloa, just south of Arizona, he and other members of the Caro Quintero clan are revered and are even the subjects of songs and legends (Bowden 1991). "Drug trafficking has been a family affair in Mexico handed down through the generations. Relatives often launder drug profits through seemingly legitimate businesses, while sons and daughters learn the tricks of the trade as armed enforcers or distributors of bribes" (Lacey 2009b: 4).

The length and remoteness of the 1,933-mile-long border between Mexico and the United States make patrolling very difficult and facilitate the transportation of drugs into Texas, California, Arizona, and New Mexico. Drugs are also secreted in a variety of motor vehicles and smuggled past official border entry points. Private aircraft make use of hundreds of small airstrips that drape the U.S.-Mexican border and dozens of larger airstrips on the Yucatán Peninsula to move heroin north.

METHAMPHETAMINE AND MARIJUANA

While in Southern California in the early 1990s, Jesus Amezcuza, at the time a low-level Mexican trafficker, discovered the growing popularity of methamphetamine, a drug whose profits do not have to be shared with Colombians. In a few years, Amezuca had established an international supply network and labs in the mountains of Mexico that could produce methamphetamine (Wallace-Wells 2009). Although latecomers to the trade, Mexican drug organizations have become dominant in the manufacture and distribution of methamphetamine whose profits are substantial, usually a tenfold return on investment (Arax and Gorman 1995). However, Mexican restrictions on precursor chemicals ephedrine and pseudo-ephedrine resulted in a decrease in methamphetamine production in Mexico and reduced the flow of the drug from Mexico to the United States. Some Mexican traffickers relocated their production operations to California, acquiring ephedrine and pseudoephedrine through large-scale smurfing operations—circumventing state and federal ephedrine sales restrictions by making numerous small-quantity ophedrine product purchases from multiple retail outlets. Others adapted their operating procedures, smuggling restricted chemicals through new routes, importing nonrestricted chemical derivatives such as Phenyl-2-propanone (P2P) instead of precursor chemicals, and diverting precursor chemicals from sources in Southeast Asia and South America (National Drug Intelligence Center 2009l).

Better organization and an extensive drug portfolio have enabled Mexican organizations to diversify by dividing operations into heroin, cocaine, marijuana, and now methamphetamine units. Although major international trafficking organizations have traditionally specialized in one substance—heroin or cocaine—in several cases commodity lines have become blurred: Colombians, historically cocaine traffickers, have become involved in the heroin business, while Mexicans, traditionally heroin traffickers, have become major cocaine dealers. The portfolio of Mexican traffickers includes marijuana that some observers believe has become their most lucrative product. Mexican traffickers have relocated many of their outdoor cannabis cultivation operations in Mexico from traditional growing areas to more remote locations in central and northern Mexico, primarily to reduce the risk of eradication and gain easier access to U.S. drug markets (National Drug Intelligence Center 2009c).

As opposed to the instability of the U.S. heroin and cocaine markets, marijuana retains its marketability and profitability. Mexican marijuana is transported to the United States in pickup trucks driven over a ramp that has been placed on border security fences, or through cross-border tunnels. Sometimes they simply throw bales of marijuana over the fence to be retrieved by confederates on the U.S. side. The 9/11 terrorist attacks led to substantial tightening of the U.S.-Mexican border that affected marijuana smuggling routes. To avoid smuggling, cartels harvest on the U.S. side where they lease fertile land such as vineyards or grow and harvest marijuana in national forests (Moore 2009). In March and April growers are driven to planting sites that were scouted during the winter. In teams of 4 to 10, the growers move into the forest with seedlings and lightweight irrigation systems and live there until autumn, often poaching deer and bear, when the crop is harvested (Verini 2007). As a result, plant growth hormones have been dumped into streams and the growing areas have become polluted with weed and bug sprays banned in the United States, and rat poison used to keep animals away from the young plants (Cone 2008). Their campfires have been blamed for wildfires including the 90,000-acre Santa Barbara wildfire in 2009 that took several weeks to be fully contained (McKinley 2009c).

GOLDEN TRIANGLE

The Golden Triangle of Southeast Asia encompasses approximately 150,000 square miles of forested highlands, including the western fringe of Laos, the four northern provinces of Thailand, and the northeastern parts of Myanmar, formerly Burma (see Figure 11.4). Myanmar accounts for about 90 percent of the total heroin production of the Golden Triangle and is the world's second largest source of heroin and opium. Myanmar is also a major producer of methamphetamine (Mydans 2003). These countries emerged from colonial rule with relatively weak central governments. Their rural areas were inhabited by bandits and paramilitary organizations such as the Shan United Army. Colonial officials, particularly the French, used these organizations and indigenous tribes against various insurgent groups, particularly those that followed a Marxist ideology. As support for overseas colonies dwindled at home, French officials in Southeast Asia utilized the drug trade to finance their anti-insurgent efforts. Golden Triangle opium was shipped to Marseilles, where the Corsican underworld processed it into heroin for distribution in the United States—the "French Connection" discussed earlier.

The French withdrew from Southeast Asia in 1955, and several years later the United States took up the struggle against Marxist groups there. The Vietnam War is part of this legacy. The U.S. Central Intelligence Agency (CIA) waged its own clandestine war. Again, heroin played a role, for many of the indigenous tribal groups that were organized by the CIA cultivated opium. In Laos and South Vietnam corrupt governments were heavily involved in heroin trafficking, making the substance easily available to U.S. soldiers (A. W. McCoy 1972, 1991). This long-standing tradition of using drugs to help finance military efforts continues in that part of the world.

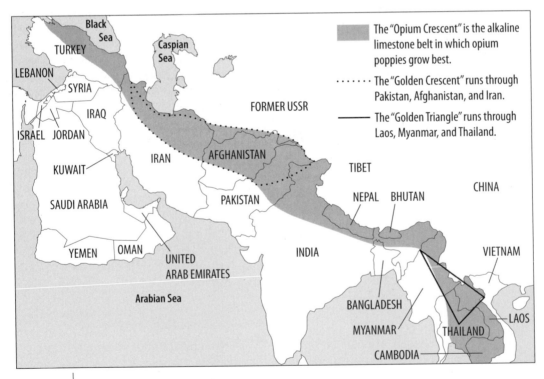

FIGURE 11.4 | MAJOR ASIAN OPIUM REGIONS

Shan United Army   The Shan States, an area somewhat larger than England, lie on a rugged, hilly plateau in the eastern part of central Burma, flanking the western border of China's Yunnan Province. Because it is located next to the Golden Triangle, China's Yunnan ("south of the clouds") province, with a population that includes twenty of the country's minority groups, has been a center for drug trafficking. High-quality heroin passes easily over borders that were opened for trade more than a decade ago, supported by rampant corruption among the police and other officials. The traffickers are well armed, gunfights are frequent, and the army has been used extensively to combat the drug gangs.

The Shan States contain an array of tribal and linguistic groupings. The largest group is the Shans, who speak Thai and therefore have more in common with their neighbors in Thailand than with Burma. The Shans are lowland rice cultivators, but hill tribes on the mountain ridges around them cultivate opium. During British colonial rule (1886–1948) the Shan States were administered independently from Burma, and the Shan princes enjoyed a great deal of autonomy. When Burma won independence in 1948, the Shans, with great misgivings, agreed to join the Union of Burma in return for statehood and guarantees of a number of ministry posts. As a final incentive the Shans were given the right to secede after 1957. Since a coup in 1962, Burma has been dominated by a repressive military dictatorship. In 1989 the country changed its name to Myanmar. Brutality against ethnic minorities and collaboration with drug trafficking continue.

The Burmese government's heavy-handed approach to the Shan States set the stage for revolution. Official Burmese financial policies were devastating to many hill farmers, who turned more and more to poppy cultivation as a cash crop outside of central government control (Delaney 1977). Shan princes (known as *sawbwas*) "had been encouraged to introduce the opium poppy to their fiefdoms by the British as far back as 1866 and opium shops had been opened throughout Burma to retail the narcotics to licensed addicts" (Bresler 1980: 67). In later years the British made a number of efforts to abolish opium cultivation in the Shan States, although they were never completely successful (A. W. McCoy 1972). In any event many Shans blamed their princes for accommodating the central government, and traditional systems of authority deteriorated.

Mong Tai Army   Originally known as the Shan United Army, the Mong Tai Army (MTA), under the leadership of Chang Chifu, who is half-Chinese, half-Shan and better known as Khun Sa, resorted to opium trafficking to purchase arms and support its independence movement (Delaney 1977). The MTA came to dominate the opium trade along the Thai-Burmese border, where about 400,000 hill tribesmen had no source of income other than heroin (Permanent Subcommittee on Investigations 1981a). The MTA was able to control both the shipments of opium and the production of heroin in its laboratories.

In the 1980s the Thai government succeeded in driving the MTA out of Thailand and back into Burma, but the group continued to dominate opium traffic, taxing drug caravans crossing their territory. In 1990 the Shans suffered significant setbacks: A U.S. federal grand jury indicted Khun Sa for drug trafficking, and the United States offered a $3 million reward for his capture and conviction in a U.S.

HEROIN'S LONG JOURNEY

In the mist-shrouded mountains along the border between China and Myanmar, where the monsoon washes away roads linking villages without electricity or running water, heroin begins its long journey to North America. By the time it reaches the streets of America's cities, the heroin will have traveled through half a dozen countries, soared at least 5,000-fold in price, and changed hands a hundred times. A kilo that will ultimately sell for more than $200,000 wholesale in New York City costs as little as $2,500 in Myanmar. The real profits in heroin are all downstream, in transportation and distribution. The first fingers to touch it, though, belong to people such as a certain 36-year-old mother of seven. She and her husband begin the harvest by scoring each poppy pod with a needlelike knife. A creamy gum oozes from the cuts, and once it turns black, it is scraped off with a crescent-shaped tool that has been in her family for as long as she can remember. It is painstaking work, and for their labor they earn $600 annually, barely enough to feed their children. Brokers come from the valley in early March to purchase the raw opium gum, which sells for about $135 a kilogram (Brzezinski 2002).

court. Also, his Mong Tai Army suffered defeats by the primitive but ferocious Wa tribesmen (Schmetzer 1990).

In 1994 a joint U.S.-Thai operation ("Tiger Trap") closed the Thai-Myanmar border in areas where the MTA operates. This cut off Khun Sa's ability to move heroin into Thailand and curtailed purchase of supplies for his forces. Later that year, Thai police arrested thirteen major MTA brokers who had been indicted by a federal grand jury in New York. The squeeze was complete in 1995 when the Myanmar army moved against Khun Sa, whose forces were low on food, ammunition, and medical treatment for their wounded. Shortly afterward, ethnic strife broke out. The rank-and-file ethnic Shans mutinied against the MTA, whose top officers are ethnic Chinese (Shenon 1996). Khun Sa began secret negotiations with Myanmar, and in 1996 a deal was made. In front of reporters from Thailand the 61-year-old Khun Sa submitted his resignation—he was retiring to raise chickens, he told them—and disbanded the MTA. The Myanmar government refused to extradite him, and until his health deteriorated—he died in 2007—Khun Sa regularly golfed with the generals against whom he had fought a protracted guerrilla war (Wren 1998a). As a result of Khun Sa's retirement the amount of Southeast Asian heroin entering the United States dropped dramatically (replaced by heroin from Colombia).

United Wa State Army   Until 1989 another formidable private army in the Golden Triangle served the Burmese Communist Party (BCP). The BCP force had in the past received support from the People's Republic of China. After Beijing cut off this aid to improve relations with Myanmar, the BCP, following a long-established precedent in the region, went into the opium business. The BCP controlled much of the poppy-producing area and received opium as a form of tax and tribute from local farmers, which the BCP then refined into heroin in its own laboratories.

In 1989 its ethnic rank-and-file Wa tribesmen—fierce warriors whose ancestors were headhunters—rebelled, and the BCP folded as an armed force (Haley 1990).

Most Wa political groups reached an accommodation with the Myanmar ruling junta, but one faction of the Wa organized as the United Wa State Army (UWSA). Headquartered on the border of China's Yunnan Province, the UWSA uses trafficking in heroin—and more recently methamphetamine—as a means of funding efforts against Burmese control (Witkin and Griffin 1994). Nearly one million Wa straddle the border between Myanmar and China, and the UWSA has an estimated strength of 20,000 men, with another 30,000 reserves, well armed with ground-to-air missiles and modern communications equipment. In 1997 a Myanmar military patrol of thirty men stumbled onto a Wa, drug caravan smuggling methamphetamine into Thailand and was wiped out. For the Wa profits from methamphetamine production and smuggling have surpassed those from heroin. Ironically, the Wa routinely executes anyone who is caught dealing heroin for local use (Wren 1998b). "The USWA maintains close ties with the People's Republic and uneasy peace with Myanmar which has unsuccessfully pressed the Wa to disarm (Moe 2009). The United States has offered $2 million for anyone who aids in the capture of the Wa drug kingpin who was born in China but has held leadership positions in the Wa government.

Whatever its source, Southeast Asian opium in the form of morphine base or almost pure heroin is usually brokered in Thailand, which has modern communications and transportation systems. A nation of 50 million people, Thailand is almost as large as France. A staunch anti-Communist ally of the United States, Thailand sent troops to fight alongside U.S. soldiers in Korea and Vietnam. In addition to its role in drug trafficking, Thailand, with an estimated 50,000 active brothels, has the reputation of being the world's biggest whorehouse (Schmetzer 1991). Thailand is also a major consumer of methamphetamine smuggled in from Myanmar (Mydans 2003). In 1991 a military coup—one of seventeen since 1932—overthrew the democratically elected Thai government, as did another coup in 2006.

> In Southeast Asia, not only did the British and French opium monopolies create massive addict populations, but they also inadvertently formed a smuggling network that was crucial to the post–World War II heroin epidemic. Although the colonial administrations reaped huge profits, they never became involved in the drug's distribution and sale. That work was left to each colony's licensed opium merchant. Invariably they were Chinese. (Posner 1988: 66)

Bangkok has a large population of Thai-born Chinese, called Haw, who are known by Thai names but maintain close ties with Chinese in Hong Kong, Yunnan province, Amsterdam, and British Columbia. From Bangkok Chinese criminal organizations have flooded their China White into major cities of Europe, Canada, and the United States. At the center of much of this drug trafficking are the Triads.

TRIADS

Secret societies have a long history in China; some date back to the beginning of the common era (Fong 1981; Chin 1990). An important part of these societies are the Triads and their American offshoots: tongs and Chinatown gangs. They draw their strength from the unique cultural dynamics of Chinese society, in which loyalty to family and friends is a moral imperative (J. Liu et al. 1998). "Chinese are born into a hierarchically organized society in which they never see themselves or others as free individuals, but as bound to others in an ever expanding web of social relations bearing mutual obligate bonds of varying strength" (W. Myers 1995: 3).

In this cultural setting, as Willard Myers (1995) notes, law is marginalized, relegated to a position well below meditative mechanisms within a particularistic social order of human relationships. These cultural manifestations, while not ipso facto criminal, facilitate criminal organization. Of particular interest are people of Cantonese and Fukienese heritage, who as immigrants throughout the world were subjected to pernicious discrimination, to which they responded by relying on cultural attributes that provided great advantages in business, both legal and illegal. And the cultural concept of *guanxi* (personal networks involving a system of favors or services) is global, providing a dynamic for international business, both legal and illegal. The Triad phenomenon is a natural extension of these cultural attributes.

The term *Triad* refers to the Chinese societies' common symbol: an equilateral triangle representing the three basic Chinese concepts of heaven, earth, and man. These groups, based in Hong Kong and Taiwan, wear distinctive dress and engage in highly ritualized behavior; secret hand signs, passwords, and blood oaths are used in elaborate initiation ceremonies (Carter 1991).

The Triad phenomenon is believed to have originated in opposition to the Ch'ing dynasty that was established by the conquering Manchus in 1644 (Fong 1981). The Ch'ing dynasty ended in 1911 with the success of Dr. Sun Yat-sen (1866–1925), who had been a Triad member. Many Triad members turned to criminal activities: gambling, loan-sharking, extortion, and trafficking in opium from the Golden Triangle of Southeast Asia. This trade was strengthened considerably by the activities of Chinese Nationalist forces in the Golden Triangle. Chiang Kai-shek, himself a Triad member, is reputed to have used Triads in his war against the Communists and labor unions. Triads were suppressed with a great deal of violence on the mainland by Mao Zedong when his Communist forces defeated Chiang's Nationalist Army in 1947. Triad members who fled to Taiwan with Chiang Kai-shek were tightly controlled by the Kuomintang (the Nationalist Party) and were unable to expand their criminal operations on the island (Chin 1990).

Thousands of other Triad members fled into the British colony of Hong Kong, which already had locally organized Triads that dated back to the early twentieth century. The indigenous Hong Kong Triads had begun as guilds and benevolent societies. They extended into criminal activities and actively collaborated with the Japanese during Japan's occupation of the colony during World War II. In the postwar era they emerged as powerful criminal societies (Chin 1995).

The drug-trafficking Triads expanded their operations during the Vietnam War, when thousands of U.S. soldiers were attracted to the potent heroin of Southeast Asia. When the Americans withdrew from Vietnam, the Triads followed the market and internationalized their drug operations. Because many soldiers were stationed in Europe, a major Triad marketplace developed there, with operations headquartered in Amsterdam.

Heroin manufactured in the Golden Triangle is smuggled into China's Yunnan Province and transported eastward to the coast and beyond. It is also smuggled through the Laos People's Democratic Republic and Vietnam into the Guangxi

Autonomous Region and Guangdong Province of China. Other important transit routes bring heroin from the Golden Triangle to major cities on the Southeast Asian peninsula, where it is sold in the illicit markets there or transported to other parts of the world. Golden Triangle heroin also feeds a sizable addict population in China. While Chinese authorities execute scores of drug traffickers and dealers each year, "they are not gaining the upper hand in the war against drug trafficking in the border areas, as more and more traffickers, many of them peasants from interior provinces of China hired as couriers (or "mules"), continue to cross the long and porous border" (Chin and Zhang 2007: 11).

GOLDEN CRESCENT

The Golden Crescent of Southwest Asia includes Afghanistan, Pakistan, and parts of Iran (see Figure 11.3). The region has limestone-rich soil, a climate and altitude that are ideal for poppy cultivation, and, like the Golden Triangle, a ready abundance of cheap labor for the labor-intensive production of opium, and the opium poppy grown in Afghanistan has a higher yield than that of Myanmar (*World Drug Report* 2008). "What crude oil is to the Middle East, poppies are to Afghanistan" (Powell 2007: 31).

Unlike Southeast Asia, Afghanistan's rugged terrain and the martial tradition of its tribes kept it free of colonialism. Western interest in this nation of about 27 million was limited until the Soviet invasion. The Pashtuns, a tribal group that populates Pakistan's Northwest Frontier Province, make up about 40 percent of the inhabitants of Afghanistan. The border dividing Pashtuns in Pakistan from their tribal brethren in Afghanistan was drawn by the British more than a century ago and is generally ignored; there are few border patrols in the region (Ahmed-Ullah 2001).

"Poppy growing is so uncontrolled that despite millions of aid dollars spent to train anti-drug forces and to help farmers grow other crops, Afghanistan is showing no signs of leaving its position as the world's biggest producer of opium." (Gall 2006a: 4). It now accounts for more than 90 percent of global opium production (Gall 2006b; Hafvenstein 2006). Afghan opium is processed into heroin in local laboratories or shipped to processing plants in Pakistan.

Afghan heroin destined for Europe is frequently transported across the forbidding Margo desert. Heavily armed convoys traveling at high speeds move their supplies into Iran where thousands of police officers have been killed battling the trade (Gall 2005). Turkey, which serves as a land bridge to markets in the West for heroin from the Golden Crescent, is fighting a similar battle. Kurdish separatists and Turkish criminal groups (*babas*) have important connections in the Western drug market. They move heroin across the highways of Turkey and into Europe where other criminal organizations, in particular Mafia and Camorra groups, distribute the drug throughout the European market.

In Pakistan the typical poppy farmer lives in a semiautonomous northern tribal area outside the direct control of the central government in Islamabad. The Pakistani authorities have little control in these areas and must appeal to tribal leaders to move against the region's dozens of illegal opium-processing laboratories. In northwest Pakistan's Karakoram Mountains an acre of poppies yields about a dozen kilos of opium gum; ten kilos of opium gum can be converted into one kilo

Though Pakistani officials have little control in the prevention of drug exportation, they do manage to seize some heroin destined for the United States. Most heroin trade in Pakistan is controlled by the Quetta Alliance.

of base morphine. The wholesaling is accomplished in lawless border towns such as Landi Kotal, which is about three miles from the Afghan border.

The United States has pressured Pakistan to move against poppy cultivation, but the infusion of hundreds of thousands of Afghan tribesmen into Pakistan has made this difficult if not impossible. Tribesmen in Pakistan are now armed with rocket-propelled grenade launchers and automatic weapons to protect miles of poppy plants, pledging to die fighting rather than give up their best cash crop. Furthermore, there is a growing domestic market for heroin in Pakistan. While most poppies now grow on the Afghan side of the border and are shipped to Europe and North America in the form of powdered heroin, Pakistan's heroin-smoking population has grown, with estimates as high as one million users.

Iran has been fighting a deadly battle against heavily armed Afghan traffickers and has lost several thousand men in the effort. The traffickers, equipped with antiaircraft missiles, night-vision goggles, and satellite telephones, are better armed than are their opponents in Iranian law enforcement (M. Moore 2001).

The nations of Central Asia that surround Afghanistan, such as Tajikistan, have a predominantly young, rapidly growing, and poverty-stricken population. Add heroin to this mix, and you get an expanding addict population and drug organizations taking advantage of porous borders and easily bribed officials. "The drug business sustains up to 50 percent of the Tajik economy and props up its currency, if only because of the great number of people it employs" (Orth 2002: 168). For many of the warlords who are part of the post-Taliban Afghan government, heroin was the way they supported their armed followers. Islamic terrorist groups also operate in this region, and heroin provides them with an invaluable source of funds. And the connection between drugs and corruption reaches into the highest ranks of the Russian military (Orth 2002).

In the wake of the 9/11 terrorist attacks and U.S. military action against the Taliban government, the poppy once again became an indispensable crop in parts of Afghanistan. A pound of raw opium can be sold for $100 or more, over one hundred times what a pound of fruits or vegetables will bring. By 2004 Afghanistan was producing more than three fourths of the world's opium—more than 4,000 tons. That same year, the rush to grow poppy caused a glut on the market and a steep decline in its price (Gall 2004; Rohde 2004). Opium is so critical to the Afghan economy—roughly one third of the country's total gross national product—that U.S. officials have been reluctant to engage in an antidrug war that could conflict with efforts to combat terrorism (Ives 2004; Schmitt 2004; Waldman 2004). America's military NATO allies in Afghanistan have been reluctant or unwilling to expand their mission into combating drug trafficking that they consider law enforcement (Shanker 2008).

Wealth from the drug trade has increased the power of regional local warlords, whose militias are a threat to the central government (Schmitt 2004). But high-ranking members of the government are also profiting from the drug trade, as are terrorist groups. Supporters of the U.S.-backed Afghan government are profiting from drugs as are Taliban (Gall 2003; Schweich 2008). In 2005 the United States criticized the Afghan leadership for the government's failure to curtail poppy cultivation. Antidrug efforts are hampered by a lack of alternative crops for impoverished farmers, and Taliban fighters have joined forces with drug smugglers against the government and Western troops (Cloud and Gall 2005; Schmitt 2006).

By 2008, it was becoming obvious that poverty was not the driving force behind the expansion of poppy cultivation whose growth has largely been confined to the wealthiest parts of Afghanistan: "The starving farmer" was a convenient myth that "allowed some European governments to avoid involvement with the antidrug effort. And," notes Thomas Schewich (2008: 60), "the Taliban loved it because their propaganda campaign consisted of trotting out farmers whose fields had been eradicated and having them say that they were going to starve." By 2009, it had become apparent that drug trafficking was sustaining the Taliban insurgency, and the United States

NOT ONLY POPPY

On June 8, 2008, as a result of a joint effort between the Drug Enforcement Administration's (DEA) Foreign-Deployed Advisory and Support Teams and the Islamic Republic of Afghanistan, 262 tons of hashish were seized—the largest of any known drug seizure. The drugs were stored in underground bunkers in Kandahar Province, a Taliban stronghold (DEA press release).

In 2009, a powerful Kandahar tribal warlord and Taliban ally, Bashir Noorzai, was sentenced to life imprisonment for drug trafficking. He had been arrested and tried in New York City to which he had been lured by federal officials (DEA press release).

announced that it was expanding military efforts in Afghanistan to include destruction of the opium crop (Filkins 2009). Then, abruptly, late in June 2009, a new policy was announced: there would be a shift away from eradication of opium fields to interdicting drug supplies. Opium farmers would be aided in making a living through alternative crops while enforcement would focus on intercepting drugs being shipped out of the country (Donadio 2009).

DOMINICANS

The Dominican Republic, with a population of 8 million, occupies about two thirds of the Caribbean island of Hispaniola, which it shares with Haiti. Although the Dominican Republic is not as depressed as pre-earthquake Haiti, in the mid-1960s political unrest and economic upheavals caused many residents to seek their fortunes by going north. In New York City Dominicans who have legally entered the United States number about 350,000; thousands more are illegal aliens. Some of these immigrants, legal and illegal, have entered the drug trade. Known as Dominican-Yorks, the traffickers keep a low profile in the United States, returning their profits to cities in the Dominican Republic such as San Francisco de Macoris, a city that is conspicuous for its wealth in a poverty-racked country. The influence of drug money on the island has been pervasive: "Office buildings, hotels, and shopping centers are springing up in Santo Domingo, Santiago, and San Francisco de Macoris—often in the gaudy style that some describe as narcodeco" (Rohter and Krauss 1998a: 6). Police corruption is widespread and often coordinated with law enforcement counterparts in Colombia.

Colombians franchised to criminals from the Dominican Republic a portion of the midlevel wholesale cocaine and heroin trade on the East Coast of the United States. Dominican organizations are also obtaining cocaine and heroin directly from Mexican sources at the Southwest Border and from sources in the Caribbean in order to lower purchase costs and increase profit margins. As a result of these relationships, Dominicans are also distributing marijuana and ice methamphetamine throughout the East Coast. Dominican traffickers also employ Mexican organizations to transport cocaine and heroin to the region on their behalf (National Drug Intelligence Center 2009e).

With drug-trafficking organizations based on familial or regional loyalties. Dominicans have demonstrated the necessary talent for moving large amounts of heroin, crack cocaine. They generally provide top-quality uncut drugs at competitive prices, avoiding the common practice of diluting the product as it passes through the distribution chain. Often operating out of grocery stores, bars, and restaurants in Latino neighborhoods, they employ a variety of marketing gimmicks to move their product. In Philadelphia they sold heroin packets with lottery tickets attached that a winner could use to claim an additional twelve packets.

Dominicans have demonstrated the necessary talent for moving large amounts of heroin, crack cocaine, and, more recently, ecstasy at the street level. They purchase heroin and cocaine directly from Asian and Colombian importers, sharing a common language and entrepreneurial values with the latter. Ecstasy is purchased in the Netherlands. Dominicans have apparently applied their well-known skills as traders and merchants to become New York City's top traffickers and have captured markets in Pennsylvania. They also control a significant portion of the cocaine trafficking in New England.

Dominicans developed a reputation as reliable dealers who pay their suppliers promptly and avoid using violence to muscle in on others or maintain exclusive control of a particular market. Instead, they competed on the basis of efficiency and pricing, allowing them to avoid high-profile violence (Pennsylvania Crime Commission 1990). However, while "early Dominican gangs were known for keen marketing techniques ... their successors in the 1990s mark out their territories" and use violence to maintain hegemony (Kleinknecht 1996: 260–261). Several Dominican groups have become noted for their excessive violence, both to maintain discipline and to deal with competitors. In one instance The Company, a Brooklyn-based gang, even lured a police officer to his death (Wren 1998c).

The center of the Dominican wholesale drug trade is the uptown Manhattan neighborhood of Washington Heights. In recent years some of the leaders have slipped out of New York and are running operations from their homeland, where corruption is endemic among airport officials and law enforcement. Until 1998 the Dominican Republic refused to extradite its citizens for crimes committed in the United States. In that year two notorious traffickers were sent to New York, where they were wanted for drug trafficking and murder.

Drug traffickers take advantage of the fact that the region of Central America and the Caribbean is located between major drug-producing areas and significant illicit drug markets, that there are hundreds of relatively small islands in the Caribbean with multitudes of cays, and that the socioeconomic situation in most of the countries in the region is difficult. The relatively weak institutional and political situations in some of the countries and the large number of political entities in the Caribbean pose challenges to efforts to ensure strategic coordination in the fight against illicit drug trafficking and abuse.

In the Caribbean a common practice is to airdrop illicit drug consignments into coastal waters and then have them picked up by speedboat. Private vessels, fishing boats, cruisers, and pleasure ships are also increasingly being used in maritime drug trafficking. Because of the increased efforts by the authorities of some countries to combat drug-related crime, drug traffickers have turned to moving their operations quickly to weaker jurisdictions. In addition, illicit drug stockpiling in isolated locations has become more common.

The Dominicans and their Colombian partners have made Haiti, which (along with the Dominican Republic) lies roughly between Colombia and Florida, the fastest-growing transit point for cocaine being shipped to the United States. Haiti has proven attractive to the traffickers because it is the poorest country in the hemisphere, making it relatively cheap to find criminal labor and bribe officials. The police force had to be created from scratch after the old force was abolished in the wake of the U.S. troop landing in 1994, and the police have limited training and resources.

Dominican drug traffickers control drug distribution in Puerto Rico; they are the principal transporters of illicit drugs into and through Puerto Rico and the U.S. Virgin Islands. Dominicans operate extensive transportation networks, often using the Netherlands Antilles, other Dutch territories, and their home island of Hispaniola as staging areas. They distribute wholesale, midlevel, and retail quantities of cocaine, Southeast Asian heroin, and marijuana throughout the region. They work closely with Puerto Rican traffickers, sometimes including members from Puerto Rican groups in their organizations (National Drug Intelligence Center 2009g: 4).

STREET-LEVEL DRUG BUSINESS

Below the wholesale level, selling cocaine or heroin is an easy-entry business, requiring only a source and funds. Any variety of groups can come together to deal heroin, such as street gangs in many urban areas. A variety of black criminal groups exist throughout the United States. Some are homegrown, such as Chicago's Gangster Disciples; others, such as Jamaican posses, are imported. There are important black criminal organizations in the heroin business, particularly in New York, Detroit, Chicago, Philadelphia, and Washington, D.C. Whereas African Americans have traditionally been locked out of many activities associated with organized crime (e.g., labor racketeering and loan-sharking) by prejudice, dope is an equal opportunity employer. African-American criminal groups made important strides in the heroin business when the Vietnam War exposed many black soldiers to the heroin markets of the Golden Triangle; previously, black drug-trafficking groups had depended on the American Mafia for their heroin. As a result of overseas experience, black organizations were able to bypass traditional organized crime and buy directly from suppliers in Thailand.

The enormous profits that accrue in the drug business are part of a criminal underworld in which violence is always an attendant reality. Drug transactions must be accomplished without recourse to the formal mechanisms of dispute resolution that are usually available in the world of legitimate business. This reality leads to the creation of private mechanisms of enforcement. The drug world is filled with heavily armed and dangerous individuals in the employ of the larger cartels, although even street-level operatives are often armed. These private resources for violence serve to limit market entry, to ward off competitors and predatory criminals, and to maintain internal discipline and security within an organization.

> Regular displays of violence are essential for preventing rip-offs by colleagues, customers, and professional holdup artists. Indeed, upward mobility in the underground economy of the street-dealing world requires a systematic and effective use of violence against one's colleagues, one's neighbors, and, to a certain extent, against oneself. Behavior that appears irrationally violent, "barbaric," and ultimately self-destructive to the outsider, can be reinterpreted according to the logic of the underground economy as judicious public relations and long-term investment in one's "human capital development." (Bourgeois 1995: 24)

Paul Goldstein (1985: 497) reports that violence in the drug trade is sometimes the result of brand deception:

> Dealers mark an inferior quality heroin with a currently popular brand name. Users purchase the good heroin, use it, then repackage the bag with milk sugar for resale. The popular brand is purchased, the bag is "tapped," and further diluted for resale.

These practices get the real dealers of the popular brand very upset. Their heroin starts to get a bad reputation on the streets and they lose sales. Purchasers of the phony bags may accost the real dealers, complaining about the poor quality and demanding their money back. The real dealers then seek out the purveyors of the phony bags. Threats, assaults, and/or homicides may ensue.

In the drug business, as Goldstein (1985) notes, norm violations—for example, a street-level dealer failing to return enough money to his superior in a drug network—often result in violence. Violence almost invariably results from the robbery of a drug dealer. No dealer who wants to remain in the business can allow himself to be robbed without exacting vengeance. Death is also the punishment for a norm violation that, although serious, is nevertheless widespread in the drug business: informing. Informing can be the means of eliminating competition or exacting vengeance for the sale of poor-quality dope, but more often, informing results from an attempt to gain leniency from the criminal justice system.

Occasionally, distinct patterns of injury can be recognized. For example, drug runners—teenagers who carry drugs and money between sellers and buyers—are seen in the emergency room with gunshot wounds to the legs and knees. A more vicious drug-related injury has emerged in the western part of the United States. In this injury, known as "pithing," the victim's spinal cord is cut, and he or she is left alive but paraplegic (De La Rosa, Lambert, and Gropper 1990).

The domestic business of cocaine requires only a connection to a Colombian source and sufficient financing to initiate the first buy. Any variety of people several steps removed from the Colombian source are involved in the domestic cocaine business. Because the cocaine clientele is traditionally at least middle-income, distributors likewise tend to come from the (otherwise) respectable middle class. The popularity of crack, however, dramatically altered the drug market at the consumer level, in particular the age of many retailers. James Inciardi and Anne Pottieger, experienced drug researchers, were shocked by the youthfulness of crack dealers compared with those involved in the heroin business: "While both patterns ensnare youth in their formative years, crack dealers are astonishingly more involved in a drug-crime lifestyle at an alarmingly younger age" (1991: 269).

In several areas of the United States, particularly in New York City and Los Angeles, the relatively stable neighborhood criminal organizations that once dominated the heroin and cocaine trade have found new competitors: youthful crack dealers. Entry into the crack trade requires only a small investment, since an ounce of cocaine can be converted to 2,500 milligrams of crack. Street gangs or groups of friends and relatives entered the market, often resulting in competition that touched off explosive violence involving the use of high-powered handguns and automatic weapons.

The dramatic drop in homicides during the 1990s has been linked to the decline of crack (Butterfield 1997). In New York City "in communities that used to have more open-air crack markets than grocery stores, where children grew up dodging crack vials and gunfire, the change from a decade ago is startling. On the surface, crack has disappeared from much of New York, taking with it the ragged and violent vignettes that were a routine part of street life" (Egan 1999c: 1). New York's experience has been replicated in other major cities that had been plagued by the crack epidemic. In a dramatic change in attitude toward crack, "crackheads" became community pariahs. The remaining crack market has moved indoors, or dealers use cellular phones to arrange sales, typically to users who are considerably older than the adolescents who once made up the core of the crack scene.

Some street gangs have also been expanding their organizations and drug markets to other states. Members of Los Angeles gangs, in particular the Crips, have moved into Seattle, Denver, Minneapolis, Oklahoma City, St. Louis, and Kansas City as well as smaller cities throughout California. Along with their smaller rival group, the Bloods, the Crips moved east with startling speed. "Neither gang is rigidly hierarchical. Both are broken up into loosely affiliated neighborhood groups called 'sets,' each with 30 to 100 members. Many gang members initially left Southern California to evade police. Others simply expanded the reach of crack by setting up branch operations in places where they visited friends or family members and discovered that the market was ripe" (Witkin 1991: 51).

Thomas Mieczkowski (1986) studied the activities of The Young Boys, Inc., a loosely organized retail heroin group in Detroit. At the center of their activities is a *crew boss*, who receives his supply of heroin from a drug syndicate lieutenant. The crew boss gives a consignment of heroin to each of his seven to twenty *runners*, young (16- to 23-year-old) African-American males whom he recruits. Each runner then takes his station on a street adjacent to a public roadway to facilitate purchases from vehicles. To avoid rip-offs and robberies, each crew is guarded by armed men, including the crew boss himself. Runners reported earning about $160 for a 10 1/2 hour workday.

> Participants in these drug networks tend to be the most serious drug delinquents who are frequently hired by adult or older adolescent street drug sellers as runners. Loosely organized into crews of 3 to 12, each boy generally handles small quantities of drugs—for example, two or three packets or bags of heroin. They receive these units "on credit," "up front," or "on loan" from a supplier and are expected to return about 50 to 70 percent of the drug's street value.

In addition to distributing drugs, these youngsters may act as lookouts, recruit customers, and guard street sellers from customer-robbers. They typically are users of marijuana and cocaine, but not heroin. Moreover, in some cities, dealers and suppliers prefer to hire distributors who do not "get high" during an operation. But their employment as runners is not generally steady; it is interspersed with other crimes including robbery, burglary, and theft.

A relatively small number of youngsters who sell drugs develop excellent entrepreneurial skills. Their older contacts come to trust them, and they parlay this trust to advance in the drug business. By the time they are 18 or 19 they can have several years of experience in drug sales, be bosses of their own crews, and handle more than $500,000 a year (Chaiken and Johnson 1988: 12).

The net profits in heroin for most participants at the street level, however, are rather modest. While dealers typically work long hours and subject themselves to substantial risk of violence and incarceration, their incomes generally range from $1,000 to $2,000 a month. Less-successful participants eke out a living that rivals that of minimum wage. Many get involved to support their own drug habits, to supplement earnings from legitimate employment, or both. The sale of cocaine and crack is carried out by thousands of small-time operators who may dominate particular local markets—a public housing complex, city blocks, or simply street corners.

Control is exercised through violence. Income is modest considering the dangers of death or imprisonment, and the sellers often work for less than minimum wage—for example, $30 a day for acting as a lookout, or 50 cents for each vial of crack sold. These may add up to $100 to $200 per week for long hours under unpleasant conditions without unemployment compensation, medical insurance, or any of the usual benefits of legitimate employment. A study in Washington, D.C., found that a majority of drug sellers in the sample did not sell drugs on a daily basis. Their median annual income was about $10,000. Those who sold daily earned about $3,600 a month (Reuter, MacCoun, and Murphy 1990).

At the retail level, sellers frequently deal several different drugs—"walking drug stores." Heroin dealers added cocaine to their portfolio when that substance started becoming popular at the end of the 1970s. Crack dealers have reflected a shift in the market by also selling heroin (Chitwood, Comerford, and Weatherby 1998). It is common for long-term users of cocaine to use a depressant to "mellow out." Alcohol is frequently used for this purpose, but cocaine users with access to it prefer heroin.

Marcia Chaiken and Bruce Johnson (1988) state that small drug sales are common among adult users and that some adolescents distribute drugs without being involved in more serious criminal activity. These dealers sell drugs to adolescent friends and relatives less than once a month to support their own drug use, and "most of these adolescents do not consider these activities 'serious' crimes" (Chaiken and Johnson 1988: 10). They rarely have contact with criminal justice agencies: "Since these youths conceal their illicit behavior from most adults, and are likely to participate in many conventional activities with children their age, criminal justice practitioners can take little direct action to prevent occasional adolescent sellers from distributing drugs and recruiting new users" (Chaiken and Johnson 1988: 11).

Like more conventional consumer items, drugs sold at the street level often carry a name and/or logo to promote "brand loyalty." "Among the more important marketing techniques are attractive packaging (stamps), name recognition (brand names), and consumer involvement and camaraderie around drug-consuming activities (product name contests). Moreover, product names ... reflect strong, positive attributes and notions of success, strength, power, excitement, and wealth, encourage consumers to make symbolic connections with these products" (Waterston 1993: 117).

ON NEW YORK'S LONG ISLAND

"The heroin being sold on Long Island is deadlier and cheaper than ever. A bag on the street costs about $6 or $7, cheaper than a pack of cigarettes. What makes the situation even more dangerous is the misconception among users that snorting or sniffing heroin, rather than injecting it, will not lead to addiction" ("Heroin on Long Island" 2009: 22).

Open-Air Markets[2]   Open-air markets represent the lowest level of the drug distribution network and operate in geographically well-defined areas at identifiable times so buyers and sellers can locate one another with ease. Some open-air markets are operated by groups with clear hierarchies and well-defined job functions. Others consist of fragmented and fluid systems populated by small groups of opportunistic entrepreneurs from a variety of backgrounds.

The nature of open-air markets makes participants vulnerable to law enforcement and rip-offs. In response to the risks of law enforcement, open markets tend to transform into closed markets where sellers do business only with buyers they know. Intensive law enforcement can quickly transform open markets into closed ones.

Drug dealing in open-air markets generates or contributes to a wide range of social disorder and drug-related crime in the surrounding community that can have a marked effect on the local residents' quality of life. However, simply arresting market participants will have little impact in reducing the size of the market or the amount of drugs consumed. This is especially true of low-level markets where if one dealer is arrested, there are, more than likely, several others to take their place. Moreover, drug markets can be highly responsive to enforcement efforts but the form of that response is sometimes an adaption that leads to unintended consequences, including displacement or increased revenue for dealers with fewer competitors.

Some researchers challenge the *displacement* thesis. They argue that police focus on a particular drug market does not cause dealers to "move around the corner." Drug dealers, like legitimate entrepreneurs such as auto dealers and restaurants, often find it advantageous to cluster. Clustering draws a larger customer base that, despite competition, profits all participants in the manner of a farmer's market. It also affords more protection than isolated dealing, the reason why buffalo herd, birds flock, and fish school. Focused police action, therefore, results in a diffusion benefit: drug trafficking becoming less profitable and smaller in size (Taniguchi, Rengert, and E. McCord 2009).

MARIJUANA

The business of drugs involves products other than cocaine and heroin. Substances such as PCP, LSD, methamphetamine, and barbiturates are produced in domestic laboratories; marijuana is also grown in the United States and Canada. Cannabis continues to dominate the world's illicit drug markets in terms of pervasiveness of cultivation, volume of production, and number of consumers (*World Drug Report* 2008). The people and groups that manufacture and traffic in these drugs are quite varied. They fit into no particular ethnic pattern; white, rural, working- and middle-class individuals are as likely to be involved as any identifiable racial or ethnic group. For example, there is little or no pattern to marijuana trafficking in the United States. It is an easy-entry business, and a number of relatives, friendship groups, and former military veterans have come together to "do marijuana."

Jamaican organizations distribute marijuana in the New York metropolitan area. They obtain supplies from Mexican distributors, either locally or in southwestern

---

[2]Edited from Harocopos and Hough (2005).

drug markets. Additionally, some transport multiton quantities of marijuana to the region from Jamaica aboard maritime conveyances. Jamaicans dominate marijuana distribution in sections of Manhattan and the Bronx, most of Queens (particularly the Jamaican section of southwestern Queens), northern Brooklyn, and sections of northern New Jersey (National Drug Intelligence Center 2009f: 5-6).

In the rural Appalachia region of the United States, a relatively high poverty rate contributes to an acceptance of cannabis cultivation as a source of income by many local residents. Some residents in impoverished communities regard marijuana production as a necessary means of supplementing low income. In many of these communities, cannabis cultivation is a multigenerational trade—young family members are introduced to the trade by older members who have produced marijuana for many years. Appalachia has a highly accessible transportation system, including major roadways that link it to many domestic drug markets.

Canadian marijuana known as "B.C. bud," a highly potent form named for British Columbia, where it is grown, is smuggled into Washington State and points east as far as Michigan. The trade is often two-way, with cocaine flowing north in exchange for marijuana flowing south. Criminal organizations that are involved in the trade include outlaw motorcycle clubs, Asian gangs, and Indo-Canadians, whose knowledge of the terrain gives them an advantage in transportation.

B.C. bud sells for about $3,000 to $3,500 a pound and is usually grown indoors. By way of contrast, marijuana smuggled across the southern border sells for about $400 to $1,000 a pound. The violence associated with the drug trade on the Mexican border has also become part of the Canadian scene. In 2005, for example, four officers of the Royal Canadian Mounted Police were murdered while searching for a marijuana-growing operation (Kershaw 2005).

METHAMPHETAMINE

Production of methamphetamine has blossomed in parts of rural America. In Texas, labs are located in rural areas and usually set up and run by local residents similar to the operation of small-scale production and distribution of moonshine whiskey during the prohibition era (Spence 1989). The number of meth labs seized in North Carolina has increased dramatically and about half have been in the rural mountain area in the western part of the state. Similar activity has been reported in rural communities in Tennessee and Georgia. In 2002 in the state of Washington's rural Snohomish County there were more methamphetamine lab seizures than in New York, Pennsylvania, and New England combined (Egan 2002). In farming communities isolation and the easy availability of one of the drug's main ingredients, anhydrous ammonia, a fertilizer, have spawned methamphetamine production (Butterfield 2004b).

Outlaw chemists have been stealing anhydrous ammonia normally used for fertilizer to use instead for conversion to methamphetamine by the "Nazi method," so called because German troops used anhydrous ammonia in World War II (Parker 1999). Anhydrous ammonia is stored as a liquid under pressure; however, it becomes a toxic gas when released to the environment. Anhydrous ammonia can be harmful to individuals who come into contact with it or inhale airborne concentrations of the gas. When stolen, the toxic gas can be unintentionally released, causing injuries to emergency responders, law enforcement personnel, the public, and the criminals themselves. While the labs are inexpensive for dealers to set up, the cost to the taxpayers for cleanup ranges from $5,000 to $100,000 per lab and is accomplished by crews wearing hazardous material suits for protection from fumes and deadly liquids (Brevorka 2002; Dewan and R. Brown 2009).

According to federal data, there are tens of thousands of contaminated residences whose victims include low-income elderly people whose homes were used surreptitiously by relatives and landlords whose tenants leave them with toxic messes. There are hundreds of vacant and quarantined properties, particularly in Western and Southern states; some purchased by buyers who discovered the contamination as a result of illnesses caused by the toxic residue (Dewan and R. Brown 2009).

As was noted earlier, there has been an increase in the involvement of Mexican cartels operating in southern California, where they produce methamphetamine in unpopulated desert areas. "Mexico has emerged as the primary supplier of methamphetamine to the USA in recent years following a substantial increase in manufacture after increased enforcement and domestic precursor controls took effect in the USA" (*Amphetamines and Ecstasy* 2008: 89). A report by the United Nations points to a change in the methamphetamine market: "Over the last few years, the methamphetamine market has moved from being a cottage-type industry (with many small-scale manufacturing operations) to more of a cocaine- or heroin-type market, characterized by a higher level of integration and involvement of organized crime groups that control the entire chain from the provision of precursors, to manufacture and trafficking of the end-product" (*Amphetamines and Ecstasy* 2008: 17).

Ecstasy

The vast majority of MDMA (ecstasy) consumed in the Unites States is produced in Europe—primarily the Netherlands and Belgium—and Canada; domestic production is limited. In recent years Israeli crime syndicates, some composed of Russian émigrés associated with Russian organized crime syndicates, have forged relationships with Western European traffickers and gained control over a significant share of the European market. The Israelis are the primary source for U.S. distribution groups.

Overseas ecstasy-trafficking organizations smuggle the drug in shipments of 10,000 or more tablets via express mail services, couriers aboard commercial airline flights, or air freight shipments from several major European cities to cities in the United States. While ecstasy costs as little as 25 cents per pill to produce, wholesale prices range from $5 to $20, and retail prices range from $10 to $50 a dose. Traffickers in ecstasy use brand names and logos as marketing tools and to distinguish their product from those of competitors. The logos are produced to coincide with holidays or special events. Among the more popular logos are butterflies, lightning bolts, and four-leaf clovers (Office of National Drug Control Policy 2004e).

LSD

Fewer than a dozen chemists are believed to be manufacturing nearly all of the LSD available in the United States. Some have probably been operating since the 1960s.

LSD manufacturers and traffickers can be separated into two groups. The first group, located in northern California, is composed of chemists (commonly referred to as "cooks") and traffickers who work together in close association; typically, they are major producers who are capable of distributing LSD nationwide. The second group is made up of independent producers who, operating on a comparatively limited scale, can be found throughout the country; their production is intended for local consumption (Drug Enforcement Administration n.d.a).

LSD chemists and top-echelon traffickers form an insiders' fraternity of sorts. They have remained at large because there are so few of them. Their exclusivity is not surprising, given that LSD synthesis is a difficult process to master. Although cooks need not be formally trained chemists, they must adhere to precise and complex production procedures. In instances in which the cook is not a chemist, the production recipe most likely was passed on by personal instruction from a formally trained chemist. At the highest levels of the traffic, at which LSD crystal is purchased in gram or multiple-gram quantities from wholesale sources of supply, it rarely is diluted with adulterants, a common practice with cocaine, heroin, and other illicit drugs. However, to prepare the crystal for production in retail dosage units, it must be diluted with binding agents or be dissolved and diluted in liquids. The dilution of LSD crystal typically follows a standard, predetermined recipe to ensure uniformity of the final product. Excessive dilution yields less-potent dosage units that soon become unmarketable (Drug Enforcement Administration n.d.).

MONEY LAUNDERING

The definition of money laundering is "to knowingly engage in a financial transaction with the proceeds of some unlawful activity with the intent of promoting or carrying on that unlawful activity or to conceal or disguise the nature, location, source, ownership, or control of these proceeds" (Genzman 1988: 1). According to the U.S. Treasury Department, money laundering is "the process by which criminals or criminal organizations seek to disguise the illicit nature of their proceeds by introducing them into the stream of legitimate commerce and finance" (Motivans 2003: 1).

Drug traffickers operating at the upper levels of the business have a serious problem: What to do with the large amounts of cash the business is continually generating? Ever since Al Capone was imprisoned for income tax evasion, successful criminals have sought to launder their illegally secured money. Further complicating the problem is that this cash is frequently in small denominations. In some cases "laundering" may simply be an effort to secure hundred-dollar bills so that the sums of money are more easily handled (500 bills weigh about one pound; $1 million in twenties weighs about 100 pounds) or to convert them into one or more cashier's checks.

To avoid Internal Revenue Service (IRS) reporting requirements under the Bank Secrecy Act, transfers of cash to cashier's checks or hundred-dollar bills must take place in amounts under $10,000 or through banking officials who, for a fee (generally 5 percent), agree not to fill out a Currency Transaction Report (CTR). A CTR is required for each deposit, withdrawal, or exchange of currency or monetary instruments in excess of $10,000. It must be submitted to the IRS within fifteen days of the transaction. In 1984 tax amendments extended the reporting requirements to anyone who receives more than $10,000 in cash in the course of a trade or business. A CMIR (Currency and Monetary Instrument Report) must be filed for cash or certain monetary instruments exceeding $10,000 in value that enter or leave the United States. Federal Reserve regulations require banks to file suspicious-activity reports when they suspect possible criminal wrongdoing in transactions. Attempts to strengthen these regulations have met vigorous opposition from the banking industry (Wahl 1999).

"Modern financial systems permit criminals to transfer instantly millions of dollars through personal computers and satellite dishes. Money is laundered through currency exchange houses, stock brokerage houses, gold dealers, casinos, automobile dealerships, insurance companies, and trading companies. The use of private banking facilities, offshore banking, free trade zones, wire systems, shell corporations, and trade financing all have the ability to mask illegal activities. The criminal's choice of money laundering vehicles is limited only by his or her creativity" (U.S. Department of State 1999: 3). The international trade in gold has proven to be an excellent vehicle for concealing the source of funds. Drug profits are used to buy gold, which is then legally exported for the jewelry trade and sold, the money returning to the original sources, that is, "laundered" (D. Kaplan 1999).

Currency exchanges (*casas de cambio*) along the Texas-Mexico border accept (illegally) large amounts of cash. They pool many customers' funds into one account and deposit the money in a domestic or foreign bank, keeping records on what is owed to each customer. When a foreign drug trafficker wants to send money to his own country, the *casa* operator wires the funds from the bank to the trafficker's foreign account or accounts. Even when a U.S. bank completes a CTR, it names the *casa* as the owner of the funds, not the actual owner. In the Houston area, in addition to *casas* there are *giro* (wire) houses. In general, the *giros* move drug money to Colombia, while the *casas* move Mexican drug money (Webster and McCampbell 1992).

The black market peso exchange (BMPE) is an informal currency exchange system in which one or more "peso brokers" serve as middlemen between, on one hand, narcotics traffickers who control massive quantities of drug money in cash in the United States, and, on the other, companies and individuals in Colombia who wish to purchase U.S. dollars outside the legitimate Colombian banking system so that they can, among other things, avoid the payment of taxes, import duties, and transaction fees owed to the Colombian government.

The BMPE system involves three steps. First, narcotics traffickers enter into contracts with peso brokers in which the brokers deliver pesos in Colombia in return for cash drug money in the United States and Canada. Second, the peso brokers use accounts in the United States or other countries outside Colombia to place the narcotics proceeds into the international banking system. Finally, the peso brokers enter into contracts with Colombian companies or individuals who deliver pesos to the brokers in Colombia in exchange for a wire transfer of dollars. Both transactions are verbal, without any paper trail, and the disconnection between the peso transactions (which generally all occur in Colombia) and the dollar transactions (which generally all occur outside Colombia) make discovery of the money laundering by international law enforcement extremely difficult. Because of these inherent advantages, the BMPE system has become one of the primary methods by which Colombian narcotics traffickers launder their illicit funds (DEA press release, May 4, 2004).

Chinese criminals are aided by an underground banking system operating through gold shops, trading companies, commodity houses, travel agencies, and money changers, managed in many countries by the same extended Chinese family. "The method of moving money is the *chop*, which is in effect a negotiable instrument. A *chop* can be cashed in Chinese gold shops or trading houses in many countries. The value and identity of the holder of the chop is a secret between the parties. The form of chop varies from transaction to transaction and is difficult to identify. In effect, the chop system allows money to be transferred from country to country instantaneously and anonymously" (Chaiken 1991: 495). For example, cash to finance a heroin deal is deposited in a San Francisco Chinatown gold shop in return for a *chop*. The *chop* is sent by courier to Hong Kong and is cashed. The owner of the *chop* receives his money from the original issuer, who is fronting for the drug deal.

A similar system, the *hawala*, is used in South Asia, where the size of the underground economies is estimated to be 50 to 100 percent the size of the documented economies. Similar to the modern practice of "wiring money," the ancient system of *hawala* was the primary money transfer mechanism used in South Asia prior to the introduction of Western banking. "Hawala operates on trust and connections ('trust' is one of the several meanings associated with the word 'hawala'). Customers trust hawala 'bankers' (known as hawaladars) who use their connections to facilitate money movement worldwide. Hawala transfers take place with little, if any, paper trail, and, when records are kept, they are usually kept in code" (U.S. Department of State 1999: 22). In Pakistan, for example, $100,000 (plus a transaction fee) is given to a hawaladar who provides a code term. Via the Internet, the hawaladar informs his broker in the Cayman Islands, where someone who provides the code term is given $100,000 to deposit in an island account. Money is never actually moved, and periodically hawaladars/brokers balance their respective transactions, usually by wire transfers using goods and invoices as a cover. In the United States, there are an estimated 20,000 informal remittance businesses working out of a variety of convenience stores, restaurants, and small shops whose owners speak languages unfamiliar to Westerners such as Arabic, Urdu, Hindu, and a variety of Chinese dialects (Freedman 2005).

In some schemes money launderers use dozens of people (known as "smurfs") to convert cash into money orders and cashier's checks that do not specify payees or that are made out to fictitious individuals. Each transaction is held to less than $10,000 to avoid the need for a CTR. One ring operating out of Forest Hills, New York, employed dozens of people who used about thirty banks in New York and New Jersey to launder about $100 million a year for the Cali cartel. The checks were pasted between the pages of magazines and shipped to Cali, Colombia; from there the money was transferred to banks in Panama. In 1989 sixteen people were indicted when one of the banks became suspicious of the unusual number of cash transactions and reported them to federal authorities (Morgan 1989). "Smurfing" has now been made a federal crime, and increased bank scrutiny has made tellers suspicious of cash transactions just under $10,000. In response, smurfs have reduced transactions to as low as $5,000 and often make dozens of transactions in a day, typically in banks that do not usually have long lines (Walter 1990).

Advances in banking technology have greatly facilitated money laundering. It has become increasingly difficult for the government to effectively monitor banking transactions. "An alternative to physically removing money from the country is to deposit the cash, then transfer the funds electronically to other domestic and foreign banks, financial institutions, or securities accounts. Swiss law enforcement officials report that when money is transferred by wire to Switzerland, it seldom comes directly from the country of origin, rather it is 'prewashed' in a third country such as Panama, the Bahamas, the Cayman Islands, or Luxembourg" (Webster and McCampbell 1992: 4). The sheer volume of wire transfers makes accounting difficult; one major bank in New York handles about 40,000 wire transfers each business day.

A customer can instruct his or her personal computer to direct a bank's computer to transfer money from a U.S. account to one in a foreign bank. The bank's computer then tells a banking clearinghouse that assists in the transfer; no human talks to another. Although depositing more than $10,000 in cash into an account requires the filing of a CTR, the government receives more than 7 million such reports annually and is hopelessly behind in reviewing them. The daily average volume of U.S. transactions is about $7 billion.

As part of an overseas laundering scheme a lawyer acting on behalf of a client creates a "paper" (or "boilerplate") company in any one of a number of countries that have strict privacy statutes, such as Panama, which has over 200,000 companies registered. The funds to be laundered are transferred physically or wired to the company's account in a local bank. The company then transfers the money to the local branch of a large international bank. The paper company is then able to borrow money from the U.S. (or any other) branch of this bank, using the overseas deposit as security (Walter 1990). An employment contract can also be set up between the launderer and his or her "paper" company for an imaginary service for which payments are made to the launderer. In some cases the lawyer may also establish a "boilerplate bank"; like the company, this is a shell. Not only does the criminal get the money laundered, but he or she also earns a tax write-off for the interest on the loan. Under the Bank Secrecy Act, wiring or physically transporting cash or other financial instruments out of the country in excess of $10,000 must be reported to U.S. customs officials. Once the money is out of the United States, however, it can be impossible for the IRS to trace it. Liechtenstein, with a population of 32,000, has 80,000 trust companies and associated banks whose transactions are protected by bank secrecy laws; the tiny principality has been a favorite for money laundering by the Sicilian Mafia, Colombian drug cartels, and Russian organized crime (Tagliabue 2000).

Another method of laundering funds without actually moving cash out of the country involves otherwise legitimate companies that import goods from the United States. Representatives of the Cali cartel in the United States paid for imported goods with dollars that went to the exporters. In return, the participating companies paid the cartel in Colombia at slightly less than the true exchange rate (C. Krauss and Frantz 1995). Instead of shipping currency, drug proceeds can also be used to purchase easily sold goods such as expensive liquor or electronic products. These are shipped to Colombia and sold at a 20–30 percent discount (Sanger 1995).

There is also use of so-called *digital gold currencies*, a type of "chop" (discussed earlier) updated for the twenty-first century. The metal does not physically change hands, but rather the transfer is a private accounting entry over the Internet in which only the designation of ownership changes. The process allows account holders to electronically manipulate funds while completely bypassing the U.S. banking system (National Drug Intelligence Center 2008b).

Our examination of the business of illegal drugs provides a framework for understanding the problems that confront law enforcement officials who are trying to constrain trafficking in dangerous drugs, the topic of the next chapter.

SUMMARY

- The business of illegal drugs shares some elements with the business of selling legal products.
- Traffickers may use circuitous routes to avoid the suspicion that is normally generated by shipments from source countries.
- The demise of the French Connection coupled with the subsequent emergence of criminal syndicates based in Colombia marked a significant evolution in the international drug trade.
- Terrorist groups use drug trafficking to further political ends.
- Colombia is the only country in the world where the three main plant-based illegal drugs—cocaine, heroin, and marijuana—are produced in significant amounts.
- In Colombia drug traffickers exemplify a lack of belief in the legitimacy of the country's political and economic institutions.
- Although it originated as a Marxist militia, in more recent years FARC has resembled organized banditry, operating its own coca farms and laboratories in rural Colombia.
- Contesting the FARC and other leftist militias are right-wing paramilitaries that often receive assistance from wealthy landowners, ranchers, and the Colombian military.
- Colombia-based cocaine trafficking groups in the United States continue to be organized around "cells" that operate within a given geographic area.

- By 1999, Colombians had become major heroin wholesalers, often selling cocaine and heroin to wholesalers as part of a package deal.
- The popular culture of Mexico is infused with songs and ballads glamorizing drug traffickers.
- The decline of the PRI and political reform in Mexico brought unintended consequences; a war on the drug cartels become an increasingly bloody campaign as the traffickers fought back ferociously.
- In the early 1990s the Mexicans struck a deal with the Colombians whose cocaine they were moving from Mexico into the United States on a contract basis.
- In poverty-wracked Mexico, large traffickers have received protection from the highest levels of government and law enforcement.
- Although they are latecomers to the trade, Mexican drug organizations have become dominant in the manufacture and distribution of methamphetamine.
- The Golden Triangle of Southeast Asia encompasses the western fringe of Laos, the four northern provinces of Thailand, and the northeastern parts of Myanmar.
- There is a long-standing tradition of using drugs to help finance military in the Golden Triangle.
- Drug-trafficking Triads expanded their operations during the Vietnam War. When the Americans withdrew from Vietnam, the

Triads followed the market and internatio-nalized their drug operations.

- The Golden Crescent of Southwest Asia includes Afghanistan, Pakistan, and parts of Iran.
- In the wake of U.S. military action against the Taliban, the poppy once again became an indispensable crop in parts of Afghanistan.
- Dominicans have come to dominate the middle echelon between the Colombians and the street dealers of cocaine and heroin in the New York City area and into New England.
- African-American criminal groups made important strides in the heroin business when the Vietnam War exposed many black soldiers to the heroin markets of the Golden Triangle. Previously they had depended on organized crime families for their heroin.
- Drug transactions must be accomplished without recourse to the formal mechanisms of dispute resolution that are usually avail-

able in the world of legitimate business. This reality leads to the creation of private mechanisms of enforcement.

- At the retail level, sellers frequently deal several different drugs.
- The heroin market has moved well past its urban roots, becoming established in America's suburbs.
- Mexican organizations have been increasing their presence in the United States, where they grow and harvest marijuana in national forests.
- Production of methamphetamine has blos-somed in parts of rural America reportedly set up and run by local residents.
- Money laundering is the process by which criminals disguise the illicit nature of their proceeds by introducing them into the stream of legitimate commerce and finance.
- Money laundering can involve modern financial systems or more primitive methods such as the *chop* and *hawala*.

Review Questions

1. What are the elements of the business of illegal drugs shared with the business of selling legal products?
2. How did the demise of the "French Connection" change the drug business?
3. What do terrorist groups and criminal organizations have in common?
4. What role does drug trafficking serve terrorist organizations?
5. What are the mutual benefits of the link between terrorists and drug traffickers?
6. What explains Colombian control over the cocaine industry?
7. In Colombia, what does the term "paramilitaries" refer to?
8. What are the advantages for drug traffickers whose organization is built around a cell structure?
9. What led to Colombian entry into the heroin business?
10. Why are *Los Zetas* such a formidable criminal organization?

11. How does the popular Mexican culture serve to support major drug traffickers?
12. What is "black tar" heroin?
13. What is the source most of the heavy weapons used by Mexican cartels?
14. What countries are part of the Golden Triangle?
15. What is the link between politics and the production of heroin in the Golden Triangle?
16. What is the role of Thailand in Golden Triangle heroin trafficking?
17. What are Triads?
18. What countries are part of the Golden Crescent?
19. Why has it proven impossible to wipe out production of opium in Afghanistan?
20. What is the role of Dominicans in the drug business?
21. When did African-American criminals make great strides in the drug business?
22. How did crack cocaine alter the drug business?

23. What are the two market systems at the retail end of the drug trade?
24. What are three typical sources of heroin in suburban areas?
25. What is the purpose of money laundering?
26. How does the black market peso exchange (BMPE) facilitate money laundering?
27. What is the *chop* used by Chinese criminals to facilitate money laundering?
28. How is the *hawala* system used for money laundering?
29. How has banking technology facilitated money laundering?

This year marks the 40th anniversary of President Richard Nixon's start of the war on drugs, and it now appears that drugs have won.

Nicholas D. Kristoff (2009: 10).

CHAPTER 12 | DRUG LAWS AND LAW ENFORCEMENT

AP Photo/Imperial Valley Press, Todd Krainin

"The most important precipitating factor in narcotic addiction is degree of access to narcotic drugs" (Ausubel 1980: 4), an assertion that is supported by research into heroin consumption (Anglin 1988). This is why narcotic use is higher in the inner city than in the suburbs and why the incidence of narcotic addiction in the United States approached the zero level during World War II. This also helps explain the relatively high level of drug abuse among physicians, in particular, anesthesiologists whose specialty offers ready access to fentanyl (McDougall 2006). "Thus, no matter how great the cultural attitudinal tolerance for addictive practices is, or how strong individual personality predispositions are, nobody can become addicted to narcotic drugs without access to them. Hence the logic of a law enforcement component in prevention" (Ausubel 1980: 4).

If drug use is seen as based on some combination of susceptibility and availability—"that drug abuse occurs when a prone individual is exposed to a high level of availability" (R. S. Smart 1980: 46)—it follows that a considerable reduction in availability can reduce drug use.[1] Availability also involves questions of cost; at some point the cost of purchasing a drug can reduce to near zero its availability to potential abusers, and law enforcement efforts can affect the cost of illegal drugs.

Before we can examine the strategies and techniques that law enforcement agencies use to deal with drug trafficking and to reduce the availability of drugs of abuse, we need to consider three issues that severely constrain law enforcement in general and drug law enforcement in particular: constitutional restraints, jurisdictional limitations, and corruption.

CONSTITUTIONAL RESTRAINTS

Law enforcement agencies in the United States operate under significant constitutional constraints, generally referred to as *due process*—literally meaning the *process that is due* a person before something disadvantageous can be done to him or her. Due process restrains government from arbitrarily depriving a person of life, liberty, or property. There is an inherent tension between society's desire for security and safety and the value we place on liberty. Herbert Packer (1968) refers to this as a conflict between two conceptual models of criminal justice: crime control and due process. (A conceptual model is a way of representing an idea that facilitates discussion and understanding of the reality represented by the model.)

CONCEPTUAL MODELS OF CRIMINAL JUSTICE

The *crime control model* "is based on the proposition that the repression of criminal conduct is by far the most important function to be performed by the criminal justice process" (Packer 1968: 158). The stress is on achieving the greatest amount of societal security and safety. Effective crime control requires a high level of efficiency; the system must be able to investigate, apprehend, prosecute, and convict a

---

[1]That is, of course, if we discount the abuse of alcohol and the possibility—or probability—that people who are unable to secure their preferred drug will switch to alcohol.

large proportion of criminal offenders. However, the system must respond to these cases with only limited resources. Consequently, efficiency demands that cases be handled speedily, with a minimum of formality and without time-consuming challenges. This efficiency can be accomplished only by a presumption of guilt: "The supposition is that the screening processes operated by the police and prosecutors are reliable indicators of probable guilt" (p. 160). To maximize crime control after this screening, the system must move expeditiously to conviction and sentencing. The crime control model is characterized by a high level of confidence in the ability of police and prosecutors to separate the guilty from the innocent. It conflicts with the due process model.

The *due process model* stresses the need for protecting individual freedoms. It assumes that the criminal justice system is deficient and stresses the possibility of error: "People are notoriously poor observers of disturbing events—the more emotion-arousing the context, the greater the possibility that recollection will be incorrect; confessions and admissions by persons in police custody may be induced by physical or psychological coercion so that the police end up hearing what the suspect thinks they want to hear rather than the truth; witnesses may be animated by a bias or interest that no one would trouble to discover except one specially charged with protecting the interests of the accused (as the police are not)" (Packer 1968: 163).

Due process confronts crime control and its need for efficiency and speed with an obstacle course of formalities, technicalities, and civil rights: "Power is always subject to abuse—sometimes subtle, other times, as in the criminal justice process, open and ugly. Precisely because of its potency in subjecting the individual to the coercive power of the state, the criminal justice process must ... be subjected to controls that prevent it from operating with maximal efficiency" (Packer 1968: 166). The due process model requires the system to slow down until it "resembles a factory that has to devote a substantial part of its input to quality control" (Packer 1968: 165)—due process guarantees.

Due process, while it protects individual liberty, also benefits the criminal population by guaranteeing the right to remain silent (Fifth Amendment), the right to counsel (Sixth Amendment), the right to be tried speedily by an impartial jury (Sixth Amendment), and the right to confront witnesses (Sixth Amendment). The Fourth Amendment and the exclusionary rule are particularly important for drug law enforcement.

THE FOURTH AMENDMENT AND THE EXCLUSIONARY RULE

The Fourth Amendment guarantees that "the right of the people to be secure in their persons, houses, papers and effects, against unreasonable searches and seizures shall not be violated, and no Warrants shall issue, but upon probable cause, supported by Oath or affirmation, and particularly describing the place to be searched, and the persons or things to be seized." In practice, information sufficient to justify a search warrant in drug cases is difficult to obtain; in contrast to such conventional crimes as robbery and burglary, there is an absence of innocent victims who will report the crime in drug cases. The exclusionary rule is the court's way of enforcing the Fourth Amendment; it provides that evidence that is obtained

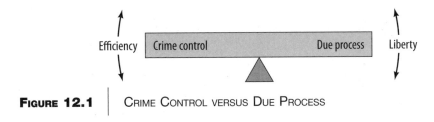

FIGURE 12.1 | CRIME CONTROL VERSUS DUE PROCESS

in violation of the Fourth Amendment cannot be entered as evidence in a criminal trial (*Weeks v. United States*, 232 U.S. 383; *Mapp v. Ohio*, 357 U.S. 643), although there are a number of exceptions that are beyond the scope of this book. The purpose of the exclusionary rule is to control the behavior of law enforcement agents, for example, making drug enforcement efforts that violate the Constitution not worth the effort. (See Figure 12.1.)

To respond effectively to drug trafficking, law enforcement officials require information about the activities of suspected traffickers. The Fourth Amendment and Title III of the Omnibus Crime Control and Safe Streets Act of 1968 (18 U.S.C. Section 2510–2520) place restraints on how the government can secure this information. Thus, to surreptitiously intercept conversations by wiretapping telephones or using electronic devices ("bugging"), officials must secure a court order that, like a search warrant, must be based on information that is sufficient to meet the legal standard of probable cause. When an order to intercept electronic communications is secured (generally referred to as a "Title III"), it is quite limited, requires extensive documentation, and demands that the people whose communications are being intercepted be notified after the order expires. These requirements make electronic surveillance expensive, in terms of personnel hours expended, and difficult to accomplish properly.

The supervision of drug law enforcement agents is also difficult, because they typically operate covertly or undercover. This means that "legal control over agents is problematic, and the circumstances of arrest are often such that there is a great temptation to perjury, violation of the exclusionary rule, misuse of informants, discretionary dropping, overlooking and altering charges, and other violations of procedural and/or legal rules" (J. Williams, Redlinger, and Manning 1979: 6). The greater the pressure on law enforcement officers "to do something about drugs," the greater is the temptation to avoid the significant constraints of due process and take unlawful (though often effective) shortcuts.

JURISDICTIONAL LIMITATIONS

The U.S. Constitution provides for a form of government in which powers are diffused horizontally and vertically. This is accomplished by three branches— legislative, judicial, and executive—and four levels of government within each branch: federal, state, county, and municipal (Figure 12.2). Although each level of government has responsibilities for responding to drug abuse and drug trafficking, there is little or no coordination among them. Each level responds to the problem of drugs independently of the others. Federalism was part of a deliberate design to

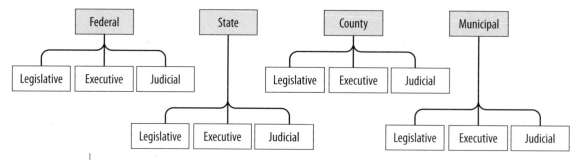

FIGURE 12.2 | GOVERNMENTAL COMPLEXITY

help protect us against tyranny; unfortunately, it also provides us with a level of in-efficiency that significantly handicaps efforts to curtail drug trafficking.

On the federal level, a host of executive branch agencies (to be examined later), ranging from the military to the Federal Bureau of Investigation, are responsible for combating drug trafficking. The separate federal judicial system is responsible for trying drug cases, and the legislative branch is responsible for enacting drug legislation and allocating funds for federal drug law enforcement efforts. At the local level are about 20,000 police agencies. Each state has state-level drug law enforcement agents, a state police or similar agency, and agencies that manage prisons and the parole system (if one exists). County government is usually responsible for prosecuting defendants, and a county-level agency, usually the sheriff, is responsible for operating jails. The county may also have a police department with drug law enforcement responsibilities under, or independent of, the sheriff's office, and almost every municipality has a police department whose officers enforce drug laws. Each of these levels of government has taxing authority and allocates resources with little or no consultation with other levels of government. The sum total is a degree of inefficiency surpassing that of most other democratic nations.

U.S. efforts against drug abuse are also limited by national boundaries: Cocaine and heroin originate where U.S. law enforcement has no jurisdiction. The Bureau of International Narcotics Matters within the Department of State has primary responsibility for coordinating international programs and gaining the cooperation of foreign governments in antidrug efforts. But the bureau has no authority to force governments to act in a manner that is beneficial to U.S. efforts in dealing with cocaine or heroin. Elaine Sciolino (1988: E3) reports that the bureau "has little influence even within the department [of State]. Foreign Service officers," she states, "readily admit that they try to avoid drug-enforcement assignments because they generally do not result in promotions." The State Department also collects intelligence on policy-level international narcotics developments, while the Central Intelligence Agency (CIA) collects strategic narcotics intelligence and is responsible for coordinating foreign intelligence on narcotics. The CIA, however, has often protected drug traffickers who have provided useful foreign intelligence. U.S. efforts against drug trafficking are often sacrificed to foreign policy (Sciolino and Engelberg 1988).

INTERNATIONAL EFFORTS

In 1988, the International Convention Against Illicit Traffic in Narcotic Drugs and Psychotropic Substances was adopted in Vienna, with two main purposes:

> First, to establish an internationally recognized set of offenses relating to drug trafficking that are to be criminalized under the domestic law of the parties to the convention; and second, to create a framework for international cooperation to enhance the prospect that traffickers and others who profit from trafficking will be brought to justice....
>
> The Convention focuses on the eradication of drugs and drug-producing laboratories; the international transportation of precursor chemicals used to produce illegal drugs; the tracing of laundered drug trade profits back to the drug cartels; and the worldwide extradition of drug criminals so that they can have no safe havens. Significantly, the Convention obligates parties to make money laundering an extraditable offense, to afford the widest measure of international mutual legal assistance in judicial proceedings, and to cooperate closely to enhance the effectiveness of law enforcement actions to suppress narcotics trafficking and related offenses. (Thornburgh 1989: 59)

In 1994 President Bill Clinton signed legislation authorizing the president to provide assistance for the prevention and suppression of international drug trafficking and money laundering. While international law (multinational treaties) provides the basis for eradicating illicit poppy and coca cultivation, adherence to treaties depends on a level of cooperation that is often sacrificed on the altar of domestic economic and political realities (discussed in Chapter 13). Under treaties, coca- and poppy-producing countries are to limit their cultivation acreage to a level that is in line with legitimate world needs. Strict controls over growers require them to deliver their crops to a government monopoly to prevent diversion to the black market. Crops growing wild are to be destroyed. The price paid by the government, however, is not competitive with that offered by traffickers, and the illegal diversion of coca or opium is the only significant source of cash for many peasant growers, whose standard of living is already marginal. Attempts to substitute other cash crops have met with only limited success because such programs cannot challenge the reality of the marketplace. As was noted in Chapter 11, coca and poppies are grown in regions where governments often have only nominal control.

Jurisdictional limitations, however, can sometimes overcome constitutional restrictions. For example, because the Bill of Rights applies only to actions of the U.S. government, the Fourth Amendment and exclusionary rule do not govern seizures in foreign countries by those nations' police. This holds even when the evidence that is seized is from U.S. citizens; thus, it would be admissible in a U.S. court (Anderson 1992). Furthermore, the Supreme Court has held that constitutional protections do not obtain in U.S. government actions against foreign nationals on foreign soil. In *United States v. Verdugo Urquidez* (110 S.Ct. 1056), a Mexican national who was suspected in the 1985 torture-murder of a Drug Enforcement Administration (DEA) agent was apprehended by Mexican police on a U.S. warrant and turned over to U.S. marshals at the California border. At the request of the DEA, Mexican police, without a warrant, searched the fugitive's two residences and seized incriminating documents, which were turned over to the DEA. The evidence was ruled admissible.

In a 1992 ruling on another case involving the DEA agent's murder, the Supreme Court ruled that kidnapping a suspect on foreign soil does not prevent the suspect from being tried in the United States. In this case (*United States v. Alvarez Machain*, 504 U.S. 655) Mexican bounty hunters kidnapped a medical doctor and took him to El Paso; they were paid $20,000 and given the right to settle with their families in the United States. The Mexican government reacted with outrage to the decision.

CORRUPTION

In Chapter 11 we examined the complex world of drug trafficking and the enormous profits that accrue to many of those involved. The easy availability of large sums of money and the clandestine nature of the business make drug law enforcement vulnerable to corruption.

Two basic strategies are available to law enforcement agencies—reactive and proactive—and many use a combination of both.

Reactive law enforcement has its parallel in firefighting: Firefighters remain in their fire stations, equipment at the ready, until they get a call for service. Reactive law enforcement encourages citizens to report crimes; the agency will then respond to the reports. This type of law enforcement is used for dealing with such conventional criminal behavior as murder, rape, assault, robbery, burglary, and theft, which are likely to be reported to the police. (It should be noted, however, that with the exception of murder and auto theft, studies indicate that most crimes of these types are *not* reported to the police.) *Proactive law enforcement* requires officers or agents to seek out indications of criminal behavior, always a necessity when the criminal violation includes victim participation (e.g., gambling, prostitution, and drugs). These crimes are often described as consensual or "victimless," although they clearly have victims who are unlikely to report the crime to the police. The problem of corruption is in part tied to the proactive strategy.

To seek out criminal activity in the most efficient manner possible, proactive law enforcement officers must conceal their identities and otherwise deceive the criminals

THE "FRENCH CONNECTION"

The French Connection heroin case was the subject of a best-selling book and an Academy Award–winning movie (Best Picture and Best Actor in 1971). In 1962, Detectives Eddie "Popeye" Egan (played in the movie by Gene Hackman) and his partner Sonny Grosso (played by Roy Scheider) smashed an international drug ring that was smuggling Turkish heroin into New York from Marseilles. That same year, the drugs seized in connection with the case—fifty-seven pounds of almost pure heroin—were vouchered with the police property clerk by Detectives Egan and Grosso.

In 1972 the Police Commissioner of the City of New York held a news conference: The French Connection heroin, he announced, had been stolen and replaced with white flour. Several days later, an inventory of the property clerk's office revealed that additional heroin was missing: A total of nearly 400 pounds of heroin and cocaine had been stolen—*by police officers* (Blumenthal 2009; Wallance 1981).

Two Hats

In 2010, the leader of a drug trafficking organization operating out of Ciudad Juárez, Mexico, was sentenced to 27 years imprisonment in a U.S. federal court. The trafficker, Jesus Manuel Fierro-Mendez, was a Juárez police officer assigned to a special counter-narcotics unit (U.S. Drug Enforcement press release, January 19, 2010).

they are stalking. As James Q. Wilson (1978: 59) points out, both reactive and proactive law enforcement officers are exposed to opportunities for graft, but the latter are more severely tested: The reactive officer, "were he to accept money or favors to act other than as his duty required, would have to conceal or alter information about a crime already known to his organization." The proactive agent, however, "can easily agree to overlook offenses known to him but to no one else or to participate in illegal transactions (buying or selling drugs) for his own rather than for the organization's advantage." Undercover officers pretending to be criminals are difficult to supervise; the agency they work often for knows only what the agents tell it.

There is also corruption in foreign countries that grow, process, or serve as transshipment stations for illegal substances. In fact, the corrupt official is an essential ingredient in the drug business, according to the President's Commission on Organized Crime (1986). The commission concluded that "[c]orruption linked to drug trafficking is a widespread phenomenon among political and military leaders, police and other authorities in virtually every country touched by the drug trade. The easily available and enormous amounts of money generated through drug transactions present a temptation too great for many in positions of authority to resist" (p. 178). In addition to corruption, there is the problem of brutality. The militaries in many drug source and transshipment countries have earned widespread condemnation for violating basic human rights.

INFORMANTS

Corruption is often intertwined with the problem of informants. Informants come in two basic categories; the "good citizen" and the "criminal." The former is such a rarity, particularly in drug law enforcement, that we will deal only with the criminal informant, the individual who helps law enforcement in order to further his or her own personal ends. These include vengeance, efforts to drive competition out of business, and/or financial rewards, but most frequently the information is given to "work off a beef"—to secure leniency for his or her own criminal activities that have become known to the authorities. Jerald Cloyd (1982: 188n) found that one federal district had a specified menu for every "beef": For each arrest resulting from informant assistance and yielding approximately the same amount of drugs that the defendant is being charged with, there is "a reduction of charges by one count. Being charged with two counts (one count of possession, one of possession with intent to sell), one arrest would get her a reduction of one count (felony possession) in exchange for an expedient plea of guilty. One good arrest and a guilty

◼ | NEWS HEADLINES

- "Ex-Cop Held in Drug Theft, Sale: Cocaine Evidence Fueled a Lavish Lifestyle." *Chicago Tribune* (February 7, 2003): Sec. 2: 1, 7.
- "2 Newark [NJ] Officers Indicted in Drug Thefts." *New York Times* (October 2, 2004): B4.
- "Retired Detective Pleads Guilty in Drug Case." *New York Times* (June 26, 2005): B3.
- "Six [NJ] Police Officers Charged with Protecting Drug Ring." *New York Times* (July 12, 2006): B3.
- "New Jersey Ex-Trooper Gets 24-Year Sentence for Involvement with Drug Gang." *New York Times* (July 15, 2006): B5.
- "Boston Officers Arrested on Drug Charges," *New York Times* (July 22, 2006): 11.
- "Ex-Detective Turned Drug Dealer Gets 6-Year Prison Sentence." *New York Times* (October 6, 2006): B3.
- "Ex-Police Lieutenant Gets Prison Term in Drug Money Case." *New York Times* (October 13, 2006): B2.
- "A Virginia Sheriff is Charged With Selling Drug Evidence." *New York Times* (November 3, 2006): 24.
- "Virginia: Ex-Officers Plead Guilty in Drug Scheme." *New York Times* (December 29, 2006): 23.
- "Three Indianapolis Metropolitan Police Officers Accused of Using Their Positions to Traffic in Marijuana." U.S. Department of Justice press release (June 16, 2008).
- "Bolivar [TN] Police Officer Charged With Possession of Hydrocodone with Intent to Distribute." U.S. Drug Enforcement Administration press release (October 21, 2008).
- "Narcotics Cop Arrested on a Drug-Run Rap." *New York Daily News* (November 17, 2008): 5.
- "Gang That Robbed Drug Dealers Included a Real Police Officer, Prosecutors Say." *New York Times* (Novmber 1, 2008): 20.
- "Customs and Border Patrol Officer Indicted for Bribery, Drug Trafficking and Alien Smuggling." U.S, Department of Justice Press Release (April 2, 2009).
- "Florida Deputy Sheriff Sentenced on Drug Charges." U.S. Department of Justice Press Release (May 14, 2009).
- "Ex-Passsaic [NJ] Sheriff's Officer Sentenced for Conspiring to Steal Cocaine from Evidence Vault." *Bergen Now* (May 18, 2009): Internet.
- "Former Benton Harbor [MI] Police Officer Sentenced After Pleading Guilty to Felony Drug Offense." FBI Press Release (June 10, 2009).
- "Corruption Charges Against Philadelphia Detective for Warning Drug Dealer of a Forthcoming Search by Federal Agents." FBI press release (June 16, 2009).
- "Former Miami-Dade County Police Officer Pleads Guilty to Aiding and Abbetting in Ecstasy Undercover Investigation." FBI press release (July 22, 2009).
- "Former Massachusetts State Trooper Sentenced on Conspiracy, Drug Charges." FBI press release (July 31, 2009).
- "Former [Starr County, TX] Sheriff Sentenced to Prison for Providing Protection to Drug Traffickers in Exchange for Cash." FBI press release (August 27, 2009).
- "Miami-Dade County Police Officer Pleads Guilty to Aiding and Abbetting in Ecstasy Undercover Investigation." FBI press release (July 22, 2009).
- "Former Starr County, TX Sheriff Sentenced to Prison for Providing Protection to Drug Traffickers in Exchange for Cash." FBI press release (August 27, 2009).

- "Florida [Miami-Dade] Police Officer Sentenced for Aiding and Abetting in Undercover Drug Operation." FBI press release (October 20, 2009).
- "Pennsylvania Police Officeer Charged with Robbery and Drug Distribution." FBI Press release (November 5, 2009).
- "Customs and Border Protection Inspector Sentenced for Alien Smuggling, Bribery, and Drug Trafficking." FBI press release (November 5, 2009).
- "Texas State Trooper Sentenced to Prison for Cocaine Trafficking." FBI press release (November 10, 2009).
- "Texas (Dallas) Deputy Sentenced on Drug and Firearms Charges." FBI press release (November 13).
- "U.S. Customs Official, Wife Sentenced on Bribery and Drug Importation Charges." FBI press release (November 25).
- "Federal Probation Officer Pleads Guily in Drug Case." *Dallas Morning News* (December 2, 2009) Internet.
- "Hired by Customs, but Working for the Cartels." *New York Times* (December 18): 1.
- "Second Texas [Hockley County] Pleads Guilty in Meth Ring." Associated Press (December 21, 2009) Internet.
- "Texas [Laredo] Police Officer and Co-Conspirator Plead Guilty to Drug Charges." FBI press release (February 17, 2010).

plea would reduce the charge to misdemeanor possession. Two good arrests would get her case dismissed."

Despite law enforcement agency regulations, often "while serving as informers, suspects are allowed to engage in illegal activity" notes Joseph Goldstein (1982: 37). "Continued use of narcotics is condoned; the narcotics detective generally is not concerned with the problem of informants who make buys and use some of the evidence themselves." Goldstein points out that although "informers are usually warned that their status does not give them a 'license to peddle,' possession of a substantial amount of narcotics may be excused" (1982: 37).

Obviously, the more involved in criminal activity the informer—"snitch" or CI (confidential informant)—is, the more useful is his or her assistance. This raises serious ethical and policy questions. Should the informant be given immunity from lawful punishment in exchange for cooperation? If so, who is to make that determination? The agent who becomes aware of the informant's activities? The agent's supervisor? The prosecutor who is informed of the situation? A trial judge? Should a murderer be permitted to remain free because he or she is valuable to law enforcement efforts against drug trafficking? Should a drug addict–informant be allowed to continue his or her abuse in order to keep in touch with traffickers? If so, doesn't this contradict the goal of drug statutes, which is to curtail drug abuse? Should the government encourage informants even if they face serious physical danger (and they usually do)? Most drug agents would argue, however, that without informants there can be no effective drug law enforcement. The issues are complex and without definitive answers.

There are other dangers. In south Florida, for example, given the number of law enforcement agencies and "given their heavy dependence on intelligence, it is inevitable that there are informants who inform on other informants, who are probably informing on them. A consequence of that is selective prosecution: arbitrary decisions made by police officers and agents as to who will go to jail and who will be allowed to remain on the street. Given the vast amounts of money at stake in the drug business, selective prosecution raises the specter of corruption" (Eddy, Sabogal, and Walden 1988: 85).

Working closely with informants is potentially corrupting. The informant helps the agent to enter an underworld that is filled with danger—as well as great financial rewards. There is always concern that the law enforcement agent might become something else to the informer—a friend, an employee, an employer, or a partner. The rewards can be considerable: Agents can confiscate money and drugs from other traffickers or receive payment for not arresting traffickers; at the same time they can improve their work record by arresting competing dealers. It is often only a small step from using drug traffickers as informants to going into business with them.

STATUTES AND LEGAL REQUIREMENTS

The legal foundation for federal drug law violations is Title II of the Comprehensive Drug Abuse Prevention and Control Act of 1970, as amended (usually referred to as the Controlled Substances Act [CSA]). Among the provisions of the CSA is a set of criteria for placing a substance in one of five schedules (Table 12.1). Following the federal model, most states have established the five-schedule system, but many "have chosen to reclassify particular substances within those five schedules. Variation also exists in the number of schedules employed by the states [North Carolina, for example, uses six] and in the purpose of these schedules" (*Illicit Drug Policies* 2002: 8). Massachusetts categorizes drugs on the basis of the penalty rather than using the federal scheme of potential for abuse and medical use. Like federal law, state statutes refer to the drug involved (e.g., cocaine or heroin), the action involved (e.g., simple possession, possession with the intent to sell, sale, distribution, or trafficking), and the number of prior offenses. Across states there is significant variation in the penalties for cocaine-, marijuana-, methamphetamine-, and ecstasy-related offenses (*Illicit Drug Policies* 2002).

People who are involved in the illegal drug business can be arrested and prosecuted for a number of different offenses: manufacture, importation, distribution, possession, or sale; conspiracy to manufacture, import, distribute, possess, or sell; or failure to pay the required income taxes on illegal income. Possession of drugs may be *actual*—for example, actually on the person, in pockets, or in a package that the person is holding; or *constructive*—not actually on the person but under his or her control, directly or through other people. Possession must be proven by a legal search, which usually requires a search warrant as per the Fourth Amendment (an important exception is at ports of entry). A search warrant requires the establishment of probable cause—providing a judge with sufficient evidence of a crime to justify a warrant. Drugs can easily be secreted in any variety of places, including inside the human body. Federal trafficking penalties are shown in Table 12.2.

In response to the Ecstasy Anti-Proliferation Act of 2000, the U.S. Sentencing Commission raised the guideline for judges' sentences for trafficking MDMA.

TABLE 12.1 | SCHEDULE OF CONTROLLED SUBSTANCES

Schedule I

A. The drug or other substance has a high potential for abuse.

B. The drug or other substance has no currently accepted medical use in treatment in the United States.

C. There is a lack of accepted safety for use of the drug or other substance under medical supervision.

Schedule II

A. The drug or other substance has a high potential for abuse.

B. The drug or other substance has a currently accepted medical use in treatment in the United States or a currently accepted medical use with severe restrictions.

C. Abuse of the drug or other substances may lead to severe psychological or physical dependence.

Schedule III

A. The drug or other substance has a potential for abuse less than the drugs or other substances in Schedules I and II.

B. The drug or other substance has a currently accepted medical use in treatment in the United States.

C. Abuse of the drug or other substance may lead to moderate or low physical dependence or high psychological dependence.

Schedule IV

A. The drug or other substance has a low potential for abuse relative to the drugs or other substances in Schedule III.

B. The drug or other substance has a currently accepted medical use in treatment in the United States.

C. Abuse of the drug or other substance may lead to limited physical dependence or psychological dependence relative to the drugs or other substances in Schedule III.

Schedule V

A. The drug or other substance has a low potential for abuse relative to the drugs or other substances in Schedule IV.

B. The drug or other substance has a currently accepted medical use in treatment in the United States.

C. Abuse of the drug or other substance may lead to limited physical dependence or psychological dependence relative to the drugs or other substances in Schedule IV.

Source: Drug Enforcement Administration.

For 800 pills, about 200 grams, the sentence increased from fifteen months to five years; for 8,000 pills, the sentence increased from forty-one months to ten years.

Enacted in 2003, the Illicit Drug Anti-Proliferation Act (sometimes known as the "Rave Act") prohibits "knowingly opening, maintaining, managing, controlling, renting, leasing, making available for use, or profiting from any place for the

TABLE 12.2

U.S Department of Justice Drug Enforcement Administration

Drug Schedule	Quantity	1st Offense	2nd Offense	Quantity	Federal Trafficking Penalties 1st Offense	2nd Offense	3rd Offense or More
Methamphetamine Schedule II	5-49 gms pure or 50-499 gms mixture	Not less than 5 yrs and not more than 40 yrs. If death or serious injury, not less than 20 or more than life. Fine of not more than $2 million if an individual, $5 million if other than an individual.	Not less than 10 yrs and not more than life. If death or serious injury, not less than life or more than life. Fine of not more than $4 million if an individual, $10 million if other than an individual.	50 gms or more pure or 500 gms or more mixture	Not less than 10 yrs and not more than life. If death or serious injury, not less than 20 or more than life. Fine of not more than $4 million if an individual, $10 million if other than an individual.	Not less than 20 yrs and not more than life. If death or serious injury, not less than life. Fine of not more than $8 million if an individual, $20 million if other than an individual.	Life Imprisonment
Heroin Schedule I	100-999 gms mixture			1 kg or more mixture			
Cocaine Schedule II	500-4,999 gms mixture			5 kgs or more mixture			
Cocaine Base Schedule II	5-49 gms mixture			50 gms or more mixture			
PCP Schedule II	10-99 gms pure or 100-999 gms mixture			100 gms or more pure or 1 kg or more mixture			
LSD Schedule I	1-9 gms mixture			10 gms or more mixture			
Fentanyl Schedule II	40-399 gms mixture			400 gms or more mixture			
Fentanyl Analogue Schedule I	10-99 gms mixture			100 gms or more mixture			
Others Schedule I & II (*Includes 1 gm or more flunitrazepam and gamma hydroxybutyric acid*)	Any	Not more than 20 yrs. If death or serious injury, not less than 20 yrs, not more than life. Fine of $1 million if an individual, $5 million if other than an individual.	Not more than 30 yrs. If death or serious injury, life. Fine of $2 million if an individual, $10 million if other than an individual.				

346

	1st Offense	2nd Offense
Others Schedules III *(Including 30 mgs-999 mgs flunitrazepam)*	Any	Not more than 5 yrs. Fine not more than $250,000 if an individual, $1 million if other than an individual.	Not more than 10 yrs. Fine not more than $500,000 if an individual, $2 million if other than an individual.
Others* Schedule IV *(Includes less than 30 mgs flunitrazepam)*	Any	Not more than 3 yrs. Fine not more than $250,000 if an individual, $1 million if other than an individual.	Not more than 6 yrs. Fine not more than $500,000 if an individual, $2 million if other than an individual.
All Schedule V	Any	Not more than 1 yr. Fine not more than $100,000 if an individual, $250,000 if other than an individual.	Not more than 2 yrs. Fine not more than $200,000 if an individual, $500,000 if other than an individual.

* Although flunitrazepam is a Schedule IV controlled substance, quantities of 30 or more milligrams of flunitrazepam are subject to greater statutory maximum penalties than the above-referenced penalties for Schedule IV controlled substances. See 21 U.S.C. §841(b)(1)(C) and (D).

purpose of manufacturing, distributing or using any controlled substance." Penalties include imprisonment for up to twenty years, criminal fines of $500,000, and civil penalties of $250,000.

CONSPIRACY

Conspiracy is an agreement between two or more individuals to commit a criminal act; the agreement becomes the *corpus* (body) of the crime. Conspiracy requires proof (beyond a reasonable doubt) that two or more individuals planned to violate drug laws and that at least one overt act in furtherance of the conspiracy was made by a conspirator (e.g., the purchase of materials to aid in the transportation or dilution of illicit drugs). Conspiracy statutes are valuable tools for prosecuting drug offenders because:

1. Intervention can occur before the commission of a substantive offense.
2. A conspirator cannot shield himself or herself from prosecution because of a lack of knowledge of the details of the conspiracy or the identity of coconspirators and their contributions.
3. An act or declaration by one conspirator committed in furtherance of the conspiracy is admissible against each coconspirator (an exception to the hearsay rule).
4. Each conspirator is responsible for the substantive crimes of coconspirators; even late joiners can be held liable for prior acts of coconspirators if the latecomer's agreement is given with full knowledge of the conspiracy's objective.

There are three basic types of conspiracy:

1. *Wheel conspiracies.* One person at the "hub" conspires individually with two or more people, who make up the "spokes" of the wheel. For the conspiracy to be (legally) complete, the wheel needs a "rim": Each spoke must be aware of and agree with the others in pursuit of one objective.
2. *Chain conspiracies.* Like the lights on a Christmas tree, each conspirator depends on the successful participation of every other member. Each member is a "link" who, to complete the conspiracy, must understand that the success of the scheme depends on everyone in the chain.
3. *Enterprise conspiracies.* Part of the RICO (Racketeer Influenced and Corrupt Organizations) statute of the Organized Crime Control Act of 1970, the enterprise conspiracy avoids the practical limitations inherent in proving wheel and chain conspiracies. The statute makes it a separate crime to conspire to violate drug laws as part of an agreement to participate in an enterprise by engaging in a pattern of racketeering activity. Members of the conspiracy need not know each other or even be aware of each other's criminal activities. All that needs to be shown is each member's agreement to participate in the organization—the "enterprise"—by committing two or more acts of racketeering, such as gambling or drug violations, within a ten-year period. The enterprise conspiracy facilitates mass trials, with each member of the enterprise subject to the significant penalties—twenty years imprisonment on each count—that can result from a conviction.

The *Continuing Criminal Enterprise* (CCE) statute is similar in purpose to RICO but targets only illegal drug activity. The statute makes it a crime to commit or conspire to commit a continuing series of felony violations of the 1970 Drug Abuse Prevention and Control Act when the violations are undertaken in concert with five or more individuals. The courts have ruled that a "series" requires three or more violations. "For conviction under this statute, the offender must have been an organizer, manager, or supervisor of the continuing operation and have obtained substantial income or resources from the drug violations" (Carlson and Finn 1993: 2). In 1999 the Supreme Court ruled (*Richardson v. United States*, 526 U.S. 813) that juries must agree on which specific illegal acts were committed by a defendant rather than simply finding that he or she committed a series of drug violations without specifying which ones. The 6–3 decision will make it harder to convict people for violating the CCE.

TAX VIOLATIONS

In 1927 the Supreme Court decided the case of *United States v. Sullivan* (274 U.S. 259), which denied the claim of self-incrimination as an excuse for failure to file income tax on illegally gained earnings. This decision enabled the federal government to successfully prosecute Al Capone and members of his organization. Drug entrepreneurs have devised ways to successfully evade taxes by, for example, dealing in cash, keeping minimal records, and setting up fronts. This is countered by the indirect method known as the *net worth theory*: "The government establishes a taxpayer's net worth at the commencement of the taxing period [which requires substantial accuracy], deducts that from his or her net worth at the end of the period, and proves that the net gain in net worth exceeds the income reported by the taxpayer" (E. Johnson 1963: 17–18). In effect, the Internal Revenue Service (IRS) reconstructs the total expenditures of the taxpayer by examining his or her standard of living and comparing it with reported income. The government can then maintain that the taxpayer did not report his or her entire income; the government does not have to show a probable source of the excess unreported gain in net worth.

MONEY LAUNDERING ACT

A U.S. Attorney General has pointed out that so much cash is involved in large, illicit drug-trafficking operations that tracking the money from these drug activities is often a more fruitful investigative endeavor than is tracking the underlying criminal activities (Thornburgh 1989). Before passage of the Money Laundering Control Act of 1986 (Title 18 U.S.C. Sections 1956 and 1957), money laundering was not a federal crime, although the Department of Justice had used a variety of federal statutes to successfully prosecute money-laundering cases. The act consolidated these statutes with the goal of increasing prosecutions for this offense. Money laundering was made a separate federal offense punishable by a fine of $500,000 or twice the value of the property involved, whichever is greater, and twenty years imprisonment. Title 18 U.S.C. Section 981 provides for the civil confiscation of any property related to a money laundering scheme.

Legislation enacted in 1988 allows the government to file a suit claiming ownership of all cash funneled through operations intended to disguise its illegal source. The courts can issue an order freezing all contested funds until the case is adjudicated (Weinstein 1988). A person is guilty of money laundering if he or she, knowing that the property involved represents the proceeds of an illegal activity, attempts to conceal or disguise the nature, location, source, ownership, or control of the proceeds or attempts to avoid a transaction-reporting requirement. Furthermore, whoever transports or attempts to transport a monetary instrument or funds out of the United States in an attempt to conceal or disguise the nature, location, source, ownership, or control of the proceeds to avoid a transaction-reporting requirement with the intent to promote an unlawful activity or with the knowledge that the monetary instrument or funds represent the proceeds of an unlawful activity shall be guilty of money laundering. For a conviction under section 1957, the prosecutor must prove:

1. That the defendant engaged in a monetary transaction in excess of $10,000,
2. That the defendant knew the money to be the fruit of criminal activity, and
3. That the money was in fact the fruit of a specified unlawful activity (Weinstein 1988).

Until 1988 the act permitted the Department of Justice to prosecute attorneys and seize fees obtained from tainted sources. Defense attorneys argued that this created a situation "in which a defendant cannot retain an attorney because of the government's threat of criminal and civil sanctions against any attorney who takes the case" (Weinstein 1988: 381). The defendant is left without a free choice of attorneys and therefore must depend on a public defender who might not be familiar with the complexities of RICO prosecutions. Supporters of this legislation argue that criminals who have grown wealthy from crime are not entitled to any greater consideration with respect to legal representation than are their less successful criminal colleagues, who are often represented by public defenders. On November 18, 1988, President Ronald Reagan signed the antidrug abuse bill, which contains an amendment to 18 U.S.C. Section 1957, effectively excepting defense attorneys' fees from the criminal money-laundering provisions. Thus, while criminal defense fees could still be subject to forfeiture, the attorney who accepts tainted fees is exempt from criminal prosecution. In 1989 the Supreme Court, in a 5–4 decision, ruled that the government, under the Comprehensive Forfeiture Act, can freeze the assets of criminal defendants before trial (*Caplin and Drysdale v. United States*, 491 U.S. 616; *United States v. Monsanto*, 491 U.S. 600).

SEIZURE AND FORFEITURE

Federal and state statutes provide for the forfeiture of property that is used in criminal activity or secured with the fruits of criminal activity. Forfeiture has proved particularly useful in dealing with drug traffickers. Section 881 of the Comprehensive Drug Abuse Prevention and Control Act of 1970 provides for the seizure of assets under certain conditions. The reach of section 881 was extended through amendments in 1978 and 1984: The statute now permits forfeiture of all profits from drug trafficking and all assets purchased with such proceeds or traded in exchange for controlled substances. It authorizes the forfeiture of all real property used in any manner to facilitate violations of drug statutes, including entire tracts of land and all improvements regardless of what portion of the property facilitated the illegal activities. Currency, buildings, land, motor vehicles, and airplanes have all been confiscated (Stahl 1992). The government also has the right to seize untainted assets as a substitute for tainted property disposed of or otherwise made unavailable for forfeiture (Greenhouse 1994).

A seizure can be made incident to an arrest or customs inspection or upon receipt of a seizure order. To obtain a seizure order (actually a warrant), the government must provide sworn testimony in an affidavit, spelling out the property to be seized and why there is reason to believe that it is being used to commit crimes or was acquired with money from criminal activity—the same process used in securing a search warrant. The filing of criminal charges against the owner is not required. The owner of the property has a right to contest the seizure only after it has occurred; he or she must prove that the money or property was earned through legal enterprise. In 1993, the Supreme Court (*United States v. Good Real Property*, 510 U.S. 43) ruled that the government cannot seize real estate without providing the owner with a notice and opportunity to contest the proposed seizure. This decision applies only to real estate and not portable possessions.

There are four types of forfeitable items:

1. *Contraband*, such as controlled substances, are illegal to possess and may be seized and destroyed without a court order.
2. *Derivative contraband* includes conveyances that are used to transport contraband, such as aircraft, vessels, and motor vehicles. While not illegal in themselves, they are classified as contraband when used in furtherance of a criminal act.
3. *Direct proceeds* are usually cash.
4. *Derivative proceeds* include real estate and stock.

In practice, vehicles and cash are the most frequently seized assets, because the pursuit of real property requires extensive financial investigation. "The investigative expense may be cost effective," however, if "the property is valuable and the potential for disrupting the criminal organization is high" (Stellwagen 1985: 5).

There are two types of forfeiture proceedings: criminal and civil. *Criminal forfeiture* is applicable only as part of a successful criminal prosecution. "The defendant in the criminal case must be convicted of the crime involving the property, or the property cannot be subject to forfeiture" (Poethig 1988: 11). Thus, the government can use criminal forfeiture to seize the home of a *convicted* drug dealer who used the home to store drugs. *Civil forfeiture*, on the other hand, does not require criminal charges; civil forfeiture can proceed even in the absence of a criminal prosecution and has certain advantages over criminal forfeiture: The level of evidence required is considerably less than that in a criminal action, and the considerable due process guarantees accruing to a criminal defendant are not applicable in a civil action. Interestingly, civil forfeiture proceedings are brought against property that is involved in a criminal offense, not against a person. "Possession of the property in and of itself may not be illegal, but the property may be subject to seizure and forfeiture because of the way it was used. No criminal charge or conviction need exist against the owner of the property for the civil case to occur" (Poethig 1988: 11). Thus, the government can use civil forfeiture to seize an automobile that is used to transport drugs (facilitation forfeiture) even if no conviction resulted from this activity.

In any number of jurisdictions, disputes have arisen over how to allocate the fruits of seized assets. Because these funds do not incur a political cost—not being linked to taxes—they are highly valued. However, "once the money reaches the local police, it often can become a political football with law enforcement and politicians squabbling over how to spend it" (Soble 1991: 23). In several California communities, for example, police officials wanted to put the money into drug law enforcement, but elected officials instead insisted on increasing the uniformed police force. There is also concern that pressure to produce revenue will encourage legally questionable activity and even alter the basic goal of drug law enforcement.

Forfeiture statutes of some states permit all seized assets to be returned to the initiating agency; others provide for distribution to all law enforcement agencies involved and the prosecutor's office; still others permit no proceeds to be returned to law enforcement and, instead, require that they be placed in an education fund. Law enforcement agencies in these states are able to bypass the requirement by having the case "adopted" by a federal agency such as the DEA or FBI, which then passes it off to the U.S. Attorney. The adoption procedure can result in up to 80 percent of the proceeds being returned to the initiating department (Worrall and Kovandzic 2008). Increased police assets via forfeiture provide an incentive for local governments to reduce their allocations for policing (Skolnick 2008). Forfeiture laws engender considerable controversy because of sharing provisions.

Intertwined with this concern is that expressed over the seizure of property owned by innocent third parties. Three fraternity houses that were seized at the University of Virginia in 1991, for example, were owned by alumni, not the current occupants, some of whom were arrested for drug violations. (Two houses were returned before the 1991–1992 school year began.) Innocent parties can be deprived of a residence, vehicle, business, or cash until they are able to prove they were not involved in law-violating activity—a reversal of the normal presumption of innocence. To get back seized property, the owner needs an attorney, and litigation can take several months without any guarantee of success. For people who make the "mistake" of traveling with large amounts of cash— particularly if they are black, Hispanic, or Asian—the results can be more than an inconvenience. A study by the *Pittsburgh Press* revealed several cases in which the cash of innocent people was seized at airports and kept for years without any criminal charges being filed (Schneider and Flaherty 1991). "Overcoming the burden of proof can be hard even for the most upright citizens. How does a mother prove she didn't know her son was using the family car to transport drugs? How does a landlord prove he didn't know a tenant was a drug dealer? ... The effort is also expensive, and even if you win, you're still out the money to pay your lawyer, which can be more than the value of the property you've recovered" (Chapman 1992: 23). In 1996 the Supreme Court determined that property can be seized even when the owner was innocent of any wrongdoing. In this case, *Bennis v. Michigan* (517 U.S. 1163), a jointly owned car was impounded after the husband used it to solicit a prostitute. In response to these criticisms, in 2000 the 1984 statute was revised to require the government to prove that confiscated property either had been used for illegal activity or was purchased with the proceeds of criminal activity.

Forfeiture has also been criticized as a plea-bargaining device for drug kingpins. There is criticism that forfeiture can distort the purpose of drug law enforcement, for example, police delaying raids until drug caches are depleted and cash maximized (Worrall and Kovandzic 2008). Or it can result in a "get out of jail free" card, a plea-bargaining device for drug kingpins. They negotiate lighter sentences by promising to reveal hidden assets and not put up court challenges to their seizure. Law enforcement agencies eager for additional funds allegedly promote leniency for those at the top of the drug trafficking ladder, while those down below, without significant hidden assets, face significant penalties (Navarro 1996).

GRAND JURY

A grand jury comprises fifteen to twenty-three citizens who have been selected to hear evidence against accused individuals and to determine whether sufficient evidence exists to bring these individuals to trial—to *indict* them. Although not all states use grand juries to indict defendants, all states and the federal government empower the grand jury to conduct investigations of criminal activity, usually pertaining to official corruption. The Organized Crime Control Act of 1970 requires that a special grand jury be convened at least every eighteen months in federal districts of more than one million people; it may also be convened at the request of a federal prosecutor, and its life may be extended to thirty-six months. The special grand jury is often used to investigate drug law violations.

The broad investigative powers of the grand jury permit jurors to consider tips and rumors as well as more substantial evidence offered by the prosecutor. Even illegally secured evidence may be used as a basis for questioning witnesses. A grand jury can issue subpoenas for documents and individuals. Federal (and most state) grand juries do not permit witnesses to be accompanied by counsel (although defendants are free to leave the grand jury room to consult with their attorneys). Testimony before a grand jury is given under oath and recorded, although the proceedings are secret until released by the court. Witnesses who invoke their constitutional right to remain silent can be granted immunity, which requires that they testify or suffer summary incarceration for the remainder of the life of the grand jury.

LAW ENFORCEMENT AGENCIES

As was noted earlier, local efforts against drug trafficking are usually directed at midlevel dealers, although most frequently it is the low-level street dealer who is arrested and prosecuted at the local level. Federal drug law enforcement seeks to

LEVELS OF DRUG LAW ENFORCEMENT

There are five levels of drug law enforcement (Kleiman 1985):

1. *Source control.* This comprises actions aimed at limiting cultivation and production of poppies and opium, coca and cocaine, and marijuana. Both the State Department and the Drug Enforcement Administration have agents assigned to foreign countries.
2. *Interdiction.* The interception of drugs being smuggled into the United States is primarily the role of the Coast Guard and Customs Service and Border Protection. (Since 2002 these two agencies have been in the Department of Homeland Security.)
3. *Domestic distribution.* The disruption of high-level trafficking is usually the responsibility of the Drug Enforcement Administration and the Federal Bureau of Investigation.
4. *Wholesaling.* The focus on midlevel dealing is usually the role of state and local law enforcement.
5. *Street sales.* Low-level dealing, often by addicts supporting their own drug habits, is usually left to local law enforcement.

disrupt illicit trafficking organizations and to reduce the availability of drugs for illicit use. This is accomplished in three ways (Comptroller General 1983: 3):

- Arrest, prosecution, and incarceration of traffickers and the immobilization of trafficking organizations eliminate some capacities for supplying illicit drugs.
- Removal of drugs from the distribution networks directly reduces supply.
- Seizure of equipment and operating resources leaves the drug networks at least inconvenienced, at best crippled.

On the federal level, because the United States, unlike most other democratic nations, does not have a national police force, the job of carrying out these objectives falls on a confusing number of agencies in several departments—Justice, Treasury, Homeland Security, Defense—whose responsibilities for enforcing drug laws often overlap. This fragmentation is the result of the ad hoc creation of law enforcement agencies at the national level; each time a particular problem arose, an agency was established without significant attention to the problem of coordination. We will discuss the agencies in the order listed in Table 12.3.

DRUG ENFORCEMENT ADMINISTRATION (DEA)

The mission of the Drug Enforcement Administration (DEA) is to enforce the controlled substances laws and regulations of the United States and bring to the criminal and civil justice system of the United States, or any other competent jurisdiction, those organizations and principal members of organizations involved in the growing, manufacture, or distribution of controlled substances appearing in or destined for illicit traffic in the United States; and to recommend and support non-enforcement programs aimed at reducing the availability of illicit controlled substances on the domestic and international markets (DEA Web site).

TABLE 12.3 | FEDERAL DRUG LAW ENFORCEMENT AGENCIES

Department of Justice

Drug Enforcement Administration

Federal Bureau of Investigation

Bureau of Alcohol, Tobacco, Firearms and Explosives

U.S. Marshals Service

Department of Homeland Security

Immigration and Customs Enforcement

Customs Service and Border Protection

Secret Service

Coast Guard

Department of the Treasury

Internal Revenue Service

Postal Service

Postal Inspection Service

The DEA evolved out of several predecessor agencies, particularly the Federal Bureau of Narcotics (see Chapter 2). It is a single-mission agency responsible for enforcing federal statutes dealing with controlled substances by investigating alleged or suspected major drug traffickers. The DEA is also responsible for regulating the legal trade in such controlled substances as morphine, methadone, oxycodone, and barbiturates. Diversion agents conduct accountability investigations of drug wholesalers, suppliers, and manufacturers. They inspect the records and facilities of major drug manufacturers and distributors, and special agents investigate instances in which drugs have been illegally diverted from legitimate sources. DEA special agents are also stationed in dozens of countries where their mission is to gain cooperation in international efforts against drug trafficking and to help train foreign enforcement officials.

The basic approach to DEA drug law enforcement is the *buy and bust* or the *controlled buy*. Typically, a drug agent is introduced to a seller by an informant. The agent arranges to buy a relatively small amount of drugs and then attempts to move farther up the organizational ladder by increasing the amount purchased. When arrests are made, DEA agents attempt to "flip" the suspect, convincing him or her to become an informant, particularly if the person has knowledge of the entire operation, so that a conspiracy case can be effected. As was discussed above, the use of informants is problematic.

The DEA's mission is to enforce the controlled substances laws and regulations and to bring to justice the organizations and principal members that are involved in the growing, manufacture, or distribution of controlled substances appearing in or destined for illicit traffic in the United States and to recommend and support

Special teams of U.S. Customs inspectors and canine enforcement officers examine cargo imported into the United States. Agents don't need probable cause or warrants to search for drugs at ports of entry.

DEA Antecedent Agencies

1973–Present: Drug Enforcement Administration
1968–1973: Bureau of Narcotics and Dangerous Drugs
1930–1968: Federal Bureau of Narcotics
1927–1930: Bureau of Prohibition
1915–1927: Bureau of Internal Revenue

nonenforcement programs aimed at reducing the availability of illicit controlled substances in the domestic and international markets. According to the DEA's Web site, the agency's primary responsibilities include:

1. Investigation and preparation for the prosecution of major violators of controlled substance laws operating at interstate and international levels.
2. Management of a national drug intelligence program in cooperation with federal, state, local, and foreign officials to collect, analyze, and disseminate strategic and operational drug intelligence information.
3. Seizure and forfeiture of assets derived from, traceable to, or intended to be used for illicit drug trafficking.

4. Coordination and cooperation with federal, state, and local law enforcement officials on mutual drug enforcement efforts and enhancement of such efforts through exploitation of potential interstate and international investigations beyond local or limited federal jurisdictions and resources.

5. Coordination and cooperation with federal, state, and local agencies and with foreign governments in programs designed to reduce the availability of illicit abuse–type drugs on the U.S. market through nonenforcement methods such as crop eradication, crop substitution, and training of foreign officials.

6. Responsibility, under the policy guidance of the Secretary of State and U.S. ambassadors, for all programs associated with drug law enforcement counterparts in foreign countries.

7. Liaison with the United Nations, Interpol, and other organizations on matters relating to international drug control programs.

FEDERAL BUREAU OF INVESTIGATION (FBI)

The FBI is as close to a federal police force as exists in the United States. Its broad investigative mandate was expanded in 1982, when the FBI was given concurrent jurisdiction with the DEA for drug law enforcement and investigation. In addition, the administrator of the DEA is now required to report to the director of the FBI, who has overall responsibility for supervising drug law enforcement efforts and policies. Despite its increased mandate, the primary role of the FBI is to deal with domestic espionage and terrorism.

IMMIGRATION AND CUSTOMS ENFORCEMENT (ICE)

Immigration and Customs Enforcement (ICE) is the result of a post-9/11 restructuring of the Immigration and Naturalization Service and the Customs Service. The primary role of the immigration enforcement arm of ICE is to prevent illegal entry into the United States and to apprehend people who have entered illegally. Uniformed Border Patrol officers check suspicious individuals within 100 miles of border areas that are likely to be used as illegal crossing points, and they often arrest people who are transporting drugs.

The Customs Service was established in 1789 to collect duties on various imports. Inspectors examine cargoes and baggage; articles worn or carried by individuals; and vessels, vehicles, and aircraft entering or leaving the United States. The frontiers of the United States, to the north and the south, "are the longest undisputed, undefended borders on earth" (T. Weiner 2002: 14).

Special teams of inspectors and canine enforcement officers concentrate on cargo and conveyances that are considered to be at high risk. In 1981 the Customs Service established the Office of Intelligence to better manage information and target suspects; it participates in several multiagency programs designed to combat organized criminal activities in drug trafficking. The service works with commercial carriers, often signing cooperative agreements, to enhance the carriers' ability to prevent their equipment from being used to smuggle drugs. Special agents are responsible for carrying out investigations into drug smuggling and currency violations as part of money-laundering schemes.

DRUG-SMUGGLING INTERCEPTIONS

- A light gray spray-painted bust of Jesus composed of molded cocaine
- 5 pounds of cocaine packed in condoms surgically implanted in a sheepdog
- 37 pounds of cocaine packed in condoms and inserted in the rectums of live boa constrictors
- 1,000 pounds of cocaine packed in hollow plaster shells shaped and painted to resemble yams
- 6,000 pounds of cocaine packed in kilo bricks inside ice-packed cases of broccoli
- 2,000 pounds of cocaine in the soles of a shipment of sneakers
- 16 tons of cocaine inside concrete fence posts
- 3,000 pounds of cocaine hidden beneath a shipment of iced fish fillets
- Mexican drug organizations were found to have smuggled cocaine into the United States secreted in tombstones engraved with the Virgin Mary.
- 12 pounds of heroin were discovered by customs officials at Newark Airport; they were in more than 100 candy bars that had been individually wrapped and packaged.
- The Postal Inspection Service uncovered a smuggling operation that shipped cocaine from Puerto Rico to New York City concealed in boxes of children's toys and puzzles.

Sources: Speart (1995), Associated Press (1999c), Lambert (2006); Associated Press (2007); U.S. Drug Enforcement Administration press release, (September 23, 2008).

ICE is not bound by Fourth Amendment protections that typically restrain domestic law enforcement. Agents do not need probable cause or warrants to engage in search and seizure at ports of entry; certain degrees of suspicion will suffice. The typical case is a "cold border bust," the result of an entry checkpoint search. Because it is impractical, if not impossible, to thoroughly search most vehicles and individuals entering the United States, agents have developed certain techniques for minimizing inconvenience to legitimate travelers and shippers while targeting those who are most likely to be involved in smuggling activity. Besides being alert to various cues that act as tip-offs, the officials at border-crossing points have computers containing information such as license plate numbers and names of known or suspected smugglers. People arrested by ICE become targets for offers of plea bargaining in efforts to gain their cooperation in follow-up enforcement efforts by the Drug Enforcement Administration; they are pressured to become informants in return for some form of leniency. As a result of the 9/11 attacks, ICE priorities have shifted to intercepting potential terrorists seeking to enter the United States.

ICE is hampered by the need to patrol more than 12,000 miles of international boundary, which more than 420 billion tons of goods and 270 million people cross each year. About half the drugs entering the United States come through commercial ports, where they are secreted in tightly sealed steel containers, twenty or forty feet long, twelve feet high, and eight feet wide, millions of which enter the country every year. Officials can inspect only a small number (about 10 percent) of these containers; and without advance information, the drugs typically pass right through the ports. Drugs that are intercepted are easily replaced.

In 2009, the Drug Enforcement Administration and ICE entered into an interagency agreement to increase the number of agents targeting international drug traffickers, improve and enhance information and intelligence sharing, and promote effective coordination between the agencies. According to the agreement, an unlimited number of ICE agents will be cross-designated to investigate violations of the Controlled Substances Act at border crossings in coordination with DEA. In addition, ICE now will be able to investigate these violations overseas while coordinating with the DEA. (DEA press release, June 19, 2009).

COAST GUARD

The Coast Guard, formerly part of the Department of Transportation and now part of the Department of Homeland Security, is responsible for drug interdiction at sea. Coast Guard personnel do not have to establish probable cause before boarding a vessel at sea. "Responsible in large part for U.S. drug interdiction efforts, the Coast Guard's strategy has been mainly directed toward intercepting mother ships as they transit the major passes of the Caribbean. To effect this 'choke point' strategy, the Coast Guard conducts both continuous surface patrols and frequent surveillance flights over waters of interest, and boards and inspects vessels at sea" (President's Commission on Organized Crime 1986: 313). In 2008, for example, a Coast Guard law enforcement detachment boarded a Panamanian flagged vessel on the Caribbean and seized 1,930 kilograms of cocaine; they also arrested the crew members (DEA press release, October 2, 2008).

Smugglers bringing drugs from Colombia across the Caribbean to the Florida coast carry extra fuel for the 700-mile round trip in boats that are thirty to forty-five feet long, capable of carrying 3,000 pounds of cocaine, and travel at nearly seventy miles per hour. In response, in 1999 the Coast Guard modernized a tactic that had last been employed during Prohibition: Helicopter-borne sharpshooters disable the engines of speedboats that refuse to follow the orders of Coast Guard vessels (Stout 1999).

INTERNAL REVENUE SERVICE (IRS)

The mission of the IRS is to encourage and achieve the highest possible degree of voluntary compliance with tax laws and regulations. When such compliance is not forthcoming or not feasible, as in the case of drug traffickers, the Criminal Investigation Division receives the case. Agents examine bank records, canceled checks, brokerage accounts, property transactions, and purchases, compiling a financial biography of the subject's lifestyle to prove that proper taxes have not been paid. As a result of the excesses that were revealed in the wake of the Watergate scandal, Congress enacted the Tax Reform Act of 1976, which reduced the law enforcement role of the IRS and made it difficult for law enforcement agencies (other than the IRS) to gain access to income tax returns. Amendments in 1982 reduced the requirements and permits the IRS to better cooperate with the efforts of other federal law enforcement agencies that are investigating drug traffickers.

U.S. MARSHALS SERVICE

The U.S. Marshals Service is the oldest federal law enforcement agency, dating back to 1789. During the period of westward expansion, the U.S. marshal played a significant role in the "Wild West." Today, marshals provide security for federal court facilities, transport federal prisoners, serve civil writs issued by federal courts, and investigate and apprehend certain federal fugitives. Marshals are responsible for seizing, managing, and disposing of forfeited properties and assets from major drug cases. The Marshals Service's most important task relative to drug trafficking is its responsibility for administering the Witness Protection Program.

Because of the potentially undesirable consequences for a witness who testifies in a drug trafficking case, efforts have been made to protect such witnesses from retribution. The *Witness Protection Program* was authorized by the Organized Crime Control Act of 1970:

> The Attorney General of the United States is authorized to rent, purchase, modify, or re-model protected housing facilities and to otherwise offer to provide for the health, safety, and welfare of witnesses and persons intended to be called as Government witnesses, and the families of witnesses and persons intended to be called as Government witnesses in legal proceedings instituted against any person alleged to have participated in an organized criminal activity whenever in his judgment testimony from, or a willingness to testify by, such a witness would place his life or person, or the life or person of a member of his family or household, in jeopardy. Any person availing himself of such an offer by the Attorney General to use such facilities may continue to use such facilities for as long as the Attorney General determines the jeopardy to his life or person continues.

The program was given over to the Marshals Service to administer. There was logic behind this arrangement (Permanent Subcommittee on Investigations 1981b: 54): "Law enforcement officers wanted the protecting and relocating agency to be in the criminal justice system but to be as far removed as possible from both investigating agents and prosecution. That way the Government could more readily counter the charge that cooperating witnesses were being paid or otherwise unjustifiably compensated in return for their testimony."

BUREAU OF ALCOHOL, TOBACCO, FIREARMS AND EXPLOSIVES (ATF)

The Bureau of Alcohol, Tobacco, Firearms and Explosives dates back to 1791, when a tax was placed on alcoholic spirits. It eventually evolved into the Prohibition Bureau, which, with the repeal of Prohibition, became known as the Alcohol Tax Unit. The bureau was given jurisdiction over federal firearms statutes in 1942 and over arson and explosives in 1970. ATF agents often encounter drug traffickers during their investigation of firearms and explosives violations. They have been particularly active in efforts against outlaw motorcycle clubs, which typically traffic in firearms and drugs.

THE MILITARY

The most controversial federal agency involved in drug law enforcement is the Department of Defense (DOD). In 1878 congressional Democrats enacted the Posse

Comitatus (literally "force of the county") Act to stop Republican presidents from using the army to further Reconstruction in the states of the erstwhile Confederacy. The act (as amended) makes it a crime to use the military as a domestic police force: "Whoever, except in cases and under circumstances expressly authorized by the Constitution or Act of Congress willfully uses any part of the Army or Air Force as a posse comitatus or otherwise to execute the laws shall be fined not more than $10,000 or imprisoned not more than two years or both" (18 USCA Section 1385). In 1956 Congress added the Air Force to the Posse Comitatus Act, while the Navy and Marines promulgated administrative restrictions.

Until 1981 DOD limited its involvement in drug law enforcement to lending equipment and training civilian enforcement personnel in the use of military equipment. In that year, as part of a new "War on Drugs," Congress amended the Posse Comitatus Act, authorizing a greater level of military involvement in civilian drug law enforcement, particularly the tracking of suspect ships and planes and the use of military pilots and naval ships to transport civilian enforcement personnel. As a result of this legislation, DOD provided surveillance and support services, using aircraft to search for smugglers and Navy ships to tow or escort vessels seized by the Coast Guard to the nearest U.S. port. The legislation authorized the military services to share information collected during routine military operations with law enforcement officials and to make facilities and equipment available to law enforcement officials.

Further amendments to the 1981 legislation led to the use of military equipment and personnel in efforts against cocaine traffickers in Bolivia, Colombia, and Peru. These amendments permit the use of such personnel and equipment if the

CORRUPTING THE NAVY ...

In 1996 twenty-one U.S. sailors were arrested in Italy by the Naval Criminal Investigative Service, whose agents were able to infiltrate a Nigerian drug ring that paid the defendants to carry bags of cocaine and heroin across European borders. A lieutenant commander was the highest-ranking member of the group ("Navy Holds 21 Sailors in Italy in Smuggling Case" 1996).

... and the Marines ...
In 2002, at the Camp Lejeune Marine base in North Carolina, the Naval Criminal Investigation Service arrested eighty-four marines and sailors and ninety-nine civilians and seized $1.4 million in drugs. The suspects were accused of trafficking in ecstasy, cocaine, LSD, and methamphetamine (Kilian and Mendell 2002). The eighty-four military personnel were convicted and sentenced to prison terms ranging from three to nineteen years ("84 Military Personnel Convicted...." 2002).

... and the Air National Guard
In 2006 a captain and a master sergeant in the Air National Guard pled guilty to importing 290,000 ecstasy pills from Germany on a military aircraft. When the captain was arrested, $700,000 in cash was found in his Bronx apartment (Preston 2005).

Secretary of State or the Secretary of Defense and the Attorney General jointly determine that an emergency exists in that the scope of specific criminal activity poses a serious threat to the interests of the United States. Combined operations involving U.S. Army Special Forces, DEA agents, U.S. Border Patrol officers, and Bolivian police and military officers have been successful in destroying hundreds of coca paste laboratories in the coca-growing Champare region of Bolivia. In 1999 a U.S. spy plane crashed in an isolated region of Colombia, killing five U.S. soldiers and revealing their controversial role in antidrug efforts. As FARC guerrillas continue to finance their revolution through trafficking in cocaine and heroin, the U.S. struggle against drug trafficking and the fight against Marxist insurgencies have become blurred.

The 1981 statute and subsequent amendments maintain the prohibition against the involvement of U.S. military personnel in arrest and seizure activities. This prohibition was based on the fear that further DOD involvement in drug law enforcement could:

- compromise U.S. security by exposing military personnel to the potentially corrupting environment of drug trafficking (Sciolino and Engelberg 1988);
- impair the strategic role of the military; and
- present a threat to civil liberties.

Despite this fear, in 1988 legislation was overwhelmingly approved to dramatically expand the role of the military and allow the arrest of civilians under certain circumstances.

The U.S. Department of State uses former military pilots to fly helicopter gunships, transport planes, and crop dusters used by U.S. and foreign drug agents in countries where U.S. military operations are barred. Early in 1990 and again in 2006, National Guardsmen, who as members of state militias are not governed by the Posse Comitatus Act, were deployed to search for drugs and illegal immigrants along the border with Mexico and at ports of entry. U.S. military officials have traditionally opposed the involvement of the armed forces in law enforcement.

POSTAL INSPECTION SERVICE

The Postal Inspection Service, among its several responsibilities, investigates the use of the U.S. mail to transport drugs.

STRIKE FORCES AND TASK FORCES

To overcome the inefficient competitive efforts and turf-protecting proclivities of enforcement agencies, since 1966 the federal government has utilized task forces in response to organized crime. That year, the Department of Justice established the "Buffalo Project" in upstate New York, bringing together personnel from a number of federal enforcement agencies. The success of the project led to the establishment of a strike force in every city that is known to have organized crime (Mafia) groups. In his 1982 "War on Drugs" speech, President Ronald Reagan announced the creation of regional Organized Crime Drug Enforcement Task Forces, and by the end of 1983 twelve such task forces were located in such core cities as

New York, Los Angeles, and Detroit. In 1984 a thirteenth, the Florida/Caribbean task force, was added.

"The Task Force Program relies largely on the Continuing Criminal Enterprise statutory provision and the Racketeer Influenced and Corrupt Organizations (RICO) statutes. The conviction rate in cases reaching disposition is approximately 95 percent. State and local officers participate in nearly one-half of the Task Force investigations" (President's Commission on Organized Crime 1985: 319). Local enforcement officers may be sworn in as special U.S. marshals, allowing them to enforce federal statutes and to cross jurisdictional boundaries that typically inhibit local enforcement agencies. Guidelines for the Organized Crime Drug Enforcement Task Force specify that a case is appropriate for Task Force adoption if it:

- appears to involve major drug trafficking figures;
- requires the resources and expertise of another agency because of possible violations other than those involving narcotics;
- has serious investigative ramifications extending to other geographical jurisdictions; and/or
- requires the assistance of an assistant U.S. attorney during the early stages of an investigation.

INTERPOL

The International Police Organization, known by its telegraphic designation INTERPOL, assists law enforcement agencies with investigative activities that transcend international boundaries. INTERPOL meant very little to the U.S. law enforcement community until 1968, when Iran announced that it was going to end its ban on opium production. At the same time there appeared to be an epidemic of drug use in the United States. A U.S. INTERPOL National Central Bureau (NCB) was quickly activated in Washington, D.C.

As of 2009, there were 187 INTERPOL members; a country becomes a member merely by announcing its intention to join. In each member country there is an NCB that acts as a point of contact and coordination with the General Secretariat, which is headquartered in Lyon, France. The General Secretariat has a staff of around 500 people, some of whom are law enforcement officers, from more than eighty different countries. INTERPOL is under the day-to-day direction of a secretary general; it is a coordinating body and has no investigators or law enforcement agents of its own.

The United States National Central Bureau (USNCB) is the entity through which the United States functions as an INTERPOL member and serves as a point of contact for U.S. federal, state, local, and tribal law enforcement for the international exchange of information. Responsibility for the management of the USNCB is shared by the the Department of Justice and the Department of Homeland Security. Senior management positions in the USNCB rotate between the two departments every 3 years.

The U.S. NCB receives about 12,000 requests for assistance from federal, state, and local law enforcement agencies each year. These are checked and coded by technical staff and entered into the INTERPOL Case Tracking System (ICTS), a computer-controlled index of people, organizations, and other crime information items. The ICTS conducts automatic searches of new entries, retrieving those that correlate with international crime. The requests are forwarded to senior staff members, who serve as INTERPOL case investigators. These are usually veteran agents from a federal agency whose experience includes work with foreign police forces. Each investigator is on loan from his or her principal agency.

Requests for investigative assistance include a whole range of criminal activity—murder, drug violations, illicit firearms traffic—and often involve locating fugitives for arrest and extradition. The bureau also receives investigative requests for criminal histories, license checks, and other ID verifications (Fooner 1985). The Financial and Economic Crime Unit at INTERPOL headquarters facilitates the exchange of information about offshore banking and money-laundering schemes. Monitoring this type of activity can sometimes lead to identifying suspects involved in drug trafficking who had previously escaped detection.

STREET-LEVEL LAW ENFORCEMENT

Efficient street-level enforcement, argues Mark Moore (1977), is a strategy worth pursuing, even if there is *displacement*—sellers moving to new locations and becoming more cautious. Jonathan Caulkins (1992) agrees that even when there is complete displacement, benefits to society accrue. Because street-level enforcement makes sellers more cautious and therefore more difficult to find, the buyer is forced to spend more time searching for a connection and less time searching for money (criminal opportunity) or actually using drugs. Under such conditions many users might be motivated to seek treatment, although there is often a shortage of available treatment programs. New users in particular will have difficulty "scoring." If this situation becomes widespread, profits from drug wholesaling will drop as if there were a drop in consumer demand.

Lorraine Mazerolle, David Sachs, and Sacha Rombout (2007) divide street-level enforcement into three generic categories:

Community-wide policing approaches involve a wide array of diverse interventions that rely on the police forging partnerships (e.g., with other police agencies, community entities, regulators, city inspectors) and implementing strategies that are targeted at relatively large areas, such as across entire communities or neighborhoods, to address drug markets. This category involves partnerships with local councils, community groups, regulators, inspectors, business groups, and other crime-control agencies such as probation and parole departments. It uses such tactics as knock-and-talks, drug patrols, local police storefronts, drug hot lines, foot and bike patrols, neighborhood revitalization, block watch, neighborhood watch, and arrest referral to drug treatment.

Geographically focused policing approaches typically involve the use of problem-solving models and/or partnerships with third parties, such as regulators, service providers, and government agencies. This category uses problem-oriented policing: partnering with nonpolice agencies in response to identified community problems such as abandoned vehicles and buildings; cooperative efforts with regulatory agencies using civil remedies; and crime control through environmental design (surveillance cameras, additional street lighting, and reconfiguring traffic patterns.)

Hot-spots policing uses traditional approaches to drug law enforcement that are unfocused and rely principally on police-only activities that are geographically focused on drug hot spots. This category uses crackdowns—abrupt escalations in law enforcement activities intended to increase the perceived or actual threat of apprehension—undercover "buy and bust" operations, and intensive/saturation patrol. "[I]t is unlikely that buy-bust operations aimed specifically at street dealers will significantly disrupt the distribution system. Sellers operating at this level are easily replaced and while buy-bust operations may result in large number of arrests, convictions rarely lead to lengthy sentences" (Hough 2005: 25).

In Lynn, Massachusetts, a drug task force made up of six state police officers and a city detective was deployed to decrease the flagrant selling of heroin in the city's High Rock area. Open drug dealing poses special threats. "Some neighborhood residents, particularly children, may become users; and … the behavior of buyers and sellers will be disruptive or worse. In poor neighborhoods, the opportunity for quick money offered by the illicit market may compete with entry-level licit jobs and divert labor-market entrants from legitimate careers. When the drug sold is heroin, residents are likely to be bothered by users 'nodding' in doorways and heroin-using prostitutes soliciting" (Kleiman 1988: 10). The goal was achieved, and drugs were harder to purchase in the area. This led to an increase in the number of people seeking treatment for drug abuse. A significant reduction in street crime was also reported for the area (Kleiman 1988). The drying up of immediate sources of heroin can potentially reduce experimentation, although long-term users will merely be inconvenienced. The time and energy required to establish new sources, however, might otherwise be spent on drug use and criminality. If treatment is available, the crackdown might serve as an incentive for entering a treatment program.

In New York City a 1984 street-level enforcement effort known as Operation Pressure Point (OPP) was designed to improve the quality of life and reduce drug-related crime in an area of the city's Lower East Side. Drug trafficking in the area had become so blatant that residents and their political representatives demanded police action. OPP instituted aggressive patrolling by uniformed officers, cleared abandoned buildings and parks of drug users, and sent out detectives to make "buy-and-bust" arrests. The risk of arrest increased dramatically for both buyers and sellers, and most of them abandoned the area and others resorted to low-profile trafficking. OPP followed up these activities with programs designed to strengthen the community and increase cooperation with and support for the police. The program achieved its goals and neighborhood residents reported being very satisfied. Similar operations in other parts of New York City, however, have not been as successful (Zimmer 1990). Mike Hough (2005) cautions that this type of drug enforcement can have the unintended consequence of increased revenue for remaining dealers, who face less competition.

Drug Market Intervention Initiative   A relatively new approach to the problem of street-level drug markets is the brainchild of David Kennedy of New York City's John Jay College of Criminal Justice. Instead of the traditional "hot spot" approach, after a particular drug market is identified, violent dealers are arrested while nonviolent ones are brought to a "call-in" where they face a roomful of law enforcement officers, social service providers, community figures, ex-offenders, and their own parents, relatives, and neighbors: "The drug dealers are told that (1) they are valuable to the community, and (2) the dealing must stop. They are offered social services. They are informed that local law enforcement has worked up cases them, but that these cases will be 'banked' (temporarily suspended). Then they are given an ultimatum: If you continue to deal, the banked cases against you will be activated" (Kennedy 2009: 13).

The "call-in" provides a forum at which everyone affected can say to the dealers: "Enough!" Dealers are told by relatives that while they are loved, their behavior is unacceptable. This is backed by law enforcement officers who explain: "We want to take a chance on you. We have done the investigation, and we have cases against you ready to go. You could be in jail today, but we do not want to ruin your life. We have listened to the community. We do not want to lock you up, but we are not asking. This is not a negotiation. If you start dealing again, we will sign the warrant, and you will go to jail."

Preliminary research into this approach, which is being used in more than 25 cities, has revealed a remarkable level of success in shutting down drug markets. Referred to as "Ceasefire," Kennedy's approach is also used to reduce gang violence (Seabrook 2009).

Street-level enforcement is expensive and, if it is to be more than briefly effective, must be combined with sufficient prison space to accommodate the increase in population. In an attempt to stem the 1985 crack epidemic in New York City, police initiated a street-level crackdown with impressive results: Crack arrests and jailings reached record levels; felony drug arrests went up 21 percent the first year and 70 percent the next. Total jail sentences for drug felonies increased by 60 percent in 1987. Nevertheless, the street price of crack dropped steadily. And in response to the stepped-up police activity, crack dealers began recruiting thousands of young addicts to make street sales, overwhelming a number of city neighborhoods as well as the city's overextended police force. Placing unusually large resources in one area also raises the possibility that the problem will be displaced into areas where law enforcement efforts are less concentrated. Furthermore, the reduction of crime in Lynn, Massachusetts, discussed earlier was short-lived, and a similar crackdown in Lawrence, Massachusetts, actually resulted in

DRUG-SNIFFING DOGS

In 2000 the Supreme Court ruled (*Indianapolis v. Edmond, et al.* 531 U.S. 32, 2000) that in the absence of any suspicion, police checkpoints that briefly detain drivers and use drug-sniffing dogs violate the Fourth Amendment. Checkpoints are permitted, however, for discovering and taking intoxicated drivers off the road because that protects public safety. In 2005, however, the Court ruled (*Illinois v. Caballes*, 543 U.S. 405) that during a routine traffic stop police may use a trained dog to sniff the car for drugs. Such drug-sniffing activity had already been ruled permissible for luggage at airports.

an increase in crime, particularly burglary and robbery (A. Barnett 1988; Bouza 1990: 47).

In New York, in response to intensive police efforts against street dealing, sellers moved away from high-profile and vulnerable street sales to mobile delivery services using pagers and/or cellular telephones. As a result of the extra costs associated with this type of drug trafficking, in terms of both the equipment and time spent making deliveries, sellers began dealing only with those who could purchase large amounts at once, with the attendant risk of increased consumption. These buyers may become dealers to their friends. This strategy can also move drug selling from urban areas into the suburbs, making drugs more accessible to those who were reluctant to purchase in neighborhoods with which they are not familiar.

Street-level enforcement efforts bring with them the specter of corruption and related abuses: "Bribery, perjured testimony, faked evidence and abused rights in the past have accompanied street-level narcotics enforcement. Indeed, it was partly to avoid such abuses that many police departments began concentrating on higher-level traffickers and restricted drug efforts to special units" (Moore and Kleiman 1989: 8). These special units have brought problems of their own. New York provides an example. In 1971, to centralize drugs, vice, and organized crime enforcement and to prevent corruption through stricter supervision, the city established the Organized Crime Bureau. Early in 1992 the police department's chief of inspectional services submitted a confidential report citing recent cases in which the bureau's narcotic officers were accused of lying to strengthen cases and to obtain search warrants; there were no accusations of corruption. The report noted: "Of all units in the department, the greatest integrity hazards and vulnerability exist in narcotics" (Raab 1992).

ISSUES IN DRUG LAW ENFORCEMENT

Besides those discussed at the beginning of this chapter, several perplexing issues complicate drug law enforcement. The first involves measuring success: How can we determine whether drug law enforcement in general or specific activities in particular are successful? What criteria can provide a standard for measuring success? The number of people arrested, convicted, or imprisoned? The amount of drugs seized? The level of purity or price of the product sold on the streets? The number of people admitted to hospital emergency rooms for drug overdoses? The number of people seeking admission to drug treatment programs? In practice, we use all of these, with often confusing results. For example, increased arrests and drug seizures have often been accompanied by declining prices and greater levels of purity. A 1983 report by the U.S. Comptroller General points out that while enhanced federal resources increased the amount of illegal drugs seized, purity at the retail level increased while prices fell. The Comptroller General also revealed that some drug seizures are counted several times by different agencies that are eager to claim credit and improve their statistics. Sometimes there is triple-counting: The Coast Guard typically turns its interdicted drugs over to Customs, while the seizure may be the result of intelligence information developed by DEA, and all three agencies include the amount in their totals.

Successful law enforcement efforts, at least in theory, should reduce the available supply of drugs while driving up the price and reducing purity. When the level of purity dips below some hypothetical level but the price remains high, the abuser will supposedly no longer find it worth his or her while to make a purchase. The abuser will either switch to a more readily available chemical—perhaps alcohol— or abandon drug use completely. In fact, successful law enforcement efforts may cause a switch from a less dangerous substance—for example, marijuana—to a more dangerous substance, such as heroin, a situation that apparently occurred when Operation Intercept at the Mexican border effectively choked off supplies of marijuana in 1969. "There was an upsurge in heroin use among urban, white, middle-class high school students shortly after Operation Intercept" (Zinberg and Robertson 1972: 210). More recent successful campaigns against marijuana might be causing an increase in the use of alcohol, particularly among adolescents. Increases in law enforcement do not necessarily translate into reductions in supply; a widely heralded (by politicians) 1986 $1.7 billion federal antidrug law resulted in an increase in drug seizures and arrests with no discernible impact on supply (J. Johnson 1987). Successful interdiction might reduce the amount of heroin and cocaine entering the United States, but if demand remains unchanged, underground chemists will be inspired to greater creativity. Indeed, experienced cocaine users cannot tell the difference between cocaine and synthetic substances that mimic cocaine, and heroin addicts often prefer the synthetic opiate fentanyl to the diluted heroin typically available on the streets.

The structure of the drug market, as was noted in Chapter 11, makes it the last refuge of laissez-faire capitalism. The Drug Enforcement Administration (2003: 7) argues that the "element of risk created by strong enforcement policies raises the price of drugs, and therefore lowers the demand." But how does law enforcement affect the price and use of illegal drugs? Mark Kleiman (1985: 69) states that the key to analyzing this question "is the response of drug purchasers to increasing drug prices." If there is a reduction in supply and a corresponding increase in price, will the amount of drug consumption remain unchanged? Is demand relatively inelastic to price? If demand is relatively elastic, consumption will decrease as price goes up. This will cause a decrease in the profits of drug traffickers. If demand is inelastic, however, drug law enforcement may actually increase the profits of traffickers, since those who elude arrest and prosecution will reap higher prices. With respect to heroin, Kleiman notes, consumption is likely to decrease in the long run as addicts, unable to keep up with the increase in price, enter drug treatment or find alternative drugs. The issue with respect to cocaine is more difficult. Cocaine has typically been relatively expensive, although the introduction of crack altered the market. Nevertheless, Kleiman argues, an increase in price as a result of law enforcement efforts is likely to increase the profits of cocaine traffickers; it is a market that is relatively impervious to price.

At the domestic distribution level, successful law enforcement efforts whittle down the number of people involved in drug trafficking. This may leave a void at certain levels of distribution that, in a seller's market, will simply attract new entrepreneurs. Furthermore, the better-organized groups resist and survive law enforcement efforts. Thus, the level of law enforcement vigor and ability determines whether or not certain groups will come to dominate the drug trade and bring a concomitant increase in profits by virtue of oligopolistic (scarcity of sellers) market circumstances. On the other hand, reduced law enforcement allows more groups to remain in business, with a corresponding reduction in profits, resulting from a more competitive market. Under such conditions, organizations that are equipped with resources for violence may be tempted to use force to reduce competition.

Another issue is the argument that the substantial investment in drug law enforcement increases criminality—drug abusers committing crimes to support habits—and diverts resources that could be better utilized to deal with more serious criminality. Police, prosecutors, and judges are occupied with drug law enforcement, and U.S. jails, prisons, and probation and parole systems are overcrowded. Our drug enforcement agents are exposed to great danger, both from a most violent class of criminals and from being around the drugs themselves.

Our "war" on drugs is really a fight against socioeconomic dynamics that are reputed to be unconquerable: the profit motive and the law of supply and demand.

In the next chapter, we will examine our policy for responding to drug abuse.

SUMMARY

- The most important precipitating factor in drug use is the degree of access.
- Constitutional restraints, jurisdictional limitations, and corruption severely constrain law enforcement in general and drug law enforcement in particular.
- Effective crime control requires a high level of efficiency; the system must be able to investigate, apprehend, prosecute, and convict a large proportion of criminal offenders.
- The *due process model* stresses the need for protecting individual freedoms.
- The exclusionary rule is the court's way of enforcing the Fourth Amendment.
- On the federal level, a host of executive branch agencies, ranging from the military to the Federal Bureau of Investigation, are responsible for combating drug trafficking.
- The easy availability of large sums of money and the clandestine nature of the business make drug law enforcement vulnerable to corruption.
- *Proactive law enforcement* requires officers or agents to seek out indications of criminal behavior, always a necessity when the criminal violation includes victim participation.
- Corruption is often intertwined with the problem of informants.

- The legal foundation for federal drug law violations is Title II of the Comprehensive Drug Abuse Prevention and Control Act of 1970, as amended (usually referred to as the Controlled Substances Act [CSA]).
- The CSA has a set of criteria for placing a substance in one of five schedules.
- People who are involved in the illegal drug business can be prosecuted for manufacture, importation, distribution, possession, or sale; conspiracy to manufacture, import, distribute, possess, or sell; or failure to pay the required income taxes on illegal income.
- Conspiracy is an agreement between two or more individuals to commit a criminal act; the agreement becomes the *corpus* (body) of the crime.
- In 1927 the Supreme Court denied the claim of self-incrimination as an excuse for failure to file income tax on illegally gained earnings.
- A person is guilty of money laundering if he or she, knowing that the property involved represents the proceeds of an illegal activity, attempts to conceal or disguise the nature, location, source, ownership, or control of the proceeds or attempts to avoid a transaction-reporting requirement.

- Federal and state statutes provide for the forfeiture of property that is used in criminal activity or secured with the fruits of criminal activity.
- There are two types of forfeiture proceedings: criminal and civil. Civil forfeiture does not require criminal charges; the level of evidence required is considerably less than that in a criminal action, and the considerable due process guarantees accruing to a criminal defendant are not applicable in a civil action.
- Forfeiture laws engender considerable controversy because of sharing provisions and concern over the seizure of property owned by innocent third parties.
- On the federal level, drug law enforcement is the responsibility of a confusing number of agencies in several departments (Justice, Treasury, Homeland Security, Defense) whose responsibilities often overlap.
- The basic approach to DEA is the *buy and bust* or the *controlled buy*. Typically, a drug agent is introduced to a seller by an informant. The agent arranges to buy a relatively small amount of drugs and then attempts to move farther up the organizational ladder by increasing the amount purchased.
- ICE is not bound by Fourth Amendment protections that typically restrain domestic law enforcement. Agents do not need probable cause or warrants to engage in search and seizure at ports of entry; certain degrees of suspicion will suffice.
- The U.S. Marshals Service is responsible for the Witness Protection Program.
- Military involvement in drug law enforcement is limited by the Posse Comitatus Act and fears of corruption.
- INTERPOL assists law enforcement agencies with investigative activities that transcend international boundaries.
- Efficient street-level enforcement, argues Mark Moore (1977), is a strategy worth pursuing even if there is *displacement*.
- There are three categories of street-level drug enforcement: community-wide, geographically-focused, and hot-spot policing.
- The drug market intervention initiative is a relatively new approach to the problem of street-level drug markets.
- Street-level drug enforcement has many unintended consequences.
- Measuring the success of drug enforcement is uncertain.
- Successful law enforcement efforts may cause a switch from a less dangerous substance to a more dangerous substance and increase the profits of some drug traffickers.

Review Questions

1. Why is heroin use higher in the inner city than in the suburbs?
2. What is the conflict between crime control and due process?
3. What is essential for the crime control model to achieve its goals?
4. How does the due process model interfere with the ability of crime control to achieve its goals?
5. What does the due process model stress?
6. What is the connection between the Fourth Amendment and the exclusionary rule?
7. Why is drug enforcement more difficult than dealing with conventional crimes such as burglary and robbery?
8. How does the U.S. form of government affect drug law enforcement?
9. Why is it necessary to use proactive law enforcement in responding to drug trafficking?
10. Why is proactive law enforcement more likely to be associated with corruption?
11. What is the connection between the use of informants and corruption in drug law enforcement?

12. How does Title II of the Comprehensive Drug Abuse Prevention and Control Act of 1970 distinguish a Schedule I drug from a Schedule II drug?

13. What are the elements of a conspiracy?

14. What are the advantages of using conspiracy statutes?

15. What is the difference between actual and constructive possession of dangerous drugs?

16. What did the Supreme Court rule with respect to the claim of self-incrimination as an excuse for failure to file income tax on illegally gained earnings?

17. What does the government have to prove in order to convict someone of money laundering?

18. What are the four types of items subject to forfeiture?

19. How does civil forfeiture differ from criminal forfeiture?

20. What are the controversies surrounding seizure and forfeiture?

21. What is the basic law enforcement approach of the Drug Enforcement Administration?

22. What is the extraordinary power enjoyed by Immigration and Customs Enforcement (ICE)?

23. What are limitations of the military in drug law enforcement?

24. What is the purpose of establishing strike or task forces for drug law enforcement?

25. What is the role of INTERPOL in drug law enforcement?

26. What are some of the unintended negative consequences of successful drug law enforcement?

27. Why is street-level drug enforcement worth pursuing even when it results in displacement?

28. What are the three categories of street-level drug enforcement?

29. What are the advantages and disadvantages of concentrating drug law enforcement efforts at the street level?

30. What are the features of the "drug market intervention initiative"?

31. What are the unintended consequences street-level drug law enforcement?

32. Why is it difficult to measure success in drug law enforcement?

According the World Health Organization, the United States leads the world in rates of experimenting with marijuana and cocaine despite strict drug laws.

Maggie Fox (2008: Reuters).

CHAPTER **13** | # DRUG USE AND ABUSE POLICY I: THE U.S. MODEL

ZHANG YAN/Xinhua/Landov

Out of the history explored in Chapter 2 developed two basic models for responding to the use of dangerous substances. The first is a *disease model*: The abuser is "helpless" and "blameless," analogous to the cancer or coronary patient. This model defines substance abuse as a disease to be prevented or treated, just like any other public health problem. The second is a *moral-legal model* that defines alcohol and other psychoactive drugs as either legal or illegal and attempts to control availability through penalties. The moral-legal model utilizes three methods to control potentially dangerous drugs in the United States:

- *Regulation.* Certain substances that may be harmful to their consumers can be sold with only minimal restrictions. These substances are heavily taxed, providing government with an important source of revenue. Alcoholic beverages and tobacco products are subjected to disproportionate taxation, and their sale is restricted to people above a certain age. Special licenses are usually required for the manufacture, distribution, and sale of regulated substances.
- *Medical auspices.* The use of certain potentially harmful substances is permitted under medical supervision. The medical profession is given control over legal access to specific substances that have medical uses because when the substances are taken under the direction of a physician, their value outweighs their danger (J. Kaplan 1983a). In this category are barbiturates, amphetamines, certain opiates (morphine and codeine), and heroin substitutes such as methadone.
- *Criminalization.* Statutory limitations make the manufacture or possession of certain dangerous substances a crime and empower specific public officials to enforce these statutes. Certain other substances are permitted under medical auspices, but punishment is specified for individuals who possess these substances outside of accepted medical practice. Thus, heroin has no permissible use in the United States—an absolute prohibition—while other psychoactive substances, such as morphine and Seconal (secobarbital sodium), are permissible for medical use but are illegal under any other circumstances.

The official response to a particular substance—regulation or law enforcement—determines the manner in which the user of that substance will be treated. Thus, the alcoholic is typically viewed according to the disease model, while the user of illegal drugs has the criminal label attached. From the Civil War to the 1920s, the U.S. response to dangerous drugs moved from permissiveness to one of rigid law enforcement—from the public health model to the moral-legal model. The practical effect of this change was "to define the addict as a criminal offender" (Schur 1965: 130), leading to the creation of a vast black market in which drug entrepreneurs quickly filled the void left by the withdrawal of lawful sources: "In the 1920s this country had a large number of addicts, but they were not regarded as criminals by the law; in general, they did not commit crimes and conducted their lives much the same way as the nonaddict population did. Clinics and private physicians were free to prescribe maintenance doses. It was the outlawing of the addictive drug that gave rise to an illegal market controlled by organized crime; and it is the exorbitant cost of the outlawed drug that has driven addicts into criminal activity to support their habit" (National Council on Crime and Delinquency 1974: 4).

Drug policy in the United States has been guided by "commonly shared simplifications"—in particular, the belief that "drug problems are largely attributable to morally compromised or pathological individuals who were not properly inculcated in childhood with normal American values such as self-control and respect for the law. These individuals must be disciplined and punished by authorities to deter them from involvement (for pleasure or profit) with inherently dangerous, addicting drugs" (Gerstein and Harwood 1990: 41).

Drug use, notes Gresham Sykes, "became defined as a fundamental affront, part of a larger pattern challenging society with an alternative view of a meaningful life." The wrongdoing of the drug user was "moved into the category of the most serious offense—treason—where the individual forsakes his society for an enemy allegiance" (Sykes 1967: 77). A "clearer case of misapplication of the criminal sanction," writes Herbert Packer (1968: 333), "would be difficult to imagine." Post–Harrison Act efforts against certain psychoactive chemicals were based on their potential to harm users. Policy has now come full circle, and it is the user who is the target of vigorous enforcement efforts: "We must focus responsibility and sanctions on illegal drug users" (White House Conference for a Drug Free America 1988: 9).

INCONGRUITIES BETWEEN FACTS AND POLICIES

Before examining the current policy, we need to return to the first chapter and recall some incongruities. Of the most widely used psychoactive drugs, heroin and cocaine (except for limited topical use) are banned; barbiturates, tranquilizers, and amphetamines are restricted; and alcohol, caffeine, and nicotine products are freely available. These inconsistencies make any response to the problem of substance abuse very difficult. How do you tell the progeny of cigarette-smoking, coffee- and alcohol-drinking, sedative-using parents that drugs should not be used for recreational purposes? "Someone who smokes tobacco is a *smoker*, but someone who smokes marijuana is a *drug user*" (Whiteacre 2005: 9). Therefore, "a major step toward developing sounder policy with respect to drugs would be to use that label for alcohol and nicotine (as the scientific literature already does), and to make an augmented Office of Drug Control Policy responsible for coordinating federal policy toward alcohol and nicotine as part of the overall national drug control strategy" (Reuter and Caulkins 1995: 1061).

To what extent does knowledge actually affect drug policy? Although nicotine and alcohol are clearly dangerous psychoactive chemicals—*drugs*—semantic fiction portrays them otherwise. Statutory vocabulary and social folklore have established the fiction that alcohol and nicotine are not really drugs at all (National Commission on Marijuana and Drug Abuse 1973). Furthermore, as the National Commission on Marijuana and Drug Abuse points out, to do otherwise would be inconsistent with our stated policy goal of eliminating drug abuse—an admission that we can never eliminate the problem. Joseph Gusfield (1975) suggests that we distinguish between *scientific* knowledge—the body of facts and theories related to drug use—and *political* knowledge, which concerns public attitudes toward drug use, including scientific knowledge. Norman Zinberg (1984: 200) states that in the field of drug use, the truth will not necessarily set one free. The scientific truth, he notes, is that not all psychoactive drug use is misuse; but because this concept contravenes formal social policy, those who present this message run the risk that "their work will be interpreted as condoning use."

Our response to easily abused substances is not based on the degree of danger inherent in their use. Indeed, measured on any dimension, alcohol is a more serious drug of abuse than marijuana, though this is not reflected in the U.S. legal system. And while marijuana smokers are subject to arrest and prosecution, people who smoke tobacco are left free of restraint save for the inconvenience posed by smoking-related cancer and emphysema. In 2006, it was determined that for some unknown reason, smoking marijuana does not increase the risk of lung cancer (Bloomberg News 2006). Furthermore, many dangerous substances, such as amphetamines, barbiturates, and a variety of sedatives, were actively promoted for use in dealing with anxiety, stress, obesity, or insomnia. Famous abusers of these substances, such as Marilyn Monroe and Elvis Presley, who have been commemorated on our postage stamps, are representative of a large abusing population that is not subjected to arrest and imprisonment. The pushers of these substances—the drug companies and their willing partners in the medical profession—are not arrested or prosecuted.

That some drugs are outlawed while others are legally and widely available is better understood in terms other than those of science or medicine: in terms of the tobacco industry, the alcoholic-beverage industry, the drug-manufacturing industry, and the dietary supplements industry. The 1994 Dietary Supplement Health and Education Act allowed manufacturers to market an array of products, many of them ephedra-based, with claims that these products will boost energy levels, improve your sex drive and performance, help you to lose weight, and cause you to gain muscle. "The law states that you don't have to prove natural supplements are safe or effective before you market them; the government has to prove that they aren't after the fact" (O'Keefe and Quinn 2005: 88). Ironically, one of the major purveyors of these products is a multimillionaire and convicted drug dealer. In 2004, supplements containing ephedra were banned by the Food and Drug Administration.

In addition to political contributions, the purveyors of legal psychoactive substances are able to protect their interests through advertising and employment of media specialists. In fact, the public's knowledge of and response to the "drug problem" is mediated through newspapers and television. Frightening news stories create pressure for more vigorous drug enforcement, which increases drug-fighting budgets, which yield more arrests (L. G. Hunt 1977). The resulting statistics are then viewed as proof of a growing drug problem. "Evidence," in fact, "has little bearing on the kind of moral beliefs many people hold: that the use of psychoactive drugs is wrong, and their sale more wrong; or that government intrusion into the drug use decision is wrong, and harsh sanctions against possession are also wrong" (Caulkins, Reuter, Iguchi, and Chiesa 2005: 2).

The "volume of attention generated when the national press converges on a story, like drugs, virtually demands a political response. In their haste, these [politicians'] reactions may not always be carefully considered" (Merriam 1989: 31). Convergence occurs when media sources discover an issue and respond to each other "in a cycle of peaking coverage, before largely dismissing the issues" (Reese and Danielian 1989: 30n). In 1989, for example, President George H. W. Bush made a major television address during which he "declared war" on drugs. For the next week, network news averaged four stories each evening on drugs, and an opinion poll indicated that 64 percent of the public viewed drugs as America's most important problem. A year later, that figure had fallen to 10 percent as new problems received presidential and media attention (Oreskes 1990).

On November 17, 1985, crack cocaine was mentioned for the first time in the major media, in the *New York Times*. In less than eleven months, every major news source had stories about crack—more than 1,000 of them—capped by specials on CBS and NBC (Inciardi, Surratt, Chitwood, and McCoy 1996). This set off an ill-conceived and, some argue, racist legislative response. Under federal law, for purposes of punishment, a given amount of crack is equivalent to 100 times that amount of powdered cocaine. In the twenty-first century it would be difficult to find mention of crack in the major media.

With these incongruities serving as a backdrop, let us critically examine U.S. drug policy on reducing the supply of drugs and reducing demand for them.

SUPPLY REDUCTION THROUGH THE CRIMINAL SANCTION

In theory, in a free-market economy, reducing the supply of a product will drive up the price and thus reduce demand and consumption. But in the drug economy, an increase in price might just raise the revenue for traffickers because there is no significant decrease in consumption. The evidence is that there is not a single documented instance in which one or a succession of high-level drug cases coincided with a substantial reduction in consumption in a city (Kleiman 1989). John DiNardo (1993: 63) failed to find "any significant effects of law enforcement on the price of cocaine faced by users" (See also Caulkins, Crawford, and Reuter 1993.). Thus, enforcement to reduce the supply of drugs might simply eliminate the less-organized criminal distributors, resulting in an increase in the profits of criminal organizations that are strong enough and ruthless enough to survive (Kleiman 1989).

An alternative strategy, focusing on lower-level dealers, presents two additional problems: the political problem of going after small wrongdoers while largely ignoring the big ones (Kleiman 1985) and the practical problem of the cost of arresting, prosecuting, and imprisoning large numbers of people. However, this approach was the mainstay of the so-called (Governor) Rockefeller Laws in New York during the 1970s. As a result, the time needed to dispose of drug cases nearly doubled between 1973 and 1976, and by mid-1976 the system was approaching collapse. Research indicates that the use of drugs increased during this time, as did drug-related crimes such as burglary, robbery, and theft (Joint Committee on New York Drug Law Evaluation 1977).

In 1987 the strategy recommended by Kleiman caused New York City to establish special courts to rapidly dispose of felony drug cases through plea bargaining because the regular criminal courts were being flooded with arrests of street-level drug dealers. Because of the volume, it was taking six to twelve months to dispose of a case, which created a chaotically overcrowded situation on Riker's Island, the city jail for people awaiting trial (Raab 1987). In the decade from 1981 to 1991, the average daily jail population in New York City increased 170 percent. The *New York*

Times concluded that "New York City's war on drugs has resulted in so many arrests that there are simply not enough prosecutors, judges, Legal Aid lawyers or probation officers to give adequate attention to each of the thousands of cases, let alone courtrooms to try the suspects in or jail cells to hold the convicts" ("Drug Arrests and the Courts' Pleas for Help" 1989: E6).

Other states followed New York's lead, with similar results. The number of people who were convicted of drug felonies in state courts increased almost 70 percent in the two-year period from 1988 to 1990. In Cook County (Chicago), Illinois, the chief criminal court judge stated that drug cases were overwhelming the county's court system (O'Connor 1990). In the federal courts, the number of drug arrests so backed up the system that judges were unable to attend to civil cases, increasing delays despite a drop in the number of civil filings. By 2004 federal prisons were operating at 140 percent of capacity, and state prisons were operating at 115 percent of capacity (*Prisoners in 2004*, 2005). Jails throughout the United States are already being operated severely over capacity, and any strategy that causes a significant increase in the inmate population could be disastrous.

The General Accounting Office (1991) found that overcrowded jails and prisons, the result of increased drug arrests and prosecutions, resulted in more offenders being placed in the probation and parole systems, which, in turn, has generally decreased the level of supervision of probationers and parolees as a result of excessive caseloads. It also led to emergency prison release programs and an increase in plea bargaining—signs of a system spinning its wheels. In 1996 and again in 1998, Arizona voters took matters into their own hands and enacted propositions that mandate treatment instead of imprisonment for drug offenders (Egan 1999b).

A RACIST DRUG WAR?

A study conducted by *USA Today* revealed that African Americans are four times as likely as whites to be arrested on drug charges, even though both groups use drugs at about the same rate; and African Americans are more likely to be imprisoned for drug charges than are non-Hispanic whites (Meddis 1993). A more recent study found that black men are nearly 12 times as likely to be imprisoned for drug convictions as adult white men (Eckholm 2008b).

Cocaine in the form of crack is most likely to be used and sold by African Americans, while powdered cocaine is often used and sold by whites. Under federal statutes, "It takes one hundred times the amount of powder cocaine to equal the same sentence as crack cocaine" (*Illicit Drug Policies*, 2002: 134). A cocaine dealer would have to sell $75,000 worth of the drug in powdered form to get the same mandatory five-year federal sentence that a crack dealer would receive for selling $750 worth. And "crack is the only drug that carries a mandatory prison term for possession, whether or not the intent is to distribute" (C. Jones 1995: 9).

The war on drugs also exacerbates racial disparities related to health and well-being in minority communities: Federal law prohibits ex-prison inmates from receiving any federal benefits for five years if their conviction was for drug possession or drug trafficking; they are also barred from Temporary Assistance to Needy Families and food stamps; and they become ineligible for one year after conviction, two years after a second conviction, and indefinitely after a third for federal education

In Black and White

Blacks in New York are seven times more likely to be arrested than Whites for marijuana possession and no more serious crime; Latinos are four times more likely (Dwyer 2009).

assistance ("How the War on Drugs Influences the Health and Well-Being of Minority Communities" 2001).

In 1991 the Minnesota Supreme Court found unconstitutional and discriminatory against African Americans a state law providing twenty years in prison for crack possession but only five years for possession of powdered cocaine. In 1988, of the people charged with crack possession in Minnesota, 96.6 percent were black, while those charged with possessing cocaine hydrochloride were 79.6 percent white (*State v. Russell* 477 N.W.2d 886).

Would Changing the Penalties Help?

What about a policy of incarceration for only the most serious criminal offenders, such as robbers, among the drug-abusing population? Unfortunately, this is not feasible. "Existing criminal justice practices would fail to detect most persons who actually are robber-dealers" (B. Johnson, Lipton, and Wish 1986a: 187). In their study, Bruce Johnson and his colleagues found that none of the high-rate addict-robbers were ever arrested for robbery. In fact, "less than 1 percent of self-reported crimes by cocaine-heroin abusers result in an arrest; the higher the crime rate, the lower the possibility of arrest per thousand crimes" (1986b: 4).

In a report to the Ford Foundation, Patricia Wald and Peter Hutt (1972: 37) recommended reducing penalties to a fine or abolishing them completely for those possessing drugs for personal use: "If this were done, drug users—but not drug traffickers—could then be handled on a public health and social-welfare basis.... Law-enforcement efforts would, and in our opinion should, continue, but they would be directed at illegal distribution. And illegal drugs would remain subject to confiscation wherever found." In Switzerland and the Netherlands (as will be discussed in Chapter 14), there has been an unofficial policy of tolerating small-time drug sellers and their customers, as long as they do not become public nuisances. At best, states Kleiman (1989: xviii), law enforcement efforts can prevent the "effective decriminalization" of drugs, the point at which trafficking "is so open and flagrant that demand increases because the apparent social disapproval is reduced."

Increasing penalties for drug trafficking seems an unrealistic strategy because sentences for trafficking are already high—forty years for a second offense—and because capital punishment (for drug transaction–related murders) has now become part of the federal effort against drugs. Severe penalties encourage in traffickers the mindset that they have little or nothing to lose by using violence in their attempts to avoid arrest and prosecution.

CHINESE DRUG TREATMENT

In response to an increasing problem with drugs, in 2008 China authorized the police to test those suspected of drug use. A positive finding results in two-to-five years in a "rehabilitation center" where residents receive substandard meals, beatings, and are allowed to shower once a month. Some centers are actually business ventures run by the police using residents as forced labor. The drug offense status of residents is noted on their national identification cards making it virtually impossible to secure post-release employment (Jacobs 2010).

China and some third-world countries execute drug dealers, but the impact of this policy is questionable. For example, although Malaysia imposes the death penalty for anyone who is found trafficking in heroin or marijuana, the substances are readily available even to foreigners traveling through that country. The People's Republic of China routinely executes drug traffickers who are found in possession of a pound or more of heroin; in 1994 more than 466 were killed in Yunnan Province alone (Tyler 1995). Every June 26th, on United Nations "International Day Against Drug Abuse," China executes drug traffickers: twenty in 2009. On one day in 1999, China executed at least seventy-one people as part of its antidrug campaign (Associated Press 1999b). Despite the executions, drug trafficking continues to thrive, particularly in Yunnan and Guangdong provinces in southern China, and the country has become a transshipment point for Golden Triangle and Golden Crescent heroin (French 2004). Draconian attempts to deal with opium and heroin abuse in Iran have proven unsuccessful. While traffickers are routinely hung, in contrast to the United States, Iran uses a harm reduction approach to heroin addicts: needle distribution, methadone maintenance, and an extensive network of government-supported treatment programs (Fathi 2008).

IMPROVING DRUG LAW ENFORCEMENT

Increasing the government's drug law enforcement ability—for example, by improving enforcement resources and centralizing the operational command structure of the executive branch—can bring its own dangers. These are stressed by Edward Jay Epstein (1977: 8), who argues that President Richard Nixon used the "war on heroin" to "set up a series of special units which, it was hoped, would conduct clandestine surveillance of both government officials and newsmen during his first administration." On the basis of an executive order, the Office of Drug Abuse Law Enforcement (ODALE) was established with agents requisitioned from the Bureau of Narcotics and Dangerous Drugs, Customs, the Internal Revenue Service, and the Bureau of Alcohol, Tobacco and Firearms. This strike force was funded by the executive branch (Law Enforcement Assistance Administration), thus bypassing the need for congressional approval. A special-action office was set up in the White House to work with ODALE; it included Watergate participants Egil Krogh, G. Gordon Liddy, and E. Howard Hunt (McWilliams 1992). Had the Watergate scandal not intervened, Epstein (1977: 252) argues, the drug superagency proposed by the administration "might have served as the strong investigative arm for domestic surveillance that President Nixon had long quested after." As was noted in Chapter 12, inefficient law enforcement is the price we pay for our constitutional form of government.

In theory, if at some point the price of drugs rises significantly and/or the amount available for consumption falls off considerably, abusers will seek treatment or give up their drug-using habits. Indeed, research has found that the amount of heroin use is related to price (Bach and Lantos 1999). But experience reveals that when drug abusers are unable to secure their preferred substance, they frequently switch to other substances that could be even more harmful. We have already seen that heroin and cocaine have analogs that are produced in the United States. As long as demand remains strong, successful interdiction will encourage the production of domestic inorganic (agonists) depressants and stimulants. However, with respect to heroin, increases in cost lead to more addicts seeking methadone treatment (Bach and Lantos 1999).

Richard Cowan (1986: 27) argues that federal efforts against cocaine led to the development of crack: "*The iron law of drug prohibition is that the more intense the law enforcement, the more potent the drug will become.* The latest stage of this cycle has brought us the crack epidemic." Free-market conditions provide an incentive for traffickers to improve the attractiveness of their product. Jeffrey Fagan and Ko-Lin Chin (1991) point out that crack was the subject of an ingenious production and marketing strategy (see also Witkin 1991). A glut of cocaine forced prices down in 1983, but even lower prices did not keep up with production: "At this point, a new product was introduced which offered the chance to expand the market in ways never before possible: crack, packaged in small quantities and selling for $5 and sometimes even less—a fraction of the usual minimum for powder— allowed dealers to attract an entirely new class of consumers. Once it took hold this change was very swift and very sweeping" (T. Williams 1989: 7).

Crack never became a mainstream drug and by 1990 the epidemic had peaked, but heroin use increased. Because heroin had lost its dominant market position to cocaine, heroin purity levels increased substantially, drawing in new users who can snort or smoke the substance instead of injecting it intravenously in the more traditional manner. But the "crack scare" of the 1980s left in its wake new laws and greater use of imprisonment, adding significantly to an already overcrowded prison system (Egan 1999a). As David Musto notes: "History shows that excessive use of a drug at one time does not mean that such a high rate will continue indefinitely; the drug may fade in esteem and usage, even to the vanishing point. Reasonable drug policies must take into account the long-term perspective. We should avoid hastily surrendering to defeat at a time of extensive use nor declare victory after a long and deep decline in drug use" (1998: 58).

Reducing the market for illegal drugs can have unpleasant outcomes because "competition will increase among dealers, perhaps violently. In addition, because selling cocaine has been the primary source of earnings for poor adult males dependent on cocaine, these individuals may turn to other forms of crime to finance their continued consumption, relying more on muggings, burglary, and shoplifting for income, just as heroin users/dealers have done for many years" (RAND Drug Policy Research Center 1992: Internet).

Insofar as drug abuse is caused by societal deficiencies in education, housing, and other quality-of-life-variables, the more we expend on law enforcement, the less we have available to deal with these social ills, which continue to foster greater drug abuse. Not only are we spinning our wheels in the mud, but the faster we go, the deeper the hole becomes. Furthermore, "when criminals are the most successful people in a community, the effect on that community's natural order is devastating. The authority of parents, schools, religious leaders, and (legal) businesspeople is undermined, and violent criminals become role models" (Boaz 1990: 3).

Steven Wisotsky (1987) argues that our law enforcement efforts have failed and will continue to do so. He certainly has the lessons of history and classical economics on his side. "Stop talking about winning drug wars," states Trebach (1987: 383). "In the broadest sense, there is no way to win because we cannot make the drugs or their abusers go away. They will always be with us. We have never run a successful drug war and never will." Nevertheless, more extreme measures are being considered, such as shooting down aircraft that are suspected of transporting drugs. Legislation to accomplish this was introduced in the Senate in 1989 but ran into a storm of opposition from pilots who feared possible mistakes. The Mexican government reports, however, that they have shot down aircraft that are suspected of carrying drugs when the planes refuse to respond to warnings. Peru has done the same, and this has cost the lives of innocent travelers on commercial airliners.

In 2005, Iowa, like nearly thirty other states, enacted a law restricting the sale of cold medicines whose pseudoephedrine can be used to make methamphetamine. As a result, during the first seven months there was a significant decrease in home-cooked methamphetamine; lab seizures went from 120 to 20, and whereas $2.8 million dollars had been spent in 2004 on treating people at the University of Iowa Burn Center whose skin had been scorched by toxic chemicals, there was a virtual absence of victims in 2005. But the bad news: more methamphetamine-dependent patients were under treatment and the seizure of the drug increased as the home-made powdered version was replaced by the more powerful Mexican crystal methamphetamine (Zernike 2006a).

In 1995, the DEA seized large quantities of precursor chemicals that disrupted the methamphetamine supply chain. As a result, the price of methamphetamine in California tripled while purity decreased from 90 to 20 percent. Within four months, however, the price returned to its original level and within eighteen months so did purity (RAND Drug Policy Research Center 2009). We must recognize a troubling aspect of drug trafficking: It operates according to the powerful forces of free-market capitalism. It is paradoxical that politicians who argue that capitalism defeated Communism in Eastern Europe also talk of defeating the business of drugs. They fail to acknowledge that these same forces operate in the drug trade—and that government cannot compete effectively with the free market. As Cali Cartel leader Gilberto Rodriguez Orejuela pointed out: "Economics has a natural law: Supply is determined by the demand. When cocaine stops being consumed, when there's no demand for it … that will be the end of the business" (Moody 1991: 36).

SUPPLY REDUCTION BY CONTROLLING DRUGS AT THEIR SOURCE

The current U.S. policy of attempting to control drugs at their source has had unintended consequences: displacement of production and human rights violations.

THE "BALLOON EFFECT" AND HUMAN RIGHTS VIOLATIONS

The successful effort to force Turkey to curtail its production of opium in the 1970s resulted in a concomitant rise in opium production in Mexico and Southeast Asia. Mexican antidrug efforts have led to a rise in poppy production in neighboring Guatemala, whose government is ill equipped to respond to the problem (Sheppard 1990). Crackdowns in Colombia succeeded in displacing the problem into other countries: Ecuador and Brazil now have cocaine-processing laboratories; Argentina, Uruguay, and Chile have emerged as major money-laundering centers; and drug-related corruption scandals have hit Argentina and Venezuela, which, along with Chile, serve as major cocaine transshipment centers.

Bolivia reduced coca cultivation by more than half, but at a price: According to the Human Rights Watch, pressure on the government of Bolivia to deal with coca cultivation led to widespread trampling of civil rights and physical abuse of citizenry (Vivanco 1995). Using similar methods, Peru has also cut coca cultivation by more than half. "Peru leads the world in documented cases of disappearances of people taken prisoner by security forces" (Brooke 1991: 6). In response to declines in these source countries, the Colombian wholesalers who bought Bolivian and Peruvian coca increased domestic production (Krauss 1999a).

Coca production in Colombia has more than doubled from 1995 to 2000; the country is now the source of more than 500 tons of cocaine a year, 90 percent of the world's supply. The breakup of the powerful Colombian Medellín and Cali drug cartels spurred coca cultivation in more remote regions of the country and resulted in alliances between new drug gangs and leftist guerillas. Added to this volatile mix are right-wing paramilitary forces who, like their left-wing enemies, are supported by the drug trade. "Feeling relatively safe on their native soil, native coca-growing syndicates have invested heavily in developing more potent strains, some of which can be harvested in as little as 60 days" (Rohter 2000b). Colombian syndicates have achieved extraordinary levels of efficiency in extracting cocaine from their coca crops. High-yielding varieties of coca are being grown in parts of Colombia. Likewise, Colombian laboratory operators became more efficient in processing coca leaf into cocaine base than they had been previously (U.S. Department of State 2000).

After Congress approved a Clinton administration allocation of $1.6 billion to help the Colombian government fight drug traffickers, an editorial in the *Chicago Tribune* (March 12, 2000: 18) argued: "This policy threatens to entangle the U.S. in a decade-old foreign guerilla war while doing nothing to dampen the engine that ultimately drives narcotrafficking: America's roughly $50 billion a year appetite for illicit drugs." The editorial, after noting the involvement of the Colombian army and its right-wing paramilitary allies in massive human rights violations, stated: "It would be repugnant to funnel American aid to a foreign army with such bloody credentials." And "the latest chapter in America's long war on drugs—a six-year, $4.7 billion effort to slash Colombia's coca crop—has left the price, quality and availability of cocaine on American streets virtually unchanged" (Forero 2006).[1]

---

[1]For an historical analysis of the U.S. relationship with Colombia and the "war on drugs," see Crandall (2008).

There is one immutable rule in the drug business: As long as demand remains strong, successful efforts against it at the source level will shift cultivation to a new location. This is what happened in Peru in 2002. In addition to shifting much production to Colombia, a tightened supply has tempted poor farmers in virgin areas to begin cultivating coca (Forero 2002). With financial support from the United States, Colombia is using more than eighty planes to spray herbicide on more than 1 million acres of coca and poppy plants. (Five planes have been shot down.) Nevertheless, cocaine prices in the United States remained stable, and purity improved (Brinkley 2005). An editorial in the *New York Times* concluded, "Forcible crop eradication moves the problem around, enriches traffickers by raising the price of their holdings, and creates turmoil in rural areas" (May 27, 2005: 22).

Economic Importance of the Coca Crop in Peru and Bolivia

In Peru and Bolivia inhabitants of coca-growing areas are strongly opposed to U.S.-inspired efforts to eradicate their most important cash crop, and both countries face Marxist insurgencies that are particularly strong in these remote regions. Unfortunately, in addition to providing a livelihood for impoverished Bolivian farmers, cocaine brings into Bolivia more money than all legal exports combined.

In Peru's Upper Huallaga Valley, which extends for 200 miles along the Huallaga River, an estimated 60,000 families depend on coca as a cash crop for their survival. Large-scale eradication, notes Alan Riding (1988: 6), could "provoke a social convulsion, forcing thousands of families to leave the area" and creating deep resentment that Marxist guerrillas exploit. And "coca is Peru's largest export, earning more than one billion dollars a year. As many as one million of the country's twenty-one million citizens are involved in the trade" (Massing 1990: 26). Under President Alberto K. Fujimori,[2] Peruvian armed forces shot down planes suspected of transporting drugs—about twenty-five aircraft have met this fate. This strategy succeeded in breaking the "air bridge," and when the price of coca leaf dropped more than 60 percent in 1995, farmers began abandoning the crop. With U.S. help, Peruvian officials began teaching farmers to raise coffee instead of coca. By 1999, however, traffickers had reopened some air routes and had replaced others with river, road, and sea channels, once again making coca profitable, and the crop rebounded (Krauss 1999b). Government anti-coca efforts in Bolivia left thousands of Indian farmers without a source of income and helped to generate violent protests that left several soldiers, police officers, and farmers dead (Associated Press 2000b).

"Not only is coca fully integrated into Andean society but it is also an integral part of the region's ecosystem—a stubborn and dismaying biological fact impeding those who would like to make it disappear. As a cultivated plant, coca is nearly ideal. It has few predators and pests.... The plant will grow in soils too poor and

---

[2] In 2009 Fujimori, who was president of Peru from 1990 until escaping to Japan in 2000 during a corruption scandal, was sentenced in Peru to 25 years imprisonment for his role in massacres by military forces during a period of guerrilla attacks in the early 1990s.

on slopes too steep to support other crops, will live for forty years or more, and will tolerate many harvests a year" (Weil 1995: 72).

Wisotsky (1987: 57) states that "in both Peru and Bolivia, the failure of coca control is not a temporary aberration but a function of culture, tradition, and the weakness and poverty of underdevelopment. These basic social conditions render effective enforcement against coca impossible. Widespread corruption in the enforcement agencies, the judiciary, and elsewhere in government is endemic. Indeed, the central governments do not necessarily control major portions of the coca-growing countryside, where the traffickers rule like feudal lords." Participation in the illicit cocaine economy, writes Edmundo Morales (1986: 157), "is inevitable. Not only is the natives' traditional way of life intertwined with coca, but their best cash crop is the underground economy for which no substitute has yet been provided."

In 1999, thirteen people, including jurists, doctors, artists, religious leaders, and three former Latin American presidents—Belisario Betancur of Colombia, Violeta Chamorro of Nicaragua, and Nobel Peace Prize Laureate Oscar Arias of Costa Rica—signed a letter stating that the U.S.-led military-style war on drugs has failed and should be changed to focus more on ending the demand for drugs and drug money. "The escalation of a militarized drug war in Colombia and elsewhere in the Americas threatens regional stability, undermines efforts towards demilitarization and democracy and has put U.S. arms and money into the hands of corrupt officials and military ... units involved in human rights abuses. It is time to admit that after two decades, the U.S. war on drugs—both in Latin America and in the United States—is a failure" (Jelinek 1999: Internet).

In 2002 President George W. Bush met with the Bolivian president at the White House. The Bolivian leader promised President Bush that he would press ahead in his campaign to eradicate the coca crop but said he needed more U.S. assistance to help ease the impact on farmers. Otherwise, Gonzalo Sánchez de Lozado stated, "I may be back here in a year seeking political asylum." Mr. Bush laughed and wished him luck. The following year, Mr. Lozado was living in exile in the United States after having been ousted by a popular uprising (Rohter 2003). In 2005, Bolivia elected a leader of *cocalero* movement, coca growers opposed to U.S. eradication efforts.

CROP ERADICATION OR SUBSTITUTION

Crop substitution programs have been part of our effort to control drugs at their source but have met with only limited success. As long as demand remains high, the price offered for poppy or coca will be many times that received for conventional crops. There are other problems: In 1991 the leader of a Peruvian coca growers association who had agreed to a crop substitution program was murdered, reputedly by corrupt government officials who earned money from the cocaine business (Strong 1992).

Attempts to eradicate the crop by cutting or burning result in healthier and more bountiful growth, and uprooting coca plants causes the soil to become unproductive for as long as eight to ten years (Morales 1989). An eradication program in the Upper Huallaga Valley was established with U.S. funding in 1982, but about forty of its workers were eventually murdered. The United States subsequently suspended the program (Massing 1990).

An alternative is the use of aerial herbicides that are either sprayed or dropped as pellets and that melt into the soil when it rains. The United States has been conducting research on a variety of environmentally safe herbicides. The most successful herbicides, however, kill many species of plants, including crop plants, and remain in the soil, affecting future plantings. Environmentalists have raised objections to the use of herbicides, and the companies that produce them are concerned about potential liability and fear that their employees in South America could become targets of retribution by trafficking organizations (Riding 1988). Furthermore, Lee McIntosh (1988: 26) has found that a "single genetic mutation can give rise to complete resistance in a similar herbicide. This implies it may be necessary continually to spray different classes of herbicides in the future." The human and political dangers inherent in this approach to drug control should serve as a restraining influence.

Successful eradication and interdiction efforts can affect both availability and price. However, because of the pattern of price markups in the cocaine business, efforts to eradicate crops or supply routes that increase the cost of the coca leaf tenfold add only 5 percent to the retail consumer price, and doubling seizures from importers increases consumer cost by only 10 percent (Passell 1990). "It costs cocaine refiners only 30 cents to purchase the coca leaf needed to produce a gram of cocaine, which sells for about $150 in the United States. Even if the price of the leaves needed for that gram of the finished produce doubled, it would be negligible. And if retail prices don't rise, then consumption in the United States will not decline" (Reuter 2000: 29).

If all of the coca that the producing countries of Latin America have publicly committed themselves to eradicate were actually eradicated, the effect in the United States would be minimal. It is likely that African, Middle Eastern, and Southeast Asian areas would be able to cultivate enough to meet consumer demand in coca indefinitely (as they have done with opium). It should be noted that coca leaf has been grown commercially in Indonesia, Malaysia, Nigeria, Sri Lanka, and Taiwan. Indeed, the crop that is grown in Java and Taiwan contains more than twice the cocaine of the varieties grown in Latin America (Karch 1998). Epstein (1988: 25) points out that "the entire cocaine market in the United States can be supplied for a year by a single cargo plane." Furthermore, as was noted in previous chapters, curtailing importation without affecting demand provides an incentive for greater domestic efforts: the production of synthetic analogs for cocaine and heroin and stronger strains of marijuana.

The highly inventive marijuana horticulturists of California are using a new, faster-growing, highly potent strain that matures in three months (older strains require four months). Cultivation of this new strain has been discovered in the national forests of Northern California. (Growing marijuana on federal lands was made a felony in 1987, punishable by a prison term of up to ten years.) Indoor cultivation of very powerful strains of marijuana has blossomed in the western Canadian province of British Columbia (B.C.). Although Canadian law is similar to the United States with respect to marijuana, attitudes in British Columbia reflect a different mindset; even wholesale growers receive light penalties, often just fines. Much of the B.C. crop is smuggled into the United States, where it fetches premium prices owing to the high level of its THC.

Aerial marijuana searches continue to locate illegal farms, but as this photo shows, clever cultivators have gone underground. Innovations can include diesel-powered lights, ventilation systems, and hydroponic technology.

In response to law enforcement efforts against imported marijuana, some innovative growers have established elaborate underground farms equipped with diesel-powered lights and ventilation systems. Their use of hydroponic technology—growing plants in water to which nutrients have been added—has helped to make marijuana the number one cash crop in the United States.

DRUG ENFORCEMENT AND FOREIGN POLICY

There is evidence that U.S. efforts against drug trafficking are often secondary to foreign policy considerations. The Anti-Drug Abuse Act of 1986, for example, requires the president to certify to Congress that producer and transshipment nations have made adequate progress in attacking drug production and trafficking. Without certification a country can lose aid, loans, and trade preferences. Elaine Sciolino (1988) reports that the law has numerous loopholes that have allowed several nations to be certified despite their failure to cooperate in the war against drugs. In 1990, of the twenty-four major drug-producing and drug-transiting countries, only four—Afghanistan, Myanmar, Iran, and Syria—were denied certification. At the other extreme, the United States turned to the military in Guatemala, a major producer of opium and a leading transshipment point for Colombian cocaine, to take the lead in efforts against trafficking. The Guatemalan military has been responsible for human rights abuses that have plagued the country (Gruson 1990).

For many years the United States tolerated the drug-trafficking activities of Central American ally General Manuel Noriega. When his politics took on a decidedly anti-U.S. tone, in 1988 the general was indicted and apprehended, following the "Operation Just Cause" invasion of Panama by the U.S. military. (For a discussion of Noriega, his relationship with the United States, and drug dealing, see Dinges [1990] and Kempe [1990].) According to Thomas A. Constantine, retired director of the DEA, the Clinton administration was more concerned about trade and other economic issues in its relationship with Mexico than with corruption and drug trafficking (Golden 1999).

Peter Andreas and his colleagues (1991–1992: 107) noted, "after more than a decade of U.S. efforts to reduce the cocaine supply, more cocaine is produced in more places than ever before. Curiously, the U.S. response to failure has been to escalate rather than reevaluate." Andreas and colleagues state: "The logic of escalation in the drug war is in fact strikingly similar to the arguments advanced when U.S. counterinsurgency strategies, undercut by ineffective and uncommitted governments and security forces, were failing in Vietnam: 'We've just begun to fight.' 'We're turning the corner.'" Andreas and his colleagues argued, "since failure can so easily be used to justify further escalation, how do we know whether we are really turning the corner or simply running around in a vicious circle?"

Demand Reduction by Criminal Prosecution for Fetal Liability The prosecution of drug-using pregnant women for fetal endangerment, delivering drugs to a minor, or child abuse dates back to the end of the 1980s, when drug abuse was high in the political consciousness of elected officials and an increasing number of "drug babies" were being reported. It is estimated that about 350,000 infants annually are exposed prenatally to some form of illegal drug (Nolan 1990). Prosecution is sometimes used to coerce women into drug treatment, although drug treatment programs might not be readily available and those that are might be unwilling or unable to provide for pregnant clients.

The first woman convicted for delivering a controlled substance to her fetus, in Florida in 1990, was sentenced to a year in a drug treatment program and fourteen years probation; her conviction was upheld by a state appeals court the following year but was later voided by the Florida Supreme Court (Lewin 1991, 1992). In 1991 the Michigan Court of Appeals ruled that a woman who took crack hours before giving birth could not be charged with delivering cocaine to her son through the umbilical cord. In response to the ruling, the Muskegon County prosecutor defended his decision to charge the woman: "This is a major health care crisis and we must use whatever means we can to reach a solution" (Wilkerson 1991: 13). Health care officials who supported the woman expressed fear that prosecuting drug-using pregnant women will drive them away from prenatal care. Courts have dismissed similar cases in Maryland, New Mexico, North Carolina, Ohio, and Florida (Lewin 1991; Nossiter 2008). In Alabama, however, women have been successfully prosecuted and imprisoned for using drugs while pregnant (Nossiter 2008).

Despite considerable concern about the high rate of cocaine use among pregnant women, studies have failed to find a homogeneous pattern of fetal effects, and there is little consensus on the adverse effects of the drug (Finnegan et al. 1994). In a study of birth outcomes and developmental growth of children who were exposed to drugs *in utero*, infants varied in their birth outcomes, a majority evidencing no significant problems (Cosden, Peerson, and Elliott 1997). An overwhelming majority of women who use cocaine also ingest other drugs, including nicotine, alcohol, marijuana, and opiates, and many suffer from sexual and physical abuse (Finnegan 1993). It is difficult to separate the effects of cocaine from other potential hazards to the fetus. "Women who use cocaine during pregnancy also engage in other behaviors, such as alcohol and tobacco use, that are risk factors for poor pregnancy outcome. In addition, they often live in circumstances that, in themselves, create an environment that fosters poor developmental outcome. To understand the unique or independent effects of cocaine exposure during pregnancy, it is critical to separate factors that correlate with prenatal cocaine use and with the outcome, both at birth and during the postpartum period" (Richardson and Day 1999: 234).

Although we know that women who abuse heroin during pregnancy frequently give birth to infants suffering from neonatal abstinence syndrome—the newborn suffers withdrawal symptoms—we do not know whether there are long-range effects that are directly attributable to the use of drugs; as with cocaine, it is difficult, if not impossible, to separate the effects of drugs from those of poverty and poor prenatal care. Furthermore, the fetus can be endangered by any number of maternal behaviors that are not related to illegal drug use, for example, "too much or too little exercise, an inadequate or harmful diet, or use of cigarettes, alcohol [6,000 to 8,000 born annually with fetal alcohol syndrome], and other [lawful] drugs" (Nolan 1990: 13–14). Other risks include the general environment and specific workplace exposures.

Research has revealed that infants (about 750,000 per year) who are exposed to a high level of cigarette smoke (one pack or more per day) *in utero* suffer from decreased birth weight, head circumference, and body length; there are also increased rates of spontaneous abortions and bleeding during pregnancy. An estimated 5,600 infants die each year as a result of smoking by their pregnant mothers. A study in 1994 revealed that mothers who smoke as few as ten cigarettes a day cause their children under age five years to test positive for cancer-causing compounds (Hilts 1994). A study of 4,400 youngsters ages six to sixteen by Kimberly Yoltan of the Cincinnati Children's Medical Center revealed that, after controlling for factors such as race, income, and parents' educational levels, children exposed to high-levels of second-hand smoke have significantly lower test scores in reading, math, and problem-solving than those with the low-levels of exposure as determined by the presence of a nicotine byproduct (cotinine) in their blood (Szabo 2005).

And what of the liability of the father who is using illegal drugs or alcohol or tobacco? Recent research suggests that psychoactive substances are hazardous to spermatozoa (Finnegan 1993), and secondhand smoke has been proven to seriously harm the health of children. Furthermore, what of the societal responsibility to provide adequate prenatal care for all pregnant women? The nonmedical use of controlled substances is only one facet of a significantly greater social problem that will not be resolved by a simplistic recourse to criminal law.

An equally pressing problem is the cost of providing for infants of drug-abusing mothers: Foster care for one child ranges from $15,000 to $20,000 a year. New York City has responded to this problem by permitting drug-abusing mothers to keep their children at home under the intensive supervision of a social worker (Treaster 1991). A study in Illinois found that although white and African American

NO LOANS FOR STUDENT DRUG OFFENDERS

U.S. Department of Education regulations, based on a law enacted in 1998, bar students who have been convicted of drug offenses from receiving federal college tuition aid. A first possession conviction bars aid for a year, and a sales conviction will bar aid for two years. Students who are convicted for a second time of possessing drugs will lose aid for two years; those who are convicted a third time lose it permanently. A student who has been convicted twice of selling drugs will lose aid permanently. Some students will be able to retain eligibility by completing a drug rehabilitation program. Students must report any drug convictions on federal financial aid forms, including Pell grants and student loans. Students who lie will have to return any aid that they have received and may be prosecuted (McQueen 1999).

women show similar rates of illegal drug use during pregnancy, "the black women are more likely to be reported to authorities" (Olen 1991: Sec. 3: 14). Illinois is one of a number of states where medical personnel are required to report suspected prenatal drug use to authorities. But there are few places in the state to care for babies born with drugs in their bloodstream, so the babies are usually sent home with their mother with some type of outpatient help and monitoring (Poe and Searcey 1996).

DEMAND REDUCTION BY EXPANDING TREATMENT

"Drug treatment … is demonstratively effective in reducing crime. Law enforcement helps 'divert' users into treatment and makes the treatment system work more efficiently by giving treatment providers needed leverage over the clients they serve. Treatment programs narrow the problem for law enforcement by shrinking the market for illegal drugs" (Office of National Drug Control Policy 2002b: 4). While the core of the U.S. response to drug use has centered on enforcement, expanding the availability of treatment might be more productive for reducing demand. There is almost universal agreement that without reduced demand, antidrug efforts will remain ineffective.

The cost-effectiveness of treatment versus law enforcement is emphasized by Peter Rydell and Susan Everingham (1994: xv). They argue that $246 million would have to be spent on domestic law enforcement to achieve the same reduction in drug use that could be achieved by spending $34 million on treatment. And no assumption is made about the long-range effect of treatment—abstinence—on the individual abuser: "The cost advantage is so large that even if the after-treatment effect is ignored, treatment is still more cost-effective than law enforcement."

It is the possession of controlled substances that constitutes a crime; an addict is not a criminal by virtue of his or her addiction. In *Robinson v. California* (370 U.S. 660, 1962), the Supreme Court ruled that individuals cannot be prosecuted for "being under the influence" or for "internal possession" of illegal drugs. In that same decision the Court upheld the civil commitment of drug addicts for purposes of treatment (similar to commitment of the mentally ill): "A state might determine that the general health and welfare require that the victims of these and other human afflictions might be dealt with by compulsory treatment, involving quarantine, confinement, or sequestration."

Some twenty-seven states have made such a determination and enacted legislation that permits the civil commitment of drug addicts (J. Kaplan 1983b). However, only California and New York made extensive use of such statutes; and in both states budgetary and political issues led to the programs being discontinued (New York in 974) or eviscerated (California). Bruce Johnson and his colleagues (1986a, 1986b) argue in favor of mandatory treatment because almost all-objective evidence suggests that drug treatment has an important impact on the criminality of heroin and cocaine abusers. The cost of such a policy, they note, would be prohibitive unless treatment were on an outpatient basis, a method that they support. Because most heroin and cocaine abusers have come into contact with the criminal justice system, all criminal defendants should be subjected to drug tests, which, if positive, should require mandatory treatment.

Johnson and colleagues argue that drug treatment should be part of any sentence for convicted drug abusers and that postrelease treatment should be a condition of probation or parole supervision, with careful monitoring of urine for at least one year (see, for example, Benedict, Huff-Corzine, and Corzine 1998). This writer supervised heroin addicts on parole in New York for several years, and their careful monitoring by a parole officer does ensure a high rate of abstinence, at least during the period of supervision. But in any number of jurisdictions, supervision in the community is superficial, with caseloads so large that clients cannot be monitored adequately. Offenders who violate the conditions of supervision by using drugs often go unnoticed or unpunished, remaining at liberty until they are arrested again for another drug offense (Abadinsky 2009).

MEASURING THE RESULTS OF POLICY CHANGES

A major problem with instituting any changes in policy is measurement of results. Increases or decreases in the number of people using illegal substances cannot be measured with any accuracy, and the statistics that are often presented as "data" are usually meaningless. There are no direct measures of the incidence or prevalence of drug use in the general population; all estimates are inferences derived from various data gathered by law enforcement or medical sources.

Patrick Biernacki (1986: 189) points out that "it cannot be determined with any degree of certainty what effect U.S. drug policy has had on the addict population. What we do know is that the indicators used to estimate the size of the addict population at any one time are unreliable. For example, if the number of hospital emergency room admissions for heroin overdoses drops, does this indicate the effectiveness of police control methods, or the successful treatment of addicts? Or can the drop in admissions be attributed to a change in drug preference? Or to an increase in the number of natural recoveries?" Natural recovery, or the abandoning of heroin use, was discovered among returning Vietnam veterans on a relatively large scale (Robins 1973, 1974; Robins, Helzer, Hesselbrock, and Wish 1980).[3]

---

[3]On natural recovery among middle-class addicts, see Granfield and Cloud (1996).

To the extent to which we have been able to measure the effect of U.S. drug policy, the results, though not necessarily the claims, have been unclear. The question remains: Should we be punishing people "simply because we are unable to demonstrate the benefits of *not* punishing them"? (Husak and de Marneffe 2005: 26). The next chapter will explore issues relating to that question.

Now that we have examined drug policy in the United States, in the next chapter we will consider more radical changes, some of which are being or have been adopted by European countries.

SUMMARY

- The *disease model* views the abuser as "helpless" and "blameless" and defines substance abuse as a disease to be prevented or treated.
- The *moral-legal model* defines psychoactive drugs as either legal or illegal and attempts to control availability through penalties. The moral-legal model utilizes three methods: regulation, medical auspices, and criminalization.
- The official response to a particular substance—regulation or law enforcement—determines the manner in which the user of that substance will be treated. Thus, the alcoholic is typically viewed according to the disease model, while the user of illegal drugs has the criminal label attached.
- Of the most widely used psychoactive drugs, heroin and cocaine (except for limited topical use) are banned; barbiturates, tranquilizers, and amphetamines are restricted; and alcohol, caffeine, and nicotine products are freely available. These inconsistencies make any response to the problem of substance abuse very difficult.
- Under federal law, for purposes of punishment, a given amount of crack is equivalent to 100 times that amount of powdered cocaine—and blacks are more likely to be involved with crack; Whites powdered cocaine.
- Enforcement to reduce the supply of drugs might simply eliminate the less-organized criminal distributors, resulting in an increase in the profits of criminal organizations that are strong enough and ruthless enough to survive.

- Focusing on lower-level dealers presents the political problem of going after small wrongdoers while largely ignoring the big ones and the practical problem of the cost of arresting, prosecuting, and imprisoning large numbers of people.
- If at some point the price of drugs rises significantly and/or the amount available for consumption falls off considerably, abusers are more likely to seek treatment. Research has found that the amount of heroin use is related to price. But experience reveals that when drug abusers are unable to secure their preferred substance, they frequently switch to other substances that could be even more harmful.
- Drug trafficking operates according to the powerful forces of free-market capitalism.
- Success against coca or poppy cultivation can result in the "balloon effect."
- In Peru and Bolivia inhabitants of coca-growing areas are strongly opposed to U.S.-inspired efforts to eradicate their most important cash crop, and both countries face Marxist insurgencies.
- Crop substitution programs have been part of our effort to control drugs at their source but have met with only limited success.
- The most successful herbicides, however, kill many species of plants, including crop plants, and remain in the soil, affecting future plantings.
- Coca has been grown commercially in Indonesia, Malaysia, Nigeria, Sri Lanka, and Taiwan, and curtailing importation without affecting demand provides an incentive for

greater domestic efforts: the production of synthetic analogs for cocaine and heroin and stronger strains of marijuana.

- There is evidence that U.S. efforts against drug trafficking are often secondary to foreign policy considerations.
- Employers are interested in having a drug-free workplace because controlled substances are presumed to be detrimental to job performance. But monitoring job performance makes more sense than drug testing, since some people will perform quite well even though their urine reveals drugs.
- Despite considerable concern about the high rate of cocaine use among pregnant women,

there is little consensus on the adverse effects of the drug because it is difficult to separate the effects of cocaine from other potential hazards to the fetus, such as alcohol and tobacco use.

- There is almost universal agreement that without reduced demand, antidrug efforts will remain ineffective.
- A major problem with instituting any changes in policy is measurement of results. Increases or decreases in the number of people using illegal substances cannot be measured with any accuracy.

Review Questions

1. What is the disease model of drug use?
2. What are the three methods used by the moral-legal model to control drugs?
3. How does the official reaction to a substance determine how the user will be labeled?
4. How did the U.S. response to dangerous drugs from permissiveness to law enforcement lead to the creation of a vast black market?
5. What are the contradictions between scientific knowledge and U.S. drug policy?
6. What led to the federal law that punishes crack as an equivalent to 100 times the same amount of powdered cocaine?
7. How can effective law enforcement increase the profits of criminal organizations?
8. What are the problems of an enforcement policy that focuses on lower-level dealers?
9. Why might one conclude that the "drug war" is racist?
10. What has the Supreme Court ruled with respect to medical marijuana?

11. What are some of the possible unpleasant outcomes of reducing the market for illegal drugs?
12. How does the iron law of capitalism work against effective drug law enforcement?
13. In trying to control drugs at their source, what is the "balloon effect"?
14. Why has coca crop eradication failed?
15. How does the economics of cocaine production limit the effectiveness of coca crop eradication?
16. How has enforcement efforts changed marijuana cultivation?
17. How do foreign policy decisions influence U.S. efforts against drug trafficking?
18. What is the controversy over criminal prosecution for fetal liability?
19. Why is drug treatment more cost-effective than drug law enforcement?
20. What have been the results of coercive treatment of drug addicts?
21. What is the most difficult part of evaluating drug policy?

The easy cynicism that has grown up around the drug issue is no accident. Sowing it has been the deliberate aim of a decades-long campaign by proponents of legalization, critics whose mantra is "nothing works," and whose central insight appears to be that they can avoid having to propose the unmentionable—a world where drugs are ubiquitous—if they can hide behind the bland management critique that drug control efforts are "unworkable."

National Drug Control Strategy (2002b: 3)

DRUG USE AND ABUSE POLICY II: DECRIMINALIZATION AND HARM REDUCTION

CHAPTER **14**

DANNY MOLOSHOK/Landov

Considerable evidence suggests that the legalization of drugs would create behavioral and public health problems to a degree that would far outweigh the current consequences of the drug prohibition.

James A. Inciardi (2002: 281)

What should we as a nation do about drug use? What are our options beyond those examined in Chapter 13? What are the policies being used in other countries?

DECRIMINALIZATION

Decriminalization refers to the absence of laws punishing people for using drugs, as is the case with alcohol and tobacco, drugs restricted only to those below a certain chronological age or only when used under certain conditions, such as driving a car. While some might argue there are distinctions between decriminalization and legalization, they will not be part of the discussion.

John Kaplan (1983b: 101) poses a policy question: "Could we not lower the total social costs of heroin use and the government response to it by allowing the drug to be freely and cheaply available in liquor stores, or as an over-the-counter drug?" Such policy would be consistent with the U.S. approach to other unhealthy habits, such as cigarette smoking, drinking alcohol, and overeating, or the approach to sports such as mountain climbing, skydiving, bull riding, football, and boxing—an acknowledgment of an individual's freedom to enjoy himself or herself or to earn money, even through activities that might be injurious to that person's health. In fact, deliberately engaging in dangerous pursuits can be explained by these activities causing release of potentially reinforcing neurotransmitters such as dopamine or endorphins.

Edward Brecher (1972: 528) notes that most of the harmful aspects of heroin use are the result of its being illegal: "Many American morphine and heroin addicts before 1914 led long, healthy, respectable, productive lives despite addiction—and so do a few addicts today. The sorry plight of most heroin addicts in the United States results primarily from the high price of heroin, the contamination and adulteration of the heroin available on the black market, the mainlining of the drug instead of safer modes of use, the laws against heroin and the ways in which they are enforced, the imprisonment of addicts, society's attitudes toward addicts, and other nonpharmacological factors." Expressing historical ignorance, Barry McCaffrey, Director of the Office of National Drug Control Policy in the Clinton administration, argued that "addictive drugs were criminalized because they are harmful; they are not harmful because they were criminalized" (press release June 15, 1999). "Our attempt to protect drug users from themselves," notes James Ostrowski (Committee on Law Reform of the New York County Lawyers Association 1987: 6), "has backfired, as it did during the prohibition of alcohol. We have only succeeded in making drug use much more dangerous and driving it underground, out of the reach of moderating social influences." Furthermore, imprisonment serves as a form of networking and recruitment for drug dealers and their clients (Currie 1993).

THE PROS

The practical advantages of a drug decriminalization policy are impressive:

1. There would be a reduction in the resources necessary for drug law enforcement. Federal, state, and local governments spend billions of tax dollars annually for drug law enforcement; additional billions are spent on

imprisonment and probation and parole supervision of drug offenders. These resources could be shifted to other areas of crime control and for drug treatment and prevention. However, if the money that is saved from not having to enforce drug prohibition were used to fund drug prevention, "even by our most optimistic estimates of prevention's effectiveness" it would not offset any increase in use resulting from relaxation of controls (Caulkins et al. 1999: xxx).

2. The low cost of psychoactive substances would curtail secondary criminality—that needed to support an expensive drug habit. It would obviate the need to trade sex for drugs, a practice that has helped to spread HIV/AIDS.

3. Criminal organizations that are supported by drug trafficking would no longer remain viable unless, of course, they moved into other criminal activities (which is what happened when Prohibition ended and major bootleggers became major racketeers).

4. The aggressive marketing by traffickers aimed at expanding their customer bases would no longer be operative. This type of marketing resulted in the widespread use of crack cocaine.

5. Those who are dependent on heroin, cocaine, or other currently illegal psychoactive substances could lead more normal lives; the time and energy needed to maintain the habit could be channeled into more constructive pursuits; and abusers would have an opportunity to become contributing members of society. For example, it is not the drug but the law that makes heroin hazardous to the addict. Opiates, like widely prescribed sedatives, provide relief from anxiety, distress, and insomnia to people who would have difficulty functioning normally in the absence of such substances. Similar arguments can be made for cocaine and other substances.

   For those who accept the disease theory of addiction—the idea that some people take heroin or cocaine to compensate for a physiological deficiency—decriminalization is a reasonable suggestion. Allowing these people to access drugs is analogous to the diabetic's need for insulin. Some researchers have found a strong correlation between poor mental health and drug abuse. People frequently self-prescribe drugs to deal with their mental problems, and psychoactive drugs do alleviate psychological discomfort, at least temporarily, enabling the person to relax and/or function more effectively.

6. Intravenous use of heroin would not necessarily involve the danger of hepatitis or AIDS because each user would have his or her own hypodermic kit. In the United States, while the incidence of AIDS among the homosexual population has stabilized, the disease is spreading among drug addicts. Decriminalization would also make many drugs available in liquid form for oral ingestion. Under government oversight drugs would be distributed in precisely measured doses, free of any dangerous contaminants. The chance of a drug overdose would thus be reduced.

7. Decriminalization would enable the use of social controls that inhibit antisocial, albeit lawful, behavior. Because drugs are illegal, users avoid detection and are shielded from social pressure. "Therefore, illicit drug users generally escape the potent forms of social control that are applied to smokers and drunk drivers" (Alexander 1990: 8).

THE CONS

There are, of course, important disadvantages:

"Those who would legalize the use of illicit drugs tend to fall back on familiar arguments, perhaps the most common of which is that we should treat illegal drugs 'like we treat alcohol or cigarettes.' They neglect to point out that there are 120 million regular drinkers in the United States and some 61 million smokers. The comparable figure for illegal drugs is about 20 million—a large number to be sure, but far smaller than would be the case if drugs were legal" (Office of National Drug Control Policy 2004c: 8; Drug Enforcement Administration 2003). "People use drugs because they are pleasurable, and because they are an effective antidote to anxiety, frustration, and feelings of inadequacy. Were drugs legal, they would be socially destigmatized and they would become easier to acquire, cheaper to purchase, and safer to use. Given the genuine psychological benefits of drug use, we can be sure that it would increase were drugs legalized" (de Marneffe 2003: 34). Robert Peterson (1991) argues that drug prohibition, as contrasted with the devastation caused by a lack of similar controls over alcohol, saves billions of dollars and thousands of lives each year. Chanoch Jacobsen and Robert Hanneman (1992) state that the illegitimacy of drug abuse allows for the activation of informal social controls through families, peers, and community that restrain drug abuse.

Cocaine, amphetamines, and heroin freely available to adults could be abused by youngsters as easily as cigarettes and alcohol are. Restrictions on these items have not proven effective in keeping the substances away from young people. Adolescents who are motivated toward drug use are unlikely to be thwarted by legislative acts and law enforcement efforts. As Zimring and Hawkins (1992: 121) point out, however: "To the extent that prohibition policies make drugs more difficult or more expensive for adults to acquire, the same policies will mean that young persons will encounter a prohibited drug less often and will often be unable to afford the purchase even when a source is located."

More people would be tempted to try legalized controlled substances and abuse-related problems might increase accordingly. As was noted in an earlier chapter, because of easier access, medical practitioners have a higher rate of drug use than among the general population. According to the President's Commission on Organized Crime (1986: 331) "legalization would almost certainly increase demand, and therefore spread this destruction." The American Academy of Psychiatrists in Alcoholism and Addictions argues against legalization of drugs because "increased availability will lead to increased use, abuse and addiction to illegal substances, and … there is no rational plan for distribution of these drugs that would not be hazardous and full of ethical problems" (American Academy of Psychiatrists in Alcoholism and Addictions Board of Directors 1990).

Decriminalizing all psychoactive substances would signal an acceptance of their use similar to the acceptance of alcohol and tobacco. While most users of alcohol do not become addicted, Kaplan (1983b) argues that we do not know whether this would hold true for such drugs as heroin. Studies indicate that rats and monkeys perform considerable amounts of work to earn injections of heroin or cocaine but do not respond so eagerly to alcohol.

Soldiers returning to the United States who used high-quality heroin while in Vietnam discontinued use when they were no longer confronted by the anxiety and depression of the war experience and when the cheap, high-quality heroin to which they had grown accustomed was no longer available (Robins 1973, 1974; Robins et al. 1980). The availability of cheap heroin in the United States, argues Wilson (1990), might have kept these veterans addicted. Indeed, by 1999 it was apparent that the increasing use of heroin in the United States was the result of the drug's becoming purer, cheaper, and more readily available for intravenous use or sniffing and smoking. New users are often white and from more affluent backgrounds than was typical of heroin addicts in the past (Wren 1999a).

The easy availability of legal heroin, cocaine, and other currently illegal psychoactive substances would reduce the incentive for those who are already addicted or habituated to enter drug treatment or otherwise to seek a drug-free existence. The legal availability of heroin, however, could prolong heroin addiction beyond the age (35 to 40 years) at which spontaneous remission typically occurs.

POLICY: FOCUS ON CAUSES

To develop a policy that answers these serious concerns, we need to understand the cause(s) of drug use. Are some people more vulnerable than others? As we saw in earlier chapters, we do not know why some people use or abuse drugs while others who have similar access do not. We do not know why some people who experiment with certain drugs become dependent while others do not. Any discussion of drug policy is conditioned on views of drug abuse and on the particular theory that one adopts:

1. Drug abuse is a disease with a physiological basis.
2. Drug abuse is a psychological condition or personality disorder.
3. Drug abuse is a response to oppressive social conditions.
4. Drug abuse is simply the pleasure-seeking activity of hedonistic individuals.

We know that there is a high correlation between urban poverty and heroin and cocaine use. A great deal of drug use, it seems, feeds on human misery. "Britain first came to experience widespread and serious problems of drug misuse amidst the economic downturn of the early 1980s which devastated the local economies of many local industrial working class communities. Subsequently, chronic drug-related problems have become established as a common feature of the social landscape in many neighborhoods in this condition. Under such circumstances, local efforts to curb drug misuse are likely to be severely handicapped unless supported by wide schemes of urban regeneration, access to jobs and training, and other initiatives to combat social exclusion" (Advisory Council on the Misuse of Drugs 1998: 40). Similarly, a serious effort to deal logically with drugs in the United States would require greater [read: expensive] efforts to reduce the social ills of urban America. The policy of "drug warriors" seldom reflects on social conditions as a source of drug misuse.

Chein and his colleagues (1964: 381) extend this argument further: "Is a society which cannot or will not do anything to alleviate the miseries which are, at least subjectively, alleviated by drugs better off if it simply prevents the victims of these miseries from finding any relief?" Recall much of the damage that is inflicted by drugs is the result of their illicit status and not from their pharmacology.

Among those who are strongly opposed to drug decriminalization, however, are many leaders of the African American community. They have expressed the view that such programs are merely schemes designed to tranquilize members of the minority community who would be attracted by the availability of cheap drugs to alleviate their social and psychological frustrations. Some members of the minority community would abandon protest and political activity for the "easy fix," and such programs would saddle the community with lifelong abusers who have been robbed of the incentive to give up drugs.

Congressman Charles B. Rangel of New York, whose district includes Harlem, while chairman of the House Select Committee on Narcotics Abuse and Control vigorously opposed any type of drug maintenance program or decriminalization. He stated that while "illegal drug-trafficking violence would end under decriminalization, a new crime source would be created by the influx of new addicts," and "hyperactive reactions to such drugs as cocaine will spur criminal behavior" (1990: 14).

Until 1988 the debate over drug decriminalization remained basically academic; that is, discussed seriously only by a few university educators and liberal or libertarian political ideologues. In that year drugs became a—possibly *the*—major political issue of the presidential campaign. In response to the obvious—antidrug efforts have not had a significant effect—*Time* magazine (30 May 1988) presented a cover article on the issue: "Should Drugs Be Made Legal?" In a balanced presentation *Time* outlined the benefits and disadvantages of such a proposal and concluded that "even though corner drug shops are not going to pop up anytime soon, nor should they, the hot new debate over legalization is a significant one. It reflects the widespread and understandable dismay over anti-drug efforts that have gone to such discomforting lengths as to call in the military without noticeably making a dent in the crime and abuse problem." In 1989, the *New York Times* reported that while popular opinion still opposed decriminalization, debate over the issue had intensified: "It has become a staple of editorial pages, letters to the editor, talk shows on television and radio and public lectures. And many who do not go as far as advocating legalization show a new interest in the subject" (Corcoran 1989: 9). The discussion of decriminalization brought a hostile response from William Bennett, then the "drug czar" (actually, federal director of drug policy). He argued that *any* public discussion of the issue only worsens the problem and undermines efforts to combat drug abuse (Sly 1989).

MODELS OF DECRIMINALIZATION

There are three broad models of decriminalization:

1. Dangerous drugs can be dispensed only through government-controlled clinics or specially licensed medical personnel and only for short-term treatment purposes; unauthorized sale or possession entails criminal penalties. Long-term maintenance is limited to the use of methadone.
2. Dangerous drugs can be prescribed by an authorized medical practitioner for treatment or maintenance; criminal penalties are imposed for sale or possession outside medical auspices.

3. Dangerous drugs can be sold and used as tobacco and alcohol products are; that is, nonprescription use by adults is permitted. This was the case in the United States before the Harrison Act.

Pat O'Malley and Stephen Mugford (1991) suggest a more limited version:

- Providing safer options by, for example, making coca tea readily available but significantly limiting cocaine and severely restricting crack, which, along with morphine and heroin, would be available only through prescription or licensing arrangements. There would be no incentives to attract new users.
- Offering and encouraging safer ingestion. For example, smoking opium would be readily available, but intravenous drug use would be severely restricted.
- Permitting cultivation and possession of small amounts of marijuana and criminalizing large-scale operations.
- Banning prodrug advertising—including that for tobacco and alcohol products—while encouraging education and antidrug advertising, which would be financed through drug-related tax revenues.

Wisotsky (1987) argues that we have continuously focused on the negatives of substances whose nonmedical use is subjected to criminal sanctions. Yet these substances provide relief from anxiety, euphoria, a sense of enhanced wellbeing, and experiences that the user obviously finds pleasing. Although these substances carry some dangers, so do a host of other substances, such as tobacco, alcohol, and even certain foods whose abuse can lead to obesity and high blood pressure, not to mention firearms, extreme martial arts, and any number of dangerous pastimes that people find pleasurable—that produce a "high." Why pick on chemicals, or rather on the specific chemicals we have chosen to control with criminal sanctions? To the person whose appetite appears insatiable, certain food (sometimes referred to as "junk food") is addicting, yet we do not restrict the intake of potentially harmful foods that have little, if any, nutritional value.

The noted economist Ludwig von Mises (1949: 728–729), a favorite of many political conservatives, argues:

> Opium and morphine are certainly dangerous, habit-forming drugs. But once the principle is admitted that it is the duty of government to protect the individual against his own foolishness, no serious objections can be advanced against further encroachments. A good case could be made out in favor of the prohibition of alcohol and nicotine. And why limit the government's benevolent providence to the protection of the individual's body only? Is not the harm a man can inflict on his mind and soul even more disastrous than any bodily evils? Why not prevent him from reading bad books and seeing bad plays? The mischief done by bad ideologies surely, is much more pernicious, both for the individual and for the whole society, than that done by narcotic drugs.

Some argue that decriminalization would send the wrong message, that drug use is acceptable. However, many activities that are wrong—breaking promises, lying to friends, cheating on a spouse or a boy- or girlfriend should not be punished by law. Only in the context of drug use is failure to punish is viewed pro-drug (Husak and de Marneffe 2005).

Nadelmann (1988: 97) adds: "There is little question that if the production, sale, and possession of alcohol and tobacco were criminalized, the health costs associated with their use and abuse could be reduced. But most Americans do not believe that criminalizing the alcohol and tobacco markets would be a good idea. Their opposition stems largely from two beliefs: that adult Americans have the right to choose what substances they will consume and what risks they will take, and that the economic costs of trying to coerce so many Americans into abstaining from those substances would be enormous and the social costs disastrous." While two out of every three Americans consume alcohol, 10 percent of the drinkers account for half of all the alcohol consumed in the United States. Because some users of psychoactive substances will become dysfunctional as a result, is that sufficient to ban their use? "It is very hard to see why one's freedoms should be held hostage this way"—why individual rights should be held hostage to the person who is most irresponsible (Shapiro 2003: 43).

"Most people," states Wisotsky (1987: 207), "will not *permit* themselves to become addicted, just as most people will not consistently overeat to the point of obesity." With respect to heroin and cocaine the "dominant pattern consists of controlled recreational use or social use, not chronic, compulsive, or obsessive use." Zinberg (1984) points out that our policies have failed to distinguish between the controlled user of psychoactive substances and the one for whom drug use has become dysfunctional. The use of drugs in the United States is widespread, and most of those who ingest psychoactive chemicals, from alcohol and marijuana to heroin and cocaine, do not become dysfunctional.

It appears irrational to give the dysfunctional alcoholic a "legal pass" while subjecting the occasional user of marijuana, heroin, or cocaine to criminal sanctions—sanctions that can result in labeling that, in itself, may be socially, psychologically, and economically debilitating. In fact, much of what society decries about drug abuse is the result of our policy of criminal sanctions. With a redefinition of the problem Wisotsky (1987: 214) asserts, "drug abuse would become like any other health problem, managed by research, prevention, education and treatment," an approach that could be funded by the considerable amount of money now spent on drug law enforcement. This approach would help to destroy heroin and cocaine cartels that threaten the integrity and stability of a number of nations while reducing the everyday dangers to which we expose the public and our drug law enforcement agents.

MEDICAL MAINTENANCE

Kaplan (1983b) argues that our inability to predict the consequences of making heroin freely available raises doubts about a policy of drug legalization. Nadelmann (1988: 91) responds: "The case for legalization [of heroin, cocaine, and marijuana] is particularly convincing when the risks inherent in alcohol and tobacco use are compared with those associated with illicit drug use." Chein and colleagues (1964) and Trebach (1982) recommend a more modest policy: placing greater trust in the medical profession and allowing physicians to treat addicts with a variety of drugs, including heroin. They recommend that clinics be established to implement this policy. Such clinics are not likely to be popular with community residents,

Any person who is shown to be addicted to heroin could receive prescriptions for the drug. Determining whether or not a person is addicted and how much heroin he or she should be given would be left to the medical profession. Trebach notes that some drugs would be diverted into the black market, but the black market in illegal heroin is already considerable.

Legalization would, of course, reduce the price of heroin, thereby reducing the incentive for dealing in the substance. This policy, Trebach argues, would attract heroin addicts in large numbers and cause significant decreases in crime. Such clinics would also offer a wide variety of social services, including help in becoming drug-free (which would be encouraged but not imposed by clinic staff).

Although cocaine abuse is a major problem, fewer researchers are calling for its decriminalization (Wisotsky 1987; O'Malley and Mugford 1991). Kaplan (1983b) notes that monkeys who become addicted to heroin will increase their dosage to a relatively high level and then stabilize the amount and work to earn food or other rewards; laboratory animals that are given unlimited access to cocaine, by contrast, will continue to increase self-injected doses of the substance until the supply is cut off or they die from debilitation (see Dworkin et al. 1987). Of course, monkeys do many things that humans do not, and this might be one of them. However, while satiety for heroin can be satisfied by substituting methadone, cocaine might induce greater craving. Thus, providing clinical doses of cocaine could stimulate rather than reduce the demand for street cocaine (National Institute on Drug Abuse 1997b). Interestingly, Brecher and the editors of Consumer Reports (1972) advocate legalizing heroin for addicts but take no similar position with respect to cocaine (or amphetamines).

MARIJUANA POLICY

Efforts to decriminalize possession of marijuana for personal use encounters a view offered by the Office of National Drug Control Policy (2008: 3):

> For far too long marijuana has represented a "blind spot" in our society. Notions carried over from the 1960s and 1970s—and perpetuated by popular culture—have characterized marijuana as a "soft" or relatively harmless drug. This view was not accurate in the past, and it is certainly not true today. It is now well-accepted that marijuana is addictive and that it can induce compulsive drug-seeking behavior and psychological withdrawal symptoms, as do other addictive drugs such as cocaine or heroin.

The cannabis policy debate "has often been represented as a forced choice between two positions: Doves who argue that cannabis use is harmless, and hence it should be legalized; and Hawks who argue that cannabis use is harmful to health, and hence should continue to be prohibited." But, argues Wayne Hall (1999: 1):

> This false antithesis has prevented a realistic appraisal of the adverse health effects of cannabis. It has meant that the public has been exposed to two polarized views of the adverse health effects of cannabis dictated by their proponents' views on the legal status of cannabis. The Doves focus on the modest health risks of intermittent cannabis use; the Hawks emphasize the worst-case interpretation of the evidence on the risks of chronic cannabis use. There seems to be an implicit agreement between Doves and Hawks that the acute health effects of intermittent cannabis use provide at best a weak justification for prohibition. The Doves stress that there is no risk of overdose from cannabis. The Hawks respond by pointing to the possibility of death or serious injury in a motor vehicle accident if cannabis users drive, and to the social consequences of engaging in risky sexual and other behavior while intoxicated by cannabis.

Possession of marijuana for personal use has been decriminalized in some states, and some authorities have proposed legalization and taxation. Although the state supreme court in Alaska decriminalized the possession of small amounts of marijuana in 1975, fifteen years later voters passed a ballot initiative making it illegal once again. (Marijuana was also recriminalized in Oregon.) There is no evidence to indicate that legal changes have resulted in a marijuana abuse problem in these states. European countries such as the Netherlands and Spain have similarly decriminalized the possession of marijuana for personal use. In the Netherlands thousands of "coffee shops" sell marijuana and hashish under government regulation (discussed later in the chapter).

In 2002 England established a policy of not arresting people for possessing small amounts of marijuana for personal use. This was apparently based on a six-month experiment in South London's Brixton area, where people who were caught smoking marijuana were given warnings rather than being arrested. The policy is not without its critics; residents complained of the openness of marijuana smoking and the fact that sellers often peddle an array of illegal substances, not just marijuana. In response Parliament increased penalties for drug selling, particularly of heroin and cocaine (Lyall 2002). A government reclassification of cannabis downward resulted in a 30 percent drop in arrests, enabling the police to increase efforts against Class A drugs such as heroin and cocaine (Home Office 2004).

In Australia, where most young people have used cannabis at some time in their lives, use decreases with age, marriage, and parenthood, and "only a small proportion use the drug for several years or more." Heavy users regularly use alcohol and are likely to have experimented with a variety of illegal drugs (Hall, Degenhardt, and Lynskey 2001: xviii).

Medical Marijuana   As noted in Chapter 6, while marijuana has some use in medicine—for example, to relieve the pressure on the eyes of glaucoma patients, to control the nausea and vomiting that accompany cancer chemotherapy, and to control the muscle spasms of multiple sclerosis patients—its use remains illegal. Since 1982, however, there has been a legally available pharmaceutical for physicians in ophthalmology and cancer treatment: **Marinol** (dronabinol), which is 98.8 percent pure THC.

There is some dispute as to whether or not oral THC is as effective as smoking marijuana (see, for example, Grinspoon [1987] and a response from Jourbert [1987]; also in opposition to smoking marijuana, see Nahas and Pace [1993]). In 1989 an administrative law judge for the DEA recommended that marijuana be placed on a less restricted schedule, one that would make it available by medical prescription. The judge called marijuana "one of the safest therapeutically active substances known to man." The DEA rejected the judge's recommendation ("U.S. Resists Easing Curb on Marijuana" 1989). In 1999 a federally commissioned report by the Institute of Medicine stated that the active ingredient in marijuana is useful for treating pain, nausea, and the severe weight loss experienced by victims of AIDS. Because the smoke emitted by marijuana is even more toxic than tobacco smoke, the report recommended use of the drug only on a short-term basis, under close supervision, for patients who failed to respond to other therapies (Stolberg 1999).

By 2010, 14 states had laws permitting medical use of marijuana. Since Proposition 215 was approved by the voters in 1996, it has been permissible in California for authorized medical patients to possess or cultivate marijuana and the law allows growers to cultivate the drug as long as he or she has been designated as a primary caregiver by the patient. A 2003 legislative amendment to the statute permits any California resident to own up to half a pound of processed seed which could be purchased from a patient's collective or cooperative. Local governments are permitted to have their own ordinances regulating marijuana, and scores have enacted outright bans (McKinley 2008). In practice, Proposition 215 has spawned a growth industry in marijuana for both legitimate medical purposes and apparent recreational use (Samuels 2008). There are an estimated 200,000 persons in California who use medical marijuana (McKinley 2008). *Time* columnist Joel Klein received a County of Los Angeles medical marijuana ID card "even though I am healthy" from a doctor after complaining of constant anxiety, insomnia, and headaches (2009: 64).

The economics of cannabis in California is compelling: The amount of space needed to grow a tomato plant will produce between one-quarter to two pounds of marijuana that when wholesaled to a dispensary will bring about $2000. Getting into the business is fascilitated by Oaksterdam University in Oakland, a company that teaches people how to grow and sell marijuana (Kuchinksas 2009).

The federal government responded to the referendum by threatening to punish doctors who advise patients that marijuana might ease some of their symptoms by revoking their DEA registration to prescribe controlled substances. Ten doctors and six patients brought a class-action lawsuit challenging that policy, and in 2002 the U.S. Court of Appeals for the Ninth Circuit ruled that the federal policy violated both the free speech of doctors and the principles of federalism. In 2003, the U.S. Supreme Court refused to consider a government appeal of the Ninth Circuit decision. Seven of the nine states in that circuit have laws permitting medical use of marijuana that nevertheless is illegal under federal law. In 2005, the Supreme Court (*Gonzales* v. *Raich*, 545 U.S. 1) upheld an appeals court decision (*Gonzales* v. *Raich,* 352 F.3d 1222) that affirmed the power of the federal government to enforce federal prohibitions against possession and use of marijuana for medical purposes even in the states that permit its use.

In 2003 five jurors in a federal trial in California that convicted a medicinal marijuana advocate issued a public apology to him and demanded that the judge grant him a new trial. The jurors said that they had been unaware that the defendant, Ed Rosenthal, was growing marijuana for medical purposes when they convicted him on three federal counts of cultivation and conspiracy. The reason for Rosenthal's marijuana cultivation was ruled inadmissible at trial (Murphy 2003). Although the government sought a two-year sentence, the judge sentenced him to only one day. The government appealed the sentence and in 2006 the conviction was overturned for juror misconduct. In 2009, Attorney General Eric H. Holder announced that the enforcement policy of the Department of Justice would be restricted to those marijuana traffickers falsely masquerading as medical dispensers.

In 2006, in a controversial statement, the FDA denied that any medical benefits result from the use of marijuana. The FDA statement was criticized for being more ideological than scientific; it did not provide any research data and ignored a report by the prestigious National Academy of Science (Joy, Watson, and Benson 1999) that the substance does provide some benefits to certain patients suffering from AIDS and chemotherapy-related nausea and vomiting (Zernike 2006b). An editorial in the *New York Times* ("Politics of Pot" 2006: 14) argued that the "Food and Drug Administration, for no compelling reason, unexpectedly issued a brief, poorly documented statement disputing the therapeutic value of marijuana." In response Henry Miller, a physician and former head of the FDA's Office of Biotechnology, wrote in support of the FDA statement stated that marijuana smoking cannot be subjected to clinical trials because it does not come in standardized doses and therefore cannot meet the accepted standards for purity, potency, and quality (H. Miller 2006). Permission to conduct clinical trials has been denied by the DEA (Harris 2010).

In 2009, Attorney General Eric H. Holder announced that the enforcement policy of the Department of Justice would be restricted to those marijuana traffickers falsely masquerading as medical dispensers. People who use marijuana for medical purposes and those who disribute it to them no longer face federal prosecution if they act in accordance with state law: "It will not be a priority to use federal resources to prosecute patients with serious illnesses or their caregivers who are complying with state laws on medical marijuana, but we will not tolerate drug traffickers who hide behind claims of compliance with state law to mask activities that are clearly illegal,"

NEEDLE EXCHANGE PROGRAMS

It was discovered that intravenous drug abusers who are also diabetic do not get AIDS. At first this appeared to be connected to their diabetes, but it was subsequently explained by their legal access to hypodermic needles (Chapman 1991a). As a result, needle-exchange programs began to gain support. In these programs intravenous drug users present their used needles, which are exchanged for unused sterile ones. In an effort to reduce the spread of AIDS among intravenous drug users and to reduce AIDS among infants of addict mothers, in 1988 a service agency in the city of Portland, Oregon, became the first to distribute free needles as part of a pilot project involving 125 addicts. Oregon has no law restricting the distribution of hypodermic needles, but addicts frequently do not have the necessary funds to purchase them. In 1992, Connecticut changed its law to permit the purchase and possession of hypodermic needles without a prescription. As a result the number of AIDS cases fell by 40 percent (G. Judson 1995). By 1992 eight U.S. cities had needle-exchange programs, half of them in the state of Washington (Navarro 1992). Opponents among law enforcement, political, religious, and drug treatment officials contend that free needles promote drug use—that making needles available suggests that the government is condoning drug use. (Similar arguments have been made about distributing condoms.) Nevertheless, at the end of 2006, New Jersey, which has one of the highest rates of HIV in the nation, became the last of the fifty states to approve legislation permitting needle-exchange programs. In 1988, Congress banned federal funds for needle-exchange programs, a

As a harm reduction measure, needle exchange programs are considered a small but important step in curbing HIV, which can spread through shared and dirty needles.

ban that was lifted 2009. In 2007, President George W. Bush signed legislation that lifted a federal ban on needle exchange programs in the District of Columbia.

Switzerland and the Netherlands distribute hypodermic needles to reduce the spread of AIDS (Bollag 1989), as does almost every other country in Western Europe. Australia has a needle- and syringe-exchange program, which has been operating in the state of New South Wales since 1986. While Australia has a relatively high number of AIDS cases and intravenous drug users, there are very few intravenous drug users with AIDS (Wodak 1990; Wodak and Lurie 1997). As part of its harm reduction approach (discussed below), the state of New Mexico distributes needles and Narcan (used in cases of overdose) to heroin addicts.

According to an editorial in the *New York Times* in support of needle-exchange programs, "Intravenous-drug users who spread disease by sharing dirty needles and engaging in unprotected sex are responsible for more than a third of all the AIDS cases in the United States and more than half of the new cases of hepatitis C" (September 24, 2004: 26). In 1995 a report by the National Academy of Sciences that was commissioned by Congress found programs that encourage drug abusers to exchange used needles for new ones greatly reduce the spread of AIDS (Leary 1995). In 1997, the American Medical Association endorsed the concept of using needle-exchange programs to combat AIDS. Nevertheless, in 1998 President Clinton, fearing criticism from congressional Republicans, refused to lift a 1989 federal ban on financing for programs that distribute clean needles to drug addicts even though government scientists reported that such programs do not encourage drug use and could save lives by reducing the spread of AIDS (Stolberg 1998).

While drug policy in the United States has changed little since the Harrison Act, in 1914, significant changes are occurring elsewhere in the world.

HARM REDUCTION

A somewhat ambiguous position between criminalization and decriminalization was adopted in Zurich, Switzerland: *containment*. Vigorous police action drove hard-core users into a park near the heart of the city, where open drug sale and use were tolerated. "Needle Park" accommodated about 400 hard-core users of heroin and cocaine and about 3,000 others who passed through daily. An AIDS prevention program was established in the park, and free needles were distributed as part of the effort. Social workers attempted to guide users into treatment programs, and volunteers provided free lunches. Because of the number of drug overdoses—an average of twelve a day—five doctors had to be stationed in the park. Urination killed off all the trees and flowers.

Drug users were drawn to the park from throughout Europe, an important factor in the park's eventual demise: In 1992 the park was shut, and it remains sealed behind a ten-foot iron fence (Treaster 1990b; R. Cohen 1992). The drug market in Zurich did not end with the closing of the park; it moved a half-mile away to a little-used railway station. There, a policy of tolerance again ensued until increasing violence, including the murder of four dealers, led to a 1995 government crackdown, and the area was closed off with razor wire and steel fencing (Cowell 1995).

Switzerland, with a population of about seven million, has about 30,000 drug addicts. In 1997 the Swiss public voted to continue a program that permits hard-core heroin addicts to receive their drugs from the government. Three times a day, enrolled addicts visit one of 23 authorized centers, where they pay a modest fee and receive heroin that they inject at antiseptic clinic tables. As part of the program, participants are enrolled in health, social, and psychological services, and abstinence programming is available (Olson 1997; Associated Press 1997b). In a review of the program, research found criminal activity among participants—drug- and non-drug related-crimes—decreased markedly, while daily ties to the drug scene were broken and lives were stabilized; however, participants had difficulties securing and maintaining employment (Güttinger et al. 2003; Ribeaud 2004). In 2008, 68 percent of Swiss voters approved making the heroin program permanent while 63 percent voted against the legalization of marijuana.

Like Switzerland, a number of other European countries have been exploring relatively new ways of responding to drug use, in particular, **harm reduction** as an alternative to the *supply reduction* strategy—aggressive law enforcement and pressure on producer nations—and the *demand reduction* strategy—treatment and prevention. This alternative recognizes that while abstinence is desirable, it is not a realistic goal. Instead, this approach examines harm from two points of view: harm to the community and harm to the drug user. The focus, then, is on lowering the amount of harm to each. "Each policy or programmatic decision is assessed for its expected impact on society. If a policy or program is expected to reduce aggregate harm, it should be accepted; if it is expected to increase aggregate harm, it should be rejected. The prevalence of drug use should play no special and separate role" (Reuter and Caulkins 1995: 1060). As Jonathan Caulkins (1996: 232) notes, however, "attempting to translate the concept of harm reduction into formal terms brings out key philosophical questions that must be addressed. How does one measure harm? How does one aggregate and compare different types of harm? Which (whose) harms count?"

PRINCIPLES OF HARM REDUCTION

At present there is no agreement in the drug literature or among practitioners as to the definition of harm reduction (Tammi 2004), but in harm reduction approaches the use of drugs is accepted as a fact, and focus is placed on reducing harm while use continues. The main characteristics or principles of harm reduction are (Conley et al. n.d.):

- *Pragmatism*: Harm reduction accepts that some use of mind-altering substances is a common feature of human experience. It acknowledges that while carrying risks, drug use also provides the user with benefits that must be taken into account if drug-using behavior is to be understood. From a community perspective containment and amelioration of drug-related harms may be a more pragmatic or feasible option than efforts to eliminate drug use entirely.
- *Humanistic values*: The drug user's decision to use drugs is accepted as fact. This does not mean approval. No moralistic judgment is made either to condemn or to support use of drugs, regardless of level of use or mode of intake. The dignity and rights of the drug user are respected.
- *Focus on harms*: The fact or extent of a person's drug use per se is of secondary importance to the risk of harms consequent to use. Harms that are addressed are related to health, social, economic, and other factors affecting the individual, the community, and society as a whole. Therefore, the first priority is to decrease the negative consequences of drug use to the user and to others rather than focusing on decreasing the drug use itself. Harm reduction neither excludes nor presumes the long-term treatment goal of abstinence. In some cases reduction of level of use may be one of the most effective forms of harm reduction. In others alteration to the mode of use may be more effective.
- *Balancing costs and benefits*: A pragmatic process of identifying, measuring, and assessing the relative importance of drug-related problems, their associated harms, and costs and benefits of intervention is carried out in order to focus resources on priority issues. The analysis extends beyond the immediate interests of users to include broader community and societal interests. Because of this rational approach, harm reduction approaches theoretically lend themselves to evaluation of impacts in comparison to some other, or no, intervention. In practice, however, such evaluations are complicated because of the number of variables to be examined in both the short and the long term.

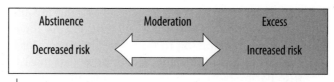

FIGURE 14.1 | RISK CONTINUUM

- *Priority of immediate goals*: Most harm-reduction programs have a hierarchy of goals, with the immediate focus on proactively engaging individuals, target groups, and communities to address their most pressing needs. Achieving the most immediate and realistic goals is usually viewed as first steps toward risk-free use or, if appropriate, abstinence.

REDUCING THE RISKY CONSEQUENCES OF DRUG USE

In the view of Alan Marlatt, Julian Somers, and Susan Tapert (1993), harm reduction seeks to avoid marginalizing drug users because more can be done to control the often destructive behavior of drug abusers when they are "normalized." While abstinence is an ultimate objective, in the continuum shown in Figure 14.1, Marlatt and colleagues posit that *any* steps that decrease risk are worthwhile goals.

The focus is on reducing the risky consequences of drug use rather than on reducing drug use per se. In place of the "war" analogy and "total victory" rhetoric, Marlatt and colleagues support even small steps that reduce harm. For example, intravenous use would be made safer through needle-exchange programs. The next step would be to encourage safer methods of ingestion. Risk would be further reduced by substituting methadone for heroin or other legal substances for cocaine and then by moderating the use of drugs—including nicotine and alcohol—en route to abstinence when this is possible. Related risk-taking behavior would also be targeted in an effort to deal with AIDS and other sexually transmitted diseases; in this case the focus of harm reduction would be on reducing the frequency of high-risk sexual activity by promoting less risky sexual practices, monogamous sex, and the use of birth control. To reduce accidental overdoses--from which more than 600 New Yorkers die every year--and the spread of HIV/AIDS, New York City health officials published and distributed a 17-page brochure—*Tips for Safer Use of Heroin*—whose first page urges users to get drug treatment and offers 24-hour hotline numbers (Hartocollis 2010).

HARM REDUCTION IN THE UNITED KINGDOM

The harm reduction approach is more easily achieved in England where controlled substances can be prescribed for those dependent on them and local governments have some flexibility in their approach to drug use. The first British drug control laws (passed in 1916) dealt with cocaine, a substance that was being used by soldiers on leave from World War I. The government had difficulty interpreting the statute for action, and in response the Ministry of Health formed a committee of physicians that moved the problem of drug abuse toward a medical response (Stimson and Oppenheimer 1982). The committee noted that some medical experts favored a program of providing diminishing doses until the patient became drug-free. Other physicians argued that some addicts will never be able to live drug-free, and for them, after all other treatment had proven unsuccessful, heroin maintenance was suggested—if not cure, then care. Most important, the committee report stated that drug abuse is a disease, not an indulgence (Trebach 1982). The British system that resulted from the committee's report gave the medical profession almost unhindered freedom to treat drug addicts by means of providing drugs.

Problems grew in the 1950s when a substantial market in heroin tablets grew in London. Most of the new addicts were young recreational users whose lifestyles were more deviant than those of the older class of addicts. A 1966 report concluded that the problem was caused by a handful of doctors who were overprescribing heroin, which was being diverted into a black market. As a result, the use of opiates and cocaine to treat addiction was restricted to specially licensed physicians and drug treatment clinics. Between the late 1970s and the early 1980s there was a large growth in the volume of smokable and injectable heroin in all parts of the United Kingdom. This problem continued throughout the 1980s, during which there was a growth in the acid house music culture, with major media coverage of MDMA (ecstasy) and other hallucinogenic drugs. In 1999 cocaine was determined to be overtaking heroin in popularity (Murray and Tendler 1999). Today, specially licensed doctors can provide heroin or cocaine for drug treatment, but this has become rare. Instead of heroin most licensed physicians and clinics prescribe methadone for oral ingestion, although any medical doctor can provide heroin as an analgesic for physical pain.

The modern British system involves two barely compatible policies operating at the same time: a political policy whose focus is on supply reduction and penal policies in the belief that elimination of drug use is possible, and a services policy whose focus is on local prevention campaigns and providing a variety of local services, including needle-exchange schemes, advice and counseling services, and a variety of prescribing options from short-term outpatient detoxification to long-term prescribing and rehabilitation. "At the heart of this approach is the view that drug use cannot be eliminated, but its most harmful consequences for the individual, society, and public health can be moderated" (Turner 1991: 184–185).

As part of a harm reduction approach to battle an alarming number of AIDS cases, physicians in Edinburgh, Scotland, are permitted to prescribe oral doses of nearly any drug craved by abusers. And there is indeed harm reduction: Great Britain has the lowest rate of AIDS in Europe (Schmidt 1993). In Britain harm reduction principles are not seen as incompatible with vigorous street policing; "indeed in many circumstances they actually require it" (Advisory Council on the Misuse of Drugs 1994: 2). While U.S. "drug warriors" have frequently denounced the harm reduction approach as capitulation (or worse), the British Advisory Council on the Misuse of Drugs, whose membership includes police executives, recommends "the wider adoption of harm reduction principles in developing law enforcement strategies" (1994: 83).

Although the United Kingdom has demonstrated greater flexibility than has the United States, basic U.K. drug policy is prohibitionary with a heavy emphasis on law enforcement (Home Office 2004). There is also extensive use of the criminal justice system to identify and treat drug users. Working out of police or custodial facilities, "Arrest Referral" counselors, many of whom are trained ex-addicts, interview and offer assistance to drug users (O'Shea and Powis 2003).

THE MERSEYSIDE MODEL

In the province of Merseyside, a severely disadvantaged region whose largest city is Liverpool, vestiges of the "old British system" remain, with addicts taking home injectable opiates. But Merseyside has also introduced a comprehensive harm reduction. Merseyside provides needle exchange, counseling, prescription of drugs including heroin, and employment and housing services. Many levels of service and a wide variety of agencies are involved, and services are integrated to provide drug users with help when they need it. Pharmacists play a vital role in the workings of the Merseyside system. Some fill prescriptions for smokable drugs in the form of "reefers," which provide an alternative to injection and produce the "buzz" that some intravenous users crave. To prepare reefers, drugs such as heroin and methadone are injected into either herbal or regular cigarettes. Clients who have received injectable prescriptions for more than ten years are now voluntarily switching to reefers in an attempt to stop injecting. In addition to reefers, pharmacists dispense drugs in the form of ampoules, liquid, and aerosols.

By no means soft on drugs, the Drug Squad of the Merseyside police force arrest and charge a greater number of people for drug offenses than all other provincial forces. Nevertheless, their focus on harm reduction means that first offenders found in possession of any drug are cautioned. Cautioning involves confiscating the drug, taking an offender to a police station, recording the incident, and formally warning the offender that any further unlawful possession of drugs will result in prosecution. The offender must also meet certain conditions, such as not having a previous drug conviction and not having an extensive criminal record. He or she is given information about treatment services in the area, including syringe exchanges. On the second and third occasions the user is sent to court and fined for possession of small quantities or sentenced for possession of large amounts. If an addict becomes registered by getting in touch with service agencies, then he or she is legally entitled to carry drugs for personal use. The overall effect of this policy is to steer users away from crime and possible imprisonment (Riley, n.d.).

Harm reduction aims at "avoiding the amplification of a drug-using career that may stem from a first conviction" (O'Hare 1992: xiv), and the Merseyside police have become national leaders in developing a cooperative harm reduction strategy with the regional health authority. The police sit on health authority drug advisory committees and employ health authority officers in police training courses involving the issue of drugs and HIV. The police have also agreed not to conduct surveillance on treatment centers, to refer arrested drug offenders to services, not to charge for possession of syringes to be exchanged, and to publicly support syringe exchange.

DUTCH DRUG POLICY

The harm reduction approach is popular throughout Europe where officials generally avoid the "drug warrior" approach. European Union countries frequently practice what can be called *unofficial harm reduction*; that is, they utilize informal police and prosecutorial practices to eliminate punishments for obtaining or possessing small amounts of an illegal drug (Böllinger 2004). In Austria, at the cost of one Euro, customers can purchase a small box containing two syringes, a condom, an antiseptic wipe, filters, and Vitamin C that breaks down drugs into a liquid so that users do not accidentally inject solid drug particles into their veins (Nilson 2007). Possession of any drugs for personal use is not a criminal offense in the Baltic States, the Czech Republic, Italy, Portugal, and Spain ("Briefing: Dealing with Drugs" 2009).

The country that is most identified with a national policy of harm reduction is the Netherlands. The Netherlands is one of the most densely populated countries in the world, a largely urban population of about 16 million people in an area about the size of South Carolina. The Dutch have a strong belief in individual freedom, and government is expected to avoid becoming involved in matters of morality and religion. At the same time there is a strong sense of responsibility for the well-being of the community. The Netherlands has a very extensive system of social security, while health care and education are accessible to everyone (Barnard 1998; Bullington 1999). Accordingly, drug treatment programs are readily available (de Kort and Cramer 1999). In contrast to the U.S. experience discussed in Chapter 2, drugs in the Netherlands have not been strongly associated with marginalized groups (Uitermark 2004).

Dutch policy is based on the idea that drug use is a fact of life and needs to be discouraged in as practical a manner as possible (Barnard 1998). In place of prohibitionism's "war on drugs" and "user accountability," the Dutch have implemented a pragmatic and nonmoralistic approach whose main objective is to minimize the risks associated with drug use, both for users themselves and for those around them. The Dutch distinguish between "soft" drugs such as marijuana and "hard" drugs such as heroin, cocaine, and ecstasy. The idea is to separate the market so that users of soft drugs are less likely to come into contact with hard drugs and will not suffer the negative consequences of labeling (discussed in Chapter 7), since young people who become stigmatized are more likely to start using more dangerous drugs (de Kort and Cramer 1999; von Solinge 2004).

During the 1970s possession or sale of small amounts of marijuana (30 grams, reduced to 5 grams in 1995) was virtually decriminalized, and the substance remains widely available in so-called "coffee shops" (MacCoun and Reuter 1997); by contrast, trafficking in hard drugs can bring a twelve-year sentence. Although drug users are rarely arrested, those involved in secondary criminality are prosecuted, and drugs are not a mitigating circumstance (Silvas 1994). "Criminalization of the consumer is considered a harmful way of discouraging drug use" (Wever 1994: 64). The "coffee shops must follow specific rules: no advertising, no nuisance, no minors (under age 18 years), no hard drugs, and total stock not exceeding 500 grams" (von Solinge 2004).

The Dutch response to ecstasy was similarly laissez faire, and MDMA was not outlawed until 1988, the result of international concern that the Netherlands might become a production site. This fear has materialized; The Netherlands reportedly produces 80 percent of the world supply of ecstasy. Nevertheless, officials do not consider the substance a major health issue, and the government provides facilities where pills can be tested, providing greater safety for the user and data for monitoring the drug market (Uitermark 2004).

Extensive social services in the Netherlands provide aid to drug abusers that is not available in many other countries, including the United States. Nevertheless, in the early 1980s downtown areas of larger Dutch cities became increasingly dominated by a highly visible population of untreated drug users. This fostered a change in approach, which had previously focused almost exclusively on promoting abstinence. Treatment was expanded to deal with the host of social and physical problems that abusers experience. Harm reduction became the focus: If abstinence is not possible, then safer use of drugs and safer sex practices should be the near-term goals. Drug abusers are now provided with health-related education and a wide variety of treatment programs are readily available, including methadone maintenance (Wever 1994), and there are sites in social service facilities where drugs may be safely ingested. This arrangement reduces neighborhood nuisances and exposes addicts to available services and drug treatment (Wolf, Linssen, and de Graaf 2003; van de Mheen and Gruter 2004).

Drug abuse prevention efforts in the Netherlands treat alcohol and tobacco, as well as heroin and cocaine, as dangerous drugs; legal versus illegal is not considered a sound basis for differentiation. This avoids the double standard that provokes cynicism in young people. The focus is on risky behavior, which also includes eating disorders. The policy seeks to deglamorize drugs and stresses individual responsibility for the consequences of substance abuse. People are cautioned against using dangerous substances while being provided with information on how to reduce the risks for those who insist on experimenting with drugs (Marshall and Marshall 1994). As was noted earlier, there are extensive treatment programs for those who become drug dependent.

Ineke Marshall and Chris Marshall note the differences between the Dutch and U.S. approaches to drugs (1994: 226): "The American mass media, public, politicians, and educators appear to devote considerably more resources and energy to issues related to drug prevention than is the case in Holland. Differences in intensity of prevention efforts reflect fundamental differences in the definition of drugs as a social problem in the U.S. and Netherlands: In the U.S., drugs are viewed as a terrible evil to be fought with heavy arms (both in terms of prevention and repression); in the Netherlands, from a policymaker's viewpoint, drugs are viewed as a 'normal' social and health risk controlled by minimal measures or even ignored (e.g., cannabis, XTC)." Marshall and Marshall conclude that the "Dutch pragmatic approach has prevented the use of radical measures such as forced treatment, drug testing at the workplace, and fear-inducing information campaigns—'solutions' which may give the appearance of a tough approach, but which frequently cause more problems than they solve" (1994: 226).

Problems Over the Past Twenty Years   The Dutch approach has had problems. From 1979 to 1983 Amsterdam permitted drug use rooms where drugs could be consumed. It eventually became obvious that drug dealers were in charge and that the group norm within these centers was aimed at maintaining high levels of drug use and criminality. In 1983 the centers were closed, and more emphasis was given to police interventions and public order problems. By the early 1990s the coffee shops were becoming increasingly commercial and multiplying rapidly. Since they operated on the margins of society, there was the very real prospect of the coffee shops becoming centers of criminal activity—receiving stolen goods, for example—and they were attracting increasing numbers of foreigners. In response, new restrictions were announced: no more than 5 grams per transaction and, owing to an increase in marijuana among school-children, a ban on those under age eighteen. Local authorities were given the power to ban or close coffee shops, and their numbers began to fall. Their regulation is now largely a local affair (de Kort and Cramer 1999).

Dutch drug policy led to an influx of heroin users from other countries. In part, this appears to have been the unanticipated result of success in lowering the use of heroin—since methadone maintenance is readily available—which caused a decrease in price and attracted users from elsewhere (Korf, Riper, and Bullington 1999). In defending the Dutch approach, Herbert Barnard (1998), counselor for health and welfare at the Netherlands Embassy in Washington, D.C., stated that the Dutch policy has kept the number of heroin addicts relatively low in comparison with the number in many countries and that the addict population is rather stable and rapidly aging. Furthermore, the number of addicts who are infected with HIV is exceptionally low. He argues that despite the fact that marijuana is readily available, the rate of cannabis use in the Netherlands is lower than that in the United States (see also von Solinge 2004). A situation that is often encountered in other nations, in which the user—in most cases a minor—runs the risk of getting into trouble with the police is seen as highly undesirable in the Netherlands.

Larry Collins (1999) disputes this view. He states that marijuana use is a serious problem in the Netherlands. However, on the basis of the figures he presents, marijuana use is actually greater in the United States. Collins argues that because of the Netherlands' liberal attitude, that country has become a Mecca for drug traffickers and drug trafficking. The Dutch have the world's biggest seaport (Rotterdam), making it attractive to shippers of unlawful goods as well as lawful ones. Its central geographical position makes it a hub for European commerce. That the liberal Dutch attitude toward drugs attracts drug traffickers is an argument "built on the assumption that (potential) drug traffickers rationally consider and compare countries in order to decide from which to operate. The reality, however, is that professional drug traffickers do not expect to be caught" (von Solinge 2004: 134). As was noted in Chapter 13, even the death penalty in several nations has not stopped drug dealing.

Collins notes that much of the ecstasy entering other European countries originates in the Netherlands. The Dutch have recognized this problem and responded by setting up a special national unit to deal combat synthetic drugs. But MDA-type synthetic drugs such as MDMA remain a problem to which the Dutch have responded with a public campaign on their dangers and, in line with the harm reduction approach, by providing first-aid resources where the substance is most likely to be used. Indeed, since certain chemical configurations of MDA are more dangerous than others, Dutch policy provides pill testing for potential consumers.

Crack cocaine has also been a problem in the Netherlands, although its use is primarily among a stable subset of polydrug users who also abuse heroin and methadone (de Kort and Cramer 1999). But despite greater visibility of drug users and the ready availability of drugs in the Netherlands, this "has not led to high(er) domestic drug use" (von Solinge 2004: 107).

PORTUGAL

The most dramatic change in Western European drug policy occurred in Portugal, a country of almost 11 million persons and a member of the European Union that shares the Iberian Peninsula with its larger neighbor to the east, Spain. Largely Catholic and socially conservative, since 2001, *all* drugs have been decriminalized: there are no criminal penalties for possession of drugs for personal use defined as up to a ten-day supply. "The law formed part of a strategic approach to drug use which aimed to focus police resources on those people who profit from the drugs trade, while enabling a public health approach to drug users"—investment in treatment and prevention doubled (C. Hughes and Stevens 2007: 2). While drug trafficking and furnishing drugs to a minor continue to be criminal offenses, possession for personal use is an administrative offense (think parking tickets), not a crime. The police are required to issue citations for drug use or possession which are referred to the *Comissões para a Dissuasão da Toxicode-pendência* (Commission for Dissuasion of Drug Addiction). These are regional three-member panels—usually a lawyer, a doctor, and a social worker or psychologist—that are responsible for adjudicating administrative drug offenses and making evaluation and treatment recommendations. They have the power to impose community work and fines, but their focus is on getting dependent drug users into treatment. While they cannot *mandate* treatment, they can suspend a license to practice a profession such as medicine, law, or being a taxi driver. In practice, many police officers do not bother issuing citations that they consider a waste of time (Greenwald 2009).

A report drafted by the libertarian Cato Institute (which favors decriminalization) states that while Portugal did not experience significant change in drug use, there was a dramatic increase in the number of drug users seeking treatment. Between 2001 and 2007, the number of persons who say they have used heroin at least once in their lives increased from 1 percent to 1.1 percent, while lifetime use of other drugs decreased. Thus the country has one of Europe's lowest rates of marijuana use ("Treating, Not Punishing" 2009). With large sums no longer expended for enforcement, prosecution, and imprisonment, funding for treatment increased and the drug dependent, freed from both stigma and prosecution, took advantage of treatment opportunities in record numbers (Greenwald 2009).

As a result of the policy change, "the general public is more likely to admit to past or present drug use and to seek or encourage other drug users to obtain assistance. On the other hand decriminalization is seen as sending the wrong message and increasing the sense of social acceptability and tolerance of drug use" (C. Huges and Stevens 2007: 7).

HARM REDUCTION ELSEWHERE

Austria   While it is a major transit point for drugs coming into Western Europe from the East, the problem of drug use in Austria is somewhat smaller than in other countries of Western Europe or North America. Chad Nilson (2007) outlines the basis for Austrian drug policy:

- There must be a balance between the use of health tools aimed at reducing demand for drugs and law enforcement tools aimed at reducing the supply of drugs.
- Drug use should not be legalized but decriminalized.
- Drug addiction should be acknowledged as a disease not an immoral life choice.
- Because the aim of a drug-free society is unrealistic, measures should be taken to reduce the social and bodily harm caused by drug use

Police officers in Austria lack the discretion common in the United States and other democracies—they must process all offenses they see or investigate, even the smallest amounts of drug possession. However, those charged with possession for personal use are sent to a municipal health authority where they must register and develop an action plan that responds to their condition—they are not charged with a criminal offense. If, after two years, there is no further contact with the police, their file is destroyed. A drug-dependent person charged with a crime faces imprisonment during which they undergo drug treatment and can be released from prison if they agree to long-term treatment in the community. The government provides funding for those without the means to pay for treatment. In a few regions in Austria, there are programs designed to reintegrate ex-abusers into the labor market by employing them in various postal services and renovation work. Other regions provide temporary housing along with employment services to recovering drug users (Nilson 2007).

Canada   Despite opposition from the United States, Canada is slowly moving in the Western European direction of harm reduction. Vancouver, a scenic city on Canada's Pacific coast, site of the 2010 Winter Olympics, serves as an entry point for Asian drugs. Its Downtown East Side has an active and open drug subculture—ten blocks with an estimated 5,000 intravenous heroin addicts and thousands of crack users, many of whom are HIV positive and/or suffer from hepatitis C. Dozens die of drug overdoses every year (Beiser 2008). The city's mayor was elected by a landslide on a platform of more treatment for addicts and regulated injection sites (C. Krauss 2003). Vancouver hosts North America's only official injection site where nurses ensure that addicts are using clean equipment and intervene in the case of an overdose (C. Krauss 2003; K. Johnson 2010).

Marijuana has been virtually decriminalized; sellers are plentiful in the neighborhood and a bimonthly slick magazine, *Cannabis Culture*, is published nearby. More than 1,200 volunteers have been trained in the use of Narcan and overdose deaths have fallen by more than two-thirds. The city hands out free syringes and clean mouthpieces for crack pipes; about 4,000 persons get prescription methadone; and there is a storefront injection site with two nurses on duty. There is a pilot project that provides heroin for some addicts and the mayor has proposed prescription alternatives to cocaine and methamphetamine. The philosophy behind this approach is what Vince Beiser (2008: 63) calls "enlightened self-interest":

> The idea is to give addicts clean needles and mouthpieces not to be nice but so they don't get HIV or pneumonia from sharing equipment and then become a burden on the public health system. Give them a medically supervised place to shoot up so they don't overdose and clog up emergency rooms, leaving their infected needles behind on the sidewalk. Give them methadone—or even heroin—for free so they don't break into cars and homes to get money for the next fix.

Since the program was initiated, rates of HIV infections have fallen by half and hepatitis C rates by two-thirds.

While there is no evidence that the program has increased the number of drug users, there is an absence of evidence that is has reduced drug use, and Vancouver continues to experience a great deal of competitive violence between groups seeking to dominate the drug trade, including the Hell's Angels Motorcycle Club, Asian, and home-grown gangs (Rodgers 2009).

Latin America   In 2009, Mexico decriminalized possession of drugs intended for personal use: a police search that reveals no more than a half-gram of cocaine, about "four lines," 5 grams of marijuana, about four cigarettes, 50 milligrams of heroin, 40 milligrams of methamphetamine, or 0.015 milligrams of LSD, will not result in incarceration (Lacey 2009d). Mexican officials say that law simply recognizes the long-standing practice of not prosecuting people caught with small amounts of drugs (Associated Press 2009b). Other Latin American countries have also moved toward decriminalization: In 2009, the Supreme Court of Argentina ruled that it is unconstitutional to arrest persons for possession of small amounts on illegal drugs, and in 2006 Brazil eliminated prison sentences for drug users in favor of treatment (Barrionuevo 2009).

Founded in 1993, the Harm Reduction Coalition in the United States (www.harmreduction.org) has been promoting public policies aimed at moving the country in the direction of European countries who have abandoned the "drug warrior" approach to drug use.

HARM REDUCTION EDUCATION

Harm reduction is a controversial approach to drug education. Instead of focusing on preventing *use*, harm reduction attempts to prevent *abuse* (J. Cohen 1996). This paradigm recognizes that people will always use psychoactive substances whether they are legal or illegal and attempts to minimize the hazards of use as a more realistic goal (Duncan et al. 1994). Supporters of this approach are critical of school and media drug education programs that present information that is intended to demonstrate the adverse consequences of drug use because of the tendency to exaggerate the dangers and to perpetuate certain convenient stereotypes. In addition, the "just say no" approach assumes, against evidence to the contrary, that a child's decision not to use drugs becomes much easier once he or she is acquainted with the consequences. In fact, evaluations have shown that information has little or no impact on whether young people use drugs. Indeed, some studies suggest that excessive use of primary prevention might actually encourage drug use by creating a sense of mystique around the subject, which appeals to children's natural curiosity.

Primary prevention approaches stress drug use as abnormal and views drug users as deficient in knowledge, self-esteem, or skills. Yet, as was noted earlier, some studies show that individuals with high self-esteem actually are more likely to experiment with drugs. Moreover, research indicates that experimentation is an extremely poor predictor of long-term use or abuse. Primary prevention approaches also ignore the pleasure and other benefits of drug use and fail to acknowledge that decisions to try drugs are often expressions of independence. "Deviancy amplification" divides users and nonusers and works against meaningful dialogue with adults. The harm reduction approach to education instead focuses on nonjudgmental information about different drugs, their properties and effects, the law and legal rights, how to reduce risks, and where to get help if needed. It helps youths to develop a wide range of skills in assessment, judgment, communication, assertiveness, conflict resolution, decision making, and safer use. Teaching begins in early years about familiar substances other than drugs and emphasizes that most of the things we consume have the potential for both harm and benefit depending on the way we use them.

Norman Zinberg (1984: 207), a psychiatrist and well-known researcher on drug use, recommends educational programs that parallel the approach that is often used to deal with adolescent sexual behavior: "although our society does not condone teenage sexual activity, it has decided that those who are unwilling to follow its precepts should be given the basic information needed to avoid disease and unwanted pregnancy." Accordingly, drug education "should provide information on how to avoid the effects of destructive drug combinations (for example, barbiturates and alcohol), the unpleasant consequences of using drugs of unknown purity, the hazards of using drugs with a high dependence liability, the dangers of certain modes of administration, and the unexpected effects of various dose levels and various settings" (Zinberg 1984: 207).

EXAMPLE: HARM REDUCTION INFORMATION ON METHAMPHETAMINE

Speed has the ability to make you feel good. You can have intense feelings of pleasure and well-being and be able to function at top speed, getting lots of work or studying done or dancing all night. Of course, with the up comes the down. There are not-so-pleasurable effects of using speed too. As with other drugs, the more you use speed, the more of it your body needs. This is called tolerance. Tolerance occurs more rapidly when speed is injected or smoked. Speed tells your body that you do not need food or sleep, so you are extremely tired and depleted when you take a break. Depression, nightmares, and insomnia are also side effects of using speed. Then there is the crash. To avoid crashing, people often take more speed, which intensifies the negative effects of the crash when it does come—and the crash always comes (Harm Reduction Coalition 1998).

The harm reduction approach contrasts markedly with U.S. policy toward another potentially addictive behavior: gambling. The United States went from outlawing most forms of gambling to aggressively promoting the behavior in search of tax revenue. Some critics might even be tempted to use the term *hypocrisy*.

CONCLUSION

Suggesting a comprehensive policy that is acceptable to mainstream America does not take a great deal of imagination, but it would take a great deal of money. The level of funding that would be required to institute most of these recommendations makes them unrealistic in the present United States. We already spend about $4 billion a year on controlling illegal drugs, more than half of that going for drug law enforcement.

Reducing the consumption of drugs by increasing law enforcement and large-scale treatment programs does not solve such significant sociological problems as lack of educational and employment opportunity and residential instability. We know that drug abuse is not randomly dispersed over the population but is concentrated in areas of poverty. Insofar as drug abuse is the result of despair, frustration, hopelessness, and alienation, programs directed only at the symptom—drug abuse—cannot succeed. Elliott Currie (1993) points out that drug abuse is not an isolated problem within stricken inner-city communities but part of a syndrome that includes family disintegration, child abuse and neglect, delinquency, and alcohol abuse. Successful treatment of individual drug abusers would not stem the tide of new entries generated by unchanged social conditions that serve as a fertile breeding ground. "Even the best, most comprehensive programs to help addicts transform their lives will inevitably be compromised if we do not simultaneously address the powerful social forces that are destroying the communities to which they must return" (Currie 1993: 279).

A COMPREHENSIVE PROGRAM FOR RESPONDING TO DRUG ABUSE

1. Institute educational programs at the elementary, high school, and college levels that fully present all aspects of the use of psychoactive chemicals, including moderation and controlled use. Unfortunately, to date there has been little evidence to indicate that educational efforts actually reduce the use of drugs, although they might encourage a more rational or controlled use.
2. Decriminalize marijuana for personal use to conserve valuable resources and to avoid stigmatizing persons unnecessarily. Breaking the connection between marijuana and hard drugs might also help to keep young people away from hard drugs. Furthermore, notes Richard Cowan (1986), effective law enforcement against marijuana drives up the price and might move users toward more readily available crack cocaine.
3. Reduce the supply of drugs by enhancing domestic law enforcement; that is, significantly increase personnel and equipment for the Coast Guard, Customs, and Drug Enforcement Administration (the Federal Bureau of Investigation should not have drug law enforcement responsibilities, because this merely

increases interagency conflict and detracts from that agency's major law enforcement role, which includes combating espionage and terrorism).

4. Reduce the supply of drugs at source countries; that is, provide more technical support and equipment and greater financing for crop substitution and eradication programs.

5. Reduce the consumer market by expanding local law enforcement efforts and place all convicted drug abusers on intensive probation supervision or incarceration followed by intensive parole supervision. This would require a significant increase in local law enforcement personnel assigned to drug law enforcement, an expansion of correctional facilities (which are already over-taxed), and a significant increase in probation and parole personnel.

6. Drastically expand the availability of treatment programs, enabling every substance abuser—including those addicted to nicotine and alcohol—to have access to treatment. Continue research efforts into the causes of substance abuse and the effectiveness of various approaches to treatment.

7. Provide educational and vocational programs for drug abusers who have enrolled in treatment programs. In addition to the problem of financing such efforts, there is the problem of equity: Should only drug abusers be entitled to receive educational and vocational services, or should these be made available to all disadvantaged individuals?

8. Enact and enforce legislation prohibiting employment discrimination against former substance abusers.

This comprehensive program would require a significant expenditure of tax dollars during a time of severe economic downturn.

No author enjoys ending a book on a note of pessimism. Defeatism is anathema to the American culture. We like to believe that Yankee ingenuity can overcome any problem, just as we have overcome the Nazis, the Communists, and a host of diseases. But reality indicates that some problems, particularly social ones like crime and poverty, can be intractable. The United States has the widest gap between rich and poor in the industrialized world, and that gap is growing (Bradsher 1995b, 1995c; Segre 2003). David Bellis (1981: xiv) states that "resolving issues like poverty, crime and addiction, especially in isolation from one another, and unmediated by economic, social and political factors may be impossible."

That our current strategies in response to drug abuse have failed is obvious. Despite the posturing and dramatic pronouncements of several administrations, we have been unable to stem the flow of heroin and cocaine into the United States and are unlikely to do so in the future. Our success against foreign marijuana has led to improvements in domestic cultivation, so pot connoisseurs now prefer the home-grown crop. There is every reason to believe that if efforts to eradicate coca and poppy cultivation in source countries and/or to improve antismuggling techniques ever succeeded, it would simply spur the domestic production of cocaine and heroin substitutes. Furthermore, as was indicated in Chapters 9 and 10, there is no evidence that widespread educational efforts have significantly reduced the number of persons using drugs, or ever will, or that treatment programs will be any more successful. There also remains the problem of widespread deprivation: "We are far from suggesting that all types and levels of drug use are at all times and in all circumstances deprivation-related. What we do, however, feel confident in asserting is that deprivation relates statistically to types and intensities of drug use which are problematic" (Advisory Council on the Misuse of Drugs 1998: 111).

Our current policy of "shared simplifications" (Gerstein and Harwood 1990) appears to reflect the popular will: allowing the majority of society to be against drug abuse while remaining free to abuse alcohol and tobacco. In other words, laws and law enforcement efforts against substances that are desired by a substantial minority of our citizenry provide symbolic opposition for the majority without actually impairing their own freedom to enjoy dangerous substances and activities—a policy that most Americans would be pleased to "drink to."

SUMMARY

- Decriminalization refers to the absence of laws punishing people for using drugs, as is the case with alcohol and tobacco.
- Most of the harmful aspects of heroin use are the result of its being illegal.
- Decriminalization would result in a reduction in the resources necessary for drug law enforcement; the low cost of psychoactive substances would curtail secondary criminality; drug trafficking organizations would no longer remain viable; those dependent drugs could lead more normal lives; and decriminalization would enable the use of social controls that inhibit antisocial, albeit lawful, behavior.
- Decriminalization, given the psychological benefits of drug use, would increase drug use; drugs freely available to adults could be abused by youngsters; decriminalization would signal an acceptance of drug use and more people would be tempted to try them; and the easy availability of currently illegal psychoactive substances would reduce the incentive to enter drug treatment or otherwise to seek a drug-free existence.
- Any discussion of drug policy is conditioned on views of drug abuse and on the particular theory that one adopts.
- There is a high correlation between urban poverty and heroin and cocaine use.
- There are three broad models of decriminalization.

- Some argue that drug prohibition is a selective infringement on rights since we do not criminalize similarly dangerous activity.
- Marijuana policy has been between those who argue that cannabis use is harmless, and hence it should be legalized; and opponents who argue that it is harmful to health, and hence should continue to be prohibited.
- Possession of marijuana for personal use has been decriminalized in some states but remains a federal crime.
- While marijuana has some use in medicine its use remains illegal. While its active ingredient (THC) is available as a prescription for certain medical treatment, there is some dispute as to whether or not oral THC is as effective as smoking marijuana.
- Needle-exchange programs exchange used needles for unused sterile ones in an effort to reduce the spread of AIDS.
- While drug policy in the United States has changed little since the Harrison Act, significant changes are occurring elsewhere in the world, in particular harm reduction whose focus is on reducing the risky consequences of drug use rather than on reducing drug use.
- European Union countries frequently practice what can be called *unofficial harm reduction*; that is, they utilize informal police and prosecutorial practices to eliminate punishments for obtaining or possessing small amounts of illegal drug.
- The country most closely identified with harm reduction is The Netherlands.

Review Questions

1. What is meant by a policy of decriminalization?
2. Why was heroin use less dangerous when it was not illegal?
3. Why are the most harmful aspects of heroin use the result of it being illegal?
4. What are the arguments for decriminalizing drugs in the United States?
5. What are the possible drawbacks of decriminalizing drugs in the United States?
6. What are the practical advantages of drug decriminalization/?
7. What are the disadvantages of drug decriminalization?
8. Why do those in the medical profession have a higher rate of drug use than the general population?
9. What are the different models of decriminalization?
10. What are the four views of drug abuse that provide the basis for policy?
11. If drug use is related to a physiological condition—an endorphin deficiency, for example—what policy implications are suggested?
12. Why does a serious effort to reduce drug abuse require a great expenditure of public money?
13. What are the issues involved in the controversy over medical marijuana?
14. What has the Supreme Court ruled with respect to medical marijuana?
15. What are the goals of a needle-exchange program?
16. Why is needle-exchange controversial?
17. What is "unofficial harm reduction"?
18. How does Dutch drug policy differ from that of the United States?

GLOSSARY

absorption Process by which elements from the outside move inside the body

abstinence Non-use of psychoactive substances

acetaldehyde A byproduct of the metabolism of alcohol

acetylcholine Neurotransmitter found in the brain where it regulates memory and in the peripheral nervous system where it regulates skeletal and smooth muscle

acute Intense and/or rapid onset

additive Two drugs that have similar actions are ingested, and the effect is cumulative $(1 + 1 = 2)$

adenosine Neurotransmitter regulating sleep for which caffeine is an antagonist

addiction A preoccupation with the use of psychoactive substances characterized by neurochemical and molecular changes in the brain

adrenaline Epinephrine; hormone secreted by the adrenal gland that arouses the sympathetic nervous system

affective processes Govern mood, feelings, and emotions

aftercare Treatment that follows discharge from a residential treatment program

agonist A substance that stimulates receptor sites

Al-Anon Mutual self-help organization for the families of alcoholics affiliated with Alcoholic Anonymous

alcohol Complex psychoactive substance that has both stimulating and depressing characteristics

Alcoholics Anonymous (AA) Original twelve-step mutual self-help organization

Amanita muscaria Hallucinogenic mushroom; fly agaric

amino acid transmitters The most prevalent neurotransmitters in the brain, these include glutamate and aspartate, which have excitatory actions, and glycine and gamma-amino butyric acid (GABA), which have inhibitory actions

amphetamine Artificially produced central nervous system stimulant

amygdala Part of forebrain that plays a role in emotional learning

amyl nitrate Volatile inhalant muscle relaxant

analgesic Substance that has the ability to reduce feelings of pain without loss of consciousness

analog Chemical compound that is similar to another drug in its effects but differs slightly in its chemical structure

anandamide Neurotransmitter that binds to cannabinoid receptors

Anesthesia Assisted Rapid Opiate Detoxification See *rapid detox*

anesthetic Agent that causes insensitivity to pain

angel dust Phencyclidine (PCP), a stimulant and hallucinogen

anhedonia Inability to feel pleasure

anomie A condition characterized by estrangement from society, the result of being unable to achieve financial success through legitimate avenues

Antabuse A drug that produces unpleasant reactions when used with alcohol

antagonist A drug that counters or blocks the effects of another drug

antagonistic Two or more drugs are taken together, and one counteracts the effects of the other(s) $(1 + 1 = 0)$

antidepressant Psychoactive drug prescribed for depressive disorders

arousal theory The theory that those whose central nervous system quickly habituates to incoming stimuli owing to a neurotransmitter malfunction are most apt to be reinforced for engaging in antisocial behavior and less likely to learn alternative behavior patterns

autonomic nervous system Part of the peripheral nervous system responsible for regulating the activity of involuntary bodily functions such as that of the heart and lungs. It includes the sympathetic and parasympathetic nervous systems

axon The fiberlike extension of a neuron by which the cell sends information to target cells

422

bad trip Slang for negative effects of hallucinogen ingestion

barbiturates CNS depressants

behavior modification Treatment approach based on learning theory

behavior processes These include voluntary movements such as walking and talking, and the autonomic bodily functions (such as those of the heart, lungs, and digestive system) are involuntary functions that are regulated by the **autonomic nervous system**

benzodiazepines Drugs that relieve anxiety or are prescribed as sedatives; among the most widely prescribed medications, including valium and librium

bind The attaching of a neurotransmitter to a receptor

blood alcohol level (BAL) Amount of alcohol in the blood: .08 or .10 is legal standard by intoxication as measured by a breathalyzer test

blood-brain barrier System that filters blood for toxins before it can enter the brain

brain stem The major route by which the forebrain sends information to and receives information from the spinal cord and peripheral nerves. It controls, among other things, respiration and regulation of heart rhythms

buprenorphine Drug that blocks the action of opiates by occupying their receptor sites

BZP A "club drug" with properties similar to amphetamine

caffeine Mild stimulant found in coffee and also used in some beverages

cannabinoid receptor Binding site for active ingredients in cannabis

cannabis Marijuana

catecholamines The neurotransmitters dopamine, epinephrine, and norepinephrine active in the brain and sympathetic nervous system

cell body (soma) Central structure of a neuron

central nervous system (CNS) Brain and the spinal vertebrae, which carry information to the brain; CNS

cerebral cortex The outermost layer of the cerebral hemispheres of the brain. It is responsible for all forms of conscious experience, including perception, emotion, thought, and planning

chasing the dragon Slang for smoking heroin

China White Southeast Asian heroin of high purity

chipper Occasional user of heroin

chronic Condition that persists over time

cirrhosis Scarring of the liver, the result of alcohol abuse

civil commitment The nonpunitive incarceration of addicts for purposes of treatment

classical conditioning Learning in which a primary stimulus that naturally produces a specific response is repeatedly paired with a neutral stimulus. With repeated pairing, the neutral stimulus becomes a conditioned stimulus that can evoke a response similar to that of the primary stimulus

Clonidine An antihypertension drug used to relieve many of the symptoms of opioid withdrawal, particularly those involving autonomic nervous system hyperactivity

club drug A term used to characterize psychoactive substances associated with dance parties or *raves*, in particular MDMA, known as ecstasy

CNS See *central nervous system*

cocaine Powerful stimulant derived from the coca plant

cocaethylene Substance produced when cocaine and alcohol are ingested together; increases the euphoric effect and the risk of sudden death

coca paste Product of the first step in extracting cocaine from coca leaves

cognition Process by which organism gains knowledge and uses that knowledge for comprehension and problem-solving

cold turkey Slang for giving up drug use without use of chemicals

contingency contracting Treatment using a mutually agreed upon contract providing privileges for compliance and negative contingencies for violations

crack Smokable form of cocaine

crank Methamphetamine

crash Slang for depression that occurs when high levels of stimulant ingestion are discontinued

craving Powerful and sometimes uncontrollable desire for psychoactive substances

cross-tolerance Tolerance to one substance that carries over to another

decriminalization Policy of not using criminal sanctions against drug users

delirium tremens (DTs) A severe symptom of alcohol withdrawal

demand reduction Strategies that reduce consumption of drugs as opposed to those that reduce supply

dendrite A treelike extension of the neuron cell body. Along with the cell body, it receives information from other neurons

depressants Sedating drugs that depress the central nervous system

depression Mental disorder characterized by depressed mood and abnormalities in sleep, appetite, and energy level

designer drugs Analog of a restricted drug that has psychoactive properties

desipramine Antidepressant used to wean cocaine users off the drug

detoxification Process of allowing the body to rid itself of a drug while managing the symptoms of withdrawal

dependence Stage of physical adaptation characterized by physical and/or psychological withdrawal symptoms when a substance is discontinued

Dextromethorphan (DXM) Active ingredient in many over-the-counter cough medicines that has hallucinogenic properties

diagnosis Classification of the nature and severity of a medical problem

dimethyltryptamine (DMT) A hallucinogenic substance that occurs naturally in many plants

disease model Explanation for drug use based on deficiencies or abnormalities in a person's physical or psychological make-up

dissociative anesthetics Anesthetics that distort perceptions of sight and sound and produce feelings of detachment

distillation Process used to extract alcohol from fermented grains or fruit

diversion Unauthorized distribution of a controlled substance from lawful sources

DMT Abbreviation for dimethyltryptamine

DXM Abbreviation for dextromethorphan

dopamine A stimulating (catecholamine) neurotransmitter present in regions of the brain that regulate movement, emotion, motivation, and feelings of pleasure; its absence results in Parkinson's disease

drug abuse Excessive use of psychoactive substances

drug court A nonadversarial approach to integrating substance abuse treatment with criminal justice case processing

ecstasy 3, 4-methylenedioxymethamphetamine (MDMA); designer drug having hallucinogenic and amphetamine-like characteristics

ego Psyche's contact with reality that maximizes gratification with a minimum of difficulties

electroencephalogram (EEG) Graphic record of electrical brain activity

EMIT Commonly used drug test

emphysema Lung disease, often caused by smoking, in which tissue deterioration results in difficult breathing and shortness of breath

employee assistance program (EAP) Help provided by employers to aid workers dealing with substance abuse

endogenous Produced by the body

endorphins Neurotransmitters produced in the brain that generate cellular and behavioral effects similar to morphine

ephedra Plant species with stimulant properties

ephedrine Stimulant used in treating allergies and cold symptoms

epinephrine A hormone, released by the adrenal medulla and the brain, that acts with norepinephrine to activate the sympathetic division of the autonomic nervous system; sometimes called adrenaline

enkephalins Neurotransmitter; endogenous opioid

fentanyl Potent opiate agonist

fermentation Process by which yeast interacts with plant sugars to produce alcohol

forebrain The largest part of the brain, which includes the cerebral cortex and basal ganglia. It is credited with the highest intellectual functions

formication Sensations, caused by cocaine and amphetamine, that insects are crawling under the skin

freebase Cocaine hydrochloride whose crystalline base is separated to enable smoking

GABA Gamma-aminobutyric acid; inhibitory neurotransmitter

gamma-amino butyric acid (GABA) An amino acid transmitter in the brain whose primary function is to inhibit the firing of neurons

gateway drug Substances that presage use of other psychoactive drugs; e.g., nicotine leading to marijuana leading to heroin

GBL (gamma-butyrolactone) A GHB precursor. Colorless, odorless, virtually tasteless, and in very low doses a CNS depressant; in higher doses can produce unconsciousness and even respiratory failure. Recalled in 1999.

GHB Similar to Rohypnol, gamma-hydroxybutyrate is colorless, odorless, virtually tasteless, and in very low doses a CNS depressant. Used by sexual predators since in addition to rendering victims unconscious, victims are often unable to recall what happened

glutamate amino acid Neurotransmitter that acts to excite neurons

half-life The time it takes for one-half of a drug to be eliminated from the body

halfway house Drug treatment residence

hallucinogens Natural or artificial chemicals that can produce distortions of reality

harm reduction Policy that seeks to reduce the harm of using drugs without requiring abstinence

hashish More potent form of marijuana

hepatitis C Liver disease spread through sexual intercourse and sharing of hypodermic needles

heroin Opiate produced from and more powerful than morphine

high Euphoria or feeling of wellbeing enjoyed by a substance user

hippocampus Section of the brain dealing with emotions, learning, and memory

homeostasis A state of equilibrium or balance achieved through the self-adjusting characteristics of the body

hypothalamus Brain structure that integrates information from a variety of

sources and is the control center of the central nervous system

id Mass of powerful drives, wishes, and urges that are energized in the form of the libido

inhalant Volatile psychoactive chemical produced for nondrug purposes

intravenous Ingestion of a drug into a vein

ions Electrically charged atoms or molecules

khat Stimulant leaves of an African plant

ketamine Surgical anesthetic related to phencyclidine (PCP)

kindling Recurring drug reaction that occurs without continued ingestion

Korsakoff's syndrome A disease associated with chronic alcoholism characterized by memory loss and psychotic behavior

LAMM Levo-alpha-acetylmethadol; synthetic opiate

learning theory Concept that behavior is shaped by its consequences

levo-alpha-acetylmethadol Opiate agonist similar to methadone used to treat heroin addiction

LSD Lysergic acid diethylamide; an hallucinogen

lysergic acid diethylamide Hallucinogen that can be produced artificially or from ergot; LSD

magnetic resonance imaging (MRI) Imaging technique for pictures of the brain

marijuana Cannabis

Marinol Trade name for pharmaceutical delta-9 tetrahydrocannabinol (THC), the active ingredient in marijuana that is used in medicine

MDMA Ecstasy

medial forebrain bundle Brain pathway that produces pleasure when stimulated

mescaline Hallucinogen found in the peyote cactus

mesolimbic system Section of the brain that generates feelings, emotions, and motivations; also important for learning and memory

metabolism Process by which the body breaks down matter into more simple components and for elimination as waste

methadone Opiate agonist used to treat heroin addiction

methamphetamine Powerful CNS stimulant

monoamine oxidase (MAO) Chemicals in the presynaptic terminals that control the level of neurotransmitters

MAO inhibitors Drugs used to treat depression by controlling the reuptake of serotonin

Minnesota model Private inpatient treatment using a twelve-step approach

morphine Opiate derivative used to relieve pain

naloxone Short-acting opiate antagonist

naltrexone Opiate agonist that is longer lasting than naloxone

narcolepsy Disorder characterized by uncontrollable episodes of deep sleep typically treated with stimulant drugs

narcotic CNS depressant derived from opiates

nativism Hostility toward foreigners

needle exchange Program that provides intravenous drug users with sterile needles

negative reinforcement Removal of a stimulus that increases the likelihood of a behavior

neuroadaption After repeated ingestion of a psychoactive drug, the CNS adjusts to its effects; tolerance

neuroenhancers Use of drugs developed for recognized medical conditions to strengthen ordinary cognition

neuron Nerve cell for the transmission of information and characterized by long fibrous projections called axons, and shorter, branch-like projections called dendrites

neurotransmitter A chemical released by neurons at a synapse for the purpose of relaying information via receptors

nicotine Tobacco plant alkaloid responsible for smoking's psychoactive and addictive effects

nitrous oxide "Laughing gas" used as an anesthetic and abused for its intoxicating effects

norepinephrine A neurotransmitter produced in the brain and in the peripheral nervous system that governs arousal and elevates mood

nucleus accumbens Located in the limbic system, provides feelings of pleasure when stimulated and nearly all psychoactice substances increase dopamine in this area

operant conditioning Repeated presentation or removal of a stimulus (reinforcer) following a behavior to increase the probability of the behavior. If the probability of a behavior increases after removal, negative reinforcement has occurred

opiates Drugs derived from opium

opioidphobia Physician fear that patients will become addicted to opioids prescribed for pain

opium Psychoactive sap of the poppy plant

overdose Ingestion of a psychoactive substance way above the level of tolerance; can be fatal

oxycodone Generic name for OxyContin

OxyContin Class II prescription opioid often diverted and abused

parasympathetic nervous system A branch of the autonomic nervous system concerned with the conservation of the body's energy and resources during relaxed states

Parkinson's disease Neurological disorder caused by a dopamine deficiency and characterized by muscular rigidity and difficulty starting movements, tremors, and loss of balance

passive smoke Product of tobacco or cannabis use—secondhand smoke—causing involuntary exposure

patent medicines Secret formulas that carried no patent and often contained coca or opiates

PCP phencyclidine, a dissociative drug

performance-enhancing drugs Chemicals used by athletes to improve physical abilities

peripheral nervous system A division of the nervous system consisting of all nerves not part of the brain or spinal cord

peyote Cactus plant whose "buttons" have hallucinogenic properties

phencyclidine (PCP) Anesthetic, dissociative drug

physical dependence Physiological state that results from a pattern of regular drug use as tolerance builds and results

in withdrawal symptoms if the drug is discontinued

placebo effect An inert compound triggering a drug-like response

polydrug use Use of more than one psychoactive drug

poppy Flowering plant from which opium is derived

positive reinforcement A stimulus that increases the likelihood that a behavior will be repeated

positron emission tomography (PET scan) Brain imaging technique

potentiating Two drugs have different actions but when taken together each enhances the effect of the other

prescription drug abuse Use of prescription drugs nonmedically

precursor Chemical that is critical to the manufacturing process and becomes part of the final drug

Prohibition Period between 1920 and 1933 when alcohol as a beverage was outlawed

psilocybin Hallucinogen found in certain mushrooms

psychedelic Hallucinogen

psychoactive Referring to a substance that affects the central nervous system

psychoanalytic theory Belief that unconscious material controls conscious behavior

psychosis Severe symptom of mental illness characterized by being out of contact with reality

psychotherapy Talk-based treatment

rapid detox A heroin- or other opiate-addicted patient is anesthetized and breathing through a respirator and receives intravenous doses of a heroin antagonist; patient experiences instant withdrawal that is complete in about four to six hours

rave Late-night dance party at which club drugs are often used

receptor sites Sites consisting of molecules on the surface or inside cells where neurotransmitters attach and exert their effects

reinforcement Consequence of a behavior that increases the likelihood that it will reoccur

relapse Reversion to drug use after abstinence and/or treatment

remission Absence of symptoms even though the underlying condition has not been cured

reuptake A process by which released neurotransmitters are absorbed for subsequent reuse

reverse tolerance Increase in the reaction to a drug that develops after chronic use; sensitization

Ritalin (methylphenidate) Stimulant used for treating attention deficit hyperactivity disorder

reward Process that reinforces behavior

Rohypnol A benzodiazepine (sedative) widely prescribed in Europe but not approved for use in the United States. Known to abusers as "roofies" or "rope," it is often ingested with alcohol or marijuana

rush How drug users describe a surge of pleasure that follows the intake of a psychoactive substance

sedative CNS depressant that can produce calm and induce sleep

selective tolerance Tolerance to one aspect of a drug's effect

self-medicating Nonmedical use of psychoactive substances in response to physiological and/or psychological difficulties

sensitization Increase in a drug's effect with repeated administration, the change being in the opposite direction of tolerance

serotonin A neurotransmitter that elevates mood; antidepressant drugs often stimulate the release of serotonin

social norms Explicit or implicit rules that guide social behavior in a given community

soma See *cell body*

speed Methamphetamine

spontaneous remission Discontinuing drug use without treatment intervention

stimulant Psychoactive chemical that activates the central nervous system and elevates mood

subcutaneous Ingesting a drug under the skin

substance abuse Harmful use of one or more psychoactive substances

superego Psychic mechanism exercising a critical influence; a sense of morality that controls behavior

symbolic interactionism Sociological perspective whose focus is on how particular people or behaviors are labeled

sympathetic nervous system A branch of the autonomic nervous system responsible for mobilizing the body's energy and resources during times of stress and arousal

synapse A gap between two neurons that functions as the site of information transfer from one neuron to another

synergistic Two drugs have similar actions but their combined effect is more than cumulative

tetrahydrocannabinol (THC) Active ingredient in marijuana

thalamus Structure deep within the brain serving as a filter and relay station for information

theory Building block for scientific knowledge that organizes events, explains past events, and predicts future events

therapeutic community Residential drug treatment program based on Alcoholics Anonymous emphasizing addicts helping one another to become socially conforming persons

thought processes Involve the ability to reason, categorize, organize, abstract, and pay attention

tobacco Dried plant leaves containing nicotine

tolerance Progressive ability of the body to adopt to the effects of a drug used at regular and frequent intervals, making the drug less effective; higher doses of a drug are required to produce the same effect

toluene Ingredient in solvents that causes intoxication when inhaled; methyl benzene

tranquilizer Prescribed drugs having a sedating effect

transporter Neuron chemical that carries a neurotransmitter back to its presynaptic terminal

tricyclic antidepressants Used to treat depression by manipulating the level of several neurotransmitters

twelve steps Principles on which Alcoholics Anonymous and similar programs are based

unconscious According to psychoanalytic theory, repressed feelings and experiences that exert an influence over conscious behavior

ventral tegmental area (VTA) Neurons containing dopamine

volatile substance Nondrug chemical inhaled for its psychoactive effects

Volstead Act Federal statute for enforcing the Eighteenth (Prohibition) Amendment

withdrawal Unpleasant symptoms that result when an addicted person fails to ingest a sufficient amount of addictive substance

REFERENCES

Abadinsky, Howard
2010 *Organized Crime*, 9th ed. Belmont, CA: Wadsworth.
2009 *Probation and Parole: Theory and Practice*, 10th ed. Upper Saddle River, NJ: Prentice Hall.
2008 *Law and Justice: An Introduction to the American Legal System*, 6th ed. Upper Saddle River, NJ: Prentice Hall.
Abel, Ernest L., ed.
1978 *The Scientific Study of Marijuana*. Chicago: Nelson-Hall.
Abrahart, David
1998 "Concerning Lysergic Acid Diethylamide (LSD) and Mental Health." Master of Arts thesis, Department of Mental Health Studies, University of Portsmouth, England.
Acker, Caroline Jean
2002 *Creating the American Junkie: Addiction Research in the Classic Era of Narcotic Control*. Baltimore: Johns Hopkins University Press.
Adams, Jane Meredith
2002 "Medical Marijuana Users Sue U.S. Officials." *Chicago Tribune* (October 10): 12.
Addiction Research Unit
1998 *Dopamine*. Internet. Buffalo: State University of New York at Buffalo.
Adler, Jerry
2007 "Rehab Reality Check." *Newsweek* (February 19): 44–46.
2003 "In the Grip of a Deeper Pain." *Newsweek* (October 20): 48–49.

Adler, Patricia A.
1985 *Wheeling and Dealing: An Ethnography of an Upper-Level Drug-Dealing and Smuggling Community*. New York: Columbia University Press.
Adrade, Xavier, Stephen J. Sifaneck, and Alan Neaigus
1999 "Dope Sniffers in New York City: An Ethnography of Heroin Markets and Patterns of Use." *Journal of Drug Issues* 22 (2): 271–98.
Advisory Council on the Misuse of Drugs
1998 *Drug Misuse and the Environment*. London, England: Home Office.
1994 *Police, Drug Misusers and the Community*. London, England: Home Office.
1993 *Drug Education in Schools: The Need for New Impetus*. London, England: Home Office.
"A Fishy Haul"
2004 *New York Daily News* (September 28): 5.
Agar, Michael
1973 *Ripping and Running: A Formal Ethnography of Urban Heroin Addicts*. New York: Seminar Press.
Ahmed-Ullah, Noreen S.
2001 "Pashtun Identity Defies Colonial Line." *Chicago Tribune* (November 6): 15.
Aicchorn, August
1963 *Wayward Youth*. New York: Viking.

Alexander, Bruce K.
1990 "Alternatives to the War on Drugs." *Journal of Drug Issues* 20 (1): 1–27.
Alford, Geary S.
1980 "Alcoholics Anonymous: An Empirical Outcome Study." *Addictive Behaviors* 5: 359–70.
Alford, Geary S., Roger A. Koehler, and James Leonard
1991 "Alcoholics Anonymous-Narcotics Anonymous Model Inpatient Treatment of Chemically Dependent Adolescents: A 2-Year Outcome Study." *Journal of Studies on Alcohol* 52 (March): 118–26.
Allen, Frederick
1998 "American Spirit." *American Heritage* (May/June): 82–92.
Altman, Lawrence K.
2005 "Cocaine Users Face Greater Risk of Aneurysm." *New York Times* (May 10): F6.
Alvarez, A.
2001 "Drugs and Inspiration." *Social Research* 68 (Fall): 779–95.
American Heart Association
1999 "More Bad News for Cocaine Users: Drug Can Triple Risk of Aneurysm." (November 9): Internet.
American Heritage Dictionary
2000 Boston: Houghton Mifflin. American Academy of Psychiatrists in Alcoholism and Addictions Board of Directors 1990 Internet.

American Psychiatric Association (APA)
1995 *Psychiatric Services for Addicted Patients.* Washington, DC: APA.
1994 *Diagnostic and Statistical Manual of Mental Disorders,* 4th ed. (DSM-IV). Washington DC: APA.

American Social Health Association
1972 *Guidelines: A Comprehensive Community Program to Reduce Drug Abuse.* Overview I. NY: American Social Health Association.

Anderson, Austin A.
1992 "Transnational Crimes: A Global Approach." *FBI Law Enforcement Bulletin* (March): 26–32.

Andrews, Edmund L.
1990 "2 Treatments for Cocaine Addiction." *New York Times* (July 21): 18.

Angier, Natalie
1995 "Variant Gene Tied to a Love of New Thrills." *New York Times* (January 2): 1, B9.
1991 "Moderate Drinking Cuts Risk of Heart Disease, Study Says." *New York Times* (August 24): 10.

Anglin, M. Douglas
1988 "The Efficacy of Civil Commitment in Treating Narcotic Addiction." Pages 8–34 in *Compulsory Treatment of Drug Abuse: Research and Clinical Practice.* Rockville, MD: National Institute on Drug Abuse.

Anglin, M. Douglas and George Speckart
1988 "Narcotics Use and Crime: A Multisample, Multimethod Analysis." *Criminology* 26 (May): 197–233.

Anglin, M. Douglas and Thomas H. Maughr II
1992 "Ensuring Success in Interventions with Drug-Using Offenders." *Annals* 521 (May): 66–90.

Anglin, M. Douglas and William McGlothlin
1985 "Methadone Maintenance in California: A Decade's Experience." Pages 219–80 in *The Year Book of Substance Use and Abuse,* edited by Leon Brill and Charles Winick. New York: Human Services Press.

Anglin, M. Douglas and Yih-Ing Hser
1990a "Legal Coercion and Drug Abuse Treatment: Research Findings and Social Policy Implications." Pages 151–76 in *Handbook of Drug Control in the United States,* edited by James A. Inciardi. Westport, CT: Greenwood.

1990b "Treatment of Drug Abuse." Pages 393–460 in *Drugs and Crime,* edited by Michael Tonry and James Q. Wilson. Chicago: University of Chicago Press.

Anglin, M. Douglas, Douglas Longshore, and Susan Turner
1999 "Treatment Alternative to Street Crime: An Evaluation of Five Programs." *Criminal Justice and Behavior* 26 (June): 168–95.

Aniskiewicz, Rick and Earl Wysong
1990 "Evaluating DARE Drug Education and the Multiple Meanings of Success." *Policy Studies Review* 9 (Summer): 727–47.

Anonymous
2006 "To Quit Heroin Cold Turkey." *Esquire* (August): 126.

Anslinger, Harry J. and William F. Tompkins
1953 *The Traffic in Narcotics.* New York: Funk and Wagnalls.

Anthony, James C. and Valerie Forman
2000 "At the Intersection of Public Health and Criminal Justice Research on Drugs and Crime." Draft of a paper for the Drugs and Crime Research Forum.

"Anti-Drug Efforts Encounter Resistance in Colombia"
1995 *New York Times* (December 12): 4.

Arax, Mark and Tom Gorman
1995 "The State's Illicit Farm Belt Export." *Los Angeles Times* (March 13): 1, 16, 17.

Archibold, Randal C.
2009a "Drug Cartel Violence Spills Over From Mexico, Alarming U.S." *New York Times* (March 23): 1, 12.
2009b "In Heartland Death, Traces of Heroin's Spread." *New York Times* (May 31): 1, 24.
2009c "15 Are Indicted in Chicago In Push on Mexican Cartel." *New York Times* (November 21): 12.
2007 "Along the Border, Smugglers Build a World Below Ground." *New York Times* (December 7): 18.

Armstrong, Andrew
2003 "Drug Courts and the De Facto Legalization of Drug Use for Participants in Residential Treatment Facilities." *Journal of Criminal Law and Criminology* 94 (Fall): 133–69.

Asbury, Herbert
1950 *The Great Illusion: An Informal History of Prohibition.* Garden City, NY: Knopf.

Ashley, Richard
1975 *Cocaine: Its History, Uses and Effects.* New York: St. Martin's Press.

Ashton, Elizabeth
2008 *Alcohol Abuse Makes Prescription Drug Abuse More Likely.* National Institute on Drug Abuse: Internet.

Associated Press
2009a "Video Shows 53 Inmates Escape Mexican Prison." *USA Today* (May 21): Internet.
2009b "Mexico Legalizes Drug Possession." *New York Times* (August 21): 12.
2009c "Four Held in Revenge Attack on Hero's Family." (December 24): Internet.
2007 "Feds Seize Candy Bars Filled with 5M in Heroin." *New York Daily News* (February 24): 10.
2006 "A Deadly Heroin Mix is Claiming Dozens of Lives." *New York Times* (May 28): 27.
2005 "Pregnancy Warning on Antidepressants." *New York Times* (May 18): 21.
2004a "Smoking and Drug Use by Teenagers Drops Again." *New York Times* (December 22): B8.
2004b "Two Drinks Can Kill Brain Cells in a Fetus, Studies Suggest." *New York Times* (February 15): 21.
2002 "Doctor I Sentenced for OxyContin Deaths." *New York Times* (March 23): 11.
2001 "Jury Awards Flight Attendant $400,000 in Drug Test Case." *New Jersey Online* (July 6): Internet.
2000a "Ex-Mexico Drug Czar Gets More Jail." (February 22): Internet.
2000b "Economic Protests Disrupt Bolivia." *Chicago Tribune* (April 10): 11.
1999a "Alcohol-Linked Road Death at Low." Internet.
1999b "China Executes at Least 71 in a Day." Internet.
1999c "Cocaine Seized in Fish Shipment." Internet.
1999d "Study Links Cigars to High Risk of Cancer." *New York Times* (June 10): 24.
1998 "Alcohol, Violence Link Still Strong, U.S. Says." *Chicago Tribune* (April 6): 5.
1997a "High Nicotine Levels Found in Smoking Moms' Babies." *Chicago Tribune* (March 20): 13.
1997b "Swiss Back Heroin Project." *New York Times* (September 29): 1.

1995 "5,600 Infant Deaths Tied to Mothers' Smoking." *New York Times* (April 13): 11.

Ausubel, David P.
1980 "An Interactional Approach to Narcotic Addiction." Pages 4–7 in *Theories on Drug Abuse: Selected Contemporary Perspectives,* edited by Dan J. Lettieri, Mollie Sayers, and Helen Wallenstein Pearson. Rockville, MD: National Institute on Drug Abuse.
1978 *What Every Well-Informed Person Should Know About Drug Addiction.* Chicago: Nelson-Hall.

Avants, S. Kelly, Arthur Margolin, Thomas R. Kosten, and Ned L. Cooney
1995 "Differences Between Responders and Nonresponders to Cocaine Cues in the Laboratory." *Addictive Behaviors* 20 (March/April): 214–24.

Bach, Peter B. and John Lantos
1999 "Methadone Dosing, Heroin Affordability, and the Severity of Addiction." *American Journal of Public Health* 5 (May): 662–65.

Baer, John S.
2002 "Student Factors: Understanding Individual Variation in College Drinking." *Journal of Studies on Alcohol* 14 (March): 40–53.

Bailey, Pearce
1974 "The Heroin Habit." Pages 171–76 in *Yesterday's Addicts; American Society and Drug Abuse, 1865–1920,* edited by Howard Wayne Morgan. Norman: University of Oklahoma Press.

Bakalar, Nicholas
2006 "Review Sees No Advantage in 12-Step Programs." *New York Times* (July 25): F6.
2005 "When the Smoke Doesn't Clear." *New York Times* (March 22): F7.

Baker, Al
2002 "Boy, 12, Flies into U.S. After Swallowing Heroin in Condoms." *New York Times* (April 12): 24.

Ball, John C., Lawrence Rosen, Ellen G. Friedman, and David N. Nurco
1979 "The Impact of Heroin Addiction upon Criminality." Pages 163–69 in *Problems of Drug Dependence 1979,* edited by Louis S. Harris. Rockville, MD: National Institute on Drug Abuse.

Balster, Robert L.
1988 "Pharmacological Effects of Cocaine Relevant to Its Abuse." Pages 1–13 in *Mechanisms of Cocaine Abuse and Toxicity,* edited by Doris Clouet, Khursheed Asghar, and Roger Brown. Rockville, MD: National Institute on Drug Abuse.

Balter, Mitchell B.
1974 "Drug Abuse: A Conceptual Analysis and Overview of the Current Situation." Pages 3–21 in *Drug Use: Epidemiological and Sociological Approaches,* edited by Eric Josephson and Eleanor E. Carroll. New York: Wiley.

Bandura, Albert
1974 "Behavior Theory and the Models of Man." *American Psychologist* 29 (December): 860–66.
1969 *Principles of Behavior Modification.* New York: Holt, Rinehart and Winston.

Barnard, Herbert P.
1998 *The Netherlands' Drug Policy: 20 Years of Experience.* Internet. Washington, DC: Royal Netherlands Embassy.

Barnett, Arnold
1988 "Drug Crackdowns and Crime Rates: A Comment on the Kleiman Paper." Pages 35–42 in *Street-Level Drug Enforcement: Examining the Issues,* edited by Marcia R. Chaiken. Washington, DC: U.S. Government Printing Office.

Barnett, Randy E.
1987 "Curing the Drug-Law Addiction: The Harmful Side Effects of Legal Prohibition." Pages 73–102 in *Dealing with Drugs: Consequences of Government Control,* edited by Ronald Hamowy. Lexington, MA: D.C. Heath.

Barrionuevo, Lexi
2009 "Latin America Weighs Less Punitive Path to Curb Drug Use." *New York Times* (August 27): 8.

Bartosiewicz, Petra
2004 "A Quitter's Dilemma: Hooked on the Cure." *New York Times* (May 2): BU8.

Batki, Steven L., Janice F. Kauffman, Ira Marion, Mark W. Parrino, and George E. Woody
2005 *Medication-Assisted Treatment for Opioid Addiction in Opioid Treatment Programs.* Rockville, MD: U.S. Substance Abuse and Mental Health Services Administration.

Baumeister, S. E. and P. Tossmann
2005 "Association Between Early Onset of Cigarette, Alcohol and Cannabis Use and Later Drug Use Patterns: An Analysis of a Survey in European Metropolises." *European Addiction Research* 11: 92–99.

Baumgartner, Werner A., Virginia Hill, and William H. Blahd
1989 "Hair Analysis for Drugs of Abuse." *Journal of Forensic Sciences* 34 (November): 1433–53.

Baumrind, Diana
1987 "Familial Antecedents of Adolescent Drug Use: A Developmental Perspective." Pages 13–44 in *Etiology of Drug Abuse: Implications for Prevention,* edited by Coryl LaRue Jones and Robert J. Battjes. Rockville, MD: National Institute on Drug Abuse.

Beck, Jerome and Marsha Rosenbaum
1994 *Pursuit of Ecstasy: The MDMA Experience.* Albany, NY: State University of New York Press.

Becker, Howard S.
1977 "Knowledge, Power, and Drug Effects." Pages 167–90 in *Drugs and Politics,* edited by Paul E. Rock. New Brunswick, NJ: Transaction Books.
1967 "History, Culture, and Subjective Experience: An Exploration of the Social Bases of Drug-Induced Experiences." *Journal of Health and Social Behavior* 8: 163–76.
1966 *Outsiders: Studies in the Sociology of Deviance.* New York: Free Press.

Beeching, Jack
1975 *The Chinese Opium Wars.* New York: Harcourt Brace Jovanovich.

Beers, Rand and Francis X. Taylor
2002 "The Worldwide Connection Between Drugs and Terror." *Testimony Before Senate Committee on the Judiciary Subcommittee on Technology, Terrorism and Government Information* (March 13): Internet.

Begley, Sharon
1999 "Hope for Snow Babies." *Pressweek* (September 29): 62–63.

Beiser, Vince
2008 "First, Reduce Harm." *Miller-McCune* (November/ December): 60–71.

Belenko, Steven
1993 *Crack and the Evolution of Anti-Drug Policy.* Westport, CT: Greenwood.

Belenko, Steven and Ko-lin Chin
1989 "Typologies of Criminal Careers Among Crack Arrestees." Paper presented at the annual meeting of the American Society of Criminology, Reno, NV, November.

Belkin, Lisa
1990 "Airport Anti-Drug Nets Snare Many People Fitting 'Profiles.'" *New York Times* (March 20): 1, 11.

Bellis, David J.
1981 *Heroin and Politicians: The Failure of Public Policy to Control Addiction in America*. Westport, CT: Greenwood.

Belluck, Pam
2003 "Methadone, Once the Way Out, Suddenly Grows as a Killer Drug." *New York Times* (February 9): 1.
2009 "High-Risk Drug is in Spotlight in Wake of High Profile Death." *New York Times* (August 7): 1, 3.

Bendavid, Naftali
2002 "Critics Decry Ads Linking Drugs, Terror." *Chicago Tribune* (March 24): 1, 17.

Benedict, William Reed, Lin Huff-Corzine, and Jay Corzine
1998 "'Clean Up and Go Straight': Effects of Drug Treatment on Recidivism Among Felony Probationers." *American Journal of Criminal Justice* 22 (2): 169–87.

Bennett, David H.
1988 *The Party of Fear: From Nativist Movements to the New Right in American History*. Chapel Hill: University of North Carolina Press.

Bennett, Trevor and Katy Holloway
2005 "The Association Between Multiple Drug Misuse and Crime." *International Journal of Offender Therapy and Comparative Criminology* 49 (1): 63–81.

Bennett, William Ira
1988 "Patterns of Addiction." *New York Times Magazine* (April 10): 60–61.

Benton, Sarah Allen
2009 *Understanding the High Functioning Alcoholic*. New York: Praeger.

Berger, Joseph
1989 "Judgment Replaces Fear in Drug Lessons." *New York Times* (October 30): 1, 8.

Berke, Richard L.
1990 "Bennett Doubts Value of Drug Education." *New York Times* (February 3): 1, 9.
1989 "Corruption in Drug Agency Called a Crippler of Inquiries and Morale." *New York Times* (December 17): 1, 22.

Berkow, Robert, ed.
1982 *The Merck Manual of Diagnosis and Therapy*. Rahway, NJ: Merck Sharp and Dohme.

Bhati, Avinash Sing, John K. Roman, and Arron Chalfin
2008 *To Treat or Not to Treat: Evidence on the Prospects of Expanding Treatment to Drug-Involved Offenders*. Washington, DC: Urban Institute.

Biernacki, Patrick
1986 *Pathways from Heroin Addiction: Recovery Without Treatment*. Philadelphia: Temple University Press.

Billeaud, Jacques
2009 "Smugglers Get Creative Sneaking Drugs into the U.S." *Philadelphia Inquirer* (November 8): K6.

Binder, Arnold and Gilbert Geis
1983 *Methods of Research in Criminology and Criminal Justice*. New York: McGraw-Hill.

Bishop, Katherine
1991 "Business Data Is Sought in Marijuana Crackdown." *New York Times* (May 24): B9.
1987 "Ex-Employee Wins Drug Testing Case." *New York Times* (October 31): 18.

Blackmore, John
1979 "Diagnosis: Heroin Addiction. Prescription: Methadone." *Corrections Magazine* 5 (December): 24–31.

Blakeslee, Sandra
2007 "A Small Part of the Brain and Its Profound Effects." *New York Times* (February 6): F6.
1998 "Two Studies Shed New Light on Cocaine's Effect on Brain." *New York Times* (May 14): 18.
1997 "Studies of Brain Find Marijuana Can Have the Same Effect as Other Drugs." *New York Times* (June 27): 13.
1994 "Yes, People Are Right. Caffeine Is Addictive." *New York Times* (October 5): B9.
1991 "Finding the Secrets of Caffeine, the Drug." *New York Times* (August 7): B6.
1989 "Crack's Toll Among Babies: A Joyless View of Even Toys." *New York Times* (September 18): 1, 12.
1988 "8-Year Study Finds 2 Sides to Teen-Age Drug Use." *New York Times* (July 21): 1, 13.

Bloom, Floyd E.
1993 "Brain Research for Today and Tomorrow: Recent Advances and Research Frontiers." Pages 9–26 in *International Research Conference on Biomedical Approaches to Illicit Drug Demand Reduction*, edited by Christine R. Hartel. Washington, DC: U.S. Government Printing Office.

Bloomberg News
2006 "Pot-Cancer Link up in Smoke—Study." *New York Daily News* (May 24): 10.

Bluhm, Judy
1987 *When You Face the Chemically Dependent Patient: A Practical Guide for Nurses*. St. Louis, MO: Ishiyaku EuroAmerica.

Blum, Kenneth, Ernest P. Noble, Peter J. Sheridan, Anne Montgomery, Terry Ritchie, Puduer Jagadeeswaran, Harou Nogami, Arthur H. Briggs, and Jay B. Cohn
1990 "Allec Association of Human Dopamine D2 Receptor Gene in Alcoholism." *Journal of the American Medical Association* 263 (April 8): 2055–60.

Blum, Richard H. and Associates
Society and Drugs. San Francisco: Jossey-Bass.

Blumenthal, Ralph
2009 "French Connection Epilogue: Mob Boss Offers a New Ending." *New York Times* (February 22): 27, 30.

Boaz, David, ed.
1990 *The Crisis in Drug Prohibition*. Washington, DC: Cato Institute.

Bolla, Karen I., Jean-Lud Cadet, and Edythe D. London
1998 "The Neuropsychiatry of Chronic Cocaine Abuse." *Journal of Neuropsychiatry* 1 (Summer): 280–89.

Bollag, Burton
1989 "Swiss-Dutch Drug Stance: Tolerance." *New York Times* (December 1): 4.

Böllinger, Lorenz
2004 "Drug Law and Policy in Germany and the European Community: Recent Developments." *Journal of Drug Issues* 34 (Summer): 419–20.

Bonnie, Richard J. and Charles H. Whitebread II
1970 "The Forbidden Fruit and the Tree of Knowledge: An Inquiry into the Legal History of American Marijuana Prohibition." *Virginia Law Review* 56 (October): 971–1203.

Bonson, Katherine R., Steven J. Grant, Carlo S. Contoreggi, Jonathan M. Links, Janet Metcalfe, Lloyd Weyl, Varughese Kurian, Monique Ernst, and Edythe D. London
2002 "Neural Systems and Cue-Induced Cocaine Craving." *Neuropsychopharmacology* 26 (3): 376–86.

Booth, William and Steve Fainaru
2009 "Mexican Cartels Recruiting Youths." *Philadelphia Inquirer* (November 8): 15.

Bourgeois, Philippe
1995 *In Search of Respect: Selling Crack in El Barrio.* Cambridge, England: Cambridge University Press.

Bouza, Anthony
1990 *The Police Mystique: An Insider's Look at Cops, Crime, and the Criminal Justice System.* New York: Plenum.

Bowden, Charles
2009 "We Bring Fear." *Mother Jones* (July/August): 29–43.
1991 "La Virgen and the Drug Lord." *Phoenix* (March): 96–103.

Bowman, Rex
2005 "Prescription for Crime." *Time* (March 28): 50–51.

Bozarth, Michael A.
1994 "Pleasure Systems in the Brain." Pages 5–16 in *Pleasure: The Politics and the Reality,* edited by D. M. Warburton. New York: John Wiley & Sons.

Bradsher, Keith
1995a "Low Ranking for Poor American Children." *New York Times* (August 14): 7.
1995b "Gap in Wealth in U.S. Called Widest in West." *New York Times* (April 17): 1, C4.
1995c "Widest Gap in Incomes? Research Points to U.S." *New York Times* (October 27): C2.

Brecher, Edward M. and the Editors of Consumer Reports
1972 *Licit and Illicit Drugs.* Boston: Little, Brown.

Brems, Christiane, Mark E. Johnson, David Neal, and Melinda Freemon
2004 "Childhood Abuse History and Substance Use Among Men and Women Receiving Detoxification Services." *American Journal of Drug and Alcohol Abuse* 30 (November): 799–822.

Bresler, Fenton
1980 *The Chinese Mafia.* New York: Stein and Day.

Brevorka, Jennifer
2002 "Meth Lab Seizures on Rise in North Carolina." *Asheville Citizen-Times* (July 22): 1, 5.

Brewington, Vincent, Michael Smith, and Douglas Lipton
1994 "Acupuncture as a Detoxification Treatment: An Analysis of Controlled Research." *Journal of Substance Abuse Treatment* 11 (4): 289–307.

"Briefing: Dealing with Drugs"
2009 *The Economist* (March 7): 30–36.

Brigham, Gregory S.
2003 "12-Step Participation as a Pathway to Recovery: The Maryhaven Experience and Implications for Treatment and Research." *Perspectives* 2 (August): 43–51.

Brinkley, Joel
2005 "Anti-Drug Gains in Colombia Don't Reduce Flow to U.S." *New York Times* (April 28): 3.

Brody, Jane E.
2009 "High Functioning, But Still Alcoholics." *New York Times* (May 5): D7.
2003 "Addiction: A Brain Ailment, Not a Moral Lapse." *New York Times* (September 30): B10.
2001 "An Old Enemy, Smoking, Hangs Tough." *New York Times* (December 11): D7.
1997 "Many Smokers Who Can't Quite Are Mentally Ill, a Study Shows." *New York Times* (August 27): B10.
1995 "Tourette Syndrome Can't Be Cured, but Knowledge Often Reduces Suffering." *New York Times* (March 1): B8.
1988 "Personal Health." *New York Times* (April 21): 24.
1987 "Role of Heredity in Alcoholism." *New York Times* (August 14): 14.

Brooke, James
1995 "Colombia's Rebels Grow Rich from Banditry." *New York Times* (July 2): 1, 4.
1991 "Marxist Revolt Grows Strong in the Shantytowns of Peru." *New York Times* (November 11): 1, 6.

Brotman, Richard and Frederic Suffet
1975 "The Concept of Prevention and Its Limitations." *Annals* 417 (January): 53–65.

Brounstein, Paul J. and Janine M. Zweig
n.d. *Understanding Substance Abuse Prevention. Toward the 21st Century: A Primer on Effective Programs.* Washington, DC: Substance Abuse and Mental Health Services Administration.

Brounstein, Paul J., Harry P. Hatry, David M. Altschuler, and Louis H. Blair
1990 *Substance Use and Delinquency Among Inner City Adolescent Males.* Washington, DC: Urban Institute.

Brown, Ethan
1999 "Clear and Present Danger." *New York* (November 22): 43–45.

Brownlee, Shanon
1999 "Inside the Teen Brain." *U.S. News and World Report* (August 9): 44–53.

Brownlee, Shanon and Joannie M. Schrof
1997 "The Quality of Mercy." *U.S. News and World Report* (March 17): 54–62, 65–67.

Brzezinski, Matthew
2002 "Re-Engineering the Drug Business." *New York Times Magazine* (June 23): 24–29, 46, 54, 56.

Buchanan, David R.
1992 "Social History of American Drug Use." *Journal of Drug Issues* 22 (Winter): 31–52.

Buckley, Cara
2009 "Young and Suburban, and Falling for Heroin." *New York Times* (September 27): LI: 1, 10.

Buckley, William F. Jr., et al.
1996 "War on Drugs Is Lost." *National Review* (February 12): 34–48.

Buckman, Robert T.
2004 *Latin America.* Harpers Ferry, WV: Sryker-Post Publications.

Budney, Alan J., Roger Roffman, Robert S. Stephens, and Denise Walker
2007 "Marijuana Dependence and Its Treatment." *Addiction Science and Clinical Practice* (December): 4–16.

Bukstein, Oscar, David A. Brent, and Yifrah Kaminer
1989 "Comorbidity of Substance Abuse and Other Psychiatric Disorders in Adolescents." *American Journal of Psychiatry* 146 (September): 1131–41.

Bullington, Bruce
1999 "Editor's Introduction: The 'Golden Age' of Dutch Drug Policy?" *Journal of Drug Issues* 29(3): 443–50.

Burgess, Robert L. and Ronald L. Akers
1969 "Differential Association-Reinforcement Theory of Criminal Behavior." Pages 291–320 in *Behavioral Sociology,* edited by Robert L. Burgess and Don Bushell Jr. New York: Columbia University Press.

Burkholz, Herbert
1987 "Pain: Solving the Mystery." *New York Times* (January 15): Internet.

Burns, R. Stanley and Alan Done
1980 "Special Management Procedures for Emergency Medical Staff." Pages 95–120 in *Phencyclidine Abuse Manual,* edited by Mary Tuma McAdams, Ronald L. Linder, Steven E. Lerner, and Richard Stanley Burns. Los Angeles, CA: University of California Extension.

Burros, Marian and Sarah Jay
1996 "Concern Is Growing over an Herb That Promises a Legal High." *New York Times* (April 10): B1, 8.

Bush, Patricia J. and Ronald Iannotti
1987 "The Development of Children's Health Orientations and Behaviors: Lessons for Substance Abuse Prevention." Pages 45–74 in *Etiology of Drug Abuse: Implications for Prevention*, edited by Coryl LaRue Jones. Rockville, MD: National Institute on Drug Abuse.

Butterfield, Fox
2005 "Fighting Illegal Drugs Through Its Legal Source." *New York Times* (January 30): 20.
2004a "Home Drug-Making Laboratories Expose Children to Toxic Fallout." *New York Times* (February 23): 1, 16.
2004b "Across Rural America, Drug Casts a Grim Shadow." *New York Times* (January 4): 10.
1997 "Drop in Homicide Rate Linked to Crack's Decline." *New York Times* (October 27): 10.

Byck, Robert, ed.
1974 *Cocaine Papers: Sigmund Freud.* New York: Stonehill.

Byrne, Andrew
2000 "Nine-year Follow-up of 86 Consecutive Patients Treated with Methadone in General Practice, Sydney, Australia." *Drug and Alcohol Review* 19 (June): 153–59.

Calefati, Jessica
2008 "Heroin Hits the Suburbs—Hard." *U.S. News and World Report* (December 15): 27–28.

California Narcotic Addict Evaluation Authority
1994 *All About the Civil Addict Program.* Norco, CA: California Narcotic Addict Evaluation Authority.

"Canadian Study Quantifies Link Between Substance Abuse and Crime: Alcohol Abuse Associated with Violent Offenses"
2002 *Alcoholism and Drug Abuse Weekly* 14 (May 13): 2–5.

Cantrell, Geoffrey
2002 "Valuable Marijuana Crop Found in Madison." *Asheville Citizen-Times* (July 24): B1.

Caputo, Philip
2009 "The Border of Madness." *The Atlantic* (December): 42–69.

Carey, Benedict
2010 "Prompt Doses Morphine Can Blunt Traumatic Stress, Study Finds." *New York Times* (January 14): 18.
2007 "In Clue to Addictive Behavior, a Brain Injury Halts Smoking." *New York Times* (January 26): 1, 18.

Carlson, Kenneth and Peter Finn
1993 *Prosecuting Criminal Enterprises.* Washington, DC: Bureau of Justice Statistics.

Carpenter, Cheryl, Barry Glassner, Bruce D. Johnson, and Julia Loughlin
1988 *Kids, Drugs, and Crime.* Lexington, MA: D.C. Heath.

Carroll, Kathleen
1998 *A Cognitive-Behavioral Approach: Treating Cocaine Addiction.* Rockville, MD: National Institute on Drug Abuse.

Carroll, Kathleen, Samuel A. Ball, Charla Nich, Patrick G. O'Connor, Dorothy A. Eagan, Tami L. Frankforter, Elisa G. Triffleman, Julia Shi, and Bruce J. Rounsaville
2001 "Targetting Behavioral Therapies to Enhance Naltrexone Treatment of Opioid Dependence." *Archives of General Psychiatry* 58 (August): 755–83.

Carroll, Linda
2003 "Alcohol's Toll on Fetuses: Even Worse than Thought." *New York Times* (November 4): F1, 6.
2002 "Marijuana's Effects: More than Munchies." *New York Times* (January 29): D6.
2000 "Genetic Studies Promise a Path to Better Treatment of Addictions." *New York Times* (November 14): D6.

Carter, Hodding IV
1991 "Day of the Triads." *M Inc.* (June): 68–73.

Cashman, Sean D.
1981 *Prohibition.* New York: Free Press.

Castillo, E. Edwardo
2009 "Slaying of Drug Hero's Family Shocks Mexico." Associated Press (December 22): Internet.

Catanzarite, Anne M.
1992 *Managing the Chemically Dependent Nurse.* Chicago: American Hospital Publishing.

Cauchon, Dennis
1992 "Michigan Drug Law: No Exceptions, No Mercy." *USA Today* (April 7): 3.

Caulkins, Jonathan P.
1997 "Is Crack Cheaper than (Powder) Cocaine?" *Addiction* 92: 1437–43.
1996 "What Does Mathematical Modeling Tell Us About Harm Reduction?" *Drug and Alcohol Review* 15: 231–35.
1994 "What Is the Average Price of an Illicit Drug?" *Addiction* 89 (July): 815–19.
1992 "Thinking About Displacement in Drug Markets: Why Observing Change of Venue Isn't Enough." *Journal of Drug Issues* 22 (Winter): 17–30.

Caulkins, Jonathan P., C. Peter Rydell, Susan S. Everingham, James Chiesa, and Shawn Bushway
1999 *An Ounce of Prevention, a Pound of Uncertainty: The Cost-Effectiveness of School-Based Drug Prevention Programs.* Santa Monica, CA: RAND.

Caulkins, Jonathan P., C. Peter Rydell, William L. Schwabe, and James S. Chiesa
1997 *Mandatory Minimum Drug Sentences: Throwing Away the Key or the Taxpayer's Money?* Santa Monica, CA: RAND.

Caulkins, Jonathan P., Gordon Crawford, and Peter Reuter
1993 "Simulation of Adaptive Response: A Model of Drug Interdiction." *Mathematical and Computer Modeling* 17 (2): 37–52.

Caulkins, Jonathan P. and H. John Heinz III
2002 "Law Enforcement's Role in a Harm Reduction Regime." *Contemporary Issues in Crime and Justice* 64 (January): 1–12.

Caulkins, Jonathan P., Patricia A. Ebener, and Daniel F. McCaffrey
1995 "Describing DAWN's Dominion." *Contemporary Drug Problems* 22 (Fall): 547–67.

Caulkins, Jonathan P., Peter Reuter, Martin Y. Iguchi, and James Chiesa
2005 *How Goes the "War on Drugs"? An Assessment of U.S. Drug Policy Problems and Policy.* Santa Monica, CA: RAND Drug Policy Research Center.

Cawley, Janet
1990 "3% Fail Drug Tests in Transit Industries." *Chicago Tribune* (July 11): 9.

Center on Addiction and Substance Abuse
1994 "Relationship Between Cigarette Smoking and Heroin, Cocaine and Crack." Press release, March 10.

Center for Substance Abuse Research
2009a "Less than 3% of Federal and State Substance Abuse Spending Goes to Prevention, Treatment, or Research." *CESAR FAX* (June 1): 1.
2009b "Marijuana, Inhalants, and Prescription Drugs Are Top Three Substances Abused by Teens." *CESAR FAX* (March 9): 1.
2009c "Friends and Family Are the Most Common Source of Prescription Amphetamines and Narcotics Used Nonmedically by 12th Graders." *CESAR FAX* (February 2): 1.

Chaiken, Jan M. and Marcia R. Chaiken
1991 "Drugs and Predatory Crime." Pages 203–39 in *Drugs and Crime,* edited by Michael Tonry and James Q. Wilson. Chicago: University of Chicago Press.

Chaiken, Marcia R. and Bruce D. Johnson
1988 *Characteristics of Different Types of Drug-Involved Offenders.* Washington, DC: National Institute of Justice.

Chambers, Carl D. and Leon Brill
1973 *Methadone: Experiences and Issues.* New York: Behavioral Publications.

Chambliss, William
1973 *Functional and Conflict Theories of Crime.* New York: MSS Modular Publications.

Chapman, Stephen
1992 "The Awful Price of Fighting the War on Drugs." *Chicago Tribune* (May 21): 23.
1991a "Do We Want to Save Addicts or Kill Them?" *Chicago Tribune* (February 21): 23.
1991b "In the Drug War, Bigger Sentences for Smaller Crimes." *Chicago Tribune* (June 9): Sec. 4: 3.
1991c "Prohibition—From Alcohol to Drugs—Is a Costly Failure." *Chicago Tribune* (September 1): Sec. 4: 3.

Chavez, Nelba and Ruth Sanchez-Way
1997 *Selected Findings in Prevention.* Washington, DC: U.S. Substance Abuse and Mental Health Services Administration.

Chavkin, Wendy
2001 "Cocaine and Pregnancy: Time to Look at the Evidence." *Journal of the American Medical Association* 285:1626–28.

Cheever, Susan
2004 *My Name is Bill. Bill Wilson: His Life and the Creation of Alcoholics Anonymous.* New York: Simon and Schuster.

Chein, Isidor, Donald L. Gerard, Robert S. Lee, and Eva Rosenfeld
1964 *The Road to H: Narcotics, Delinquency, and Social Policy.* New York: Basic Books.

Chen, David W.
2007 "Five Arrested in New Jersey in Illegal Sales of Painkillers." *New York Times* (January 27): B4.
2006 "No Compromise in Sight on Plan to Fight H.I.V." *New York Times* (June 4): 37, 40.

Chermack, Stephen T. and Stuart P. Taylor
1995 "Alcohol and Human Physical Aggression: Pharmacological Versus Expectancy Effects." *Journal of Studies on Alcohol* 56 (July): 449–56.

Cheung, Yuet W., Patricia G. Erickson, and Tammy C. Landau
1991 "Experience of Crack Use: Findings from a Community-Based Sample in Toronto." *Journal of Drug Issues* 21 (Winter): 121–40.

Childress, Ann Rose
1993 "Medications in Drug Abuse Treatment." Pages 73–75 in *NIDA Second National Conference on Drug Abuse Research and Practice: An Alliance for the 21st Century.* Rockville, MD: National Institute on Drug Abuse.

Childress, Anna Rose, A. Thomas McLellan, and Charles P. O'Brien
1985 "Behavioral Therapies for Substance Abuse." *International Journal of the Addictions* 20: 947–69.

Childress, Ann Rose, Anita V. Hole, Ronald N. Ehrman, Steven J. Robbins, A. Thomas McLellan, and Charles P. O'Brien
1993 "Cue Reactivity and Cue Reactivity Interventions in Drug Dependence." Pages 73–95 in *Behavioral Treatments for Drug Abuse and Dependence,* edited by Lisa Simon Onken, John D. Blaine, and John J. Boren. Rockville, MD: National Institute on Drug Abuse.

Childress, Anna Rose, P. David Mozley, William McElgin, Josh Fitzgerald, Martin Reivich, and Charles P. O'Brien
1999 "Limbic Activation During Cue-Induced Cocaine Craving." *American Journal of Psychiatry* 156 (January): 11–18.

Chin, Ko-lin
1995 "Triad Societies in Hong Kong." *Transnational Organized Crime* 1 (Spring): 47–64.
1990 *Chinese Subculture and Criminality: Non-traditional Crime Groups in America.* Westport, CT: Greenwood.

Chin, Ko-lin and Jeffrey Fagan
1990 "The Impact of Crack on Drug and Crime Involvement." Paper presented at the annual meeting of the American Society of Criminology, Baltimore, November.

Chin, Ko-lin and Sheldon X. Zhang
2007 *The Chinese Connection: Cross-border Drug Trafficking Between Mynamar and China.* Newark, NJ: Rutgers University.

Chitwood, Dale D., James E. Rivers, and James A. Inciardi
1996 *The American Pipe Dream: Crack Cocaine and the Inner City.* Ft. Worth, TX: Harcourt Brace.

Chitwood, Dale D., Mary Comerford, and Norman L. Weatherby
1998 "The Initiation of the Use of Heroin in the Age of Crack." Pages 51–76 in *Heroin in the Age of Crack-Cocaine,* edited by James A. Inciardi and Laura D. Harrison. Thousand Oaks, CA: Sage.

Christian, Sue Ellen
2000 "Teen's Death Sheds Light on a Volatile Party Drug." *Chicago Tribune* (February 7): 1, 34.

Cintron, Myrna
1986 "Coca: Its History and Contemporary Parallels." Pages 25–51 in *Drugs in Latin America,* edited by Edmundo Morales. Williamsburg, VA: College of William and Mary.

Clay, Rebecca A.
2004 "Peer-to-Peer Program Promotes Recovery." *SAMHSA News* 12 (September/October): 1–4.

Clines, Francis X. and Barry Meier
2001 "Cancer Painkillers Pose New Abuse Threat." *New York Times* (February 9): 1, 18.

Cloninger, Susan C.
1993 *Theories of Personality: Understanding Persons.* Upper Saddle River, NJ: Prentice Hall.

Cloud, David S. and Carlota Gall
2005 "U.S. Memo Faults Afghan Leader on Heroin Fight." *New York Times* (May 22): 1, 12.

Cloward, Richard A. and Lloyd E. Ohlin
1960 *Delinquency and Opportunity.* New York: Free Press.

Cloyd, Jerald W.
1982 *Drugs and Information Control: The Role of Men and Manipulation in the Control of Drug Trafficking.* Westport, CT: Greenwood.

Clymer, Adam
1994 "Senate Told That Cigarettes Are Entry into Hard Drugs." *New York Times* (March 11): 12.

Coffey, Thomas A.
1975 *The Long Thirst: Prohibition in America, 1920–1933.* New York: Norton.

Cohen, Albert K.
1965 *Delinquent Boys.* New York: Free Press.

Cohen, Julian
1996 "Drug Education: Politics, Propaganda and Censorship." *The International Journal of Drug Policy* 7 (3): Internet.

Cohen, Peter J.
2002 "Untreated Addiction Imposes an Ethical Bar to Recruiting Addicts for Non-Therapeutic Studies of Addictive Drugs." *Journal of Law, Medicine and Ethics* 30 (Spring): 73–83.

Cohen, Roger
1992 "Amid Growing Crime, Zurich Closes a Park It Reserved for Drug Addicts." *New York Times* (February 11): 11.

Coker, J. Kelly
2001 "Four-fold prevention: strategies to prevent substance abuse among elementary school-aged children." *Professional School Counseling* 5 (October): 70–75.

Collins, James J., Robert L. Hubbard, and J. Valley Rachel
1985 "Expensive Drug Use and Illegal Income: A Test of Explanatory Hypotheses." *Criminology* 23 (November): 743–64.

Collins, Larry
1999 "Holland's Half-Baked Drug Experiment." *Foreign Affairs* 78 (May/June): 82–98.

"Colombian Heroin May Be Increasing"
1991 *New York Times* (October 27): 10.

Colombia's New Armed Groups
2007 Bogotá, Colombia: International Crisis Group.

Colorado Alcohol and Drug Abuse Division.
1987 *Drug Use Trends in Colorado.* Denver.

Comings, David E.
1996 "Genetic Factors in Drug Abuse and Dependence." Pages 16–38 in *Individual Differences in the Biobehavioral Etiology of Drug Abuse,* edited by Harold W. Gordon and Meyer D. Glantz. Rockviille, MD: National Institute on Drug Abuse.

1987 "Coming To Grips With Alcoholism." *U.S. Press and World Report* (November 30): 56–63.

Committee on Law Reform of the New York County Lawyers Association
1987 *Advisory Reports. Part I: Why Cocaine and Heroin Should Be Decriminalized. Part II: Why Cocaine and Heroin Should Not Be Decriminalized.* New York: Photocopied.

Compton, Beaulah and Burt Galaway
1979 *Social Work Processes,* 2nd ed. Homewood, IL: Dorsey Press.

Comptroller General
1988 *Controlling Drug Abuse: A Status Report.* Washington, DC: General Accounting Office.

1983 *Federal Drug Interdiction Efforts Need a Strong Central Oversight.* Washington, DC: General Accounting Office.

Conant, Eve
2005 "Ecstasy: A Possible New Role for a Banned Club Drug." *Newsweek* (May 2): 11.

Condor, Bob
2002a "Getting a Grip." *Chicago Tribune* (June 30): Sec. 13: 1, 4–5.
2002b "Learning to Sip: A New Program Helps Problem Drinkers Cut Back on Alcohol" *New York Daily News* (August 12): 42–44.

Cone, Tracie
2008 "Mexican Marijuana Cartels Sully US Forests, Parks." Associated Press (October 11): Internet.

Conley, Peter, David Hewitt, Wayne Mitic, Christiane Poulin, Diane Riley, Robin Room, Ed Sawka, Eric Single, and John Topp
n.d. "Harm Reduction: Concepts and Practice: A Policy Discussion Paper." Ottawa: Canadian Centre on Substance Abuse (CCSA) National Working Group on Policy: Internet.

Cook, Christopher C. H.
1988a "The Minnesota Model in the Management of Drug and Alcohol Dependency: Miracle, Method or Myth? Part I. The Philosophy and the Programme." *British Journal of Addiction* 83: 625–34.
1988b "The Minnesota Model in the Management of Drug and Alcohol Dependency: Miracle, Method or Myth? Part II. Evidence and Conclusions." *British Journal of Addiction* 83: 735–48.

Cook, L. Foster and Beth A. Weinman
1988 "Treatment Alternatives to Street Crime." Pages 99–105 in

Compulsory Treatment of Drug Abuse: Research and Clinical Practice, edited by Carl G. Leukefeld and Frank M. Tims. Rockville, MD: National Institute on Drug Abuse.

Coomber, Ross
1999 "The Cutting of Heroin in the United States in the 1990s" *Journal of Drug Issues* 29: 17–36.

Cooper, James
1998 "Statement Presented at the Joint New York Assembly Committee on Alcoholism and Drug Abuse and Committee on Health Hearings, New York City." December 11.

Cooper, Michael
1998 "Police Raid Wrong Apartment in Brooklyn." *New York Times* (May 8): 17.

Corcoran, David
1989 "Legalizing Drugs: Failures Spur Debate." *New York Times* (November 27): 9.

Cosden, Merith, Stacey Peerson, and Katherine Elliott
1997 "Effects of Prenatal Drug Exposure on Birth Outcomes and Early Child Development." *Journal of Drug Issues* 27: 525–39.

Costa, Antonio Maria
2009 "Preface." *Drug Control 1909–2009: A Positive Balance Sheet.* Vienna, Austria: United Nations Office on Drugs and Crime.

Courtwright, David T.
1982 *Dark Paradise: Opiate Addiction in America Before 1940.* Cambridge, MA: Harvard University Press.

Cowan, Richard C.
1986 "A War Against Ourselves: How the Narcs Created Crack." *National Review* (December 5): 26–31.

Cowell, Alan
1997 "Zurich's Open Drug Policy Goes into Withdrawal." *New York Times* (March 12): 3.

Cox, W. Miles
1985 "Personality Correlates of Substance Abuse." Pages 209–46 in *Determinants of Substance Abuse: Biological, Psychological, and Environmental Factors,* edited by Mark Galizio and Stephen A. Maisto. New York: Plenum.

Crabbe, John C.
2002 "Generic Contributions to Addiction." Pages 435–62 in *Annual Review of Psychology,* Vol. 53. Palo Alto, CA: Annual Reviews.

Craig, Robert J.
1987 "The Personality Structure of Heroin Addicts." Pages 25–36 in *Neurobiology of Behavioral Control in Drug Abuse,* edited by Stephen I. Szara. Rockville, MD: National Institute on Drug Abuse.

Crandall, Russell
2008 *Driven by Drugs: U.S. Policy Toward Colombia,* 2nd ed. Boulder, CO: Lynne Rienner, Publishers.

Crank, John P. and Lee R. Rehm
1992 "From Drug Courier Profiles to Officer Awareness: A Study of a State Drug Interdiction Program." Paper presented at the annual meeting of the Academy of Criminal Justice Sciences, Pittsburg, March.

Crits-Christoph, Paul, Lynne Siqueland, Jack Blaine, Arlene Frank, Lester Luborsky, Lisa S. Onken, Larry R. Muenz, Michael E. Thase, Roger Weiss, David R. Gastfriend, George E. Woody, Jacques P. Barber, Stephen F. Butler, Dennis Daley, Ihsan Salloum, Sarah Bishop, Lisa M. Najavits, Judy Lis, Delinda Mercer, Margaret L. Griffin, Karla Moras, and Aaron T. Beck
1999 "Psychosocial Treatments for Cocaine Dependence." *Archives of General Psychiatry* 56 (June): 493–502.

Crowley, Geoffrey
1996 "Herbal Warning." *Pressweek* (May 6): 60–67.

Crowley, Thomas J.
1981 "The Reinforcers for Drug Abuse: Why People Take Drugs." Pages 367–81 in *Classic Contributions in the Addictions,* edited by Howard Shaffer and Milton Earl Burglass. New York: Brunner/Mazel.

Currie, Elliott
1993 *Reckoning: Drugs, the Cities, and the American Future.* New York: Hill and Wang.

Cushman, Paul Jr.
1974 "Relationship Between Narcotic Addiction and Crime." *Federal Probation* 38 (September): 38–43.

Danaceau, Paul
1974 *Methadone Maintenance Programs: The Experience of Four Programs.* Washington, DC: Drug Abuse Council, Inc.

Davenport-Hines, Richard
2002 *Pursuit of Oblivion: A Global History of Narcotics.* New York: Norton.

Davey, Monica
2005 "Grisly Effect of One Drug: 'Meth Mouth.'" *New York Times* (June 11): 1, 10.

Davis, Debra P.
2008 *Combination Treatment Extends Marijuana Abstinence.* Rockville, MD: National Institute on Drug Abuse.

Davis, Joel
1984 *Endorphins: New Waves in Brain Chemistry.* Garden City, NY: Doubleday.

DeJong, William
1987a *Arresting the Demand for Drugs: Police and School Partnership to Prevent Drug Abuse.* Washington, DC: National Institute of Justice.
1987b "A Short Term Evaluation of Project DARE: Preliminary Indications of Effectiveness." *Journal of Drug Education* 17: 279–94.

de Kort, Marcel and Ton Cramer
1999 "Pragmatism Versus Ideology: Dutch Drug Policy Continued." *Journal of Drug Issues* 29 (3): 473–92.

De Lama, George
1988 "Besieged Colombia Becoming the Lebanon of Latin America." *Chicago Tribune* (November 20): 5.

Delaney, William P.
1977 "On Capturing an Opium King: The Politics of Law Sik Han's Arrest." Pages 67–88 in *Drugs and Politics,* edited by Paul E. Rock. New Brunswick, NJ: Transaction Books.

De La Rosa, Mario, Elizabeth Y. Lambert, and Bernard Gropper, eds.
1990 *Drugs and Violence: Causes, Correlates, and Consequences.* Rockville, MD: National Institute on Drug Abuse.

Delbanco, Andrew and Thomas Delbanco
1995 "A.A. at the Crossroads." *New Yorker* (March 20): 50–63.

De Leon, George
2000 *The Therapeutic Community: Theory, Model, and Method.* New York: Springer.
1995 "Residential Therapeutic Communities in the Mainstream: Diversity and Issues." *Journal of Psychoactive Drugs* 27 (1): 3–15.
1994 "The Therapeutic Community: Toward a General Theory and Model." Pages 16–53 in *Therapeutic Community: Advances*

in Research and Application, edited by Frank M. Tims, George De Leon, and Nancy Jainchill. Rockville, MD: National Institute on Drug Abuse.
1990 "Treatment Strategies." Pages 115–38 in *Handbook of Drug Control in the United States,* edited by James A. Inciardi. Westport, CT: Greenwood.
1986a "The Therapeutic Community for Substance Abuse: Perspective and Approach." Pages 5–18 in *Therapeutic Communities for Addictions,* edited by George De Leon and James T. Ziegenfuss Jr. Springfield, IL: Charles C Thomas.
1986b "Program-Based Evaluation Research in Therapeutic Communities." Pages 69–87 in *Drug Abuse Treatment Evaluation: Strategies, Progress, and Prospects,* edited by Frank M. Tims and Jacqueline P. Ludford. Rockville, MD: National Institute on Drug Abuse.

De Leon, George, James A. Inciardi, and Steven S. Martin
1995 "Residential Drug Abuse Treatment Research: Are Conventional Control Designs Appropriate for Assessing Treatment Effectiveness?" *Journal of Psychoactive Drugs* 27 (1): 85–91.

DeLong, James V.
1972 "Treatment and Rehabilitation." Pages 173–254 in *Dealing with Drug Abuse: A Report to the Ford Foundation.* New York: Praeger.

de Marneffe, Peter
2003 "Against the Legalization of Heroin." *Criminal Justice Ethics* 22 (Winter/Spring): 34–40.

Dembo, Richard, Linda Williams, Alan Getreu, Lisa Genung, James Schmeidler, Estrellita Berry, Eric D. Wish, and Lawrence Voie
1991 "A Longitudinal Study of the Relationship Among Marijuana/ Hashish Use, Cocaine Use, and Delinquency in a Cohort of High Risk Youths." *Journal of Drug Issues* 21: 271–312.

De Quincey, Thomas
Confessions of an English Opium-Eater. London: J. M. Dent. Originally published in 1821.
1995 Dettling, Michael, Andreas Heinz, Peter Dufeu, Hans Rommelspacher, Klaus-Jürgen Gräf, and Lutz G. Schmid

1995 "Dopaminergic Responsivity in Alcoholism: Trait, State, or Residual Marker?" *American Journal of Psychiatry* 152 (9): 1317–21.

Dew, Brian J., Kirk W. Elifson, and Claire E. Sterk
2006 "Treatment Implications for Young Adult Users of MDMA." *Journal of Addictions and Offender Counseling* 26 (April): 84–99.

Dewan, Shaila and Robbie Brown
2009 "Illness Afflict Homes with a Criminal Past." *New York Times* (July 14): 1, 16.

Dickson, Donald T.
1977 "Bureaucracy and Morality: An Organizational Perspective on a Moral Crusade." Pages 31–52 in *Drugs and Politics,* edited by Paul E. Rock. New Brunswick, NJ: Transaction Books.

Dillon, Sam
1999a "Mexico's Troubadors Turn from Amor to Drugs." *New York Times* (February 19): 4.
1999b "Ruling Party, at 70, Tries Hard to Cling to Power in Mexico." *New York Times* (March 4): 1, 12.
1996 "Mexicans Tire of Police Graft as Drug Lords Raise Stakes." *New York Times* (March 21): 3.
1995 "Speed Carries Mexican Drug Dealer to the Top." *New York Times* (December 27): 6.

DiNardo, John
1993 "Law Enforcement, the Price of Cocaine and Cocaine Use." *Mathematical and Computer Modelling* 17 (2): 53–64.

Dinges, John
1990 *Our Man in Panama: How General Noriega Used the United States—and Made Millions in Drugs and Arms.* New York: Random House.

Dishion, Thomas J., Gerald R. Patterson, and John R. Reid
1988 "Parent and Peer Factors Associated with Drug Sampling in Early Adolescence: Implications for Treatment." Pages 69–93 in *Adolescent Drug Abuse: Analyses of Treatment Research,* edited by Elizabeth R. Rahdert and John Grabowski. Rockville, MD: National Institute on Drug Abuse.

Dole, Vincent P.
1980 "Addictive Behavior." *Scientific American* 243: 138–54.

Dole, Vincent P. and Marie F. Nyswander

1966 "Rehabilitation of Heroin Addicts After Blockade with Methadone." *New York State Journal of Medicine* 66 (April): 2011–17.
1965 "A Medical Treatment for Diacetylmorphine (Heroin) Addiction." *Journal of the American Medical Association* 193 (August): 146–50.

Donadio, Rachel
2009 "U.S. Plans New Course for Antidrug Efforts in Afghanistan." *New York Times* (June 28): 12.

Donovan, Dennis M.
1988 "Assessment of Addictive Behaviors: Implications of an Emerging Biopsychosocial Model." Pages 3–48 in *Assessment of Addictive Behaviors,* edited by Dennis M. Donova and G. Alan Marlatt. New York: Guilford.

Dotson, James W., Deborah L. Ackerman, and Louis Jolyon West
1995 "Ketamine Abuse." *Journal of Drug Issues* 25 (Fall): 751–57.

Downes, Lawrence
2009 "Songs Without Borders." *New York Times* (August 16): TR1, 6–7.

Doyle, A. Conan
1899 *Memoirs of Sherlock Holmes.* New York: Harper and Brothers.

"Drug Arrests and the Courts' Pleas for Help"
1989 *New York Times* (April 9): E6.

Drug Enforcement Administration (DEA)
2008 *Prescription for Disaster: How Teens Abuse Medicine.* Washington, DC: DEA.
2003 *Speaking Out Against Drug Legalization.* Washington, DC: DEA.
1994a *Crack Cocaine.* Washington, DC: DEA.
1994b *Trends in Heroin.* Washington, DC: DEA.
1991 *Worldwide Heroin Situation.* Washington, DC: DEA.
1989 *Drugs of Abuse.* Washington, DC: DEA.
n.d.a *LSD Manufacture.* Internet.
n.d.b *LSD Use and Effects.* Internet.

Drugs Prevention Initiative
1999 London, England: Home Office.

Duenwald, Mary
2001 "Fresh Look at a Fast Way to Kick a Heroin Habit." *New York Times* (December 4): D6, 8.

Duncan, David F., Thomas Nicholson, Patrick Clifford, Wesley Hawkins, and Rick Petosa

1994 "Harm Reduction: An Emerging New Paradigm for Drug Education." *Journal of Drug Education* 24 (4): 281–90.

Dunwiddie, Thomas V.
1988 "Mechanisms of Cocaine Abuse and Toxicity: An Overview." Pages 337–53 in *Mechanisms of Cocaine Abuse and Toxicity,* edited by Doris Clouet, Khursheed Asghar, and Roger Brown. Rockville, MD: National Institute on Drug Abuse.

DuPont, Robert L. and John P. McGovern
1994 *A Bridge to Recovery: An Introduction to 12-Step Programs.* Washington, DC: American Psychiatric Press.

Duster, Troy
1970 *The Legislation of Morality: Law, Drugs, and Moral Judgment.* New York: Free Press.

Duterte, Micheline, Kristin Hemphill, Terrence Murphy, and Sheigla Murphy
2003 "Tragic Beauties: Heroin Images and Heroin Users." *Contemporary Drug Problems* 30 (Fall): ProQuest.

Duzán, Maria
1994 *Death Beat.* New York: HarperCollins.

Dworkin, Steven I. and Raymond C. Pitts
1994 "Use of Rodent Self-Administration Models to Develop Pharmaco-Therapies for Cocaine Abuse." Pages 88–112 in *Neurobiological Models for Evaluating Mechanisms Underlying Cocaine Addiction,* edited by Lynda Erinoff and Roger M. Brown. Rockville, MD: National Institute on Drug Abuse.

Dworkin, Steven I., Nick E. Goeders, John Grabowski, and James E. Smit
1987 "The Effects of 12-Hour Limited Access to Cocaine: Reduction in Drug Intake and Mortality." Pages 221–25 in *Problems of Drug Dependence, 1986,* edited by Louis S. Harris. Rockville, MD: National Institute on Drug Abuse.

Dwyer, Jim
2009 "Whites Smoke Pot, but Blacks Are Arrested." *New York Times* (December 23): 24.

Eaglin, James B.
1986 *The Impact of the Federal Drug Aftercare Program.* Washington, DC: Federal Judicial Center.

Eckhold, Erik
2010 "Border Tribe Feels Stuck in Middle of Drug War." *New York Times* (January 25): 1, 10.
2008a "Innovative Courts Give Some Addicts Chance to Straighen Out." *New York Times* (October 15): 1, 18.
2008b "Reports Find Persistent Racial Gap in Drug Arrests." *New York Times* (May 6): 21.
2008c "Grim Tradition and a Long Struggle to End It." *New York Times* (April 2): 18, 22.

Eckholm, Erik and Olga Pierce
2010 "Border Tribe Feels Stuck in Middle of Drug War." *New York Times* (January 25): 1, 10.
2008 "Methadone Rises as a Painkiller with Big Risks." *New York Times* (August 17): 1, 17.
2008b "Reports Find Persistent Racial Gap in Drug Arrests." *New York Times* (May 6): 21.

Eddy, Paul, Hugo Sabogal, and Sara Walden
1988 *The Cocaine Wars.* New York: Norton.

Egan, Timothy
2006 "Youthful Binge Drinking Fueled by Boredom of the Open West." *New York Times* (September 2): 1, 12.
2004 "Taking Aim at the Professional Rodeo Circuit's Drug of Choice." *New York Times* (June 11): 14.
2002 "Meth Building Its Hell's Kitchen in Rural America." *New York Times* (February 6): 14.
1999a "The War on Crack Retreats, Still Taking Prisoners." *New York Times* (February 28): 1, 20–21.
1999b "In States' Anti-Drug Fight, A Renewal for Treatment." *New York Times* (June 10): 1, 22.
1999c "A Drug Ran Its Course, Then Hid with Its Users." *New York Times* (September 19): 1, 27.

"84 Military Personnel Convicted in Drug Case at Camp Lejeune"
2002 *New York Times* (July 4): 8.

Eiler, Kathryn, Melodie R. Schaefer, and Daniel Salstrom
1995 "Double-Blind Comparison of Bromocriptine and Placebo in Cocaine Withdrawal." *American Journal of Drug and Alcohol Abuse* 21 (1): 65–79.

Eitle, David, R. Jay Turner, and Tamela McNulty Eitle
2003 "The Deterrence Hypothesis Reexamined: Sports Participation and Substance Use Among Young Adults." *Journal of Drug Issues* 33 (Winter): 193–222.

Ellickson, Phyllis L.
1995 "Schools." Pages 93–120 in *Handbook on Drug Prevention,* edited by Robert H. Coombs and Douglas Ziedonis. Boston: Allyn and Bacon.

Ellickson, Phyllis L. and Robert M. Bell
1990 "Drug Prevention in Junior High: A Multi-Site Longitudinal Test." *Science* 247 (March 16): 1299–1305.

Ellickson, Phyllis L., Daniel F. McCaffrey, Bonnie Ghosh-Dastidar, and Douglas L. Longshore
2003 "New Inroads in Preventing Adolescent Drug Use: Results from a Large-Scale Trial of Project ALERT in Middle Schools." *American Journal of Public Health* 93 (11): 1830–36.

Elliott, Stuart
2003 "Thanks to Cable, Liquor Ads Find a TV Audience." *New York Times* (December 15): C1, 11.

Ellis, Lee
1990 "Universal Behavioral and Demographic Correlates of Criminal Behavior: Toward Common Ground in the Assessment of Criminological Theories." Pages 36–49 in *Crime in Biological, Social, and Moral Contexts,* edited by Lee Ellis and Harry Hoffman. Westport, CT: Praeger.

Elsasser, Glen
1989 "Suspicion Is Ruled Ample Basis for Drug Search." *Chicago Tribune* (April 4): 3.

Engel, Madeline H.
1974 *The Drug Scene.* Rochelle Park, NJ: Hayden Book Co.

Ennett, Susan T., Nancy S. Tobler, Christopher L. Ringwalt, and Robert L. Flewelling
1994 "How Effective Is Drug Abuse Resistance Education? A Meta-Analysis of Project DARE Outcome Evaluations." *American Journal of Public Health* 84 (9): 1394–1401.

Epstein, Edward Jay
1988 "The Dope Business." *Manhattan, inc.* (July): 25–27.
1977 *Agency of Fear: Opiates and Political Power in America.* New York: G.P. Putnam's Sons.
1974 "Methadone: The Forlorn Hope." *The Public Interest* 36 (Summer): 3–24.

Epstein, Joan F. and Joseph C. Gfroerer
1997 *Heroin Abuse in the United States.* Substance Abuse and Mental Health Services Administration: Internet.

Erikson, Kai T.
1966 *Wayward Puritans.* New York: Wiley.

Fagan, Jeffrey and Ko-lin Chin
1991 "Social Processes of Initiation into Crack." *Journal of Drug Issues* 21: 313–43.

Fahmy, Dalia
2007 "Aiming for a Drug-Free Workplace." *New York Times* (May 10): C6.

Fathi, Nazila
2008 "Iran Fights the Scourge of Addiction in Plain View, Stressing Treatment." *New York Times* (June 27): 6, 7.

Farabee, David, Vandana Joshi, and M. Douglas Anglin
2001 "Addiction Careers and Criminal Specialization." *Crime and Delinquency* 47 (April): 196–220.

"Far East Sopranos"
2003 *U.S. News and World Report* (January 27): 34.

Faupel, Charles E. and Carl B. Klockars
1987 "Drugs-Crime Connections: Elaborations from the Life Histories of Hard-Core Heroin Addicts." *Social Problems* 34 (February): 54–68.

Fay, Peter Ward
1975 *The Opium War: 1840–1842.* Chapel Hill: University of North Carolina Press.

"FDA: Date-Rape Drug Has Medical Use"
2002 *Chicago Tribune* (July 18): 16.

Feldman, Harvey
1977 "Street Status and Drug Use." Pages 207–22 in *Drugs and Politics,* edited by Paul E. Rock. New Brunswick, NJ: Transaction Books.

Felson, Richard B., Brent Teasdale, and Keri B. Buchfield
2008 "The Influence of Being Under the Influence: Alcohol Effects on Adolescent Violence." *Journal of Research in Crime and Delinquency* 45 (May): 119–41.

Fenichel, Otto
1945 *The Psychoanalytic Theory of Neuroses.* New York: Norton.

Feuer, Alan
2000 "U.S. Colonel Is Implicated in Drug Case." *New York Times* (April 4): 20.

Fields, Richard
2001 *Drug in Perspective,* 4th ed. New York: McGraw-Hill.

Filkins, Dexter
2009 "U.S. Sets Fight in the Poppies to Stop Taliban." *New York Times* (April 29): 1, 8.

Finestone, Harold
1964 "Cats, Kicks, and Color." Pages 281–97 in *The Other Side*, edited by Howard S. Becker. New York: Free Press.

Finnegan, Loretta
1993 "Discussant and Discussion." Pages 189–207 in *International Research Conference on Biomedical Approaches to Illicit Drug Demand Reduction*, edited by Christine R. Hartel. Washington, DC: U.S. Government Printing Office.

Finnegan, L. P., A. P. Streissguth, G. Koren, D. Neuspiel, and K. Kaltenbach
1994 "The Teratogenicity of the Drugs of Abuse: A Symposium." Pages 51–54 in *Problems of Drug Dependence, 1993*. Vol. I, edited by Louis S. Harris. Rockville, MD: National Institute on Drug Abuse.

Fiorentine, Robert
1999 "After Drug Treatment: Are 12-Step Programs Effective in Maintaining Abstinence?" *American Journal of Drug and Alcohol Abuse* 25 (February): Internet.

Fischer, Benedikt
2003 "Doing Good with a Vengeance: A Critical Assessment of the Practices, Effects and Implications of Drug Treatment Courts in North America." *Criminal Justice* 3 (3): 227–48.

Fischer, Benedikt, Jude Gittins, and Jürgen Rehm
2008 "Characterizing the 'Awakening Elephant' of Prescription Opioid Use in North America: Epidemiology, Harms, Interventions." *Contemporary Drug Problems* 35 (Summer): 397–428.

Fishbein, Diana H. and Susan E. Pease
1990 "Neurological Links Between Substance Abuse and Crime." Pages 218–43 in *Crime in Biological, Social, and Moral Contexts*, edited by Lee Ellis and Harry Hoffman. Westport, CT: Praeger.

Fishbein, Diana H., David Lozovsky, and Jerome H. Jaffe
1989 "Impulsivity, Aggression, and Neuroendocrine Responses to Serotonergic Stimulation in Substance Abusers." *Biological Psychiatry* 25: 1049–66.

Flores, Philip J.
1988 *Group Psychotherapy with Addicted Populations*. New York: Haworth.

Flores, Phillip J. and Jeffrey M. Georgi
2005 *Substance Abuse Treatment: Group Therapy*. Rockville,

MD: Substance Abuse and Mental Health Services Administration.

Foltin, Richard W. and Marian W. Fischman
1994 "Cocaine: Self-Administration Research: Treatment Implications." Pages 139–62 in *Neurobiological Models for Evaluating Mechanisms Underlying Cocaine Addiction*, edited by Lynda Erinoff and Roger M. Brown. Rockville, MD: National Institute on Drug Abuse.

Fong, Mak Lau
1981 *The Sociology of Secret Societies: A Study of Chinese Secret Societies in Singapore and Peninsular Malaysia*. Oxford, England: Oxford University Press.

Fooner, Michael
1985 *A Guide to Interpol*. Washington, DC: U.S. Government Printing Office.

Forero, Juan
2006 "Colombia's Coca Survives U.S. Plan to Uproot It." *New York Times* (August 19): 1, 8.
2005 "Turbulent Bolivia Is Producing More Cocaine, the U.N. Reports." *New York Times* (June 15): 5.
2005d "U.S. Voicing Fears of Tampered Elections, Is Rebuked by Colombia." *New York Times* (December 18): 25.
2002 "Farmers in Peru Are Turning Again to Coca Crop." *New York Times* (February 14): 3.
2001a "New Challenge to the Bogotá Leadership." *New York Times* (May 6): 8.
2001b "Where a Little Coca Is as Good as Gold." *New York Times* (July 8): Sec. 4: 12.
2001c "Ranchers in Colombia Bankroll Their Own Militia." *New York Times* (August 8): 1, 6.

Forrest, Gary G.
1985 "Psychodynamically-Oriented Treatment of Alcoholism and Substance Abuse." Pages 307–36 in *Alcoholism and Substance Abuse: Strategies for Clinical Intervention*, edited by Thomas E. Bratter and Gary G. Forrest. New York: Free Press.

Fortini, Amanda
2008 "Special Treatment: The Rise of Luxury Rehab." New *Yorker* (December 1): 40–47.

Fowler, Joanna S., Nora D. Volkow, Cheryl A Kassad, and Linda Chang
2007 "Imaging the Addicted Human Brain." *Science and Practice Perspectives* (April): 4–16.

Fox, Maggie
2008 "U.S. Leads World in Substance Abuse, WHO Finds." *Reuters* (July 1): Internet.

Frank, Blanche, Gregory Rainone, Michael Maranda, William Hopkins, Edmundo Morales, and Alan Kott
1987 "A Psycho-Social View of 'Crack' in New York City." Paper presented at the American Psychological Association Convention, New York City, August 28.

Franklin, Stephen
1987 "Detroit Wages All-Out War Against Crack." *Chicago Tribune* (December 13): 29.

Frawley, P. Joseph and James W. Smith
1990 "Chemical Aversion Therapy in the Treatment of Cocaine Dependence as Part of a Multimodal Treatment Program: Treatment Outcome." *Journal of Substance Abuse Treatment* 7: 21–29.

Frazier, Thomas L.
1962 "Treating Young Drug Abusers: A Casework Approach." *Social Work* 7 (July): 94–101.

Freed, Christopher R.
2007 "Addiction Medicine and Addiction Psychiatry in America: The Impact of Physicians in Recovery on the Medical Treatment of Addiction." *Contemporary Drug Problems* 34 (Spring): 111–37.

Fredlund, Eric V., Richard T. Spence, Jane C. Maxwell, and Jennifer A. Kavinsky
1990 *Substance Abuse Among Youth Entering Texas Youth Commission Facilities, 1989: Final Report*. Austin: Texas Commission on Alcohol and Drug Abuse.

Freedman, Michael
2005 "The Invisible Bankers." *Forbes* (October 17): 94–104.

French, Edward D., Stefanie Levenson, and Angelo Ceci
1990 "Characterization of the Actions of Phencyclidine Midbrain Dopamine Neurons." Pages 255–63 in *Problems of Drug Dependence 1989*, edited by Louis S. Harris. Rockville, MD: National Institute on Drug Abuse.

French, Howard W.
2004 "A Corner of China in the Grip of a Lucrative Heroin Habit." *New York Times* (December 23): 4.
1991 "Filthy Rich with a Drug Connection." *New York Times* (August 6): 6.

Freud, Sigmund
1961 *A General Introduction to Psychoanalysis.* New York: Washington Square Press. Originally published in 1924.

Freudenheim, Milt
1985 "Specialty Health Care Booms." *New York Times* (November 24): 25, 26.

Friedman, David P.
1993 "Introduction to the Brain: A Primer on Structure and Function of the Brain's Reward Circuitry." Pages 53–62 in *International Research Conference on Biomedical Approaches to Illicit Drug Demand Reduction,* edited by Christine R. Hartel. Washington, DC: U.S. Government Printing Office.

Frisher, Martin and Helen Beckett
2006 "Drug Use Desistance." *Criminology and Criminal Justice* 6 (1): 127–45.

Galaif, Elisha and Steve Sussman
1995 "For Whom Does Alcoholics Anonymous Work?" *International Journal of the Addictions* 30 (2): 161–84.

Gall, Carlotta
2006a "Opium Harvest at Record Level in Afghanistan." *New York Times* (September 3): 1, 30.
2006b "Another Year of Drug War, and the Poppy Crop Flourishes." *New York Times* (February 17): 4.
2005 "Armed and Elusive, Afghan Drug Dealers Roam Free." *New York Times* (January 2): 3.
2004 "Afghan Poppy Growing Reaches Record Level, U.N. Says." *New York Times* (November 19): 3.
2003 "U.N. Aide Says Afghan Drug Trade Pays for Terrorist Attacks." *New York Times* (September 5): 5.

Gandossy, Robert P., Jay R. Williams, Jo Cohen, and H. J. Harwood
1980 *Drugs and Crime: A Survey and Analysis of the Literature.* Washington, DC: U.S. Government Printing Office.

Gardner, Stephen E., Paul J. Brounstein, and Deborah Stone
2001 *Promising and Proven Substance Abuse Prevention Programs.* Washington, DC: Substance Abuse and Mental Health Administration.

Gawin, Frank H., M. Elena Khalsa, and Everett Elinwod Jr.
1994 "Stimulants." Pages 111–39 in *The American Psychiatric Press Textbook of Substance Abuse Treatment,* edited by Marc Galanter

and Herbert D. Kleber. Washington, DC: American Psychiatric Press.

Gay, Bruce
1999 "Drug education programs fail in Houston." *Society* 36 (January–February): Internet.

Geary, Nori
1987 "Cocaine: Animal Research Studies." Pages 19–47 in *Cocaine Abuse: New Directions in Treatment and Research,* edited by Henry I. Spitz and Jeffrey S. Rosecan. New York: Brunner/Mazel.

Gebelein, Richard S.
2000 "The Rebirth of Rehabilitation: Promise and Perils of Drug Courts." *Sentencing and Corrections* 6 (May): 1–7.

Gelernter, Joel, David Goldman, and Neil Risch
1993 "The Al Allele at the D2 Dopamine Receptor Gene and Alcoholism." *Journal of the American Medical Association* 269 (April 7): 1673–77.

General Accounting Office (GAO)
1998 *Drug Abuse Treatment Data Limitations Affect the Accuracy of National and State Estimates of Need.* Washington, DC: GAO.
1993 *Drug Use Measurement: Strengths, Limitations, and Recommendations for Improvement.* Washington, DC: GAO.
1991 *The War on Drugs: Arrests Burdening Local Criminal Justice Systems.* Washington, DC: GAO.
1987 *Drug Abuse Prevention: Further Efforts Needed to Identify Programs that Work.* Washington, DC: GAO.

Genzman, Robert W.
1988 "Press Release." October 11.

George, William H. and Jeanette Norris
n.d. "Alcohol, Disinhibition, Sexual Arousal, and Deviant Sexual Behavior." *Health and Research World* posted by the Indiana Prevention Resource Center: Internet.

George, William H. and Susan A. Stoner
2000 "Understanding Acute Alcohol Effects on Sexual Behavior." *Annual Review of Sex Research* 11: 92–122.

Gerstein, Dean R.
1994 "Outcome Research: Drug Abuse." Pages 45–64 in *The American Psychiatric Press Textbook of Substance Abuse Treatment,* edited by Marc Galanter

and Herbert D. Kleber. Washington, DC: American Psychiatric Press.

Gerstein, Dean R. and Henrick J. Harwood, eds.
1990 *Treating Drug Problems, Vol. I: A Study of the Evolution, Effectiveness, and Financing of Public and Private Drug Treatment Systems.* Washington, DC: National Academy Press.

Ghazi, Katayon
1991 "Drug Trafficking Is Thriving in Iran." *New York Times* (December 4): 7.

Gilbert, R. M.
1981 "Drug Abuse as Excessive Behavior." Pages 382–95 in *Classic Contributions in the Addictions,* edited by Howard Shaffer and Milton Earl Burglass. New York: Brunner/Mazel.

Gilbert, Susan
1997 "Youth Study Elevates Family's Role." *New York Times* (September 10): B10.
1996 "Doctors Found to Fail in Diagnosing Addictions." *New York Times* (February 14): B4.

Gilham, Steven A., Wayne L. Lucas, and David Sivewright
1997 "The Impact of Drug Education and Prevention Programs: Disparity Between Impressionistic and Empirical Assessments." *Evaluation Review* 21 (October): 589–613.

Ginzburg, Harold M.
1985 *Naltrexone: Its Clinical Utility.* Rockville, MD: National Institute on Drug Abuse.

Giuffrida, Greg
2002 "Schools Use Testing to Smoke Out Tobacco Use." *Chicago Tribune* (October 8): 8.

Glassman, Alexander H. and George F. Koob
1996 "Psychoactive Smoke." *Nature* 379 (February 22): 677–78.

Glassner, Barry and Julia Loughlin
1989 *Drugs in Adolescent Worlds: Burnouts to Straights.* Houndmills, England: Macmillan.

Glenny, Misha
2008 *McMafia: A Journey Through the Global Criminal Underworld.* New York: Knopf.

Goering, Laurie
1998 "In Peru, Battle Against Flow of Drugs Moves to Amazon River Maze." *Chicago Tribune* (June 30): 6.

Goffman, Erving
1961 *Asylums: Essays on the Social Situation of Mental Patients and Other Inmates*. Garden City, NY: Doubleday.

Gold, Mark S.
1994 "Neurobiology of Addiction and Recovery: The Brain, the Drive for the Drug, and the 12-Step Fellowship." *Journal of Substance Abuse Treatment* 11 (2): 99–97.

Gold, Mark S., Charles A. Dackis, A. L. C. Pottash, Irl Extein, and Arnold Washton
1986 "Cocaine Update: from Bench to Bedside." *Advances in Alcohol and Substance Abuse* 5 (Fall/Winter): 35–60.

Gold, Steven
1980 "The CAP Control Theory of Drug Abuse." Pages 8–11 in *Theories on Drug Abuse: Selected Contemporary Perspectives*, edited by Dan J. Lettieri, Mollie Sayers, and Helen Wallenstein Pearson. Rockville, MD: National Institute on Drug Abuse.

Goldberg, Jeff
1988 *Anatomy of a Scientific Discovery*. New York: Bantam.

Golden, Tim
1999 "U.S. Brushed Aside Mexican Role, Former Drug Chief Says." *New York Times* (November 26): 12.
1997 "Mexico and Drugs: Was the U.S. Napping?" *New York Times* (July 11): 1, 10.

Goldstein, Avram
2001 *Addiction: From Biology to Drug Policy*, 2nd ed. New York: Oxford University Press.

Goldstein, Joseph
1982 "Police Discretion Not to Invoke the Criminal Process." Pages 33–42 in *The Invisible Justice System: Discretion and the Law*, 2nd ed., edited by Burton Atkins and Mark Pogrebin. Cincinnati, OH: Anderson.

Goldstein, Paul J.
1985 "The Drugs/Violence Nexus: A Tripartite Conceptual Framework." *Journal of Drug Issues* 15 (Fall): 493–506.

Goldstein, Paul J., Patricia Bellucci, Barry J. Spunt, and Thomas Miller
1991 "Volume of Cocaine Use and Violence: A Comparison Between Men and Women." *Journal of Drug Issues* 21: 345–67.

Goleman, Daniel
1990 "Scientists Pinpoint Brain Irregularities in Drug Addicts." *New York Times* (June 26): B5.
1989 "Lasting Costs for Child Are Found from a Few Early Drinks." *New York Times* (February 16): 20.
1988 "Psychologists and Psychiatrists Clash Over Hospital and Training Barriers." *New York Times* (May 17): 21.
1987 "Physicians Said to Persist in Undertreating Pain and Ignoring the Evidence." *New York Times* (December 31): 10.

Golub, Andrew and Bruce D. Johnson
1994 "Cohort Differences in Drug-Use Pathways to Crack Among Current Crack Abusers in New York City." *Criminal Justice and Behavior* 21 (December): 403–22.

Gomez-Cespedes, Alejandro
1999 "The Federal Law Enforcement Agencies: An Obstacle in the Fight Against Organized Crime in Mexico." *Journal of Contemporary Criminal Justice* 15 (November): 352–69.

Gomez, Linda
1984 "America's 100 Years of Euphoria and Despair." *Life* (May): 57–68.

Goode, Erich
1989 *Drugs in American Society*, 3rd ed. New York: Knopf.
1972 *Drugs in American Society*. New York: Knopf.

Goodstadt, Michael S.
n.d. *Drug Education*. Rockville, MD: National Institute of Justice.

Grady, Denise
1998 "Hardest Habit to Break: Memories of the High." *New York Times* (October 27): D1, 9.
1996 "Engineered Mice Mimic Drug Use and Mental Illness." *New York Times* (February 20): B5, B8.

Granfield, Robert and William Cloud
1996 "The Elephant That No One Sees: Natural Recovery Among Middle-Class Addicts." *Journal of Drug Issues* 26 (Winter): 45–61.

Greenberg, Brigitte
1999 "Study: Alcohol Cuts Stroke Risk." Associated Press (November 17): Internet.

Greenfeld, Lawrence A.
1998 *Alcohol and Crime*. Washington, DC: Bureau of Justice Statistics.

Greenhouse, Linda
1994 "Supreme Court Supports U.S. on Seizures in Drug Cases." *New York Times* (November 8): 13.
1990 "Use of Illegal Drugs as Part of Religion Can Be Prosecuted, High Court Says." *New York Times* (April 18): 10.
1989 "High Court Backs Airport Detention Based on Profile." *New York Times* (April 4): 1, 10.

Greenspan, Stanley I.
1978 "Substance Abuse: An Understanding from Psychoanalytic Developmental and Learning Theory Perspectives." Pages 73–87 in *Psychodynamics of Drug Dependence*, edited by Jack D. Blaine and Demetrious A. Julius. Rockville, MD: National Institute on Drug Abuse.

Greenwald, Glenn
2009 "Drug Decriminalization in Portugal: Lessons for Creating Fair and Successful Drug Policies." Washington, DC: Cato Institute.

Griffiths, Roland R.
1990 "Caffeine Abstinence Effects in Humans." Pages 129–30 in *Problems of Drug Dependence 1990*, edited by Louis S. Harris. Rockville, MD: National Institute on Drug Abuse.

Griffiths, Roland R., Suzette M. Evans, Stephen J. Heisman, Kenzie L. Preston, Christine A. Sannerud, Barbara Wolf, and Phillip P. Woodson
1990 "Low-Dose Caffeine Physical Dependence in Humans." *Journal of Pharmacology and Experimental Therapeutics* 255 (3): 1123–32.

Grinspoon, Lester
1987 "Cancer Patients Should Get Marijuana." *New York Times* (July 28): 23.
1979 *Psychedelic Drugs Reconsidered*. New York: Basic Books.

Grinspoon, Lester and James B. Bakalar
1985 *Cocaine: A Drug and Its Social Evolution: Revised Edition*. New York: Basic Books.
1976 *Cocaine: A Drug and Its Social Evolution*. New York: Basic Books.

Grinspoon, Lester and Peter Hedblom
1975 *The Speed Culture: Amphetamine Use and Abuse in America*. Cambridge, MA: Harvard University Press.

Groopman, Jerome
2001 "Eyes Wide Open." *New Yorker* (December 3): 52–57.

Gross, Jane
2008 "Rise Seen in Trafficking in Enahnced Ecstasy." *New York Times* (January 9): 11.

2007 "On Florida Coast, Addicts Find Home in an Oasis of Sobriety." *New York Times* (November 16): 1, 24.

Grosswirth, Marvin
1982 "Medical Menace: Doctors Hooked on Drugs." *Ladies Home Journal* (February): 94, 141–44.

Gruson, Lindsey
1990 "U.S. Pinning Hopes on Guatemalan Army for Stability and War Against Drugs." *New York Times* (July 5): 4.

Guardia, José, Ana M. Catafau, Fanny Batlle, Juan Carlos Martin, Lidia Segura, Begona Gonzalvo, Gemma Prat, Ignasi Carrió, and Miguel Casas
2000 "Striatal Dopaminergic D2 Receptor Density Measured by [123] Iodobenzamide SPECT in the Prediction of Treatment Outcome of Alcohol-Dependent Patients." *American Journal of Psychiatry* 157 (1): 127–29.

Guillermoprieto, Alma
2002 "Waiting for War." *New Yorker* (May): 48–55.

Gulley, Joshua M., Cecelia McNamara, Thomas J. Barbera, Mary C. Ritz, and Frank R. George
1995 "Selective Serotonin Reuptake Inhibitors on Ethanol-Reinforced Behavior in Mice." *Alcohol* 12 (May/June): 177–81.

Guo, Jie, Karl G. Hill, J. David Hawkins, Richard F. Catalano, and Robert D. Abbott.
2002 "A developmental Analysis of Sociodemographic, Family, and Peer Effects on Adolescent Illicit Drug Initiation." *Journal of the American Academy of Child and Adolescent Psychiatry* 41 (July): 838–46.

Gusfield, Joseph R.
1975 "The (F)Utility of Knowledge? The Relation of Social Science to Public Policy Toward Drugs." *Annals* 417 (January): 1–15.
1963 *Symbolic Crusade: Status Politics and the American Temperance Movement.* Urbana, IL: University of Illinois Press.

Güttinger, Franziska, Patrick Gschwend, Bernd Schulte, and Jürgen Rehm
2003 "Evaluating Long-Term Effects of Heroin-Assisted Treatment: The Results of a 6-Year Follow-Up." *European Addiction Research* 9: 73–79.

Hafvenstein, Joel
2006 "Afghanistan's Drug Habit." *New York Times* (September 30): 27.

Haggerty, Kevin, Rick Kosterman, Richard F. Catalano, and J. David Hawkins
1999 *Preparing for the Drug Free Years.* Washington, DC: Office of Juvenile Justice and Delinquency Programs.

Haley, Bruce
1990 "Burma's Hidden Wars." *U.S. News and World Report* (December 10): 44–47.

Halkitis, Perry N., Jeffrey T. Parsons, Leo Wilton
2003 "An Exploratory Study of Contextual and Situational Factors Related to Methamphetamine Use Among Gay and Bisexual Men in New York City." *Journal of Drug Issues* 33 (Spring): Internet.

Hall, Kevin G.
2000 "Drug Chemicals Difficult to Target." *Chicago Tribune* (November 23): 36.

Hall, Trish
1990 "New Way to Treat Alcoholism Discards Spiritualism of A.A." *New York Times* (December 24): 1, 10.

Hall, Wayne
1999 "Appraisals of the Adverse Health Effects of Cannabis Use: Ideology and Evidence." *Drug Policy Analysis Bulletin*: Internet.

Hall, Wayne, Louisa Degenhardt, and Michael Lynskey
2001 *The Health and Psychological Effects of Cannabis Use.* Canberra, Australia: Commonwealth Department of Health and Aging.

Hallstone, Michael
2002 "Updating Howard Becker's Theory of Using Marijuana for Pleasure." *Contemporary Drug Problems* 29 (Winter): 821–47.

Hanes, W. Travis and Frank Sanello
2005 *The Opium Wars: The Addiction of One Empire and the Corruption of Another.* New York: Barnes and Noble.

Hanson, David J.
1980 "Drug Education: Does It Work?" Pages 251–82 in *Drugs and the Youth Culture,* edited by Frank S. Scarpitti and Susan K. Datesman. Beverley Hills, CA: Sage.

Hanson, Glen R.
2002a "Drug Abuse, Gender Matters." *NIDA Notes* 17 (2): 3, 4.
2002b "New Insights into Relapse." *NIDA Notes* 17 (3): 3–4.
2001 "Looking the Other Way: Rave Promoters and Club Drugs." Hearing before the Senate Caucus on International Narcotics Control (December 4).

Hargreaves, William A.
1986 "Methadone Dosage and Duration for Maintenance Treatment." Pages 19–79 in *Research on the Treatment of Narcotic Addiction: State of the Art,* edited by James R. Cooper, Fred Altman, Barry S. Brown, and Dorynne Czechowicz. Rockville, MD: National Institute on Drug Abuse.

Harm Reduction Coalition
1998 "Effects, Tolerance & Addiction." Internet.

Harocopos, Alex and Mike Hough
2005 *Drug Dealing in Open-Air Markets.* Washington, DC: U.S. Department of Justice.

Harris, Gardiner
2010 "Researchers Find Study of Medical Marijuana Discouraged." *New York Times* (January 19): 14.
2009 "F.D.A. Threatens to Ban Caffeinated Alcoholic Drinks." *New York Times* (November 14): 11.
2007 "Study on Nicotine Levels Stirs Calls for New Controls." *New York Times* (January 19): B1.

Harris, Louis S., ed.
1999 *Problems of Drug Abuse, 1998.* Rockville, MD: National Institute on Drug Abuse.

Harris, Louis S.
1993 "Opiates: A History of Opiates and Their Use in Treatment." Pages 85–90 in *International Research Conference on Biomedical Approaches to Illicit Drug Demand Reduction,* edited by Christine R. Hartel. Washington, DC: U.S. Government Printing Office.

Hartel, Christine R., ed.
International Research Conference on Biomedical Approaches to Illicit Drug Demand Reduction. Washington, DC: U.S. Government Printing Office.

Hartocollis, Anemona
2010 "City Urged to Withdraw Flier on 'Safer' Heroin Use That Some See as How-to-Guide." *New York Times* (January 6): 17.

Harwood, Henrick J. and Tracy G. Myers
2004 *New Treatments for Addiction: Behavioral, Ethical, Legal, and Social Questions.* Washington, DC: National Academies Press.

Hawkins, Dana
2002 "Tests on Trial: Jobs and Reputations Ride on Unproven Drug Screens." *U.S. News and World Report* (August 12): 46–48.

Hawkins, J. David, Denise M. Lishner, and Richard F. Catalano
1987 "Childhood Predictors and the Prevention of Adolescent Substance Abuse." Pages 75–126 in *Etiology of Drug Abuse,* edited by Coryl LaRue Jones and Robert J. Battjes. Rockville, MD: National Institute on Drug Abuse.

Hawley, Thersa Lawton, Tamara G. Halle, Ruth E. Drasin, and Nancy G. Thomas
1995 "Children of Addicted Mothers: Effects of the 'Crack Epidemic' on the Caregiving Environment and the Development of Preschoolers." *American Journal of Orthopsychiatry* 65 (July): 364–79.

Hays, Tom
2000 "Army Colonel to Plead Guilty." Associated Press (April 4): Internet.

Hedgepath, William
1989 "Mule Skinner." *Atlanta* (March): 61–62, 93–101.

Heinz, Andreas, Sabine Löber, Alexander Georgi, Jana Wrase, Derik Hermann, Eibe-R. Rey, Stefan Wellek, and Karl Mann
2003 "Reward Craving and Withdrawal Relief: Assessment of Different Motivational Pathways to Alcohol Intake." *Alcohol and Alcoholism* 38 (1): 35–39.

Helmer, John
1975 *Drugs and Minority Oppression.* New York: Seabury Press.

Henderson, Leigh A.
1994a "About LSD." Pages 37–53 in *LSD: Still with Us After All These Years,* edited by Leigh A. Henderson and William J. Glass. New York: Lexington Books.
1994b "Adverse Reactions to LSD." Pages 55–75 in *LSD: Still with Us After all These Years,* edited by Leigh A. Henderson and William J. Glass. New York: Lexington Books.

Hendler, Harold I. and Richard C. Stephens
1977 "The Addict Odyssey: From Experimentation to Addiction." *International Journal of the Addictions* 12: 25–42.

Hepburn, John R. and Angela N. Harvey
2007 "The Effect of the Threat of Legal Sanction on Program Retention and Completion: Is That Why They Stay in Drug Court?" *Crime and Delinquency* 53 (April): 255–80.

Hepburn, John R., C. Wayne Johnston, and Scott Rogers
1994 *Do Drugs. Do Time: An Evaluation of the Maricopa County Demand Reduction Program.* Washington, DC: National Institute of Justice.

"Heroin on Long Island"
2009 *New York Times* editorial (July 31): 22.

Hester, Reid K. and William R. Miller
1988 "Empirical Guidelines for Optimal Client-Treatment Matching." Pages 27–38 in *Adolescent Drug Abuse: Analyses of Treatment Research,* edited by Elizabeth R. Rahdert and John Grabowski. Rockville, MD: National Institute on Drug Abuse.

Higgens, Stephen T. and Alan Budney
1993 "Treatment of Cocaine Dependence Through the Principles of Behavior Analysis and Behavioral Psychology." Pages 97–121 in *Behavioral Treatments for Drug Abuse and Dependence,* edited by Lisa Simon Onken, John D. Blaine, and John J. Boren. Rockville, MD: National Institute on Drug Abuse.

Higginbotham, Adam
2007 "Fentanyl." *Details* (April): 212–17.

Hilts, Philip J.
1994 "Survey Finds Surge in Smoking by Young." *New York Times* (July 20): C19.
1990 "How the Brain Is Stimulated by Marijuana Is Discovered." *New York Times* (July 21): 1, 5.

Himmelstein, Jerome L.
1983 *The Strange Career of Marijuana: Politics and Ideology of Drug Control in America.* Westport, CT: Greenwood.

Hinson, Riley E.
1985 "Individual Differences in Tolerance and Relapse." Pages 101–24 in *Determinants of Substance Abuse: Biological, Psychological, and Environmental Factors,* edited by Mark Galizio and Stephen A. Maisto. New York: Plenum.

Hirschi, Travis
1969 *Causes of Delinquency.* Berkeley: University of California Press.

Hoaken, Peter N. S., Tavis Campbell, Sherry H. Stewart, and R. O. Phil
2003 "Effects of Alcohol on Cardio-vascular Reactivity and the Mediation of Aggressive Behavior in Adult Men and Women." *Alcohol and Alcoholism* 38 (1): 84–92.

Hobson, Katherine
2006 "Conquering Cravings." *U.S. News and World Report* (October 23): 64–66.
2002 "Danger at the Gym." *U.S. News and World Report* (January 21): 59.

Hoffmann, Norman G., Patricia A. Harrison, and Susan G. Streed
1991 "Outcome Evaluation." Pages 137–54 in *Substance Abuse Services: A Guide to Planning and Management,* edited by Joseph Westermeyer and Ronald S. Krug. Chicago: American Hospital Association.

Holinger, Paul C.
1989 "A Developmental Perspective on Psychotherapy and Psychoanalysis." *American Journal of Psychiatry* 146 (November): 1404–12.

Hollon, Tom
2002 "Phenotype Offers New Perception on Cocaine: Researchers Say Glutamate is More Essential to Addiction than Dopamine." *The Scientist* 16 (January 21): 16–17.

Holloway, Marguerite
1991 "Rx for Addiction." *Scientific American* (March): 94–103.

Home Office (HO)
2007 *Identifying and Exploring Young People's Experiences of Risk, Protective Factors and Resilience to Drug Use.* London, UK: HO.
2004 *Tackling Drugs Changing Lives. Keeping Communities Safe from Drugs.* London, UK: HO.

Hormes, Joseph T., Christopher M. Filley, and Neil L. Rosenberg
1986 "Neurologic Sequelae of Chronic Solvent Vapor Abuse." *Neurology* 36 (May): 698–702.

Horowitz, Craig
1996 "The No-Win War." *New York Times* (February 5): 23–33.

Horton, Terry and Suzanne McMurphy
2004 "Phoenix House, A Therapeutic Community." *Perspectives* 2 (August): 27–29.

Hough, Mike
2005 *Drug Dealing in Open-Air Markets.* Washington, DC: U.S. Department of Justice.

"How the War on Drugs Influences the Health and Well-Being of Minority Communities"
1999 DPRC (Drug Police Research Center) *Newsletter* (June): 1–3.

Howe, Benjamin Ryder
2000 "Out of the Jungle." *nn* (May): 32–38.

Hser, Yih-Ing, Christine E. Grella, Robert L. Hubbard, Shih-Chao Hsieh, Bennett W. Fletcher, Barry S. Brown, and M. Douglas Anglin
2001 "An Evaluation of Drug Treatments for Adolescents in 4 U.S. Cities." *Archives of General Psychiatry* 58 (July): 689–95.

Hubbard, Robert L., Mary Ellen Marsden, J. Valley, Rachel Henrick, J. Harwood, Elizabeth R. Cavanaugh, and Harold M. Ginsberg
1989 *Drug Abuse Treatment: A National Study of Effectiveness.* Chapel Hill: University of North Carolina Press.

Hughes, Caitlin and Alex Stevens
2007 "The Effects of Decriminalization of Drug Use in Portugal." Briefing paper, Beckley Foundation Drug Policy Programme, London.

Hughes, John R.
1990 "Nicotine Abstinence Effects." Page 123 in *Problems of Drug Dependence 1989,* edited by Louis S. Harris. Rockville, MD: National Institute on Drug Abuse.

Hughes, Patrick H.
1977 *Behind the Wall of Respect.* Chicago: University of Chicago Press.

Huizinga, David H., Scott Menard, and Delbert S. Elliott
1989 "Delinquency and Drug Use: Temporal and Developmental Patterns." *Justice Quarterly* 6 (September): 419–55.

Humphries, Drew and David F. Greenberg
1981 "The Dialectics of Crime Control." Pages 209–54 in *Crime and Capitalism,* edited by David F. Greenberg. Palo Alto, CA: Mayfield.

Hunt, Leon Gibson
1977 *Assessment of Local Drug Abuse.* Lexington, MA: D.C. Heath.

Hunt, Walter A.
1983 "Ethanol and the Central Nervous System." Pages 133–63 in *Medical and Social Aspects of Alcohol Abuse,* edited by Boris Tabakoff, Patricia B. Sutker, and Carrie L. Randall. New York: Plenum.

Husak, Douglas and Peter de Marneffe
2005 *The Legalization of Drugs.* New York: Cambridge University Press.

Hyman, Steven E. and Eric J. Nestler
1996 "Initiation and Adaptation: Paradigm for Understanding Psychotropic Drug Action." *American Journal of Psychiatry* 153 (February): 151–62.

Ihde, Aaron J.
1982 "Food Controls Under the 1906 Act." Pages 40–50 in *The Early Years of Federal Food and Drug Control,* edited by James Harvey Young. Madison, WI: American Institute of the History of Pharmacy.

Ikonomidou, Chrysanthy, Petra Bittigau, Masahiko J. Ishimaru, David F. Wozniak, Christan Koch, Kerstin Genz, Madelon T. Price, Vanya Stefovska, Friederlke Hörster, Tanya Tenkova, Krikor Dikranian, and John W. Olney
2000 "Ethanol-Induced Apoptotic Neurodegeneration and Fetal Alcohol Syndrome." *Science* 287 (February 11): 1056–60.

Illicit Drug Policies: Selected Laws from the 50 States
2002 Chicago, IL: Robert Wood Johnson Foundation.

Iliff, Laurence
2005 "Nuevo Laredo Officers Charged With Organized-Crime Activities." *Dallas Morning News* (September 6): Internet.

Illinois Criminal Justice Authority
1999 "Drug Court Provides Treatment Alternative to Incarceration." *On Good Authority* 2 (April): 1–4.

Inciardi, James A.
2002 *The War on Drugs III: The Continuing Saga of the Mysteries and Miseries of Intoxication, Addiction, Crime, and Public Policy.* Boston: Allyn and Bacon.
1986 *The War on Drugs: Heroin, Cocaine, Crime, and Public Policy.* Palo Alto, CA: Mayfield.
1981 "Heroin Addiction and Street Crime." Pages 53–60 in *International Narcotics Trafficking, hearings before the Permanent Subcommittee on Investigations, November 10, 11, 12, 13, 17, and 18.* Washington, DC: U.S. Government Printing Office.

Inciardi, James A. and Anne E. Pottieger
1991 "Kids, Crack, and Crime." *Journal of Drug Issues* 21: 257–70.

Inciardi, James A., Duane McBride, and Hilary L. Surratt
1998 "The Heroin Street Addict: Profiling a National Population." Pages 31–50 in *Heroin in the Age of Crack-Cocaine,* edited by James A. Inciardi and Laura D. Harrison. Thousand Oaks, CA: Sage.

Inciardi, James A., Hilary I. Surratt, Dale D. Chitwood, Clyde B. McCoy
1996 "The Origins of Crack." Pages 1–14 in *The American Dream: Crack Cocaine and the Inner City,* edited by Dale D. Chitwood, James E. Rivers, and James A. Inciardi. New York: Harcourt Brace.

Institute for the Study of Drug Dependence (ISDD)
1987 *Drug Abuse Briefing.* London: ISDD.

International Narcotics Control Strategy Report, 1999
2000 Bureau for International Narcotics and Law Enforcement Affairs, U.S. Department of State. Washington, DC, March 2000.

Inverarity, James M., Pat Lauderdale, and Barry Field
1983 *Law and Society: Sociological Perspectives on Criminal Law.* Boston: Little, Brown.

Irwin, John
1970 *The Felon.* Englewood Cliffs, NJ: Prentice Hall.

Ives, Nat
2004 "Flavored Kool Cigarettes Are Attracting Criticism." *New York Times* (March 9): C11.

Izenwasser, Sari and Ellen M. Unterwald
1994 "Sensitization and Tolerance to Cocaine." Pages 71–73 in *Problems of Drug Dependence, 1993,* edited by Louis S. Harris. Rockville, MD: National Institute on Drug Abuse.

Jacob, Peyton III and Alexander Shulgin
1994 "Structure-Activity Relationships of the Classic Hallucinogens and Their Analogs." Pages 74–91 in *Hallucinogens: An Update,* edited by Geraline C. Lin and Richard A. Glennon. Rockville, MD: National Institute on Drug Abuse.

Jacobs, Andrew
2010 "China Turns Drug Rehab into a Punishing Ordeal." *New York Times* (January 8): 4.

Jacobsen, Chanoch and Robert A. Hanneman
1992 "Illegal Drugs: Past, Present and Possible Futures." *Journal of Drug Issues* 22 (Winter): 105–20.

Jamieson, Anne, Alan Glanz, and Susanne MacGregor
1984 *Dealing with Drug Misuse: Crisis Intervention in the City.* London, England: Tavistock.

Jelinek, Pauline
1999 "Latin Leaders: U.S. Drug War Failed." Associated Press (November 3).

Johannessen, Koreen, Carolyn Collins, Beverly Mills-Novoa, and Peggy Glider
1999 *A Practical Guide to Alcohol Abuse Prevention: A Campus Case Study in Implementing Social Norms and Environmental Management Approaches.* Tucson, AZ: University of Arizona.

Johnson, Bruce D., Andrew Golub, and Jeffrey Fagan
1995 "Careers in Crack, Drug Use, Drug Distribution, and Nondrug Criminality." *Crime and Delinquency* 41 (July): 275–95.

Johnson, Bruce D., Douglas S. Lipton, and Eric D. Wish
1986a *Facts About the Criminality of Heroin and Cocaine Abusers and Some New Alternatives to Incarceration.* New York: Photocopied.
1986b *Facts About the Criminality of Heroin and Cocaine Abusers and Some New Alternatives to Incarceration* (Research Summary). New York: Narcotic and Drug Research, Inc.

Johnson, Bruce D., Eric C. Wish, James Schmeidler, and David Huizinga
1991 "Concentration of Delinquent Offending: Serious Drug Involvement and High Delinquency Rates." *Journal of Drug Issues* 21: 205–29.

Johnson, Bruce D., Kevin Anderson, and Eric C. Wish
1989 "A Day in the Life of 105 Drug Addicts and Abusers: Crimes Committed and How the Money Was Spent." *Sociology and Social Research* 72: 185–91.

Johnson, Bruce D., Paul J. Goldstein, Edward Preble, James Schmeidler, Douglas S. Lipton, Barry Spunt, and Thomas Miller
1985 *Taking Care of Business: The Economics of Crime by Heroin Abusers.* Lexington, MA: D.C. Heath.

Johnson, Bruce D., Terry Williams, Koja A. Dei, and Harry Sanabria
1990 "Drug Abuse in the Inner City: Impact on Hard-Drug Users and the Community." Pages 9–67 in *Drugs and Crime,* edited by Michael Tonry and James Q. Wilson. Chicago: University of Chicago of Press.

Johnson, C. Anderson, Mary Ann Pentz, Mark D. Weber, James H. Dwyer, Neal Baer, David P. MacKinnon, William B. Hansen, and Brian R. Flay
1990 "Relative Effectiveness of Comprehensive Community Programming for Drug Abuse Prevention with High-Risk and Low-Risk Adolescents." *Journal of Consulting and Clinical Psychology* 58 (August): 447–56.

Johnson, Earl Jr.
1963 "Organized Crime: Challenge to the American Legal System." *Criminal Law, Criminology, and Police Science* 54 (March): 1–29.

Johnson, Julie
1987 "Two Reagan Officials Report Limited Success in Drug War." *New York Times* (December 9): 53.

Johnson, Kelly Dedel
2004 *Underage Drinking.* Washington, DC: U.S. Department of Justice.

Johnson, Kevin
2010 "Vancouver's 'Safe House' for Drug Addicts Draws Controversy." *USA Today* (February 15): Internet.

Johnson, Kirk
2006 "Officials Seeking Source of Lethal Heroin Mixture." *New York Times* (June 15): 14.

Johnson, Patrick B., Sharon M. Boles, and Herbert D. Kleber
2000 "The Relationship Between Adolescent Smoking and Drinking and Likelihood Estimates of Illicit Drug Use." *Journal of Addictive Diseases* 19 (2): 75–81.

Joint Committee on New York Drug Law Evaluation
1977 *The Nation's Toughest Drug Law: Evaluation of the New York Experience.* New York: Association of the Bar of the City of New York.

Jones, Allison North
2002 "Strong Views, Pro and Con, on Ads Linking Drug Use to Terrorism." *New York Times* (April 2): C7.

Jones, Charisse
1995 "Crack and Punishment: Is Race the Issue?" *New York Times* (October 16): 1, 9.

Jones, Coryl LaRue and Robert J. Battjes
1987 "The Context and Caveats of Prevention Research on Drug Abuse." Pages 1–12 in *Etiology of Drug Abuse: Implications for Prevention,* edited by Coryl LaRue Jones and Robert J. Battjes. Rockville, MD: National Institute on Drug Abuse.

Jones, Hendrée E.
2004 "Practical Considerations for the Clinical Use of Buprenorphine." *Perspectives* 2 (August): 4–24.

Jones, Kenneth L., Louis W. Shainberg, and Curtis O. Byer
1979 *Drugs and Alcohol,* 3rd ed. New York: Harper and Row.

Jordon, Mary and Kevin Sullivan
2005 "Border Police Chief Only Latest Casualty in Mexico Drug War." *Washington Post Foreign Service* (June 16): 1.

Jourbert, Lucien
1987 "The Oral Dose Is Safer," Letter to the *New York Times* (August 15): 14.

Joy, Janet E., Stanley J. Watson Jr., and John A. Benson Jr., eds.
1999 *Marijuana and Medicine: Assessing the Science Base.* Washington, DC: National Academy Press.

Judson, Barbara A. and Avram Goldstein
1986 "Uses of Naloxone in the Diagnosis and Treatment of Heroin Addiction." Pages 1–18 in *Research on the Treatment of Narcotic Addiction: State of the Art,* edited by James R. Cooper, Fred Altman, Barry S. Brown, and Dorynne Czechowicz. Rockville, MD: National Institute on Drug Abuse.

Judson, George
1995 "Study Finds AIDS Risk to Addicts Drops if Sale of Syringes is Legal." *New York Times* (August 30): 1, 12.

Kajdasz, D. K., J. W. Moore, H. Donepudi, C. E. Cochrane, and R. J. Malcolm
1999 "Cardiac and Mood-Related Changes during Short-Term Abstinence from Crack Cocaine: The Identification of Possible Withdrawal Phenomena." *American Journal of Drug and Alcohol Abuse* 25 (4): 629–37.

Kampman, Kyle M.
2008 "The Search for Medications to Treat Stimulant Dependence." *Addiction Science and Clinical Practice* (June): 28–35.

Kandel, Denise K.
1974 "Interpersonal Influences on Adolescent Illegal Drug Use." Pages 207–40 in *Drug Use: Epidemiological and Sociological Approaches,* edited by Eric Josephson and Eleanor E. Carroll. New York: Wiley.

Kandel, Denise K. and Mark Davies
1991 "Friendship Networks, Intimacy, and Illicit Drug Use in Young Adulthood: A Comparison of Two Competing Theories." *Criminology* 29 (August): 441–67.

Kaplan, David
1999 "The Golden Age of Crime." *U.S. News & World Report* (November 29): 42–44.
Kaplan, John
1983a "Drugs and Crime: Legal Aspects." Pages 643–52 in the *Encyclopedia of Crime and Justice,* edited by Sanford H. Kadish. New York: The Free Press.
1983b *The Hardest Drug: Heroin and Public Policy.* Chicago: University of Chicago Press.
Karch, Steven B.
1998 *A Brief History of Cocaine.* Boca Raton, FL: CRC Press.
1996 *The Pathology of Drug Abuse: Second Edition.* Boca Raton, FL: CRC Press.
Katcher, Leo
1959 *The Big Bankroll: The Life and Times of Arnold Rothstein.* New York: Harper & Brothers.
Katel, Peter
1995 "Justice: The Trouble with Informants." *Pressweek* (January 30): 48.
Kauffman, Eda, Martha Morrison Dore, and Lani Nelson-Zlupko
1995 "The Role of Women's Therapy Groups in the Treatment of Chemical Dependence." *American Journal of Orthopsychiatry* 65 (July): 355–63.
Kaufman, Edward
1994 *Psychotherapy of Addicted Persons.* New York: Guilford Press.
Kay, David C.
1973 "Federal Civil Commitment in the Federal Medical Program for Opiate Addicts." Pages 17–35 in *Yearbook of Drug Abuse,* edited by Leon Brill and Earnest Harms. New York: Behavioral Publications.
Kempe, Frederick
1990 *Divorcing the Dictator: America's Bungled Affair with Noriega.* New York: Putnam's Sons.
Kenneally, Scott
2007 "Use as Directed." *Details* (February): 61–62.
Kennedy, David
2009 "Drug, Race and Common Ground: Reflections on the High Point Intervention." *NIJ Journal* 292: 12–17.
Kennedy, Randy
1995 "Death Highlights Drug's Lethal Allure to Doctors." *New York Times* (November 11): 1, 10.

Kerr, Peter
1988 "Crime Study Finds High Drug Use at Time of Arrest." *New York Times* (January 22): 1, 9.
Kershaw, Sarah
2006 "Through Indian Lands, Drugs' Shadowy Trail." *New York Times* (February 19): 1, 26–27.
2005 "Violent New Front in Drug War Opens on the Canadian Border." *New York Times* (March 5): 1, 8.
Kertzner, Robert M.
1987 "Individual Psychotherapy of Cocaine Abuse." Pages 138–55 in *Cocaine Abuse: New Directions in Treatment and Research,* edited by Henry I. Spitz and Jeffrey S. Rosecan. New York: Brunner/Mazel.
Khantzian, Edward J.
1985 "The Self-Medication Hypothesis of Addictive Disorders: Focus on Heroin and Cocaine Dependence." *American Journal of Psychiatry* 142: 1259–64.
1980 "An Ego/Self Theory of Substance Dependence: A Contemporary Psychoanalytic Perspective." Pages 29–33 in *Theories on Drug Abuse: Selected Contemporary Perspectives,* edited by Dan J. Lettieri, Mollie Sayers, and Helen Wallenstein Pearson. Rockville, MD: National Institute on Drug Abuse.
Khantzian, Edward J., John E. Mack, and Alan F. Schatzberg
1974 "Heroin Use as an Attempt to Cope: Clinical Observations." *American Journal of Psychiatry* 131 (February): 160–64.
Kidorf, Michael and Maxine L. Stitzer
1996 "Contingent Use of Take-Home and Split Dosing to Reduce Illicit Drug Use of Methadone Patients." *Behavior Therapy* 27 (Winter): 41–51.
Kilian, Michael and David Mendell
2002 "$1 Million in Drugs Seized in Base Sting." *Chicago Tribune* (July 3): 10.
King, Rufus
1969 *Gambling and Organized Crime.* Washington, DC: Public Affairs Press.
Kinlock, Timothy W., Thomas E. Hanlon, and David N. Nurco
1998 "Heroin Use in the United States: History and Present Developments." Pages 1–30 in *Heroin in the Age of Crack-Cocaine,* edited by James A. Inciardi

and Laura D. Harrison. Thousand Oaks, CA: Sage.
Kirkey, Sharon
2006 "Second-hand Smoke Linked to Behaviour Problems." *Ottawa Citizen* (May 1): Internet.
Kirsebbaum, Susan
2002 "Darling, pass the Xanax: Trading Prescription Painkillers and Sedatives Is the Latest Trend at Parties." *Harper's Bazaar* (May): 108–10.
Klam, Matthew
2001 "Experiencing Ecstasy." *New York Times Magazine* (January 21): 38–43, 64, 68, 78–79.
1999 "Experiencing Ecstasy." *New York Times Magazine* (January 21): 38–43, 64, 68, 78–79.
Klebe, Kelli J. and Maureen O'Keefe
2004 *Outcome Evaluation of the Crossroads to Freedom House and Peer 1 Therapeutic Communities.* Washington, DC: U.S. Department of Justice.
Kleiman, Mark A. R.
1992 *Against Excess: Drug Policy for Results.* New York: Basic Books.
1989 *Marijuana: Costs of Abuse, Costs of Control.* New York: Greenwood Press.
1988 "Crackdowns: The Effects on Intensive Enforcement on Retail Heroin Dealing." Pages 3–18 in *Street-Level Drug Enforcement: Examining the Issues,* edited by Marcia R. Chaiken. Washington, DC: U.S. Government Printing Office.
1985 "Drug Enforcement and Organized Crime." Pages 67–87 in *The Politics and Economics of Organized Crime.* Lexington, MA: D.C. Heath.
Klein, Joel
2009 "Save the Pot Dealers!" *Time* (November 16): 64.
Kleinknecht, William
1996 *The New Ethnic Mobs: The Changing Face of Organized Crime in America.* New York: Free Press.
Kocieniewski, David
1998 "In Drug War, Risky Tactic Yields a Fatality." *New York Times* (January 21): 18.
Kolata, Gina
1996 "The Unwholesome Tale of the Herb Market." *New York Times* (April 21): 6E.
1989a "Medications May Ease Craving for Cocaine." *New York Times* (March 7): 21, 23.

1989b "Experts Finding New Hope on Treating Crack Addicts." *New York Times* (August 24): 1, 9.

Koob, George F., Barak Caine, Athina Markou, Luigi Pulvirenti, and Freidbert Weiss
1994 "Role for the Mesocortical Dopamine System in the Motivating Effects of Cocaine." Pages 1–16 in *Neurobiological Models for Evaluating Mechanisms Underlying Cocaine Addiction,* edited by Lynda Erinoff and Roger M. Brown. Rockville, MD: National Institute on Drug Abuse.

Korf, Dirk J., Heleen Riper, and Bruce Bullington
1999 "Windmills in Their Minds? Drug Policy and Drug Research in the Netherlands." *Journal of Drug Issues* 29 (3): 451–72.

Kornblut, Anne E.
2006 "All (Puff) in Favor (Puff) Say Aye (Wheeze)." *New York Times* (February 12): WK 3.

Kosten, Thomas R.
1993 "Clinical and Research Perspectives on Cocaine Abuse: The Pharmacology of Cocaine Abuse." Pages 48–56 in *Cocaine Treatment: Research and Clinical Perspectives,* edited by Frank M. Tims and Carl G. Leukefeld. Rockville, MD: National Institute on Drug Abuse.

Kotulak, Ronald
2002a "Experts Say Love of Nicotine is all in the Mind." *Chicago Tribune* (March 14): 1, 18.
2002b "Traffic Signal: Red Light, Green Light and Booze." *Chicago Tribune* (September 29): Sec. 2: 1, 7.
1997 "Unlocking Secrets of Alcohol's Grip." *Chicago Tribune* (August 24): 1, 16.

Krauss, Clifford
2003 "Canada Parts with the U.S. on Drugs." *New York Times* (May 19): 1.
2000 "Bolivia Wiping out Coca, at a Price." *New York Times* (October 23): 10.
1999a "Bolivia, at Some Risk, Is Making Big Gains in Eradicating Coca." *New York Times* (May 9): 6.
1999b "Peru's Drug Successes Erode as Traffickers Adapt." *New York Times* (August 19): 3.

Krauss, Clifford and Douglas Frantz
1995 "Cali Drug Cartel Using U.S. Business to Launder Cash." *New York Times* (October 30): 1, 13.

Kreek, Mary Jeanne
1997 "Goals and Rationale for Pharmacotherapeutic Approach in Treating Cocaine Dependence: Insights from Basic and Clinical Research." Pages 5–35 in *Medication Development for the Treatment of Cocaine Dependence: Issues in Clinical Efficacy Trials.* Rockville, MD: National Institute on Drug Abuse.
1987 "Tolerance and Dependence: Implications for the Pharmacological Treatment of Addiction." Pages 53–62 in *Problems of Drug Dependence,* 1986, edited by Louis S. Harris. Rockville, MD: National Institute on Drug Abuse.

Kristoff, Nicholas D.
2009 "Drugs Won the War." *New York Times* (June 14): 10.
1999 "1492: The Prequel." *New York Times Magazine* (June 6): 80–86.

Krystal, Henry and Herbert A. Raskin
1970 *Drug Dependence: Aspects of Ego Function.* Detroit: Wayne State University Press.

Kuchinskas, Susan
2009 "The Buds of Wrath." *Miller-McCune* (November-December): 19–21.

Kummer, Corby
1999 "Smoky Scotch." *Atlantic Monthly* (December): 115–19.

Labaton, Stephen
1989 "New Tactics in the War on Drugs Tilt Scales of Justice Off Balance." *New York Times* (December 29): 1, 14.

Lacey, Marc
2009a "For Some Taxi Drivers, a Different Kind of Traffic." *New York Times* (March 2): 10.
2009b "Drug Gangs' Kin, Guilty or Not, Are Ensnared in Mexico Crackdown." *New York Times* (May 30): 4.
2009c "Mexico's Drug Traffickers Continue Trade in Prison." *New York Times* (August 11): 1, 6.
2009d "In the Streets of Mexico, Ambivalence on a Drug Law." *New York Times* (August 24): 4, 9.
2009e "Mexican Lawmen Outmatched by Drug Violence." *New York Times* (October 17): 1, 7.
2006 "Keystone Kops? No Kenyans, but Often Similarly Inept." *New York Times* (April 18): 4.

Lambert, Bruce
2006 "Law Enforcement Agencies Break 2 Major Drug Rings." *New York Times* (March 31): B3.

1996 "Fears Prompting Crackdown on Legal Herbal Stimulant." *New York Times* (April 23): 12.

Lamour, Catherine and Michael R. Lamberti
1974 *The Second Opium War.* London, England: Allen Lane.

Lang, Alan R.
1983 "Addicting Personality: A Viable Construct?" Pages 157–235 in *Commonalities in Substance Abuse and Habitual Behavior,* edited by Peter K. Levison, Dean R. Gerstein, and Deborah R. Maloff. Lexington, MA: D.C. Heath.

Latessa, Edward J. and Melissa M. Moon
1992 "The Effectiveness of Acupuncture in an Outpatient Drug Treatment Program." *Journal of Contemporary Criminal Justice* 8 (December): 317–31.

Latimer, Dean and Jeff Goldberg
1981 *Flowers in the Blood: The Story of Opium.* New York: Franklin Watts.

Law Commission of Canada (LCC)
2003 *What is a Crime? Challenges and Alternatives. Discussion Paper.* Quebec, Canada: LCC.

Lawson, Gary W.
1992 "A Biopsychological Model of Adolescent Substance Abuse." Pages 3–10 in *Adolescent Substance Abuse,* edited by Gary W. Lawson and Ann W. Lawson. Gaithersburg, MD: Aspen Publications.

Leary, Warren E.
1995 "Report Endorses Needle Exchanges as AIDS Strategy." *New York Times* (September 20): 1, 14.

Ledwith, William E.
2000 "Statement Before the House Government Reform Committee, Subcommittee on Criminal Justice, Drug Policy, and Human Resources." February 15.

Lee, Rensselaer III
1995 "Drugs in Communist and Former Communist Countries." *Transnational Organized Crime* 1 (Summer): 193–205.

Legrand, Lisa N., William G. Iacono, and Matt McGue
2005 "Predicting Addiction: Behavioral Genetics Uses Twins and Time to Decipher the Origins of Addiction and Learn Who is Most Vulnerable." *American Scientist* 93 (March–April): 140–48.

Lemert, Edwin M.
1951 *Social Pathology.* New York: McGraw-Hill.

Lerner, Steven E.
1980 "Phencyclidine Abuse in Perspective." Pages 13–23 in *Phencyclidine Abuse Manual,* edited by Mary Tuma McAdams, Ronald L. Linder, Steven E. Lerner, and Richard Stanley Burns. Los Angeles: University of California Extension.

Leshner, Alan I.
1997 "Addiction Is a Brain Disease and It Matters." *Science*: 278: 45–47.
1999a "Editorial: Science is Revolutionizing Our View of Addiction—and What to Do About It." *American Journal of Psychiatry* 156 (January): 1–3.
1999b "Research Shows Effects of Prenatal Cocaine Are Subtle But Significant." *NIDA Notes* 14 (3): 3–4.

Letcher, Andy
2007 *Shroom: A Cultural History of the Magic Mushroom.* New York: Ecco/HarperCollins.

Leukefeld, Carl C. and Frank M. Tims, eds.
1988 *Compulsory Treatment of Drug Abuse: Research and Clinical Practice.* Rockville, MD: National Institute on Drug Abuse.

Levine, Michael
1990 *Deep Cover.* New York: Delacorte.

Levinthal, Charles F.
1988 *Messengers of Paradise: Opiates and the Brain.* Garden City, NY: Doubleday.

Lewin, Tamar
2002 "With Court Nod, Parents Debate School Drug Tests." *New York Times* (September 29): 1, 27.
1992 "Drug Verdict over Infants is Voided." *New York Times* (July 24): B6.
1991 "Guilt Upheld for Drug Delivery by Umbilical Cord." *New York Times* (April 20): 1, 6.

Li, Guohua, Gordon S. Smith, and Susan P. Baker
1994 "Drinking Behavior in Relation to Cause of Death Among U.S. Adults." *American Journal of Public Health* 84 (9): 1402–6.

Lidz, Charles W. and Andrew L. Walker
1980 *Heroin, Deviance and Morality.* Beverley Hills, CA: Sage.

Lin, Geraline and Richard A. Glennon, eds.
1994 *Hallucinogens: An Update.* Rockville, MD: National Institute on Drug Abuse.

Linder, Ronald L., Steven E. Lerner and R. Stanley Burns
1981 *PCP: The Devil's Dust.* Belmont, CA: Wadsworth.

Lindesmith, Alfred C.
1968 *Addiction and Opiates.* Chicago: Aldine.

Lindesmith, Alfred C. and John H. Gagnon
1964 "Anomie and Drug Addiction." Pages 158–88 in *Anomie and Deviant Behavior,* edited by Marshall B. Clinard. New York: Free Press.

Lipton, Douglas S.
1995 *The Effectiveness of Treatment for Drug Abusers Under Criminal Justice Supervision.* Washington, DC: National Institute of Justice.

Liu, Jainhong, Dengke Zhou, Allen E. Liska, Steven F. Messner, Marvin D. Krohn, Lening Zhang, and Zhou Lu
1998 "Status, Power, and Sentencing in China." *Justice Quarterly* 15 (June): 289–300.

Liu, Liang Y.
1994 *Substance Use Among Youths at High Risk of Dropping Out: Grades 7–12 in Texas, 1992.* Austin: Texas Commission on Alcohol and Drug Abuse.

Lo, Celia C.
2003 "An Application of Social Conflict Theory to Arrestees' Use of Cocaine and Opiates." *Journal of Drug Issues* 33 (Winter): 237–67.

London, Perry
1964 *The Modes and Morals of Psychotherapy.* New York: Holt Rinehart and Winston.

Lubasch, Arnold H.
1990 "Trial Shows the Rich Rewards of a Federal Drug Informant." *New York Times* (November 4): 23.

Luft, Kerry
1995 "For Busted Drug Lord, Terror Too Crass." *Chicago Tribune* (June 15): 3.

Lukas, Scott E.
1996 *Proceedings of The National Consensus Meeting on the Use, Abuse and Sequelae of Abuse of Methamphetamine with Implications for Prevention, Treatment and Research.* Rockville, MD: U.S. Department of Health and Human Services Substance Abuse and Mental Health Services.

Lupsha, Peter A.
1991 "Drug Lords and Narco-Corruption: The Players Change But the Game Continues." *Crime, Law and Social Change* 16: 41–58.
1990 "The Geopolitics of Organized Crime: Some Comparative Models from Latin American Drug Trafficking Organizations." Paper presented at the annual meeting of the American Society of Criminology, Baltimore, November.

Lurigio, Arthur J.
2008 "The First 20 Years of Drug Treatment Courts: A Brief Description of Their History and Impact." *Federal Probation* (June): 13–17.

Lyall, Sarah
2002 "Easing to Marijuana Laws Angers Many Britons." *New York Times* (August 12): 3.

Lyman, Rick
1998 "Rights Query on Killing of Immigrant." *New York Times* (October 21): 18.

Mabry, Donald J.
1995 "The U.S. Military and the War on Drugs." Pages 43–60 in *Drug Trafficking in the Americas,* edited by Bruce M. Bagley and William O. Walker III. New Brunswick, NJ: Transaction Publishers.

MacCoun, Robert and Peter Reuter
1997 "Interpreting Dutch Cannabis Policy: Reasoning by Analogy in the Legalization Debate." *Science* 278 (October): 47–52.

MacCoun, Robert, Beau Kilmer, and Peter Reuter
2002 "Research on Drug-Crime Linkages: The Next Generation." Drugs and Crime Research forum draft.

MacDonald, James and Michael Agar
1994 "What Is a Trip—and Why Take One?" Pages 9–36 in *LSD: Still with Us After All These Years,* edited by Leigh A. Henderson and William J. Glass. New York: Lexington Books.

MacKenzie, Doris Layton
2006 *What Works in Corrections: Reducing the Criminal Activities of Offenders and Delinquents.* New York: Cambridge University Press.

Maddux, James F. and David P. Desmond
1981 *Careers of Opioid Users.* New York: Praeger.

Magura, Stephen, Cathy Casriel, Douglas S. Goldsmith, David L. Strug, and Douglas S. Lipton
1988 "Contingency Contracting with Polydrug-Abusing Methadone

Patients." *Addictive Behaviors* 13: 113–18.

Magura, Stephen, Sung-Yeon Kang, and Janet L. Shapiro
1995 "Measuring Cocaine Use by Hair Analysis Among Criminally-Involved Youth." *Journal of Drug Issues* 25 (Fall): 683–701.

Males, Mike
2006 "This is Your Brain on Drugs, Dad." *New York Times* (January 3): 21.

Malkin, Elisabeth
2009 "Police Posts in Mexico Attacked After Arrest." *New York Times* (July 13): 6.

Maltzman, Irving
1994 "Why Alcoholism Is a Disease." *Journal of Psychoactive Drugs* 26 (January/March): 13–31.

Manderson, Desmond
1999 "Symbolism and Racism in Drug History." *Drug and Alcohol Review* 18 (2): 179–86.

Mann, Arnold
2004a "Successful Trial Caps 25-Year Buprenorphine Development Effort." *NIDA Notes* 19 (3): 7–9.
2004b "Cocaine Abusers' Cognitive Deficits Compromise Treatment Outcomes." *NIDA Notes* 19 (1): 4–5.

Mann, Robert E., Reginald G. Smart, and Richard Govoni
2004 *The Epidemiology of Alcoholic Liver Disease.* Bethesda, MD: National Institute on Alcohol Abuse and Alcoholism.

Mansnerus, Laura
1996 "Timothy Leary, Pied Piper of Psychedelic 60's, Dies at 75." *New York Times* (June 1): 1, 11.

Manzoni, Patrik, Benedikt Fischer, and Jurgen Rehm
2007 "Local Drug-Crime Dynamics in a Canadian Multi-Site Sample of Untreated Opioid Users." *Canadian Journal of Criminology and Criminal Justice.* 49 (3): 341–73.

Marion, Ira J.
2005 "Methadone Treatment at Forty." *Science and Practice Perspectives* 3 (December): 25–31.

Markel, Howard
2002 "For Addicts, Relief May Be an Office Visit Away." *New York Times* (October 27): WK 14.

Marlatt, G. Alan, Julian M. Somers, and Susan F. Tapert
1993 "Harm Reduction: Application to Alcohol Abuse Problems." Pages 147–66 in *Behavioral Treatments*

for Drug Abuse and Dependence, edited by Lisa Simon Onken, John D. Blaine, and John J. Boren. Rockville, MD: National Institute on Drug Abuse.

Marlowe, Ann
1999 *How to Stop Time: Heroin from A to Z.* New York: Basic Books.

Marriott, Michael
1989 "Struggle and Hope from the Ashes of Drugs." *New York Times* (October 22): 1, 22.

Marshall, Donnie
2001 "Testimony Before the U.S. House of Representatives Committee on the Judiciary Subcommittee on Crime," March 29.

Marshall, Ineke Haen and Chris E. Marshall
1994 "Drug Prevention in the Netherlands: A Low Key Approach." Pages 205–31 in *Between Prohibition and Legalization: The Dutch Experiment in Drug Policy,* edited by Ed. Leuw and I. Haen Marshall. Amsterdam: Kugler Publications.

Martin, B. R., S. Childers, A. Howlett, R. Mechoulam, and R. Pertwee
1994 "Cannabinoid Receptors: Pharmacology, Second Messenger Systems and Endogenous Ligands." Pages 55–60 in *Problems of Drug Dependence, 1993.* Vol. I, edited by Louis S. Harris. Rockville, MD: National Institute on Drug Abuse.

Martin, Douglas
1990 "A Big Bribe Helps Mothers Flee the Seduction of Crack." *New York Times* (March 7): 13.

Martin, Susan E., Christopher D. Maxwell, Helene R. White, and Yan Zhang
2004 "Trends in Alcohol Use, Cocaine Use, and Crime: 1989–1998." *Journal of Drug Issues* 34 (Spring): 333–60.

Martino, Michael M. Jr.
2009 "Buy Heroin Here." *Long Island Press* (July 9-15): 10–15.

Marzulli, John
2005 "Jury Convicts 3 in JFK Drug Ring." *New York Daily News* (June 14): XQ 1.

Massing, Michael
1999 "The Real Methadone Problem." *New York* (January 11): 40–43, 102.
1990 "In the Cocaine War, the Jungle Is Winning." *New York Times Magazine* (March 4): 26, 88, 90, 92.

Mathias, Robert
2003 "School Prevention Program Effective with Youths at Risk for Substance Abuse." *NIDA Notes* 18 (5): 12–13.
2002 "Chronic Solvent Abusers Have More Brain Abnormalities and Cognitive Impairments than Cocaine Abusers." *NIDA Notes* 17 (4): 5–6, 12.
2000 "Methamphetamine Brain Damage in Mice More Extensive than Previously Thought." *NIDA Notes* 15 (4): 1, 10.
1999 "Study Shows How Genes Can Help Protect from Addiction." *NIDA Notes* 14 (March): 5, 9.

Mathias, Robert and Patrick Zickler
2001 "NIDA Conference Highlights Scientific Findings on MDMA/ Ecstasy." *NIDA Notes* 16 (5): 1, 5–8, 12.

Mattison, J. B.
1883 "Opium Addiction Among Medical Men." *Medical Record* 23 (June 9): 621–23. Reproduced in Morgan, 1974, pages 62–66.

May, Clifford D.
1988a "Drug Enforcement: Once-Lonely Voice Finds an Audience." *New York Times* (June 6): 12.
1988b "Coca-Cola Discloses an Old Secret." *New York Times* (July 1): 25, 29.

Mayes, Linda G.
1992 "Prenatal Cocaine Exposure and Young Children's Development." *Annals* 521 (May): 11–27.

Mazerolle, Lorraine, David W. Soole, and Sacha Rombouts.
2007 *Crime Prevention Research Reviews No. 1: Disrupting Street-Level Drug Markets.* Washington, DC: U.S. Department of Justice Office of Community-Oriented Policing Services.

McBride, Duane C. and Clyde B. McCoy
1981 "Crime and Drug-Abusing Behavior." *Criminology* 19 (August): 281–302.

McCance, Elinore F.
1997 "Overview of Potential Treatment Medications for Cocaine Dependence." Pages 36–72 in *Medication Development for the Treatment of Cocaine Dependence: Issues in Clinical Efficacy Trials,* edited by Betty Tai, Nora Chiang, and Peter Bridge. Rockville, MD: National Institute on Drug Abuse.

McConnaughey, Janet
2000 "Study: Smoking' Dangers Immediate." Associated Press (March 9): Internet.

McCoy, Alfred W.
1991 *The Politics of Heroin: CIA Complicity in the Global Heroin Trade.* Brooklyn, NY: Lawrence Hill Books.
1972 *The Politics of Heroin in Southeast Asia.* New York: Harper and Row.

McCoy, H. Virginia, Christine Miles, and James A. Inciardi
1995 "Survival Sex: Inner-City Women and Crack-Cocaine." Pages 172–77 in *The American Drug Scene: An Anthology,* edited by James A. Inciardi and Karen McElrath. Los Angeles: Roxbury.

McCurley, Carl and Howard N. Snyder
2008 "Co-Occurrence of Substance Use Behaviors in Youth." *Juvenile Justice Bulletin* (November): 1–8.

McDougall, Christopher
2006 "The Junkie in the O. R." *Men's Health* (November): 186–91, 193.

McElrath, Karen
1995 "Alcoholics Anonymous." Pages 314–17 in *The American Drug Scene: An Anthology,* edited by James A. Inciardi and Karen McElrath. Los Angeles: Roxbury.

McFadden, Robert D.
2005 "Drug Suspect in Afghan Ring Is Sent to U.S." *New York Times* (October 25): B1, 2.

McFarland, George C.
1989 *Drug Abuse Indicators Trend Report, District of Columbia.* Washington, DC: Alcohol and Drug Abuse Services Administration.

McGehee, Daniel S., Mark J. S. Heath, Shari Gelber, Piroska Devay, Lorna W. Role
1995 "Nicotine Enhancement of Fast Excitatory Synaptic Transmission in CNS by Presynaptic Receptors." *Science* 269 (September 22): 1692–96.

McGlothlin, William H., M. Douglas Anglin, and B. D. Wilson
1978 "Narcotic Addiction and Crime." *Criminology* 16: 293–315.

McIntosh, Lee
1988 "Letter to the Editor." *New York Times* (June 39): 26.

McKim, William A.
1991 *Drugs and Behavior: An Introduction to Behavioral Pharmacology,* 2nd ed. Englewood Cliffs, NJ: Prentice Hall.

McKinley, James C. Jr.
2009a "U.S. Is a Vast Arms Bazaar for Mexican Cartels." *New York Times* (February 26): 1, 18.
2009b "Drug Cartels in Mexico Lure American Teenagers as Killers." *New York Times* (June 23): 1, 18.
2009c "Deep in California Forests, An Illicit Business Thrives." *New York Times* (August 22): 9.
2009d "Vast Drug Case Tries to Disrupt Cultlike Cartel." *New York Times* (October 23): 1, 24.
2009e "Rights Group Report Faults Mexican Army's Conduct in Drug War." *New York Times* (December 8): 12.
2009f "Rights Group Report Faults Mexican Army's Conduct in Drug War." *New York Times* (December 8): 12.
2008 "Marijuana Hotbed Retreats on Medicinal Use." *New York Times* (June 9): 1, 17.
2008a "After Massacre, a Mexican Towns Left in Terror of Drug Violence." *New York Times* (May 31): 1, 8.
2008b "Drug War Causes Wild West Blood Bath, Killing 210 in a Mexican Town." *New York Times* (April 16): 10.
2008c "Mexican Federal Agents Seize Millions and Arrest 6." *New York Times* (April 4): 8.
2008d "Mexican Forces Clash with Drug Cartel Gunmen in Tijuana." *New York Times* (January 18): 5.
2008e "Mexico Hits Drug Gangs with Full Fury of War." *New York Times* (January 22): 1, 9.
2008f "Mexico's War Against Drugs Kills Its Police." *New York Times* (May 26): 1, 9.
2008g "6 Charged in Shooting Death of a Police Chief in Mexico." *New York Times* (May 13): 8.
2008h "3 Americans Arrested in Gang Battle with Mexican Police." *New York Times* (January 9): 5.
2007 "Mexico's Latest War on Drug Gangs Is Off to a Rapid Start." *New York Times* (January 27): 10.
2006 "With Beheadings and Attacks, Drug Gangs Terrorize Mexico." *New York Times* (October 26): 1, 12.

McKinley, James C. Jr., and Marc Lacey
2009 "Torrent of Cash Flows Where the U.S. and Mexico Meet." *New York Times* (December 26): 1, 12.

McKinley, Jesse
2006 "Marijuana Fight Envelops Wharf in San Francisco." *New York Times* (July 3): 1, 13.

McMillan, Brian and Mark Conner
2002 "Drug Use and Cognitions About Drug Use Amongst Students: Changes Over the University Career." *Journal of Youth and Adolescence* 31 (June): 221–30.

McNeil, Donald G. Jr.
2003 "Research on Ecstasy Is Clouded by Errors." *New York Times* (December 2): F1, 4.
2002 "Study in Primate Show Brain Damage from Doses of Ecstasy." *New York Times* (September 27): 26.

McQueen, Anjetta
1999 "No Loans for Student Drug Offenders." Associated Press (October 26). Internet.

McWilliams, John C.
1992 "Through the Past Darkly: The Politics and Policies of America's Drug War." Pages 5–41 in *Drug Control Policy: Essays in Historical and Comparative Perspective,* edited by William O. Walker III. University Park, PA: Pennsylvania State University.

Meddis, Sam
1993 "Is the Drug War Racist?" *USA Today* (July 23): 1, 2.

Meier, Barry
2007 "Narcotic Maker Guilty of Deceit Over Marketing." *New York Times* (May 11): 1, C4.

Meier, Barry and Melody Peterson
2001 "Sales of Painkiller Grew Rapidly, but Success Brought a High Cost." *New York Times* (March 5): 1, 15.

Meltzer, Herbert L.
1979 *The Chemistry of Human Behavior.* Chicago: Nelson-Hall.

Melzack, Ronald
1990 "The Tragedy of Needless Pain." *Scientific American* 262 (February): 27–33.

Mendelson, Bruce D. and Linda Harrison
1989 *Drug Use in Denver and Colorado.* Denver: Colorado Alcohol and Drug Use Division.

Mendelson, Jack H. and Nancy K. Mello
1995 "Alcohol, Sex, and Aggression." Pages 50–56 in *The American Drug Scene: An Anthology,* edited by James A. Inciardi and Karen McElrath. Los Angeles: Roxbury.

Merlin, Mark David
1984 *On the Trail of the Ancient Opium Poppy.* Rutherford, NJ: Fairleigh Dickinson University Press.

Merriam, John E.
1989 "National Media Coverage of Drug Issues, 1983–1987." Pages 21–28 in *Communication Campaigns About Drugs: Government, Media, and the Public,* edited by Pamela J. Shoemaker. Hillside, NJ: Lawrence Erlbaum Associates.

Merton, Robert
1964 "Anomie, Anomia, and Social Interaction." Pages 213–42 in *Anomie and Deviant Behavior,* edited by Marshall B. Clinard. New York: Free Press.

Mieczkowski, Thomas
1995 *Hair Analysis as a Drug Detector.* Washington, DC: National Institute of Justice.
1986 "Geeking up and Throwing Down: Heroin Street Life in Detroit." *Criminology* 24 (November): 645–66.

Miller, Henry I.
2006 "Reefer Medicine." *New York Times* (April 28): 23.

Miller, Norman S.
1995 *Addiction Psychiatry: Current Diagnosis and Treatment.* New York: Wiley.

Miller, Norman S. and Mark S. Gold
1990 "Benzodiazepines: Reconsidered." *Advances in Alcohol and Substance Abuse* 8 (3/4): 67–81.

Miller, Walter B.
1958 "Lower Class Culture as a Generating Milieu of Gang Delinquency." *Journal of Social Issues* 14: 5–19.

Miller, William R. and Reid K. Hester
1980 "Treating the Problem Drinker: Modern Approaches." Pages 11–141 in *The Addictive Behaviors,* edited by William R. Miller. New York: Pergamon.

Milloy, Ross E.
2002 "A Forbidding Landscape That's Eden for Peyote." *New York Times* (May 7): 14.

Minnesota Department of Human Services
1987 *Chemical Dependency Program Division Biennial Report.* St. Paul, MN: Department of Human Services.

Mintz, John
1997 "Getting a Financial High from Rope." *Washington Post National Weekly Edition* (January 13): 18–19.

Miron, Jeffrey A.
2001 "The Economics of Drug Prohibition and Drug Legalization." *Social Research* 68 (Fall): 835–57.

Misner, Dinah L. and Jame M. Sullivan
1999 "Mechanism of Cannabinoid Effects on Long-Term Potentiation and Depression in Hippocampal CA1 Neurons." *Journal of Neuroscience* 19 (August): 6795–6805.

Missouri Division of Alcohol and Drug Abuse (MDADA)
1999 *Status Report on Missouri's Alcohol and Drug Abuse Problems.* Jefferson City, MO: MDADA.

Moe, Wai
2009 "UWSA Leader Calls for 'Solid United' Wa State." *The Irrawaddy* (April 17): Internet.

Molgaard, Virigina K., Richard L. Spoth, and Cleve Redmond
2000 *Competency Training.* Washington, DC: Office of Juvenile Justice and Delinquency Prevention.

Molotsky, Irvin
1999 "Study Links Teen-Age Substance Abuse and Parental Ties." *New York Times* (August 31): 14.

Moody, John
1991 "A Day with the Chess Player." *Time* (July 1): 34–36.

Moore, Mark H.
1977 *Buy and Bust: The Effective Regulation of an Illicit Market in Heroin.* Lexington, MA: D.C. Heath.

Moore, Mark H. and Mark A. R. Kleiman
1989 *The Police and Drugs.* Washington, DC: U.S. Government Printing Office.

Moore, Molly
2001 "Iranians Wage War on Afghan Drugs." *Chicago Tribune* (July 19): 10.

Moore, Solomon
2009a "Border Proves No Obstacle for Mexican Cartels." *New York Times* (February 2): 1, 10.
2009b "How U.S. Became Turf for Mexican Drug Feud." *New York Times* (December 9): 1, 26.

Morales, Edmundo
1989 *Cocaine: White Gold Rush in Peru.* Tucson: University of Arizona Press.
1986 "Coca and Cocaine Economy and Social Change in the Andes of Peru." *Economic Development and Social Change* 35: 144–61.

Moras, Karla
1993 "Substance Abuse Research: Outcome Measurement Conundrums." Pages 217–48 in *Behavioral Treatments for Drug Abuse and Dependence,* edited by Lisa Simon Onken, John D. Blaine, and John J. Boren. Rockville, MD: National Institute on Drug Abuse.

Morgan, Howard Wayne
1981 *Drugs in America: A Social History, 1800–1980.* Syracuse, NY: Syracuse University Press.

Morgan, Howard Wayne, ed.
1974 *Yesterday's Addicts: American Society and Drug Abuse, 1865–1920.* Norman: University of Oklahoma Press.

Morgan, Thomas
1989 "16 Charged in Scheme to Launder Millions." *New York Times* (May 14): 24.

Morgenthau, Robert M.
1988 "We Are Losing the War on Drugs." *New York Times* (February 16): 27.

Morojele, Neo K. and Judith S. Brook
2001 "Adolescent Precursors of Intensity of Marijuana and Other Illicit Drug Use Among Adult Initiators." *Journal of Genetic Psychology* 162 (December): 430–51.

Moss, Andrew
1977 "Methadone's Rise and Fall." Pages 135–53 in *Drugs and Politics,* edited by Paul E. Rock. New Brunswick, NJ: Transaction Books.

Motivans, Mark
2003 *Money-Laundering Offenders, 1994–2001.* Washington, DC: Bureau of Justice Statistics.

Murphy, Dean E.
2003 "Jurors Who Convicted Marijuana Grower Seek New Trial" *New York Times* (February 5): 13.

Murray, Ian and Stewart Tendler
1999 "Cocaine Deaths on the Increase." *London Times* (August 9): 6.

Musto, David
1998 "The American Experience with Stimulants and Opiates." Pages 51–78 in *Perspectives on Crime and Justice: 1997–1998 Lecture Series.* Washington, DC: National Institute of Justice.
1987 *The American Disease: Origins of Narcotic Control, Expanded Edition.* New York: Oxford.
1973 *The American Disease: Origins of Narcotic Control.* New Haven, CT: Yale University Press.

Mydans, Seth
2003 "Thailand Police Crack Down in Deadly Fight Against Drugs." *New York Times* (February 17): 6.

Myers, Linnet
1995 "Europe Finds U.S. Drug War Lacking in Results." *Chicago Tribune* (November 2): 1, 24, 25.

Myers, Willard H. III
1995 "Orb Weavers—The Global Webs: The Structure and Activities of Transnational Ethnic Chinese Groups." *Transnational Organized Crime* 1 (Winter): 1–36.

Nadelmann, Ethan A.
1988 "U.S. Drug Policy: A Bad Export." *Foreign Policy* 70 (Spring): 83–108.

Nagourney, Eric
2008 "Despite Dangers, Hookahs Gain Favor." *New York Times* (May 20): F6.

Nahas, Gabriel and Nicholas A. Pace
1993 "Marijuana as Chemotherapy Aid Poses Hazards." Letter to the *New York Time* (December 4): 14.

Nash, Nathaniel C.
1992 "Cocaine Invades Chile, Scorning the Land Mines." *New York Times* (January 23): 6.

Nathan, Peter E.
1988 "The Addictive Personality is the Behavior of the Addict." *Journal of Consulting and Clinical Psychology* 56 (April): 183–88.

National Center on Addiction and Substance Abuse
1998 *Behind Bars: Substance Abuse and America's Prison Population.* New York: National Center on Addiction and Substance Abuse at Columbia University.

National Commission on Marijuana and Drug Abuse
1973 *Drug Abuse in America: Problem in Perspective.* Washington, DC: U.S. Government Printing Office.

National Council on Crime and Delinquency
1974 "Drug Addiction: A Medical, Not a Law Enforcement Problem." *Crime and Delinquency* 20 (January): 4–9.

National Drug Intelligence Center (NDIC)
2009a *National Drug Threat Assessment.* Johnstown, PA: NDIC
2009b *National Prescription Drug Threat Assessment.* Johnstown, PA: NDIC.
2009c *Domestic Cultivation Assessment 2009.* Johnstown, PA: NDIC
2009d *North Texas High Intensity Drug Trafficking Area.* Johnstown, PA: NDIC.

2009e *Philadelphia/Camden High Intensity Drug Trafficking Area.* Johnstown, PA: NDIC.
2009f *New York/New Jersey High Intensity Drug Trafficking Area.* Johnstown, PA: NDIC.
2009g *Puerto Rico/U.S. Virgin Islands High Intensity Drug Trafficking Area.* Johnstown, PA: NDIC.
2009h *Northwest High Intensity Drug Trafficking Area.* Johnstown, PA: NDIC.
2009i *Rocky Mountain High Intensity Drug Trafficking Area.* Johnstown, PA: NDIC.
2009j *Appalachia High Intensity Drug Trafficking Area.* Johnstown, PA: NDIC.
2009k *California Border Alliance Group.* Johnstown, PA: NDIC.
2009l National Methamphetamine Threat Assessment. Johnstown, PA: NDIC.
2009m *Central Valley California High Intensity Drug Trafficking Area.* Johnston, PA: NDIC.
2008a *Indian Country: Drug Threat Assessment.* Johnstown, PA: NDIC.
2008b *Money Laundering in Digital Currencies.* Johnstown, PA: NDIC.
2007 *Methadone Diversion, Abuse, and Misuse: Deaths Increasing at Alarming Rate.* Johnstown, PA: NDIC
n.d. *Yaba Fast Facts.* Johnstown, PA: NDIC.

National Institute on Alcohol Abuse and Alcoholism (NIAAA)
2004 *Alcohol's Damaging Effects on the Brain.* Bethesda, MD: NIAAA.
2003 *Genetics of Alcoholism. NIAAA* 60 (July): Internet.
1997 *Ninth Special Report to the U.S. Congress on Alcohol and Health.* Rockville, MD: NIAAA.

National Institute on Drug Abuse (NIDA)
2009 "Drug Abusing Offenders Not Getting Treatment They Need in Criminal Justice System." Press release, January 13.
2008a *Understanding Drug Abuse and Addiction.* Bethesda, MD: NIDA.
2008b *Cocaine.* Bethesda, MD: NIDA
2008c *Stimulant ADHD Medications: Methylphenidate and Amphetamines.* Bethesda, MD: NIDA.
2008d *Treatment Approaches for Drug Addiction.* Bethesda, MD: NIDA.
2007 *Salvia.* Bethesda, MD: NIDA.
2006 *MDMA Abuse.* Bethesda, MD: NIDA.

2005 *Prescription Drugs: Abuse and Addiction.* Bethesda, MD: NIDA: Internet.
2004 *Cigarettes and Other Nicotine Products.* Bethesda, MD: NIDA: Internet.
2003a *Preventing Drug Use Among Children and Adolescents.* Bethesda, MD: NIDA.
2003b *Drug Addiction Treatment Methods.* Rockville, MD: NIDA.
2002a "Methamphetamine: Abuse and Addiction." NIDA: Internet.
2002b "Therapeutic Community." *National Institute on Drug Abuse Research Report.* Washington, DC: U.S. Department of Human Services.
2001a *Crack and Cocaine.* Washington, DC: NIDA.
2001b *Inhalants.* Bethesda, MD: NIDA: Internet.
2001c *Lessons from Prevention Research.* Washington, DC: NIAA
2001d "Nicotine Addiction." *NIDA Research Report.* Rockville, MD: NIDA.
2001e "Ritalin." NIDA Infofax: Internet.
2000 "Update on Nicotine Addiction and Tobacco Research." *NIDA Notes* 15 (5): 15.
1999a "Hallucinogens and Dissociative Drugs." *NIDA Research Report.* Rockville, MD: NIDA.
1999b *Methamphetamine Abuse and Addiction.* Rockville, MD: NIDA.
1999c *Rohypnol and GHB.* Bethesda, MD: NIDA.
1999d "Thirteen Principles of Effective Drug Addiction Treatment." *NIDA Notes.* Rockville, MD: NIDA: Internet.
1999e Press release, June 22.
1999f Press release, September 1.
1999g Press release, August 1.
1998a "Methamphetamine Abuse and Addiction." *Research Report Series.* Washington, DC: NIDA.
1998b *Nicotine Addiction.* Bethesda, MD: NIDA.
1998c Press release, May 6.
1998d Press release, February 3.
1997a *Drug Abuse Prevention for At-Risk Individuals.* Rockville, MD: NIDA.
1997b *Problems of Drug Dependence 1997.* Rockville, MD: NIDA.
1997c Press release, June 24.
1991 *Drug Abuse and Drug Abuse Research.* Rockville, MD: NIDA.
1987 *Drug Abuse and Drug Abuse Research.* Rockville, MD: NIDA.

1985 "Cocaine Use in America." *Prevention Networks* (April): 1–10.

National Institute of Justice

2002 *An Honest Chance: Perspectives on Drug Courts: Executive Summary.* Internet.

1995a *Fact Sheet: Drug Related Crime 1994.* Washington, DC: National Institute of Justice.

1995b *The Drug Court Movement.* Washington, DC: National Institute of Justice.

National Narcotics Intelligence Consumers Committee

1998 The *Supply of Illicit Drugs to the United States.* Washington, DC: National Narcotics Intelligence Consumers Committee.

Navarro, Mireya

1996 "When Drug Kingpins Fall, Illicit Assets Buy a Cushion." *New York Times* (March 19): 1, C19.

1995 "Drug Sold Abroad by Prescription Becomes Widely Abused in U.S." *New York Times* (December 12): 1, 9.

1992 "New York City Resurrects Plan on Needle Swap." *New York Times* (May 14): 1, B8.

1996 "Navy Holds 21 Sailors in Italy in Smuggling" *New York Times* (May 29): 13.

Nelson, Jack E., Helen W. Pearson, Mollie Sayers, and Thomas J. Glynn

1982 *Guide to Drug Abuse Research Terminology.* Washington, DC: Government Printing Office.

Nestler, Eric J.

2005 "The Neurobiology of Cocaine Addiction." *Science and Practice Perspectives* 5 (December): 4–10.

Newcomb, Michael D. and Peter M. Bentler

1989 "Substance Use and Abuse Among Children and Teenagers." *American Psychologist* 44 (February): 242–48.

1988 *Consequences of Adolescent Drug Use.* Newbury Park, CA: Sage.

1986 "Cocaine Use Among Adolescents: Longitudinal Associations with Social Context, Psychopathology, and Use of Other Substances." *Addictive Behavior* 11: 263–73.

"New Drug Law Leaves No Room for Mercy"

1989 *Chicago Tribune* (October 5): 28.

"New Hazard of Drinking in Pregnancy Is Found"

1996 *New York Times* (January 3): 9.

Newman, Robert G.

1977 *Methadone Management, Findings, and Prospects for the Future.* New York: Academic Press.

New York State Division of Substance Abuse Services

1986 *Annual Report.* Albany, NY: State Division of Substance Abuse Services.

Nichols, David E. and Robert Oberlender

1989 "Structure-Activity Relationships of MDMA-like Substances." Pages 1–28 in *Pharmacology and Toxicology of Amphetamine and Related Designer Drugs,* edited by Khursheed Asghar and Errol De Souza. Rockville, MD: National Institute on Drug Abuse.

Nielson, Amie L. and Frank R. Scarpitti

1997 "Changing the Behavior of Substance Abusers: Factors Influencing the Effectiveness of Therapeutic Communities." *Journal of Drug Issues* 27 (Spring): 279–98.

Nieves, Evelyn

1991 "Tainted Drug's Death Toll Rises to 10, Officials Say." *New York Times* (February 4): C11.

Nilson, Chad

2007 "Treatment First, Punishment Second: The Health and Criminal Justice Consensus in Austrian Drug Policy." *Crime and Justice International* 23 (January/February): 4–9

Noble, Barbara Presley

1992 "Testing Employees for Drugs." *New York Times* (April 12): F27.

Nolan, Kathleen

1990 "Protecting Fetuses from Prenatal Hazards: Whose Crimes? What Punishment?" *Criminal Justice Ethics* 9 (Winter/Spring): 13–23.

Northern, Helen

1969 *Social Work with Groups.* New York: Columbia University Press

Nossiter, Adam

2008 "Rural Alabama County Cracks Down on Pregnant Drug Users." *New York Times* (March 15): 10.

Nunes, Edward V. and Jeffrey S. Rosecan

1987 "Human Neurobiology of Cocaine." Pages 48–94 in *Cocaine Abuse: New Directions in Treatment and Research,* edited by Henry I. Spitz and Jeffrey S. Rosecan. New York: Brunner/Mazel.

Nurco, David N., John C. Ball, John W. Shaffer, and Thomas Hanlon

1985 "The Criminality of Narcotic Addicts." *Journal of Nervous and Mental Disorders* 173: 94–102.

Nyre, George F.

1985 *Final Evaluation Report, 1984–1985: Project DARE.* Los Angeles: Evaluation and Training Institute.

Oakie, Susan

2009 "The Epidemic That Wasn't." *New York Times* (January 27): D1, 6.

O'Brien, Charles P., Arthur Alterman, Dan Walter, Anna Rose Childress, and A. T. McLellan

1990 "Evaluation of Treatment for Cocaine Dependence." Pages 78–83 in *Problems of Drug Dependence 1989,* edited by Louis S. Harris. Rockville, MD: National Institute on Drug Abuse.

O'Brien, John and Jan Crawford Greenburg

1996 "Raids Reveal How Little Guys Climb the Drug Ladder." *Chicago Tribune* (May 3): 1, 21.

O'Brien, Robert and Sidney Cohen

1984 *Encyclopedia of Drug Abuse.* New York: Facts on File.

O'Connor, Anahad

2005 "Scientists Explore Meth's Role in Immune System." *New York Times* (February 23): F7.

2004 "New Ways to Loosen Addiction's Grip." *New York Times* 9(August 3): F1, 6.

O'Connor, Matt

1990 "Drug Court a Success, but It's Not Enough." *Chicago Tribune* (February 22): 1, 2.

O'Day, Patrick and Rex Venecia

1999 "Cazuelas: An Ethnographic Study of Drug Trafficking in a Small Mexican Border Town." *Journal of Contemporary Criminal Justice* 15 (November): 421–43.

O'Donnell, John A.

1969 *Narcotic Addicts in Kentucky.* Washington, DC: U.S. Government Printing Office.

Oetting, E. R. and Fred Beauvais

1990 "Adolescent Drug Use: Findings of National and Local Surveys." *Journal of Consulting and Clinical Psychology* 58 (August) 385–94.

Office of National Drug Control Policy (ONDCS)

2009a *National Drug Control Strategy: 2009 Annual Report.* Washington, DC: ONDCS.

2009b *National Southwest Border Counternarcotics Strategy,* Washington DC: ONDCS.

2008 *National Drug Control Strategy: 2008 Annual Report.* Washington, DC: ONDCS.

2004a *Pulse Check: Trends in Drug Abuse*. Washington, DC: ONDCS.
2004b *Predicting Heavy Drug Use*. Washington, DC: ONDCS.
2004c *The Challenge in Higher Education: Confronting and Reducing Substance Abuse on Campus*. Washington, DC: ONDCS.
2004d *National Drug Control Strategy*. Washington, DC: ONDCS.
2004e *National Synthetic Drugs Action Plan*. Washington, DC: ONDCS.
2002a *MDMA (Ecstasy)*. Washington, DC: ONDCS.
2002b *National Drug Control Strategy*. Washington, DC: ONDCS.
2002c *Rohypnol*. Washington, DC: ONDCS.
2002d *What You Need to Know About Drug Testing in Schools*. Washington, DC: ONDCS.
2001 *National Drug Control Strategy: 2001 Report*. Washington, DC: ONDCS.
2000 *National Drug Control Strategy: 2000 Report*. Washington, DC: ONDCS.
1998 *Rohypnol*. Washington, DC: ONDCS.
1995 *Pulse Check: National Trends in Drug Abuse*. Washington, DC: ONDCS.
1989 *National Drug Strategy*. Washington, DC: Office of National Drug Control Policy.
n.d. *Who's Really in Prison for Marijuana?* Washington, DC: ONDCS.
n.d. *What Americans Need to Know About Marijuana*. Washington DC: ONDCS.

Office on Drugs and Crime
2008 *The Threat of Narco-Trafficking in the Americas*. New York: United Nations.

Ogborne, Alan C. and Frederick B. Glaser
1985 "Evaluating Alcoholics Anonymous." Pages 176–92 in *Alcoholism and Substance Abuse,* edited by Thomas E. Bratter and Gary G. Forrest. New York: Free Press.

O'Hare, P. A.
1992 "Preface: A Note on the Concept of Harm Reducation." Pages xiii–xvii in *The Reduction of Drug Related Harm,* edited by P. A. O'Hare, R. Newcome, A. Matthews, E. C. Buning, and E. Drucker. London: Routledge.

O'Keefe, Michael and T. J. Quinn
2005 "Beating the Heat." *New York Daily News* (December 25): 88–91.

Olen, Helaine
1991 "Racial Tinge to Drug Testing of New Moms." *Chicago Tribune* (December 19): 14.

Olson, Elizabeth
1997 "Swiss to Weigh Fate of Clinics Offering Legal Heroin." *New York Times* (September 28): 3.

O'Malley, Pat O. and Stephen Mugford
1991 "The Demand for Intoxicating Commodities: Implications for the 'War on Drugs.'" *Social Justice* 18 (Winter): 49–75.

O'Neil, John
2006 "A Warning on Hazards of Smoke on Others." *New York Times* (June 28): 14.

Orenstein, Peggy
2002 "Staying Clean." *New York Times Magazine* (February 10): 34–39, 50–51, 74–75.

Oreskes, Michael
1990 "Drug War Underlines Fickleness of Public." *New York Times* (September 6): 12.

Orth, Maureen
2002 "Afghanistan's Deadly Habit." *Vanity Fair* (March): 150–52, 165–77.

Oscar-Berman, Marlene and Ksenija Marinkovic
2004 *Alcoholism and the Brain: An Overview*. Bethesda, MD: National Institute on Alcohol Abuse and Alcoholism.

O'Shea, Joanne and Beverly Powis
2003 *Drug Arrest Referral Schemes: A Case Study of Good Practice*. London, UK: Home Office.

"OxyContin: Prescription Drug Abuse—2008 Revision"
2008 *Substance Abuse Treatment Advisory* 7 (Summer): 1–7.

Pace, Eric
1988 "Lois Burnham Wilson, a Founder of Al-Anon Groups, Is Dead at 97." *New York Times* (October 4): 15.

Packer, Herbert L.
1968 *The Limits of the Criminal Sanction*. Stanford, CA: Stanford University Press.

Padgett, Tim
2005 "The Killers Next Door." *Time* (April 18): 140–41.
2009 "On the Bloody Border." *Time* (May 4): 36–41.

Paik, Leslie
2006 "Organizational Interpretations of Drug Test Results." *Law and Society Review* 40 (4): 931–62.

Palacios, Marco
2007 *Between Legitimacy and Violence: A History of Colombia, 1875–2002*. Durham: Duke University Press. Translated by Richard Stoller.

Palfai, Tibor and Henry Jankiewicz
1991 *Drugs and Human Behavior*. Dubuque, IA: William C. Brown.

Palmquiest, Matt
2009 "The Ecstasy and the Agony." *Miller-McCune* 2 (5): 36–40.

Parker-Pope, Tara
2008 "Social Smoking Takes a Lasting Toll." *New York Times* (October 8): Internet.

Parker, Suzi
1999 "Ammonia's New Cachet." *U.S. Press & World Report* (September 27): 37.

Parrott, Andy C.
1999 "Does Cigarette-Smoking Cause Stress?" *American Psychologist* 54 (October): 817–20.

Parsons, Loren H., Friedbert Weiss, and George F. Koob
1998 "Serotonin1B Receptor Stimulation Enhances Cocaine Reinforcement." *Journal of Neuroscience* 18 (December): 10078–89.

Passell, Peter
1990 "Policy: Gauging Success." *New York Times* (June 6): C2.

Payne, Malcolm
1997 *Modern Social Work Theory,* 2nd ed. Chicago: Lyceum.

Peachey, J. E. and H. Lei
1988 "Assessment of Opioid Dependence with Naloxone." *British Journal of Addiction* 83: 193–201.

Pearson, Geoffrey
1987 *The New Heroin Users*. Oxford, England: Basil Blackwell.

Peele, Stanton
1995 *Diseasing of America*. San Francisco: Jossey-Bass.
1985 *The Meaning of Addiction: Compulsive Experience and Its Interpretation*. Lexington, MA: D.C. Heath.
1980 "Addiction to an Experience: A Social-Psychological Theory of Addiction." Pages 142–44 in *Theories of Drug Abuse: Selected Contemporary Perspectives,* edited by Dan J. Lettieri, Mollie Sayers, and Helen Wallenstein Pearson. Rockville, MD: National Institute on Drug Abuse.

Pennsylvania Crime Commission (PCC)
1990 *Organized Crime in Pennsylvania: A Decade of Change, 1990 Report.* Conshohocken, PA: PCC.

Pentz, Mary Ann
1985 "Social Competence and Self-Efficacy as Determinants of Substance Abuse in Adolescence." Pages 117–42 in *Coping and Substance Abuse,* edited by Saul Shiffman and Thomas Ashby Wills. Orlando, FL: Academic Press.

Pérez-Peña, Richard
2003 "New Drug Promises Shift in Treatment." *New York Times* (August 11): 1, B7.

Perl, Raphael
2000 "Organized Crime, Drug Trafficking, and Terrorism in a Changing Global Environment." Statement before the House Judiciary Committee, Subcommittee on Crime, December 13.

Permanent Subcommittee on Investigation, U.S. Senate
1981a *International Narcotics Trafficking.* Washington, DC: U.S. Government Printing Office.
1981b *Witness Security Program.* Washington, DC: U.S. Government Printing Office.

Peterson, Robert C., ed.
1980 *Marijuana Research Findings: 1980.* Rockville, MD: National Institute on Drug Abuse.

Peterson, Robert E.
1991 "Legalization: The Myth Exposed." Pages 324–55 in *Searching for Alternatives: Drug Control Policy in the United States,* edited by Melvyn B. Krauss and Edward P. Lazear. Stanford, CA: Hoover Institution.

Pfaelzer, Jean
Driven Out: The Forgotten War Against Chinese Americans. New York: Random House.

"Pharmacy Update: How Addiction Occurs"
2003 *Chemist and Druggist* (December 20): 17.

Physicians' Desk Reference
1988 Oradell, NJ: Medical Economics Company.
1987 Oradell, NJ: Medical Economics Company.

Pickens, Roy W. and Travis Thompson
1984 "Behavioral Treatment of Drug Dependence." Pages 53–67 in *Behavioral Intervention Techniques in Drug Dependence Treatment,* edited by John Grabowski, Maxine L. Stitzer, and Jack E. Henningfield. Rockville, MD: National Institute on Drug Abuse.

Platt, Jerome J. and Christina Labate
1976 *Heroin Addiction: Theory, Research, and Treatment.* New York: John Wiley.

Platt, Jerome J., Mindy Widman, Victor Lidz, and Douglas Marlowe
1998 "Methadone Maintenance Treatment: Its Development and Effectiveness After 30 Years." Pages 160–87 in *Heroin in the Age of Crack-Cocaine,* edited by James A. Inciardi and Laura D. Harrison. Thousand Oaks, CA: Sage.

Poe, Janita and Dionne Searcey
1996 "Few Options Are Open for Drug Babies." *Chicago Tribune* (January 31): Sec. 2: 1, 4.

Poethig, Margaret
1988 "Q & A: Seizing the Assets of Drug Traffickers." *The Compiler* 8 (Winter): 11–12.

"Politics of Pot"
2006 *New York Times* (April 22): 14.

Pollan, Michael
1993 "How Pot Has Grown." *New York Times Magazine* (February 19): 31–35, 44, 50, 56–57.
2008 "Moral, Prudential, and Political Arguments About Harm Reduction." *Contemporary Drug Problems* 35 (Summer): 211–41.

"Poor Man's Heroin"
2001 *U.S. News and World Report* (February 12): 27.

Posner, Gerald L.
1988 *Warlords of Crime: Chinese Secret Societies—The New Mafia.* New York: McGraw-Hill.

Post, Robert M. and Susan R. B. Weiss
1988 "Psychomotor Stimulant vs. Local Anesthetic Effects of Cocaine: Role of Behavioral Sensitization and Kindling." Pages 217–38 in *Mechanisms of Cocaine Abuse and Toxicity,* edited by Doris Clouet, Khursheed Asghar, and Roger Brown. Rockville, MD: National Institute on Drug Abuse.

Powell, Bill
2007 "Inside the Afghan Drug War." *Time* (February 19): 29–37.

Preble, Edward and John J. Casey
1995 "Taking Care of Business—The Heroin Addict's Life on the Street." Pages 121–32 in *The American Drug Scene: An Anthology,* edited by James A. Inciardi and Karen McElrath. Los Angeles: Roxbury.

Préfontaine, D. C. and Yvon Dandurand
2004 "Terrorism and Organized Crime: Reflections on an Illusive Link and Its Implications for Criminal Law Reform." Paper presented at the annual meeting of the International Society for Criminal Law Reform, Montreal, August 8–12.

Prendergzast, Michael, David Farabee, Jerome Cartier, and Susan Henkin
2002 "Involuntary Treatment Within a Prison Setting: Impact on Psychosocial Change During Treatment." *Criminal Justice and Behavior* 29 (February): 5–26.

Prescott, Carol A. and Kenneth S. Kendler
1999 "Genetic and Environmental Contributions to Alcohol Abuse and Dependence in a Population-Based Sample of Male Twins." *American Journal of Psychiatry* 156 (January): 34–40.

"Prescription Drugs Abuse and Addiction"
2005 *Research Report.* Rockville, MD: National Institute on Drug Abuse.

President's Commission on Organized Crime
1986 *America's Habit: Drug Abuse, Drug Trafficking, and Organized Crime.* Washington, DC: U.S. Government Printing Office.
1985 *Organized Crime and Heroin Trafficking.* Washington, DC: U.S. Government Printing Office.
1984 *Organized Crime and Cocaine Trafficking.* Washington, DC: U.S. Government Printing Office.

Preston, Julia
2005 "2 Charged with Smuggling Ecstasy Pills of Military Jet." *New York Times* (April 14): B6.

Principles of Drug Dependence Treatment
2008 United Nations Office on Drugs and Crime.

"Principles of Nerve Cell Communication"
1997 Alcohol *Health and Research World* 21 (2): 107–8.

Prisoners in 2005
Washington, DC: Bureau of Justice Statistics.

"Propofol Abuse Growing Problem for Anesthesiologists"
2007 *Anesthesiology News* 33 (May): Internet.

Quadagno, Jill S. and Robert J. Antonio
1975 "Labeling Theory as an Oversocialized Conception of Man: The Case of Mental Illness." *Sociology and Social Research* 60 (October): 30–41.

Querna, Elizabeth
2005 "The Newest War on Drugs." *U.S. News and World Report* (February 21): 52–54.
"Quitting Caffeine Can Bring on the Blahs"
1991 *Chicago Tribune* (August 18): 24.
Raab, Selwyn
1992 "Chief Seeks Action on Narcotics Unit." *New York Times* (January 9): B8.
1987 "New York Establishes Special Courts to Hasten Disposal of Drug Cases." *New York Times* (June 7): 17.
Rabin, Roni C.
2009 "Alcohol's Good for You? Some Scientists Doubt It." *New York Times* (June 16): D1, 6.
Rachlin, Howard
1991 *Introduction to Modern Behaviorism.* New York: W.H. Freeman.
Rado, Sandor
1981 "The Psychoanalysis of Pharmacothymia (Drug Addiction)." Pages 77–94 in *Classic Contributions in the Addictions,* edited by Howard Shaffer and Milton E. Burglass. New York: Brunner/Mazel.
"Raising Nicotine Doses, on the Sly"
2006 *New York Times* editorial (August 31): 24.
RAND Drug Policy Research Center
2009 "Major Methamphetamine Supply Disruption Had Temporary Market Effects and Little Influence on Crime." *DPRC Insights* (4) 3.
1992 *Cocaine: The First Decade.* Issue Paper 1. Santa Monica, CA: RAND Drug Policy Research Center.
Rangel, Charles B.
1990 "Letter to the Editor: 'What's Wrong with Legalizing Drugs?'" *New York Times* (July 24): 14.
Rannazzisi, Joseph T.
2008 "Online Pharmacies and the Problem of Internet Drug Abuse." Statement presented before the House Subcommittee on Crime, Terrorism, and Homeland Security, June 24.
Ray, Oakley
1978 *Drugs, Society, and Human Behavior.* St. Louis: C.V. Mosby.
Reese, Joel
2000 "Problem Drug." *Chicago* (April): 51–60.
Reese, Stephen D. and Lucig H. Danielian
1989 "Intermedia Influence and the Drug Issue: Converging on Cocaine." Pages 29–45 in *Communication Campaigns About Drugs: Government, Media, and the Public,* edited by Pamela J. Shoemaker. Hillsdale, NJ: Lawrence Erlbaum Associates.
Reid, T. R.
2005 "Caffeine." *National Geographic* (January): 2–33.
Reiff, Phillip
1963 *Freud, Therapy and Techniques.* New York: Crowell-Collier.
Rettig, Richard P., Manuel J. Torres, and Gerald R. Garrett
1977 *Manny: A Criminal Addict's Story.* New York: Houghton-Mifflin.
Reuter, Peter
2001 "Supply-Side Drug Control." *Milken Institute Review* (First Quarter): 14–23.
2000 "One Tough Plant." *New York Times* (March 31): 29.
1999 "Drug Use Measures: What Are They Really Telling Us?" *National Institute of Justice Journal* (April): 12–19.
Reuter, Peter and Jonathan P. Caulkins
1995 "Redefining the Goals of National Drug Policy: Recommendations from a Working Group." *American Journal of Public Health* 85 (August): 1059–63.
Reuter, Peter, Robert MacCoun, and Patrick Murphy
1990 *Money from Crime: A Study of the Economics of Drug Dealing in Washington, D.C.* Santa Monica, CA: RAND.
Reuters
2006 "Colombia: Soldiers Arrested in Killing of Policemen." *New York Times* (June 2): 6.
2004a "Gunmen Free 29 Inmates From Mexico Jail." *New York Times* (January 6): 6.
Reyna, Valerie F. and Frank Farley
2006 "Is the Teen Brain Too Rational?" *Scientific American Mind* (December): 59–65.
Rhodes, Jean E. and Leonard Jason
1990 "A Social Stress Model of Substance Abuse." *Journal of Consulting and Clinical Psychology* 58 (August): 395–401.
Rhor, Monica
1991 "Nearly Undetectable Cocaine Found." *Chicago Tribune* (June 27): 31.
Ribeaud, Denis
2004 "Long-Term Impacts of the Swiss Heroin Prescription Trials on Crime of Treated Users." *Journal of Drug Issues* 34 (Winter): 163–95.
Richardson, Gale A. and Nancy L. Day
1999 "Studies of Prenatal Cocaine Exposure: Assessing the Influence of Extraneous Variables." *Journal of Drug Issues* 29 (2): 225–36.
Richey, Warren
1991 "Prosecutors' Deal with Criminals: Testify Against Noriega and Go Free." *Chicago Tribune* (November 27): 4.
Riding, Alan
1988 "Dispute Impeding U.S. War on Coca." *New York Times* (June 28): 1, 6.
1987 "Colombia's Drugs and Violent Politics Make Murder a Way of Life." *New York Times* (August 23): E3.
Riley, Diane
n.d. "The Harm Reduction Model: Pragmatic Approaches to Drug Use from the Area Between Intolerance and Neglect." Canadian Centre on Substance Abuse: Internet.
Roberton, Robert J.
1986 "Designer Drugs: The Analog Game." Pages 91–96 in *Bridging Services: Drug Abuse, Human Services and the Therapeutic Community,* edited by Alfonso Acampora and Ethan Nebelkopf. New York: World Federation of Therapeutic Communities.
Robertson, Nan
1988a "The Changing World of Alcoholics Anonymous." *New York Times Magazine* (February 21): 40–44, 47, 57, 92.
1988b *Getting Better: Inside Alcoholics Anonymous.* New York: William Morrow.
Robins, Lee N.
1974 *The Vietnam Drug User Returns.* Washington, DC: U.S. Government Printing Office.
1973 *A Follow-up of Vietnam Drug Users.* Washington, DC: U.S. Government Printing Office.
Robins, Lee N., John E. Helzer, Michi Hesselbrock, and Eric Wish
1980 "Vietnam Veterans Three Years After Vietnam: How Our Study Changed Our View of Heroin." Pages 213–30 in *The Yearbook of Substance Use and Abuse,* Vol. II, edited by Leon Brill and Charles Winick. New York: Human Services Press.
Robinson, Linda
1998a "Is Colombia Lost to Rebels?" *U.S. News and World Report* (May 11): 38–42.

1998b "Land for Peace in Colombia." *U.S. News and World Report* (November 23): 37.

Robinson, T. Hank
2006 *Moving Past the Era of Good Intentions: Methamphetamine Treatment Study*. Omaha, NE: University of Nebraska.

Robinson, Terry and Kent C. Berridge
2003 "Addiction." *Annual Review of Psychology* (54): 25–54.

Rocha, Beatriz, Kimberly Scearce-Levie, José J. Lucas, Noboru Hiroi, Nathalie Castanon, John C. Crabbe, Eric J. Nestler, and René Hen
1998 "Increased Vulnerability to Cocaine in Mice Lacking the Serotonin-1B Receptor." *Nature* 393 (May 14): 175–78.

Rodgers, Paul
2009 "From Heaven to Hell: 18 Die as Drug War Rages on Streets of Vancouver." *The Independent* (April 5): Internet.

Roffman, Roger A. and William H. George
1988 "Cannabis Abuse." Pages 325–63 in *Assessment of Addictive Behaviors*, edited by Dennis M. Donovan and G. Alan Marlatt. New York: Guilford.

Rohde, David
2004 "Poppies Flood Afghanistan: Opium Tide May Yet Turn." *New York Times* (July 1): 13.

Rohter, Larry
2003 "Bolivian Leader's Ouster Seen as a Warning on U.S. Drug Policy." *New York Times* (October 23): 1, 14.

2000a "Driven by Fear, Colombians Leave in Droves." *New York Times* (March 5): 8.

2000b "Weave of Drugs and Strife in Colombia." *New York Times* (April 21): 1, 10, 11.

1999a "Colombia Tries, Yet Cocaine Thrives." *New York Times* (November 20): 6.

1999b "Colombian Army Hopes to Get Fighting Fit, No Easy Task." *New York Times* (December 5): 17.

Rohter, Larry and Clifford Krauss
1998a "Dominicans Allow Drugs Easy Sailing." *New York Times* (May 10): 1, 6.

1998b "Dominican Drug Traffickers Tighten Grip on the Northeast." *New York Times* (May 11): 12, 17.

Romach, Myroslava K., Paul Glue, Kyle Kampman, Howard L. Kaplan, Gail R. Somer, Sabrina Poole, Laura Clarke,

Vicki Coffin, James Cornish, Charles P. O'Brien, and Edward M. Sellers
1999 "Attenuation of the Euphoric Effects of Cocaine by the Dopamine D1/D5 Antagonist Ecopipam." *Archives of General Psychiatry* 56 (December): 1101–6.

Romero, Simon
2010 "Colombian Paramilitaries' Successors Called a Threat." *New York Times* (February 4): 11.

2009a "Wider Drug War Threatens Colombian Indians." *New York Times* (April 22): 1, 3.

2009b "Cocaine Trade Helps Rebels Reignite War in Peru." *New York Times* (March 18): 1, 11.

2007 "Colombian Government is Ensnared in a Paramilitary Scandal." *New York Times* (January 21): 15.

Romoli, Kathleen
1941 *Colombia*. Garden City, NY: Doubleday, Doran.

Ropero-Miller, Jeri D. and Peter R. Stout
2009 "Analysis of Cocaine Analytes in Human Hair: Concentration Ratios in Different Hair Types, Cocaine Sources, Drug-User Populations, and Surface-Contaminated Specimens." Research report funded by the U.S. Department of Justice, Document 225531.

Rosecan, Jeffrey S. and Edward V. Nunes
1987 "Pharmacological Management of Cocaine Abuse." Pages 255–70 in *Cocaine Abuse: New Directions in Treatment and Research,* edited by Henry I. Spitz and Jeffrey S. Rosecan. New York: Brunner/Mazel.

Rosecan, Jeffrey S., Henry I. Spitz, and Barbara Gross
1987 "Contemporary Issues in the Treatment of Cocaine Abuse." Pages 299–323 in *Cocaine Abuse: New Directions in Treatment and Research,* edited by Henry I. Spitz and Jeffrey S. Rosecan. New York: Brunner/Mazel.

Rosenbaum, Marsha
1981 *Women on Heroin*. New Brunswick, NJ: Rutgers University Press.

Rosenbaum, Ron
1988 "High Life: The Social Rise of Timothy Leary." *Vanity Fair* (April): 132–44, 154.

Rosenberg, Tina
2007 "Doctor or Drug Pusher." *New York Times Magazine* (June 17): 48–55, 64, 68, 71.

Rosenfeld, Richard and Scott H. Decker
1999 "Are Arrest Statistics a Valid Measure of Illicit Drug Use? The Relationship Between Criminal Justice and Public Health Indicators of Cocaine, Heroin, and Marijuana Use." *Justice Quarterly* 16 (September): 685–99.

Rosenkranz, Keith
2003 "High Fliers." *New York Times* (January 23): 27.

Rosenthal, Elisabeth
1993 "Patients in Pain Find Relief, Not Addiction, in Narcotics." *New York Times* (March 28): 1, 11.

Rosenthal, Mitchel
1984 "Therapeutic Communities: A Treatment Alternative for Many but Not All." *Journal of Substance Abuse Treatment* 1: 55–58.

1973 "New York City Phoenix House: A Therapeutic Community for the Treatment of Drug Abusers and Drug Addicts." Pages 83–102 in *Yearbook of Drug Abuse*, edited by Leon Brill and Earnest Harms. New York: Behavioral Publications.

Rothman, Richard B.
1994 "A Review of the Effects of Dopaminergic Agents in Humans: Implications for Medication Development." Pages 67–87 in *Neurobiological Models for Evaluating Mechanisms Underlying Cocaine Addiction*, edited by Lynda Erinoff and Roger M. Brown. Rockville, MD: National Institute on Drug Abuse.

Rowell, Earle A. and Robert Rowell
1939 *On the Trail of Marijuana: The Weed of Madness*. Mountain View, CA: Pacific Press.

Royal College of Psychiatrists
1987 *Drug Scenes: A Report on Drug Dependence*. London: Gaskell.

Rubin, Elizabeth
2006 "Inside the Land of the Taliban." *New York Times Magazine* (October 22): 86–97, 172–73, 175.

Russell, Francis
1975 *A City in Terror—1919—The Boston Police Strike*. New York: Viking.

Rydell, C. Peter and Susan S. Everingham
1994 *Controlling Cocaine: Supply Versus Demand Programs*. Santa Monica, CA: RAND.

Sack, Kevin and Brent McDonald
2008 "Popularity of a Hallucinogen May Thwart Its Medical Use." *New York Times* (September 9): 1, 24.

Sackman, Bertram S., M. Maxine
Sackman, and G. G. DeAngelis
1978 "Heroin Addiction as an
Occupation: Traditional Addicts
and Heroin-Addicted Polydrug
Users." *International Journal of the
Addictions* 13: 427–41.

SAMHSA News
2006 Vol. 14 (September/October).

Samuels, David
2007 "Dr. Kush: How Medical
Marijuana Is Transforming the Pot
Industry." *New Yorker* (July 28):
49–61.

Sanger, David E.
1995 "Money Laundering, New and
Improved." *New York Times*
(December 24): E4.

Santana, Rosa Maria
1996 "Drinking Blamed for Death of
Teenager." *Chicago Tribune*
(January 3): Sec. 2: 6.

Santora, Marc
2006 "17 Deaths Tied to Resurgence of
Deadly Drug Mix in New York."
New York Times (August 30): B2.

Savitt, Robert A.
1963 "Psychoanalytic Studies on
Addiction: Ego Structure in Narcotic
Addiction." *Psychoanalytic
Quarterly* 32: 43–57.

Sawyers, June
1988 "When Opium Was Really the
Opiate of the Masses." *Chicago
Tribune Magazine* (January 3): 5.

Schemo, Diana Jean
2003 "A Study of Colleges Critical of
Antidrinking Drives." *New York
Times* (July 24): 16.
1999 "Bogotá Sees Drug War as Path to
Peace." *New York Times* (January
6): 11.
1997 "Players Are Main Danger in
Noisy Colombian Game." *New
York Times* (December 26): 10.

Schemo, Diana Jean and Tim Golden
1998 "Bogotá Aid: To Fight Drugs or
Rebels?" *New York Times* (June 2):
1, 12.

Schiffer, Frederic
1988 "Psychotherapy of Nine
Successfully Treated Cocaine
Abusers: Techniques and
Dynamics." *Journal of Substance
Abuse Treatment* 5: 131–37.

Schmetzer, Uli
1991 "Slave Trade Survives, Prospers
Across Asia." *Chicago Tribune*
(November 15): 1, 18.
1990 "'Prince of Death' Is a Wanted
Man." *Chicago Tribune* (March
21): 21.

Schmidt, William E.
1993 "To Battle AIDS, Scots Offer
Drugs to Addicts." *New York
Times* (February 8): 3.

Schmitt, Eric
2009 "Diverse Sources Pour Cash into
Taliban's War Chest." *New York
Times* (October 19): 1, 9.
2006 "Springtime for Killing in
Afghanistan." *New York Times*
(May 28): Sec. 4: 1, 3.
2004 "Afghans' Gains Face Big Threat
in Drug Traffic." *New York Times*
(December 11): 1, 6.

Schneider, Andrew and Mary Pat
Flaherty
1991 "Drug Law Leaves Trail of
Innocents." *Chicago Tribune*
(August 11): 1, 13.

Schnoll, Sidney H.
1979 "Pharmacological Aspects of
Youth Drug Abuse." Pages 255–75
in *Youth Drug Abuse*, edited by
George M. Beschner and Alfred S.
Friedman. Lexington, MA: D.C.
Heath.

Schuckit, Marc A.
1985 "Genetics and the Risk for
Alcoholism." *Journal of the
American Medical Association* 254:
2614–17.

Schur, Edwin H.
1973 *Radical Non-Intervention:
Rethinking the Delinquency
Problem.* Englewood Cliffs, NJ:
Prentice Hall.
1965 *Crimes Without Victims: Deviant
Behavior and Public Policy.
Abortion, Homosexuality, Drug
Addiction.* Englewood Cliffs, NJ:
Prentice Hall.

Schuster, Charles R.
1993 "A Natural History of Drug
Abuse." Pages 37–51 in
*International Research Conference
on Biomedical Approaches to Illicit
Drug Demand Reduction,* edited by
Christine R. Hartel. Washington,
DC: U.S. Government Printing
Office.

Schweich, Thomas
2008 "Is Afghanistan a Narco-State?"
New York Times Magazine
(July 27): 45–47, 60–62.

Science of Addiction, The
2007 Rockville, MD: National Institute
on Drug Abuse.

Sciolino, Elaine
1988 "Diplomats Do Not Hurry
to Enlist in the War on Drugs."
New York Times (February
21): E3.

Sciolino, Elaine and Stephen Engelberg
1988 "Narcotics Effort Foiled by U.S.
Security Goals." *New York Times*
(April 10): 1, 10.

Scott, Michael S.
2002 *Rave Parties.* Washington, DC:
U.S. Department of Justice.

Seabrook, John
2009 "Annals of Crime: 'Don't Shoot.'"
New Yorker (June 22): 32–41.

Segre, Sandro
2003 *Controlling Illegal Drugs: A
Comparative Study.* New York:
Aldine de Gruyer. Translated by
Nora Stern.

Selden, Lewis W., William L. Woolverton,
Stanley A. Lorens, Joseph E. G. Williams,
Rebecca L. Corwin, Norio Hata, and
Mary Olimski
1993 "Behavioral Consequences of Partial
Monoamine Depletion in the CNS
After Methamphetamine-Like Drugs:
The Conflict Between Pharmacology
and Toxicology." Pages 34–51 in
*Assessing Neurotoxicity in Drugs of
Abuse,* edited by Lynda Erinoff.
Rockville, MD: National Institute on
Drug Abuse.

Seligmann, Jean and Patricia King
1996 "'Roofies': The Date-Rape Drug."
Pressweek (February 26): 54.

Semple, Kirk
2001 "Colombia's Cocaine Frontier."
Mother Jones (November/
December): 58–63.

Senay, Edward C.
1986 "Clinical Implications of Drug
Abuse Treatment Outcome." Pages
139–50 in *Drug Abuse Treatment
Evaluation: Strategies, Progress,
and Prospects,* edited by Frank M.
Tims and Jacqueline P. Ludford.
Rockville, MD: National Institute
on Drug Abuse.
2000 "Sexual Dysfunction and Addiction
Treatment" *Addiction Treatment
Forum* 9 (Spring): 1, 6–8.

Shanker, Thom
2008 "Obstacle Seen in Bid to Curb
Afghan Trade in Narcotics." *New
York Times* (December 23): 6.

Shapiro, Daniel
2003 "Individual Rights, Drug Policy,
and the Worst-Case Scenario."
Criminal Justice Ethics 22 (Winter/
Spring): 41–45.

Sharps, Phyllis, Jacquelyn C. Campbell,
Doris Campbell, Faye Gary, and Daniel
Webster
2003 "Risky Mix: Drinking, Drug Use,
and Homicide." *NIJ Journal* 250
(November): 1–6.

Shenk, Joshua Wolf
1999 "America's Altered States." *Harper's Magazine* (May): 38–52.

Shenon, Philip
1996 "Opium Baron's Rule May End with Surrender in Myanmar." *New York Times* (January 6): 4.

Sheppard, Nathaniel Jr.
1990 "Guatemalan Climate: Good for Poppy Fields, Drug Traffickers." *Chicago Tribune* (September 23): 12.

Sher, Kenneth J.
1991 *Children of Alcoholics: A Critical Appraisal of Theory and Research*. Chicago: University of Chicago Press.

Sherman, Carl
2005 "Dopamine Enhancement Underlies a Toluene Behavioral Effect." *NIDA Notes* 19 (5): 4–5.

Shiffman, Saul and Mark Balabanis
1995 "Associations Between Alcohol and Tobacco." Pages 17–36 in *Alcohol and Tobacco: From Basic Science to Clinical Practice*. Bethesda, MD: National Institute on Alcohol Abuse and Alcoholism.

Short, James F. Jr.
1968 *Gang Delinquency and Delinquent Subculture*. New York: Harper and Row.

Siegal, Harvey A., Richard C. Rapp, Casey W. Kelliher, James H. Fisher, Joseph H. Wagner, and Phyllis A. Cole
1995 "The Strengths Perspective of Case Management: A Promising Inpatient Substance Abuse Treatment Enhancement." *Journal of Psychoactive Drugs* 27 (1): 67–72.

Siegel, Ronald K.
1989 *Intoxication: Life in Pursuit of Artificial Paradise*. New York: E. F. Dutton.

Silvas, Jos
1994 "Enforcing Drug Laws in the Netherlands." Pages 41–58 in *Between Prohibition and Legalization: The Dutch Experiment in Drug Policy*, edited by Ed. Leuw and I. Haen Marshall. Amsterdam: Kugler Publications.

Simpson, Dwyne
2002 "We Know it Works; Now Let's Make it Better." *Drugs and Alcohol Findings* 7: 7.

Simpson, Edith E.
1989 "Adherence to Cigarette, Marijuana, and Cocaine Treatment Programs: A Survival Analysis."

Paper presented at the annual meeting of the American Society of Criminology, Reno, NV, November.

Sinclair, Andrew
1962 *The Era of Excess: A Social History of the Prohibition Movement*. Boston: Little, Brown.

Sinclair, Upton
1981 *The Jungle*. New York: Bantam. Originally published in 1906.

Skinner, B. F.
1974 *About Behaviorism*. New York: Knopf.

Sly, Liz
1989 "Bennett Attacks Drug Legalization." *Chicago Tribune* (December 14): 24.

Smart, Frances
1970 *Neurosis and Crime*. New York: Barnes and Noble.

Smart, Reginald S.
1980 "An Availability-Proneness Theory of Illicit Drug Abuse." Pages 46–49 in *Theories on Drug Abuse: Selected Contemporary Perspectives*, edited by Dan J. Lettieri, Mollie Sayers, and Helen Wallenstein Pearson. Rockville, MD: National Institute on Drug Abuse.

Smith, Craig
2008 "Albert Hofmann, the Father of LSD, Dies at 102." *New York Times* (April 30): B7.

Smith, David E.
1986 "Cocaine-Alcohol Abuse: Epidemiological, Diagnostic and Treatment Considerations." *Journal of Psychoactive Drugs* 18 (April–June): 117–29.

Smith, David E., ed.
1979 *Amphetamine Use, Misuse, and Abuse*. Boston, MA: G. K. Hall and Co.

Smith, David E. and Donald R. Wesson
1994 "Benzodiazepines and Other Sedative-Hypnotics." Pages 179–90 in *The American Psychiatric Press Textbook of Substance Abuse Treatment*, edited by Marc Galanter and Herbert D. Kleber. Washington, DC: American Psychiatric Press.

Snyder, Solomon H.
1989 *Brainstorming: The Science of Politics and Opiate Research*. Cambridge, MA: Harvard University Press.
1986 *Drugs and the Brain*. New York: Scientific American.
1977 "Opiate Receptors and Internal Opiates." *Scientific American* (March): 44–56.

Soble, Ronald L.
1991 "Seized Assets Underwrite the War on Drugs." *Los Angeles Times* (April 16): 3, 23.

Society for Neuroscience (SNS)
2002 *Brain Facts: A Primer on the Brain and Nervous system*. Washington, DC: SNS.

Speaker, Susan L.
2001 "'The Struggle of Mankind Against Its Deadliest Foe': Themes of Counter-Subversion in Anti-Narcotic Campaigns, 1920–1940." *Journal of Social History* 34 (Spring): Internet.

Speart, Jessica
1995 "The New Drug Mules." *New York Times Magazine* (June 11): 44–45.

Speckart, George and M. Douglas Anglin
1987 "Narcotics Use and Crime: An Overview of Recent Research Advances." *Contemporary Drug Problems* 16 (Winter): 741–69.
1985 "Narcotics and Crime: An Analysis of Existing Evidence for a Causal Relationship." *Behavioral Sciences and the Law* 3: 259–82.

Spence, Richard T.
1989 *Current Substance Abuse Trends in Texas*. Austin, TX: Commission on Alcohol and Drug Abuse.

Spitz, Henry I.
1987 "Cocaine Abuse: Therapeutic Group Approaches." Pages 156–201 in *Cocaine Abuse: New Directions in Treatment and Research*, edited by Henry I. Spitz and Jeffrey S. Rosecan. New York: Brunner/Mazel.

Spitz, Henry I. and Jeffrey S. Rosecan
1987 "Overview of Cocaine Abuse Treatment." Pages 97–118 in *Cocaine Abuse: New Directions in Treatment and Research*, edited by Henry I. Spitz and Jeffrey S. Rosecan. New York: Brunner/Mazel.

Spohn, Cassia and David Holleran
2001 "The Effect of Imprisonment on Recidivism Rates of Felony Offenders: A Focus on Drug Offenders." *Criminology* 40 (May): 329–57.

Spoth, Richard L., Scott Clair, Chungycol Shin, and Cleve Redmond
2006 "Long-Term Effects of Universal Preventive Interventions on Methamphetamine Use Among Adolescents." *Archives of Pediatric Adolescent Medicine* 160: 876–82.

Spotts, James V. and Franklin C. Shontz
1980 "A Life-Theme Theory of Chronic Drug Abuse." Pages 59–70 in *Theories on Drug Abuse: Selected Contemporary Perspectives*, edited by Dan J. Lettieri, Mollie Sayers, and Helen Wallenstein Pearson. Rockville, MD: National Institute on Drug Abuse.

Stahl, Marc B.
1992 "Asset Forfeiture, Burdens of Proof and the War on Drugs." *Journal of Criminal Law and Criminology* 83: 274–337.

Starkweather, C. Woodruff
1982 "Techniques of Therapy Based on Cognitive Learning Theory." Pages 37–47 in *Communication Disorders: General Principles of Therapy*, edited by William H. Perkins. New York: Thieme-Stratton.

Stearns, Peter N.
1998 "Dope Fiends and Degenerates: The Gendering of Addiction in the Early Twentieth Century." *Journal of Social History* 31 (Summer): 809–14.

Stellwagen, Lindsey D.
1985 *Use of Forfeiture Sanctions in Drug Cases*. Washington, DC: National Institute of Justice.

Stevens, Jay
1987 *Storming Heaven: LSD and the American Dream*. New York: Atlantic Monthly Press.

Stimson, Gerry V. and Edna Oppenheimer
1982 *Heroin Addiction: Treatment and Control in Britain*. London: Tavistock.

Stitzer, Maxine L., George E. Bigelow, Ira A. Liebson, and Mary E. McCaul
1984 "Contingency Management of Supplemental Drug Use During Methadone Maintenance Treatment." Pages 84–103 in *Behavioral Intervention Techniques in Drug Abuse Treatment*, edited by John Grabowski, Maxine L. Stitzer, and Jack E. Henningfield. Rockville, MD: National Institute on Drug Abuse.

Stitzer, Maxine L., George E. Bigelow, and Mary E. McCaul
1985 "Behavior Therapy in Drug Abuse Treatment: Review and Evaluation." Pages 31–50 in *Progress in the Development of Cost-Effective Treatment for Drug Abusers*, edited by Rebecca S. Ashery. Rockville, MD: National Institute on Drug Abuse.

Stocker, Steven
1999 "Studies Link Stress and Drug Addiction." *NIDA Notes* 14 (April): 12–15.

Stolberg, Sheryl Gay
1999 "Government Study of Marijuana Sees Medical Benefits." *New York Times* (March 18): 1, 20.
1998 "President Decides Against Financing Needle Programs." *New York Times* (April 21): 1, 18.

Stout, David
1999 "Coast Guard Using Sharpshooters to Stop Boats." *New York Times* (September 14): 16.

Strong, Simon
1992 "Peru Is Losing More than the Drug War." *New York Times* (February 17): 11.

Stryker, Jeff
2001 "For Partygoers Who Can't Say No, Experts Try to Reduce the Risks." *New York Times* (September 25): D5.

Stuart, Richard B.
1974 "Teaching Facts About Drugs: Pushing or Preventing?" *Journal of Educational Psychology* 66 (April): 189–201.

Stutman, Robert M. and Richard Esposito
1992 *Dead on Delivery: Inside the Drug Wars, Straight from the Street*. New York: Warner.

Substance Abuse and Mental Health Services Administration
2001 *Guide to Science-Based Practices*. Washington, DC: Substance Abuse and Mental Health Services Administration.

Substance Abuse Resource Center
1999 "Study Says Community Partnerships Can Reduce Drug Use." (December 23): Internet.

Sunderwirth, Stanley G.
1985 "Biological Mechanisms: Neurotransmission and Addiction." Pages 11–19 in *The Addictions: Multidisciplinary Perspectives and Treatments*, edited by Harvey B. Milkman and Howard J. Shaffer. Lexington, MA: DC Heath.

Sutherland, Edwin
1973 *On Analyzing Crime*, edited by Karl Schuessler. Chicago: University of Chicago Press.

Swadi, Harith and Harry Zeitlin
1987 "Drug Education for School Children: Does It Really Work?" *British Journal of Addiction* 82: 741–46.

Swan, Neil
n.d. "Researchers Probe Which Comes First: Drug Abuse or Antisocial Behavior." *Drug Abuse Prevention Research and the Community*. Washington, DC: National Institute on Drug Abuse.

Sykes, Gresham M.
1967 *Crime and Society*, 2nd ed. New York: Random House.

Szabo, Liz
2005 "Study Links Kids' Lower Test Scores to Secondhand Smoke." *USA Today* (January 3): Internet.

Szasz, Thomas
1974 *Ceremonial Justice: The Ritual Persecution of Drugs, Addicts, and Pushers*. Garden City, NY: Doubleday.

Tackett, Michael
1990 "Minor Drug Players Are Paying Big Prices." *Chicago Tribune* (October 15): 1, 9.

Tagliabue, John
2000 "The Prince and His Black Sheep: This is No Liechtenstein Fairy Tale." *New York Times* (April 8): 4.

Talbot, Margaret
2009 "Brain Gain: The Underground World of 'Neuroenhancing' Drugs." *New Yorker* (April 27): 32–43.

Tamayo, Juan O.
2001 "Colombia's Heroin Trade Is Flourishing." *Chicago Tribune* (August 24): 6.

Tammi, Tuuka
2004 "The Harm-Reduction School of Thought: Three Factions." *Contemporary Drug Problems* 31 (Fall): 381–400.

Tancer, Manuel and Charles R. Schuster
1997 "Serotonin and Dopamine System Interactions in the Reinforcing Properties of Psychostimulants: A Research Strategy." *Pressletter of the Multidisciplinary Association for Psychedelic Studies* 7 (Summer): Internet.

Taniguchi, Travis A., George F. Rengert, and Eric S. McCord
2009 "Where Size Matters: Agglomeration Economies of Illegal Drug Markets in Philadelphia." *Justice Quarterly* 26 (December): 670–94.

Tapper, Andrew R., Sheri L. McKinney, Raad Nashmi, Johannes Schwarz, Purnima Deshpande, Cesar Labarca, Paul Whiteaker, Michael J. Marks, Allan C. Collins, and Henry A. Lester

2004 "Nicotine Activation of [alpha]4* Receptors: Sufficient for Reward, Tolerance, and Sensitization." *Science* 306 (November 5): 1029–33.

Tarter, Ralph E.
1988 "Are There Inherited Behavioral Traits That Predispose to Substance Abuse?" *Journal of Consulting and Clinical Psychology* 56 (April): 189–96.

Tarter, Ralph E., Arthur I. Alterman, and Kathleen L. Edwards
1985 "Vulnerability to Alcoholism in Men: A Behavior-Genetic Perspective." *Journal of Studies on Alcohol* 46 (July): 329–56.

Taylor, David
2002 "Drugs on the Brain." *Meanjean* 61 (June): 138–44.

Terry, Charles E. and Mildred Pellens
1928 *The Opium Problem.* New York: The Committee on Drug Addictions in Collaboration with the Bureau of Social Hygiene, Inc.

"33-Year Study Shows Severe Long-Term Effects of Heroin"
2001 *Brown University Digest of Addiction Theory and Application* 20 (June): 16–20.

Thomas, Josephine
2001 "Maternal Smoking During Pregnancy Associated with Negative Toddler Behavior and Early Smoking Experimentation." *NIDA Notes* 16 (1): 1, 4–5.

Thompson, Ginger
2005 "Drug Violence Paralyzes a City, and Chills the Border." *New York Times* (May 24): 4.

Thornburgh, Dick
1989 *Drug Trafficking: A Report to the President.* Washington, DC: U.S. Government Printing Office.

Thoumi, Francisco E.
2002 "Illegal Drugs in Colombia: From Illegal Economic Boom to Social Crisis." *Annals* 582 (July): 102–16.

1995 "The Size of the Illegal Drug Industry." Pages 77–96 in *Drug Trafficking in the Americas,* edited by Bruce M. Bagley and William O. Walker III. New Brunswick, NJ: Transaction Publishers.

Tilson, Hugh A.
1993 "Neurobehavioral Methods Used in Neurotoxicology." Pages 1–33 in *Assessing Neurotoxicity in Drugs of Abuse,* edited by Lynda Erinoff. Rockville, MD: National Institute on Drug Abuse.

Tindall, George B.
1988 *America: A Narrative History,* Vol. 2. New York: Norton.

Tobacco Addiction
2009 Rockville, MD National Institute on Drug Abuse.

Torriero, E. A.
2002 "Afghan Officials Struggle to Stop Opium Bonanza." *Chicago Tribune* (March 3): 6.

Tortora, Gerard J.
1983 *Principles of Human Anatomy,* 3rd ed. New York: Harper and Row.

Treaster, Joseph B.
1991 "Plan Lets Addicted Mothers Take Their Newborns Home." *New York Times* (September 19): 1, 16.

1990a "Bypassing Borders, More Drugs Flood Ports." *New York Times* (April 29): 1, 18.

1990b "At City's Heart, Carnival for Haunted." *New York Times* (September 27): 4.

"Treating, Not Punishing"
2009 *The Economist* (August 31): Internet.

Trebach, Arnold S.
1987 *The Great Drug War: A Radical Proposal That Could Make America Safe Again.* New York: Macmillan.

1982 *The Heroin Solution.* New Haven, CT: Yale University Press.

Truitt, Linda
2007 *The Impact of a Mature Drug Court Over 10 Years of Operation: Recidivism and Costs.* Portland, OR: NPC Research.

Tullis, LaMond
1995 *Unintended Consequences: Illegal Drugs and Drug Policies in Nine Countries.* Boulder, CO: Lynne Reinner.

Tuma, Dan J. and Carol A. Casey
2004 *Dangerous Byproducts of Alcohol Breakdown—Focus on Adducts.* Bethesda, MD: National Institute on Alcohol Abuse and Alcoholism.

"12 Mexican Intelligence Agents Tortured, Slain"
2009 *USA Today* (July 14): Internet.

Tyler, Patrick E.
1995 "China Battles a Spreading Scourge of Illicit Drugs." *New York Times* (November 15): 1, 7.

1991 "Teheran Convicts Nine in Opposition." *New York Times* (September 22): 9.

Tymoczco, Dmitri
1996 "The Nitrous Oxide Philosopher." *Atlantic Monthly* (May): 93–101.

Uelmen, Gerald F. and Victor G. Haddox, eds.
1983 *Drug Abuse and the Law.* New York: Clark Boardman.

Uitermark, Justus
2004 "The Origins and Future of the Dutch Approach Towards Drugs." *Journal of Drug Issues* 34 (Summer): 511–33.

United Nations Office on Drugs and Crime
2008 *Amphetamines and Ecstasy: 2008 Global ATS Review.* New York: UNODC.

2007 *Cocaine Trafficking in West Africa: The Threat to Stability and Development (with Special Reference to Guinea-Bissau).* New York: UNODC.

U.S. Department of Justice
2009 *The United States National Central Bureau of INTERPOL.* Washington, DC: Office of the Inspector General.

U.S. Department of State (USDS)
2008 *International Narcotics Control Strategy Report. Volume 1: Drug and Chemical Control.* Washington, DC: USDS.

2000 *Policy and Program Overview for 1999.* Washington, DC: Bureau for International Narcotics and Law Enforcement Affairs.

1999 *Money Laundering and Financial Crimes.* Washington, DC: Bureau for International Narcotics and Law Enforcement Affairs.

"U.S. Resists Easing Curb on Marijuana."
1989 *New York Times* (December 31): 14.

Vaillant, George E.
1983 *The Natural History of Alcoholism.* Cambridge, MA: Harvard University Press.

1970 "The Natural History of Narcotic Drug Addiction." *Seminars in Psychiatry* 2 (November): 486–98.

Valenzuela, C. Fernando
1997 "Alcohol and Neurotransmitter Interactions." *Alcohol Health and Research World* 21 (2): 144–48.

van de Mheen, Dike and Paul Gruter
2004 "Interventions on the Supply Side of the Local Hard Drug Market: Towards a Regulated Hard Drug Trade? The Case of the City of Rotterdam." *Journal of Drug Issues* 34 (Winter): 145–62.

Van Dyke, Craig and Robert Byck
1982 "Cocaine." *Scientific American* 246 (March): 128–41.

Varisco, Raymond
2000 "Drug Abuse and Conduct Disorder Linked to Maternal Smoking During Pregnancy." *NIDA Notes* 15 (5): 5.

Verhovek, Sam Howe
1995 "Young, Carefree and in Love with Cigarettes." *New York Times* (July 30): 1, 10.

Verini, James
2007 "A Budding Invasion." *Men's Vogue* (March/ April): 71, 74, 78, 80, 86.

Vest, Jason
1997 "DEA to Florists: The Poppies Are Unlovely." *U.S. News and World Report* (March 17): 49.

"Victims of Botched U.S. Drug Sting Sue"
1995 *Chicago Tribune* (January 24): 7.

Visher, Christy A.
1990 "Linking Criminal Sanctions, Drug Testing, and Drug and Drug Abuse Treatment: A Crime Control Strategy for the 1990s." *Criminal Justice Policy Review* 3: 329–43.

Vivanco, José Miguel
1995 "Letter to the New York Times: 'U.S. Aids Bolivia in Trampling Rights.'" *New York Times* (July 18): 14.

Vogt, Amanda
2003 "Now Many 'Just Say No' to DARE." *Chicago Tribune* (January 26): 1, 14.

Volkow, Nora D.
2006 "NIDA Director's Report to CPDD Meeting: Progress, Priorities, and Plans for the Future." Pages 70–79 in *Problems of Drug Dependence 2005*. Bethesda, MD: National Institute on Drug Abuse.

Volkow, Nora D., Gene-Jack Wang, Joanna S. Fowler, Jean Logan, Samuel J. Gatley, Andrew Gifford, Robert Hitzemann, Yu-Shin Ding, and Naomi Pappas
1999 "Prediction of Reinforcing Responses to Psychostimulants in Humans by Brai Dopamine2 Receptor Levels." *American Journal of Psychiatry* 156 (September): 1440–43.

Volkow, Nora D., Gene-Jack Wang, Joanna S. Fowler, Jean Logan, Samuel J. Gatley, Christopher Wong, Robert Hitzemann, and Naomi R. Pappas
1999 "Reinforcing Effects of Psychostimulants in Humans Are Associated with Increases in Brain Dopamine and Occupancy of D2 Receptors." *Journal of*

Pharmacology and Experimental Therapeutics 291 (October): 409–15.

Volkow, Nora D., L. Chang, Gene-Jack Wang, Joanna S. Fowler, M. Leonido-Yee, D. Franceschi, M. J. Sedler, Samuel J. Gatley, Robert Hitzemann, YuShin Ding, Jean Logan, C. Wong, and E. N. Miller
2001 "Association of Dopamine Transporter Reduction with Psychomotor Impairment in Methamphetamine Abusers." *American Journal of Psychiatry* 158 (March): 377–82.

von Mises, Ludwig
1949 *Human Action: A Treatise on Economics*. New Haven, CT: Yale University Press.

von Solinge, Tim Boekhout
2004 *Dealing with Drugs in Europe: An Investigation of European Drug Control Experience: France, the Netherlands and Sweden*. The Hague: BJu Legal Publishers.

von Zielbauer, Paul
2003 "Court Treatment System Is Found to Help Drug Offenders Stay Clean." *New York Times* (November 9): 33.

Vorenberg, James and Irving F. Lukoff
1973 "Addiction, Crime, and the Criminal Justice System." *Federal Probation* 37 (December): 3–7.

Wahl, Melissa
1999 "Hitting a Wall of Opposition." *Chicago Tribune* (February 4): Sec. 3: 1, 4.

Wald, Matthew
2002 "Hidden Plague of Alcohol Abuse by the Elderly." *New York Times* (April 2): D7.

Wald, Patricia M. and Annette Abrams
1972 "Drug Education." Pages 123–72 in *Dealing with Drug Abuse: A Report to the Ford Foundation*. New York: Praeger.

Wald, Patricia M. and Peter Barton Hutt
1972 "The Drug Abuse Survey Project: Summary of Findings, Conclusions, and Recommendations." Pages 3–61 in *Dealing with Drug Abuse: A Report to the Ford Foundation*. New York: Praeger.

Waldman, Amy
2004 "Afghan Route to Prosperity: Grow Poppies." *New York Times* (April 10): 1, 5.

Waldorf, Dan
1973 *Careers in Dope*. Englewood Cliffs, NJ: Prentice Hall.

Wallace, John
1993 "Modern Disease Models of Alcoholism and Other Chemical Dependencies: The New Biopsychosocial Models." *Drugs and Society* 8 (1): 69–87.

Wallace-Wells, Ben
2009 "Six Ways of Looking at the Drug War." *Mother Jones* (July/August): 53, 80.

Wallance, Gregory
1981 *Papa's Game*. New York: Ballantine.

Walter, Ingo
1990 *Secret Money: The World of International Financial Secrecy*. New York: Harper Business.

Walters, John
2003 *Dialogue with John Walters, Director, White House Office of National Drug Control Policy*. Washington, DC: Center for Strategic and International Studies.

Washton, Arnold M.
1989 *Cocaine Addiction: Treatment, Recovery, and Relapse Prevention*. New York: Norton.

Washton, Arnold M. and Mark S. Gold
1987 "Recent Trends in Cocaine Abuse as Seen from the '800-Cocaine Hotline.'" Pages 10–22 in *Cocaine: A Clinicians Handbook*, edited by Arnold M. Washton and Mark S. Gold. New York: Guilford Press.

Washton, Arnold M. and Nanette Stone-Washton
1993 "Outpatient Treatment of Cocaine and Crack Addiction: A Clinical Perspective." Pages 15–30 in *Cocaine Treatment: Research and Clinical Perspectives*, edited by Frank M. Tims and Carl G. Leukefeld. Rockville, MD: National Institute on Drug Abuse.

Washton, Arnold M., Nannette S. Stone, and Edward C. Henrickson
1988 "Cocaine Abuse." Pages 364–89 in *Assessment of Addictive Behaviors*, edited by Dennis M. Donovan and G. Alan Marlatt. New York: Guilford.

Waterston, Alisse
1993 *Addicts in the Political Economy*. Philadelphia: Temple University Press.

Watlington, Dennis
1987 "Between the Cracks." *Vanity Fair* (December): 146–51, 184.

Watson, Russell
1999 "Coke and Mrs. Colonel." *Pressweek* (August 16): 37.

Waxman, Sharon
2007 "Stars Check In, Stars Check Out." *New York Times* (June 17): ST1, 10.

Webster, Barbara and Michael S. McCampbell
1992 *International Money Laundering: Research and Investigation Join Forces*. Washington, DC: National Institute of Justice.

Weil, Andrew
1995 "The New Politics of Coca." *New Yorker* (May 15): 70–80.

Weiner, Tim
2002 "Border Customs Agents Are Pushed to the Limit." *New York Times* (July 25): 14.

Weinstein, Adam K.
1988 "Prosecuting Attorneys for Money Laundering: A New and Questionable Weapon in the War on Crime." *Law and Contemporary Problems* 51 (Winter): 369–86.

Weisheit, Ralph A.
1990 "Cash Crop: A Study of Illicit Marijuana Growers." Working draft for the National Institute of Justice.

Weisheit, Ralph and William L. White
2009 *Methamphetamine: Its History, Pharmacology, and Treatment*. Center City, MN: Hazelden.

Weiss, Roger D. and Steven M. Mirin
1987 *Cocaine*. Washington, DC: American Psychiatric Press.

Welsh, Wayne N.
2007 "A Multisite Evaluation of Prison-Based Therapeutic Community Drug Treatment." *Criminal Justice and Behavior* 34 (November): 1481–98.

2003 *Evaluation of Prison-Based Therapeutic Community Drug Treatment Programs in Pennsylvania*. Philadelphia, PA: Temple University.

Weppner, Robert S.
1983 *The Untherapeutic Community: Organizational Behavior in a Failed Addiction Treatment Program*. Lincoln: University of Nebraska.

Wesson, Donald R. and David E. Smith
1985 "Cocaine: Treatment Perspectives." Pages 193–203 in *Cocaine Use in America: Epidemiologic and Clinical Perspectives*, edited by Nicholas J. Kozel and Edgar H. Adams. Rockville, MD: National Institute on Drug Abuse.

1977 *Barbiturates: Their Use, Misuse, and Abuse*. New York: Human Sciences Press.

Wever, Leon
1994 "Drugs as a Public Health Problem." Pages 59–74 in *Between Prohibition and Legalization: The Dutch Experiment in Drug Policy*, edited by Ed. Leuw and I. Haen Marshall. Amsterdam: Kugler Publications.

Wexler, Harry K., Douglas S. Lipton, and Kenneth Foster
1985 "Outcome Evaluation of a Prison Therapeutic Community for Substance Abuse Treatment: Preliminary Results." Paper presented at the American Society of Criminology, San Diego, CA, November.

Wexler, Harry K., George DeLeon, George Thomas, David Kressel, and Jean Peters
1999 "The Amity Prison TC Evaluation: Reincarceration Outcomes." *Criminal Justice and Behavior* 26 (June): 147–67.

Wexler, Harry K., Gregory P. Falkin, and Douglas S. Lipton
1990 "Outcome Evaluation of a Prison Therapeutic Community for Substance Abuse Treatment." *Criminal Justice and Behavior* 15: 71–92.

Wexler, Harry K. and Ronald Williams
1986 "The Stay 'N Out Therapeutic Community: Prison Treatment for Substance Abusers." *Journal of Psychoactive Drugs* 18 (July-September): 221–30.

"What Kind of Drug Use Does School-Based Prevention Prevent?"
2002 *Drug Policy Research Center Newsletter* (June): Internet.

Wheat, Sue and Philip Withers Green
1999 "Leaf in the Lurch." *Geographical* (September): 42–48.

White House Conference for a Drug Free America
1988 *Final Report*. Washington, DC: U.S. Government Printing Office.

White, Peter
1989 "Coca–An Ancient Herb Turns Deadly." *National Geographic* (January): 3–47.

White, William L.
1998 *Slaying the Dragon: The History of Addiction Treatment and Recovery in America*. Bloomington, IN: Chestnut Health Systems.

Whiteacre, Kevin W.
2005 "Criminal Constructions of Drug Users." Pages 3–13 in *Cocktails and Dreams: Perspectives on Drug and Alcohol Use*, edited by Wilson R. Palacios. Upper Saddle River, NJ: Prentice Hall.

Whiteacre, Kevin W. and Hal Pepinsky
2002 "Controlling Drug Use." *Criminal Justice Policy Review* 13 (March): 21–31.

Whitlock, Rod Van, Howard Collings, and Cathleen Burnett
1990 "Relationship Between Cocaine Use and Severity of Crime." Paper presented at the annual meeting of the American Society of Criminology, Baltimore, November.

Whitten, Lori
2007a "Behavioral Response to Novelty Foreshadows Neurological Response to Cocaine." *NIDA Notes* 21 (3): 1, 6.

2007b "Serotonin System May Have Potential as a Target for Cocaine Medications." *NIDA Notes* 21 (3): 12–13.

2006a "Court-Mandated Treatment Works as Well as Voluntary." *NIDA Notes* (July): 1, 6.

2006b "Study Finds Rapid Withdrawal No Easier with Ultrarapid Opiate Detox." *NIDA Notes* (October): 4–5.

2006c "Low-Cost Incentives Improve Outcomes in Stimulant Abuse Achievement." *NIDA Notes* 21 (October): 1, 6.

2005 "Cocaine-Related Environmental Cues Elicit Physiological Stress Responses." *NIDA Notes* (August): 1, 6–7.

Wicker, Tom
1987 "Drugs and Alcohol." *New York Times* (May 13): 27.

Wilbanks, William
1990 "The Danger in Viewing Addicts as Victims: A Critique of the Disease Model of Addiction." *Criminal Justice Policy Review* 3: 407–22.

Wilkerson, Isabel
1991 "Court Backs Woman in Pregnancy Drug Case." *New York Times* (April 3): 13.

Williams, Jay R., Lawrence J. Redlinger, and Peter K. Manning
1979 *Police Narcotics Control: Patterns and Strategies*. Washington, DC: U.S. Government Printing Office.

Williams, Jill Schlabig
2004 "The Neurobehavioral Legacy of Prenatal Tobacco Exposure." *NIDA Notes* 18 (6): 8–9, 13.

Williams, Terry
1989 *The Cocaine Kids: The Inside Story of a Teenage Drug Ring.* Reading, MA: Addison-Wesley.

Willoughby, Alan
1988 *The Alcohol Troubled Person: Known and Unknown.* Chicago: Nelson-Hall.

Wilson, James Q.
1990 "Against the Legalization of Drugs." *Commentary* 89 (February): 21–28.
1978 *The Investigators: Managing FBI and Narcotics Agents.* New York: Basic Books.
1975 *Thinking About Crime.* New York: Basic Books.

Winerip, Michael
1998 "Binge Nights: The Emergency on Campus." *New York Times Education Life* (January 4): 28–31, 42.

Winger, Gail
1988 "Pharmacological Modifications of Cocaine and Opioid Self-Administration." Pages 125–36 in *Mechanisms of Cocaine Abuse and Toxicity,* edited by Doris Clouet, Khursheed Asghar, and Roger Brown. Rockville, MD: National Institute on Drug Abuse.

Winick, Charles
1961 "Physician Narcotic Addicts." *Social Problems* 9: 174–86.

Winter, Greg
2003 "Study Finds No Sign That Testing Deters Students' Drug Use." *New York Times* (May 17): 1, 14.

Winter, Jerrold C.
1994 "The Stimulus Effects of Serotonergic Hallucinogens in Animals." Pages 157–82 in *Hallucinogens: An Update,* edited by Geraline C. Lin and Richard A. Glennon. Rockville, MD: National Institute on Drug Abuse.

Winters, Ken C. and George Henly
1988 "Assessing Adolescents Who Abuse Chemicals: The Chemical Dependency Adolescent Assessment Project." Pages 4–18 in *Adolescent Drug Abuse: Analyses of Treatment Research,* edited by Elizabeth R. Rahdert and John Grabowski. Rockville, MD: National Institute on Drug Abuse.

Wish, Eric
n.d. *Drug Testing.* Rockville, MD: National Institute of Justice.

Wish, Eric D. and Bruce Johnson
1986 "The Impact of Substance Abuse on Criminal Careers." Pages 52–88 in *Criminal Careers and Career Criminals,* edited by Alfred Blumstein, Jacqueline Cohen, Jeffrey A. Roth, and Christy A. Visher. Washington, DC: National Academy Press.

Wishart, David
1974 "The Opium Poppy: The Forbidden Crop." *Journal of Geography* 73 (January): 14–25.

Wisotsky, Steven
1987 *Breaking the Impasse in the War on Drugs.* Westport, CT: Greenwood.

Witkin, Gordon
1991 "The Men Who Created Crack." *U.S. Press and World Report* (August 19): 44–53.

Witkin, Gordon and Jennifer Griffin
1994 "The New Opium Wars." *U.S. News & World Report* (October 10): 39–44.

Wodak, Alex
1990 "Needle Exchange Succeeding in Australia." Letter to the *New York Times* (March 26): 14.

Wodak, Alex and Peter Lurie
1997 "A Tale of Two Countries: Attempts to Control HIV Among Injecting Drug Users in Australia and the United States." *Journal of Drug Issues* 27: 117–34.

Wolf, Judith, Loes Linssen, and Ireen de Graaf
2003 "Drug Consumption Facilities in the Netherlands." *Journal of Drug Issues* 33 (Summer): Internet.

Wolfe, Tom
1968 *The Electric Kool-Aid Acid Test.* New York: Farrar, Straus and Giroux.

Wolfgang, Marvin E. and Franco Ferracuti
1967 *The Subculture of Violence: Toward an Integrated Theory in Criminology.* London: Tavistock.

Wolvier, Robbie, Michael Martino, Jr., and Timothy Bolger
2009 "Long Highland. Heroin: It's 'This Generation's Drug of Choice.'" *Long Island Press* (June 26): 8–15.

Wood, Daniel
1991 "Bar Lab Challenges the Alcohol Mystique." *Chicago Tribune* (February 24): Sec. 5: 6.

Wood, Roland W.
1973 "18,000 Addicts Later: A Look at California's Civil Addict Program." *Federal Probation* 38 (March): 26–31.

Woodiwiss, Michael
1988 *Crime, Crusades and Corruption: Prohibition in the United States, 1900–1987.* Totawa, NJ: Barnes and Noble.

Woods, James R. Jr.
1993 "Effects of Drugs of Abuse on Mother and Fetus." Pages 179–87 in *International Research Conference on Biomedical Approaches to Illicit Drug Demand Reduction,* edited by Christine R. Hartel. Washington, DC: U.S. Government Printing Office.

Woody, George E., Lester Lubrosky, A. Thomas McLellan, Charles P. O'Brien, Aren T. Beck, Jack Blaine, Ira Herman, and Anita Hole
1983 "Psychotherapy for Opiate Addicts: Does It Help?" *Archives of General Psychiatry* 40 (June): 639–45.

World Drug Report
2008 New York: United Nations.

Worral, John L.
2008 "Is Policing for Profit? Answers from Asset Forfeiture." *Criminology and Public Policy* 7 (May): 219–244.
2008 *Asset Forfeiture.* Washington, DC: U.S. Department of Justice.

Worth, Robert F.
2003 "20 Airport Workers Held in Smuggling of Drugs for Decade." *New York Times* (November 26): 1, B4.
2002 "Judge's Ruling on Statements to A.A. Is Overturned." *New York Times* (July 18): 19.

Wren, Christopher S.
1999a "A Purer Form of Heroin Lures New Users to a Long, Hard Fall." *New York Times* (May 9): 27.
1999b "Bid for Alcohol in Antidrug Ads Hits Resistance." *New York Times* (May 31): 1, 8.
1999c "In Battle Against Heroin, Scientists Enlist Heroin." *New York Times* (June 8): D1, 6.
1998a "Road to Riches Starts in the Golden Triangle." *New York Times* (May 11): 8.
1998b "Afghanistan's Opium Output Drops Sharply, U.N. Survey Shows." *New York Times* (September 27): 11.
1998c "Drug Officials Sense a Shift in Dominicans." *New York Times* (August 14): 16.
1996 "Mexican Role in Cocaine Is Exposed in U.S. Seizure." *New York Times* (May 3): C19.

Wright, Fred D., Aaron T. Beck, Cory F. Newman, and Bruce S. Liese
1993 "Cognitive Therapy of Substance Abuse: Theoretical Rationale." Pages 123–46 in *Behavioral*

Treatments for Drug Abuse and Dependence, edited by Lisa Simon Onken, John D. Blaine, and John J. Boren. Rockville, MD: National Institute on Drug Abuse.

Wurmser, Leon
1978 "Mr. Pecksniff's Horse? (Psychodynamics in Compulsive Drug Use)." Pages 36–72 in *Psychodynamics of Drug Dependence,* edited by Jack D. Blaine and Demetrios A. Julius. Rockville, MD: National Institute on Drug Abuse.

Wysong, Earl, Richard Aniskiewicz, and David Wright
1994 "Truth and DARE: Drug Education to Graduation and as Symbolic Politics." *Social Problems* 41 (August): 448–72.

Ynclan, Nery
2002 "Web Site Gives Addicts Support on the Road." *Chicago Tribune* (October 13): Sec. C10.

Yorke, Clifford
1970 "A Critical Review of Some Psychoanalytic Literature on Drug Addiction." *British Journal of Medical Psychology* 43: 141–59.

Young, Douglas
2002 "Impact of Perceived Legal Pressure on Retention in Drug Treatment." *Criminal Justice and Behavior* 29 (February): 27–55.

Young, James Harvey
1961 *The Toadstool Millionaires: A Social History of Patent Medicines in America Before Federal Regulation.* Princeton, NJ: Princeton University Press.

Zahniser, Nancy R., Joanna Peris, Linda P. Dwoskin, Pamela Curella, Robert P. Yasuda, Laurie O'Keefe, and Sally J. Boyson
1988 "Sensitization to Cocaine in the Nigrostriatal Dopamine System." Pages 55–77 in *Mechanisms of Cocaine Abuse and Toxicity,*

edited by Doris Clouet, Khursheed Asghar, and Roger Brown. Rockville, MD: National Institute on Drug Abuse.

Zambito, Thomas
2005 "Afghani Heroin King Denies Rap." *New York Daily News* (October 25): 8.

Zernike, Kate
2006a "Potent Mexican Meth Floods in as States Curb Domestic Variety." *New York Times* (January 23): 1, 17.
2006b "F.D.A.'s Report Illuminates Wide Divide on Marijuana." *New York Times* (April 22): 11.
2001 "Antidrug Program Says It Will Adopt a New Strategy." *New York Times* (February 15): 1, 23.
2000 "New Tactic on College Drinking: Play It Down." *New York Times* (October 3): 1, 21.

Zezima, Katie
2009a "Cigarettes With No Smoke, Tar or, as It Happens, U.S. Assent." *New York Times* (June 2): 1, 3.
2009b "Analysis Finds Toxic Substances in Electronic Cigarettes." *New York Times* (July 23): 22.

Zickler, Patrick
2006 "Animal Research Shows GHB Act on GHB Receptors." *NIDA Notes* 20 (April): 9–10.
2004 "In Chronic Drug Abuse, Acute Dopamine Surge May Erode Resolve to Abstain." *NIDA Notes* 19 (1): 1, 6–7.
2003 "Genetic Variation May Increase Nicotine Craving and Smoking Relapse." *NIDA Notes* 18 (3): 1, 6.
2002 "Study Demonstrates That Marijuana Smokers Experience Significant Withdrawal." *NIDA Notes* 17 (3): 7, 10.
2001 "Cues for Cocaine and Normal Pleasures Activate Common Brain Sites." *NIDA Notes* 16 (2): 1, 5, 7.
2000a "Brain Imaging Studies Show Long-term Damage from

Methamphetamine Abuse." *NIDA Notes* 15 (3): 11, 13.
2000b "Nicotine Craving and Heavy Smoking May Contribute to Increased Use of Cocaine and Heroin." *NIDA Notes* 15 (5): Internet.
1999 "Twin Studies Help Define the Role of Genes in Vulnerability to Drug Abuse." *NIDA Notes* 14 (4): 1, 5, 8.

Zielbauer, Paul
2000 "New Campus High: Illicit Prescription Drugs." *New York Times* (March 24): 1, 19.

Zimmer, Lynn
1990 "Proactive Policing Against Street-Level Drug Trafficking." *American Journal of Police* 9: 43–74.

Zimring, Franklin E. and Gordon Hawkins
1992 *The Search for Rational Drug Control.* New York: Cambridge University Press.

Zinberg, Norman E.
1984 *Drug, Set, and Setting: The Basis for Controlled Intoxicant Use.* New Haven, CT: Yale University Press.

Zinberg, Norman E. and John A. Robertson
1972 *Drugs and the Public.* New York: Simon and Schuster.

Zinberg, Norman E., Wayne M. Harding, Shirley M. Stelmack, and Robert A. Marblestone
1978 "Patterns of Heroin Abuse." Pages 10–24 in *Recent Developments in Chemotherapy of Narcotic Addiction,* edited by Benjamin Kissin, Joyce H. Lowinson, and Robert B. Millman. New York: New York Academy of Sciences.

Zuckerman, Laurence
2000 "Workers Get Greater Drug Test Protection." *New York Times* (December 15): 20.

NAME INDEX

SUBJECT INDEX

A

Academy of Addiction Psychiatry, 66
Adderall, 183
Addiction, 4, 6
Adolescents and drugs. *See* Drugs and
    adolescents
Alcohol, 2, 3, 107–118
    blood alcohol level, 111–114
    dangers of, 116–118
    effects of, 110–115
    fetal alcohol syndrome (FAS), 118
    genetics and, 114–115
    high functioning alcoholic (HFA), 189
    history of, 29–31. *See also* Prohibition
    numbers who use, 17–18
    pharmacology, 107–110
    psychology. *See* Drug abuse/use, psycho-
        logical explanations of
    sex and, 110–111
    stages of use, 189
    tolerance for, 115–116
    types of, 107–109
    violence and, 107
    Wernicke-Korsakoff Syndrome, 117
    withdrawal from, 115–116
Alcoholics Anonymous (AA)/Twelve Step
        Programs. *See* Treatment, Alcoholics
        Anonymous (AA)/Twelve Step
        Programs
Alpert, Richard, 59–60
Amanita muscaria, 161–162
American Bar Association, 48
American Board of Psychiatry and Neurology,
    66
American Medical Association (AMA), 40,
    43, 47, 55, 66
American Pharmaceutical Association, 40, 43
American Protective Association, 30
American Psychiatric Association,
    2, 4

American Society of Addiction Medicine, 66,
    195
American Temperance Union, 29
Amphetamines, 135–143
    dangers of, 141–143
    effects of, 138
    history of, 57–58
    medical uses of, 140–141
    methamphetamines,
        67, 136–143, 308, 381
    military uses of, 141
    pharmacology, 138–140
    sex and, 139–140
    tolerance for, 140
    types of, 136
    withdrawal from, 140
"Angel Dust". *See* Phencyclidine
Anomie. *See* Drug abuse, sociological
    explanations
Anslinger, Harry J., 48, 55, 61, 62
Anti-Drug Abuse Act of 1986, 120, 386
Anti-Drug Abuse Act of 1988, 65
Anti-Saloon League, 30
Arias, Oscar, 384
Armed Forces. *See* Law enforcement, agen-
    cies, Department of Defense
Army disease, 34
Arousal theory, 77
Arrestee Drug Abuse Monitoring (ADAM),
    12, 16–17

B

Bank Secrecy Act, 330
Barbiturates, 101–110
    dangers of, 104
    effects of, 101–103
    history of, 58
    medical uses of, 103–104

pharmacology, 102–103
    tolerance for, 103
    withdrawal from, 103
Batista, Fulgencio, 294
Bayer, 35
Beatles, 60
Behaviorism. *See* Drug abuse/use,
        psychological explanations; Treat-
        ment, behavior modification
Behavior modification. *See* Treatment, be-
        havior modification
Bennett, William J., 66, 398
Bennis v. Michigan, 352
Benzedrine, 57
Benzodiazepines, 104–107
    dangers of, 106–107
    effects of, 105
    history of, 58–59
    medical uses of, 105–106
    tolerance for, 106
    withdrawal from, 106
Betancur, Belisario, 384
Bias, Len, 65, 130
Bible, 29
Black market peso exchange
        (BMPE), 328
Board of Education v. Earls, 242
Boggs Act, 62
Brain, 79–84. *See also* Central Nervous Sys-
        tem (CNS)
Brent, Henry Charles, 41
Buprenorphine, 255
Bureau of Customs. *See* Law
        enforcement, agencies, Bureau
        of Customs
Bureau of Drug Abuse Control, 64
Bureau of Narcotics and Dangerous Drugs
        (BNDD), 64, 379
Burma. *See* Drug trafficking, Golden Triangle/
        Southeast Asia,
        Myanmar (Burma)

471